The Routledge Companion to Behavioural Accounting Research

Behavioural research is well established in the social sciences, and has flourished in the field of accounting in recent decades. This far-reaching and reliable collection provides a definitive resource on current knowledge in this new approach, as well as providing a guide to the development and implementation of a Behavioural Accounting Research project.

The Routledge Companion to Behavioural Accounting Research covers a full range of theoretical, methodological and statistical approaches relied upon by behavioural accounting researchers, giving the reader a good grounding in both theoretical perspectives and practical applications. The perspectives cover a range of countries and contexts, bringing in seminal chapters by an international selection of behavioural accounting scholars, including Robert Libby and William R. Kinney, Jr.

This book is a vital introduction for Ph.D. students as well as a valuable resource for established behavioural accounting researchers.

Theresa Libby is the Ernst & Young Professor of Accounting in the Kenneth G. Dixon School of Accounting, University of Central Florida, USA.

Linda Thorne is Professor of Accounting at the Schulich School of Business, York University, Canada.

Routledge Companions in Business, Management and Accounting

For a full list of titles in this series, please visit www.routledge.com

Routledge Companions in Business, Management and Accounting are prestige reference works providing an overview of a whole subject area or sub-discipline. These books survey the state of the discipline including emerging and cutting edge areas. Providing a comprehensive, up to date, definitive work of reference, Routledge Companions can be cited as an authoritative source on the subject.

A key aspect of these Routledge Companions is their international scope and relevance. Edited by an array of highly regarded scholars, these volumes also benefit from teams of contributors which reflect an international range of perspectives.

Individually, Routledge Companions in Business, Management and Accounting provide an impactful one-stop-shop resource for each theme covered. Collectively, they represent a comprehensive learning and research resource for researchers, postgraduate students and practitioners.

Published titles in this series include:

The Routledge Companion to Behavioural Accounting Research

Edited by
Theresa Libby and Linda Thorne

LONDON AND NEW YORK

First published 2018
by Routledge
2 Park Square, Milton Park, Abingdon, Oxon OX14 4RN

and by Routledge
52 Vanderbilt Avenue, New York, NY 10017

First issued in paperback 2020

Routledge is an imprint of the Taylor & Francis Group, an informa business

British Library Cataloguing-in-Publication Data
A catalogue record for this book is available from the British Library

Library of Congress Cataloging-in-Publication Data
Names: Libby, Theresa, editor. | Thorne, Linda, 1956– editor.
Title: The Routledge companion to behavioural accounting research / edited by
    Theresa Libby and Linda Thorne.
Description: Abingdon, Oxon ; New York, NY : Routledge, 2018. |
    Includes index.
Identifiers: LCCN 2017028250 | ISBN 9781138890664 (hbk)
Subjects: LCSH: Accounting—Psychological aspects.
Classification: LCC HF5625 .R6969 2018 | DDC 657.01/9—dc23
LC record available at https://lccn.loc.gov/2017028250

ISBN 13: 978–0–367–58102–2 (pbk)
ISBN 13: 978–1–138–89066–4 (hbk)

Typeset in Bembo
by Apex CoVantage, LLC

In the course of preparing this edited volume, our good friend and mentor Bryan Church passed away unexpectedly. Bryan and Lucy Ackert contributed Chapter 14 to this volume. Bryan will be sorely missed not only by his family and friends, but also by the Behavioural Accounting Research community of which he was an important part. We dedicate this volume to the memory of our wonderful colleague Bryan.

Contents

Contents

Contents

Figures

Figures

Tables

Contributors

Lucy F. Ackert is a Professor of Finance at the Michael J. Coles College of Business, Kennesaw State University. Dr. Ackert holds a Ph.D. in Financial Economics from Emory University. Her research interests include individuals' use of information and financial market reaction to information.

Lindsay M. Andiola is an Assistant Professor of Accounting in the School of Business, Virginia Commonwealth University. Dr. Andiola holds a Ph.D. in Accounting from Bentley University. Her research interests focus on auditor interactions, specifically those involving performance feedback, coaching and training of auditors.

Vicky Arnold is the Ernst & Young Professor of Accounting in the Kenneth G. Dixon School of Accounting, University of Central Florida. Dr. Arnold holds a Ph.D. in Accounting from the University of Arkansas. Her research interests include judgment and decision-making and the impact of information technology systems designed to support these judgments.

Jean C. Bedard is the Timothy B. Harbert Professor of Accountancy in the Department of Accountancy at Bentley University. Dr. Bedard holds a Ph.D. in Accounting from the University of Wisconsin-Madison. Her research interests include individual auditor decision quality, risk assessment and adjustment in audit engagements, and the effects of computerization on the audit process.

Marco Bellucci (Ph.D.) is Research Fellow in Accounting at the Department of Economics and Management of the University of Florence (Italy). His main research interests include stakeholder theory, sustainability reporting, social enterprises and third sector organizations.

Donna Bobek is an Associate Professor of Accounting in the School of Accounting, Darla Moore School of Business, University of South Carolina. Dr. Bobek holds a Ph.D. in Accounting from the University of Florida. Her research interests include taxation, tax policy, judgment and decision-making of taxpayers and tax professionals, as well as ethical decision-making.

J.F.M.G. (Jan) Bouwens is a Professor of Accounting in the Faculty of Economics and Business, at the University of Amsterdam. Professor Bouwens holds a Ph.D. in Accountancy from Tilburg University. His research interests include performance measurement and the impact of control system design on individual and organizational performance.

Frank A. Buckless is a Professor of Accounting in the Poole College of Management at North Carolina State University. Dr. Buckless holds a Ph.D. from Michigan State University. His research interests include auditing, research methods and accounting education.

Ian Burt is an Assistant Professor of Accounting in the College of Business Administration, at Niagara University. Dr. Burt holds a Ph.D. in accounting from the University of Waterloo. His research interests include employee incentives, the pros and cons of the internal auditor's organizational identity, ethics in tax and management tools used in athletic departments.

Ariela Caglio is an Associate Professor of Accounting in the Department of Accounting at the University of Bocconi. Dr. Caglio holds a Ph.D. from the University of Bocconi. Her research interests include management accounting and controls in inter-organizational relationships and networks, the accounting profession and CFO and top executives' compensation.

Bryan K. Church is a Professor of Accounting in the Scheller College of Business at Georgia Tech. Dr. Church holds a Ph.D. in accounting from the University of Florida. His research interests include audit judgment, experimental economics and behavioural finance.

Andrew D. Cuccia is the Steed Professor and Grant Thornton Faculty Fellow at the Michael F. Price College of Business at the University of Oklahoma. Dr. Cuccia holds a Ph.D. in accounting from the University of Florida. His research interests include professional judgment and taxpayer compliance.

Angelo Ditillo is an Associate Professor of Accounting in the Department of Accounting at the University of Bocconi. Dr. Ditillo holds a Ph.D. from the University of Bocconi. His research interests include business planning and control of private equity agreements, management control of creative and innovative organizations, inter-organizational control of private and public partnerships and modes of control in knowledge-intensive firms.

Mary Parlee Durkin is an Assistant Professor of Accountancy in the School of Business at the University of San Diego. Dr. Parlee holds a Ph.D. from Bentley University. Her research interests include financial statement auditing, auditor judgment and decision-making and professional skepticism.

Jonathan Farrar is an Associate Professor in the Ted Rogers School of Management at Ryerson University. Dr. Farrar holds a Ph.D. in business administration from York University. His research interests include understanding taxpayer compliance decisions including how fairness, revenge and guilt influence taxpayer decision-making.

Dennis D. Fehrenbacher is a Senior Lecturer in the Accounting Department at Monash University. Dr. Fehrenbacher holds a Ph.D. from Stuttgart University. His research interests include behavioural accounting and the study of how information systems impact individual behaviour.

James Gaa is Professor Emeritus of Accounting in the School of Business at the University of Alberta. Dr. Gaa holds a Ph.D. in Accounting from the University of Illinois at Urbana-Champaign and a Ph.D. in Philosophy from the Washington University in St. Louis. His research interests include business and professional ethics.

Pujawati Mariestha (Estha) Gondowijoyo is a Ph.D. student in the Smith School of Business at Queen's University (Canada). Her research interests include behavioural management accounting, management control and risk management.

George C. Gonzalez is an Assistant Professor of Accounting in the Faculty of Management at the University of Lethbridge. Dr. Gonzalez holds a Ph.D. in Accounting from the University of Pittsburgh. His research interests include behavioural issues in management accounting and information systems.

Irene M. Gordon is the CGA-BC Research Fellow and Professor of Accounting in the Beedie School of Business at Simon Fraser University. Dr. Gordon holds a Ph.D. from Simon Fraser University. Her research interests include financial accounting theory, accounting education and corporate social responsibility.

Lan Guo is an Associate Professor of Accounting at the Lazaridis School of Business and Economics at Wilfrid Laurier University. Dr. Guo holds a Ph.D. in accounting from Washington State University. Her research interests include performance measurement, incentive designs and other behavioural topics in management accounting.

Matthew Hall is a Professor in the Accounting Department at Monash University. Dr. Hall holds a Ph.D. in Accounting from Monash University. His research interests include the impact of management accounting, performance measurement and evaluation, particularly in the nongovernmental and social sectors.

Clark Hampton is an Assistant Professor in the Darla Moore School of Business at the University of South Carolina. Dr. Hampton holds a Ph.D. in Accounting from the University of Central Florida. His research interests include assurance and risk assessment, the use and impact of accounting information systems in organizations. Dr. Hampton has a special interest in examining the appropriate use of statistical methods, especially structural equation modelling.

Frank G.H. Hartmann is a Professor of Management Accounting and Control in the Rotterdam School of Management at Erasmus University. Professor Hartmann holds a Ph.D. from Maastricht University. His research interests are in management control system design.

Jean-François Henri is a Professor of Accounting in the Faculty of Business Administration at Laval University. Dr. Henri holds a Ph.D. in Management Accounting from HEC (Montréal). His research interests include the design and use of performance measurement and management control systems, especially environmental management accounting and eco-control.

Candice T. Hux is a Ph.D. candidate in the Department of Accountancy at Bentley University. Her research interests include auditors' decision-making processes and improvements to audit education.

Jeannine Jeitziner is an Audit Assistant FS with PwC Switzerland. Ms. Jeitziner holds a master's degree in Accounting, Control and Finance from HEC Lausanne.

Radzi Jidin is a Lecturer in the School of Accounting, UNSW Business School at the University of New South Wales. Dr. Jidin holds a Ph.D. from the Australian National University. His research interests are in the areas of judgment and decision-making in auditing and financial accounting.

Jennifer Joe is the Whitney Family Professor of Accounting in the Alfred Lerner College of Business and Economics at the University of Delaware. Dr. Joe holds a Ph.D. in Accounting from the University of Pittsburgh. Her research interests focus on judgment and decision-making in auditing.

S. Jane Jollineau is a Distinguished Professor of Accounting in the School of Business at the University of San Diego. Dr. Jollineau holds a Ph.D. in Accounting from Duke University. Her research interests include the effects of human behaviour on decision-making, financial reporting and auditing.

Kathryn Kadous is a Professor of Accounting in the Goizueta Business School at Emory University. Dr. Kadous holds a Ph.D. in Accounting from the University of Illinois at Urbana-Champaign. Her research interests include judgment and decision-making issues in auditing and accounting.

Steven E. Kaplan is the KPMG Professor of Accountancy at the W.P. Carey School of Business at Arizona State University. Dr. Kaplan holds a Ph.D. from the University of Illinois at Urbana-Champaign. His research interests include behavioural and ethical issues in decision-making involving accounting and tax information among managers, auditors, tax preparers and financial statement users.

William R. Kinney, Jr., is Professor Emeritus of Accounting in the McCombs School of Business at the University of Texas at Austin. Dr. Kinney holds a Ph.D. in Accounting from Michigan State University. His research interests include auditing and financial reporting.

Ethan G. LaMothe is a Ph.D. candidate specializing in Accounting in the Darla Moore School of Business at the University of South Carolina. His research interests include behavioural issues in taxpayer compliance.

Robert Libby is the David A. Thomas Professor of Management in the Samuel Curtis Johnson School of Management at Cornell University. Dr. Libby holds a Ph.D. from the University of Illinois at Urbana-Champaign. His research centres on the interplay among managers' financial reporting decisions, financial analysts' forecasts and auditors' assurance strategies.

Theresa Libby is Ernst & Young Professor of Accounting in the Kenneth G. Dixon School of Accounting, University of Central Florida. Dr. Libby holds a Ph.D. in Accounting from the University of Waterloo. Her research interests include behavioural issues in management accounting and control.

R. Murray Lindsay is a Professor of Accounting in the Faculty of Management at the University of Lethbridge. Dr. Lindsay holds a Ph.D. from Lancaster University. His research interests include statistical issues in accounting research and the role of management control systems in facilitating strategic adaptation.

Anne M. Magro is an Associate Professor of Accounting in the School of Business at George Mason University. Dr. Magro holds a Ph.D. in Accountancy from University of Illinois at Urbana-Champaign. Her research interests include cognition and judgment/decision-making of accountants and users of accounting information, especially tax professionals.

Giocomo Manetti is an Associate Professor in the Department of Economics and Management at the University of Florence. Dr. Manetti holds a Ph.D. in Planning and Control from the University of Florence. His research interests include stakeholder theory, corporate social responsibility, sustainability reporting and assurance, third sector and accounting history.

Mary Marshall is a Ph.D. candidate in the Darla Moore School of Business at the University of South Carolina. Her research interests include judgment and decision-making research in taxation, primarily policy implications related to the behaviour of tax professionals, taxpayers and investors.

Martin Messner is a Professor of Management Control at the University of Innsbruck. Professor Messner holds a Ph.D. from the University of Innsbruck. His research interests include the use of performance measures for strategy implementation, the relationship between financial and strategic objectives in new product development and the evolution of the Beyond Budgeting approach.

Anette Mikes is a Professor in the Department of Accounting and Control at HEC Lausanne. Dr. Mikes holds a Ph.D. from the London School of Economics and Political Science. Her research interests include risk management and control, man-made disasters, social and organizational practices of accounting.

Gary S. Monroe is a Professor of Accounting at the UNSW Business School, University of New South Wales. Dr. Monroe holds a Ph.D. from the University of Massachusetts. His research interests include auditing with an emphasis on auditor judgment and decision-making and the economics of auditing, business ethics, banking, fund management and financial reporting.

Daniel Oyon is a Professor in the Department of Accounting and Control at HEC Lausanne. Dr. Oyon holds a Ph.D. from HEC Lausanne. His research interests include management control with a focus on the importance of formal control systems for business strategy development.

Robin R. Radtke is an Assistant Professor of Accounting in the College of Business at Clemson University. Dr. Radtke holds a Ph.D. from the University of Florida. Her research interests include behavioural and ethical issues in accounting.

Susan Pickard Ravenscroft is the Roger P. Murphy Professor of Accounting in the College of Business at Iowa State University. Dr. Ravenscroft holds a Ph.D. from Michigan State University. Her research interests include managerial accounting and incentives and accounting education.

Jacob M. Rose is a Professor of Accounting at Oregon State University. Dr. Rose holds a Ph.D. in Accounting from Texas A&M University. His research interests include accounting, auditing and governance issues using experimental methods.

Kristian Rotaru is a Senior Lecturer in the Department of Accounting at Monash University. Dr. Rotaru holds a Ph.D. in Economics and a Ph.D. in Information Systems and Risk Management from Monash University. His research interests include behavioural/experimental accounting and finance, risk modelling and decision-making.

Stephen B. Salter is a Professor in the Department of Accounting, Jones College of Business, Middle Tennessee State University. Dr. Salter holds a Ph.D. from the University of South Carolina. His research interests include management accounting and international business.

Steven E. Salterio is a Professor and Stephen J.R. Smith Chair of Accounting and Auditing in the Smith School of Business, Queen's University. Dr. Salterio holds a Ph.D. in Accounting from the University of Michigan. His research interests include corporate governance and the role of the audit committee and external auditor, negotiations between auditor and client management on financial reporting issues and judgmental effects of performance measurement systems.

Janet A. Samuels is a Clinical Associate Professor in the W.P. Carey School of Accountancy at Arizona State University. Dr. Samuels holds a Ph.D. from Arizona State University. Her research interests include accounting information, incentives and motivation issues in managerial contexts.

Kimberly M. Sawers is the Joseph C. Hope Professor of Leadership and Ethics in the School of Business, Government and Economics at Seattle Pacific University. Dr. Sawers holds a Ph.D. in Accounting from the University of Washington. Her research interests include decision-making in the managerial accounting context drawing on theories from accounting, economics, psychology and organizational behaviour.

Axel K.-D. Schulz is a Professor of Accounting in La Trobe Business School at La Trobe University. Dr. Schulz holds a Ph.D. in Accounting from the University of New South Wales. His research interests include design of management control systems and the effects of performance measurement systems and incentive system design on performance.

Linda Thorne is a Professor of Accounting in the Schulich School of Business at York University. Dr. Thorne holds a Ph.D. in Accounting from McGill University. Her research interests include understanding the ethical decisions and decision process of professionals, and in particular professional accountants.

Anis Triki is an Assistant Professor in the College of Business Administration at the University of Rhode Island. Dr. Triki holds a Ph.D. from the University of Central Florida. His research interests are in behavioural accounting, especially nonprofessional investors' judgment and decision-making.

Kim Trottier is an Associate Professor of Accounting in the Beedie School of Business at Simon Fraser University. Dr. Trottier holds a Ph.D. in Accounting from the University of British Columbia. Her research interests include econometrics, mathematical modelling, capital markets and information economics.

Yuepin (Daniel) Zhou is a Ph.D. Candidate in the Goizueta Business School at Emory University. Mr. Zhou's research interests include judgment and decision-making in accounting and auditing.

Section 1
Overview

Introduction

Theresa Libby and Linda Thorne

In 1967, Becker presented the notion of "behavioural accounting" as the application of methods and approaches from the behavioural sciences in investigating the interface between accounting and human behaviour (Birnberg and Shields 1989). Today Behavioural Accounting Research (BAR) can be defined as the systematic observation of people creating, reporting and/or responding to accounting data. Behavioural accounting researchers evaluate behaviours, judgments, decisions, cognitive and physiological responses to accounting information and disclosures individually and in the aggregate.

The field and approaches relied upon by behavioural accounting researchers have expanded in the 50 years since its inception to include theories and techniques adapted from psychology, sociology, ethics as well as economics via behavioural economics. Although historically, the BAR methodology has been considered to be synonymous with the use of traditional psychological experiments, BAR has "moved beyond the lab" as it has evolved to encompass surveys, interviews, case studies, field studies and more recently neuroscientific approaches.

This volume provides a compilation of existing approaches that are used in BAR to provide an archive for experienced and budding researchers. The aim of this volume is to provide an overview of the theories, methodologies and data collection techniques relied upon in BAR. In so doing, we believe that this volume presents an invaluable resource for established researchers seeking a single repository on the current state of BAR methods, debates and relevant literature as well as for graduate students and scholars for their initial introduction and exploration of the array of theories, techniques and methodologies used in BAR.

Content and structure

This volume contains 32 chapters, which are organized into seven thematic sections loosely based upon the structure of the predictive validity framework (fondly known by BAR researchers as "Libby boxes") (See Figure 1.1). We have reprinted Chapter 1 of Libby (1981) (currently out-of-print) due to the prominence and widespread adoption of the ideas expressed in that chapter throughout the field. "Libby boxes" are not only a useful framework for the organization and evaluation of BAR research, but are valuable as an organizing framework for all types of empirical research.

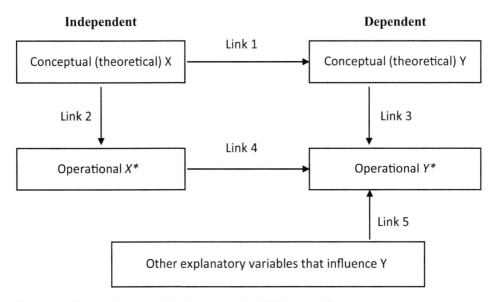

Independent

Dependent

Conceptual (theoretical) X

Link 1

Conceptual (theoretical) Y

Link 2

Link 3

Operational X*

Link 4

Operational Y*

Link 5

Other explanatory variables that influence Y

Figure 1.1   The predictive validity framework (or "Libby boxes")

The Libby framework identifies five key links as being critical to validity in Behavioural Accounting Research design (see Figure 1.1). Link 1 captures the role of theory as the foundation of rigorous research. Theory describes, a priori, the relationship between two variables or constructs: the independent variable that is the catalyst to a causal relationship, and the dependent variable that captures the impact or effect of the causal relationship. Link 2 evaluates the operationalization of the independent variable, which involves an evaluation of how well the measurement of the independent variable captures the theoretical constructs as described in the theory. Link 3 evaluates the operationalization of the dependent variable, which involves an evaluation of how well the measurement of the dependent variable captures the theoretical constructs as described in the theory. Link 4 evaluates the association between the dependent and independent variables and assesses the extent to which the operationalization of the association in the research captures the theoretical relationship as described in Link 1. Link 5 is the assessment of contextual variables and controls, which considers how context and other factors may be unique to a particular study.

This volume is organized consistent with the links in the predictive validity framework as follows. The first section of this volume includes three overview chapters. The first chapter is this Introduction. The second chapter is a particularly important contribution to this volume as it presents William Kinney's framework on how to plan a study. Many of us have already been introduced to "Kinney's three paragraphs" which he uses as an important organizational approach to the initiation of Behavioural Accounting Research. The third chapter is the reprint of the original Libby (1981) chapter as discussed above.

The second section of this volume focuses on Link 1 of the predictive validity framework by presenting an overview of five theoretical perspectives relied upon by behavioural accounting researchers. Chapter 4 describes the BAR literature specifically grounded in the judgment and decision-making (JDM) research based on a cognitive psychological perspective. Chapter 5 describes the foundation and the current state of social-psychological BAR research. Chapter 6 presents an overview of various theoretical frameworks in ethics, morality and philosophy as applied to BAR. Chapter 7 outlines the two dominant sociological theories used in BAR research: stakeholder and legitimacy theories. Chapter 8 describes the dominant economic theory, agency theory, as applied to BAR questions. All five theoretical perspectives have been used extensively in BAR research.

The third section of this volume focuses on Link 2 and Link 3 of the predictive validity framework by identifying how to operationalize the theoretical constructs, which applies to both the independent variable (Link 2) and the dependent variable (Link 3). There are three chapters in this section. Chapter 9 describes how to create valid and reliable measures of accounting constructs. Chapter 10 discusses the development and use of manipulation and attention checks in Behavioural Accounting Research. Chapter 11 examines the impact of and potential controls for social desirability in accounting measures.

Link 4 evaluates the extent to which the operationalization of the relation under study captures the theoretical relationship. It captures both methodological and data analysis choices. More specifically, Link 4 choices include the selection of a study design, choices made in the implementation of a study and data analysis. Accordingly, we have devoted three separate sections of this volume to the choices inherent in Link 4: (a) Link 4a are the study design choices that are considered in the fourth section of this volume; (b) Link 4b are study implementation choices that are considered in the fifth section of this volume and (c) Link 4c are data analysis choices that are considered in the sixth section of this volume.

The fourth section includes six chapters that focus on Link 4a, study design choices. Chapter 12 discusses the potential for diversity in methodological approaches to Behavioural Accounting Research. Chapter 13 examines judgment and decision-making (JDM) research methods and design choices. Chapter 14 illustrates how experimental economics theories and approaches can be applied to BAR. Chapter 15 introduces the complexities and necessities related to survey research. Chapter 16 presents an overview of field research techniques for behavioural accounting researchers, while Chapter 17 specifically discusses the techniques and importance of case study research for BAR. Chapter 18 presents new technologies that have only recently been adopted in BAR. These include MRI imaging, retinal scans and other physiological responses to the presentation of accounting information.

The fifth section includes four chapters that present important considerations for study implementation inherent in Link 4b. Chapter 19 considers ethical aspects of conducting BAR, which includes getting ethics approval, priming subjects and deception. Chapter 20 considers the use of student subjects and introduces Mechanical Turk (MTurk), which is Amazon's computer workforce database that has been increasingly useful in BAR. Chapter 21 introduces the importance of sample size and the notion of power for BAR.

The sixth section addresses Link 4c in five chapters that consider the choices inherent in data analysis of BAR. Chapter 22 outlines preliminary data analysis and data cleansing techniques in BAR. Chapter 23 compares and contrasts the appropriateness of ANOVA as compared to regression in BAR, and considers simple effects analysis. Chapter 24 discusses tests for mediation and moderation, as well as mediated moderation, in BAR. Chapter 25 outlines structural equation analysis and its use in BAR. Chapter 26 presents specialized and emerging multivariate approaches in BAR including cluster analysis, Logit and Probit techniques.

The seventh section addresses contextual controls within Link 5, which considers how context and other factors that may be unique to a particular BAR study impacts validity of the data collected. We specifically include three chapters that consider distinctive contexts in BAR. Chapter 27 specifically considers BAR in the tax context. Chapter 28 presents an overview of specialized considerations for cross-cultural BAR research. Chapter 29 considers special aspects of risk management in BAR research.

The final and eighth section presents three chapters that address publication considerations. Chapter 30 presents a framework and an approach to writing a literature review. Chapter 31 outlines an approach and considerations in writing a BAR article review for a journal. Chapter 32 discusses the importance of replication in BAR. We truly hope the readers will find this volume comprehensive and helpful in their own Behavioural Accounting Research.

References

Birnberg, J.G. and Shields, J.F., 1989, 'Three decades of behavioural accounting research: A search for order', *Behavioral Research in Accounting* 1, 23–74.

Libby, R., 1981, *Accounting and Human Information Processing: Theory and Applications*, Prentice Hall, Upper Saddle River, NJ.

2

Planning for research success by answering three (universal) questions

William R. Kinney, Jr.

So, you have some possible insights about accounting – how the world works, what causes what, or how to fix what's broken. How can you convince others – research consumers and your critics (editors/reviewers/competitors) – that you are right? What evidence must you obtain to convincingly "stress test" your ideas, and how should you write up what you did (and found) and why does it matter?

This chapter can help you as a student or new scholar address these questions using three structured paragraphs. Using the approach, you customize the content of three related paragraphs with defined objectives for efficiently and effectively communicating the essentials of your research. The pre-set objectives are almost universal in that they address questions your readers will be asking. Using the approach helps you *plan what you do* in conducting your own research while you also *plan to be successful* because you will preemptively identify and may resolve some issues likely to be raised by others when they read your work.

We'll support the three paragraphs with a few basic statistical relationships (but omitting proofs and details) and add research concepts I've gleaned from others that can help build your intuition about how to structure and refine your own ideas.[1] There is no rigorous review of philosophy of science or a generic research design template able to accommodate all types of empirical accounting-related research ideas (Kinney 1986, 1992). Also, there is nothing original here, save maybe the combination of the elements – all of which need not appear in every paper.

Instead, the approach is simply a way to help you articulate the intuition behind your implicit research plan, anticipate what others will ask you, and systematically evaluate and improve your chances for research success ex ante. The answers are based on the conceptual thinking underlying four types of operational variables and basic statistics for stress tests, plus five boxes to help you evaluate (and modify as needed) your own plan via a format for assessing research validity or "believability".

You can apply the three-paragraph approach iteratively as your research progresses. Plus, your peers can help you and you can help them by presenting only three short and structured paragraphs to each other – before doing the hard work of implementing the plans.[2] We begin by discussing three universally asked questions about a research project followed by an example to illustrate it and the logic or reasoning behind the approach. The remainder of the chapter provides a checklist for research tasks and matters to include in your writing to assist reader understanding as well as helpful hints and insights.

Three universal questions for translating research

Let's jump right in. If you are at the dissertation stage, someone has probably already asked you three questions: "What are you trying to find out? Why would anyone care about that? How will you do it/what did you find?" These initial questions are natural and commonly asked by those interested in you or in the subject matter. The questions will be asked by reader/consumers, your advisors and other experts who can help you make your research better, your critics who must evaluate and approve of your work and those interested in the results as they relate to their own backgrounds, such as practice, policy setting or their own research. By anticipating the questions, you can prepare a more precise and focused study that keeps your reader on the right track and avoids unnecessary backtracking to explain what you are trying to do.

Your promising dissertation or article idea is about "what causes what" in accounting based on your experiences and knowledge from your courses in accounting, other disciplines and statistics. You've thought about factual data you might obtain to test your idea and possible abstract theories or policy alternatives regarding accounting that explain or predict the relation of one set of facts to another set of facts. An example might be a reasoned prediction of why or how a voluntary or mandated accounting method choice or a change in method would likely affect real-world outcomes such as valuation, performance or perceived risk. You also have ideas about whether to use archival data from a particular domain and time period or from another accounting regime that applies different accounting methods – or whether you'll need to create your own environment in an experiment with perhaps hypothetical accounting treatments and randomly assign participants to a particular treatment.

But how should you put all your ideas on paper in a few well-chosen words? Context and communication are key, and Figure 2.1 outlines the connecting links. The cloud on the left represents what is in your head and the box on the right is the audience with whom you may want to communicate, get advice from and/or convince. Each party has a particular background, expertise and interests. The remarkable thing is, by following the universal format, you can better explain what your research is about so that most readers will understand enough to be able to

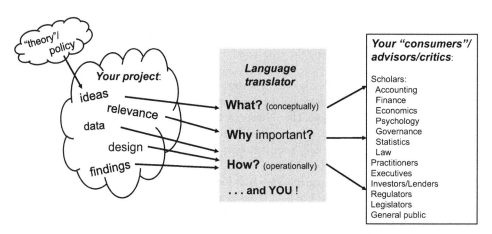

Figure 2.1 Universal research language

assess relevance and research quality – and also advise you how to make it better. Furthermore, the translation attempt may also help you, on your own, to see what's missing!

The communication vehicle is a structured response to the three natural and almost universally asked questions that helps you translate.[3] Responding to the questions will help you cover all bases, and help others help *you* by making the three answers clear. Further, writing the three paragraphs will preempt some of the readers' questions about what you have omitted or left out (because the questions are indeed universal).

The three universally asked questions (summarized in Figure 2.2):

1 **What are you trying to find out?** (What, exactly, is your research question?)

   The response is usually expressed as a theory or policy positing a "causal" connection or relation between conceptual factor (X) that "causes" an effect on another conceptual factor (Y) that may apply across multiple real-world contexts (or $X \rightarrow Y$).

2 **Why is an answer important?** (Who cares about your answer and why should they care?)

   Importance usually depends on the magnitude and direction of δ, the relation between concepts (X and Y) as measured (X and Y) in the context studied, or that can be reasonably generalized or extended to other contexts and settings.

3 **How do you find the answer/what did you find?** (What research method and data do you use, and if available, what are your empirical results?)

   The research methods applied (e.g., experiment vs. archival), the context or setting, and the operational X to measure X, and the operational Y to measure Y as well as the statistical methods used to calculate the covariation of X and Y, other things equal (or $X \rightarrow Y \mid Vs$ and Zs).[4]

If you are like most new researchers, you want to talk about your paragraph 3. Most students focus on paragraph 3 because they feel strongly about the particular experiment or the regression model they want to run. They often ask, "How can I improve my experiment/regression model?" But the best answer for how to improve your operationalization in paragraph 3 depends on what you are trying to find out conceptually as stated in 1, or why it is important to find out as stated in 2. Others will often help you refine paragraph 3 – if they understand your first two.

Paragraph 1 is usually key – if all else fails, try theory. And paragraph 2 is a close second. You know that authors get more scholarly credit for illuminating important theoretical or policy-based ideas that have broad application. So careful articulation in paragraph 1 of what you are

---

1 What are you trying to "find out"?
(does **X** "cause" **Y** to vary) (conceptual)
2 Why is it important to find out?
(effect of X (δ) is large or opposite sign) (operational/conceptual)
3 How do *you* find out/what do you find? (operational)
(sources of X and Y/does X covary with Y|Vs, Zs as predicted?)

Figure 2.2 Three universal research questions

trying to find out – in conceptual or policy terms – is critical to designing your particular experiment or regression to best address the question you want to answer.

Paragraph 2 is the most overlooked by beginning researchers. Ironic, because before you read an accounting research paper, don't you ask yourself (subconsciously), "What's in it for me?" Others do, too, and you can help yourself by telling them what's in it for them. Students usually have pretty good ideas, but don't think through why they are important for others. I've often heard, "Bill, I have a good paragraph 1 and paragraph 3 and *no one has ever examined* the association of *this* particular X and Y combination, but I just can't think why an answer is important – can you help me?" My answer is, "Sometimes."

Sometimes you can reasonably explain why others haven't tested the particular empirical association – because others didn't have the benefit of your new theory or data or design and estimation skills. Sometimes you just need to think beyond the particular context in paragraph 3 and reflect on the broader conceptual implications underlying paragraph 1 to address importance in paragraph 2. That is, apply the dictum: "If all else fails, try theory." In some cases, your subconscious knows the answer and after passage of time, your subconscious will "reveal" the underlying importance – especially if you try hard and take a break as a distractor. But if *you* can't figure out a good reason why your planned research is important for others to read, then you might decide to abort the project as "unlikely to pay off for me because I can't explain why it should be important to someone else".

More important, what's in paragraphs 1, 2 and 3 are needed to articulate and convey *your own unique contribution* to knowledge. Think about it: the only thing you have to sell, your raison d'être, is your unique insight into some slice of understanding for the accounting domain. What is it? What is new and unique – is it your theory, data or estimation (that's about all there is)? Why is it important? Say it short and sweet in a few well-chosen words.

An example using the three universal questions

Now, let's apply the three questions and structured responses to an example that, in three sentences, combines accounting, auditing and professional structure based on Kinney, Palmrose, Scholz (KPS) (2004). The example is an archival study motivated by a late nineteenth-century assertion of the SEC chairman and other critics that "independent" audit firms accept poor quality accounting by their audit clients who also pay the audit firm large consulting fees for non-audit services and audit firms supposedly come to depend on these other fees. As a result, some consulting services for an audit client were proscribed by the Sarbanes–Oxley Act in 2002. So, the "theoretical" basis for predicting a relation of "lucrative consulting fees" to poor financial reporting quality is an authority's suspicion of a dependent behavioural relationship and eventually, an assumption at least implicit in an act of Congress.

Let's see how far the title and structured three-paragraph response approach can take us applying the universal research language in Figure 2.1 (emphasis added).

> *"Auditor independence and non-audit services: Was the US government right?"*
>
> *Kinney, Palmrose, and Scholz (2004)*

> (para. 1) Does an audit firm's *dependence* on fees for financial information system design and implementation, internal audit and certain other services to an audit client reduce *financial reporting quality*?

(para. 2) The answer is *important because* (a) the Sarbanes-Oxley Act presumes so, banning some services to audit clients, and (b) some registrants now voluntarily restrict tax and other legally permitted services, perhaps with adverse effects, and if the presumption is false, then banning or restricting such consulting services may reduce *financial reporting quality* and raise assurance, consulting and enforcement *costs*.

(para. 3) Using confidential fee data from 1995–2000 for 432 registrants subsequently restating their 10-K filings and 512 similar registrants not restating, we find no consistent association between *fees* for financial information system design and implementation or internal audit services with future *restatements*, but find significant positive association between unspecified services *fees* and *restatements* and significant negative association between *tax fees* and *restatements*.

The paper's ten-word title captures some of the research idea and the question of whether the government was right suggests controversy. Setting the stage helps the reader know what to expect in the next few words. So, after reading the title and three paragraphs (but before proceeding), let's have a reality check: Are you skeptical about whether using the three-paragraph approach can possibly help the author articulate the essence of a research project and make the reader more amenable to what follows? If you are, then take five minutes to run in your head two mental experiments posed in the Appendix (one with you as the subject and the other a reviewer at a scholarly journal) and to consider a common alternative presentation format. These three exercises may help your thinking about how the research establishment works – even if you don't like the three paragraphs.

Now let's probe the content and origins of KPS to set up what is to follow. KPS asks a conceptual question about whether an audit firm that depends on fees for certain non-audit services is lax in its audits and allows poor financial reporting ($\mathbf{X} \to \mathbf{Y}$). The answer is important because, as of 2002, federal law effectively presumes so as do some directors, and if the presumption is false, restricting these services may harm all parties. So the question is, what is the sign and statistical significance of the association of non-audit fees with quality? KPS address the conceptual question empirically by relating non-audit fees received by large audit firms (X) that, as of 2002, were not publicly available and hand-collected subsequent financial *re*statement data (Y). We match 432 restating firms with 512 similar non-restating firms (to account for Vs), include a contemporaneous acquisitions indicator (as a Z) and calculate the correlation of non-audit fees and future restatements ($\mathbf{X} \to \mathbf{Y} \mid \text{Vs and Zs}$).

Clearly, the unique feature of KPS is our access to then non-public audit firm fees – and the three paragraphs make this uniqueness apparent (it also was clear to an editor who asked us to consider the *Journal of Accounting Research* for publication).[5]

Research validity assessment using the three paragraphs

Let's drill down on the underlying conceptual and empirical structure of the three paragraphs and our example application. Doing so will allow us to consider five commonly applied measures of research validity summarized as the links in Figure 2.3. Part A of Figure 2.3 is general and is based on Runkel and McGrath (1972) and Libby (1976, 1981, Ch. 1 [appears as Ch. 3 below]). Part B uses the KPS example and the numbered arrows track five validities from Shadish, Cook and Campbell (2002).

Paragraph 1 is based on the presumed cause and effect relation between abstract theoretical concepts or policy prescriptions ($\mathbf{X} \to \mathbf{Y}$), and because the relation is conceptual, its essence

A. In general:

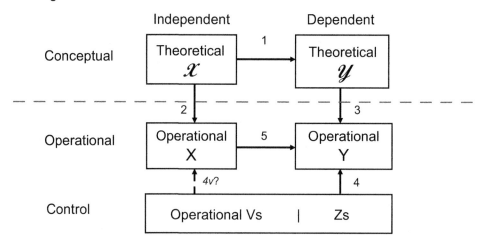

B. KPS example:

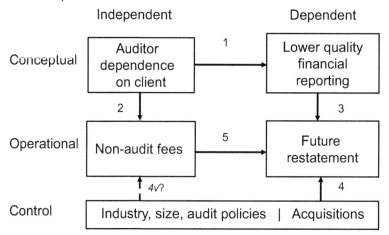

Figure 2.3 Analyze *threats to validity* using predictive validity boxes

may apply to other real-world contexts, locations and time periods. The generalizability of the relation to predict outcomes in other settings determines the *external validity* of the empirical research (Link 1 in Figure 2.4).[6]

Paragraph 2 regarding importance connects the concepts in paragraph 1 and the empirical operations in paragraph 3. The importance of the research is typically reflected by the magnitude of the theoretical implications or consequences of the operational (measured) research outcome (estimate of δ, the effect of X on Y described in paragraph 3 (X → Y, other things equal) to evaluate whether the predicted response 1 (**X → Y**) is supported.

Paragraph 3 characterizes the research method and data used to operationalize "X → Y, other things equal", including the (operational) measures of **X** (denoted X) and **Y** (denoted Y) for

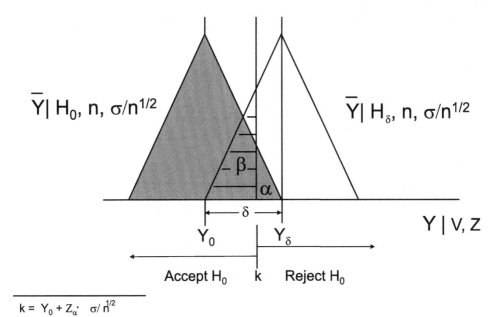

$$k = Y_0 + Z_\alpha \cdot \sigma / n^{1/2}$$

Figure 2.4   Testing H_0 vs. H_δ

the particular research context. The plausibility of choices of how to measure the underlying concepts $\mathbf{X} \rightarrow$ X and $\mathbf{Y} \rightarrow$ Y determine the *construct validity of the cause* (Link 2) and *construct validity of the effect* (Link 3).

Internal validity (Link 4), depends whether the observed correlation or effect on Y is caused by X, i.e., X $\rightarrow$ Y, and not by something else, which, in turn, depends on a research design that rules out or otherwise accounts for possible causes other than X. Timing of measurement is a factor in internal validity. If measurement Y is obtained at t = 1 and X is obtained at t = 0, then $Y_1 \rightarrow X_0$ can be logically ruled out. And factors other than your measured "new cause", X_0, also have a timing aspect. Some other causes of Y_1 may have occurred prior to t = 0 (denoted Vs, subscripted V_{-1}) or at t = 0 (denoted Zs, or Z_0). To increase internal validity, systematic identification of important prior Vs and concurrent Zs can begin by asking conceptual and operational advice from experts in other disciplines such as those listed in the right-hand box of Figure 2.1.

Link "4v?" and its dashed arrow requires some elaboration. KPS didn't include Link 4v, but it's important to consider the question "How did the X get there?" This is a primary distinction between experiments and archival research. The answer for an experimenter may be "I randomly assigned participants to the accounting treatments" and argue that any V effects are randomly distributed among treatments. It is hard for an archival researcher to argue that accounting method choice is random – and still argue that accounting choice is important. An archivalist may have to consider modelling the X choice and perhaps rule out the Vs that may have caused the X choice to better model the effect on Y, perhaps via path analysis.

Finally, *statistical conclusion validity* (Link 5) depends on "doing the statistics right" and includes the study's estimate of the effect size, δ, and its standard deviation (denoted σ) to complete the three related paragraphs (Shadish, Cook and Campbell 2002). If statistical assumptions are met and X and Y are correlated in the direction predicted by your theory ($\mathbf{X} \to \mathbf{Y}$), then belief in your theory is increased, other things equal.

To summarize the role of validity underlying the three-paragraph approach empirically, it "more believable" that $\mathbf{X} \to \mathbf{Y}$ if:

- X and Y are correlated (Link 5: statistical conclusion validity)
- Other-than-X causes (Vs and Zs) are ruled out by design, including (Link 4: internal validity)

  - $Y \to X$
  - X and Y caused by omitted Vs or Zs

- There is reason to believe

  - Y reasonably measures $\mathbf{Y}$ (Link 3: construct validity of effect)
  - X reasonably measures $\mathbf{X}$ (Link 2: construct validity of cause)

- There is reason to believe $X \to Y$ generalizes to other people, times and settings (Link 1: external validity).

Application to Kinney, Palmrose and Scholz

External validity

The conceptual basis for prediction in paragraph 1 is very specific and suggests a causal link between two *theoretical* constructs: X, audit firm *dependence on consulting* fees from audit clients leads to reduced audit quality, and thus reduces Y, *financial reporting quality*. Such a linkage in behaviours might generalize and apply to other audit firm services and apply in other countries. However, the ideas of dependence (and independence) of independent auditors hired by the auditee to attest to the auditee's assertions would seem to have limited generalizability (or validity of prediction) beyond the context studied empirically.

Construct validity of cause and construct validity of effect

Paragraph 3 notes various types of consulting fees (X) and financial restatements (Y) are the chosen measures of dependence and financial reporting quality. As to the cause, "lucrative consulting fees" taken by audit firms were often mentioned in speeches of the late 1990s by critics of audit firms, and particularly by the SEC Chairman. For the effect, there are alternative empirical measures of financial reporting quality, including multiple models of unexpected accruals and issuance of going concern exceptions. But restatements are the only publicly available source for known accounting misstatements that are so egregious that they required restatement of original filings. Thus, there is some construct validity based on logical reasoning.

But there is a further reason for these measurement choices based on what is the best "stress test" to resolve the matter in the minds of others. We choose non-audit fees and restatements because those suggesting the relation would more likely be convinced by empirical tests using these variables. In addition to the SEC chairman's speeches, a senior SEC staff member at the time privately stated a belief that consulting fees (such as tax services fees) from an audit client are correlated with restatements filed with the Commission. Others argued that tax consultations might lead to better audits and fewer restatements – and that buying consulting from their own audit firm might lower total costs. In response, the staff member said something like, "Some professors should get fee data from the firms and run a regression on fees and restatements – I believe they would find a positive correlation."

I took the challenge and enlisted Zoe-Vonna and Suzan because they had restatement expertise and the biggest restatement data file available. I began contacting large audit firms to get audit firm fees for audits and six categories of consulting services to audit clients we selected. Because access to confidential audit firm fees was the main source of KPS's unique contribution, I'll elaborate on dealing with the firms and requesting a substantial investment on their part by providing access to specific and detailed confidential information on a large number of clients.

The responses of the firms were almost identical. Their approximate response was:

> We don't want to provide the data, but we will. We too want to know the answers and we know that releasing our data is the only way to do it. We trust the research team not to break confidentiality with respect to individual clients and we understand and agree that, other than confidentiality, we cannot constrain the research or its outcome.

Again, note the self-interest aspect: the firms were willing to incur the cost of retrieving fee amounts and accept the outcome risk because they believed that knowing the answer to the empirical part of question 3 was in their interest and the interests of others.

Internal validity

Prior research shows that financial restatements (Y) are associated with issuer size, issuer industry and possibly the rigour of the audit firm's policies, other things equal. So, it makes sense to account for these differences. Also, acquisition of a new business component often causes accounting mistakes that require a restatement. Because the data had to be obtained from the audit firms, we selected restatement firm years and matched each by year, industry and audit firm to the non-restatement firm closest in total revenues (Vs) and to account for acquisition effects, we noted acquisitions during the year that was eventually restated (our only Z). Thus, there is reason to believe that the variation in restatement probability (tracked by Y) is due to variation in non-audit fees (X). For example, the consistently observed negative correlation (i.e., $\delta < 0$) between tax-consulting fees and restatements suggests that buying tax advice from the firm's auditor does not reduce and may even improve financial reporting quality.[7]

As to Link 4v for KPS, we did not try to account for why some firms choose to buy non-audit services from their financial statement audit firm and choose to buy a little or a lot. In retrospect, the possible endogeneity should have been considered in evaluating the $X \rightarrow Y \mid Vs$ and Zs link.

Statistical conclusion validity

Paragraph 2 says the KPS question is important because the sign of the ban's actual effect, δ, may be of the opposite sign from that presumed and the ban may thus reduce reporting quality and raise costs. Thus, potentially, the government and others may have been wrong and have, via a misguided presumption, set policy that has the opposite effect from the intent and may also raise total cost of public issuers. KPS did not try to estimate the size of δ, the magnitude of the effect of non-audit fees on the probability of restatement. Thus, we may overemphasize statistical significance for correlation (related to α) and ignore the economic importance of effect magnitude (δ and 1- β regarding power) (Ziliak and McCloskey 2008).

The accounting researcher's problem: α, β, δ, σ, n and planning

To build intuitive understanding of the three universal questions and predictive validity, let's relate them to the researcher's problem in general and to the vexing problems for research about accounting-related topics. A simple illustration will help visualize the empirical elements for Links 4 and 5 as well as the particular risks of an incorrect conclusion about your theory. It uses a regression model consistent with the three paragraphs and five boxes where a dichotomous variable $X_0 = 1$ indicates an observation where the "new" accounting treatment is used, and V_{-1} and Z_0 measure the only other prior and contemporaneous causes of Y_1. The equation regression equation is:

$$Y_1 = a + b X_0 + c V_{-1} + d Z_0 + e.$$ Eq. 1

In Eq. 1, b is δ, the effect of X, c and d are the effects of "other things" on Y_1, and the standard deviation of the e's reflects σ.

For simplicity, assume the researcher (you) is using Eq. 1 to test a simple null hypothesis: H_0: treatment effect = 0 against a simple alternative H_δ: treatment effect = δ. You face and must deal with five variables that are related through a single equation. The variables are:

  α the "risk" that your data (incorrectly) "supports" your new theory,
  β the "risk" that your data (incorrectly) rejects your new theory,
  δ the true (but unknown) size of treatment effect of X on Y,
  σ residual variation in Y, given your research design (e.g., minus V and Z effects), and
  n the available sample size.

The equation combining all five variables can be written with any of the variables on the left side. You, of course, are vitally interested in β, the risk that, even though your theory is correct, the data you obtain will suggest it is incorrect. Putting Z_β on the left yields:[8]

$$\mathbf{Z}_{\beta} = \mathbf{Z}_{\alpha} + \frac{(\delta n^{1/2})}{\sigma}$$ Eq. 2.

where the bold Z_α and Z_β are obtained from a standard normal distribution table. So β will be small when α, δ, and n are large, and when σ is small. Unfortunately, most of us don't even think about β and δ ex ante – but Nature does.

Here is the scholarly researcher's problem: everything but β is fixed or semi-fixed ex ante, so the β for your research may be huge and you won't find out until after you've run your experiment or collected your data. Journal editors cause a "small α" problem by effectively setting it at 0.05 or 0.10 (ask yourself why a self-interested editor would have such a policy). Most researchers face a "small n" problem due to lack of archival data or qualified subjects for participation in experiments. And Nature sets δ, which results in an acute "small δ" problem for accounting researchers because "how the accounting is done" is usually a second-order effect at best,

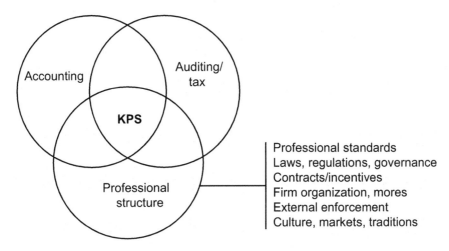

Figure 2.5 Accounting research domain

meaning that the accounting researcher faces a "large σ" problem due to the first-order business, behavioural, regulatory and behavioural effects in the business setting. This makes identification and incorporation of Vs and Zs critical for accounting research studies.

Figure 2.4 diagrams the elements in Eq. 1 and Eq. 2 using triangles to represent normal probability densities. Your research will yield one sample outcome and where it falls along the horizontal axis determines your fate as dictated by H_0, α, k. In this illustration, you can quantify β for when your theory is correct and it appears to be about 0.25 in Figure 2.4. Are you willing to work for a year with a 0.25 risk of failing, even when you are correct? Unfortunately, many accounting studies face β much greater than 0.25. Try redrawing Figure 2.4, but halving triangle heights and doubling their bases (keeping the area constant) and locate the new k. You'll find β is well above 0.50. This is what happens when $\sigma/ n^{1/2}$ is large.

So what can you do? New theories, new estimation methods, new or especially relevant data access can help, as can recognizing new questions and contexts.[9] And given the prime role of σ, so can thoughtful attention to finding new Vs and Zs – perhaps facilitated by knowledge and expertise of the disciplines represented in Figure 2.1 and Figure 2.5 below. Also, you can plan better by at least pondering what might be a reasonable (or the maximum) value for δ – and then draw Figure 2.4 using your δ estimate and flatten or raise the distributional triangles based on prior research or a preliminary sample to approximate your estimate of $\sigma/ n^{1/2}$. Then relocate k and see how β is affected. And, if you can't improve your design, you should think about dropping the research project if β is above, say, 0.30 or 0.40. Don't willingly run costly tests when your β risk is greater than 0.50.

Closing thoughts

Finally, let's think broadly about accounting research and how we can best focus on what our work may add to the mix. The diagram in Figure 2.5 shows intersecting circles comprised of accounting matters, auditing or tax matters, and multiple other factors labelled as "professional structure" within which the accounting takes place. The diagram reminds us that each of the circles are complex and their combinations will be especially so. But mind-numbing complexity is the nature of our chosen beast.

Somehow, we've got to exploit our comparative advantage from knowledge of technical accounting, auditing and tax matters to provide insights within a complex and varied environment. And somehow we've got to explain the uniqueness, importance and value of our work via the editorial review process. This requires effective writing that both translates and explains conceptually what the accounting, auditing and tax complexities mean to the broader audience of non-accounting experts.

The diagram also reminds us that the intersections are likely to be deemed more important to more audiences. KPS was a success, in part, because it combined accounting, auditing and professional structures. Specifically, it used unique data that professional firms willingly provided because they were interested in the result. Also, the diagram also reminds us that professional structures as well as accounting and auditing vary around the world. So, we should think about "elaborating" our theory testing (per R. A. Fisher) to use other contexts to make predictions about what results should be, both positively and negatively if, indeed, our theories describe real-world phenomena.

Finally, to be successful (at least in 2017), you must explain things to others in writing. Writing answers to the three universal research questions – and rewriting them as your thinking develops – is one structured and systematic way to analyze, express and refine your ideas and to quickly evaluate ideas of others.

Notes

1 This chapter is based on my experiences over 50 years. These began when I was studying agricultural research designs and business at Oklahoma State and Michigan State and continued as I taught MAcc and beginning Ph.D. students at Iowa, Michigan and Texas to think broadly and intuitively about how to design, conduct, and evaluate research related to accounting – and the value of communicating efficiently as well as effectively.

2 Readers outside your area (even relatives) can be especially helpful because you must explain the essence of technical matters to someone "outside the box" you inhabit. Briefly reframing your ideas for them may help you see what is unique and important about your project – and maybe help you drop a project with little chance of success.

3 I have used these paragraphs since before 1986 (footnote 23 of Kinney 1986) and believe they work because the method translates what is in your head into what might be called "universal research language", which people listed in the right-hand box of Figure 2.1 can understand in varying degrees and therefore quickly come to a practical conclusion that may help you.

4 "Other things equal" typically means after accounting for prior and other concurrent causes of Y (denoted Vs and Zs, respectively) (Simon and Burstein 1985).

5 After KPS began collecting the fee data, the SEC mandated audit and less aggregated non-audit fee disclosures, starting in 2000. In 2003, based on KPS evidence, the SEC decided not to ban tax consulting under SOX.

6 Link 1 has two roles: initially, it describes the direction of causality hypothesized by the researcher's theory or presumed by a policy setter, and after evaluating links 2–5, it addresses whether the same correlation can be extended to predict outcomes from other contexts.

7 Three of the other four services fees correlations were not significantly different from zero and one, "unspecified services" other than audit-related, tax, internal control, or internal auditing" was sometimes significantly positive.

8 Auditors use a variation of this formula by placing n on the left side to calculate the required sample size to test whether an account is misstated by the "material amount" = δ. For audit use, small δ requires a large n.

9 Irish agricultural economics principle states: "One gets the biggest potatoes on the *first pass* through the field" (at least according to Frank O'Connor, my economist friend at Iowa). The idea is not to search for big potatoes, but to be aware of potentially new fields – that are expected to have new and big potatoes to be found. Keeping up with expanding horizons could be part of your comparative advantage or uniqueness.

10 Also think about using the approach yourself to plan your work (and self-evaluate it), and to write it up to be convincing to your readers. You can also use the approach to "pick out" the essential elements of a research paper for an Accounting Workshop – and do it quickly and easily. You will be able to get a "big picture" view quickly and then can fine-tune as you process details.

References

Kinney, W., 1986, 'Empirical accounting research design for Ph.D. students', *The Accounting Review* 61(2), 338–350.

Kinney, W., 1992, 'Issues in accounting research design education', *Critical Perspectives in Accounting* 3(1), 93–97.

Kinney, W., 2003, 'New accounting scholars – Does it matter what we teach them?', *Issues in Accounting Education* 18(1), 37–47.

Kinney Jr., W.R. and Libby, R., 2002, 'The relation between auditors' fees for non-audit services and earnings quality: Discussion', *The Accounting Review* 77 (Supplement, Quality of Earnings Conference, 107–114.

Kinney Jr., W.R., Palmrose, Z. and Scholz, S., 2004, 'Auditor independence, non-audit services, and restatements: Was the U.S. government right?', *Journal of Accounting Research* 42(3), 561–588.

Libby, R., 1976, 'Discussion of cognitive changes induced by accounting changes: Experimental evidence of the functional fixation hypothesis', *Journal of Accounting Research* 14(Supplement), 18–24.

Libby, R., 1981, *Accounting and Human Information Processing: Theory and Applications*, Prentice-Hall, Englewood Cliffs, NJ.

Runkel, P. and McGrath, J., 1972, *Research on Human Behavior – a Systematic Guide to Method*, Holt, Rinehart, and Winston, Inc., New York.

Shadish, W., Cook, T. and Campbell, D., 2002, *Experimental and Quasi-Experimental Designs for Generalized Causal Inference*, Wadsworth, Belmont, CA.

Simon, J. and Burstein, P., 1985, *Basic Research Methods in Social Science* (3rd ed.). Random House, New York.

Ziliak, S. and McCloskey, D., 2008, *The Cult of Statistical Significance*. University of Michigan Press, Ann Arbor.

Appendix

Two thought experiments and an alternative presentation format

Before analyzing the paragraphs' structure and content, let's have some communication reality checks. I'll start by asking you to run a thought experiment about your reaction to the KPS abstract then a second thought experiment about how a scholarly journal reviewer would react to KPS. This is followed by consideration of an alternative three-paragraph format that parallels many abstracts in journals today.

Your reaction: For you as a first-time reader, do these three *sentences* in KPS give *you* enough information to understand the basic concepts, relations and consequences at issue, why it is important to know the answer, and how the authors go about answering the question as well as what they find? With your background, could you now ask the authors two or three sensible questions – based solely on KPS's title and three sentences? Would you also be willing to read the paper's introduction and perhaps its tables and conclusions for possible interest? If your answers are yes to all three questions, then continue reading.[10]

A scholarly reviewer: Now assume you are a financial reporting expert who has been asked by a scholarly journal's editor to evaluate the entire KPS paper for possible publication. How would you react? It's an honour to be asked, but as an expert you are busy and have your own work to do and a limited time budget for reviews. Most self-interested reviewers want to know answers to the three questions *before* seriously investing in a 40- to 60-page scholarly paper. For KPS, your first impression is from the title and three paragraphs. First impressions matter – have you already come to a tentative conclusion about the quality of KPS? If yes, then your eventual reviewer will likely do the same when reading your title and abstract.

If a paper claims to use reasonable theory to address a matter of practical or theoretical importance/consequences, and also uses new data (as in KPS) or a new estimation method, or an experiment uses especially relevant participants or is cleverly designed to isolate a critical theoretical or policy factor, then the expert reviewer is motivated to give the paper more careful consideration. With such a start, the reviewer's main jobs are a technical review to see if the empirical work is valid and make suggestions for substantive improvement. The author, reviewer, editor and readers all win.

The sequence of responses and outcomes is important because most reviewers who understand what you are trying to find out (para. 1) and believe what you are doing is important (para. 2) will also be willing help you (and the editor) improve para. 3 – maybe tighten the theory, or even suggest other contexts or consequences that could be added. If you don't pose the right questions, then it may be very hard (and too expensive) for the reviewer to decode what you are doing and be able to help you. So, it is in your interest to help yourself by helping the reviewer see value in what you do – and the checklist implicit in the three questions can help.

An alternative format: Now a final reality check. Let's consider an alternative format for the abstract or introduction. A format in common use today reorders the three responses and leaves sorting out issues and putting things together to the whims of the reader. The structure is:

1   I run a regression of [operational X] and [operational Y] and find significant positive correlation.
2   These results are *consistent with* [Insert label] theory that more [conceptual **X**] causes more [conceptual **Y**].
3   The findings have important [unstated] implications for standards setters and regulators.

What's wrong with this format? First, the chosen regression model, data and findings (a) seem to be the starting point for the study and being "consistent with" underlying conceptual theory (b) sounds as it was determined *after* the regression result is known. The study's results precede the conceptual reasoning and readers are left to their own devices to figure out (c), the implications for standard setters and regulators and why the results are important for them.

Using this alternative format, it is possible that the regression you chose may be the best way to test your theory, your results may have huge and specific implications, and you may explain all these important matters later in the paper. But, these critical elements are left for *your reader* to find and assess. Can you depend on the reader to be diligent and figure out what is missing regarding answers to the three questions? Can you afford to take such chances?

3

Accounting and human information processing[1]

Robert Libby

Introduction

Decision behaviour forms much of the basis for general standards of accounting and auditing practice. Consider, for example, such questions as the following:

1   What changes in the income statement and balance sheet accounts would alter a user's decision?
2   How are decisions affected by changes in accounting principles?
3   What internal control attributes affect the auditor's reliance on the overall system?
4   When will standardized procedures improve audit decisions?
5   Will traditional auditing methods be cost effective in detecting fraud?
6   Do "Big 8" accounting firms dominate the decisions of accounting policy boards?
7   Which changes in accounting report format will affect performance evaluations by managers?

The first two questions are of major concern to the Financial Accounting Standards Board (FASB) in its attempts to develop materiality standards and to eliminate accounting alternatives. Questions 3 and 4 are being examined by numerous public accounting firms attempting to improve their audit programs. Questions 5 and 6 form the basis for regulatory action being considered by both Congress and the Securities and Exchange Commission. The answer to the last question has a major impact on the designers of management information systems.

Answers to these questions have traditionally been supported by an informal consensus of practitioners' experience. It is only in recent years that accounting researchers have endeavoured to provide systematic evidence which bears on these basic issues. Researchers have discovered that similar questions have been examined in other disciplines, such as economics, finance and psychology. Those who attempt to answer questions which require descriptions of individual behaviour have turned to a branch of psychology called *behavioural decision theory*, which has its roots in cognitive psychology, economics and statistics.

Given the importance of decision-making in all phases of human endeavour, it is not surprising that a vital literature in psychology has developed.[2] Further, decision-making is being studied in the context of a variety of applied disciplines, such as engineering, law, medicine, marketing and accounting. The goal of much of this work is to describe actual decision behaviour, evaluate its quality, and develop and test theories of the underlying psychological processes which produce the behaviour. In addition, these descriptions reveal flaws in the behaviour and often suggest remedies for these deficiencies.

General framework for analyzing decision-making

The purpose of this chapter is to demonstrate what research in judgment and decision-making[3] offers to accountants. To meet this goal, a very basic question must first be addressed: *Why should accountants be interested in individual judgment and decision-making?* The general answer is that decision-making is an intrinsic part of the current practice of accounting. Decision-making is the basis for the demand for accountants' services and is involved in many of their more difficult duties. First, the demand for the accountant's product, *information*, is generated by those who believe the accounting information will aid them in their decision-making. Investors, lenders, employees, government and the management of a firm are affected by the information choices accountants make. For example, when reports are developed for a manager who makes production-planning decisions, the choice of level of data aggregation, number of periods, report format and accuracy of the information might all affect the decision maker's performance. Since the impact of the accountant's choice will be, in part, a function of how the information is processed by the decision maker, the accountant must learn how users' decisions are made.

Second, accountants themselves are called upon to make countless complex decisions. For example, the accountant must (a) determine the content of reports provided to decision makers, (b) estimate, in the context of giving tax and accounting advice, how different regulations will be interpreted by authorities, (c) decide how to combine the results of various parts of an audit to produce an appropriate audit report and (d) predict the demand for audit services in order to plan personnel needs. The quality of these decisions, among others, will determine the account- ant's success in the marketplace. Whether accountants are concerned with their own or others' decisions, the focus of their concern is on the *improvement* of decisions.

Improving decisions

What, then, are the available options for improving decisions? Figure 3.1 illustrates three basic options:

1   Changing the information (area A).
2   Educating the decision maker to change the way he or she processes information (area B).
3   Replacing the decision maker with a model (area C).

In addition, some combination of these three options might be employed. In Figure 3.1, these combinations are represented by areas D, E, F and G.

Accountants have traditionally tended toward the first approach, changing the information. However, the impact of this option is not unaffected by decisions regarding the other choices. The impact of a change in information will be determined, at least in part, by how the infor- mation is used. Further, the characteristics of the information will in turn affect the way the

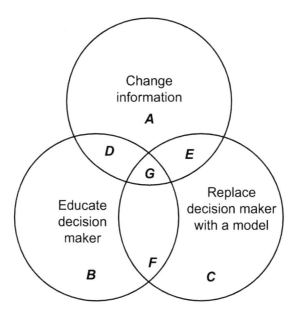

Figure 3.1 Decision improvement options
Source: Libby (1976, Figure 1).

information is processed. Stated more simply, the information set and the method chosen to process the information have an interactive effect on the quality of decisions.

Some would argue that there is no need to understand how information is being used, but on the optimal way different sets of information can be processed and the best combination of information and processing methods. However, before one can decide that a change is necessary, a baseline is needed to measure the incremental benefits of the change. This calls for an understanding of how decisions are currently being made and a measure of current decision performance. Perhaps more important is that knowledge of how decisions are being made highlights flaws and inconsistencies in the process, which are clues to specific methods of improving decisions. Our first step toward this ultimate goal of *improving decisions* is to study a general framework for describing how decisions are made.

A structure for representing decision situations

In most decision-making situations, judgments about the environment must be made in the absence of direct contact with the object or event to be judged. In such circumstances, "most likely" judgments are formed on the basis of information or cues whose relationships to the object or event of interest are imperfect or probabilistic. That is, judgments and decisions are made under conditions of *uncertainty* about the relationships between cues and events. For example, bankers evaluating a loan application must predict whether or not the customer will default on loan payments in the future. They must make this judgment on the basis of such indicators as financial statements, interviews, plant visits and loan history, which both individually and collectively are imperfectly related to the future default-nondefault.

Let us examine a situation of decision-making under uncertainty with which most readers should be familiar – the graduate business school admissions decision. Figure 3.2 presents

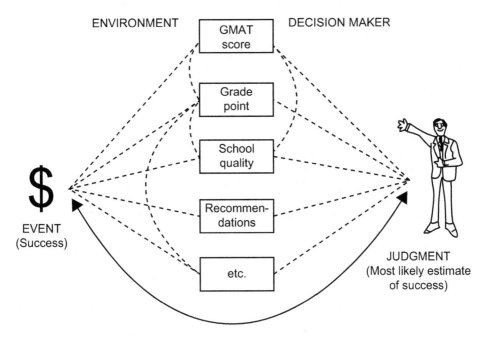

Figure 3.2 The simple lens model

a general structure which highlights the important features of this situation. When making this decision, the admissions committee (decision maker) attempts to predict an applicant's future success as a student and in the job market. Future success will be represented by $. However, the committee cannot judge this future event directly, as it has yet to take place. As in most situations, the decision maker is separated from the event of interest by space or time.

On what basis, then, can this judgment of future success be made? The applicant usually provides a number of cues, including GMAT scores, grade point average (GPA), quality of the undergraduate school attended, recommendations, participation in extracurricular activities and answers to subjective questions. None of these individual cues or combinations are perfect indicators of future success. Some of them, however, may be probabilistically related to this event. In Figure 3.2, these imperfect relationships are denoted by broken lines.

One would also expect that in most cases these cues will come in related bundles; that is, some of the cues will contain information redundant with that provided by other cues. For example, one could speculate that the school quality index will be negatively related to GPA and that GMAT scores will be positively related to both GPA and school quality. In Figure 3.2 the relationships between cues are expressed with broken lines.

On the basis of these cues, the committee will make a rating which indicates their most likely estimate of the candidate's success. The cues will be used to varying degrees, and the relative reliance on different cues is likely to change over time as a result of fatigue, special circumstances, learning and so on. The resulting probabilistic relationship between each cue and the judgment is also represented in Figure 3.2 by broken lines.

The final relationship in Figure 3.2, which will be called judgmental *achievement*, is the focus of our schematic representation of decision-making under uncertainty. The achievement measure comprises two factors: (a) measurement of the accuracy of the judgments and (b) determination of the consequences of any error. The accuracy of the judgments can be measured after the student has completed his or her education by comparing estimated and actual performance. The consequences of the error will be a function of the action or choice which results from the judgment and the decision maker's preferences for outcomes.

To review, the model in Figure 3.2, which is an adaptation of Brunswick's (1952) lens model, portrays the decision maker as (a) being separated from the event of interest by time or space, (b) faced with multiple overlapping cues which are imperfect predictors of the environmental state and (c) probabilistically combining these cues to form a judgment. In effect, the environment is observed through a "lens" of imperfect cues.

The focus of the model is on judgmental achievement. The model suggests that judgmental achievement will be a function of *both* the environment (the model's left side) and the decision maker (the right side). This dual effect implies that a complete understanding of decision-making requires that the decision maker and the environment be studied jointly.

This structure is very general and can be applied to almost any decision-making scheme. Again, consider a simplified commercial lending decision in which the principle task of the loan officer is to predict loan default. Loan default-nondefault is mainly a function of the future cash flows which will be available to the customer to service the debt. The customer provides a number of cues, some of which are probabilistically related to future cash flows. These include indicators of liquidity, leverage and profitability drawn from financial statements, management evaluations resulting from interviews, plant visits, discussions with other knowledgeable parties and outside credit ratings. No individual cue or combination of cues is a perfect predictor of future cash flows, and there is overlap in the information (e.g., credit ratings are closely associated with profitability and liquidity measures). In making this judgment, the loan officer combines these cues into a prediction of future cash flows. Even if the banker's judgmental policy is highly stable over time, some inconsistencies are likely to arise, which will result in a probabilistic relationship between the cues and the final judgment. At the end of the term of each loan, the officer's prediction of cash flows can be compared with the actual event, and any resulting losses can be computed to measure achievement. While this example is highly simplified, it illustrates the generality of the framework and its importance for accountants. The model's principal concern with information-processing *achievement* in an uncertain world coincides both with accountants' interest in *improving* the decisions made by users of accounting information and their more recent attention to the quality of their own decisions.

Basic questions about decision-making

This simplified lens model portrays the individual interacting with the uncertain environment. The relationships in the model suggest the following research questions,[4] which are fundamental to an understanding of decision-making:

1   What information about the event is available to decision makers?
2   How accurate is the information?
3   How is the information combined in forming judgments?
4   How accurate are the judgments?
5   What attributes of the information set, the context and the decision maker affect the quality of the judgment?
6   How might the quality of judgments be improved?

INPUT ⟶ PROCESS ⟶ OUTPUT

I. Information set (cues) II. Judge (decision maker) III. Judgment-prediction-decision

Variables of interest
A. Scaling
   1. Level of measurement
      (nominal, ordinal, etc.)
   2. Discrete or continuous
   3. Deterministic or
      probabilistic
B. Statistical properties of the
   information set
   1. Number of cues
   2. Distributional
      characteristics
   3. Interrelationships of cues
   4. Underlying dimensionality
C. Information content
   (predictive significance)
   1. Bias (systematic error)
   2. Reliability (random error)
   3. Form of relationship to
      criterion
D. Method of presentation
   1. Format (numerical,
      graphical, verbal)
   2. Sequence
   3. Aggregated or
      disaggregated
      (precombination of data)
E. Context
   1. Physical viewing conditions
   2. Instructions
      a) Objective
      b) Costs and rewards
      c) Information about cue
         attributes
   3. Task characteristics
      a) Type
      b) Response modes
      c) Social influences
      d) Uniformity of
         information cues
   4. Feedback

Variables of interest
A. Judge characteristics
   1. Human-mechanical
   2. Number of judges
   3. Personal characteristics
      a) Intellectual ability
      b) Personality
      c) Cognitive structure
      d) Attitudes
      e) Demographics (e.g.,
         age, sex)
   4. Task-related characteristics
      a) Prior experience-stored
         information
      b) Interest and
         involvement

B. Characteristics of decision rule
   1. Form (linear, configural,
      compensatory, etc.)
   2. Cue usage (weighting)
   3. Stability (change-learning)
   4. Heuristics

Variables of interest
A. Qualities of judgment
   1. Accuracy (validity)
   2. Speed
   3. Reliability
      a) Consistency
      b) Consensus
      c) Convergence
   4. Response bias
   5. Predictability
B. Self-insight
   1. Subjective cue usage
   2. Perceived decision quality
   3. Perceptions of
      characteristics of
      information set

Figure 3.3 Classification of information-processing variables

Source: Libby and Lewis (1977, Figure 1)

The first two questions address the nature of the decision environment. Questions 3 and 4 pertain to a particular decision maker's process. Question 5 asks how characteristics of the environment and decision process interact in affecting the decisions. Finally, the last question suggests the goal of applied decision research – improvement in the quality of judgments. The general model presented therefore provides both a method of integrating these questions and a systematic method for structuring decision-related accounting issues.

Each of the preceding questions is composed of subparts, which are presented in Figure 3.3 under the headings of the information set, the decision maker and his or her judgments. Although this listing is not exhaustive, these are many of the subparts or attributes which make up the substance of most accounting research questions. Accountants addressed many questions about decision-making before they began applying behavioural decision theory, but they did not look upon these "accounting problems" as being composed of a series of underlying information-processing variables. Viewing the problem of interest in terms of the underlying variables leads the research to the appropriate psychological theory and evidence which can help to set expectations about what might be found in the accounting situation. Methodologies which have proved useful in similar situations may also be discovered.

Fortunately, psychologists have studied many of the variables in which we are interested, situations very similar to those which characterize the practice of accounting. For example, a number of studies of individual accounting behaviour have examined the impact on decisions of adding supplementary inflation-adjusted information to traditional financial statement presentations (see Dyckman 1975, for a review). Not one of these studies made any prediction about the potential effects of this change. This deficiency can probably be attributed to the failure of the researchers to analyze the alterations in the underlying information environment caused by the accounting change. Had they done so, they might have examined the change in potentially important variables, such as the number of cues, their interrelationships and their predictive ability. Further, the literature suggests that the effects of the change might be mediated by the decision maker's lack of experience with this type of data. These issues have been studied extensively in the multiple-cue probability learning literature. The findings of the psychological research could have helped set the early accounting researchers' expectations, which would have guided them in their conceptualization of the problem and in their experimental design. Further, methodologies which are more suitable for addressing these issues than those used in the early studies have since been developed.

Before the specific approaches to the study of judgment and decision-making are examined, we will make a small investment in discussing the experimental approach to hypothesis testing to illustrate how it relates to other research approaches. This section is of principal interest to more advanced readers. The discussion will aid in an understanding of the strengths and weaknesses of the specific research studies we will later evaluate. In keeping with the purpose of this book, the discussion will be in summary form. Those requiring a more detailed presentation are referred to standard methodology texts, such as that by Kerlinger (1973).

Theory validation

A general framework for theory validation will help to illustrate the research process. This framework is usually called the *predictive validity* model. In its simplest form, a theory specifies relationships between concepts. For example, concept A, intelligence, is assumed to affect concept B, academic achievement. Researchers who might attempt to test this theory are faced with a problem. Neither of these two concepts, intelligence and academic achievement, can be

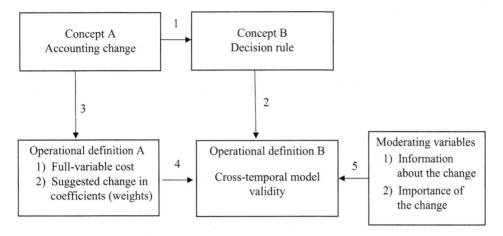

Figure 3.4 Conceptual framework

directly measured, because concepts themselves are not observable. The researcher must therefore develop operational or observable definitions of these concepts. For example, scores on an IQ test might be used as the operational definition of intelligence, and school grades might be used as the operational definition of academic achievement. In addition, the researcher must be concerned with other factors, such as social background, that could affect or moderate the relationship.

Accounting researchers who attempt to test theoretical relationships are faced with the same problems. Figure 3.4 illustrates the conceptual network implicit in a study by Ashton (1976). Ashton hypothesized that decision rules (concept B) would be insufficiently adjusted in response to changes in accounting rules (concept A). He studied this question in a product pricing decision context. The independent variable, change in accounting rule, was operationally defined as a change from full to direct cost inventory accounting, or vice versa. The change in decision rule, the dependent variable, was operationally defined as a change in a certain statistical indicator called "cross-temporal model validity".[5] Ashton also controlled for two moderating variables: information about the change in accounting rules and the importance of the change.

Again, because a researcher can never directly test the relationship between two concepts (Link 1 in Figure 3.4), the theory must be tested by assessing the relationship between the operational definitions of the independent and dependent variables (Link 4 in Figure 3.4). Implicit in this framework are the assumptions that Links 2 and 3, which relate the concepts to the operational definitions, are valid, and that other factors that might affect the dependent variable (Link 5) either have been controlled for or have no effect.

The evaluation of the validity of a study will then be a function of the appraisal of Links 1, 2, 3, and 5. Once it has been determined that a logically consistent theoretical framework is being employed (Link 1), the evaluator should look closely at the ways in which variables are operationalized (Links 2 and 3) and other factors are controlled for (Link 5). If there is a major flaw in the theoretical relationship, or if the operationalization and control are not appropriate, the results of the study are of little value no matter how clever the procedures or how sophisticated the analysis.

Experimental design

Next, the design of the experiment must be considered.[6] The major purpose of experimental design is to arrange observations of effects and causes or treatments so that we can be sure that observed effects are the result of our treatments, thereby producing what is called *internal validity*. In the example in Figure 3.4, the researcher would attempt to arrange observations of decision rule changes and accounting changes to ensure that any changes in the former were caused by changes in the latter. A second important goal of experimental design is *external validity*, or the ability to generalize results beyond the specific tasks, measurement methods and actors of a specific study. Both internal and external validity are affected by how the variables in a study are treated. In any research study, the principal variables of interest can be treated in the following ways:

$X =$ independent variable or treatment. The values of independent variables are established prior to execution of the study. They can either be systematically manipulated, as they normally are in experiments, or they can be measured in natural settings, as they normally are in econometric studies.

$O =$ dependent variable or observation. The dependent variable, which is allowed to vary freely in response to the independent variable, is measured. This is the place in the study where new information is gathered.

The remaining variables in the study can be treated by the following:

$K =$ holding constant. The variable is held constant at one value across all values of the independent variables.

$M =$ matching. Matching assures that the distribution of the variable is equal across levels of the independent variables.

$R =$ randomizing. Randomizing ensures that the distribution of the variable is unbiased or is equally probable across levels of the independent variables.

$Z =$ ignoring (intentionally or unintentionally). Variables are ignored intentionally if we have thought about them and have decided they logically should have no effect.

These six modes of treatment of variables can be used to compare two often-used accounting research approaches: econometric studies and experimental studies. Our framework for

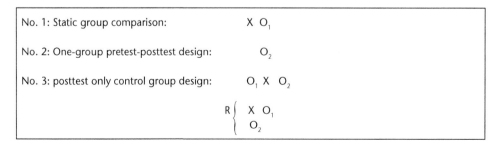

Figure 3.5 Some experimental and quasi-experimental designs
Adapted from Campbell et al. (1963)

Figure 3.6 Design 1: Static group comparison

comparing different experimental designs is based on Campbell et al.'s (1963) scheme. Three of these designs are presented in Figure 3.5.

Most studies of stock-price reactions to actual accounting changes ("efficient markets" studies) use either designs 1 or 2 (see Dyckman, Downes and Magee 1975, for a review). We will first examine design 1, the static-group comparison design as presented in Figure 3.6. In this design, the effect of the treatment variable, the accounting change, is determined by comparing certain attributes of security returns between a group of companies exhibiting one level of the independent variable and a group exhibiting a second level of the independent variable. Note that the *measured* independent variable (*X*) and the observation (*O*) are *not* the only modes of treatment used in these studies. A re-examination of the predictive validity framework depicted in Figure 3.4 will indicate that, while the independent and dependent variables have been specified, we have yet to consider the other potential moderating factors which might affect the dependent variable. How can these remaining variables be treated in a stock-price study? Some may be held constant (*K*); for example, we can decide to consider only firms with certain characteristics (e.g., New York Stock Exchange firms only). The two groups can also be matched (*M*) on certain variables (e.g., size or industry). The remaining variables are treated by *Z*; they are ignored. Often, the decision to consciously ignore certain variables is based upon the results of prior research. Other times, these variables are *assumed* to be randomly distributed across levels of the independent variables. Because it is impractical to hold constant or match many variables, a large number of potentially relevant factors must be ignored in stock-price studies.

Accounting studies using the static-group comparison design face two major problems in determining the effect of the treatment. Each problem creates a competing hypothesis which could explain observed differences in behaviour. First, even before receiving the treatment, the groups may be systematically different on some variables which were ignored or ineffectively matched. This results in what are called *selection biases*. Second, even if the groups are assumed from the beginning to be equivalent, they may experience *differential mortality*; that is, the drop-out rate may be different between the two experimental groups. For example, more of the firms using one accounting method may drop out of a sample as a result of failure or merger.

Many efficient market studies employ a second design, the one-group pretest-posttest design (Figure 3.5, design 2). In this design, the same dependent variable (relating to stock returns) is observed both before and after receipt of the treatment (accounting change) to determine its effect. The variable observed is usually some measure of portfolio returns which is "preobserved" when the portfolio is formulated. This design faces different threats to internal validity, the most important of which, to accountants, is *history*. History becomes a rival hypothesis when other change-producing events occur between the pretest and posttest observations. For example, a change in government regulations may take place contemporaneously with the accounting

Figure 3.7 Design 3: posttest only control group

event of interest. This design would not allow the effect of the accounting change to be disentangled from the effect of the change in government regulation. Other threats to internal validity intrinsic to these designs are discussed by Campbell et al. (1963).

In contrast, laboratory and field experiments investigating individual decisions use a different design. In this case, design 3, the posttest-only control group design presented in Figure 3.7 is commonly used. Note that this design is very similar to design 1, except that variables which are not held constant or matched are not ignored, but are randomized. Instead of *assuming* that other important variables are randomly distributed, such a distribution is assured by randomly assigning participants to the experimental groups. This design eliminates the remaining threats to internal validity. Experiments based on this design also tend to use more of mode *K*, holding moderating variables constant, to simplify the experimental task.

Note the major differences between designs 1 and 2, which are employed in stock-price studies, and design 3, which is used in experimental studies. In stock-price studies, by necessity, a number of variables are treated with mode *Z*; they are ignored. Treating variables in this fashion threatens the *internal validity* of the study. Recent studies of the effects of the new oil and gas accounting standards on drilling companies illustrate these problems. In most stock-price studies, the effects of other potentially relevant events are assumed to be distributed randomly across levels of our independent variable (whether the company used full-cost or successful-efforts accounting before the change). However, mode *Z* does not assure this distribution. In the oil and gas case, there is some evidence that companies with different economic characteristics choose different accounting methods. This produces potential *selection biases*. Events relevant to drillers' stock prices, such as the issue of a new government regulation or a change in oil prices, may have also occurred contemporaneously with the issue of the new accounting standard. In instances where accounting choices and economic attributes may be related, one cannot expect that the effects of these other events will be randomly distributed. As a result, there will be no method for discriminating between the effects on stock prices of our independent variable, the accounting-policy change, and these contemporaneous events. In capital-market studies, however, the treatment variable (*X*) is *measured* in the real world, the actors and context are also observed in the real world and diverse populations are usually sampled (little *K* is used). All these factors minimize threats to external validity.

Alternatively, experimental studies treat many variables by holding them constant and employ a *manipulated* independent variable, which, by its nature, is in part contrived. These practices and questions about the representativeness of contexts and subjects create important threats to *external validity* for experimental studies. However, since variables which are not matched, held constant or treated as independent variables are controlled for through randomization, most threats to the internal validity of these studies are eliminated.

A likely question to arise at this point is "Must *all* potential sources of invalidity, both internal and external, be eliminated for a study to make a contribution?" The answer is "Definitely not." However, given the different strengths and weaknesses of the two research approaches that have been discussed, it should be clear that they are complementary.[7] This complementarity supports the view of research as an interactive process of evidence gathering in which the use of various methodologies with different strengths and weaknesses increases the diagnostic value of the findings.

Notes

1 Originally appeared as Chapter 1 of *Accounting and Human Information Processing: Theory and Applications* (Libby 1981). Reprinted with permission.
2 Hogarth (1980) and Nisbett and Ross (1980) illustrate the breadth of this literature.
3 The terms *judgment* and *decision-making* are often used interchangeably. When distinguished, judgment usually refers to the process of estimating outcomes and their consequences, while decision-making involves an evaluation of these consequences which leads to a choice among the alternatives. Judgment, as well as tastes and preferences, provides the input for decisions. The differences in meaning become more evident as we progress through the book.
4 See Newell (1968) for a more extensive set of questions.
5 This statistic measured the change in a linear representation of the subject's decision process.
6 Campbell et al. (1963) is the primary reference on this subject.
7 Stock-prices studies and individual-decision studies also differ greatly in their goals, as the relationship between individual and aggregate market behaviour is quite complex. This example was chosen only to illustrate the different experimental design problems faced by the two types of research.

References

Ashton, R.H., 1976, 'Cognitive changes induced by accounting changes: Experimental evidence on the functional fixation hypothesis', *Journal of Accounting Research* 14, 1–17.
Brunswick, E., 1952, *The Conceptual Framework of Psychology*, University of Chicago Press, Chicago.
Campbell, D.T., Stanley, J.C. and Gage, N.L., 1963, *Experimental and Quasi-Experimental Designs for Research*, Houghton Mifflin, Boston, MA.
Dyckman, T.R., 1975, 'The effects of restating financial statements for price-level changes: A comment', *The Accounting Review* 50(4), 796–808.
Dyckman, T.R., Downes, D.H. and Magee, R.P., 1975, *Efficient Capital Markets and Accounting: A Critical Analysis*, Prentice-Hall, Englewood Cliffs, NJ.
Hogarth, R.M., 1980, *Judgment and Choice: The Psychology of Decision*, Wiley, New York.
Kerlinger, F.N., 1973, *Foundations of Behavioural Research* (2nd ed.), Holt, Rinehart and Winston, New York.
Libby, R., 1976. 'Prediction achievement and simulated decision makers as an extension of the predictive ability criterion: a reply'. *The Accounting Review* 51(3), pp. 672–676.
Libby, R. and Lewis, B.L., 1977. 'Human information processing research in accounting: The state of the art'. *Accounting, Organizations and Society* 2(3), pp. 245–268.
Libby, R., 1981, *Accounting and Human Information Processing: Theory and Applications*, Prentice Hall, Englewood Cliffs, NJ.
Newell, A., 1968, Judgment and its representation. In B. Kleinmuntz (ed.), *Formal representation of human judgment*, New York: Wiley, pp. 1–16.
Nisbett, R.E. and Ross, L., 1980, *Human Inference: Strategies and Shortcomings of Social Judgment*, Prentice Hall, Englewood Cliffs, NJ.

Section 2

Theoretical perspectives as applied to Behavioural Accounting Research (Link 1)

4

Understanding and improving judgment and decision-making in accounting

S. Jane Jollineau and Mary Parlee Durkin

Introduction

Judgment and decision-making (JDM) research has its roots in cognitive psychology. Cognitive psychology studies how the human mind works, including attention, perception, processing and problem solving. JDM research is interested in *how*, and *how well*, individuals make judgments and decisions (Ashton 1982). Judgments are evaluations or predictions regarding some *target*[1] or event, while decisions are actions that usually follow judgments. For example, an auditor might evaluate the likelihood that a business will continue to exist for the next year and, based on that judgment, decide whether to issue a going concern opinion. Understanding how individuals make judgments and decisions encompasses understanding how an individual searches for information, how information is processed to render a judgment and how judgments translate into decisions.

Although the study of JDM is important in its own right in psychology, it has been adopted by accounting researchers because professionals such as auditors, accountants, managers, analysts, bankers and investors use financial and non-financial information to make important judgments and decisions that affect the welfare of their stakeholders, themselves personally and the economy as a whole. Knowing *how*, and *how well*, these professionals make judgments and decisions helps us understand how these judgments and decisions can be *improved*. Identifying ways to improve judgments and decisions is a key goal of JDM research in accounting (Ashton 1982; Ashton and Ashton 1995; Bonner 2008; Libby 1981).

In this chapter, we begin with a brief discussion of early JDM research. Next, we discuss the concept of *dual processing* and outline how individuals use automatic (*heuristic*) and effortful (*analytic*) processes to make judgments and decisions, and when these processes result in *biased* judgments and decisions. Biased judgment refers to systematic judgment errors as opposed to random errors or missteps. Finally, we consider a framework that classifies judgment errors and suggests how judgments may be improved. We selectively review research in accounting that examines ways to avoid or mitigate these errors, particularly when such errors can result in poor judgments and decisions, and the consequences of poor judgments are important.[2]

Pioneering work in JDM

Early JDM research in accounting began with Ashton (1974), who studied auditors' internal control judgments, and Libby (1975), who examined loan officers' bankruptcy predictions. Their research was inspired by policy-capturing research in psychology that attempted to model individuals' judgments and decisions by examining the statistical relations between input information (i.e., cues) and outputs (i.e., judgments or decisions). Ashton (1974) examined how well auditors processed six cues related to internal control strength by measuring consistency within auditors and consensus across auditors. He found that some auditors exhibited inconsistency in this relatively simple judgment task and that there was not uniform consensus on which cues to use. Libby (1975) also looked at cue usage by asking loan officers to evaluate five ratios for 60 companies, half of which had filed for bankruptcy. His focus was on *how well* loan officers were able to predict bankruptcy as measured by consistency, consensus, confidence and accuracy. He found that loan officers' opinions on how well they performed did not reliably predict their actual performance, indicating that their confidence was misplaced. These early works by Ashton (1974) and Libby (1975) laid the groundwork for JDM research in accounting today.

A second inspiration for JDM research in accounting came from the pioneering work on heuristics and biases by Daniel Kahneman and Amos Tversky in the late 1970s. Their work, summarized in *Judgment under Uncertainty: Heuristics and Biases* (Kahneman, Slovic and Tversky 1982), identifies common cognitive shortcuts, called heuristics, which individuals use to make probabilistic judgments and decisions. The heuristics identified were *availability*, *anchoring* and adjustment, and *representativeness*. Availability refers to the tendency for individuals to use the ease with which something can be brought to mind to guide their judgments about the frequency or likelihood of an event occurring (e.g., buying flood insurance after watching news coverage of floods elsewhere). Anchoring and adjustment refers to the tendency to start an evaluation with an initial belief or data item (anchor) and adjust from that point to a final evaluation. The implication is that different anchors (e.g., the listing price of real estate) can yield different final evaluations (e.g., the assessed value of real estate) even when the anchor is irrelevant or when the information set is identical but presented in different orders. Representativeness refers to the tendency to organize objects or events into categories based on similarity. However, similarity may not be the key attribute, e.g., a whale may resemble a fish more than it resembles other mammals. Although they considered these heuristics to be largely functional and efficient, Tversky and Kahneman (1974) documented systematic and predictable errors or departures from *normative* standards, which they called biases, that result from use of heuristics in certain conditions.

Because concurrent research in many fields, e.g., economics, relies upon the premise that human judgment is generally unbiased, rational and efficient, Kahneman and Tversky's research was initially criticized as being an artefact of using college students and/or lay people who did not face economic consequences for their poor judgments nor any incentive to correct judgment "errors". Behavioural researchers in accounting seized the opportunity to study whether these biases would be found in professional judgments where knowledge is extensive and incentives for high-quality judgments are pervasive. Ex ante, it was far from clear that knowledgeable professionals charged with decisions that involved potentially large economic consequences would exhibit the same JDM biases as the college students and lay people used in Kahneman and Tversky's experiments. Interestingly, early JDM work in accounting revealed that professionals also exhibited these judgment biases although not always to the same extent as found in psychology (e.g., Joyce and Biddle 1981a, 1981b; Burgstahler and Jiambalvo 1986; Moser 1989).

Understanding good judgments and decisions

JDM research from the early 1980s to the late 1990s switched its focus from recognizing deficiencies in judgment to identifying determinants of good judgment, specifically the judgments of experienced auditors and users of financial information. The belief was that by understanding how experts learn to perform, we learn how to best impart that knowledge to less experienced judges and thus improve judgments. Libby and Luft (1993) summarized the contribution of this literature and set the agenda for further research with an equation: Performance $= f$ (Ability, Knowledge, Environment, Motivation). Each element influences performance directly or indirectly by interacting with the other elements. Knowledge mediates the effects of experience on performance (see also Bonner 1990 and Frederick 1991). Ability is directly related to performance and also facilitates the role of knowledge in performance (Bonner and Lewis 1990). The authors exhorted researchers to identify knowledge necessary to complete a task, when and how that knowledge would be acquired and the processes through which it would be brought to bear on the task. They emphasized the need to design research such that it was possible to predict and observe different results depending on whether that knowledge was or was not applied, and to manipulate the task stimuli or context such that predictions could be made about when knowledge would and would not affect performance so that alternative explanations could be ruled out. These recommendations for experimental design became known as "the expertise paradigm".[3]

Libby and Luft (1993) discuss key environmental factors that vary in accounting settings and have been shown to influence JDM, e.g., learning opportunities, guidance and decision aids (technology), prior knowledge, hierarchical group settings and multiple judgments over time. Some of these characteristics change the knowledge required to perform a task, e.g., technology or decision aids, whereas other characteristics influence the level of effort brought to bear on the task, i.e., motivation to perform. Moreover, these factors may interact. For example, Ashton (1990) found that decision aids, feedback, monetary incentives and justification requirements each improved performance in a bond rating task. However, when feedback, monetary incentives or justification requirements were paired with a decision aid, performance did not improve because the decision aid set a performance threshold that constrained the strategies that had been used when only one of the other three factors were in place. Two other papers (among many) that demonstrate the complex nature of the accounting setting on JDM performance are McDaniel (1990), who studied the interaction of audit structure and time pressure, and Glover (1997), who studied the interaction of time pressure and accountability.

System 1 and System 2 processing

By the beginning of the new millennium, JDM research in cognitive psychology had developed considerable consensus on a dual-processing framework for cognition (Evans 2008), more popularly referred to as *System 1* and *System 2* processing (Kahneman 2011; Kahneman and Frederick 2002).[4] Gilovich, Griffin and Kahneman (2002) summarize the application of this framework to the heuristics and biases literature, essentially generalizing it beyond probabilistic judgments to all intuitive judgments and decisions. We believe that the dual systems framework could be useful for understanding current accounting and auditing research and guiding future research (see also Griffith, Kadous and Young 2016), provided it considers the unique features of accounting tasks and the accounting environment. We discuss it next.

The concept of dual processing distinguishes between fast, automatic, unconscious processes (System 1) and slow, deliberative, analytic processes that use working memory (System 2). System

1, often called the heuristic system, provides fast, reflexive, largely functional responses to stimuli based on prior knowledge and beliefs. Examples of System 1 processing are: recognizing someone you know, doing simple arithmetic, stopping at stop signs, completing word pairs such as "bread and . . .". System 2, often referred to as the analytic system, involves logical reasoning. For example, it solves more complex arithmetic problems, searches memory for where we may have seen a somewhat familiar face before, monitors social interactions, and helps us drive on a slippery road or in heavy traffic (Kahneman 2011). Recent research provides evidence that the systems run in parallel and are interdependent (Evans 2006). System 1 suggests default responses (i.e., mental models or plausible hypotheses) based on knowledge and beliefs. System 2 provides shallow analytic monitoring for the faster, more automatic System 1 (De Neys and Glumicic 2008). The intuitive judgments of System 1 are expressed when endorsed by System 2. If conflicts are detected, i.e., System 2 does not endorse the intuitive judgments of System 1, System 2 activates deeper cognitive processing. This processing can override or correct the intuitive judgments of System 1. Errors occur when System 2 (a) does not recognize a conflict, (b) detects a conflict, but the judge/decision maker is unable to inhibit or override the heuristic response of System 1 or (c) makes a judgment error despite cognitive effort. System 1 can have more influence on behaviour when System 2 is cognitively busy. See Figure 4.1.

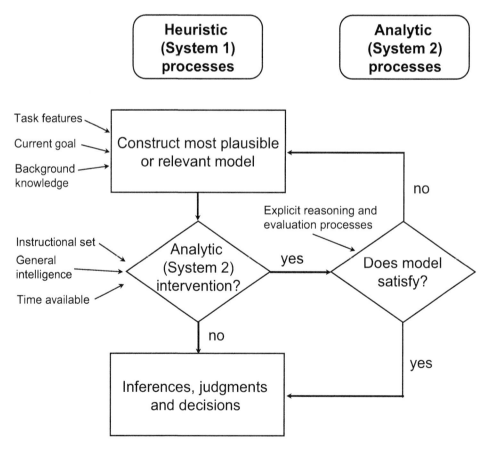

Figure 4.1 Heuristic (System 1) vs. analytic (System 2) cognitive processing

Intervention by System 2 to halt the default response and revise or replace default models depends on the judge, the task and the environment. We begin with discussion of the judge. Working memory capacity and cognitive ability must be sufficient for performance on all tasks. However, capacity and ability levels are not fixed. As individuals learn and practice, some tasks become easier and more automatic, i.e., the judgment process migrates from System 2 to System 1, freeing System 2 for other demands. Individuals also differ in their cognitive style. Some individuals are more intuitive thinkers and are predisposed to accept default responses less critically, while others are more analytic thinkers who tend to evaluate their default responses with explicit reasoning. More intuitive thinkers rely more on System 1's default responses because it subjects the default response to less scrutiny. An individual's goals can also influence the level of analysis brought to bear on a particular task. An individual with high-performance goals in a particular task will rely less on a default response, preferring instead to undertake a critical analysis.

Task and environment features such as importance, time constraints, structure, availability of decision aids and instructions also influence the activation of System 2 when such features stimulate more abstract or logical thinking. And of course, judge, task and environment features may interact. For instance, although System 2 operates more effectively in those with higher general intelligence and knowledge, factors such as stress, distraction and *cognitive load* can undermine System 2's effectiveness, such that increased errors result (Kahneman and Frederick 2002). Time pressure may work against the effectiveness of the relatively slow System 2. A more analytical approach to the problem may be desirable, but generally takes more time.

Some judgment errors resulting from System 1 have been called cognitive illusions because, similar to optical illusions, they are compelling responses to stimuli. For example, consider the well-known Muller-Lyer illusion in Figure 4.2 below. If asked which line is longer, the quick automatic response is the bottom line. However, the lines are virtually the same size, with the bottom line being slightly *shorter*. System 2 may detect a conflict with the automatic response and urge the judge to measure it. More likely however, the judge finds the automatic response so compelling that the act of measuring is deemed unnecessary. Successful suppression of such compelling responses requires effort. Moreover, if the individual were to see the same figure again, say the next day, it would provoke the identical automatic response.

Errors of intuitive judgment in the dual-processing system beg the questions "What features of System 1 create the errors?" and "Why did System 2 not detect and correct the

Figure 4.2 Muller-Lyer illusion

error?" (Kahneman and Frederick 2002). We will first consider System 1 in more depth and then turn to System 2.

What features of System 1 create judgment errors?

System 1 effortlessly accesses our beliefs and knowledge. It also acts on emotion, makes causal connections, deals with concrete and specific concepts and spontaneously evaluates similarity. System 1 often provides intuitive answers to more difficult questions by answering simpler questions. Kahneman and Frederick (2002) call this *attribute substitution*. They consider judgments to be made heuristically when a judge substitutes a heuristic attribute, i.e., one that comes more readily to mind, for the target attribute. This substitution can work well if evaluations of the target attribute correlate highly with evaluations of the heuristic attribute, but this may not always be the case. We provide some examples below of System 1 features that create judgment errors.

System 1 feature: perceiving feelings as information

With System 1, our emotions guide our evaluations and our feelings are often treated as information (Schwartz 2002). The use of feelings as information is particularly likely when feelings are relevant to the judgment at hand. For example, if we are happy when we look at a rental apartment because its high ceilings and large windows make us feel good, and these features are what we value most highly in a living space, this heuristic is functional. The problem occurs when we misattribute feelings that have arisen from some other experience as a reaction to the target, and evaluate the target more (or less) favourably than we would based on the truly relevant factors. If we are attracted to a rental apartment because we smell bread baking in the oven and hear our favourite music playing on the sound system (a trick allegedly used by realtors), we may make a choice based on the positive *affect* (induced by scent and sounds) without placing appropriate weight on more relevant factors (e.g., location, space and functionality).

Kadous, Leiby and Peecher (2013) provide an example of System 1's tendency towards feelings-as-information in a professional context. They find that auditors rely heavily on advice from a colleague they like, regardless of the quality of that advice, but are more discerning regarding advice from someone with whom they have no social relationship. The functionality of *"choosing by liking"* depends on how closely our affective response corresponds to the actual value or utility of the target (Frederick 2002). Problems occur when the affective response (a) is to co-occurring but irrelevant stimuli (hence, the success of advertising), (b) is heightened by familiarity and (c) does not consider other relevant aspects such as reliability, durability or probability. Interestingly, research by Schwartz (2002) has found that happy moods foster heuristic processing (System 1's natural assessments), whereas sad moods foster systematic processing (System 2's analytic processing). Consistent with Schwartz (2002), Cianci and Bierstaker (2009) find that auditors in a negative mood state outperform auditors in a positive mood state on a hypothesis generation task that requires explaining fluctuations in ratios (i.e., System 2 processing). However, auditors in positive mood states perform better on two ethics tasks. Although the authors do not explain this result in terms of System 1's default response, it raises an interesting question about whether our automatic responses are more ethical than our analytical responses.

System 1 feature: substituting an easy question for a difficult question

System 1 also uses *fluency* – the ease with which we perceive our experiences – to influence judgments and decisions. When faced with a question, System 1 spontaneously generates answers and may substitute the question asked for one that can be more easily answered because of associations that come to mind. For example, when evaluating candidates for an assistant professor position, System 1 might respond to the key question "How likely is this individual to be successful?" with a response to an alternative (easier) question "How much did I like the paper she presented?" or "How impressive did I find her presentation?" (Kahneman and Frederick 2002). Likewise, auditors may respond to the key question "Can I trust management to faithfully represent the financial condition of this company in its financial statements?" with a response to the easier question "Has management ever lied to us before?"

System 1 feature: valuing causal reasoning over statistical reasoning

In addition, System 1 will ignore information that does not seem to be causally connected. In his book, *Thinking, Fast and Slow*, Kahneman (2011) observed, "System 1 can deal with stories in which the elements are causally linked, but it is weak in statistical reasoning." Causal interpretations have a stronger effect on our thinking than non-causal information. Statistical *base rates* will be underweighted and are often entirely ignored when there is case-specific information available, unless base rates are clearly related to a causal story. Individuals are also more likely to infer, invent or misremember causal details in order to make a story coherent. For these reasons (among others), eyewitness testimony is inherently unreliable (Bell and Loftus 1989).

We retain a rich and detailed model of the world in our *associative memory*, and System 1 is very adept in distinguishing surprising events from normal or expected occurrences in this world. When surprises are detected, System 1 attempts to find a causal interpretation of the events. Research finds that individuals are willing to generalize from surprising individual cases (anecdotes) and change their view of the world, but they are unlikely to deduce from the general to the specific (Kahneman 2011). For example, we are more likely to conclude that swimming in the ocean is dangerous after we hear stories about recent, but statistically rare, shark bites. In contrast, we find it difficult to believe that, despite a recent shark bite, it is highly likely safe to swim in the ocean today because millions of people swim every day and do not get attacked.

System 1 feature: making spontaneous similarity judgments – the desire to categorize

Similarity judgments are made spontaneously by System 1, and substitute for more difficult judgments of category membership. For example, if asked to name a mammal most individuals would not spontaneously name a whale, although most individuals know that a whale is a mammal. Instead one might say "dog" or "horse" because these are more similar to the prototypical mammal. System 1 forms categories with "normal" or "similar" examples of what would comprise that category. A robin would be a normal example of the bird category, but an ostrich would not. Judging category membership by similarity is largely functional but may lead to *base rate neglect, conjunction errors* and failure to appreciate sample size as many studies have demonstrated (Tversky and Kahneman 1973). Of course, stereotyping is an example of judging by similarity in a social context. The law prohibits hostile stereotyping in hiring, promotion, college admissions, etc., because it leads to undesirable behaviour toward certain groups. Nevertheless, such assessments are the result of System 1, and it takes conscious monitoring and suppression by System 2 to recognize when such judgments are inappropriate.

Auditors have the challenge of resisting similarity substitution much of the time and embracing it other times. For example, auditors must resist the generalization that most accounts are properly stated, that most managers are honest, and that management's explanations can usually be corroborated. They must test account balances and management's explanations with a skeptical mindset, even though the risk of misstatement may be extremely low, ex ante. On the other hand, when auditors find errors, they must generalize. If there is one error, there may be more. Even if an auditor can rule out additional errors of the specific type found, the auditor should project to the population (and not isolate the error) because it is not the individual characteristic of the error that is relevant, but the fact that the error exists (Burgstahler and Jiambalvo 1986).

Why did System 2 not detect and correct the error?

Because System 1 generates default responses based on knowledge, beliefs and emotion, it has difficulty with unfamiliar or novel problems. Complex problems require simulations from the slow, sequential but capacity-limited System 2. System 2 has been described as a "lazy monitor" (Kahneman 2011). Evans (2006) explained this with two principles: the singularity principle and the satisficing principle. The first principle implies that only one model or hypothesis is considered at a time, and this model tends to be biased towards prior beliefs.[5] The second principle implies that System 2 will accept representations from System 1 that are "good enough". Realistically, decisions have to be made without endless scrutiny and analysis of all possibilities. Thus, the consequences of accepting "good enough" representations are occasional endorsements of fallacious inferences in deductive reasoning, *confirmation biases* in hypothesis testing, and other such lapses (Evans 2006). Individuals tend to test one hypothesis at a time with positive test strategies (i.e., look for confirming evidence) and update beliefs as they learn whether the hypothesis considered was correct. If incorrect, a new hypothesis is formed. Most people treat verification and falsification as equivalent justifications for a hypothesis. System 2 accepts the heuristic default from System 1 that cases that *could be* true *are* true. In addition, System 2 does not spontaneously construct counter-examples. So, a hypothesis is accepted until there is compelling reason to give it up. Obviously, when System 2 is stressed, the standard for "good enough" representations may be lower.

Improving judgments and decisions

A logical extension of the research on heuristics and biases in accounting, and in psychology, is the process of debiasing, i.e., the extent to which specific interventions can help to avoid or mitigate judgment errors, particularly when such errors can be costly. Various debiasing frameworks have been proposed in psychology (e.g., Arkes 1991; Fischhoff 1982) as well as in accounting (e.g., Bonner 2008; Kennedy 1993). Although it appears that the burden is largely on System 2 to prevent, detect or correct errors in judgment, using interventions or altering environmental factors can ease this burden and make it more likely that System 1 judgments will be functional (Evans 2008; Kahneman 2011; Kahneman and Frederick 2002).

Fischhoff (1982) proposed that debiasing requires attention to the judge, the task and the interaction of the two. Intelligence and skill are positively correlated with judgment and decision performance. However, judgment can also improve with training, practice and feedback (Bonner 2008). As people acquire more skills, they require less effort to complete tasks that use those skills. Memory holds these skills; System 1 accesses memory to automatically provide intuitive responses that originally required the attention of System 2. For example, when first learning to drive around curves, you have to focus on when to decelerate and brake. However, after some practice, the process becomes automatic and you hardly notice curves in the road. The conditions under which this happens are ideal because you receive immediate and unambiguous feedback. Complex cognitive operations migrate from System 2 to System 1 as proficiency is acquired (Kahneman and Frederick 2002). This migration frees capacity for other tasks that require attention and effort from System 2. Thus, extensive feedback and training may help individuals make better judgments and decisions with System 1. Unfortunately though, many judgments have delayed feedback or none at all and thus are not ideal candidates for learning.

A framework for improving judgments: Arkes (1991)

Arkes (1991) proposed classifying judgment errors as (a) association-based, (b) psychophysically-based or (c) strategy-based. These classifications consider the nature of the error and recognize that different types of errors require different types of remedies. The remainder of this chapter discusses these three types of judgment errors within the context of System 1 and System 2 processing and summarizes select accounting research that examines the correction or avoidance of these judgment errors.

Association-based errors

Association-based errors are caused when associations in memory are activated and influence cognition, but these associations are irrelevant or counterproductive to the task. System 1 effortlessly activates these associations, which for the most part are highly useful. However, the psychology literature is replete with examples of when they are not. *Availability bias, explanation bias, hindsight bias, confirmation bias* and *overconfidence bias* are all association-based errors that can result in poor judgments generated by System 1 processing. System 1 spontaneously links effects to causes, things to properties and things to categories (Kahneman 2011). Therefore, correcting association-based errors requires altering, or redirecting associations, actively or passively. For example, prompting individuals to think about why they might be wrong, or to argue for outcomes that did not occur reduces overconfidence and hindsight bias. This is effective because System 1 makes new associations and creates new causal chains. Ironically, the same processes that create the bias can be used to reduce the bias.

Association-based errors are conceptually similar to what Wilson, Centerbar and Brekke (2002) refer to as "*mental contamination*" – an unconscious or uncontrollable mental process that results in unwanted judgments, emotions or behaviour. In order to correct the contamination, they argue that individuals must be aware the contamination exists, be aware of the direction and magnitude, and have the mental control to adjust their response. Strategies could be pre-emptive or after-the-fact. Pre-emptive strategies would limit exposure to the contaminating information. For example, auditors who must predict account balances in an analytical review could be prohibited from looking at the actual account balance until their expectations are formed. They cannot be influenced by an outcome they have not seen. However, limiting exposure may not be possible. In that case, individuals could employ after-the-fact strategies to resist (prevent encoding), remediate (perform mental operations that undo the bias such as *counterfactual reasoning*) or prevent themselves from acting on their beliefs. System 1 forms associations with contaminated information so quickly and effortlessly that resistance is likely ineffective. Thus, any corrections from individual decision makers would likely have to come from the monitoring, intervention and prohibition aspects of System 2. It is far from clear that individuals appreciate the extent of their association-based errors, and potential interventions may over or under correct the bias. For example, Frank and Hoffman (2015) find that when auditors are informed that their subordinates' judgments are biased by their positive or negative affect towards the client, they seem to rely more on their subordinates' judgments rather than less. The authors refer to this as the "ironic rebound effect" – where judges trying not to rely on information ironically end up relying on it more. As Wilson et al. (2002) say, "contaminated judgments do not smell" thus they are hard to detect and correct. We should worry most about mental contamination when we make decisions with consequences that affect us in important ways.

Correcting or mitigating association-based errors in accounting research

Experimental research in accounting has examined many of the errors classified as association-based errors. In particular, outcome and hindsight bias and confirmation bias have been identified as biases commonly affecting audit professionals, tax professionals and investors. It is important to note that the use of incentives to eliminate association-based errors is ineffective (Arkes 1991). Incentives are unlikely to improve association-based errors because motivated subjects will merely perform the suboptimal behaviour with more enthusiasm. Some experimental studies in accounting that use alternative strategies are summarized next.

Heiman (1990) uses an analytical-review task wherein auditors judge the likelihood that a hypothesized cause of an unexpected fluctuation in the client's financial statements is the correct cause. She finds that when at least two *alternative* explanations for the fluctuation are considered, auditors reduce their likelihood judgments that the hypothesized cause is correct, and a larger number of alternative causes increase this difference. In a similar vein, Koonce (1992) finds that when auditors are instructed to explain why a hypothesized cause may be correct (incorrect) their beliefs in that cause increase (decrease). When asked to explain and then counter-explain, or to counter-explain and then explain, the beliefs are revised downward. Thus, considering other alternatives or thinking about why something might *not* be true does not seem to be spontaneous, but when prompted is helpful for curbing tendencies to accept initial hypotheses uncritically (Lipe 1991).

The debiasing effect of counterfactual thinking can also be accomplished with less explicit intervention. Parlee (2016) uses a simple, non-conscious *prime* to activate a counterfactual mindset, i.e., individuals ponder the "what if" and "if only" aspects of a scenario with more than one potential outcome, to reduce confirmation bias in a subsequent audit task. She primes a counterfactual mindset by using a short story (unrelated to the audit judgment task) that describes an event that nearly occurred. Despite monetary incentives to reward efficiency and induce confirmation bias in the subsequent audit judgment task, the presence of a counterfactual prime appears to foster the search for and reliance on disconfirming information. Presumably, triggering a counterfactual mindset activates System 2 processing, inducing skepticism about the dominant hypothesis and encouraging the consideration of alternatives (Kray and Galinsky 2003; Galinsky and Moskowitz 2000).

Psychophysically-based errors

Psychophysically-based errors occur when individuals map nonlinear physical stimuli on to psychological responses (e.g., how high is your pain on a scale of 1 to 10?). Because extreme stimulus ranges (e.g., very high or very low temperatures, sounds or light) are experienced less frequently, individuals are less sensitive to or less able to discriminate differences at these extremes. For example, when you are extremely cold, you are not sensitive to a one degree fluctuation in temperature. System 1 is again the "culprit" because, while it discriminates remarkably well within the range of stimuli that it most frequently encounters, it does not do well with extreme stimuli that are outside the normal experience. To be able to discriminate fine changes in the extremes would impose tremendous costs on the system.

As with physical stimuli, individuals are also insufficiently sensitive to extremes in non-physical stimuli, e.g., gains and losses in wealth. Kahneman and Tversky (1979) proposed a descriptive theory that captures how individuals respond to changes in wealth when making judgments and decisions. See Figure 4.3. Prospect theory replaces the utility function in normative expected utility theory with value functions that are "S-shaped" over losses and gains. Losses and gains are defined relative to some reference point. The upper part of the "S" captures responses to gains and the lower part of the "S" captures responses to losses. The response to further gains (i.e., moving to the right) flattens out more quickly than a response to further losses (i.e., moving to the left of the reference point). Formally, the value function is concave in gains and convex in losses, and the absolute response to a given magnitude of loss is greater than the absolute response to a given magnitude of gain.

This behaviour leads to predictable "mental accounting" errors that are classed as psycho-physically-based errors by Arkes (1991). For example, individuals who make an expensive purchase, such as a vehicle, often add additional features that cost relatively little in comparison to the price of the car (e.g., floor mats). However, in isolation or when lumped with small purchases, the same individual is far less likely to purchase the item, considering it too expensive or unnecessary. Another example is when individuals continue to invest in losing projects because they have already invested so much that further investment seems relatively minor, and may turn the project around. Individuals find it difficult to ignore past expenditures and consider only the best use of the current investment funds.

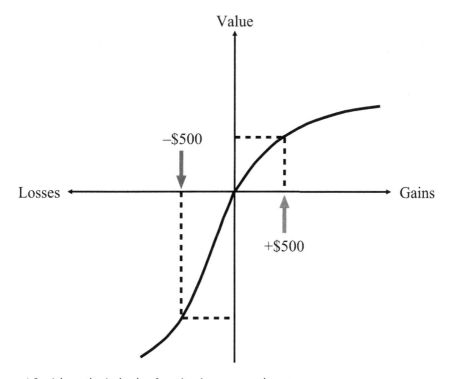

Figure 4.3 A hypothetical value function in prospect theory

Correcting or avoiding psychophysically-based errors in accounting research

Solutions for psychophysically-based errors are to reframe the problem to be within a familiar range, or to reset reference points, so that System 1 can do what it does well. For example, some organizations that try to help with behaviours such as over-eating, smoking and drinking have recognized that resetting reference points with "today is the first day of the rest of your life" help individuals get back on track after they have lapsed on their diets, smoked or taken a drink after a period of sobriety. Similarly, we make resolutions on New Year's Eve in anticipation of a new year, i.e., resetting the reference point to zero.

The "sunk cost" fallacy, a tendency to continue to invest in losing projects in order to justify past expenditures, can by eliminated by changing the reference point from how much has been invested in the past (a large loss) to zero (no loss). At "zero" new projects can be considered and only future cash flows are relevant, allowing better decisions. Professional training and standard procedures can also help avoid some psychophysically-based errors. For instance, an accountant is less likely to fall prey to the sunk cost effect in their professional decisions (although they may still be susceptible in their personal decisions) because they have received specific training and have standard templates for problems that do not incorporate sunk costs, e.g., net present value of future cash flows for capital budgeting (Arkes 1991).

Next, we highlight two experimental studies in accounting that use such strategies. Fukukawa and Mock (2011) examine the effect of framing on auditors' risk assessments. Their participants read financial statement assertions (i.e., existence, valuation and accuracy) that are framed either positively (e.g., accounts receivable on the balance sheet exist) or negatively (e.g., a material amount of accounts receivable does not exist but is included on the balance sheet). They find that auditors who receive negatively framed audit assertions assess the risk of material misstatement higher than auditors who receive positively stated assertions. Thus, audit firm procedures could be framed to elicit the desired audit effort and thereby increase audit quality.

Farrell, Krische and Sedatole (2011) show that when making decisions related to their stock-options, employees commonly anchor on three readily available values, two of which lie below cost (zero value, intrinsic value) and one of which lies above (stock price). They find that a stock option education program that changes employees' focus from simple anchors (reference points) to relevant features that consider the time-value component of their options leads to better decisions. This result is consistent with Arkes's (1991) recommendation that professional training and instruction can provide decision makers with the tools needed to reach more appropriate judgments and decisions.

Strategy-based errors

Strategy-based errors occur when individuals use lower cognitive effort to solve problems that require higher cognitive effort for correct solutions. The lower effort is supplied because the perceived cost of more effort outweighs the perceived benefit of greater accuracy. Individuals are satisfied with this trade-off when the stakes are low. System 1 will supply the low-effort solution, but if accuracy is important, System 2 should intervene and supply the requisite (higher-effort) analysis to arrive at a higher quality response. Of course, a necessary condition is that the decision maker has the ability to solve the problem. To illustrate, in the Cognitive Reflection Test, Frederick (2002) poses a simple problem: *A bat and a ball cost $1.10. The bat costs one dollar more than the ball. How much does the ball cost?* Spend a minute to solve this problem. The intuitive answer supplied by most individuals who are asked this question is 10 cents. It is appealing, effortless and wrong. However, individuals who supply this intuitive answer are likely capable of solving the problem correctly.[6] If we offered rewards for reaching the correct response, we would expect more correct responses for this type of problem. System 2 would be more inclined to check whether the default response fit the two conditions or rules in the problem.

Correcting or avoiding strategy-based errors in accounting research

Monetary incentives can be used to induce effort, which may improve task performance. Bonner and Sprinkle's (2002) conceptual framework posits a positive relation between monetary incentives and greater effort, where greater effort can refer to the direction, duration or intensity of effort, and to strategy development. The latter results in delayed improvements in performance whereas increases in effort direction, effort duration and effort intensity can lead to immediate improvements in performance, provided the judge has the requisite skill to perform the task. Accounting research has examined both monetary incentives and accountability as two potential interventions for improving judgments. We discuss two experimental papers that use these mechanisms next.

Farrell, Goh and White (2014) investigate the extent to which performance-based incentive contracts activate System 2 processing and mitigate the effects of emotion (i.e., affect) on decisions. Using functional magnetic resonance imaging (fMRI), they observed evidence of activity in managers' brains while they made investment decisions that were in emotion-laden or emotion-free contexts under both fixed and performance-based incentive contracts. Emotion was induced by descriptions of colleagues that proposed the investment choices, and pairs of choices were designed so that decisions based on emotion would be less economically desirable. They found greater response in System 1 regions of the brain when emotion-laden choices were introduced compared to when emotion-free choices were introduced. This response of System 1 to emotion is present regardless of performance contract type. Most interesting, they found that the greatest level of System 2 processing, according to the activated region of the brain, was with combined performance-based contracts *and* emotion-laden investment alternatives. The activation of System 2 was greater under the incentive contract when the context was emotion-laden than when it was not, providing evidence that performance contracts induce analytical processing when it is needed most, when affective reactions could be costly. However, the influence of affect on processing and decisions was reduced but not eliminated by the performance incentive.

Increasing the level of *accountability* experienced by the individual is another method for improving judgments when performance is effort sensitive. Kennedy (1993) proposed that individuals who were asked to evaluate a series of evidence items to judge the likelihood that a business would survive would ease the cognitive burden of this unfamiliar task by using a cognitive strategy that results in recency, i.e., the tendency to overweight the latest evidence items (Hogarth and Einhorn 1992).[7] She hypothesized that accountability would motivate participants to use a more effortful strategy to integrate evidence before updating initial beliefs, which would reduce or eliminate recency. Her results were consistent with that prediction. However, she also proposed that accountability would *not* be effective for biases that were not effort related (data-related biases in her framework). She found that outcome bias, an association-based error in Arkes's (1991) framework, was immune to accountability but was reduced with counter-explanation, i.e., explaining why a particular outcome might not occur (Kennedy 1995). The counter-explanation redirected associative networks to other possible outcomes.

Future research

As the dual-process model continues to increase its significance in the broader JDM literature, Griffith et al. (2016) propose questions for auditing research using the dual-processing model. While written for auditing research, we believe these questions could be useful for accounting JDM research more generally. We adapt some of these research questions below and add additional questions to the list:[8]

- What are the likely default responses of System 1 in the accounting-related context?
- Which accounting tasks or judgments of those who use accounting information require System 2 processes? ★
- Are there accounting tasks for which intuitive System 1 responses are more appropriate than System 2 responses, e.g., judging the reliability of others? ★
- How important are individual characteristics in determining accounting judgments and decisions? ★
- Which individual characteristics are crucial to performance quality, e.g., ability? Which accounting-related tasks should be assigned based on characteristics of the judge or decision maker? ★
- For which tasks are performance-related incentives likely to be helpful?
- For which tasks is training likely to be effective?
- How can judges and decision makers be encouraged to avoid relying on invalid System 1 responses? How can judges and decision makers be encouraged or guided to generate the appropriate analytical response? ★
- Do certain aspects of the accounting environment help (or hinder) the judgment process because they invoke (or discourage) System 1 or System 2 processing?
- Are judgments and decisions in the accounting setting overly influenced by the associations that System 1 spontaneously generates? Can these associations be broken or replaced with more appropriate associations?
- Are accounting-related judgments overly influenced by affect in the context of interest? Can (negative) affect be used to stimulate System 2 processing in the particular accounting task or setting of interest?

Conclusions

JDM research has its roots in cognitive psychology and is an important subfield in accounting research. JDM research studies how and how well judgments and decisions are made with a view to improving those judgments and decisions.

Early JDM research in accounting began with Ashton (1974) who studied auditors' internal control judgments, and Libby (1975) who studied the decisions of credit managers. Both were inspired by the policy-capturing literature in psychology and documented that, while professional judgments exhibited consistency over time and consensus across judges, professional judgment could improve.

A second inspiration for JDM research in accounting came from the pioneering work on heuristics and biases by Daniel Kahneman and Amos Tversky. Their work, summarized in *Judgment under Uncertainty: Heuristics and Biases* (Kahneman et al. 1982), identifies common cognitive shortcuts, called heuristics, which individuals use to make probabilistic judgments and decisions. A number of studies in accounting found that while professional judges might exhibit less bias in their judgments, they also relied on heuristics such as representativeness, anchoring and adjustment, and availability, and thus were susceptible to biased judgments that might result (Joyce and Biddle 1981a, 1981b; Burgstahler and Jiambalvo 1986).

In the late 1980s the focus of JDM research in accounting shifted to studying how experienced and expert users of financial information made judgments and decisions. The inputs to good performance were identified as experience, knowledge, ability and motivation. The fit between the judge and the accounting task was emphasized. Aspects of the environment such as monetary incentives (e.g., Ashton 1990; Awasthi and Pratt 1990), time pressure (e.g., McDaniel 1990; Glover 1997), accountability (e.g., Anderson, Kaplan and Reckers 1992; Kennedy 1993; Peecher 1996; Tan 1995), feedback (Ashton 1990), decision aids or technology (e.g., Ashton 1990; Kachelmeir and Messier 1990; Davis and Ashton 2002) and group processes (Solomon 1987) were identified as moderators of performance because they often changed the nature of the task, the motivation to perform, or both.

A recent third wave of JDM research in accounting is inspired by the dual-processing framework (Griffith et al. 2016). The concept of dual processing distinguishes between fast, automatic, unconscious processes (heuristic System 1) and slow, deliberative, analytic processes that use working memory (analytical System 2). Gilovich et al. (2002) summarize this work, which primarily relies on psychology research (Evans 2008; Kahneman 2011; Kahneman and Frederick 2002). The automatic processing of System 1 comes from beliefs and knowledge formed by experience, practice and instruction and relies primarily on memory. System 2 is the "lazy monitor" that decides when more analytic processing is necessary and can override the automatic responses of System 1. However, System 2 becomes compromised by simultaneous demands, noise, fatigue, distractions and stress. The key insight is that System 1 often, but not always, offers the best response. System 2 often, but not always, monitors System 1 and supplies the appropriate analysis when needed. When System 2 fails to detect or prohibit an inappropriate response from System 1, poor judgment or decisions result.

We believe that the dual systems framework is useful for understanding current accounting and auditing research and guiding future accounting and auditing research projects. It generalizes a great deal of the work that preceded its formalization, e.g., the heuristics and biases literature. We stress the importance of applying this within the accounting setting though, i.e., understanding the nature of accounting tasks and the factors that influence JDM in the accounting environment.[9] We believe that the framework offered by Arkes (1991) is a useful complement to the dual-processing framework for determining how to identify and correct deficiencies with System 1 and System 2 processing in accounting contexts.

Finally, we adapt and add to a list of research questions posed for auditing researchers by Griffith et al. (2016) that we believe will be helpful to behavioural accounting researchers in general with respect to this framework. Our intention with this chapter is to assist new researchers that rely on behavioural theories in their examinations of relevant JDM issues in accounting. We encourage researchers to consider the professional judgments or decisions of interest in the context of the dual-process model but we recognize that it is not relevant to all JDM research and that it is not the only framework. However, for many accounting judgments of interest, research could benefit by recognizing the heuristic and analytic processes at work, and identifying what invokes or prohibits these processes. In doing so, we can increase our understanding of JDM in accounting and suggest new methods for improving JDM.

Notes

1 Selected terms denoted in *italics* are defined in the glossary at the end of the chapter.
2 We do not attempt to summarize the JDM research in accounting, which is large and varied, and beyond the scope of this chapter. For an excellent review of JDM in accounting, we refer the reader to Bonner

(2008). We apologize to the many whose work is relevant to our discussion but has not been cited due to space constraints.

3 The expertise paradigm is essentially a set of guidelines for good experimental design (Libby 1989; Frederick and Libby 1986).

4 Because these are dual *processes* and not separate *systems* these labels are somewhat misleading. Evans and Stanovich (2013) encourage researchers to change the names to Type 1 and Type 2 processes. Although we agree with their concern we are reluctant to change that terminology given our audience of doctoral students. Type 1 and Type 2 often refer to errors in hypothesis testing and we do not want to confuse the two. Thus, we stay with the popular terms System 1 and System 2 for these processes.

5 This principle may originate from basic survival instincts. If primitive man hears a rustle in the grass, which potentially signals a dangerous predator or may just be the wind (null hypothesis), a Type 1 error (changing direction or route when there is no predator) is less costly than a Type 2 error (staying in the danger zone when a predator is present).

6 The answer is 5 cents.

7 Interestingly, recency was not predicted for auditors because this task (i.e., judging the ability of a firm to continue as a going concern) was familiar to auditors and thus had migrated to more automatic processing (System 1).

8 Questions marked with an asterisk are adapted from Griffith et al. (2016, p. 4).

9 This is not a call for incorporating mundane realism in accounting experiments but rather exploiting our advantage as accounting researchers in knowing what makes the accounting judgment context unique or different from everyday tasks for individuals in general settings (Gibbins and Swieringa 1995).

References

Anderson, J.C., Kaplan, S.E. and Reckers, P.M.J., 1992, 'The effects of output interference on analytical procedures judgment', *Auditing: A Journal of Practice & Theory* 11(2), 1–13.

Arkes, H.R., 1991, 'Costs and benefits of judgment errors: Implications for debiasing', *Psychological Bulletin* 110(3), 486–498.

Ashton, R.H., 1974, 'An experimental study of internal control judgments', *The Journal of Accounting Research* (Spring), 143–157.

Ashton, R.H., 1982, 'Human information processing in accounting', *Studies in Accounting Research #17*, American Accounting Association, Sarasota, FL.

Ashton, R.H., 1990, 'Pressure and performance in accounting decision settings: Paradoxical effects of incentives, feedback, and justification', *Journal of Accounting Research* (Supplement), 28, 148–180.

Ashton, R.H. and Ashton, A.H. (eds.), 1995, *Judgment and Decision Making Research in Accounting and Auditing*, Cambridge University Press, Cambridge.

Awasthi, V. and Pratt, J., 1990, 'The effects of monetary incentives on effort and decision performance: The role of cognitive characteristics', *The Accounting Review* 65(4), 797–811.

Bell, B. and Loftus, E.F., 1989, 'Trivial persuasion in the courtroom: The power of (a few) minor details', *Journal of Personality and Social Psychology* 56, 669–679.

Bonner, S., 1990, 'Experience effects in auditing: The role of task-specific knowledge', *The Accounting Review* 65(1), 72–92.

Bonner, S., 2008, *Judgment and Decision Making in Accounting*, Pearson Education, Inc., Upper Saddle River, NJ.

Bonner, S. and Lewis, B., 1990, 'Determinants of auditor expertise', *Journal of Accounting Research* 28(Supplement), 1–20.

Bonner, S. and Sprinkle, G., 2002, 'The effects of monetary incentives on effort and task performance: Theories, evidence, and a framework for research', *Accounting, Organizations, and Society* 27(4–5), 303–345.

Burgstahler, D. and Jiambalvo, J., 1986, 'Sample error characteristics and projection of error to audit populations', *The Accounting Review* 61(2), 233–248.

Cianci, A.M. and Bierstaker, J.L., 2009, 'The impact of positive and negative mood on the hypothesis generation and ethical judgments of auditors', *Auditing: A Journal of Practice & Theory* 28(2), 119–144.

Davis, E.B. and Ashton, R.H., 2002, 'Threshold adjustment in response to asymmetric loss functions: The case of auditors' "substantial doubt" thresholds', *Organizational Behavior and Human Decision Processes* (November), 1082–1099.

De Neys, W. and Glumicic, T., 2008, 'Conflict monitoring in dual process theories of thinking', *Cognition* 106, 1248–1299.

Einhorn, Hillel J., and Hogarth, Robin M., 1981, 'Behavioral decision theory: Processes of judgement and choice', *Annual Review of Psychology* 32(1), 53–88.

Evans, J. St. B.T., 2006, 'Dual system theories of cognition: Some issues', Proceedings of the 28th Annual Meeting of the Cognitive Science Society, Vancouver, Canada, www.cogsci.rpi.edu/CSJarchive/proceedings/2006/docs/p202.pdf.

Evans, J. St. B.T., 2008, 'Dual-processing accounting of reasoning, judgment, and social cognition', *Annual Review of Psychology* 59, 25–78.

Evans, J. St. B.T. and Stanovich, K.E., 2013, 'Dual-process theories of higher cognition: Advancing the debate', *Perspectives on Psychological Science* 8(3), 223–241.

Farrell, A.M., Goh, J.O. and White, B.J., 2014, 'The effect of performance-based incentive contracts on System 1 and System 2 processing in affective decision contexts: fMRI and behavioral evidence', *The Accounting Review* 89, 1979–2010.

Farrell, A.M., Krische, S.D. and Sedatole, K.L., 2011, 'Employees' subjective valuations of their stock options: Evidence on the distribution of valuations and the use of simple anchors', *Contemporary Accounting Research* 28(3), 747–793.

Fischhoff, B., 1982, 'Debiasing', in *Judgment Under Uncertainty: Heuristics and Biases*, D. Kahneman, P. Slovic and A. Tversky (eds.), Cambridge University Press, Cambridge.

Frank, M. and Hoffman, V., 2015, 'How audit reviewers respond to an audit preparer's affective bias – the ironic rebound effect', *The Accounting Review* 90(2), 559–577.

Frederick, D.M., 1991, 'Auditors' representation and retrieval of internal control knowledge', *The Accounting Review* 66, 240–258.

Frederick, D.M. and Libby, R., 1986, 'Expertise and auditors' judgments of conjunctive events', *Journal of Accounting Research* (Autumn), 270–290.

Frederick, S., 2002, 'Automated choice heuristics', in T. Gilovich, D. Griffin and D. Kahneman (eds.), *Heuristics and Biases: The Psychology of Intuitive Judgment*, 548–558, Cambridge University Press, Cambridge.

Fukukawa, H. and Mock, T.J., 2011, 'Audit risk assessments using belief versus probability', *Auditing: A Journal of Practice and Theory* 30(1), 75–99.

Galinsky, A.D. and Moskowitz, G.B., 2000, 'Counterfactuals as behavioral primes: Priming the simulation heuristic and consideration of alternatives', *Journal of Experimental Social Psychology* 36, 257–383.

Gibbins, M. and Swieringa, R.J., 1995, 'Twenty years of judgment research in accounting and auditing', in R.H. Ashton and A.H. Ashton (eds.), *Judgment and Decision Making Research in Accounting and Auditing*, Cambridge University Press, Cambridge.

Gilovich, T., Griffin, D. and Kahneman, D., 2002, *Heuristics and Biases: The Psychology of Intuitive Judgment*, Cambridge University Press, Cambridge.

Glover, S.M., 1997, 'The influence of time pressure and accountability on auditors' processing of nondiagnostic information', *Journal of Accounting Research* 35(2), 213–226.

Griffith, E.E., Kadous, K. and Young, D., 2016, 'How insights from the "new" JDM research can improve auditor judgment: Fundamental research questions and methodological advice', *Auditing: A Journal of Practice & Theory* 35(2), 1–22.

Heiman, V.B., 1990, 'Auditors' assessments of the likelihood of error explanations in analytical review', *The Accounting Review* 65, 875–890.

Hogarth, R.M. and Einhorn, H.J., 1992, 'Order effects in belief updating: The belief adjustment model', *Cognitive Psychology*, 24(1), 1–55.

Joyce, E. and Biddle, G., 1981a, 'Anchoring and adjustment in probabilistic inference in Auditing', *Journal of Accounting Research* (Spring), 120–145.

Joyce, E. and Biddle, G., 1981b, 'Are auditors' judgments sufficiently regressive?', *Journal of Accounting Research* (Autumn), 323–349.

Kachelmier, S. and Messier Jr., W., 1990, 'An investigation of the influence of a nonstatistical decision aid on auditor sample size decisions', *The Accounting Review* 65(1), 209–226.

Kadous, K., Leiby, J. and Peecher, M.E., 2013, 'How do auditors weight informal contrary advice? The joint influence of advisor social bond and advice justifiability', *The Accounting Review* 88(6), 2061–2087.

Kahneman, D., 2011, *Thinking, Fast and Slow*, Farrar, Straus and Giroux, New York.

Kahneman, D. and Frederick, S., 2002, 'Representativeness revisited: Attribute substitution in intuitive judgment', in T. Gilovich, D. Griffin and D. Kahneman (eds.), *Heuristics and Biases: The Psychology of Intuitive Judgment*, 49–81, Cambridge University Press, Cambridge.

Kahneman, D., Slovic, P. and Tversky, A., 1982, *Judgment Under Uncertainty: Heuristics and Biases*, Cambridge University Press, Cambridge.

Kahneman, D. and Tversky, A., 1979, 'Prospect theory: An analysis of decision under risk', *Econometrica* 47, 263–291.

Kennedy, J., 1993, 'Debiasing audit judgment with accountability: A framework and experimental results', *Journal of Accounting Research* 31, 231–245.

Kennedy, J., 1995, 'Debiasing the curse of knowledge in audit judgment', *The Accounting Review* 70, 249–273.

Koonce, L., 1992, 'Explanation and counterexplanation during audit analytical review', *The Accounting Review* 67, 59–76.

Kray, L.J. and Galinsky, A.D., 2003, 'The debiasing effect of counterfactual mind-sets: Increasing the search for disconfirmatory information in group decisions', *Organizational Behavior and Human Decision Processes* 91, 69–81.

Libby, R., 1975, 'Accounting ratios and the prediction of failure', *The Journal of Accounting Research* (Spring), 150–161.

Libby, R., 1981, *Accounting and Human Information Processing: Theory and Applications*, Prentice Hall, Englewood Cliffs, NJ.

Libby, R., 1989, 'Experimental research and the distinctive features of accounting settings', in T. Frecka (ed.), *The State of Accounting Research as We Enter the 1990s*, University of Illinois, Champaign.

Libby, R. and Luft, J., 1993, 'Determinants of judgment performance in accounting settings: Ability, knowledge, motivation, and environment', *Accounting, Organizations and Society* 18(5), 425–450.

Lipe, M., 1991, 'Counterfactual reasoning as a framework for attribution theories', *Psychological Bulletin* 109(3), 456–471.

McDaniel, L.S., 1990, 'The effects of time pressure and audit program structure on audit Performance', *Journal of Accounting Research* 28(2), 267–285.

Moser, D.V., 1989, 'The effects of output interference, availability, and accounting information on investors' predictive judgments', *The Accounting Review* 64(3), 433–448.

Parlee, M.C., 2016, 'Can professional skepticism be primed when the incentive structure rewards efficiency?', *Working paper*, University of San Diego.

Peecher, M., 1996, 'The influence of auditors' justification processes on their decisions: A cognitive model and experimental evidence', *Journal of Accounting Research* 34(1), 125–140.

Schwartz, N., 2002, 'Feelings as information: Moods influence judgments and processing Strategies', in T. Gilovich, D. Griffin and D. Kahneman (eds.), *Heuristics and Biases: The Psychology of Intuitive Judgment*, 534–547, Cambridge University Press, Cambridge.

Solomon, I., 1987, 'Multi-auditor judgment/decision making research', *Journal of Accounting Literature* 6, 1–25.

Tan, H., 1995, 'Effects of expectations, prior involvement, and review awareness on memory for audit evidence and judgment', *Journal of Accounting Research* 33(1), 113–135.

Tversky, A. and Kahneman, D., 1973, 'Availability: A heuristic for judging frequency and probability', *Cognitive Psychology* 5(2), 207–232.

Tversky, A. and Kahneman, D., 1974, 'Judgment under uncertainty: Heuristics and biases', *Science* 185, 1124–1131.

Wilson, T., Centerbar, D. and Brekke, N., 2002, 'Mental contamination and the debiasing Problem', in T. Gilovich, D. Griffin and D. Kahneman (eds.), *Heuristics and Biases: The Psychology of Intuitive Judgment*, 185–200, Cambridge University Press, Cambridge.

Appendix
Glossary

Affect.   Affect is negative or positive emotions, feelings or mood (arousal and motivational intensity) associated with stimuli in the decision setting.

Analytic processing.   Logical reasoning or cognition that extends beyond default responses.

Anchor (anchoring).   Anchoring refers to the tendency to rely on an initial belief or data item (the anchor) when making decisions.

Associative memory.   Mental connections between ideas, events and people.

Attribute substitution.   When a decision maker substitutes a cognitively less complex attribute assessment for a cognitively more complex target assessment. An example is substituting grade assessment for intelligence assessment.

Availability bias.   Availability refers to the tendency for individuals to use the ease with which something could be brought to mind to guide their judgments about the frequency or likelihood of an event occurring.

Base rate.   A base rate is the unconditional probability of an outcome based on its occurrence in the population, also referred to as a prior probability.

Base rate neglect.   Failure to appreciate or incorporate the base rate in likelihood judgments.

Bias.   Bias represents a systematic error or departure from normative reasoning.

Choosing by liking.   Judgments are influenced by positive or negative affect.

Cognitive load.   Current demands on a decision maker's mental capacity, which is influenced by stress, task requirements, time pressure and ability.

Conjunction errors.   Error in judgment where the intersection of two events is considered more likely than either event separately, i.e., failure to recognize the $p(A \cap B)$ [$p(A)$ or $p(B)$].

Confirmation bias.   Confirmation bias is the tendency to seek, interpret, overweight or recall information in a way that that supports or confirms one's prior beliefs.

Counterfactual reasoning (counter-explanation).   Counterfactual reasoning occurs when the decision maker considers why alternative outcomes could occur or why a hypothesized cause of an outcome may not be valid.

Debias.   Debiasing mechanisms are ways to mitigate or remove bias in judgments or decisions.

Dual processing (System 1 and System 2).   Dual processing distinguishes between fast, automatic, unconscious processes (System 1) and slow, deliberative, analytic processes that use working memory (System 2).

Explanation bias.   Explanation bias occurs when the process of explaining how the outcome may have occurred makes the outcome seem more likely or more valid to the decision maker.

Fluency.   Fluency is the ease with which a decision maker perceives their real or imagined experiences.

Framing.   Framing occurs when contextual features of the task presentation influence judgments or decisions, e.g., describing probabilities in terms of mortality versus survival.

Heuristic.   A rule of thumb or cognitive shortcut.

Hindsight bias.   Hindsight bias occurs when events are judged more likely or predictable in hindsight than they were in foresight. This may be called "the knew it all along" effect or "outcome" bias.

Mental contamination.   Mental contamination is when a judge is unable to ignore normatively irrelevant information when making a judgment or decision.

Motivated reasoning.   Motivated reasoning is the tendency to interpret or overweight information in a way that that supports or confirms one's preferred conclusion.

Normative.   Normative judgments or decisions are those that are theoretically correct in that they are logically coherent or adhere to normative principles.

Overconfidence bias.   Overconfidence bias exists when one subjectively believes they are more accurate than their objective accuracy merits, i.e., people tend to overestimate performance.

Prime (priming).   Priming occurs when a response is unconsciously stimulated by an earlier prompt, suggestion or stimulus.

Representativeness.   Representativeness refers to the tendency to organize objects or events into categories based on similarity, even when similarity may not be the key attribute in the decision problem. Probabilities of membership or occurrence are based on similarity to a prototype.

Target.   Target is the focus of interest in the judgment or decision setting.

Similarity judgments.   Judging category membership based on how similar the target appears to prominent members of the category.

Sunk cost.   Costs incurred in the past and that are normatively irrelevant to future decisions.

5

Social psychology theories as applied to Behavioural Accounting Research

Steven E. Kaplan, Janet A. Samuels and Kimberly M. Sawers

Introduction

Social psychology focuses on "how the thought, feeling and behavior of individuals are influenced by the actual, imagined or implied presence of others" (Allport 1985: 3). The study of social psychology typically begins with exploration of the self and social psychologists argue that the job of the self is to garner social acceptance and then secure and improve its position in the social group (Baumeister 2010). Thus, how an individual feels about others (e.g., interpersonal affect) or perceives others (e.g., accountability, attribution) may influence that individual's behaviour. In addition, it is important for individuals to be perceived well by others and, as a result, they will act to maintain or improve their own self-perception as well as the perception of others (e.g., accountability, social comparison). Social psychology encompasses a broad and wide ranging set of theories, such that it is not possible to comprehensively cover and discuss the entire field of social psychology in a relatively short chapter. Accordingly, we focus this chapter on the most applicable theories by first getting an overview of the themes found in social psychology, organizing them into broad categories and then examining how these categories and themes have been or could be applied to behavioural accounting. More specifically, in this chapter we focus on four specific subfields within social psychology that have been applied by behavioural accounting researchers:

1 Interpersonal Affect
2 Accountability
3 Attribution
4 Social Comparison.

For each of these subfields we provide a brief discussion of its theoretical underpinnings, an overview of the Behavioural Accounting Research findings and open questions.

Interpersonal affect[1]

Interpersonal affect is defined as an individual's generalized feelings, positive or negative, toward another person (Lobo and Casciaro 2008). Social psychology researchers have been interested in interpersonal affect for decades (Bovard 1951), and researchers in this area generally examine how an affective reaction to another person (e.g., liking or disliking the person) influences judgments and behaviours. Zajonc (1980) was one of the first researchers to contend that affect precedes cognition, and, consequently, affect influences both cognition and behaviour (Isen, Johnson, Mertz and Robinson 1985; Robbins and DeNisi 1994). Robbins and DeNisi (1994) suggest an affect-consistency bias that predisposes individuals to attend to and use information that is consistent with the affect towards a person (e.g., information that confirms the positive or negative affect towards another individual). Interpersonal affect is theorized to influence cognitive processing at the acquisition, encoding, recall and weighting of information stages. For example, during the information-acquisition stage, an individual with positive/negative interpersonal affect towards another person may seek out information consistent with their preconceived perception of another person. Thus, if one has positive affect towards person A, there will be a tendency to seek out information that reflects positively on the person A. During the encoding stage, an individual may disregard information that is not consistent with preconceived affective perceptions as being an exception or not meaningful to the decision or judgment. Thus, if one has positive affect towards person A and acquires information that reflects negatively on person A, there will be a tendency for the information not to be included in the information set or schema about person A. Consistent with this view, research has found that individuals are more likely to recall information about others that is consistent with the affective perceptions they have of others (Murphy, Gannett, Herr and Chen 1986).

Behavioural accounting researchers' interest in interpersonal affect is relatively recent (Bhattacharjee and Moreno 2002; Kida, Moreno and Smith 2001; Moreno, Kida and Smith 2002). Kida et al. (2001) examine capital-budgeting decisions. Participants, in the role of divisional managers, were asked to select one of two proposed capital-budgeting projects. Given the firm's cost of capital, one project's net present value (NPV) was greater than the other project. However, the study manipulated whether the preferred NPV project was submitted by a manager with negative interpersonal affect. As expected, participants' choice was significantly associated with interpersonal affect such that projects submitted by a manger with negative interpersonal affect were significantly less likely to be selected. Moreno et al. (2002) extended this research by investigating the influence of interpersonal affect on risky choices. Risky choices were framed as either gains or losses, which have consistently been found to influence individual decision-making. In contrast, Moreno et al. (2002) predict and find that framing effects on decision-making for risky choices is mitigated by interpersonal affect. Bhattacharjee and Moreno (2002) differ from the previous studies by examining likeability within an auditing decision context and whether experience mitigates the influence of interpersonal affect on auditor judgment.

Because accounting-based scenarios often involve another person, subsequent research has considered a wide range of settings and tasks to examine the influence of interpersonal affect on judgments and decision-making. In this regard, more recent behavioural research on interpersonal affect has investigated the following research settings: subordinate performance evaluation based on balanced scorecard performance reports (Kaplan, Petersen and Samuels 2007), auditors' whistle-blowing in response to another auditor's wrongdoing (Robertson, Stefaniak and Curtis 2011), managers' whistle-blowing in response to a fraudulent act (Kaplan, Pope and Samuels 2015); auditors' inventory obsolescence judgments (Bhattacharjee, Moreno and Riley 2012), and managers' agreement with an internal auditor's financial reporting recommendation (Fanning and Piercey 2014).

Typically, these more recent experimental studies on interpersonal affect are interested in better understanding how interpersonal affect interacts with other task attributes. Thus, these studies are able to contribute to the accounting as well as social psychology literatures. As an example, Bhattacharjee et al. (2012) examine whether and how interpersonal affect and source reliability influence auditors' inventory obsolescence judgments. While they find that interpersonal affect significantly influences auditors' judgments under low-source reliability, interpersonal affect is not associated with auditors' judgments under high-source reliability. Their findings indicate that high-source reliability represents a boundary condition for interpersonal affect. As a second example, Robertson et al. (2011) examine whether and how a wrongdoer's interpersonal affect and performance history influence managers' whistle-blowing intentions. Results from their study show a significant interaction between the two variables such that interpersonal affect influences auditors' intentions to take action against the wrongdoer when the wrongdoer had a poor performance history but not when the wrongdoer had a good performance history.

Interpersonal affect continues to be a promising topic for further Behavioural Accounting Research. For example, behavioural researchers in accounting have not, to our knowledge, considered tax settings. For example, would taxpayers' perceptions of tax evasion differ between likeable and non-likeable peer taxpayers and how might this subsequently influence the individual's compliance with tax law? If so, would other attributes of the tax-reporting environment moderate this relationship? In addition, there has been limited, if any, research by behavioural researchers examining whether and how a senior executive's interpersonal affect influences investors' judgments and decisions. For example, based on prior research, one might expect that a CEO's interpersonal affect would have a stronger influence when the firm's financial performance is weak rather than strong. Further, could interpersonal affect influence cooperation or truthful reporting in a budgeting or managerial context? How might interpersonal affect influence favourable terms within a supply chain? Overall, while behavioural researchers in accounting have begun examining issues related to interpersonal affect, further work is warranted.

Accountability

Lerner and Tetlock (1999: 255) define accountability as the "implicit or explicit expectation that one may be called on to justify one's beliefs, feelings and actions to others". Implicit in this expectation is the idea that individuals know in advance that they will be accountable to identifiable others, and that individuals are motivated to generate explanations and justifications that are likely to be effective to the identifiable others (Tetlock 1983). While individuals are generally able to identify others who they are accountable to, they may or may not know the views of these identifiable others. Accountability theory holds that individuals are likely to increase task-related effort when they do not know the views of the person to whom they are accountable. In this regard, when accountable to someone with unknown views, one is likely to attend to more information and process information more vigilantly. More effort is expected to improve both the decision as well as one's ability to explain and justify the decision.

Initial accountability-related research in accounting by Johnson and Kaplan (1991) and Kennedy (1993) examined settings where the views of the person to whom one was accountable were unknown to participants. For example, in Johnson and Kaplan (1991), auditor-participants in the accountable condition were told that their responses would be reviewed by the researchers in conjunction with staff at the national office and they would then be asked to explain the reasoning behind their judgment in small group breakout sessions. Thus, in this manipulation, participants were accountable to others with unknown views. Under the non-accountable condition, auditor-participants were not told that their work would be reviewed or that they would be asked to explain their reasoning. Johnson and Kaplan (1991) predicted that accountable auditors, relative to unaccountable auditors, would engage in more effort, which in turn, would increase consensus and self-insight among accountable auditors. Results from their study provided support for both predictions. In another example, Kennedy (1993) examined the role of accountability and its timing on the extent to which individuals exhibit an information-processing bias known as the recency effect. She predicted that accountability would mitigate the recency effect, but only under pre-accountability (e.g., participants were told they would be accountable at the beginning of the task) and not under post-accountability (e.g., participants were told they would be accountable after they received relevant task-related information, but before making task-related judgments). Results from her experiment provided support for her hypotheses.

When individuals know the views of the person to whom they are accountable, account-ability theory holds that individuals will shift their views to match the person(s) to whom they are accountable. By shifting their views to correspond to those of their audience, indi-viduals can expect that their views will be easier to explain and justify to the person to whom they are accountable. Tetlock (1985) refers to this tendency as the acceptability heuristic. Lord (1992) provides evidence consistent with auditors applying the acceptability heuristic. Under the accountable condition, auditors were told that they were accountable to the partner in charge of the audit. While participants were not explicitly told the views of the partner, based on participants auditing experience, Lord (1992) contended that conservative behaviour (e.g., recommending a qualified rather than an unqualified audit opinion) would generally be consid-ered more defensible, and consequently, he predicted and found that accountable auditors were more likely to recommend a qualified rather than an unqualified audit opinion.

Subsequently, researchers extended Lord (1992) by explicitly manipulating accountability to include the known views of the accountable audience (Peecher 1996; Tan, Jubb and Houghton 1997; Brown, Peecher and Solomon 1999; Turner 2001; Wilks 2002). This work recognized that auditors generally work for specific known supervisors, and that auditors commonly know the views of their supervisors. As expected, results from these studies generally found that an individual's judgments were shaped by knowing a superior's views before making their own judgment. For example, Peecher (1996) examined the influence of known preferences of the firm ("justifiee preference") on auditors' assessed likelihood that the client's explanation was what substantially caused a non-error account balance fluctuation. Justifiee preference was manipulated as the firm expressing concerns that (a) auditors may not be fully utilizing the client's insights, (b) auditors may not be considering all of the information or misinterpreting the evidence and (c) auditors may not be skeptical enough of client-provided explanations. Peecher (1996) also manipulated client integrity and a requirement to list competing explana-tions. Peecher found that justifiee preferences influenced auditor likelihood assessments that the client-provided explanation was what substantially caused a fluctuation.

Peytcheva and Gillett (2011) examined how learning a superior's views *after* an individual makes his/her own judgment (rather than before) influences his/her recollection of that original judgment. The study had a fixed asset capitalization/expense scenario with three conditions: participants never learned the partner's preferred treatment; participants learned the partner's view in part one of the study (prior to making their own judgment); and participants learned the partner's view in part two of the study after they made their own judgment in part one (but prior to recording that judgment). Part two of the study required participants to write down the judgment that they made regarding the capital expenditures and participants were told that their responses would be reviewed by an evaluative audience. Peytcheva and Gillett (2011) found that participants who learned the partner's views prior to reaching a judgment were influenced by those views; however, they also found that participants who learned the partner's views after reaching their own judgment were subsequently influenced by those views and their reported original judgment was significantly more aligned with the partner's views compared to a control group that never learned the partner's views. The study suggests that "auditor judgment under accountability is also subject to post-decisional malleability" (Peytcheva and Gillett 2011: 298).

The research reviewed so far focuses on accountability with respect to one individual. In contrast, auditors may be accountable to multiple parties (e.g., manager, partner, the firm, the public, the client) which is referred to as "complex accountability" (Gibbins and Newton 1994). A limited amount of auditing research has examined the effects of auditors being accountable to multiple parties (e.g., a client manager and a superior at the auditing firm). Gramling (1999) and Bierstaker and Wright (2001) examine auditors' responses to competing accountabilities – both a within-firm superior and an external source of accountability, client management. Using audit managers as participants who decided on the degree to which the engagement would rely on the work of the client's internal auditors, Gramling (1999) manipulated partner and client accountability preferences (quality versus efficiency/fee pressures). Gramling (1999) found that both client and partner preferences influenced planned reliance on the client's internal audit department; however, there was not an interactive effect between these two sources of accountability. Bierstaker and Wright (2001) had auditors plan the revenue cycle audit with client fee pressure (present or absent) and partner efficiency pressure (present or absent). Bierstaker and Wright (2001) found that auditors reduced total hours in response to client fee pressure and reduced planned tests in response to partner efficiency pressure. They also found that the combined accountability resulted in reduced budgeted hours of more experienced staff which resulted in greater cost savings. Jensen (2004; cited in Nelson and Tan 2005) demonstrates that under conflicting accountability conditions, auditors are likely to spend more time, consult with others and make less extreme decisions. Bagley (2010) manipulated accountability at three levels as follows: no accountability, accountability to a within-firm manager with unknown views, and multiple accountabilities (to a within-firm manager desiring both quality and efficiency, a possible within-firm partner review with unknown preferences and the remote possibility of a Public Company Accounting Oversight Board [PCAOB]-type review). She found that participants with multiple accountabilities experienced greater negative affect compared to participants with no accountability or those accountable to a manager with unknown views.

Finally, accountability research in accounting has considered process accountability in addition to outcome accountability. Process accountability requires individuals to justify their decision-making process while outcome accountability has individuals justify their decision outcome(s) (Lerner and Tetlock 1999). Libby, Salterio and Webb (2004) found that the requirement to justify balanced scorecard performance evaluations to a superior reduced common measure bias compared to no process accountability. More recently, Chang, Cheng and Trotman (2013) found that negotiators held accountable for the negotiation process achieved superior joint performance compared to negotiators held accountable for the negotiation outcome.

Accountability research can involve several different experimental manipulations of accountability including the actual or implied presence of another individual, identifiability of views or performance, assessment of performance and justification or the expectation that they will need to give reasons for what they say or do (Lerner and Tetlock 1999). In auditing research, these generally take the form of a review by a superior, the justification of a decision to a superior and the formal evaluation feedback on their decisions and/or justification. DeZoort, Harrison and Taylor (2006) note that many accounting studies examining accountability use one of these methods. However, DeZoort et al. (2006) suggested that these are increasing levels of accountability and the effects of each accountability level may differ. In their study, auditors had two materiality tasks and those with either justification or feedback requirements provided more conservative materiality judgments compared to auditors with only review or no accountability.

DeZoort et al. (2006) also found that the amount of time spent on the task, and the amount of explanation and consideration of qualitative factors all increased as accountability pressure increased (from no accountability to review to justification to feedback).

Accountability, the expectation that one may be called on to justify one's beliefs or actions to others, shares some similarity to other social psychology constructs such as social identity and social norms. Social identity theory (Tajfel and Turner 1985) posits that individuals organize themselves and others into social categories or groups (in-group and out-group). The theory further posits that all members of the in-group are perceived to be more similar and are liked more than members of the out-group. Group members are more likely to internalize the groups' norms and values as well as be more accepting of group members' positions. While accountability can influence an individual's judgment based on the expectation of justifying oneself to others, social identity can influence an individual's judgment based on perceived group identity or affiliation. Thus, who an individual is accountable to is important. For example, studies have found that auditors who identify with a client develop elevated and perhaps unwarranted trust of the client (King 2002) and are more likely to acquiesce to a client-preferred position (Bamber and Iyer 2007; Bauer 2015). However, this client bias has been found to be neutralized when auditors belong to or identify with another group, such as with an audit firm or professional group, that creates social pressure to conform to the group's norms (King 2002; Bamber and Iyer 2007; Bauer 2015).

Social norms are characterized as "rules and standards that are understood by members of a group, and that guide and/or constrain social behavior without the force of laws" (Cialdini and Trost 1998: 152). Similar to accountability, social norms can affect behaviour and decision-making because individuals tend to seek the respect of others as well as avoid social stigma of non-compliance. While the field of accounting is dominated by standards and laws (tax), social norms can still influence the level of compliance, honest reporting and opportunistic behaviour. For example, studies related to tax compliance have found that individual behaviour/ethical beliefs and the perceptions about the expectations of close others directly influence tax compliance decisions (Bobek, Hageman and Kelliher 2013; Blanthorne and Kaplan 2008; Lui 2014). Social norms can also influence behaviour within managerial settings such as the choice of negotiation strategies (Fisher, Frederickson and Peffer 2000), creation of budgetary slack (Stevens 2002; Hobson, Mellon and Stevens 2011), and the level of honest reporting (Evans, Hannan, Krishnan and Moser 2001; Hannan, Rankin and Towry 2006; Maas and Van Rinsum 2013).

There are rich opportunities for further research related to accountability, social identity and social norms within accounting. Teams and groups are increasingly important in business and accounting decision-making and, as such, understanding how team/group identity and accountability might influence various outcomes is encouraged. For example, how might group membership (department team versus cross-functional team) and/or perceptions of accountability influence creation of budgetary slack? Further, how might accountability and/or social norms serve to mitigate opportunistic behaviour? Or, how might accountability and/or social norms influence corporate culture, tone at the top, adoption of voluntary disclosure, organizational citizenship or pro-social behaviour?

Attribution

Attribution theory is about how people explain and respond to events that involve their own and others' behaviour (Heider 1958). Thus, attribution theory is used to examine how an individual's observations about another's behaviour affects their beliefs about why the behaviour occurred and how those beliefs affect the individual's subsequent actions. Attribution theory holds that individuals are motivated to better understand the causal structure of their environment, and consequently, seek information in an effort to better understand why events have occurred (Kelley 1973). Individuals make causal attributions by rationally interpreting and analyzing information about what has happened and why. Attribution theory applies to events and behaviours in which causality is uncertain, which is generally the case for most accounting-related events and behaviours. Broadly speaking, attribution theory views individuals as engaging in a process that ascribes cause along a continuum with two end points: dispositional causes on one end (e.g., something internal to the individual, such as ability, skill or effort) and situational causes on the other end (e.g., something external to the individual, such as task difficulty, environmental circumstances or other people) (Heider 1958). Further, attribution theory identifies three types of information individuals use to make causal attributions: consistency information, distinctiveness information and consensus information (Kelley 1967). Consistency and distinctiveness information refer to whether an individual's current behaviour is similar to or different from the individual's behaviour in the past on similar and different tasks, respectively. Consensus information refers to whether the individual's current behaviour is similar to or different from the behaviour of others on the same or similar task.

Ross (1977: 183) identified the "fundamental attribution error", which he defined as "the tendency for attributors to underestimate the impact of situational factors and to overestimate the role of dispositional factors in controlling behavior." For example, using an attitude-attribution paradigm, participants are presented with written or spoken opinion statements that they are told have been made by another person under conditions of high or low choice (e.g., Jones and Harris 1967; Jones, Riggs and Quattrone 1979). In these studies, participants attribute a significant degree of alignment between the opinion statement and the person's perceived actual attitude even when participants are informed that the other person had low (or no) choice in choosing that opinion.

Jones and Nisbett (1971) identified what they refer to as the "actor-observer difference". As proposed, "pervasive and systematic differences distinguish how one attributes causality to one's own actions from how one attributes it to another's identical behavior" (Watson 1982: 682). While individuals exhibit the fundamental attribution error when explaining either their own or others' behaviour, the fundamental attribution error is substantially stronger when explaining others' behaviour. An individual is in the role of actor when explaining one's own behaviour and in the role of an observer when explaining the behaviour of others.

Many of the accounting studies to date have focused on actor-observer situations and the fundamental attribution error. Attribution theory and the "actor-observer difference" was initially introduced into the accounting literature by Birnberg, Frieze and Shields (1977). Based on attribution theory, the paper presented a new model of the management control process, with particular focus on feedback in the form of employee performance reports. Subsequently, Shields, Birnberg and Frieze (1981) extended their earlier work by conducting two experiments to empirically test several propositions from their model. Specifically, the experiments tested propositions related to individuals' information search behaviour and systematic differences between the causal attributions made by participants assigned to the role of superior versus those assigned to the role of subordinate (namely that there would be an actor-observer bias such that superiors attributed a subordinate's performance to internal attributions while subordinates attributed their own performance to external attributions). Their results provided support for their predictions and suggest that causal attributions represent a source of friction between superiors and subordinates. Kaplan and Reckers (1985) conducted an early study applying attribution theory to examine auditors' performance evaluations. The experimental study examined auditor performance evaluation with a hypothetical subordinate auditor exceeding budgeted hours by a substantial percentage and missing a client deadline. The experiment manipulated one client-related dimension (stable versus high-growth client) and one subordinate auditor-related dimension (good or poor work history). These dimensions were hypothesized to influence superiors' causal attributions and subsequent action-response. Results from their experiment provided support for their predictions such that internal attributions were greater when the subordinate had a poor work history and when the client was stable. Additionally, internal (external) attributions were highly correlated with the action-response of directing the response at the subordinate auditor (client) trying to change something about the person (client situation).

Attribution theory has been used to study financial reporting issues. For example, Koonce, Williamson and Winchel (2010) examine situations where managers misestimate earnings forecasts (either honestly or an intentional misestimation). They suggest (and find) that nonprofessional investors will assume that the communications from others are their true beliefs (an internal attribution) rather than a communication intended to mislead the investment community (an external attribution). They also hypothesize and find that nonprofessional investors who observe forecast estimate inaccuracies and have data that other firms have better forecast accuracy are more likely to attribute the cause of the inaccuracy to management's intentional behaviour. These differential attributions affect behaviour in the form of valuation; for example, forecast inaccuracy attributed to management's intentional behaviour results in lower firm valuation.

Individuals may make self-serving attributional statements in an attempt to influence others' attributions. Accounting research has examined whether self-serving attributions are relied upon by others. For example, managers may provide causal explanations to investors for earnings news with either internal explanations (for good news) or external explanations (for bad news). Presumably, managers offer these explanations so that investors will causally attribute the good (bad) news to the company (environment) and will develop expectations that earnings will persist (dampen), which, in turn, should affect market reactions. Barton and Mercer (2005) examine the effect of these self-serving attributions by managers in forecasts and stock valuations. As expected, they find that participants make higher forecasts of future earnings when managers provide a plausible external attribution to explain why the firm reported bad earnings news. More recently, Kimbrough and Wang (2014) provide further archival evidence on the extent to which investors accept managers' self-serving attributions. They found that investors neither fully ignore nor accept these self-serving attributions but assess their plausibility by relying on industry and firm-specific information.

In the management accounting literature, Coletti, Sedatole and Towry (2005) used the fundamental attribution error perspective to examine the effects of control systems on perceived trustworthiness. Using an experiment, Coletti et al. (2005) manipulated the presence or absence of a control system and measured perceived trustworthiness and cooperation. The control system was designed to induce cooperation. They hypothesized (and found) that when a collaborator cooperates with a participant in the presence of a control system, the participant (observer) is likely to partially attribute this situationally induced cooperation to the collaborator having a dispositional trait of trustworthiness. This increased perception of trustworthiness mediates the effect of the control system on cooperation.

What an individual believes about (attributes to) a person could potentially have a wide-ranging impact on future beliefs and decisions regarding that person. For example, could attributions influence the amount of effort exerted to help, or potentially harm, another employee or manager? Could attributions influence individuals' willingness to cooperate with other organizational members or the amount and/or quality of the information they provide to other organizational members? In an audit setting, could attributions influence the level of information search conducted or the level to which supervisors' vigorously review or rely on that person's work? In a tax setting, could attributions about the tax-related behaviours of other taxpayers influence one's own tax compliance or willingness to take on a potential risky tax position?

Social comparison

Social-comparison theory holds that individuals have a drive to self-evaluate their own abilities and opinions, which, in turn, affects their self-image (Festinger 1954). Mettee and Smith (1977: 69–70) state that social-comparison theory is about "our quest to know ourselves, about the search for self-relevant information and how people gain self-knowledge". While individuals may use objective, nonsocial information, self-knowledge also comes about through comparisons with others. As originally introduced, Festinger (1954) highlighted individuals' desire to know one's capabilities; however, over time, the theory has evolved to incorporate individuals' motivations to maintain a positive self-image (Beach and Tesser 1995). Individuals have an innate desire to achieve positive social distinction (Frey 2007). While social comparisons tend to be used to enhance one's self-image, depending on the circumstances, one could be motivated to make an upward comparison (e.g., to others who are better off), a downward comparison (e.g., to others who are worse off) or to avoid making a social comparison. Beyond who is likely to be included in one's comparison group, social-comparison theory also considers how individuals interpret, distort or ignore information gained by social comparisons for self-enhancement. Also, under social-comparison theory, individuals may cope with a threat to their self-image in one area by affirming their competence in another area (self-affirmation theory, Steele 1988).

In general, social-comparison theory posits that individuals engage in comparisons with others, and such comparisons lead to self-enhancement or self-protecting behaviour. As a result, this theory is relevant to any accounting setting where individuals have information about the behaviour or performance of others or anticipate that their own behaviour or performance will be seen by others. One line of research in auditing investigates how well one is able to assess and/or predict another auditor's technical knowledge (Han, Jamal and Tan 2011; Kennedy and Peecher 1997; Tan and Jamal 2006). In an initial study, Kennedy and Peecher (1997) examine the ability of auditors to accurately assess their own as well as their subordinates' technical knowledge. They contend that auditing supervisors are prone to overestimate their own knowledge, and that one's self-estimate will be used to estimate their subordinates' knowledge. Based on this intuition, they predict and find that auditing supervisors are overconfident in their self and assessments of others' technical knowledge. Han et al. (2011) extend this work by examining auditors' estimates of another individual auditor versus a group of other auditors and task difficulty. They find that overconfidence is larger for more difficult tasks and this tendency is similar when assessing another individual or a group of other auditors.

Social-comparison theory has also been applied to examine how auditors differentially assess and weight contrary advice from advisors with whom they share a strong social bond as compared to a weak social bond (Kadous, Leiby and Peecher 2013). Kadous et al. (2013) hypothesize and find that auditors rely on a trust heuristic when assessing and weighing the advice from an advisor with whom they have a strong social bond. However, they find that specialists are more likely to discount contrary advice from a strong social bond advisor even though it is of high quality. They suggest that this is because the task is within their specialty and the contrary advice from a strong social bond advisor will trigger a negative social comparison that makes the specialist feel threatened by the advisor, become defensive and discount the advice.

One area of managerial accounting research that relies on social-comparison theory is the work surrounding relative performance information (RPI) (Frederickson 1992; Hannan, Krishnan and Newman 2008; Tafkov 2013; Hannan, McPhee, Newman and Tafkov 2013). In an RPI environment, individuals generally have knowledge of others' performance and others have knowledge of their performance. Social-comparison theory predicts that RPI will affect motivation and effort, even in cases when employees' compensation is not tied to the performance of their peers and that people also compete for non-monetary rewards such as performance-pride and self-image enhancement (Smith 2000; Frederickson 1992). For example, Tafkov (2013) predicted and found that RPI positively affects performance under two compensation contracts (individual performance, flat-wage). He also found that this positive effect is greater under an individual performance-based contract than under a flat-wage contract and that while both private and public RPI improve performance, the effect is greater for public RPI. In addition, Hannan et al. (2013) found that RPI increases a participant's effort level and his/her task choice or effort allocation and that both effects were magnified when the RPI is public rather than private. Further, in a multi-task environment, participants distorted their effort allocations away from firm-preferred proportions in order to do well on some tasks even if it means that they do worse on other tasks. Other researchers have examined how RPI influenced performance with individual versus tournament incentive schemes (Hannan et al. 2008), whether framing the RPI feedback as positive or negative influences performance (Murthy and Schafer 2011) and whether perceived usefulness of the RPI is influenced by the relative standing (better or worse) of the RPI and this, in turn, influences attitudes toward the organization providing the RPI (Mahlendorf, Kleinschmit and Perego 2014).

The desire for self-enhancement, a desire to see oneself in the most positive light (e.g., more talented and hardworking), may inflate the amount of effort employees expect of themselves. This desire, however, may be stronger or weaker depending on the type of incentive system. For example, an incentive system that bases a bonus on all performance measures (comprehensive system) may create less of a desire to self-enhance than a system that bases a bonus only on strategic performance measures (strategic system). Cianci, Kaplan and Samuels (2013) found the total hours that managers planned to work were more than the total hours their supervisors expected the manager to work, indicating self-enhancement. In addition, the type of incentive system and the type of performance measure moderated managers' tendency to engage in self-enhancement. Self-enhancement was greater under a strategic incentive system than under a comprehensive system. Further, participants engaged in self-enhancement for planned strategic hours but not for planned general hours.

Based on social-comparison theory, Brown (2014) recently examined managers' decisions to engage in earnings management. He contends that mangers who engage in earnings management activities are motivated to rationalize their behaviour. Further, he predicts that one's ability to rationalize will be greater when exposed to a more egregious example of earnings management rather than a less egregious example of earnings management. Exposure to earnings management induces managers to make a comparison. Importantly, when exposed to an egregious example, managers are more likely to engage in earnings management, in part, because they are better able to rationalize their questionable behaviour.

Farrar, Libby and Thorne (2015) examined social-comparison theory in a group setting, hypothesizing that even for a task with low interdependence and little or no interaction among group members, the simple presence of group members will allow for feelings of social comparison and increase feelings of social responsibility to the group. They find that when group members are given "groupcentric" goals (e.g., a goal for average group production), they outperform groups given individual goals or individual plus additive group goals.

Two related streams of research that draw on social-comparison theory are equity theory and distributive justice theory. Both of these theories suggest that our perceptions of fairness are often based on social comparisons (Adams 1965). For example, behavioural accounting researchers have examined how equity perceptions influence honesty in managerial and tax reporting (Matuszewski 2010; Finocchiaro-Castro and Rizzo 2014). Other behavioural accounting researchers have examined whether perceptions of organizational justice influence auditors' perceptions of promotion and turnover intentions (Parker, Nouri and Hayes 2011), whether perceptions of justice in the budget process and outcome influence task satisfaction and task performance (Lindquist 1995), and whether public accountants' attitudes and beliefs toward alternative work arrangements are influenced by perceptions about procedural and distributive justice (Johnson, Lowe and Reckers 2012).

While incentive and performance measurement systems are an obvious area of continued and future research, social comparisons also are relevant to audit settings (e.g., work performance, number of hours worked or planned), information disclosures (e.g., CEO compensation), benchmarking and balanced scorecards, and pro-social behaviour. Additionally, social-comparison theory could be used to study voluntary reporting for both financial and social responsibility reporting. That is, a company manager or investor could see that managers from other companies in the same industry are voluntarily disclosing certain information and/or disclosing information in a certain way, and therefore expect all companies in the same industry to disclose or report information in the same way.

Summary

In this chapter, we provided an overview of several key subfields within social psychology that have been applied by behavioural accounting researchers. In particular, our chapter on social psychology focused on the following subfields: interpersonal affect, accountability, attribution and social comparison. For each subfield, we discuss the theoretical underpinnings, provide a review of relevant Behavioural Accounting Research applying the theoretical underpinnings and identify open questions and suggest further research. As reflected in our chapter, these subfields have stimulated a substantial amount of Behavioural Accounting Research, and, perhaps, based, in part, on our open questions and suggestions, we expect behavioural accounting scholars will continue to find social psychology theories meaningful and relevant to their research.

Note

1 Affect is a feeling or emotion. Moods, a distinct type of affect, represent a general emotional state (e.g., positive mood or negative mood) (Chung, Cohen and Monroe 2008). Separate from moods are affective reactions which can be triggered by many things. For example, individuals can have affective reactions to the positive or negative valence of data (Kida and Smith 1995), to a net payment or refund tax position (Bhattacharjee, Moreno and Salbador 2015) or to corporate social responsibility performance (Elliott, Jackson, Peecher and White 2014). These studies all examine an affective reaction to data or a situation. In contrast, interpersonal affect is defined as an individual's generalized feelings, positive or negative, toward another person (Casciaro and Lobo 2008).

References

Adams, J., 1965, 'Inequity in social exchange', in L. Berkowitz (ed.), *Advances in Experimental Social Psychology*, 267–299, Academic Press, New York.
Allport, G.W., 1985, 'The historical background of social psychology', in G. Lindzey and E. Aronson (eds.), *The Handbook of Social Psychology*, 1–46, McGraw-Hill, New York.

Bagley, P.L., 2010, 'Negative affect: A consequence of multiple accountabilities in auditing', *Auditing: A Journal of Practice & Theory* 29(2), 141–157.

Bamber, E.M. and Iyer, V.M., 2007, 'Auditors' identification with their clients and its effect on auditors' objectivity', *Auditing: A Journal of Practice & Theory* 26(2), 1–24.

Barton, J. and Mercer, M., 2005, 'To blame or not to blame: Analysts reactions to explanations of poor management performance', *Journal of Accounting and Economics* 39(3), 509–533.

Bauer, T., 2015, 'The effects of client identity strength and professional identity salience on auditor judgments', *The Accounting Review* 90(1), 95–114.

Baumeister, R., 2010, 'The self', in R. Baumeister and E.J. Finkel (eds.), *Advanced Social Psychology: The State of Science*, 139–176, Oxford University Press, Oxford.

Beach, S. and Tesser, A., 1995, 'Self-esteem and the extended self-evaluation maintenance model: The self in social context', in M. Kernis (ed.), *Efficacy, Agency, and Self-Esteem*, 145–170, Plenum Press, New York.

Bhattacharjee, S. and Moreno, K.K., 2002, 'The impact of affective information on the professional judgments of more experienced and less experienced auditors', *Journal of Behavioral Decision Making* 15(4), 361–377.

Bhattacharjee, S., Moreno, K.K. and Riley, T., 2012, 'The interplay of interpersonal affect and source reliability on auditors' inventory judgments', *Contemporary Accounting Research* 29(4), 1087–1108.

Bhattacharjee, S., Moreno, K.K. and Salbador, D.A., 2015, 'The impact of multiple tax returns on tax compliance behavior', *Behavioral Research in Accounting* 27(1), 99–119.

Bierstaker, J.L. and Wright, A., 2001, 'The effects of fee pressure and partner pressure on audit planning decisions', *Advances in Accounting* 18, 25–46.

Birnberg, J. G, Frieze, L.H. and Shields, M.D., 1977, 'The role of attribution theory in control systems', *Accounting, Organizations and Society* 2(3), 189–200.

Blanthorne, C. and Kaplan, S., 2008, 'An egocentric model of the relations among the opportunity to underreport, social norms, ethical beliefs, and underreporting behavior', *Accounting, Organizations and Society* 33(7/8), 684–703.

Bobek, D.D., Hageman, A.M. and Kelliher, C.F., 2013, 'Analyzing the role of social norms in tax compliance behavior', *Journal of Business Ethics* 115(3), 451–468.

Bovard Jr., E.W., 1951, 'The experimental production of interpersonal affect', *The Journal of Abnormal and Social Psychology* 46(4), 521–528.

Brown, C.E., Peecher, M.E. and Solomon, I., 1999, 'Auditor's hypothesis testing in diagnostic inference tasks', *Journal of Accounting Research* 37(Spring), 1–26.

Brown, T.J., 2014, 'Advantageous comparison and rationalization of earnings management', *Journal of Accounting Research* 52(4), 849–876.

Casciaro, T. and Lobo, M. S., 2008. 'When competence is irrelevant: The role of interpersonal affect in task-related ties', *Administrative Science Quarterly* 53(4), 655–684.

Chang, L.J., Cheng, M.M. and Trotman, K.T., 2013, 'The effect of outcome and process accountability on customer-supplier negotiations', *Accounting, Organizations and Society* 38(2), 93–107.

Chung, J.O., Cohen, J.R. and Monroe, G.S., 2008, 'The effect of moods on auditors' inventory valuation decisions', *Auditing: A Journal of Practice & Theory* 27(2), 137–159.

Cialdini, R. and Trost, M.R., 1998, 'Social influence: Social norms, conformity, and compliance', in D.T. Gilbert, S.T. Fiske and G. Lindzey (eds.), *The Handbook of Social Psychology*, 2, 151–192, Oxford University Press, New York.

Cianci, A.M., Kaplan, S.E. and Samuels, J.A., 2013, 'The moderating effects of the incentive system and performance measure on managers' and their superiors' expectations about the managers' effort', *Behavioral Research in Accounting* 25(1), 115–134.

Coletti, A.L., Sedatole, K.L. and Towry, K.L., 2005, 'The effect of control systems on trust and cooperation in collaborative environments', *The Accounting Review* 80(2), 477–500.

Curtis, M.B., 2011, 'Does wrongdoer reputation matter? Impact of auditor-wrongdoer performance and likeability reputations on fellow auditors' intention to take action and choice of reporting outlet', *Behavioral Research in Accounting* 23(2), 207–234.

DeZoort, T., Harrison, P. and Taylor, M., 2006, 'Accountability and auditors' materiality judgments: The effects of differential pressure strength on conservatism, variability and effort', *Accounting, Organizations and Society* 31(4/5), 373–390.

Elliott, W.B., Jackson, K.E., Peecher, M.E. and White, B.J., 2014, 'The unintended effect of corporate social responsibility performance on investors' estimates of fundamental value', *The Accounting Review* 89(1), 275–302.

Evans III, J.H., Hannan, R.L., Krishnan, R. and Moser, D., 2001, 'Honesty in managerial reporting', *The Accounting Review* 76(4), 537–559.

Fanning, K. and Piercey, M., 2014, 'Internal auditors' use of interpersonal likability, arguments, and accounting information in a corporate governance setting', *Accounting, Organizations and Society* 39(8), 575–589.

Farrar, J., Libby, T. and Thorne, L., 2015, 'Groupcentric budget goals, budget-based incentive contracts, and additive group tasks', *Review of Accounting and Finance* 14(2), 189–206.

Festinger, L., 1954, 'A theory of social comparison processes', *Human Relations* 7(2), 117–140.

Finocchiaro-Castro, M. and Rizzo, I., 2014, 'Tax compliance under horizontal and vertical equity conditions: An experimental approach', *International Tax and Public Finance* 21(4), 560–577.

Fisher, J.G., Frederickson, J.R. and Peffer, S.A., 2000, 'Budgeting: An experimental investigation of the effects of negotiation', *The Accounting Review* 75(1), 93–114.

Frederickson, J.R., 1992, 'Relative performance information: The effects of common uncertainty and contract type on agent effort', *The Accounting Review* 67(4), 647–669.

Frey, B.S., 2007, 'Awards as compensation', *European Management Review* 4(1), 6–14.

Gibbins, M. and Newton, J.D., 1994, 'An empirical exploration of complex accountability in public accounting', *Journal of Accounting Research* 32(2), 165–186.

Gramling, A.A., 1999, 'External auditors' reliance on work performed by internal auditors: The influence of fee pressure on this reliance decision', *Auditing: A Journal of Practice & Theory* 18(Supplement), 117–135.

Han, J., Jamal, K. and Tan, H.-T., 2011, 'Auditors' overconfidence in predicting the technical knowledge of superiors and subordinates', *Auditing: A Journal of Practice & Theory* 30(1), 101–119.

Hannan, R.L., Krishnan, R. and Newman, A.H., 2008, 'The effects of disseminating relative performance feedback in tournament and individual performance compensation plans', *The Accounting Review* 83(4), 893–913.

Hannan, R.L., McPhee, G.P., Newman, A.H. and Tafkov, I.D., 2013, 'The effect of relative performance information of performance and effort allocation in a multi-task environment', *The Accounting Review* 88(2), 553–575.

Hannan, R.L., Rankin, F.W. and Towry, K.L., 2006, 'The effect of information systems on honesty in managerial reporting: A behavioral perspective', *Contemporary Accounting Research* 23(4), 885–918.

Heider, F., 1958, *The Psychology of Interpersonal Relations*, Wiley, New York.

Hobson, J.L., Mellon, M.J. and Stevens, D.E., 2011, 'Determinants of moral judgments regarding budgetary slack: An experimental examination of pay scheme and personal values', *Behavioral Research in Accounting* 23(1), 87–107.

Isen, A.M., Johnson, M.M., Mertz, E. and Robinson, G.F., 1985, 'The influence of positive affect on the unusualness of word associations', *Journal of Personality and Social Psychology* 48(6), 1413–1426.

Johnson, E.N., Lowe, D.J. and Reckers, P.M.J., 2012, 'Measuring accounting professionals' attitudes regarding alternative work arrangements', *Behavioral Research in Accounting* 24(1), 47–71.

Johnson, V.E. and Kaplan, S.E., 1991, 'Experimental evidence on the effects of accountability on auditor judgments', *Auditing: A Journal of Practice & Theory* 10(Supplement), 96–107.

Jones, E.E. and Harris, V.A., 1967, 'The attribution of attitudes', *Journal of Experimental Social Psychology* 3, 1–24.

Jones, E.E. and Nisbett, R.E., 1971, 'The actor and the observer: Divergent perceptions of the causes of the behavior', in E.E. Jones, D.E. Kanouse, H.H. Kelley, R.E. Nisbet, S. Valins and B. Weiner (eds.), *Attribution: Perceiving the Causes of Behavior*, 79–94, General Learning Press, Morristown, NJ.

Jones, E.E., Riggs, J.M. and Quattrone, G., 1979, 'Observer bias in the attitude of attribution paradigm: Effects of time and information order', *Journal of Personality and Social Psychology* 37(7), 1230–1238.

Kadous, K., Leiby, J. and Peecher, M.E., 2013, 'How do auditors weight informal contrary advice? The joint influence of advisor social bond and advice justifiability', *The Accounting Review* 88(6), 2061–2087.

Kaplan, S.E., Petersen, M. and Samuels, J.A., 2007, 'Effects of subordinate likeability and balanced scorecard format on performance-related judgments', *Advances in Accounting* 23, 85–111.

Kaplan, S.E., Pope, K.R. and Samuels, J.A., 2015, 'An examination of the effects of managerial procedural safeguards and managerial likeability on intentions to report fraud to a manager', *Behavioral Research in Accounting* 27(2), 77–94.

Kaplan, S.E. and Reckers, P.M.J., 1985, 'An examination of auditor performance evaluation', *The Accounting Review* 60(3), 477–487.

Kelley, H.H., 1967, 'Attribution theory in social psychology', in D. Levine (ed.), *Nebraska Symposium on Motivation*, 15, 192–238, University of Nebraska Press, Lincoln, NE.

Kelley, H.H., 1973, 'The processes of causal attribution', *American Psychologist* 28(2), 107–128.

Kennedy, J., 1993, 'Debiasing audit judgment with accountability', *Journal of Accounting Research* 31(2), 231–245.

Kennedy, J. and Peecher, M.E., 1997, 'Judging auditors' technical knowledge', *Journal of Accounting Research* 35(2), 279–293.

Kida, T.E., Moreno, K.K. and Smith, J.F., 2001, 'The influence of affect on managers' capital-budgeting decisions', *Contemporary Accounting Research* 18(3), 477–494.

Kida, T.E. and Smith, J.F., 1995, 'The encoding and retrieval of numerical data for decision making in accounting contexts: Model development', *Accounting, Organizations and Society* 20(7/8), 585–610.

Kimbrough, M.D. and Wang, I.Y., 2014, 'Are seemingly self-serving attributions in earnings press releases plausible? Empirical evidence', *The Accounting Review* 89(2), 635–667.

King, R.A., 2002, 'An experimental investigation of self-serving biases in an auditing trust game: The effect of group affiliation', *The Accounting Review* 77(2), 265–284.

Koonce, L., Williamson, M.G. and Winchel, J., 2010, 'Consensus information and nonprofessional investors' reaction to the revelation of estimate inaccuracies', *The Accounting Review* 85(3), 979–1000.

Lerner, J.S. and Tetlock, P.E., 1999, 'Accounting for the effects of accountability', *Psychological Bulletin* 125(2), 255–275.

Libby, T., Salterio, S.E. and Webb, A., 2004, 'The balanced scorecard: The effects of assurance and process accountability on managerial judgment', *The Accounting Review* 79(4), 1075–1094.

Lindquist, T.M., 1995, 'Fairness as an antecedent to participative budgeting: Examining the effects of distributive justice, procedural justice and referent cognitions on satisfaction and performance', *Journal of Management Accounting Research* 7, 122–147.

Lord, A.T., 1992, 'Pressure: A methodological consideration for behavioral research in accounting', *Auditing: A Journal of Practice & Theory* 11(2), 90–108.

Lui, X., 2014, 'Use tax compliance: The role of norms, audit probability, and sanction severity', *Academy of Accounting and Financial Studies Journal* 18(1), 65–80.

Maas, V.S. and Van Rinsum, M., 2013, 'How control system design influences performance misreporting', *Journal of Accounting Research* 51(5), 1159–1180.

Mahlendorf, M. D, Kleinschmit, F. and Perego, P., 2014, 'Relational effects of relative performance information: The role of professional identify', *Accounting, Organizations and Society* 39(5), 331–347.

Matuszewski, L.J., 2010, 'Honesty in managerial reporting: Is it affected by perceptions of horizontal equity?', *Journal of Management Accounting Research* 22, 233–250.

Mettee, D.R. and Smith, G., 1977, 'Social comparison and interpersonal attraction: The case for dissimilarity', in J.M. Suls and R.L. Miller (eds.), *Social Comparison Processes: Theoretical and Empirical Perspectives*, 69–101, Hemisphere Publishing Company, Washington, DC.

Moreno, K., Kida, T. and Smith, J.F., 2002, 'The impact of affective reactions on risky decision making in accounting contexts', *Journal of Accounting Research* 40(5), 1331–1349.

Murphy, K.R., Gannett, B.A., Herr, B.M. and Chen, J.A., 1986, 'Effects of subsequent performance on evaluations of previous performance', *Journal of Applied Psychology* 71(3), 427–431.

Murthy, U.S. and Schafer, B.A., 2011, 'The effects of relative performance information and framed information systems feedback on performance in a production task', *Journal of Information Systems* 25(1), 159–184.

Nelson, M. and Tan, H.-T., 2005, 'Judgment and decision making research in auditing: A task, person, and interpersonal interaction perspective', *Auditing: A Journal of Practice & Theory* 24(Supplement), 41–71.

Parker, R. J, Nouri, H. and Hayes, A.F., 2011, 'Distributive justice, promotion instrumentality, and turnover intentions in public accounting firms', *Behavioral Research in Accounting* 23(2), 169–186.

Peecher, M.E., 1996, 'The influence of auditors' justification processes on their decisions: A cognitive model and experimental evidence', *Journal of Accounting Research* 34(1), 125–140.

Peytcheva, M. and Gillett, P.R., 2011, 'How partners' views influence auditor judgment', *Auditing: A Journal of Practice & Theory* 30(4), 285–301.

Robbins, T.L. and DeNisi, A.S., 1994, 'Interpersonal affect and cognitive processing in performance appraisal: Towards closing the gap', *Journal of Applied Psychology* 79(3), 341–350.

Robertson, J.C., Stefaniak, C.M. and Curtis, M.B., 2011. 'Does wrongdoer reputation matter? Impact of auditor-wrongdoer performance and likeability reputations on fellow auditors' intention to take action and choice of reporting outlet'. *Behavioral Research in Accounting* 23(2), pp. 207–234.

Ross, L., 1977, 'The intuitive psychologist and his shortcomings: Distortions in the attribution process', in L. Berkowitz (ed.), *Advances in Experimental Social Psychology*, 10, 173–220, Academic Press, New York.

Shields, M.D., Birnberg, J.G. and Frieze, I.H., 1981, 'Attributions, cognitive processes and control systems', *Accounting, Organizations and Society* 6(1), 69–93.

Smith, R., 2000, 'Assimilative and contrastive emotional reactions to upward and downward social comparisons', in J. Suls and L. Wheeler (eds.), *Handbook of Social Comparison: Theory and Research*, 173–200, Kluwer Academic/Plenum Publishers, New York.

Steele, C., 1988, 'The psychology of self-affirmation: Sustaining the integrity of the self', in L. Berkowitz (ed.), *Advances in Experimental Social Psychology*, 21, 261–302, Academic Press, San Diego, CA.

Stevens, D., 2002, 'The effects of reputation and ethics on budgetary slack', *Journal of Management Accounting Research* 14, 153–171.

Tafkov, I.D., 2013, 'Private and public relative performance information under different compensation contracts', *The Accounting Review* 88(1), 327–350.

Tajfel, H. and Turner, J.C., 1985, 'The social identity theory of intergroup behavior', in S. Worchel and W.G. Austin (eds.), *Psychology of Intergroup Relations* (2nd ed.), 7–24, Nelson-Hall, Chicago, IL.

Tan, C.E.L., Jubb, C.A. and Houghton, K., 1997, 'Auditor judgments: The effects of the partner's views on decision outcomes and cognitive effort', *Behavioral Research in Accounting* 9(Supplement), 157–175.

Tan, H.-T. and Jamal, K., 2006, 'Managing perceptions of technical competence: How well do auditors know how others view them?', *Contemporary Accounting Research* 23(3), 761–787.

Tetlock, P.E., 1983, 'Accountability and complexity of thought', *Journal of Personality and Social Psychology* 45(1), 74–83.

Tetlock, P.E., 1985, 'Accountability: The neglected social context of judgment and choice', in B. Staw and L. Cummings (eds.), *Research in Organizational Behavior*, 1, 297–332, JAI Press, Greenwich, CT.

Turner, C.W., 2001, 'Accountability demands and the auditor's evidence search strategy: The influence of reviewer preferences and the nature of the response (belief vs. action)', *Journal of Accounting Research* 39(3), 683–706.

Watson, D., 1982, 'The actor and the observer: How are their perceptions of causality divergent?', *Psychological Bulletin* 92(3), 682–700.

Wilks, T.J., 2002, 'Predecisional distortion of evidence as a consequence of real-time audit review', *The Accounting Review* 77(1), 51–72.

Zajonc, R.B., 1980, 'Feelings and thinking: Preferences need no inferences', *American Psychologist* 35(2), 151–175.

6

Theoretical frameworks in ethics, morality and philosophy applied to Behavioural Accounting Research

James Gaa

Introduction

The ethical standards of the accounting profession have been a prominent issue in the professional literature for many decades. The codes of ethics of various organizations of professional accountants are formal statements of the duties of professional accountants to other parties. The Preamble of the Code of Professional Conduct of the American Institute of Certified Accountants is explicit about the range of these duties that go beyond, but are also constrained by, the requirements of laws and regulations (AICPA 2016, 0.300.010 Preamble .01).[1] Duties are owed to a variety of groups, including the public, clients and colleagues; in addition, it is explicitly clear that the Code requires a commitment that "honorable behaviour" may require sacrifice to one's "personal advantage" (AICPA 2016, 0.300.010 Preamble .02). In more general terms, the first sentence of the Handbook of the Code of Ethics for Professional Accountants states that: "a distinguishing mark of the accountancy profession is its acceptance of the responsibility to act in the public interest" (IESBA 2015: section 100).[2]

The next section addresses some basic issues underlying ethics and ethical behaviour (and provides a link to the practice of accounting) that are relevant to understanding professional accounting ethics, and to advancing research in ethics. The third section presents a brief description of the primary types of ethical theories.

Foundational issues

Role morality

People in general and accountants in particular often find themselves in situations where their actions have an impact on themselves and others, and where there is no feasible course of action which will be most in the interest of all affected parties. In such cases, deciding which of the competing or conflicting stakeholder interests is to be given priority over the others requires a governing principle or criterion. Norms provide guidance (and possibly, incentives provided through their enforceability), by indicating actions that are required, permitted or forbidden in a given situation.

Ethical norms are important because they are special forms of social control (Baier 1965: v) and provide key determinants of how people ought to behave. They not only provide guidance in deciding what they ought to do, they help in judging the actions of both ourselves and others. Norms also serve to explain actions to others, and to justify or criticize actions. In addition, they may be enforceable, either through social pressure or legal action. Norms may take the form of basic principles, specific rules, mores, customs, laws and regulations (Baier 1965), and may be based in religion, law, intellectual thought or cultural tradition.

Norms have two main functions. On the one hand, they provide criteria to evaluate situations and actions. On the other hand, they provide guides for action, helping people decide which action is appropriate or correct to perform. Following from both of these functions, norms also may provide standards for enforcing certain types of behaviour.[3] Ethical norms often become enforceable as statutes or government regulations, or common law rules.[4]

Bayles (1989) identifies two types of norms. Universal norms are norms that apply to people in a society merely by virtue of their membership in that society. Examples include general prohibitions against lying and deception, and inflicting harm gratuitously. Such norms are universal because they are regarded as applying to everybody, not because they hold without exception.

People are also subject to the second type of norms, role-related norms (Bayles 1989: 22–25). In the case of the accounting profession, most of the norms in codes of professional conduct are role-related norms because they apply to accountants by virtue of the particular role they play in society.[5] Confidentiality (IESBA 2015: section 140), objectivity (IESBA 2015: section 120) and independence in audit and assurance engagements (IESBA 2015: sections 290, 291) appear to be the most important role-related norms of the public accounting profession. Since independence is the only ethical norm that relates specifically to the role of auditor, it and the standards that accompany it (IESBA 2015: sections 290, 291) as well as auditing and assurance standards (IAASB 2015) define and distinguish the auditor's role within the more general role of accountant.

The concepts of professional roles and role-related norms are crucial to understanding the ethics of all professions, including the accounting profession. Held (1984: 30) makes the connection between roles and norms clear:

> A role is also a set of norms or rules concerning behavior. In accepting a role, we accept these norms. In being a lawyer, we put ourselves in a condition of "being a lawyer", but this should not be understood merely in terms of making the empirical description "that person is a lawyer" true . . . we are accepting the norms constituting the role of the lawyer in that society as valid norms.

Voluntary acceptance of a role is a matter of ethical import because it means that persons adopting it agree to act in accordance with the norms (and, as will be discussed later, the rights and duties underlying these norms) that define these latter roles (Andre 1991). For example, role-related norms establish how accountants should resolve conflicts of interest by the fundamental principle (norm) of objectivity (IESBA 2015: section 120.1). Similarly, the duty of confidentiality is a complex duty that is central to the practice of a number of professions, including accountancy (IESBA 2015: section 140.1). Therefore, information an accountant may learn on the job about his or her employer or client must be kept confidential even if the information might help family, friends or other organizations with which the accountant has important relationships. Professional standards of confidentiality specify how conflicts of interest relating to secret information known to the accountants are to be resolved. Likewise, the standards governing auditor independence adjudicate the conflicts of interest that arise (for example) when it might be economically advantageous to the client to have the auditor (or audit firm) provide non-audit services (IESBA 2015: section 290.154).

Identifying and clarifying roles facilitate ethical decision-making in specific situations, because the norms associated with a role are more easily understood and applied than those associated with universal norms because they are often too general to allow for efficient ethical decision-making in specific situations. Also, the number of factors to consider when applying universal norms can be enormous. If it were not for the role-related norms regarding confidentiality, accountants would be faced with far more complex decisions because of insufficient guidance. While the existence of role-related norms reduces vagueness and ambiguity, the acceptance of a role does not absolve the occupant from critically examining the norms themselves. As Held states, "(w)e view morality to guide us in acting in the roles we occupy, and to recommend to us how we ought to give-up, take on, revise, and restructure the roles into which society is organized" (1984: 31).

Special obligations

As written, the IESBA Code (2015) focuses on the obligations or duties of professional accountants. Thus, for example, professional accountants have obligations to be objective (IESBA section. 120), maintain confidentiality (IESBA 2015: section 140) and to be independent of their clients in audit and assurance engagements (IESBA 2015: sections 290, 291). Such obligations, in view of the special relationship between accountants and those whom their actions are supposed to benefit, are special obligations (Jeske 2014) and comprise the bulk of the IESBA Code.[6] The IESBA Code does contain at least one natural obligation, i.e., an obligation that holds for all persons in virtue simply of being persons: the duty "to comply with relevant laws and regulations" (IESBA 2015: section 150.1).[7] The special obligations of professional accountants identified in the IESBA Code include specific standards included because of their specificity, standards in Parts B and C are more clearly enforceable by the profession and regulatory agencies.[8]

In large part, accounting ethically may be defined in terms of the special obligations derived from the roles accountants play. The recognition and evaluation of special obligations is helpful when, as is often the case, they are in conflict. For example, there are many stakeholders to a decision about requiring the disclosure of information that will be important to the public but damaging to the client. Accountants have varying duties to a variety of these stakeholders, but their special obligation to the public generally would take priority and guide ethical behaviour.

One of the fundamental issues of professional ethics is when and why special obligations derived from the accountant's role take precedence over natural obligations that hold for people generally (Bayles 1989). The standards governing confidentiality (IESBA 2015: section 140; IESBA 2016) are examples where information about an organization may be of interest to the public (and therefore disclosure may be in the public interest), the IESBA Code nevertheless specifies (IESBA 2015: section 140.7) that professional accountants have a special obligation to employers and clients to protect confidential information, including information about the commission of acts that violate laws and regulations (IESBA 2015: section 140). The norms relating to confidentiality are discussed later in this chapter.

Rights and duties

A critical question about the obligation-focused codes of ethics is what are the foundations of these obligations. That is, where do the special obligations "come from"? A widely recognized and accepted theory of rights, developed by Hohfeld (1919), provides a convincing way of sorting out the structure of rights and duties in accounting, and in particular to identify the source of the special obligations that accompany the role of professional accountant. Furthermore, Hohfeld's theory provides the logical basis for the actions of standard setters (such as the IESBA and other ethics bodies to create standards governing accountants' actions) and employers and clients to create and modify accountants' obligations in particular situations. The most relevant aspects of Hohfeldian rights (and duties) are discussed below.[9]

Hohfeld (1919) distinguishes four types of rights. Following Wenar (2015), the four types of rights are:

1 Claims: *A* has a claim that *B* φ *if and only if B* has a duty to *A* to φ.
2 Privilege: *A* has a privilege to φ *if and only if A* has no duty not to φ.
3 Power: *A* has a power *if and only if A* has the ability to alter her own or another's Hohfeldian incidents.
4 Immunity: *B* has an immunity *if and only* if *A* lacks the ability to alter *B*'s Hohfeldian incidents.

In these statements, "φ" stands for an action or non-action; "A" and "B" stand for persons, organizations, groups or the public at large, as appropriate; and a Hohfeldian incident is one of the four types of right.

A number of distinctions among types of rights relate to Hohfeld's framework. Claims and privileges are primary rights because they concern an agent's actions or refraining from actions. Powers and immunities are secondary rights because they concern the creation, modification and waiving of incidents (including both primary and secondary rights). Although the specific obligations that are the core of professional ethics as incorporated in the IESBA Code (2015) are (according to Hohfeld's analysis) correlative to the claims of others, it will be seen below that all these types of incidents are incorporated in the special obligations.

Three other distinctions are important for understanding the structure of specific obligations of professional accountants. First, passive rights (claims and immunities) relate to the actions of others, while active rights (privileges and powers) concern one's own actions. In addition, passive rights may be negative or positive: claims may be either positive (because claimants are entitled to the provision of an action or service) or negative (because they are entitled to non-interference [non-action] from others);[10] immunities are only negative.[11] Third, claims may be either *in personam* and *in rem*. An *in personam* right is correlated with duties of a specific or identifiable person, while an *in rem* right of a person is correlated with duties of a whole class of persons.

The following examples of rights and duties in accounting show how rights are often "molecular rights", i.e., complex combinations of simple (atomic) Hohfeldian incidents. All of them relate directly or indirectly to the special obligations that govern the actions and non-actions of accountants to act (or not to act) in the interest of others.[12]

- Ethics standard setting:[13] The public in general has an *in rem* claim that standards boards will use their powers in the public interest. The standard setters have the power to create and modify claims that create duties of accountants to act or to refrain from acting in certain ways, and to create privileges for accountants. Standard setters are also immune from accountants and reporting entities modifying the duties formulated by the standard setters (i.e., accountants lack the power to modify their duties to others). Accountants have duties to act in the interest of clients, employees, the public and specifically a duty to act in accordance with the standards (when doing so does not conflict with the duty to comply with applicable laws and regulations).

- Confidentiality: Employers and clients of professional accountants have an *in personam* negative claim against accountants (who have a duty) to maintain the confidentiality of sensitive information about it (IESBA 2015: section 140). But this duty is nuanced. Clients and employers also have the power to specify a range of actions that accountants may or may not take in relation to confidentiality. For example, they may exercise their power to direct accountants to disclose confidential information to other parties. In addition, accountants have a legal and moral duty to disclose information when directed to do so as part of a legal proceeding, and have a privilege or a duty to disclose information in the context of the proceedings of professional or legal bodies.

- Violations of laws and regulations: Continuing with the duty of confidentiality, when accountants obtain evidence of acts by their client that may violate laws and regulations they have (in specific and restrictive circumstances) a privilege to disclose the information to an appropriate body (IESBA 2016) and, consistent with Hohfeld's framework, no duty not to disclose it. In such a case, the auditor also has an immunity from the client, i.e., the client has no power to create a duty of the auditor to not disclose the information. At the same time, an auditor does not have a privilege of disclosing information to other parties, such as journalists. The client/employer has a positive *in personam* claim and the accountant has a duty not to make such a disclosure. The accountant also has a second privilege of not disclosing the information, which means that the public has no claim (and the accountant no duty) to disclose.

Trust

For Baier (1994), the fostering of relationships among individuals, organizations and institutions is a virtue of social institutions. This general point of view suggests that relationships are fundamentally important in every aspect of our lives, and therefore also in the practice of accounting. A fundamental type of relationship is trust. This general claim is even more clearly the case for people who are carrying out professional roles, such as accounting. Li (2012) describes four kinds of situations in which trust is most important:

> when the uncertainty (e.g., complexity and ambiguity) of unmet expectations is high;
> when the vulnerability of control (e.g. failure of formal contract) is high;
> when the stakes (e.g. financial loss) of unmet expectations or control failure are high;
> when long-term interdependence (e.g. reciprocal relationship) is high.

Since all four of these conditions clearly apply to the practice of accounting (especially in the domains of auditing and of financial reporting for the use of external parties), trust in professional accountants by others is central to accounting ethics. In spite of this, trust has been almost completely ignored in the accounting literature. In the area of practice, for example, it (and related concepts such as trustworthiness) does not appear in the IESBA Code (2015). Although it has been prominent in other fields (e.g., Bachmann and Inkpen 2011; Bachmann and Zaheer 2013; Lewicki et al. 1998; Li 2012; Mayer, Davis and Schoorman 1995; Van de Walle and Six 2014), there is very little research on trust in the accounting literature.

In spite of its long history in the law of trusts and fiduciaries, a moral theory of trust has not emerged until relatively recently (Baier 1994: Ch. 6–8). According to Baier (1994: 105), trust is "letting other persons (natural or artificial, such as firms, nations, etc.) take care of something the truster cares about, where such 'caring for' involves some exercise of discretionary powers."[14]

Implicit in the trust relationship is that the power granted to trustee also confers the ability to harm the truster. Such a conferral of power requires a belief (or presumption) that the trustee is able to but will not harm the truster; otherwise, it would be unreasonable to grant such powers voluntarily. Note that a trust relationship involves the creation of a positive claim for the truster and a duty for the trustee.

Ethical theories

When people reason about ethical issues, they tend to use a small number of basic concepts and principles. These concepts and principles help individuals organize their thoughts and thus help them to analyze and evaluate situations and actions, and make a decision about what is the most ethically appropriate course of action. Most important, they help individuals in situations where norms need to be evaluated either because they are in conflict with other norms, because they need to be interpreted in order to be applicable to a specific situation or because the ethical appropriateness of the norm itself is in question. Having some sort of theoretical framework thus helps us make our choices more systematic and consistent. In addition, a theoretical or conceptual framework may help us in trying to explain and justify our actions to others and thus help us to convince others of the rightness of our actual or proposed actions, especially when our actions require their agreement or support. Seen in this way, ethical theories are considered to be formalizations of the basic concepts and principles that people commonly use to consider ethical issues, in order to develop them rigorously and in detail, and in particular to identify and deal with theoretical problems that are identified as the theory is developed. It is generally agreed that ethical theories fall into three main types. They may be considered as formal theories that develop the details and work out the difficulties of focusing solely on one kind of ethical consideration. They are briefly described below.

Consequentialist ethics

In many cases, we are concerned with the expected consequences of our actions. That is, we evaluate the actions of ourselves and of others, and make judgments and choices among alternative actions based on what we expect will result from them, and how these results affect us and others. With its exclusive focus on outcomes of actions, this framework that dates to the Enlightment (Mill and Bentham 1789; Sinnott-Armstrong 2014), adopts an approach similar to the models of rational decision-making found more recently in such fields as economics and finance. However, it takes a very different tack from these non-ethical approaches to rational choice. These normative (Thaler 2015) but non-ethical theories of rational decision-making assume, for the most part, that agents are self-interested utility maximizers. Consequentialist ethical theories take a very different view, that the consequences for all moral beings taken together count, and count equally. Carrying out the action that benefits the community most (given that some members may gain and some may lose) is in accordance with the moral point of view. This implies in particular that sometimes one's evaluation of the consequences will lead to the conclusion that the best overall consequences are produced by an action which is not in one's own self-interest.[15]

There are two basic forms of consequentialism (Sinnott-Armstrong 2014; Hooker 2015). According to direct consequentialism, every individual action should be evaluated according to its expected consequences and choose the one that maximizes "the Good" for all beings. Indirect consequentialism provides for the existence of rules and practices that, when followed, are intended to maximize the Good. Then individuals are relieved from the requirement of considering and weighing all the consequences of all alternative actions in terms of the interest of all individuals. Rather, their actions are to be evaluated according to whether they are in accordance with rules and practices (rather than their consequences), and the rules and practices should be evaluated and the action chosen that maximizes the collective interests of all. If indirect consequentialism were the foundation of the IESBA code, the IESBA would develop and promulgate the fundamental principles and the more specific standards on the basis of what will maximize the Good for all of society, and practicing accountants would have a duty to act in accordance with the Code. It is important to note that although indirect consequentialism would make it a duty for an accountant to act in accordance with special obligations contained in the Code, the fact that the Code lacks complete specificity with respect to the special obligations of accountants, the Code requires that accountants use judgment in order to apply the Code to specific situations. A consequentialist approach would provide that accountants will fulfill their duty by considering the consequences of their choices for relevant parties.

Deontological ethics

Deontological ethics is the ethics of duty: actions are right or wrong according to their conformity with fundamental moral norms that specify actions as obligatory (i.e., mandatory or forbidden) or permitted. The rightness of actions is not determined by their consequences; indeed, the actual or expected consequences of one's actions are irrelevant in making moral judgments. Thus, even if a right action (according to deontological considerations) also produces the most good in terms of its consequences, the rightness of the action rather than its goodness is the reason it is morally superior to other possible actions.

Like consequentialism, deontological ethics dates to the enlightenment. The most influential deontological theory is that of Kant (1785; Johnson and Cureton 2016), according to whom there is only one fundamental duty: the Categorical Imperative.[16] All other duties, including the special obligations of accountants, are logically deducible from the Categorical Imperative. An important implication of this view is that since more specific duties are derived from the Categorical Imperative, they are logically consistent with each other, and therefore no two duties can conflict with each other. Kant discussed one particular example of a duty that is particularly pertinent to accounting that many people find unacceptable: that people should never lie. For Kant, this proscription follows from the Categorical Imperative, and any possible consequences of truth telling are completely irrelevant. The Kantian approach implies a duty that accountants may never lie to, or mislead, others, and there is no duty to anyone else that conflicts with this duty. For example, accountants should always be truthful in their reporting even if the consequences of doing so would lead to the demise of the organization. As noted above, this obligation holds regardless of the consequences of deception or being truthful.[17]

Other deontologists (for example Ross 1930) have differed from Kant, and recognized that duties may conflict. The IESBA Code (2015) implicitly recognizes the existence of conflicting duties, such as duties to protect the interests of clients and employing organizations, but have an overriding obligation, as noted above, to the public at large (IESBA 2015: section 100.1). The analysis of the duty of confidentiality reveals the existence of conflicting duties. As discussed above, if an accountant has evidence relating to the violation of a law or regulation, he or she has a duty to consider whether to exercise his or her privilege to disclose the information to an appropriate authority. The Code identifies the conflicting duties and provides some guidance (IESBA 2016), but the accountant must still resolve the conflict in the specific circumstances. A central issue for deontological theories is the basis for determining the duties that people have. Several approaches to this question are presented here. According to Kant (1785), the Categorical Imperative (and therefore every duty) is based on reason alone and is independent of empirical matters. Ross (1930; Skelton 2012) claimed that there are five basic duties, and that they are based on self-evident intuitions of real people, developed over generations (Alexander and Moore 2015).[18] Another approach, which may be attractive in the context of role morality, and the centrality of professional duties that serve the rights or interests of others is patient-centred theory. The focus of patient-centred theories is on those to whom a duty is owed, rather than on the moral agent who has the duty (Alexander and Moore 2015). More specifically, the focus is on the rights of "patients" (i.e., the passive recipients) that are correlative to duties. Thus, rights become central to these theories. The centrality of rights in determining the duties of accountants discussed above is reinforced by patient-centred deontological theories.

Character ethics

According to the ancient Greeks, in particular Plato and Aristotle, the fundamental question of ethics is: How should a person live? This question is captured by a related question: what sort of person should a person be? That is, what character traits, or virtues, should a person possess in order to be considered a moral agent? The agent focus of virtue theory constitutes a very different orientation towards ethical issues from the act-focused theoretical frameworks. With their focus on right actions and the consequences of actions, deontological and consequentialist theories de-emphasize this question.

Virtue is about the character of a person. A common definition of virtue is the following: "The concept of a virtue is the concept of something that makes its possessor good: a virtuous person is a morally good, excellent or admirable person who acts and feels well, right, as she should" Hursthouse (2013). Virtues are positive attributes of character, character traits such as honesty, courage and trustworthiness which individuals acquire because they are brought up in communities that value them. Virtuous individuals learn how to act in accordance with these attributes. For a virtuous person, pursuing virtues is its own reward, and external consequences (such as money and reputation) are not the goal of a virtuous person's actions even if they are an outcome of his or her actions.

In addition, the focus on the agent means that virtue ethics places little emphasis on identifying special obligations. At most, a code would specify the "special virtues" that are especially important for the role morality of accountants. It might appear that the Code does this because it mentions some virtues: Accountants are supposed to have integrity and to be honest (IESBA 2015: section 110) and to be objective and not compromise their judgment via "the undue influence of others" (IESBA 2015: section 120).[19] So it may appear that the Code is a virtue-based code at least in part. But it is important to note that the focus of the Code, including these principles, is on actions and not on the possession of these virtues. A basic tenet of virtue ethics is that acting in the same way as a virtuous person would act is a good thing and may be a good guide to action, but acting in such a way is not the same as possessing these virtues (Hursthouse 2013).

Concluding remarks

In light of the ongoing challenges to the ethical standards of the accounting profession, it is important for researchers to attend to the ethical behaviour of professional accountants. This chapter presents a brief introduction to the basic concepts and principles and to the types of ethical theories that provide the conceptual foundations of ethical behaviour in the accounting profession. This is relevant to behavioural research in accounting, based on the commonplace idea that good research needs to be based on theory and so good behavioural research on ethical behaviour requires an understanding of the fundamental normative concepts and principles. In addition, this introduction presents the normative foundations to support research into ethical judgment and behaviour. One way of using ethical theory is analogous to recent work in behavioural economics, as characterized by Thaler (2015, 2016). According to Thaler, neoclassical economic theory provides a normative standard for rational economic decision-making by "econs", thus providing a standard against which the actual behaviour of humans may be examined. Likewise, ethical theories provide standards of ethical behaviour against which the actual ethical behaviour of humans can be compared. To the extent that codes of ethics provide a single set of standards and principles governing accountants' ethical behaviour, and are consistent with ethical theory, they (the codes) provide a more specific normative base for behavioural ethics in accounting.[20] In addition to research into behavioural ethics in accounting, empirical research may inform ethical theory, and may result in progress in both psychology and philosophy (Doris and Stich 2014; Alfano and Loeb 2014).

Notes

1 Sections 260 and 350 (discussed below in this chapter) of the IESBA Code (2016) demonstrate the interplay between ethical and legal norms. According to the Code, accountants are obligated to act in accordance with applicable laws and regulations. In some jurisdictions, accountants have a legal obligation to disclose some kinds of illegal acts; in other jurisdictions, accountants have a legal obligation to maintain confidentiality regarding illegal acts. In such situations, the legal obligations conflict with and override the privileges contained in the Code.

2 As of the date of publication of this chapter, the International Ethics Standards Board for Accountants (IESBA) is engaged in restructuring the code. Although no changes in content are involved, the resulting structure and organization of the code will be different. All references to the code in this chapter are to the 2015 code (IESBA 2015) and one addition to it (IESBA 2016), i.e., the code in its unrestructured form.

3 In order to have value in this regard, they must be explicitly formulated, and sufficiently precise to allow people to determine readily whether their actions are or would be in accordance with the norm.

4 And vice versa, new laws and regulations may result in a shift in moral judgments.

5 Not all norms are ethical. For example, auditors are subject to a variety of role-related norms, including a number of sources of generally accepted accounting principles (GAAP) and generally accepted auditing standards (GAAS) (IAASB 2015). Although no norm is value-free, these norms are not directly or explicitly ethical; rather, they specify certain role obligations and efficient ways of performing one's duties (GAAS, for the most part) or specify standard methods of accounting and reporting (GAAP, for the most part).

6 In this chapter, a number of references are made to articles in the *Stanford Encyclopedia of Philosophy* (plato.stanford.edu/). They are recommended because they are topic-specific, of high quality, up to date and highly accessible.

7 The principle of integrity (IESBA 2015, section 110.1), "an obligation on all professional accountants to be straightforward and honest in all professional and business relationships", which "implies fair dealing and truthfulness" appears to be a natural duty. Since it is included as an explicit part of a code relating to the role of professional accountant, it is interpreted here as a special obligation of professional accountants to others.

8 This is especially the case for section 290 on independence, which is formulated to clarify the enforceable conduct mandated by the standard. The current (as of the time of publication, see endnote 1 above) the IESBA restructuring project is being conducted at the behest of the International Organization of Securities Commissions (IOSCO) and the Public Interest Oversight Board (PIOB), in order to make the enforceable standard of conduct explicit.

9 For a more complete description of Hohfeld's analysis and discussion of other aspects of rights, see Hursthouse (2013).

10 Libertarian theories place primary emphasis on negative, since their emphasis is the freedom to act (or not act) without interference.

11 Privileges and powers are neither positive nor negative.

12 These examples are somewhat extensive, but are still incomplete specifications of all the rights and duties (special obligations) of professional accountants in these particular circumstances.

13 The focus here is on ethics standards boards, such as the IESBA and the AICPA Professional Ethics Executive Committee (PEEC). But other standard setters (e.g., the IAASB and the International Accounting Standards Board (IASB) have similar duties.

14 "Caring for" does not imply or require that the trustee and trustor have a personal relationship.

15 Thus, the statement in the preamble of the AICPA Code of Conduct (AICPA 2016), quoted at the beginning of this chapter is a commitment to the moral point of view.

16 Kant stated the Categorical Imperative in three ways that he thought were equivalent. The preponderance of commentators regard them as related but different. See, e.g., Waluchow (2003).

17 For an extended analysis of the ethical issues relating to lying and deception, see Bok (1989).

18 Note the parallel to moral psychology in Ross's appeal to the moral intuitions of real people. But note also that Ross is not doing psychology in the conventional social-scientific sense.

19 It is noteworthy that the IESBA code does not mention many character traits that might be important in the practice of accounting. Major examples include courage and trustworthiness.

20 Every accountant who is a member of a professional association of accountants that is a member of the International Federation of Accountants (IFAC) is required (to the extent that the professional associations has responsibility in its jurisdiction for ethical standards) to act in accordance with an enforceable code of ethics (and a just and effective enforcement mechanism) of that association (IFAC 2012, SMO 7). Each of these professional associations must have a code that is the same as, equivalent to or more stringent than the Code of Ethics for Professional Accountants published by the International Ethics Standards Board for Accountants (IFAC 2012, SMO 4). Thus, the IESBA Code creates a degree of universality for professional accountants around the world. In the case of the United States, the AICPA Code of Ethics applies to all professional accountants who are members of the AICPA; the rules of the Public Companies Accounting Oversight Board (PCAOB) apply to audits of public interest entities (i.e., SEC registrants). Because of the IFAC statement of member obligations, the IESBA Code will be referenced below.

References

Alexander, L. and Moore, M., 2015, 'Deontological ethics', in E.N. Zalta (ed.), *The Stanford Encyclopedia of Philosophy* (Spring 2015 ed.), http://plato.stanford.edu/archives/spr2015/entries/ethics-deontological/.

Alfano, M. and Loeb, D., 2014, 'Experimental moral philosophy', in E.N. Zalta (ed.), *The Stanford Encyclopedia of Philosophy* (Summer 2014 ed.), http://plato.stanford.edu/archives/sum2014/entries/experimental-moral/.

American Institute of Certified Public Accountants (AICPA), 2016, *AICPA Code of Professional Conduct*, http://pub.aicpa.org/codeofconduct/Ethics.aspx#.

Andre, J., 1991, 'Role morality as a complex instance of ordinary morality', *American Philosophical Quarterly* 28(1), 73–80.

Bachmann, R. and Inkpen, A.C., 2011, 'Understanding institutional-based trust building processes in inter-organizational relationships', *Organization Studies* 32(2), 281–301.

Bachmann, R. and Zaheer, A. (eds.), 2013, *Handbook of Advances in Trust Research*, Edward Elgar Pub, Dulles, VA.

Baier, A., 1994, *Moral Prejudices*, Harvard University Press, Cambridge.

Baier, K., 1965, *From a Moral Point of View* (2nd ed.), Random House, New York.

Bayles, M., 1989, *Professional Ethics* (2nd ed.), Wadsworth, Belmont, CA.

Bok, S., 1989, *Lying* (3rd ed.), Random House, New York.

Doris, J. and Stich, S., 2014, 'Moral psychology: Empirical approaches', in E.N. Zalta (ed.), *The Stanford Encyclopedia of Philosophy* (Spring 2014 ed.), http://plato.stanford.edu/archives/spr2014/entries/moral-psych-emp/.

Held, V., 1984, *Rights and Goods: Justifying Social Action*, University of Chicago Press, Chicago.

Hohfeld, W., 1919, *Fundamental Legal Conceptions*, Yale University Press, New Haven.

Hooker, B., 2015, 'Rule consequentialism', in E.N. Zalta (ed.), *The Stanford Encyclopedia of Philosophy* (Winter 2015 ed.), http://plato.stanford.edu/archives/win2015/entries/consequentialism-rule/.

Hursthouse, R., 2013, 'Virtue ethics', in E.N. Zalta (ed.), *The Stanford Encyclopedia of Philosophy* (Fall 2013 ed.), http://plato.stanford.edu/archives/fall2013/entries/ethics-virtue/.

International Auditing and Assurance Standards Board (IAASB), 2015, '2015 handbook of international quality control, auditing, review, other assurance, and related services pronouncements', www.ifac.org/publications-resources/2015-handbook-international-quality-control-auditing-review-other-assurance.

International Ethics Standards Board for Accountants (IESBA), 2015, *Handbook of the Code of Ethics for Professional Accountants* (2015 ed.), International Federation of Accountants, New York, www.ethicsboard.org/iesba-code/table-contents.

International Ethics Standards Board for Accountants (IESBA), 2016, 'Responding to non-compliance to laws and regulations', www.ifac.org/publications-resources/responding-non-compliance-laws-and-regulations.

International Federations of Accountants (IFAC), 2012, 'Statements of membership obligations (SMOs) 1–7 (Revised)', www.ifac.org/publications-resources/statements-membership-obligations-smos-1-7-revised.

Jeske, D., 2014, 'Special Obligations', in E.N. Zalta (ed.), *The Stanford Encyclopedia of Philosophy* (Spring 2014 ed.), http://plato.stanford.edu/archives/spr2014/entries/special-obligations/.

Johnson, R. and Cureton, A., 2016, 'Kant's moral philosophy', in E.N. Zalta (ed.), *The Stanford Encyclopedia of Philosophy* (Spring 2014 ed.), http://plato.stanford.edu/archives/fall2016/entries/kant-moral/.

Kahneman, D., 2011, *Thinking, Fast and Slow*, Doubleday Canada, Toronto.

Kant, I., 1785, 'Groundwork of the metaphysics of morals', in M.J. Gregor (ed.), (1996), *Practical Philosophy*, Cambridge University Press, Cambridge.

Lewicki, R.J., McAllister, D.J. and Bies, R.J., 1998, 'Trust and distrust: New relationships and realities', *Academy of Management Review* 23(3), 438–458.

Li, P. P., 2012, 'When trust matters the most: The imperatives for contextualizing trust research', *Journal of Trust Research* 2(2), 101–106.

Mayer, R.C., Davis, J.H. and Schoorman, F.D., 1995, 'An integrative model of organizational trust', *Academy of Management Review* 20, 709–734.

Mill, J. S. and Bentham, J., 1789, *An Introduction to the Principles of Morals and Legislation*, Doubleday, Garden City.

Ross, W., 1930, *The Right and the Good*, Oxford University Press, Oxford.

Sinnott-Armstrong, W., 2014, 'Consequentialism', in E.N. Zalta (ed.), *The Stanford Encyclopedia of Philosophy* (Spring 2014 ed.), http://plato.stanford.edu/archives/spr2014/entries/consequentialism/.

Skelton, A., 2012, 'William David Ross', in E.N. Zalta (ed.), *The Stanford Encyclopedia of Philosophy* (Summer 2012 ed.), http://plato.stanford.edu/archives/sum2012/entries/william-david-ross/.

Thaler, R.H., 2015, *Misbehaving*, W.W. Norton, New York.

Thaler, R.H., 2016, *Behavioral Economics: Past, Present and Future*, http://ssrn.com/abstract=2790606.

Van de Walle, S. and Six, F., 2014, 'Trust and distrust as distinct concepts: Why studying distrust in institutions is important', *Journal of Comparative Policy Analysis* 16(2), 158–174.

Waluchow, W., 2003, *The Dimensions of Ethics*, The Broadview Press, Toronto.

Wenar, L., 2015, 'Rights', in E.N. Zalta (ed.), *The Stanford Encyclopedia of Philosophy* (Fall 2015 ed.), http://plato.stanford.edu.login.ezproxy.library.ualberta.ca/archives/fall2015/entries/rights/.

7

Stakeholder and legitimacy frameworks as applied to Behavioural Accounting Research

Giacomo Manetti and Marco Bellucci

Stakeholder and legitimacy theories and behavioural accounting

Behavioural Accounting Research is defined as the study of the behaviour of accountants, with special emphasis on how non-accountants are influenced by accounting functions, reports and information (Hofstedt and Kinard 1970; Kaufman and Englander 2011).

According to Hofstedt and Kinard (1970), three perspectives can be applied to the study of accounting relative to behaviour:

1   The influence of the accountant's technical functions on behaviour (e.g., personal behaviours during an audit);
2   The behaviour of accountants (e.g., how accountants behave when making a decision on materiality);
3   The influence of accounting information on those receiving the information (e.g., the effects sustainability reports have on a reader).

As the process of communication between organizations and users of accounting information is a crucial point, the second and third perspectives are very relevant to both stakeholder and legitimacy theory. Two questions arise. The first is: *how do the expectations and values of stakeholders and communities affect the behaviour of organizations and their accounting and disclosure practices?*

Behavioural Accounting Research can investigate how society or stakeholders' perceptions influence accounting and disclosure policies. This is increasingly important given the emphasis on accountability, corporate social responsibility (CSR), and social, environmental and sustainability (SES) reporting that has emerged in the last few decades. For example, one may wonder why some entities voluntarily include details of their environmental performance and others do not. This behaviour might be motivated, on the one hand, by the willingness of the organization to demonstrate that it pursues something more than financial gain; on the other hand, this behaviour could also be motivated by a demand for legitimacy, by the willingness of an organization to align its reputation with the expectations of stakeholders and the wider community. SES reporting is conducted because different stakeholders require information for their decisions that are not available in financial reports and other company communications.

From a stakeholder theory perspective (Freeman 1984), the normative approach (Donaldson and Preston 1995) assumes that accountants have a duty to primary stakeholders. Thus, reporting is assumed to be a responsibility rather than a requirement. By contrast, the instrumental approach (Donaldson and Preston 1995; Clarkson 1995) suggests that reporting is an opportunity to improve relationships with numerous stakeholders, thereby consolidating or improving the organization's reputation and performance.

Behavioural accounting methods can be used to investigate the behaviour and criteria followed by accountants in defining the set of primary stakeholders while also explaining the most effective tools to engage them. This is important because it helps us understand how the informational demands and relative power of particular stakeholder groups can influence organization accounting and disclosure policies. Legitimacy theory (Gray, Owen and Adams 1996; Deegan 2002; Mathews 1993) stresses the idea that a social contract exists between the firm and the internal and external stakeholders. Since the terms of the social contract consider that acceptability of various activities, the legitimacy perspective focuses on a firm's willingness to demonstrate that its activities are acceptable to society and that the contract is legitimate. This chapter addresses a range of stimulating and noteworthy academic works that have contributed to this line of research (see, for example, Gray 2000; Parmar, Freeman, Harrison, Wicks, Purnell and De Colle 2010; Roberts 1992; Wood and Ross 2006; Neu, Warsame and Pedwell 1998).

The second general question that arises is: *what are the results of different accounting and reporting practices on the behaviour of communities and stakeholders?* In other words, when an entity – a stakeholder, a citizen or a structured/unstructured organization – looks at one company, this entity will consciously or unconsciously ascribe to this company a series of basic expectations. The extent to which these subjective expectations are satisfied is one of the factors that defines the legitimacy levels of that particular organization. Thus, behavioural research on accounting could employ stakeholder and legitimacy theories to explain how different accounting and reporting practices influence the behaviour of stakeholders, their expectations and their view of the company. Although some efforts have already been made to tackle this second question (see, for example, Dermer 1990; Greenwood and Van Buren 2010), further contributions are needed.

Introduction to stakeholder theory

Stakeholder theory is an organizational and management approach, originally elaborated by Freeman (1984), that gives each stakeholder a significant voice in making important decisions: "That is, each of these stakeholder groups has a right not to be treated as a means to some end, and therefore must participate in determining the future direction of the firm in which they have a stake" (Evan and Freeman 1993: 255; see also Stieb 2009 and Miles 2012). The stakeholder concept was also discussed in the works of Rhenman and Stymne (1965) in Sweden, and the Stanford Research Institute (1982) and Ansoff (1965) in the United States (Carroll and Näsi 1997).

Stakeholder theory is rooted in strategic management (e.g., Clarkson 1995; Freeman 1984; J. Freeman 1999), but in the last 20 years it has found expression in the fields of organization theory (e.g., Donaldson and Preston 1995; Jones 1995; Rowley 1997), business ethics (e.g., Phillips and Reichart 2000; Starik 1995) and accounting theory (Thorne, Mahoney and Manetti 2014). Stakeholder theory also figures prominently in the study of social, environmental and sustainability issues (e.g., Wood 1991a, 1991b). Moreover, in the last decade it has gained traction among scholars who study sustainable development (e.g., Sharma and Henriques 2005; Steurer, Langer, Konrad and Martinuzzi 2005).

Freeman (1984) initially offered a rational approach to strategic management, urging firms to recognize stakeholders in order to achieve better results and improve general performance. Whereas the traditional "shareholder view" suggests that companies have a binding fiduciary duty to give priority to shareholders' expectations, Freeman's stakeholder approach argues that several groups and individuals should be involved in the process of managing an organization, including employees, customers, suppliers, financiers, the community, governmental and non-governmental organizations, political groups and trade unions.

According to Laplume, Sonpar and Litz (2008), "stakeholder theory is timely yet adolescent, controversial yet important." It is timely because it affects "the dominant institutions of our time", oftentimes discovering misconduct or environmental wrongdoing by firms. At the same time, the theory is "adolescent" because its empirical validity has not yet been established (e.g., Jones 1995). Stakeholder theory is also controversial because it questions the traditional idea that profits are the primary measure of a firm's success, a phenomenon that Jensen (2002: 237) refers to as a "single-valued objective". In other words, stakeholder theory is relevant because it seeks to address how organizations affect the societies in which they operate (Hinings and Greenwood 2003; Stern and Barley 1996).

Laplume et al. (2008) also believe that, despite its detractors – see, for example, Margolis and Walsh (2003) and Jensen (2002) – the emergence of stakeholder theory is a product of its emotional resonance – its ability to move people (Weick 1999). As such, Freeman claims that stakeholder theory recalls the "emergence of concerns with 'vision and values,' and 'a sense of purpose' in the mainstream conversations about business" (2000: 170). Even detractors such as Jensen acknowledge that "stakeholder theory taps into the deep emotional commitment of most individuals to the family and tribe" (2002: 243). In this sense, stakeholder theory should be given priority in the study of behavioural economics and deserves to be the focus of future scholarship.

The diverse aspects of stakeholder theory

Donaldson and Preston (1995) argue that stakeholder theory features three distinct categories of analysis: descriptive, instrumental and normative. From a descriptive point of view, stakeholder theory is used to explain the characteristics and behaviours of companies and other organizations, including how they are managed, how the board of directors addresses the needs and demands of multiple constituencies, how they create and implement various management strategies, and the nature of the organization itself. The instrumental approach tries to identify the potential or effective connections that exist between stakeholder management and the achievement of organization goals and aims. This includes the links between better stakeholder management and profitability, as well as the enhancement of an organization's reputation within the community. Finally, the normative approach presumes that organizations have a duty to identify and involve stakeholders who have specific interests with the organization, identifying the "moral or philosophical guidelines for the operation and management of the corporation" (Donaldson and Preston 1995: 71).

The normative approach

Drawing inspiration from the proposals of Donaldson and Preston (1995), some scholars believe that stakeholder theory is primarily a moral theory and that much of the research focuses on finding moral bases to support its major ideas (Donaldson and Preston 1995; Goodpaster 1991; Boatright 1994). In keeping with the normative point of view, stakeholder theory implies the presence of specific duties and obligations that companies ought to address among various stakeholders. More recently, supporters of the normative approach have tried to classify the relational models between organizations and stakeholders by assuming a gradual growth of stakeholder involvement and participation (Svendsen 1998; Waddock 2002). First, the organization identifies and maps its stakeholders, if possible distinguishing between primary parties (those who are strategic in the middle- to long-term) and secondary parties (stakeholders who do not affect its sustainability) (Clarkson 1995: 92–117). Second, it tries to manage stakeholders' expectations and the claims they support in accordance with their salience (Mitchell, Agle and Wood 1997), while also balancing these various positions through a process of stakeholder management (O'Dwyer 2005). During the final step, organizations try to engage primary stakeholders in various decision-making processes, making them participants in organizational management and governance, sharing information, dialoguing and creating a model of mutual responsibility. The stakeholder engagement phase, unlike the stakeholder mapping and management phase, "creates a dynamic context of interaction, mutual respect, dialogue and change, not a unilateral management of stakeholders" (Andriof, Waddock, Husted and Rahman 2002: 9). As a result, the main feature of stakeholder engagement is not to encourage the mere involvement of stakeholders in order to "mitigate" or manage their expectations, but to create a network of mutual responsibility (Andriof et al. 2002: 15; Manetti and Bellucci 2016; Unerman and Bennett 2004; Voss, Voss and Moorman 2005; Windsor 2002: 138). Jones and Wicks (1999) and R.E. Freeman (1999) and J. Freeman (1999) explicitly reject the idea that it is possible to separate the branches of stakeholder theory, arguing that all of these branches overlap with each other. Thus, stakeholder theory is simultaneously descriptive, instrumental and normative.

The classification of stakeholders

Studying stakeholder theory from a managerial point of view, Mitchell et al. (1997) tried to classify the various stakeholder categories based on the attributes of power (the ability of a stakeholder group to impose its will in the relationship with the organization), legitimacy (how specific stakeholder group expectations and claims are socially accepted in line with expected structures or behaviours) and urgency (time sensitivity or criticality of the stakeholder interests). Management must shape the relationships between stakeholders and the organization and among stakeholders in order to maximize value and decide how wealth is distributed (Freeman 1984). Since there is often conflict among various stakeholder interests, executives must reconsider problems and find a way to satisfy the widest range of stakeholder needs, thereby enhancing the value that may be created for each category or sub-category (Harrison, Bosse and Phillips et al. 2010). According to Harrison, Bosse and Phillips (2010), "if tradeoffs have to be made then executives must figure out how to make the tradeoffs, and then work on improving the tradeoffs for all sides" (Parmar et al. 2010: 406).

Stakeholder theory and agency theory

The conflict between agency and stakeholder theories has long been debated in management literature (Shankman 1999). These two theories are often described as polar opposites, since many scholars argue that their assumptions and points of view are irreconcilable and cannot be made compatible. For instance, Jensen characterizes stakeholder theory as a challenge to nearly two centuries of economic theory and research, arguing that "stakeholder theory plays into the hands of special interests who wish to use the resources of firms for their own ends" and that "multiple objectives is no objective" (Jensen 2002: 243). According to Jensen, stakeholder theory increases agency costs in the economic system because it expands the power of managers in an unproductive way. This happens because stakeholder theory distracts managers from their main duty: the maximization of the firm's value. Therefore, Jensen affirms that the only aim of any company should be to maximize total market value, while recognizing, at the same time, that stakeholder satisfaction represents a strategic element for meeting this objective. To explain his argument further, Jensen introduces the concept of "enlightened value maximization", which represents the long-term market value of any firm that is maximized when stakeholders' preferences are fulfilled.

However, there are also many scholars who believe in a broader and more relevant reconciliation between the two theories. For instance, Shankman (1999) believes that agency theory is not inconsistent with the general stakeholder model, claiming that:

- stakeholder theory is the necessary outcome of agency theory and is thus a more appropriate way of conceptualizing other theories;
- agency theory, when properly adapted, can act as a narrow form of stakeholder theory;
- the assumptions about opportunistic human behaviour and motivation implicit in agency theory are contradictory;
- all theories must guarantee an implicit moral minimum that includes certain fundamental rights and principles and assumptions of human behaviour that may very well require other traditional theories to be modified or even reconceived.

Stakeholder theory, Shankman believes, complements rather than undermines agency theory.

Another possible means of reconciling stakeholder theory and agency theory is provided by Phillips, Freeman and Wicks (2003). Supporters of agency theory believe that agents (managers) must act solely in the interest (value maximization) of the principals (shareholders), and that stakeholder theory appears to be "immoral" because it ignores this relationship. However, Phillips et al. (2003) affirm that "this criticism of stakeholder theory is a version of the evil genie argument." Of course, managerial opportunism is a problem in many corporations, but there are many reasons to believe that stakeholder theory is more resistant to managerial self-dealing. For instance, the authors cite Hill and Jones (1992) who, in presenting their version of the "stakeholder-agency theory", argue that managers' interest in organizational growth (citing motivations such as remuneration, power, job security and status) is often contrary to not only shareholder interests, but also to the interests of stakeholders. The claims of different groups may conflict, but "each group can be seen as having a stake in the continued existence of the firm" (Hill and Jones 1992: 145). According to Phillips et al. (2003), managers serve only the interests of the organization.

The core problem in reconciling the two theories is the moral discourse involved in company management. As Quinn and Jones (1995) explain, the adoption of the agency perspective leads to a discourse based on self-interest, whereas the adoption of stakeholder theory leads to a discourse of "duty" and social responsibility. Thus, the managerial discourse cannot be expected to combine fully the extremes of profit-seeking self-interest and moral responsibility to society. According to Sternberg (1998: 28),

> the only realistic compromise solution to this problem is to adopt the business case, rather than the pure ethics case. The business case for managers to adopt a stakeholder-oriented approach is based on the notion that "good ethics" is "good business" and the employing ethics as a strategic management tool increases the present value of the firm.

Meanwhile, Quinn and Jones (1995) speak of "instrumental ethics", whereby managers adopt an ethos of corporate social responsibility in order to maximize shareholder wealth. Finally, Hill and Jones (1992) suggest that answering multiple constituencies doesn't increase accountability, as stakeholder groups will often maintain managerial accountability because diverse groups tend to monitor both management as well as each other.

All of the above considerations are synthesized in Table 7.1, which is dedicated to the differences and elements of reconciliation between agency and stakeholder theories. Table 7.1 also provides a synthetic comparison of stakeholder theory and agency theory.

Table 7.1 The differences and elements of reconciliation between stakeholder and agency theories

Differences	Authors	Elements of possible reconciliation
• Stakeholder theory increases agency costs in the economic system. • Stakeholder theory distracts managers from their main duty (value creation). • The two theories differ in their assumptions about human behaviour, levels of analysis, theories of motivation, and compliance. • Agency theory is based on organizational economics, which contrasts with the more humanistic or ethics-based approaches associated with stakeholder theory.	Jensen (2002)	• Stakeholder satisfaction represents an assumption that obtaining market value maximization is the primary goal of individual firms. • Firms often adopt an ethos of "enlightened value maximization", an approach that is based on the idea that the long-term market value of the firm cannot be met without stakeholder expectation fulfilment.
• The agency perspective acts as the primary theoretical basis of many management theories. • Stakeholder theory is not appreciated by political economists, while agency theory has achieved "managerial supremacy". • Stakeholder theory is a controversial approach in market economies. • The adoption of the agency perspective leads to a discourse based on self-interest, whereas adoption of the stakeholder theory leads to a discourse of "duty" and social responsibility.	Shankman (1999) Hill and Jones (1992)	• Stakeholder theory is the necessary outcome of agency theory. • Agency theory can act as a narrow form of stakeholder theory. • The assumptions about opportunistic human behaviour and motivation implicit in agency theory are contradictory. • All theories, even agency theory, must guarantee an implicit moral minimum that is included in stakeholder theory. • Good ethics practices represent a strategic management tool that increases the value of the firm. • Answering multiple constituencies doesn't increase accountability because diverse stakeholder groups often monitor both management and each other.

Differences	Authors	Elements of possible reconciliation
	Phillips et al. (2003)	• There are many reasons to believe that stakeholder theory is more resistant to managerial self-dealing. • Managers' interest in organizational growth is contrary not only to shareholder interests, but also to the interests of stakeholders. • Each stakeholder group can be seen as having a stake in the continued existence of the firm. • Managers serve only the interests of the organization.

Introduction to legitimacy theory

While profit has traditionally been the first and only measure of a firm's success, public expectations have changed in the last 30 years in such a way as to encourage organizations to take into account other social and environmental issues (Deegan 2002; Deegan, Rankin and Tobin 2002; Gray et al. 1996; Thorne et al. 2014). Moreover, the community and society at large have come to be seen as increasingly important stakeholders (Mitchell et al. 1997). As a result, societal aims and perceptions can influence the policies of organizations, as corporate entities are influenced by and often influence the society in which they operate.

Striving for legitimacy

Organizations want to operate within the boundaries and norms of society in order to ensure that their activities are seen as legitimate. According to Lindblom (1994), legitimacy is the condition or status which exists when an entity's value system is congruent with the value system of the larger social system of which the entity is a part. When a disparity, real or perceived, exists between the two value systems, there is a threat to the entity's legitimacy. In other words, legitimacy can be viewed as a generalized perception or assumption that the actions of an entity are desirable, proper or appropriate within a socially constructed system of norms, values, beliefs and definitions (Suchman 1995). This definition implies that legitimacy is a desirable social good, that it is something more than a matter of optics, and that it may be defined and negotiated at various levels of society (Mitchell et al. 1997).

Organizations are thought to be legitimate when they pursue socially acceptable goals in a socially acceptable manner. Given this normative quality, performance and economic efficiency alone are insufficient in terms of obtaining or maintaining an organization's legitimacy (Chen and Roberts 2010; Epstein and Votaw 1978). Thus, legitimacy is not entirely synonymous with economic achievement or legality. Economic success is just one facet of legitimacy. while the legal system often enforces, rather than creates, changes in social values (Deegan 2002; Lindblom 1994).

Suchman (1995) depicts legitimacy as a complex concept, comprising various dimensions in which distinctions are made between pragmatic, moral and cognitive legitimacy. Pragmatic legitimacy depends on the extent to which organizational behaviour positively affects its audience's well-being; moral legitimacy involves any attempt to judge the rightness of what an organization is actually doing and cognitive legitimacy depends on the capacity of the organization to render its actions and behaviour predictable (Monfardini, Barretta and Ruggiero 2013). As Buhr (1998) suggests, there are two dimensions at play in an organization's efforts to attain legitimacy: action (whether the organization's activities are congruent with social values) and presentation (whether the activities *appear* to be congruent with social values). Of course, the actions of an organization may deviate extensively from societal norms, but because the divergence goes unnoticed, the organization retains its legitimacy (Chen and Roberts 2010). Legitimacy is also a dynamic concept, as expectations can change over time and particular events might occur that adversely affect the reputation of the company, its legitimacy and perhaps even its very existence (Lindblom 1994; Makela and Nasi 2010).

The "social contract"

Maurer (1971) states that legitimization is the process whereby an organization justifies to a peer or super-ordinate system its right to exist. This latter process can be directly related to the concept of a "social contract" – or "social licence" – which contains the implicit and explicit expectations that society has on how an entity should conduct its operations. As reported by Deegan (2002), the social contract idea is not new, having been discussed by philosophers such as Thomas Hobbes (1588–1679), John Locke (1632–1704) and Jean-Jacques Rousseau (1712–1778). These early thinkers in the field viewed the social contract primarily as a political theory, insofar as it explained the supposed relationship between government and its constituencies (Rawls 1971). In the modern era, however, the social contract has been extended to include businesses and other institutions (Campbell 2000).

Gray et al. (1996) suggest that legal requirements provide the explicit terms of the contract, while other non-legislated societal expectations embody the implicit terms of the contract. This is an important point for companies, if only because they are allowed to continue their operations only insofar as they meet societal expectations. An organization's survival can be threatened if society believes that the organization has breached the social contract; when society is not satisfied that the organization is operating in an acceptable, or legitimate, manner, then it will effectively revoke the organization's "contract" to continue operating (Deegan 2002). This phenomenon is illustrated through consumers who reduce or eliminate demand for certain products, factor suppliers eliminating the supply of labour and financial capital or constituents lobbying government for increased taxes, fines or regulations to prohibit actions that do not conform with societal expectations (Deegan 2002).

This is consistent with Mathews (1993), who states that the social contract exists between organizations and individual members of society; society, as a collection of individuals, provides organizations with their legal standing, the authority to own and use natural resources, and the right to hire employees. The organization has no inherent claim to these benefits, and in order to validate a company's existence, society expects the benefits to exceed the costs (Mathews 1993). Of course, companies may take a host of actions to legitimize their activities. Dowling and Pfeffer (1975) suggest that an organization that is struggling to establish a measure of legitimacy can:

- adapt its output, goals and methods of operation to conform to prevailing definitions of legitimacy;
- attempt, through communication, to alter the definition of social legitimacy so that it conforms to the organization's present practices, output and values;
- try, again through communication, to become identified with symbols, values or institutions that have a strong base of legitimacy.

The main characteristics of legitimacy theory

Legitimacy theory focuses on whether the value system of an organization is congruent with the value system of society, and whether the objectives of organizations meet social expectations. Like stakeholder theory, legitimacy theory has its antecedent in the study of political economy (Deegan 2002), which claims that economic issues cannot be divorced from their political, social and institutional contexts (Gray et al. 1996). Political economy theory explicitly recognizes the power conflicts that exist within society and the struggles that occur between various groups within society. By considering political economy in one's work, scholars are better able to consider broader societal issues that have an impact on how organizations operate and what information they elect to disclose (Deegan 2002). Consistent with this view, supporters of legitimacy theory argue that organizations do not have any inherent right to resources or, in fact, to exist. Organizations exist to the extent that society considers them legitimate (Deegan 2002).

Legitimacy is often considered as a resource among supporters of legitimacy theory. On the one hand, organizations are dependent on this resource for survival (Dowling and Pfeffer 1975); on the other hand, organizations can manipulate how society perceives their behaviour and activities (Woodward, Edwards and Birkin 2001). Like resource dependence theory (Pfeffer and Salancik 1978), legitimacy theory suggests that managers will pursue strategies to ensure the continued supply of resources whenever the supply of that particular resource is deemed vital to organizational survival (Deegan 2002). Legitimacy theory, however, does not specify that these strategies ought to be formulated and implemented (Chen and Roberts 2010); organizations may, instead, try to control or collaborate with other parties who are considered legitimate or engage in targeted disclosures of information (Fiedler and Deegan 2007; Guthrie and Parker 1989; Oliver 1990).

Legitimacy theory and stakeholder theory

As we noted earlier in this chapter, legitimacy theory and stakeholder theory are both derived from political economy theory. At a very general level, it is possible to say that both theories provide a framework for programs and actions that aim to influence the relationships between organizations and other interested parties. Legitimacy theory stresses the alignment between the value system of an organization and the value system of society, as well as the objectives of an organization and social expectations. The scholarly literature defines legitimacy as the desirable congruence between an organization's value system and that of the larger social system of which it is a part. Indeed, the organization is said to be unable to prosper or even survive if it is not seen to espouse outputs, goals and methods that society finds acceptable (De Villiers and Van Staden 2006).

Stakeholder theory is closely aligned with legitimacy theory, as the two are often used to complement each other (Deegan 2002). However, according to Gray et al. (1996), stakeholder theory stipulates that the organization is part of a wider social system. This perspective takes into consideration the different stakeholder groups within society and the organization itself, and why and how they should best be managed if the organization is to survive.

While stakeholder theory often addresses which groups in society corporations should be responsible to, Phillips (2003) argues that the concept of legitimacy remains imprecise within the stakeholder literature. For instance, do all stakeholders have an equally "legitimate" claim on the resources of the corporation? Stakeholder legitimacy has been a central concern since Freeman's seminal work, *Strategic Management: A Stakeholder Approach*, was published in 1984.

> Stakeholder connotes legitimacy, and while managers may not think that certain groups are "legitimate" in the sense that their demands on the firm are inappropriate they had

better give "legitimacy" to these groups in terms of their ability to affect the direction of the firm. Hence, legitimacy can be understood in a managerial sense implying that it is legitimate to spend time and resources on stakeholders, regardless of the appropriateness of their demands.

(Freeman 1984: 45)

The ambiguity regarding stakeholder legitimacy manifests itself in the "broad vs. narrow" debate (Freeman and Reed 1983; Mitchell et al. 1997), which hinges on whether stakeholders can be defined as any group that is affected by the achievement of the firm's objectives (broad), or only those groups to whom a moral obligation is owed (narrow). Phillips (2003: 40) claims that "the distinction between normative, derivative, and non-stakeholders is vital to both scholars and managers." "Normative legitimacy" applies to those stakeholders for whose benefit the firm is managed, and to whom the organization has a moral obligation, while "derivative legitimacy" applies to those groups whose actions and claims must be accounted for by managers due to their potential effects upon the organization and its normative stakeholders. Phillips (2003) claims that managers have distinct ethical obligations to normative stakeholders that may not exist among derivative stakeholders or non-stakeholders. These obligations, moreover, necessitate a different sort of managerial behaviour, attention and treatment.

Table 7.2 provides a synthetic comparison of legitimacy theory and stakeholder theory.

Table 7.2 The differences and elements of reconciliation between legitimacy and stakeholder theories

Differences	Authors	Elements of possible reconciliation
• The focal point of legitimacy theory is that the alignment between organizations' behaviour and social expectations acts a strategic resource, while the focal point of stakeholder theory is that stakeholders have the right to be involved in their organization's decisions. • Both theories provide a framework for programs and actions that aim to influence the relationships between the organization and other interested parties. However, stakeholder theory also focuses on the reciprocal relationship with relevant stakeholders, while legitimacy theory focuses on a more general "licence to operate" that is issued by society as a whole.	Deegan (2002)	• Stakeholder theory is closely aligned with legitimacy theory, and the two are often used to complement each other. • Legitimacy and stakeholder theory are both products of political economic theory, which argues that economic issues cannot be divorced from their political, social and institutional contexts.
• Legitimacy theory stresses the alignment between, on the one hand, the value system of an organization and the value system of society, and, on the other hand, the objectives of an organization and social expectations. The organization is said to be unable to prosper or even survive if it does not espouse outputs, goals and methods that society finds acceptable.	Gray et al. (1996)	• By considering political economy in their research, scholars are better able to consider broader societal issues that have an impact on how organizations operate and what information they elect to disclose.

Differences	Authors	Elements of possible reconciliation
• Stakeholder theory stipulates that the organization is also considered to be part of a wider social system. This perspective takes into consideration the different stakeholder groups within society and the organization itself, and why and how they should best be managed if the organization is to survive. • While both theories take into account the expectations of society, stakeholder theory tends to focus on the expectations of the specific stakeholders of the organization. However, it is not always easy to define who the legitimate stakeholders of an organization actually are. • The concept of legitimacy remains imprecise within the stakeholder literature. It is important to ask, for instance, whether all stakeholders have an equally "legitimate" claim on the resources of any given organization.	Fiedler and Deegan (2007); Guthrie and Parker (1989); De Villiers and Van Staden (2006) Freeman (1984) Phillips (2003)	• Organizations may try to control or collaborate with other parties who are considered legitimate, be they internal or external stakeholders. • At the same time, they sometimes engage in targeted disclosures of information towards stakeholders and external parties. • Stakeholder legitimacy has been a central concern since Freeman published *Strategic Management: A Stakeholder Approach* in 1984. • He asks whether all stakeholders have an equally "legitimate" claim on the resources of any given corporation. • While stakeholder theory often addresses which groups in society corporations should be responsible to, the concept of legitimacy remains imprecise within the stakeholder literature. • Managers have distinct ethical obligations towards normative stakeholders that may not exist among derivative stakeholders or non-stakeholders. • These different obligations dictate a different brand of managerial behaviour, attention and treatment.

The contribution of stakeholder and legitimacy theories to accounting studies

Stakeholder theory has been a part of the accounting literature since its formulation during the 1980s. For instance, Dermer (1990) compared organizations to ecosystems in order to demonstrate the importance of accounting to strategic and management decisions. In such an ecosystem, organization stakeholders compete to control and/or influence corporate strategies, and accounting systems become tools for assessing the risks of "investing their stakes" with a particular firm (Greenwood and Van Buren 2010).

In 1988, while examining the annual reports of several American corporations, Meek and Gray (1988) argued that value-added statements can be useful for a wide range of stakeholder groups. Furthermore, according to Parmar et al. (2010), accounting scholars have been debating issues on SES accounting and reporting since at least the 1970s (Gray, Kouhy and Lavers 1995). The influence of stakeholder theory on SES accounting continued to grow in subsequent decades. For instance, Roberts (1992) used stakeholder theory to predict levels of corporate social disclosure. He demonstrated how stakeholder power, strategic posture and economic performance are all related to disclosure levels, especially among North American corporations. During this same period, studies on SES reporting also began to refer to stakeholder theory on a fairly regular basis (Rubenstein 1992; Ilinitch, Soderstrom and Thomas 1998). Among stakeholder categories there is some evidence that financial stakeholders and government regulators can be most effective in demanding CSR disclosure (Neu et al. 1998). In the last decade, meanwhile, Campbell, Moore and Shrives (2006) have demonstrated that community disclosures are a function of stakeholder information needs, while Boesso and Kumar (2007) have similarly claimed that social disclosure is influenced by four factors:

- the information needs of investors;
- the attention companies pay to stakeholder management;
- the relevance of intangible assets;
- market complexity.

In another relatively recent study, Wood and Ross (2006) found that stakeholders' opinions are a more powerful mechanism for influencing managerial attitudes towards SES voluntary disclosures than subsidization, regulatory costs or mandatory disclosure. Thus, research on stakeholder influence and SES reporting shows that the quantity and quality of voluntary reporting depends on several related factors.

Manetti (2011) emphasizes the role of stakeholder engagement in defining the contents of SES reports. Stakeholder engagement is strictly connected to the principles of materiality and relevance for defining the content of these reports (Manetti and Bellucci 2016). These principles suggest that stakeholder engagement determines which information and data should be included in the document (Gray 2000: 249–250). International standards and guidelines for social reporting require stakeholder engagement as a compulsory stage in order to produce a complete and useful document (AccountAbility 2011; Global Reporting Initiative 2013). Many scholars over the last decade have also collected empirical evidence regarding unprecedented levels of stakeholder dialogue in social reporting, while also questioning the sincerity and the impact of these practices (UNEP and Sustainability 1999; Miles, Hammond and Friedman 2002; Downey 2002; ACCA 2005).

Furthermore, many studies over the past 20 years have investigated the role of stakeholders in influencing financial disclosure, such as earnings management (Richardson 1997), earning announcements (Bowman, Johnson, Shevlin and Shores 1992), financial reporting approaches (Scott, McKinnon and Harrison 2003) and "creative accounting" practices (Shaw 1995). In 2003 Ashbaugh and Warfield found that several diverse stakeholder categories can have an effect on the choice of firm auditors, while Chen, Carson and Simnett (2007) demonstrated that particular stakeholder characteristics often influence the extent to which firms voluntarily disclose short-term financial information. Meanwhile, Winston and Sharp (2005) investigated the influence of stakeholders on the process of setting international financial reporting standards. There are also studies that demonstrate how auditors spend time and energy on aspects of reporting that are irrelevant to several stakeholder categories (Ohman, Hackner, Jansson and Tschudi 2006).

Even proponents of legitimacy theory claim that various accounting disciplines overlap with each other on a regular basis. Parker (2005: 846) suggests that legitimacy theory "suffers from problems that include apparent conceptual overlap with political economy accounting theory and institutional theory, lack of specificity, uncertain ability to anticipate and explain managerial behaviour and a suspicion that is still privileges financial stakeholders in its analysis." Nevertheless, legitimacy theory has contributed to accounting theory in several important ways over the past 40 years, especially in the field of SES accounting. Early accounting theory identified the users of accounting information as financial stakeholders – for example, creditors and shareholders (Magness 2006). Disclosures in annual reports were directed primarily at those groups and were designed to discharge stewardship obligations in order to ensure ongoing access to financial markets (Gray et al. 1995). Over time, the concept of the stakeholder expanded to include suppliers, insurers, consumer associations, regulators, environmental groups and media (Canadian Institute of Chartered Accountants 1997; Magness 2006), while the objectives of accounting expanded to include social and environmental interests (Gray et al. 1995; Magness 2006). This put considerable pressure on managers to find ways to respond to a diversity of interests. Legitimacy theory, for example, was subsequently integrated into the accounting literature as a means of explaining what, why, when and how certain items are addressed by corporate management in their communication with outside audiences (Magness 2006).

Legitimacy theory is often used to motivate CSR and the voluntary disclosure of non-financial information. According to the legitimacy perspective, organizations issue SES reports to reduce their external costs or diminish pressures that are being imposed by external stakeholders or regulators (Adams 2002; Caron and Turcotte 2009; Tate, Ellram and Kirchoff 2010). SES disclosure has often been seen as a tool of legitimization (Lindblom 1994; Patten 2005). Voluntary disclosure of sustainability issues is often done for strategic reasons, as organizations use these reports to influence (or even manipulate) stakeholder perceptions of their image, performance and impact (Coupland 2006; Deegan 2002; Guidry and Patten 2010).

Conclusions

In this chapter, we discussed stakeholder and legitimacy theory, and explained how both theories contribute to the fields of accounting studies and behavioural research in accounting. The stakeholder approach claims that organizations are not only accountable to their shareholders, but should also balance a multiplicity of stakeholder interests that can affect (or be affected by) organizational objectives (Freeman 1984). Legitimacy theory examines whether the value system of an organization is congruent with the value system of society, and whether the objectives and means of an organization meet societal expectations.

The relationship between stakeholder and legitimacy theory and behavioural research on accounting is in need of further exploration, as is the impact of stakeholders and society on the behaviour of accountants and the impact of accounting practices on the behaviours of internal and external stakeholders. These topics should be tackled employing innovative methodologies such as "neuroaccounting" or "neuroeconomics", both of which analyze the neurological basis of individual decision-making and behaviour.

The practical implications of these fields of study are vast due to the growing emphasis on CSR and SES accounting and reporting over the past 30 years. All three areas of research examine the management of legitimacy and stakeholder's expectations by companies and other organizations. For example, it has been shown that societal perceptions can influence and be influenced by the disclosure policies of an organization. In order to uphold its part of the "social contract", an organization could, on the one hand, adjust its aims and means; on the other hand, it could also revise its disclosure policies, re-orienting them in a way that enhances the organization's legitimacy. The focus here is on the communication process between the organization (and their accounting practices and disclosure policies) and its various stakeholders.

Further research should focus on studying why and how the expectations and values of stakeholders and communities affect the behaviour of companies and their accounting and disclosure practices. Similarly, the consequences of different accounting and reporting practices on the behaviour of stakeholders and communities is also worth examining in greater detail.

References

ACCA, 2005, *Improving Stakeholder Engagement Reporting: An ACCA and the Environment Council Workshop*, Certified Accountants Educational Trust, London.

AccountAbility, 2011, *AA1000 Stakeholder Engagement Standard 2011: Final Exposure Draft*, AccountAbility, London.

Adams, C.A., 2002, 'Internal organisational factors influencing corporate social and ethical reporting: Beyond current theorising', *Accounting, Auditing & Accountability Journal* 15(2), 223–250.

Andriof, J., Waddock, S., Husted, B. and Rahman, S., 2002, *Unfolding Stakeholder Thinking: Theory Responsibility and Engagement*, Greenleaf Publishing, Sheffield.

Ansoff, H.I., 1965, *Corporate Strategy: An Analytic Approach to Business Policy for Growth and Expansion*, McGraw-Hill, New York.

Ashbaugh, H. and Warfield, T.D., 2003, 'Audits as a corporate governance mechanism: Evidence from the German market', *Journal of International Accounting Research* 2, 1–21.

Boatright, J.R., 1994, 'Fiduciary duties & the shareholder-management relation: Or, what's so special about shareholders', *Business Ethics Quarterly* 4(4), 393–407.

Boesso, G. and Kumar, K., 2007, 'Drivers of corporate voluntary disclosure', *Accounting, Auditing & Accountability Journal* 20(2), 269–296.

Bowman, R.M., Johnson, M.F., Shevlin, T. and Shores, D., 1992, 'Determinants of the timing of quarterly earnings announcement', *Journal of Accounting, Auditing & Finance* 7, 395–422.

Buhr, N., 1998, 'Environmental performance, legislation and annual report disclosure: The case of acid rain and Falconbridge', *Accounting, Auditing & Accountability Journal* 11(2), 163–190.

Campbell, D.J., 2000, 'Legitimacy theory or managerial reality construction? Corporate social disclosure in Marks and Spencer Plc corporate reports', Paper presented at the Accounting Forum.

Campbell, D., Moore, G. and Shrives, P., 2006, 'Cross-sectional effects in community disclosure', *Accounting, Auditing & Accountability Journal* 19(1), 96–114.

Canadian Institute of Chartered Accountants, 1997, *Full Cost Accounting From an Environmental Perspective*, Canadian Institute of Chartered Accountants, Toronto, Canada.

Caron, M.A. and Turcotte, M.F.B., 2009, 'Path dependence and path creation: Framing the extra-financial information market for a sustainable trajectory', *Accounting, Auditing & Accountability Journal* 22(2), 272–297.

Carroll, A.B. and Näsi, J., 1997, 'Understanding stakeholder thinking: Themes from a Finnish conference', *Business Ethics: A European Review* 6(1), 46–51.

Chen, J.C. and Roberts, R.W., 2010, 'Toward a more coherent understanding of the organization-society relationship: A theoretical consideration for social and environmental accounting research', *Journal of Business Ethics* 97(4), 651–665.

Chen, L., Carson, E. and Simnett, R., 2007, 'Impact of stakeholder characteristics on voluntary dissemination of interim information & communication of its level of assurance', *Accounting & Finance* 47, 667–691.

Clarkson, M.B.E., 1995, 'A stakeholder framework of analyzing and evaluating corporate social performance', *Academy of Management Review* 20(1), 92–117.

Coupland, C., 2006, 'Corporate social and environmental responsibility in web-based reports: Currency in the banking sector?', *Critical Perspectives on Accounting* 17(7), 865–881.

Deegan, C., 2002, 'Introduction: The legitimising effect of social and environmental disclosures-a theoretical foundation', *Accounting, Auditing & Accountability Journal* 15(3), 282–311.

Deegan, C., Rankin, M. and Tobin, J., 2002, 'An examination of the corporate social and environmental disclosures of BHP from 1983–1997: A test of legitimacy theory', *Accounting, Auditing & Accountability Journal* 15(3), 312–343.

Dermer, J., 1990, 'The strategic agenda: Accounting for issues & support', *Accounting, Organizations & Society* 15, 67–76.

De Villiers, C. and Van Staden, C.J., 2006, 'Can less environmental disclosure have a legitimising effect? Evidence from Africa', *Accounting, Organizations and Society* 31(8), 763–781.

Donaldson, T. and Preston, L.E., 1995, 'The stakeholder theory and the corporation: Concepts, evidence and implications', *Academy of Management Review* 20(1), 65–91.

Dowling, J. and Pfeffer, J., 1975, 'Organizational legitimacy: Social values and organizational behavior', *Pacific Sociological Review* 18(1), 122–136.

Downey, P.R., 2002, 'The essential stakeholder dialogue', *Corporate Social Responsibility and Environmental Management* 9(1), 37–45.

Epstein, E.M. and Votaw, D., 1978, *Rationality, Legitimacy, Responsibility: Search for New Directions in Business and Society*, Gold Leaf Pub. Co, Birmingham, UK.

Evan, W. and Freeman, R.E., 1993, 'A stakeholder theory of the modern corporation: Kantian capitalism', in T. Beauchamp and N. Bowie (eds.), *Ethical Theory & Business*, Prentice Hall, Englewood Cliffs, NJ.

Fiedler, T. and Deegan, C., 2007, 'Motivations for environmental collaboration within the building and construction industry', *Managerial Auditing Journal* 22(4), 410–441.

Freeman, J., 1999, 'Stakeholder influence strategies', *Academy of Management Journal* 24(2), 191–205.

Freeman, R.E., 1984, *Strategic Management: A Stakeholder Approach*, Pitman Publishing, Boston.

Freeman, R.E., 1999, 'Divergent stakeholder theory', *Academy of Management Review* 24(2), 233–236.

Freeman, R.E., 2000, 'Business ethics at the millennium', *Business Ethics Quarterly* 10(1), 169–180.

Freeman, R.E. and Reed, D., 1983, 'Stockholders and stakeholders: New perspective on corporate governance', in C. Huizinga (ed.), *Corporate Governance: A Definitive Exploration of the Issues*, UCLA Extension Press, Los Angeles.

Global Reporting Initiative-GRI, 2013, *G4 Sustainability Reporting Guidelines*, GRI, Amsterdam.

Goodpaster, K.E., 1991, 'Business ethics and stakeholder analysis', *Business Ethics Quarterly* 1(1), 53–73.

Gray, R., 2000, 'Current developments and trends in social and environmental auditing reporting and attestation: A review and comment', *International Journal of Auditing* 4, 247–268.

Gray, R., Kouhy, R. and Lavers, S., 1995, 'Corporate social and environmental reporting: A review of the literature and a longitudinal study of UK disclosure', *Accounting, Auditing & Accountability Journal* 8(2), 47–77.

Gray, R., Owen, D. and Adams, C., 1996, *Accounting & Accountability: Changes and Challenges in Corporate Social and Environmental Reporting*, Prentice Hall, Upper Saddle River, NJ.

Greenwood, M. and Van Buren, H.J., 2010, 'Trust and stakeholder theory: Trustworthiness in the organisation – stakeholder relationship', *Journal of Business Ethics* 95(3), 425–438.

Guidry, R.P. and Patten, D.M., 2010, 'Market reactions to the first-time issuance of corporate sustainability reports: Evidence that quality matters', *Sustainability Accounting, Management and Policy Journal* 1(1), 33–50.

Guthrie, J. and Parker, L.D., 1989, 'Corporate social reporting: A rebuttal of legitimacy theory', *Accounting and Business Research* 19(76), 343–352.

Harrison, J.S., Bosse, D.A. and Phillips, R.A., 2010, 'Managing for stakeholders, stakeholder utility functions & competitive advantage', *Strategic Management Journal* 31(1), 58–74.

Hill, C.W.L. and Jones, T.M., 1992, 'Stakeholder-agency theory', *Journal of Management Studies* 29, 131–154.

Hinings, C.R. and Greenwood, R., 2003, 'Disconnects and consequences in organization theory?', *Administrative Science Quarterly* 47, 411–422.

Hofstedt, T.R. and Kinard, J.C., 1970, 'A strategy for behavioral accounting research', *The Accounting Review* 45(1), 38–54.

Ilinitch, A.Y., Soderstrom, N.S. and Thomas, T.E., 1998, 'Measuring corporate environmental performance', *Journal of Accounting & Public Policy* 17, 383–407.

Jensen, M.C., 2002, 'Value maximization, stakeholder theory, and the corporate objective function', *Business Ethics Quarterly* 12(2), 235–256.

Jones, T.M., 1995, 'Instrumental stakeholder theory: A synthesis of ethics and economics', *Academy of Management Review* 20(2), 404–437.

Jones, T.M. and Wicks, A.C., 1999, 'Convergent stakeholder theory', *Academy of Management Journal* 24(2), 206–221.

Kaufman, A. and Englander, E., 2011, 'Behavioral economics, federalism, and the triumph of stakeholder theory', *Journal of Business Ethic* 102(3), 421–438.

Laplume, A.O., Sonpar, K. and Litz, R.A., 2008, 'Stakeholder theory: Reviewing a theory that moves us', *Journal of Management* 34(6), 1152–1189.

Lindblom, C.K., 1994, 'The implications of organizational legitimacy for corporate social performance and disclosure', Paper presented at the Critical Perspectives on Accounting Conference, New York.

Magness, V., 2006, 'Strategic posture, financial performance and environmental disclosure: An empirical test of legitimacy theory', *Accounting, Auditing and Accountability Journal* 19(4), 540–563.

Makela, H. and Nasi, S., 2010, 'Social responsibilities of MNCs in downsizing operations: A Finnish forest sector case analysed from the stakeholder, social contract and legitimacy theory point of view', *Accounting Auditing & Accountability Journal* 23(2), 149–174.

Manetti, G., 2011, 'The quality of stakeholder engagement in sustainability reporting: Empirical evidence and critical points', *Corporate Social Responsibility & Environmental Management* 18(2), 110–122.

Manetti, G. and Bellucci, M., 2016, 'The use of social media for engaging stakeholders in sustainability reporting', *Accounting, Auditing & Accountability Journal* 29(8), 986–1011.

Margolis, J.D. and Walsh, J.P., 2003, 'Misery loves companies: Rethinking social initiatives by business', *Administrative Science Quarterly* 48(2), 268–305.

Mathews, M.R., 1993, *Socially Responsible Accounting*, Chapman & Hall, London.

Maurer, J.G., 1971, *Readings in Organization Theory: Open-System Approaches*, Random House, New York.

Meek, G.K. and Gray, S.J., 1988, 'The value-added statement: An innovation for U.S. companies?', *Accounting Horizons* 2(2), 73–81.

Miles, S., 2012, 'Stakeholders: Essentially contested or just confused?', *Journal of Business Ethics* 108(3), 285–298.

Miles, S., Hammond, K. and Friedman, A.L., 2002, *ACCA Research Report No. 77: Social and Environmental Reporting and Ethical Investment*, Certified Accountants Educational Trust, London.

Mitchell, R.K., Agle, B.R. and Wood, D.J., 1997, 'Toward a theory of stakeholder identification and salience: Defining the principle of who and what really counts', *Academy of Management Review* 22(4), 853–886.

Monfardini, P., Barretta, A.D. and Ruggiero, P., 2013, 'Seeking legitimacy: Social reporting in the healthcare sector', *Accounting Forum* 37(1), 54–66.

Neu, D., Warsame, H. and Pedwell, K., 1998, 'Managing public impressions: Environmental disclosures in annual reports', *Accounting, Organizations and Society* 23(3), 265–282.

O'Dwyer, B., 2005, 'The construction of a social account: A case study in an overseas aid agency', *Accounting Organizations and Society* 30(3), 279–296.

Ohman, P., Hackner, E., Jansson, A. and Tschudi, F., 2006, 'Swedish auditor's view of auditing: Doing things right versus doing the right things', *European Accounting Review* 15, 89–114.

Oliver, C., 1990, 'Determinants of interorganizational relationships: Integration and future directions', *Academy of Management Review* 15(2), 241–265.

Parker, L.D., 2005. 'Social and environmental accountability research: A view from the commentary box'. *Accounting, Auditing & Accountability Journal* 18(6), pp. 842–860.

Parmar, B., Freeman, R., Harrison, J., Wicks, A., Purnell, L. and De Colle, S., 2010, 'Stakeholder theory: The state of the art', *The Academy of Management Annals* 4(1), 403–445.

Patten, D.M., 2005, 'The accuracy of financial report projections of future environmental capital expenditures: a research note', *Accounting, Organizations and Society* 30(5), 457–468.

Pfeffer, J. and Salancik, G.R., 1978, *The External Control of Organizations: A Resource Dependence Perspective*, Harper and Row, New York.

Phillips, R., 2003, 'Stakeholder legitimacy', *Business Ethics Quarterly* 13(1), 25–41.

Phillips, R.A., Freeman, R.E. and Wicks, A.C., 2003, 'What stakeholder theory is not', *Business Ethics Quarterly* 13(4), 479–502.

Phillips, R.A. and Reichart, J., 2000, 'The environment as a stakeholder? A fairness-based approach', *Journal of Business Ethics* 23, 185–197.

Quinn, D.P. and Jones, T.M., 1995, 'An agent morality view of business policy', *Academy of Management Review* 20(1), 22–42.

Rawls, J., 1971, *A Theory of Justice*, Cambridge, Harvard University Press.

Rhenman, E. and Stymne, B., 1965, *Företagsledning i en föränderlig värld [Corporate Management in a Changing World]*, Aldus/Bonniers, Stockholm.

Richardson, V.J., 2000, 'Information asymmetry & earnings management: Some evidence', *Review of Quantitative Finance & Accounting* 15, 325–347.

Roberts, R.W., 1992. 'Determinants of corporate social responsibility disclosure: An application of stakeholder theory'. *Accounting, Organizations and Society* 17(6), pp. 595–612.

Rowley, T.J., 1997, 'Moving beyond dyadic ties: A network theory of stakeholder influences', *Academy of Management Journal* 22(4), 887–910.

Rubenstein, D.B., 1992, 'Bridging the gap between green accounting & black ink', *Accounting, Organizations & Society* 17, 501–508.

Scott, J.E.M., McKinnon, J.L. and Harrison, G.L., 2003, 'Cash to accrual & cash to accrual: A case study of financial reporting in two NSW hospitals 1857 to post-1975', *Accounting, Auditing & Accountability Journal* 16, 104–125.

Shankman, N.A., 1999, 'Reframing the debate between agency and stakeholder theories of the firm', *Journal of Business Ethics* 19(4), 319–334.

Sharma, S. and Henriques, I., 2005, 'Stakeholder influence on sustainability practices in the Canadian forest products industry', *Strategic Management Journal* 26, 159–180.

Shaw, A.K., 1995, 'Accounting policy choice: The case of financial instruments', *European Accounting Review* 4, 397–399.

Stanford Research Institute, 1982, *Changes Images of Man*, Author, Stanford, CA.

Starik, M., 1995, 'Should trees have managerial standing? Toward stakeholder status for non-human nature', *Journal of Business Ethics* 14, 207–217.

Stern, R.N. and Barley, S.R., 1996. 'Organizations and social systems: Organization theory's neglected mandate'. *Administrative Science Quarterly*, pp. 146–162.

Sternberg, E., 1998, *Corporate Governance: Accountability in the Marketplace*, Institute of Economic Affairs, London.

Steurer, R., Langer, M.E., Konrad, A. and Martinuzzi, A., 2005, 'Corporations, stakeholders and sustainable development: A theoretical exploration of business-society relations', *Journal of Business Ethics* 61, 263–281.

Stieb, J.A., 2009, 'Assessing Freeman's stakeholder theory', *Journal of Business Ethics* 87(3), 401–414.

Suchman, M.C., 1995, 'Managing legitimacy: Strategic and institutional approaches', *Academy of Management Review* 20(3), 571–610.

Svendsen, A., 1998, *The Stakeholder Strategy: Profiting From Collaborative Business Relationships*, Berett-Koehler, San Francisco.

Tate, W.L., Ellram, L.M. and Kirchoff, J.F., 2010, 'Corporate social responsibility reports: A thematic analysis related to supply chain management', *Journal of Supply Chain Management* 46(1), 19–44.

Thorne, L., Mahoney, L.S. and Manetti, G., 2014, 'Motivations for issuing standalone CSR reports: A survey of Canadian firms', *Accounting, Auditing & Accountability Journal* 27(4), 686–714.

UNEP and Sustainability, 1999, *The Social Reporting Report*, SustainAbility, London.

Unerman, J. and Bennett, M., 2004, 'Increased stakeholder dialogue and the internet: Towards greater corporate accountability or reinforcing capitalist hegemony?', *Accounting Organizations and Society* 29(7), 685–707.

Voss, Z.G., Voss, G.B. and Moorman, C., 2005, 'An empirical examination of the complex relationships between entrepreneurial orientation and stakeholder support', *European Journal of Marketing* 39(9/10), 1132–1150.

Waddock, S.A., 2002, *Leading Corporate Citizens: Vision Values Value Added*, McGraw-Hill, Boston, MA.

Weick, K.E., 1999, 'That's moving: Theories that matter', *Journal of Management Inquiry* 8(2), 134.

Windsor, D., 2002, 'Stakeholder responsibilities: Lessons for managers', in J. Andriof, S. Waddock, B. Husted and S. Rahman (eds.), *Unfolding Stakeholder Thinking: Theory Responsibility and Engagement*, Greenleaf Publishing, Sheffield.

Winston, C.C.K. and Sharp, D., 2005, 'Power & international accounting standard setting: Evidence from segment reporting & intangible assets projects', *Accounting, Auditing & Accountability Journal* 18, 74–99.

Wood, D.J., 1991a, 'Corporate social performance revisited', *Academy of Management Review* 16(4), 691–718.

Wood, D.J., 1991b, 'Social issues in management: Theory and research in corporate social performance', *Journal of Management* 17(2), 383–406.

Wood, D. and Ross, D.G., 2006, 'Environmental social controls & capital investments: Australian evidence', *Accounting & Finance* 46, 677–695.

Woodward, D., Edwards, P. and Birkin, F., 2001, 'Some evidence on executives' views of corporate social responsibility', *The British Accounting Review* 33(3), 357–397.

8

Agency theory

Applications in Behavioural Accounting Research

Irene M. Gordon and Kim Trottier

Introduction

This paper outlines the existing and potential relationship between Behavioural Accounting Research (BAR) and agency theory. On the surface this seems an easy task but issues arise when defining behavioural accounting. An oft-cited definition comes from Hofstede and Kinard (1970: 43), "Behavioural accounting research may be defined as the study of the behaviour of accountants or the behaviour of non-accountants as they are influenced by accounting functions and reports." Lord (1989) found this definition to be too broad and excluded two topics (agency theory and market-based research)[1] from his historical development of behavioural accounting thought. A different approach to deciding what BAR covers comes from Birnberg (2011: 2) who acknowledges that over the previous two decades the lines between BAR and other accounting research areas blurred. As with Birnberg, we concentrate on individual behaviours and a single firm but we develop and examine those aspects of agency theory that may be related to BAR.

We begin our paper by describing agency theory and explaining its origins. We follow this by introducing a diagram and providing a description of some of the key papers[2] that relate to various segments of research. We link BAR to agency theory by explaining the role compensation, information, contracts and monitoring play in agency theory. We also provide a sample of research that illustrates how behavioural accounting researchers have employed agency theory in their papers. Finally, we indicate possible research directions that may be useful for behavioural accounting researchers.

Agency theory: origins and meaning

Jensen and Meckling (1976) are often credited with the version of agency theory used in accounting research. In this version, an organization is described as a "nexus of contracts" between those who supply resources (i.e., principals) and those that employ resources for productive purposes (i.e., agents). Both of these groups want to be compensated for their contributions, principals for use of their resources and agents for their work in producing goods and services. In deciding each group's compensation, formal or informal contracts will be struck. In a large organization such as a corporation, these multiple and related contracts are the "nexus of contracts" that represent an opportunity to increase the welfare of both the principals and agents.

Agency theory grew out of economics, particularly that portion known as consumer theory. The viewpoint espoused in agency theory is most often associated with such Chicago School economists as Friedman (1953) and Stigler and Becker (1977). This view relies on several assumptions including that markets are perfectly competitive, that is, a situation where no single individual seller or buyer is able to influence market prices. Additionally, in this economic world people (a) are able to maximize their utility (or welfare) subject to the constraint of their incomes, (b) know their tastes or preferences (which do not change), (c) act rationally (e.g., they will maximize utility or profit), (d) have access to the same information, (e) are able to compare the costs and benefits of all possible actions and (f) incur no costs when searching for information or engaging in transactions. In such a world, there would be optimal contracting[3] between parties by definition.

Agency theory is also related to the economics of property rights, which has been linked to Coase (1937) and Alchian and Demsetz (1972). When one group owns resources, another group wishes to use those resources and both groups wish to maximize their utilities (e.g., wealth), property rights leads to a discussion of how to remunerate the users of the resources, and results in various contract forms. Such contracts might give the user access to resources for a fixed rent paid to the resource owner with all profits going to the user. Alternatively, the resource owner could pay the user a fixed salary with all profits going to the owner. These two contracts represent the end points in a risk-sharing arrangement and typically neither would maximize both the resource owner's and user's utilities. That is, at one end point a fixed rent means that all the risk is borne by the user who may work hard but due to circumstances (e.g., weather, the economy) be unable to pay the fixed rent. At the other end point (owner pays user a fixed salary), all the risk is borne by the owner since the user may not work hard to ensure the resources are employed productively. Compared to the two end points, a better contract would be one where both parties bear some risk and this in turn maximizes both parties' utility.

Agency theory addresses how to overcome or minimize the effects of two types of information asymmetry, moral hazard and adverse selection (Fama and Jensen 1983; Nilakant and Rao 1994). Moral hazard describes the situation when one party (principal) to a transaction or contract is unable to observe or know the effort put into completion of the contract by the other party (agent). Adverse selection depicts where one party (agent) has an information advantage over the other party (principal) to the transaction and employs this information advantage to his/her benefit. A simple example of moral hazard is where a CEO is hired to manage the firm (maximizing the owner's resources), but becomes motivated to shirk or spend time, effort and corporate resources on his/her pet projects (maximizing his/her own utility). An example of adverse selection occurs when shareholders (through their board of directors) contemplate the hiring of a CEO, but are unable to differentiate the high-quality candidates from the low-quality ones given the information supplied.[4]

While adverse selection is less well examined in Behavioural Accounting Research, the impact of moral hazard has been explored considerably through analytical work (i.e., the formal modelling in mathematical terms) such as Christensen and Feltham (2006). The basic model has two parties (one principal and one agent) and two time periods. To do away with the complexity of maximizing multiple utility functions, the problem is simplified by assuming (without loss of generality) a compensation contract is written where the agent gets exactly his or her reservation utility in expectation, and all excess utility accrues to the principal. This makes optimization simpler and allows an evaluation of the change in utility resulting from changes in the setting. Starting with the First Best solution (which is the solution obtained in the absence of moral hazard), modelling can quantify the loss in utility when information asymmetry is added to the setting.

Similarly, modelling can quantify the gain in utility from using information such as accounting to reduce moral hazard, where the increase in utility can be thought of as the value of accounting information. Generally, the principal is modelled as being risk-neutral (imagine a well-diversified shareholder) such that optimizing his/her utility is equivalent to optimizing his wealth from firm profits, while the agent is risk-averse. Without moral hazard, the optimal solution is for the principal to bear all the risk and pay a fixed salary that provides the agent his/her reservation utility. In the presence of moral hazard, the principal seeks performance measures that provide information on the agent's efforts. To the extent accounting numbers are informative about agent effort (i.e., earnings reflect CEO effort), using them in a compensation contract where the agent gets paid on these performance measures (such as an earnings-based bonus) increases agent effort, thereby increasing the principal's expected wealth. However, even if implementing a bonus program is optimal in the setting, variable compensation schemes such as a performance-based bonus inflict uncertainty on the risk-averse agent (earnings are affected by many other factors in addition to agent effort) resulting in a need for higher overall compensation and a reduction in the principal's wealth. This can be thought of as the "cost" of moral hazard.

Theoretical compensation models can be designed to explore many aspects of agency theory, from delving deeper into the characteristics of performance measures to expanding the setting to include multiple agents and/or time periods. While these models serve as a foundation for much of the empirical research, they have been criticized as overly simplistic and unrealistic.

The compensation contract is one of many ways to address the moral hazard problem through the employment relationship. Information systems, allocation of duties, giving the agent an ownership share, and the use of budgets may all be used to reduce agency costs. Additionally, some level of monitoring, whether by auditors or through corporate governance, is believed to reduce agency issues.

While resource owners and users (e.g., shareholders and managers) are most often the parties involved in the agency relationship, additional agency relationships can exist in an organizational setting. An example of another agency relationship relevant to accounting research is that found between shareholders and creditors. When the principal is a creditor, agency costs may be reduced through the lending contract by specifically preventing the agent from taking certain actions, such as increasing debt above a given level or distributing assets to shareholders via dividends.

Agency theory and theories related to it have been criticized because of the perfect market assumptions that underlie them. In the perfect markets world transactions costs do not exist. However, as Demski (1988: 625–626) indicates, "Accounting is most (or perhaps only) interesting when markets are not pristine." If there were no costs associated with supplying financial statement information, then all managers would have to do would be to post all detailed accounts on their companies' web pages. However, these actions might incur costs ranging from a loss of competitive advantage to information overload for users. Additionally, the idea of utility maximization has been questioned by at least one Nobel Laureate, Herbert Simon. Simon (1963) has argued that individuals "satisfice" by making choices that are satisfactory rather than obtaining the absolute maximum in terms of utility. Researchers who choose to use agency theory should be aware of such criticisms and understand how failure of the assumptions might affect their results.

Agency theory and Behavioural Accounting Research

Behavioural Accounting Research stemming from agency theory is the focus of this section. Throughout this chapter, we concentrate on how the *individual* is influenced by accounting processes and reports, rather than on how accounting leads to outcomes based on the aggregate behaviour of market participants. Figure 8.1 outlines our view of agency theory and how accounting and auditing mitigate problems caused by information asymmetry. We provide an overview of the extant research for each box in the figure, followed by guidance on how these areas could benefit from further research in the behavioural accounting area.

Most areas are best explored using one of the three techniques found in accounting research: theoretical models, archival/databases or surveys/experiments. The difference in techniques used for management and financial accounting is generally straightforward. Since management accounting provides information to people within the organization, it is useful for monitoring and motivating managers. From a research perspective management accounting data are mostly proprietary and therefore difficult to obtain, making surveys or experiments a more practical means of testing what goes on within the firm. Financial accounting provides audited reports to people outside the firm, making this information reasonably consistent across companies within accounting standard regimes and easier for researchers to obtain. Consequently, financial accounting questions lend themselves to archival/database research. Theoretical models can complement either technique or stand alone in a paper.

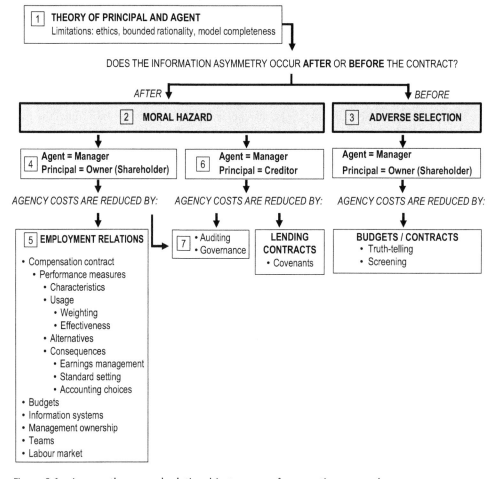

Figure 8.1 Agency theory and relationship to areas of accounting research

Our overview of the agency theory literature begins at Box #1, with the background that underpins this area of accounting research. This box refers to articles mainly written in the early days of behavioural research, such as Eisenhardt (1985) and Baiman (1990) who explain agency theory in an accounting context, and Levinthal (1988) who provides an analytical framework. Their setting has an agent who will make an effort choice that maximizes his/her expected utility (or sometimes wealth) in a setting of information asymmetry. The assumption of wealth maximization has been debated on the premise that ethics likely play a role in reducing the agent's self-interest (Noreen 1988; Booth and Schulz 2004; Rutledge and Karim 1999). The expected utility paradigm has been questioned by Uecker, Schepanski and Shin (1985), who believe people have bounded rationality among other information-processing limitations, and Larson (1977) who proposes that non-economic rewards play a motivating role, and suggests the agency model is incomplete. Research on agency assumptions, including synthesizing agency with other behavioural frameworks as in Beasley, Carcello, Hermanson and Neal (2009), Morris (1987) and Baiman (1990) could potentially lead to better models.

Moving from Box #1, we ask whether the information asymmetry in our setting leads to moral hazard (Box #2) or adverse selection (Box #3). The majority of the adverse selection literature is considered market-based, and looks at situations where the manager has inside information about the true prospects of the firm so shareholders run the risk of investing in suboptimal firms. A smaller subset of this literature examines how creditors deal with this type of information asymmetry. From a behavioural perspective (i.e., one individual and one firm) adverse selection occurs when the manager has private information about his/her own skills or productivity, or asymmetric knowledge about firm productivity or the state of nature. Sharing this information would allow the owner to maximize firm value, but the manager uses it instead to create budgetary slack for his/her benefit. Literature in this area examines factors that affect budgetary slack, ways to enable truthful revelation of private information (truth-telling), and whether budget-based incentive contracts can serve as a screening mechanism for attracting skilled employees (Sprinkle and Williamson 2006).

Much of Behavioural Accounting Research examines the moral hazard branch of information asymmetry (Box #2), with prevalence towards the friction between manager and owner (Box #4), and how this is mitigated through the employment relationship (Box #5). Compensation contracts feature prominently in this area. The owner cannot observe the manager's effort but can use "performance measures" to gauge it, and motivate higher effort with performance-based compensation as a second-best alternative. Analytical papers that explore desirable characteristics of performance measures show that manager effort is improved when the measure is precise and sensitive (Banker, Datar and Maindiratta 1989; Engel, Hayes and Wang 2003), congruent with the principal's payoff (Feltham and Xie 1994) and time horizon (Dechow and Sloan 1991), and used in conjunction with incrementally informative measures such as change in share price (Bushman and Indjedikian 1993). Recent work suggests objective effort measures are better than subjective ones (Ittner, Larcker and Meyer 2003; Ahn, Hwang and Kim 2010).

In evaluating agent performance, one of two things is measured: the behaviour of the agent or the outcomes of those behaviours (Eisenhardt 1985). If the agent's tasks can be explicitly defined and accurately measured, then monitoring is accomplished with behaviour-based performance measures such as product knowledge, number of active client accounts, closing ability and/or calls made. If the goal can be clearly stated, then outcome-based performance measures are more appropriate, for example sales volume, revenues, product turnover or profit margins. The basic idea is that one can monitor the result of a process (i.e., outcome) or the individual stages (i.e., behaviours) in a process, and sometimes both. Whether in the form of a budget or financial statement, accounting information is generally an outcome-based measure.

Audited financial accounting numbers such as earnings serve well as an outcome-based performance measure. They are informative about the manager's performance, sensitive to his/her effort, fairly objective and readily available. Incorporating earnings in a compensation contract is a cost-effective way to align the manager's goals with the owner's objective of increasing earnings and firm value. Consequently, much of the literature explores the use of earnings in executive compensation contracts. Data on executive compensation contracts have become more easily available to academics, making this a popular area of research. Results show most contracts are comprised of a base salary, a bonus based on financial accounting numbers, some form of equity and deferred compensation. Consistent with theory, contracts typically use multiple measures, weight them based on sensitivity and precision and include short- and long-horizon components (Lambert and Larcker 1987; Bushman, Indjedikian and Smith 1996; Ittner, Larcker and Rajan 1997; Core, Guay and Verrecchia 2003). A related stream of research explores whether earnings is an effective performance measure. Jensen and Murphy (1990) are among the first to explore pay-performance sensitivity; that is whether executive compensation is correlated with the firm's performance measures such as firm's earnings and share price. The findings on pay-performance sensitivity have been mixed.

Compensation contracts sometimes incorporate non-financial performance measures, as in the balanced scorecard (BSC) popularized by Kaplan and Norton (1992). The BSC establishes non-financial targets such as customer satisfaction, employee satisfaction, growth and increased market share, but typically also includes financial accounting constructs such as return on equity and profit margins. The BSC is an example of a tool that combines behaviour and outcome-based metrics. Although BSCs are widely used,[5] data on these incentive mechanisms are not easily obtained since they tend to be used for internal purposes. However, Ullrich and Tuttle (2004) find the BSC influences how managers direct their attention, and evidence suggests they work at motivating managers (Malina and Selto 2001; Davis and Albright 2004). When BSC-related research focuses on non-financial targets, its role in accounting research may be somewhat limited.

Ironically, reducing the agency problem through compensation contracts has the potential to create a different set of problems with accounting. To the extent that the agent's wealth is now a function of accounting numbers, there is an incentive to manipulate those numbers through earnings management or selective use of accounting policies. A peripheral issue is how standard setters help or hinder this process through their work. These consequences of compensation contracts comprise a large portion of the accounting literature, but are not the focus of this chapter.

The employment relationship comprises more than just a compensation contract, and provides other means of reducing moral hazard. From a managerial accounting perspective, the use of budgets is an outcome-based mechanism that could be employed to set performance targets for managers. Research in this area explores how much the agent participates in setting the budget, how difficult their budgets are to achieve, and the consequences of not achieving them. Some literature contemplates the role of honesty in the budgeting process (Rankin, Schwartz and Young 2008). Chow, Cooper and Waller (1988) show that in the presence of information asymmetry, a truth-inducing contract can be designed that reduces budgetary slack.

Other facets of the manager/owner employment relationship can mitigate agency issues. Well-designed information systems can improve manager effort by providing the owner with information on manager performance. Information systems can also promote honest reporting. Giving the manager an ownership role will naturally improve the alignment between his/her and the owners' goals. Working in teams can reduce moral hazard through mutual monitoring, although perhaps at the cost of free-riding or collusion. Even the managerial labour market itself can mitigate inappropriate behaviour, as the manager contemplates how his/her behaviour could affect his/her future employment prospects. This non-exhaustive list of features of an employment relationship are not always accounting in nature, but can improve or complement the ability of earnings and budgets to reduce agency problems.

An area that has garnered less focus is the agency problem between managers and creditors, as shown in Box #6. Here, the creditor may have an information disadvantage both in terms of moral hazard (lending to a manager who will make choices that are not in the creditor's interest) and adverse selection (lending to a firm that has undisclosed problems). In this research, lending contracts are meant to protect creditors' interests. Covenants in these lending (or debt) contracts are meant to reduce risks to the creditor. These risks include managers paying out all assets as dividends, investing in overly risky projects, and issuing debt with higher repayment priority than the existing debt. To control these risks, lending contracts specify financial ratios that must be maintained before dividends may be paid or new debt issued, and these ratios are based on accounting numbers. Research in this area includes exploring the lender perception of reporting reliability (Holder-Webb and Sharma 2010), or examining the manipulation of accruals (DeFond and Jiambalvo 1994) and accounting flexibility (Beatty, Ramesh and Weber 2002) to prevent debt covenant violations.

We finally arrive at Box #7, which lists some corporate-wide initiatives that reduce moral hazard, and (to some extent) adverse selection: auditing and governance. In addition to providing assurance on accounting numbers, external auditors can help reduce the negative effect of compensation contracts. Research shows that auditors consider aspects of the employment relationships when evaluating audit risk and the likelihood of misstatements (Dikolli, McCracken and Malawski 2004) and increase their fees when CEO and CFO incentive risks are higher (Kannan, Skantz and Higgs 2014). However, this increased oversight can lead managers to change auditors (Marten 1994). Internal audit can also play a role in mitigating moral hazard (Adams 1994), as can organizational controls (Eisenhardt 1985). Corporate governance also plays a role in reducing agency issues. Research shows the composition of the board affects the effectiveness of performance measures (Hermalin and Weisbach 1991), the disclosure quality (Forker 1992) and the financial performance of the firm.

Future research directions and conclusion

As a theoretical construct, agency theory may form the basis for a variety of future BAR papers. For example, researchers may find creative ways to use agency theory to address current issues, such as explaining how CSR reporting can be beneficial to the manager (Ness and Mirza 1991) or examining how truthfulness can be used to overcome agency problems within organizations (Chow et al. 1988).

Recent papers cited have made suggestions for future research where agency theory may provide either the theory behind the research or may help explain the results. Dikolli et al. (2004) suggest examining the relationship between compensation based on a BSC and required audit procedures. These authors suggest that future researchers will need to determine whether using the BSC requires more (or less) audit procedures than a compensation contract based on non-financial procedures. Additionally, Dikolli et al. indicate researchers may need to explain whether a compensation contract based on the BSC requires more audit procedures because the scorecard encompasses both financial and non-financial measures.

Ullrich and Tuttle (2004) propose that researchers might examine how managers allocate their time when provided different economic incentives (i.e., short-term and long-term incentives). Such future research might examine the influence of incentives where managers face a multiple task situation in which goal difficulty and feedback cues may influence total effort as applied to the tasks.

Researchers interested in experiments may consult Sprinkle (2003), who proposes expanding the scope of our models to multiple tasks or single tasks with multiple dimensions, or considering other perspectives such as employer moral hazard. He suggests the role of accounting in incentivizing workgroups and teams has been underexplored, and therefore remains a rich area for future research.

Other researchers suggest that there is a need for certain types of replication. Holder-Webb and Sharma (2010) suggest examining questions similar to those they asked (i.e., examination of lenders) but using different settings (e.g., geographical location) or multiple industries where lenders' industry expertise is matched to the industry setting.

Finally, other researchers suggest explorations of BAR in different ethical environments. Booth and Schulz (2004) propose examination of how managers' ethical predispositions interrelate with the environmental setting when making project continuation decisions. To follow this suggestion two samples of managers would be necessary, those involved and those not involved in setting ethical policies.

Agency theory could play a role in setting the stage for this future research or in interpreting the findings. For example, additional self-interested motives may influence how managers choose to act. However, there is also recognition in the research suggestions that other factors (e.g., truthfulness, CSR, geography, setting of ethics policies) may influence the behaviour of managers. Future BAR research that employs or tests agency motives holds out both opportunities and challenges for interested researchers.

Notes

1 Market-based research (also known as capital-markets research) examines the share price reaction to accounting information being released to the public. While the share price moves as a result of individual beliefs and decisions, this movement is aggregated across multiple investors and hence usually not considered behavioural in the narrower sense of BAR literature.
2 We realize there are many papers that may be deemed "key" papers related to agency and BAR. We have chosen to use papers that are highly cited or important to the development of BAR.
3 "Optimal contracting" is defined as an agreement (or contract) between parties that minimizes the costs associated with that agreement (or contract) and that arise due to the parties having asymmetric information. Typical costs associated with such agreements when asymmetric information exists include monitoring, contracting and misbehaviour on the part of any of the parties.
4 Moral hazard is sometimes called "hidden action" while adverse selection is "hidden information".
5 Maqbool (2015) notes that the percentage of firms using BSC ranges from 26% to 98% of firms depending on the setting examined.

References

Adams, M.B., 1994, 'Agency theory and the internal audit', *Managerial Auditing Journal* 9(8), 8–12.
Ahn, T.S., Hwang, I. and Kim, M.I., 2010, 'The impact of performance measure discriminability on ratee incentives', *Accounting Review* 85(2), 389–417.
Alchian, A.A. and Demsetz, H., 1972, 'Production, information costs, and economic organization', *American Economic Review* 62(5), 777–795.
Baiman, S., 1990, 'Agency research in managerial accounting: A second look', *Accounting, Organizations and Society* 15(4), 341–371.
Banker, R.J., Datar, S.M. and Maindiratta, A., 1989, 'Unobservable outcomes and multiattribute preferences in the evaluation of managerial performance', *Contemporary Accounting Research* 5(1), 96–124.

Beasley, M.S., Carcello, J.V., Hermanson, D.R. and Neal, T.L., 2009, 'The audit committee oversight process', *Contemporary Accounting Research* 26(1), 65–122.

Beatty, A., Ramesh, K. and Weber, J., 2002, 'The importance of accounting changes in debt contracts: The cost of flexibility in covenant calculations', *Journal of Accounting and Economics* 33(2), 205–227.

Birnberg, J.G., 2011, 'A proposed framework for behavioral accounting research', *Behavioral Research in Accounting* 23(1), 1–43.

Booth, P. and Schulz, A.K.D., 2004, 'The impact of an ethical environment on managers' project evaluation judgments under agency problem conditions', *Accounting, Organizations and Society* 29(5), 473–488.

Bushman, R.M. and Indjedikian, R.J., 1993, 'Accounting income, stock price, and managerial compensation', *Journal of Accounting and Economics* 16(1–3), 3–23.

Bushman, R.M., Indjedikian, R.J. and Smith, A., 1996, 'CEO compensation: The role of individual performance evaluation', *Journal of Accounting and Economics* 21(2), 161–193.

Chow, C.W., Cooper, J.C. and Waller, W.S., 1988, 'Participative budgeting: Effects of a truth-inducing pay scheme and information asymmetry on slack and performance', *Accounting Review* 63(1), 111–122.

Christensen, P.O. and Feltham, G., 2006, *Economics of Accounting: Performance Evaluation*, 2, Springer Science & Business Media, Berlin, Germany.

Coase, R.H., 1937, 'The nature of the firm', *Economica* 4(16), 386–405.

Core, J.E., Guay, W.R. and Verrecchia, R.E., 2003, 'Price versus non-price performance measures in optimal CEO compensation contracts', *Accounting Review* 78(4), 957–981.

Davis, S. and Albright, T., 2004, 'An investigation of the effect of balanced scorecard implementation on financial performance', *Management Accounting Research* 15(2), 135–153.

Dechow, P.M. and Sloan, R.G., 1991, 'Executive incentives and the horizon problem: An empirical investigation', *Journal of Accounting and Economics* 14(1), 51–89.

DeFond, M.L. and Jiambalvo, J., 1994, 'Debt covenant violation and manipulation of accruals', *Journal of Accounting and Economics* 17(1), 145–176.

Demski, J., 1988, 'Positive accounting theory: A review article', *Accounting, Organizations and Society* 13, 623–629.

Dikolli, S.S., McCracken, S.A. and Malawski, J.B., 2004, 'Audit-planning judgements and client-employee compensation contracts', *Behavioral Accounting Research* 16, 45–61.

Eisenhardt, K.M., 1985, 'Control: Organizational and economic approaches', *Management Science* 31(2), 134–149.

Engel, E., Hayes, R.M. and Wang, X., 2003, 'CEO turnover and properties of accounting information', *Journal of Accounting and Economics* 36, 197–226.

Fama, E. and Jensen, M.C., 1983, 'Separation of ownership and control', *Journal of Law & Economics* 26(2), 301–325.

Feltham, G.A. and Xie, J., 1994, 'Performance measure congruity and diversity in multi-task principal/agent relationships', *Accounting Review* 69(3), 429–453.

Forker, J.J., 1992, 'Corporate governance and disclosure quality', *Accounting and Business Research* 22(86), 111–124.

Friedman, M., 1953, 'The methodology of positive economics', in *Essays in Positive Economics*, 3–43, University of Chicago Press, Chicago.

Hermalin, B.E. and Weisbach, M.S., 1991, 'The effects of board composition and direct incentives on firm performance', *Financial Management* 20(4), 101–112.

Hofstede, T.R. and Kinard, J.C., 1970, 'A strategy for behavioral accounting research', *Accounting Review* 45(1), 38–54.

Holder-Webb, L. and Sharma, D.S., 2010, 'The effect of governance on credit decisions and perceptions of reporting reliability', *Behavioral Research in Accounting* 22(1), 1–20.

Ittner, C.D., Larcker, D.F. and Meyer, M.W., 2003, 'Subjectivity and the weighting of performance measures: Evidence from a balanced scorecard', *Accounting Review* 78(3), 725–758.

Ittner, C.D., Larcker, D.F. and Rajan, M.V., 1997, 'The choice of performance measures in annual bonus contracts', *Accounting Review* 72(2), 231–255.

Jensen, M.C. and Meckling, W.H., 1976, 'Theory of the firm: Managerial behavior, agency costs and ownership structure', *Journal of Financial Economics* 3(4), 305–360.

Jensen, M.C. and Murphy, K.J., 1990, 'Performance pay and top-management incentives', *Journal of Political Economy* 98(2), 225–264.

Kannan, Y.H., Skantz, T.R. and Higgs, J.L., 2014, 'The impact of CEO and CFO equity incentives on audit scope and perceived risks as revealed through audit fees', *Auditing: A Journal of Practice & Theory* 33(2), 111–139.

Kaplan, R.S. and Norton, D.P., 1992, 'The balanced scorecard – measures that drive performance', *Harvard Business Review* 70(1), 71–79.

Lambert, R.A. and Larcker, D.F., 1987, 'An analysis of the use of accounting and market measures of performance in executive compensation contracts', *Journal of Accounting Research* 25(Supplement), 85–125.

Larson, M., 1977, *The Rise of Professionalism*, University of California Press, Berkeley, CA.

Levinthal, D., 1988, 'A survey of agency models of organizations', *Journal of Economic Behavior & Organization* 9(2), 153–185.

Lord, A.T., 1989, 'The development of behavioral thought in accounting, 1952–1981', *Behavioral Research in Accounting* 1, 124–149.

Malina, M.A. and Selto, F.H., 2001, 'Communicating and controlling strategy: An empirical study of the effectiveness of the balanced scorecard', *Journal of Management Accounting Research* 13(1), 47–90.

Maqbool, M.H., 2015, 'A consolidated model for putting balanced scorecard into action in Pakistan's textile industry', *Journal of Strategy and Performance Management* 3(1), 40–46.

Marten, K.U., 1994, 'Auditor change: Results of an empirical study of the auditing market in the context of agency theory', *European Accounting Review* 3(1), 168–171.

Morris, R.D., 1987, 'Signalling, agency theory and accounting policy choice', *Accounting and Business Research* 18(69), 47–56.

Ness, K.E. and Mirza, A.M., 1991, 'Corporate social disclosure: A note on a test of agency theory', *The British Accounting Review* 23(3), 211–217.

Nilakant, V. and Rao, H., 1994, 'Agency theory and uncertainty in organizations: An evaluation', *Organization Studies* 15(5), 649–672.

Noreen, E., 1988, 'The economics of ethics: A new perspective on agency theory', *Accounting, Organizations and Society* 13(4), 359–369.

Rankin, F.W., Schwartz, S.T. and Young, R.A., 2008, 'The effect of honesty and superior authority on Raki proposals', *Accounting Review* 83(4), 1083–1099.

Rutledge, R.W. and Karim, K.E., 1999, 'The influence of self-interest and ethical considerations on managers' evaluation judgments', *Accounting, Organizations and Society* 24(2), 173–184.

Simon, H., 1963, 'Problems of methodology: Discussion', *American Economic Review, Papers and Proceedings* 53, 229–231.

Sprinkle, G.B., 2003, 'Perspectives on experimental research in managerial accounting', *Accounting, Organizations and Society* 28(2), 287–318.

Sprinkle, G.B. and Williamson, M.G., 2006, 'Experimental research in managerial accounting', *Handbook of Management Accounting Research* 1, 415–444.

Stigler, G. and Becker, G., 1977, 'De Gustibus non est Disputandum', *American Economic Review* 67(2), 76–90.

Uecker, W., Schepanski, A. and Shin, J., 1985, 'Toward a positive theory of information evaluation: Relevant tests of competing models in a principal-agency setting', *Accounting Review* 60(3), 430–457.

Ullrich, M.J. and Tuttle, B.M., 2004, 'The effects of comprehensive information reporting systems and economic incentives on managers' time-planning decisions', *Behavioral Research in Accounting* 16, 89–105.

Section 3

Operationalization of theoretical constructs (Links 2 and 3)

9

The development of behavioural measures of accounting constructs

Linda Thorne

Introduction

According to Stevens (1951: 22), "Measurement is the assignment of numbers to objects or events according to rules" and psychometric measures are attempts to assign numbers to psychometric properties of individuals. Accounting-specific instruments are attempts to develop valid and reliable measures of accounting constructs, which are hypothetical concepts, specific to the accounting context, which cannot be directly observed or measured (Cronbach and Meehl 1955). For example, one of the earliest accounting constructs specifically considered in accounting research is the concept of "accounting conservatism" (Devine 1963).

Behavioural Accounting Research may be defined as the study of the behaviour of accountants or the behaviour of non-accountants as they are influenced by accounting functions and reports (Hofstede and Kinard 1970: 43). While considerable research and measures have been developed throughout the many domains in the social sciences, the unique attributes of accountants and/or the accounting context renders a specific examination of accounting constructs, using accounting-specific measures, of value. The specific challenge in Behavioural Accounting Research (BAR) is the measurement of psychometric properties of accountants or the behaviour of non-accountants as they are influenced by accounting. These psychometric properties are not readily observed and specific to the accounting domain. Consequently, behavioural accounting researchers have been developing accounting-specific measures of accounting constructs since initially engaging in BAR (Lord 1989). One early example of an accounting-specific measure is provided in the first edition of *Behavioural Research in Accounting* by Chen and Olson (1989) who considered the importance of cognitive complexity in the accounting domain and presented an accounting-specific measure of cognitive complexity.

The primary objective of this paper is to outline the key steps used in the development of quality accounting-specific measures, and, in addition, to provide a catalogue of some of the accounting-specific measures that have been developed and used in recent Behavioural Accounting Research. The second section of this paper presents six steps identified as critical to the development of valid and reliable measures of accounting constructs. When available, an illustration of how each step has been conducted by previous accounting research is provided. The third section of the paper provides a partial inventory or catalogue of accounting-specific measures published in accounting journals in the past ten years to facilitate future accounting research. The final section presents a brief discussion and conclusions.

Six steps to the development of an accounting-specific measure

Behavioural Accounting Research generally relies on the use of constructed measures of accounting constructs that attempt to evaluate accountants' psychometric properties or the psychometric properties associated with users of accounting information. Measurement involves the quantification of a construct through the assignment of numbers to qualities representative of its attributes (Nunnally 1978). A construct is a latent concept that cannot be measured directly (Kerlinger and Lee 1964). The quality of the measure is a function of the degree to which the construct is captured by the measure (Churchill 1979). Generally, an assessment of the measure's quality is made through consideration of the reliability and validity of the measure.

There are several seminal sources in the social sciences that together provide a roadmap for the steps involved in the development of high-quality measures of applied constructs (see for example, DeVellis 1991; Churchill 1979; Clark and Watson 1998; Carmines and Zeller 1979; Nunnally 1978). Taken together they suggest the following six steps that are involved in the development of valid and reliable measures, which may be applied to the development of measures of accounting constructs: (a) Identification of the construct to be measured; (b) Generation of a sample of items to be included in the measure; (c) Determination of which items are in the domain of the construct; (d) Purification of the measure; (e) Validity and reliability testing and (f) Evaluation and validation of the empirical and theoretical construct. Each will be discussed in turn, with an illustration from the accounting literature that shows how previous research has addressed this step.

Step 1: identification of the construct to be measured

Before construction of an accounting-specific measure, a review of the literature is needed to ensure that a previously used accounting-specific measure does not already exist, and whether or not there exists a "universal" measure of a similar, but universal construct.[1] Universal measures are those measures that have applicability beyond the accounting domain, but by the very nature of the uniqueness of the accounting domain or the nature of accountants, tailoring of the universal measure may be appropriate. For example, Thorne (2000) presented a measure of accountants' moral reasoning and Libby and Thorne (2004, 2007) developed an applied measure of auditors' virtue. In these examples, the researchers started with the "universal" measure and adapted it to the specifics of the accounting domain. By the adoption of the universal measure as a starting point, the researcher implicitly adopts the theoretical domain upon which the universal measure is based.

Given that the researcher determines that a universal measure as a starting point is not appropriate, the first step of measure construction starts with a literature review of the underlying theoretical underpinnings of the construct, as well as the applied theoretical applications of the underlying theory (Churchill 1979). This step would involve an examination of the theoretical basis upon which the research is based, and an identification of the latent construct. A latent construct is a theoretical construct that cannot be directly measured. One unique latent accounting construct is accounting conservatism. In the introduction to his seminal paper on accounting conservatism, Devine (1963) outlined the construct as follows:

> Accountants have held tenaciously to a combination of attitudes that they consider to be conservative. Yet, there has been little precision and clarity in setting forth the goals they are

trying to achieve. For example, the moth-eaten adage: "Anticipate no profits and provide for all possible losses," is a typical instruction that has often been used by older generations to impart wisdom to the new. This handy nostrum, if taken literally, would require the immediate write down of all prospects to zero and would lead to the immediate liquidation of a substantial portion of the accounting profession. Certainly, the admonition to "anticipate no profits" is worthless unless it is supplemented with instructions for deciding when profits are or are not anticipated. We must have a starting point for determining when we anticipate, and we need a base line and a measuring scale for determining how much we anticipate.

(127)

Thus, Devine (1963) substantiates the need for a construct of accounting conservatism that is separate from that of conservatism used in other domains. Moreover, he continues by clarifying that integral to the construct of accounting conservatism and its measurement are the identification of a referent "baseline" that captures when profits or losses are anticipated, in addition to the measurement of the amount that is anticipated.

Step 2: generate a sample of items that potentially may be included in the domain of the construct

The second step in measure construction involves an identification of those potential items that may be included in the domain of the accounting-specific construct. Nunnally (1978) defines an item as a statement that is intended to be a reflection of a theoretical construct. Items are facets, elements and/or considerations that are included in a given construct. To the extent the items included in a construct are representative and comprehensively capture the domain of the construct, the construct has content validity (Carmines and Zeller 1979). The initial generation of the sample of items involves not only the delineation of the domain of the construct, but also the consideration of how items included in the accounting-specific construct may differ and be similar from those items included in a universal measure.

One example that specifically shows the relationship between universal items and applied items to be included in an accounting-specific construct is outlined by Libby and Thorne (2004, 2007) who created an auditor specific measure of virtue. Their initial list of items to be included was based upon Pincoffs's (1986) universal inventory and categorization of the virtues, which were examined and revised semantically to be applicable to the accounting domain. Libby and Thorne (2004) used a panel of experts to ensure the comparability of the items between the Pincoffs universal inventory of virtue items and those applicable to the accounting domain.

If the researcher is not adapting a universal measure, but doing the initial generation of a list of items that may be included in an applied construct, the items can be identified/derived from the theoretical underpinnings of the construct and/or by ascertaining which items are used in the field. This may involve the use of qualitative research methods including observation, interviews of experts in the field or transcript analysis in an attempt to ascertain those items that are a reflection of the theoretical construct.

Step 3: determine the appropriate items to include in the domain-specific measure

The third step involves the determination of whether and which items appropriately represent the domain of the construct. While step 2 involves the generation of items to be potentially included in the construct, step 3 involves the evaluation of which items are appropriate. This evaluation takes place on two levels: the first level is an evaluation of the breadth of the items to be included in the measure (complete and comprehensive) and the second level is an evaluation of whether the items, as included in the measure, would be interpreted appropriately by those in the accounting-specific domain. The first level of evaluation ensures that all aspects of the construct are included: whether the items cover the full range of the construct and the extent to which there are items included in the construct which may not belong. The second level of evaluation involves ensuring that items included in the applied accounting-specific measure are interpreted appropriately by those in the applied domain. Instrument equivalence considers whether items are interpreted similarly in the applied context as compared to the universal context (Singh 1995).

This step and further steps in instrument development are similar for both applied measures and for measures being constructed from scratch. The practical determination of which items to include in the measure often involves the use of "experts" or a panel of experts. For example, Thorne (2000) developed two audit-specific measures of moral reasoning based upon the Defining Issues Test (DIT) (Rest 1979), a widely used universal measure of moral reasoning. After the identification of the potential items to be included in the audit-specific measure, Thorne (2000) attempted to ensure that the stage scoring of the accounting-specific items would be equivalent to that of the universal measure. She asked an expert panel of judges to evaluate the "stage score" of all items included in the measure according to Rest's definition of moral reasoning stage. After each judge independently evaluated the stage scores of each item in the audit-specific DIT, the final assignment of a moral stage for measure items was determined according to a decision rule requiring the agreement of three out of four experts.

Step 4: measure purification

Step 4 involves the purification of the measure. Measure purification involves the evaluation of the extent to which the instrument under development captures the underlying theoretical construct through the administration and analysis of the measure and its properties after it is administered to a target sample. The analysis of the findings is undertaken to assess the extent to which that the factors (items) captured by the instrument under development corresponds to the underlying structure of the theoretical construct. Measure purification generally involves two stages (Churchill 1979; Anderson and Gerbing 1988).

The first stage involves the administration of the preliminary instrument to a sample of participants from the target group to evaluate the factor structure, the internal consistency and the validity of the items. Often, but not ideally, the first stage of measure purification involves the use of student subjects albeit with an appropriate level of accounting expertise. Students may be appropriate for this first stage of instrument development if they possess similar knowledge or skill sets as the target sample, and access to the target sample is limited. Data from this first step is analyzed using exploratory factor analysis and computation of Cronbach's alpha (Cronbach 1951). Exploratory factor analysis identifies factors as items that are highly correlated with each other (i.e., significant positive correlations higher than 0.60), and allows for an evaluation of whether the unique aspects of the underlying construct are empirically present in the sample (Kerlinger and Lee 1964). For example, in the first stage of measure purification, Libby and Thorne (2007) eliminated several items that were highly correlated with each other to reduce redundancy in their measure. Furthermore, they also examined whether the order in which items were presented in the measure influenced results using students (order effect).

The second stage of measure purification involves the administration of the instrument to an appropriate sample to confirm the empirical structure underlying the instrument under development as reflecting that of the theoretical construct (McCall and Bobko 1990). Thus, confirmatory factor analysis is used to confirm that the underlying empirical factor structure corresponds to that of the theoretical construct. Structural Equation Modelling is often used at the confirmatory factor analysis stage since it is superior to alternate approaches (Homburg and Rudolph 2001) because of its less restrictive assumptions (Anderson and Gerbing 1988; Bagozzi, Youjae and Phillips 1991). This second sample often is also used to evaluate the validity and reliability of the final instrument. For example, after distributing their expert validated measure of auditors' virtue to 376 auditors, Libby and Thorne (2007) used structural equation modelling to refine their measure through an assessment of the degree to which their empirical model "fits" the underlying theoretical structure of auditors' virtue (Bollen 1989). The goodness of fit of their empirical model was assessed (e.g., Hair, Black, Babin, Anderson and Tatham 2006) and documentation of several "goodness of fit" measures were included in their paper. Generally, the second stage of measure purification involves the administration of the instrument using a representative target sample.

Step 5: confirmation of the measure on target population

Step 5 involves further validation and reliability of the measure that often is conducted to ensure and to establish that the measure is stable and meets acceptable levels of statistical legitimacy (Anderson and Gerbing 1988). While many statistical properties of the measure may be assessed through Structural Equation Modelling, many instrument development papers also report internal consistency, reliability, discriminant and convergent/divergent validity using traditional measures. In practice, the establishment of validity and reliability is done using a target sample that is representative of the population under investigation.

Reliability determines the stability of the "collection of items" used to capture the construct in question. A measure's internal consistency involves the calculation of the average correlations among the items in the instrument, adjusted for the variance between the items and is reported as the scale's Cronbach alpha (Cronbach 1951). DeVellis (1991) indicates that Cronbach's alpha scores ranging from .80 and .90 indicate very good reliability of the items in a measure, whereas Cronbach's alpha scores between .70 and .80 are in a respectable range for reliability, and Cronbach's alpha scores of between .65 and .70 are in a minimally acceptable range. While reliability assesses the stability of a measure, validity assessment involves whether the measure is accurately measuring what it is purporting to measure. For examine, if a person gets on a scale and it always says they weigh 1,000 pounds, the scale would be reliable, but would be low on validity.

Discriminant validity assesses how different constructs, measured in similar ways, compare to one another. A priori, we might expect one measures scores to be lower than another. This may be the case for universal versus domain-specific measures. For example, Thorne (2000) tested her audit-specific instruments' discriminant validity by comparing its mean scores to that of the universal instrument of ethical reasoning (Rest 1979), and as expected individuals received lower scores on the applied audit-specific DIT as compared to the universal DIT. This result gave some confidence that the two measures were discriminating between two similar, but different constructs.

Testing for convergent validity is often coupled with tests for divergent validity. Convergent validity occurs when similar scores are assigned to measures of similar constructs, whereas divergent validity occurs when divergent scores are assigned to differing, conflicting or unrelated constructs. In a test of convergent validity, Thorne (2000) compared the correlations between her audit-specific measures and that of the Defining Issues Test (DIT) (Rest 1979) based on her assumption that universal ethical reasoning scores would be associated with audit-specific ethical reasoning scores. In a test of divergent validity, Libby and Thorne (2007) compared auditors' virtue scores with the same individuals' scores on the Machiavellianism scale, which captures the extent to which individuals tend to deceive and manipulate others (Christie and Geis 1970). The a priori expectation, which was consistent with the findings, was that auditors that scored high on the virtue scale would score low on the Machiavellianism scale.

Step 6: evaluate the construct empirically and theoretically

Step 6 is the evaluation of the acceptability of the empirical measure that has been developed. From the empirical perspective, the development of a measure is a reiterative process, and Steps 2 to 5 are likely to be performed several times before obtaining acceptable levels of validity and reliability. To ensure that the full usable or available sample is not exhausted, Steps 2 to 5 are often first performed on a sample of students as a pretest, and then on a sample of the target population after a preliminary refinement of the measure.

Accounting measures used in Behavioural Accounting Research

Tables 9.1–9.3 present the results of a review of *The Accounting Review*; *Accounting, Organizations and Society*; *Contemporary Accounting Research*; *Behavioural Research in Accounting* and *Auditing: A Journal of Practice and Theory* to identify the behavioural accounting measures used in accounting research in the past ten years.

Table 9.1 presents 14 papers that include psychometric measures of auditors or the audit process. Of the 14 papers, one paper was from *The Accounting Review*, nine papers were from *Behavioural Research in Accounting* and four papers were from *Auditing: A Journal of Practice and Theory*. Of the 14 papers presented on Table 9.1, ten papers specifically measured psychometric properties of auditors including attitudes toward work arrangements (Johnson et al. 2012), professional commitment (Smith and Hall 2008), locus of control (McKnight and Wright 2011), ethical reasoning (Massey and Thorne 2006), Machiavellianism (Wakefield 2008), predisposition toward handling own errors (Groneworld and Donle 2011), dispositional need for closure (Bailey et al. 2011) and skepticism (Hurtt 2010; Rose 2007; Nelson 2008). The remaining four papers examine the audit process, including identification with clients (Bamber and Iyer 2006; Stefaniak et al. 2011), reputation (Robertson et al. 2011) and brainstorming quality (Brazel, Carpenter and Jenkins 2010).

Table 9.2 presents five papers that include measures of psychometric properties of auditors' clients. Of the five papers presented in Table 9.2, three papers are published in *Behavioural Research in Accounting* and two papers are published in *Auditing: A Journal of Practice and Theory*. Of the five papers, three papers specifically measured psychometric properties of auditors' clients including moral reasoning, cognitive style and trust, while two papers specifically measured factors that captured the extent to which auditors' clients relied upon auditors including confidence and overconfidence in auditors.

Table 9.3 presents four papers that include psychometric measures of managers that rely on accounting information. All four papers were published in *Behavioural Research in Accounting*, and they looked at work style, financial values and altruism, creativity and cognitive orientation.

Table 9.1 Measures of auditors

	Full reference	Finding
Auditors' attitudes toward work arrangements.	Johnson, E, Lowe, D & Reckers, P., 2012. Measuring Accounting Professionals' Attitudes Regarding Alternative Work Arrangements, Behavioral Research in Accounting, vol. 24. iss. 1, pp. 25–46.	Developed 20 item scale. Internal consistency = .72.
Professional skepticism.	Hurtt, R 2010. Development of a Scale to Measure Professional Skepticism, Auditing: A Journal of Practice and Theory, vol. 29, iss. 1, May, pp. 149–171.	Developed 30 item scale with Internal consistency = .86.
Professional commitment.	Smith, D & Hall, M 2008. An Empirical Examination of a Three-Component Model of Professional Commitment among Public Accountants, Behavioral Research in Accounting, vol. 20, iss. 1, pp. 45–74.	Internal consistency above .7.
Identification with their client.	Bamber, M & Iyer, V 2006. Auditors' Identification with their clients and its effect on auditors' objectivity, Auditing, vol. 25, issue 2, Pages 85–94.	Identification with client is associated with auditor acquiescence for external auditors.
Identification with client.	Stefaniak, C, Houston, R &Cornell, R 2011. The effect of Employer & Client Identification on Internal and External Auditors' Evaluations of Internal Control Deficiencies, Auditing, vol. 30, iss. 4, pp. 273–283.	Identification with client is associated with less lenient control evaluations for internal auditors.
Brainstorming quality.	Brazel, J, Carpenter, T & Jenkins, J 2010, Auditors' use of Brainstorming in the Consideration of Fraud: reports from the Field, The Accounting Review, vol. 85, iss. 2, pp. 289–417.	Brainstorming quality moderates the association between fraud risk assessment and testing.
Ethical reasoning.	Massey, D & Thorne, L 2006. The impact of Task information Feedback on Ethical reasoning, Behavioral Research in Accounting, vol. 18, pp. 65–83.	Task Information Feedback is effective in promoting ethical reasoning of auditors and accounting students.
Skepticism.	Rose, J 2007, Attention to Evidence of Aggressive Financial Reporting and Intentional Misstatement Judgments: Effects of Experience and Trust, Behavioral Research in Accounting, vol. 19, pp. 133–159.	Auditors' trust and skepticism is related to their attention to aggressive reporting.
Professional skepticism.	Nelson, M 2008., A Model and Literature Review of Professional Skepticism in Auditing Author: Nelson, Auditing, vol. 27, iss. 2, pp. 109–136.	Auditors' pre-existing knowledge, traits and incentives all combine (and potentially trade off or interact) to affect the amount of Professional Skepticism in audit judgment and audit actions.

(Continued)

Table 9.1 (Continued)

	Full reference	Finding
Machiavellianism.	Wakefield, R 2008. Accounting and Machiavellianism, Behavioral Research in Accounting, vol. 20, iss. 1, pp. 93–113.	Machiavellianism is not required to achieve success in auditing.
Dispositional need for closure.	Bailey, C, Daily, C & Phillips, T 2011, Auditors levels of Dispositional need for Closure and Effects on Hypothesis Generation and Confidence, Behavioral Research in Accounting, vol. 23, iss. 1, pp. 131–160.	DNFC is related to hypothesis generation and confidence in auditors.
Predisposition toward handling own errors.	Gronewold, U & Donle, M 2011. Organizational Climate and Auditors' predispositions toward Handling Errors. pp. 27–50. Behavioral Research in Accounting, vol. 23, iss.2	Auditors' organizational climate is associated with predisposition toward handling errors.
Reputation.	Robertson, J, Stefaniak, C & Curtis, M 2011. Does Wrongdoer Reputation Matter? Impact of Auditor-Wrongdoer Performance and Likeability Reputations on Fellow Auditors' Intention to take action and choice of Reporting outlet, Behavioral Research in Accounting, vol. 23, iss. 2, pp. 147–167.	Actions are more likely to be taken against less likeable, poor performers.
Locus of control.	McKnight, C & Wright, W 2011, Auditing, Characteristics of Relatively High-Performance Auditors, Auditing, vol 30, iss. 1, pp. 149–171.	Auditors with higher internal locus of control were associated with higher levels of job performance, as compared to those with external locus of control.

Table 9.2 Measures of clients

	Full reference	Finding
Confidence in and reliance in no-assurance engagements.	Reinstein, A, Green, B, & Miller, C 2006. Evidence of Perceived Quality of Plain Paper statements, Auditing, vol. 25 iss. 1, pp. 49–67.	Greater confidence and reliance on financial statements with CPA association.
Confidence in auditors' technical knowledge.	Han, J, Jamal, K & Tan, H 2011. Auditors' Overconfidence in Predicting the Technical Knowledge of Superiors and Subordinates, Auditing, vol 30, iss. 1, pp. 1–20.	Overconfidence in superiors' and subordinates' knowledge is a function of task difficulty.
Moral reasoning.	Maroney, J & McDevitt, R 2008, The Effects of Moral Reasoning on Financial Reporting Decisions in a Post Sarbanes-Oxley Environment, Behavioral Research in Accounting, vol. 20, iss. 2, pp. 55–71.	Sox mitigates financial statement overstatement for lower levels of moral reasoning but not for higher levels of moral reasoning.

	Full reference	Finding
Cognitive style.	Bryant, S, Murthy, U & Wheeler, P 2009. The Effects of Cognitive Style and feedback type on Performance in an Internal control Task, Behavioral Research in Accounting, vol. 1. iss. 1, pp. 19–35.	Cognitive style combines with outcome feedback to improve performance.
Trust	Rose, A., Rose J & Dibben, M 2010. The Effects of Trust and management Incentives on Audit Committee judgments, Behavioral Research in Accounting, vol. 22, iss. 2, pp. 51–67.	Trust influences perceptions of managements potential for deception, and in turn increases auditor support.

Table 9.3 Measures of managers

	Full reference	Finding
Work style.	Xu, Y & Tuttle, B 2005. The Role of Social Influence in using accounting Performance information to evaluate Subordinates, Behavioral Research in Accounting, vol. 17, pp. 175–189.	Work style is associated with performance evaluation.
Creativity.	Bryant, S, Stone, D & Weir, B 2010. An Exploration of Accountants, Accounting work and Creativity, Behavioral Research in Accounting, vol. 22, iss. 2, pp. 105–132.	Lower creativity in accounting students versus MBAs; however, creativity is NOT related to ethics.
Cognitive orientation.	Naranjo-Gil, D, Cuevas-Rodrigues, G, Lopez-Cabrales, A & Sanchez, J 2012. The Effects of Incentive System and Cognitive Orientation on Teams' Performance, Behavioral Research in Accounting, vol. 24, iss. 2, pp. 153–175.	Effectiveness of incentive design is a function to dominant cognitive orientation of team.
Financial values and financial altruism.	Stone, D, Bryant, S & Weir, B 2013. Why are financial incentive effects unreliable? An extension of Self-Determination Theory, Behavioral Research in Accounting, vol. 22, iss. 2, pp. 87–103.	Financial values influence the effectiveness of incentives as motivators.

Discussion and conclusion

This paper outlines the steps necessary for the development of quality behavioural accounting measures, and provides an inventory of the measures used in Behavioural Accounting Research over the past ten years from selected journals. The importance of the development of high-quality measures of latent accounting constructs should not be overlooked as the significance of findings in Behavioural Accounting Research is ultimately a function of the validity and reliability of the instrument that measures the underlying constructs being considered (cf., Jacoby 1978). Although outside the scope of this chapter, also of importance for accounting measure construction are the design choices for the rating scale used in the measure. Eutsler and Lang

(2015) convincingly argue that there should be seven points included in every scale to maximize variance, and that each point in a rating scale should be labelled, and not just the end points of the scale.

Tables 9.1–9.3 together provide a partial inventory of the psychometric accounting-specific measures published in accounting journals in the past ten years. Nevertheless, only one measure was published in a top-tier journal: *The Accounting Review* (Brazel et al. 2010). Furthermore, with only two exceptions, the papers identified in those tables investigated new accounting constructs and developed new psychometric measures. Thus, there does not appear to be a willingness by either accounting academics or accounting journals to amass a body of research relying upon a valid and reliable psychometric measure of a particular accounting construct.

One of the most alarming revelations emerging from this investigation was, with the exception of three papers (i.e., Johnson et al. 2012; Hurtt 2010; Smith and Hall 2008), most of the measures used in Behavioural Accounting Research, as identified on Tables 9.1–9.3 failed to document the steps used in their development and/or failed to reveal the extent to which their measure complied with existing standards of validity and reliability. The comparability and insights obtained from Behavioural Accounting Research in the future will benefit from the inclusion of documentation of the development of steps undertaken in the development of quality accounting measures, and from the adopting of best practices such as structural equation modelling (Homburg and Rudolph 2001) in the development of measures.

An understanding of steps needed to develop reliable and valid accounting-specific measures, by necessity, entails relying upon the seminal work of universal social science researchers, which although useful, fails to consider the impact of applied contexts, nor do they consider the extent to which levels of quality, including validity and reliability, are appropriate to the accounting domain. In some circumstances, the decision to undertake to measure a construct in the accounting domain may involve the identification of a universal construct and measure, and consideration of how the universal construct may or may not apply to the accounting domain, and the refinement of the universal measure to the accounting domain. In other circumstances, the development of an accounting-specific measure must be done "from scratch" as the underlying construct is unique to the accounting domain. Not surprisingly, the actual procedures undertaken to adapt a universal measure are not exactly the same as the procedures involved in the development of an accounting-specific construct "from scratch". It is hoped that this paper will therefore facilitate the development and enhance the documentation of reliable and valid accounting measures.

Note

1 As accounting constructs may be similar to a universal construct, a determination can be made of the extent to which the accounting-specific and the universal constructs are equivalent. Construct equivalence involves functional and conceptual equivalence. Construct equivalence is the determination of whether "the construct serves the same function and is expressed similarly" (Singh 1995: 602), which has implications for the comparability and validity of inferences made from the measure.

References

Anderson, J. and Gerbing, D., 1988, 'Structural equation modeling in practice: A review and recommended two step approach', *Psychological Bulletin* 103(3), 411–420.

Bagozzi, R., Youjae, Y. and Phillips, L., 1991, 'Assessing construct validity in organizational research', *Administrative Science Quarterly* 35(3), 421–458.

Bailey, C., Daily, C. and Phillips, T., 2011, 'Auditors levels of dispositional need for closure and effects on hypothesis generation and confidence', *Behavioral Research in Accounting* 23(1), 131–160.

Bamber, M. and Iyer, V., 2006, 'Auditors' identification with their clients and its effect on auditors' objectivity', *Auditing: A Journal of Practice and Theory* 25(2), 85–94.

Bollen, K., 1989, *Structural Equations With Latent Variables*, Wiley, New York.

Brazel, J., Carpenter, T. and Jenkins, J., 2010, 'Auditors' use of brainstorming in the consideration of fraud: Reports from the field', *The Accounting Review* 85(2), 289–417.

Bryant, S., Murthy, U. and Wheeler, P., 2009, 'The effects of cognitive style and feedback type on performance in an internal control task', *Behavioral Research in Accounting* 1, 19–35.

Bryant, S., Stone, D. and Weir, B., 2010, 'An exploration of accountants, accounting work and creativity', *Behavioral Research in Accounting* 22(2), 105–132.

Carmines, E. and Zeller, R., 1979, *Reliability and Validity Assessment*, London, Sage Publications.

Chen, K. and Olson, S., 1989, 'Measuring cognitive complexity in the accounting domain', *Behavioral Research in Accounting* 1, 160–182.

Christie, R. and Geis, F., 1970, 'How devious are you? Take the Machiavelli test to find out', *Journal of Management in Engineering* 15(4), 17–30.

Churchill, G., 1979, 'A paradigm for developing better measures of marketing constructs', *Journal of Marketing Research* 16(1), 64–73.

Clark, L. and Watson, D., 1998, *Constructing Validity: Basic Issues in Objective Scale Development*, American Psychological Association, Washington, DC.

Cronbach, L., 1951, 'Coefficient alpha and the internal structure of tests', *Psychometrika* 16(3), 297–334.

Cronbach, L. and Meehl, P., 1955, 'Construct validity', *Psychological Bulletin* 52, 281–302.

DeVellis, R., 1991, *Scale Development: Theory and Applications: Applied Social Research Methods Series*, Sage Publications, Thousand Oaks, CA.

Devine, C., 1963, 'The role of conservatism re-examined', *Journal of Accounting Research* 1(Autumn), 127–138.

Eutsler, J. and Lang, B., 2015, 'Rating scales in accounting research: The impact of scale points and labels', *Behavioral Research in Accounting* 27(2), 35–51.

Gronewold, U. and Donle, M., 2011, 'Organizational climate and auditors' predispositions toward handling errors', *Behavioral Research in Accounting* 23(2), 27–50.

Hair, J., Black, W., Babin, B., Anderson, R. and Tatham, R., 2006, *Multivariate Data Analysis*, Pearson-Prentice Hall, Upper Saddle River, NJ.

Han, J., Jamal, K. and Tan, H., 2011, 'Auditors' overconfidence in predicting the technical knowledge of superiors and subordinates', *Auditing: A Journal of Practice and Theory* 30(1), 1–20.

Hofstede, T. and Kinard, J., 1970, 'A strategy for behavioral accounting research', *The Accounting Review* 45(1), 38–54.

Homburg, C. and Rudoph, B., 2001, 'Customer satisfaction in industrial markets: Dimensional and multiple role issues', *Journal of Business Research* 52, 15–33.

Hurtt, R.K., 2010, 'Development of a scale to measure professional skepticism', *Auditing: A Journal of Practice and Theory* 29(1), 149–171.

Jacoby, J., 1978, 'Consumer research', *Journal of Marketing* 42(April), 87–96.

Johnson, E., Lowe, D. and Reckers, P., 2012, 'Measuring accounting professionals' attitudes regarding alternative work arrangements', *Behavioral Research in Accounting* 24(1), 25–46.

Kerlinger, F. and Lee, H., 1964, *Foundations of Behavioural Research: Educational and Psychological Inquiry*, Holt, Rinehart and Winston, New York.

Libby, T. and Thorne, L., 2004, 'The identification and categorization of auditors' virtues', *Business Ethics Quarterly* 14(3), 479–498.

Libby, T. and Thorne, L., 2007, 'The development of a measure of auditors' virtue', *Journal of Business Ethics* 71(1), 89–99.

Lord, A. T. (1989). The development of behavioral thought in accounting, 1952–1981. *Behavioral Research in Accounting*, 1(s 124).

Maroney, J. and McDevitt, R., 2008, 'The effects of moral reasoning on financial reporting decisions in a post Sarbanes-Oxley environment', *Behavioral Research in Accounting* 20(2), 55–71.

Massey, D. and Thorne, L., 2006, 'The impact of task information feedback on ethical reasoning', *Behavioral Research in Accounting* 18, 65–83.

McCall, M.W. and Bobko, P., 1990, 'Research methods in the service of discovery', in *Handbook of Industrial and Organizational Psychology*, 1, 381–418.

McKnight, C. and Wright, W., 2011, 'Characteristics of relatively high-performance auditors', *Auditing: A Journal of Practice and Theory* 30(1), 149–171.

Naranjo-Gil, D., Cuevas-Rodrigues, G., Lopez-Cabrales, A. and Sanchez, J., 2012, 'The effects of incentive system and cognitive orientation on teams' performance', *Behavioral Research in Accounting* 24(2), 153–175.

Nelson, M., 2008, 'A model and literature review of professional skepticism in auditing', *Auditing: A Journal of Practice and Theory* 27(2), 109–136.

Nunnally, J., 1978, *Psychometric Methods*, McGraw Hill, New York.

Pincoffs, E., 1986, *Quandaries and Virtues*, University of Kansas Press, Lawrence, KS.

Reinstein, A., Green, B. and Miller, C., 2006, 'Evidence of perceived quality of plain paper statements', *Auditing: A Journal of Practice and Theory* 25(1), 49–67.

Rest, J., 1979, *Development in Judging Moral Issues*, University of Minnesota Press, Minneapolis, MN.

Robertson, J., Stefaniak, C. and Curtis, M., 2011, 'Does wrongdoer reputation matter? Impact of auditor-wrongdoer performance and likeability reputations on fellow auditors' intention to take action and choice of reporting outlet', *Behavioral Research in Accounting* 23(2), 147–167.

Rose, A., Rose, J. and Dibben, M., 2010, 'The effects of trust and management incentives on audit committee judgments', *Behavioral Research in Accounting* 22(2), 51–67.

Rose, J., 2007, 'Attention to evidence of aggressive financial reporting and intentional misstatement judgments: Effects of experience and trust', *Behavioral Research in Accounting* 19, 133–159.

Singh, J., 1995, 'Measurement issues in cross-national research', *Journal of International Business Studies* 26(3), 597–619.

Smith, D. and Hall, M., 2008, 'An empirical examination of a three-component model of professional commitment among public accountants', *Behavioral Research in Accounting* 20(1), 45–74.

Stefaniak, C., Houston, R. and Cornell, R., 2011, 'The effect of employer and client identification on internal and external auditors' evaluations of internal control deficiencies', *Auditing: A Journal of Practice and Theory* 30(4), 273–283.

Stevens, S., 1951, 'Mathematics, measurement and psychophysics', in S. Stevens (ed.), *Handbook of Experimental Psychology*, 1–49, John Wiley, New York.

Stone, D., Bryant, S. and Weir, B., 2013, 'Why are financial incentive effects unreliable? An extension of self-determination theory', *Behavioral Research in Accounting* 22(2), 87–103.

Thorne, L., 2000, 'The development of two measures to assess accountants' prescriptive and deliberative moral reasoning', *Behavioral Research in Accounting* 12, 139–170.

Wakefield, R., 2008, 'Accounting and Machiavellianism', *Behavioral Research in Accounting* 20(1), 93–113.

Xu, Y. and Tuttle, B., 2005, 'The role of social influence in using accounting performance information to evaluate subordinates', *Behavioral Research in Accounting* 17, 175–189.

10

Manipulation and attention checks in Behavioural Accounting Research

Jacob M. Rose

Terminology

A significant problem to overcome regarding *manipulation checks* in accounting research is the lack of consistent and accurate terminology. In social psychology and most fields of psychology research, the term *manipulation check* has historically referred to a measurement that is designed to capture whether or not an experimental treatment causes the desired change to the underlying theoretical construct of interest. For example, if a researcher is interested in studying the effects of investors' beliefs about the objectivity of the audit committee on investors' decisions to invest in a company, the researcher might manipulate whether or not the audit committee members are described as close friends of the CEO. The objectivity of audit committee members is the underlying theoretical construct, and the experimental treatment is a statement in the instrument that manipulates whether or not the CEO is a friend of audit committee members. Following the classic definition, a *manipulation check* would involve measuring participants' perceptions of the objectivity of the audit committee and determining whether the two treatment conditions caused statistically significant differences in participants' assessments of objectivity.

Over time, and particularly in accounting research, the term *manipulation check* has been used to describe more than measures of the effects of treatment conditions on theoretical constructs. A large percentage of experimental studies in accounting employ measures that are used to determine whether participants have attended to the experimental treatment conditions. Using the example above, a researcher could ask participants to indicate whether or not the audit committee members are friends of the CEO. This measurement would typically be collected after participants have responded to dependent variable measures, and it would serve to provide evidence that participants read and understood the experimental treatment. The terminology for such procedures varies across different literatures. In accounting, authors have referred to these measures of attention as *manipulation checks*, while in other disciplines they are termed *attention checks, comprehension checks, recall checks* or *treatment measures*. Describing these measures of attention as *manipulation checks* is inappropriate, and accounting research needs to better distinguish *manipulation checks* from other checks.

Before discussing when *manipulation checks* (and other checks) are needed and how they should be employed, I first present a simple framework that describes appropriate terminology (see Figure 10.1) and a figure displaying the audit committee objectivity example using this framework (Figure 10.2). Accounting researchers and journals will benefit considerably from the adoption of more precise terminology regarding *manipulation checks* because this will prevent confusion during review processes and promote consistency with other disciplines. The

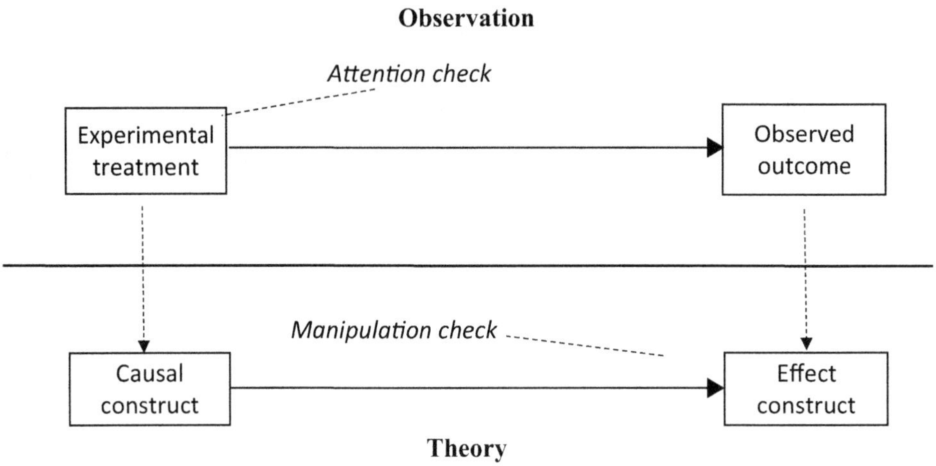

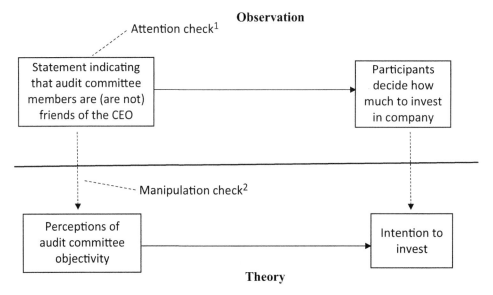

Figure 10.1   Manipulation check terminology

Observation

1) Attention check: Ask participants to recall whether or not audit committee members are friends of the CEO.

2) Manipulation check: Measure participants' perceptions of audit committee objectivity and verify that these perceptions are significantly different across treatment conditions.

Figure 10.2   Audit committee objectivity example

framework in Figure 10.1 displays the relationship between a researchers' observations (measured variables) and the theoretical constructs of interest, and it shows how attention checks and *manipulation checks* fit into the research process.

In brief, *attention checks* are used to demonstrate that participants have read and attended to the experimental treatment (e.g., participants noticed that audit committee members were described as friends of the CEO). *Manipulation checks* are used to measure the effects of treatments on theoretical constructs, such as the effects of friendships on beliefs about audit committee objectivity. An experiment provides evidence for a relationship between causal constructs and effect constructs by demonstrating a causal relationship between experimental treatments and outcome measures. *Manipulation checks* support the existence of a relationship between causal and effect constructs by providing evidence of construct validity. There are also other potential checks not presented in the framework (e.g., suspicion checks, awareness checks and instructional *manipulation checks*), and these are discussed in the *Additional considerations* section. The following section describes attention and *manipulation checks* in more detail.

Purposes of attention and *manipulation checks* in experimental research

Attention and *manipulation checks* have specific purposes that are relevant to different research questions, but are not relevant to all research questions. Thus, *manipulation checks* and attention checks are NOT always required for experimental research, and it is inappropriate to claim that the absence of these measures is a fatal flaw in a research design. The necessity of checks and types of checks required depend upon the research questions being addressed by the experiment. This section describes when the different checks are most important and when they should be employed based on the discretion of the researcher.

Attention checks

Attention checks should generally be considered discretionary, but recent discussions with colleagues and editors reveals that many accounting papers are rejected for not including attention checks. I believe that this has stemmed largely from the confounding of terminology for attention checks and *manipulation checks* in the literature, and cleansing our terminology will be beneficial for both authors and journals. The primary purpose of an attention check is to increase statistical power by reducing noise. Using the example of audit committee objectivity, if some participants in the experiment did not read the experimental treatment, then it is certain that their perceptions of audit committee objectivity and their decisions to invest were not caused by the experimental treatment. The purpose of an experiment is to evaluate the causal effects of treatments on a dependent measure and associated relationship between causal constructs and effect constructs. The causal chain is undeniably broken when participants are unaware of the experimental treatments. An attention check is included such that participants who have not attended to treatments can be removed from the data prior to statistical analyses.

While attention checks are useful, they are not substitutes for *manipulation checks*, and many accounting studies have inappropriately described and employed attention checks as checks on manipulations. To see this distinction, let's continue with the audit committee objectivity example. If we know that participants attended to the treatment, and they correctly recall that audit committee members were (or were not) friends of the CEO, this tells us nothing about participants' perceptions of the objectivity of the audit committee. If the theoretical construct of interest is objectivity, and the purpose of the research is to examine how perceptions of objectivity influence investors' decisions, then including an attention check fails to provide evidence that the experimental treatment involves objectivity.

Even when there is evidence that participants attended to a manipulation, and it appears obvious that attention to the manipulation should influence the theoretical construct of interest, an attention check still fails to provide evidence of a relationship between treatments and causal constructs. There are numerous factors that can interfere with the effectiveness of experimental treatments, even when the treatments are well-designed and of high quality. Treatments can fail because participants: are fatigued, recognize the purpose of the experiment, experience anxiety, intentionally attempt to interfere with the experiment, doubt the validity of statements made in the treatment or experience any number of unanticipated effects. Without a *manipulation check*, the experimenter will find it difficult to meet the requirements for construct validity (Shadish, Cook and Campbell 2002).

One might be tempted to argue that attention checks are also necessary to insure that treatment designs are appropriate, even if attention checks do not substitute for *manipulation checks*. But this conclusion would be incorrect. In the audit committee example, it is an indisputable matter of fact that one treatment group was told that audit members were friends of the CEO, and one treatment group was told that audit committee members were not friends of the CEO. The difference in the treatments is not in doubt, and attention checks do not provide evidence regarding the quality or design of the treatments. Attention checks only serve to identify participants that failed to attend or did not attend enough to recall the experimental manipulations, and they are discretionary tools for reducing noise in sample data.

In addition to the fact that attention checks are not essential to a valid research design, they also have limitations. The failure of a participant to respond correctly to an attention check is not a guarantee that the participant did not attend to the experimental treatment. Participants can react subconsciously to a treatment without being able to recall it. In such circumstances, an attention check could lead a researcher to ignore valuable data. Further, responses to most attention checks are collected after participants respond to dependent variables. It is therefore possible that participants who attended to a treatment and were influenced by it will forget the description of the treatment by the time attention checks are completed. Attention checks can reduce noise, but they have weaknesses.

Manipulation checks

While attention checks should be viewed as a choice of the researcher, *manipulation checks* are generally beneficial for drawing conclusions about causal relationships between theoretical constructs. The need for *manipulation checks* ultimately depends upon the research purpose and other features of the study's design. The purpose of a study may be to examine the effects of treatments on outcomes, rather than to examine latent (i.e., unobservable) theoretical constructs. Consider the inherent differences between a pharmaceutical study and a social psychology study. In many pharmaceutical experiments, the primary research purpose is to investigate the effect of Drug A versus Drug B versus a placebo on patient survival durations. Such research focuses on the relationship between treatments and survival outcomes, and the research question does not involve an underlying psychological construct affected by the drugs. There may be little or no interest in how the drugs actually operate when investigating direct effects of drugs on survival. Thus, the purpose of research can be to examine the existence of a causal relationship between a treatment and an outcome. In a study of this type, there is no place for *manipulation checks*.

Such checks would not serve a purpose and would certainly not be considered a requirement of good research design.

The pharmaceutical example may appear far removed from accounting research, but there are many examples of accounting research that are primarily interested in treatment-outcome relationships. Continuing with our audit committee example, it is not difficult to imagine that researchers or regulators would be primarily interested in measuring the effects of friendships on investors' decisions to invest. Perhaps it does not matter whether the effects of friendships on investment decisions are related to perceptions of objectivity or some other theoretical construct, and the researcher wants to know if friendships affect investors' decisions. In this case, much like the pharmaceutical experiment, there is no need for a *manipulation check*. The study is not examining an underlying psychological construct, and it is focused on a practical relationship between a treatment condition that mimics real-world relationships and decisions made by investors. A study of this type will typically make fewer contributions to theory development, but it would be inappropriate to conclude that *manipulation checks* are needed or that their absence is a design flaw.

Experimental research that is interested in the causal relationships between latent theoretical constructs usually benefits from *manipulation checks*. I say "usually" because there are exceptions, and examples of these exceptions are discussed in the *Additional Considerations* section. The importance of *manipulation checks* to research involving psychological constructs is most apparent when reading social psychology journals, which emphasize the understanding of causal relationships between psychological constructs. Sigall and Mills (1998) found that the use of *manipulation checks* in social psychology journals increased dramatically between the 1960s and 1990s, and handbooks for social psychology research stress the need for *manipulation checks* in experiments (e.g., Sansone, Morf and Panter 2004: 244). When a researcher is drawing conclusions about the causal effects of a construct like objectivity on outcomes like investor decisions, it is important to provide evidence that the treatment is related to the construct. Without establishing this association, there is only evidence of the treatment-outcome relationship, and evidence of construct validity is lacking.

How to best perform *manipulation checks* is dependent upon the treatment and construct of interest, and there is no one-size-fits-all approach. In some cases, *manipulation checks* may involve complex measurements, such as existing (and potentially multiple) psychological instruments. Other checks can be very simple, such as a response to one Likert-type scale. A construct like perceived objectivity could be measured with a response scale where participants rate the objectivity of the audit committee on a scale of 1 (very low) to 7 (very high). The researcher would expect higher ratings of objectivity when there are no friendships between committee members and the CEO relative to when there are friendships. A statistically significant difference in perceived objectivity between the treatment conditions would indicate that the treatment was at least partially effective.

Determining whether a manipulation is truly effective can require more than a simple test of mean differences, particularly when there are plausible alternative effects of treatments on constructs and there are multiple independent variables. In multiple-factor designs, it is important to remember that a treatment should *only* affect the construct that the treatment is intended to influence, and experimental treatments should not affect constructs that are supposed to relate to other treatments. If a treatment influences constructs that should be related to other independent variables, this is evidence that the independent variables are not orthogonal and that statistical results are not reliable. For example, a researcher might be interested in the effects of both the objectivity of the audit committee and audit committee power on investors' decisions. To experimentally manipulate objectivity, the researcher employs the existence of friendships with the CEO, and to manipulate audit committee power, the researcher varies the expertise of the audit committee members. If *manipulation checks* reveal that both the friendship manipulation and the expertise manipulation significantly influence participants' perceptions of audit committee objectivity, this indicates a potential problem with concluding that relationships between the treatments and outcomes indicate the existence of relationships between causal constructs and effect constructs.

Review of behavioural research in the major accounting journals suggests that researchers usually perform simple mean difference tests for each *manipulation check* to determine whether mean responses differ at different levels of the treatment, and they do not include tests to determine whether each experimental treatment influences only the construct it is designed to affect. Accounting researchers need to consider this important facet of *manipulation checks*. The potential for treatments to influence more than one construct of interest indicates that analyses of *manipulation checks* should employ full-factorial ANOVA models, rather than individual tests of mean differences.

The timing of *manipulation checks* is also important. Most often, *manipulation checks* are placed after measures of the dependent variables in experimental instruments. This is intended to reduce demand effects, and is generally good practice. However, the most important timing issue to consider involves the timing of checks related to the experiment itself. It is essential to perform *manipulation checks* before the experiment is ever conducted – during pilot testing. This allows a researcher to determine whether treatments affect the latent constructs of interest before risking a failure of the experiment and wasting data collection efforts. Performing *manipulation checks* during pilot testing can also overcome many of the undesirable effects of *manipulation checks* that can make them problematic (discussed further in the next section).

Measuring constructs to demonstrate that they are influenced by treatments should not be the end of researcher's consideration of a *manipulation check*. Researchers often consider only the treatments during data analyses, even when the research questions involve theoretical constructs. When a research question involves theoretical constructs, then there is a need to examine the effects of constructs on outcomes. For example, responses to a Likert-type scale that captures perceptions of objectivity should also be employed in additional analyses that directly examine the relationship between perceptions of objectivity and investors' decisions. These analyses would provide evidence for a relationship between the causal construct and effect construct. Data analyses in experimental accounting research tend to rely heavily on ANOVA, which necessarily concentrates hypotheses testing on the effects of experimental treatments on dependent measures. Such an approach makes perfect sense when the purpose of an investigation is to study the effects of treatments on outcome variables. But when the research is intended to investigate constructs, data analyses should go beyond the treatment effects. Regardless of the measurement approach used to perform *manipulation checks*, these measures are valuable resources for more complete analyses of experimental data.

Social-psychological researchers sometimes ignore treatments entirely during data analyses (O'Keefe 2003). Instead, analyses only examine the effects of psychological constructs on outcomes. In studies that are truly focused on psychological constructs, experimental treatments can be viewed as laboratory methods for inducing desired levels of a construct, and the treatments themselves are not considered relevant to the research question. Ignoring treatments in accounting research would generally not be appropriate given the practical importance and high ecological validity of most treatment conditions, but researchers need to examine both treatment effects and the effects of constructs on outcome measures.

Additional considerations

Online research

The emergence of online data collection through services such as Amazon Mechanical Turk have spawned new techniques and terminology, particularly with regards to attention checks. There is evidence that online participants pay less attention to experimental stimuli than do more traditional participants such as students (e.g., Goodman, Cryder and Cheema 2013), and this has led to techniques designed specifically to identify online participants who are not attending to experimental stimuli.

The primary differences between attention checks seen in controlled laboratory experiments and online experiments/surveys involves the placement of the attention check and its structure. Given that participants of online experiments/surveys are often paid for completion of an instrument, researchers have desires to quickly identify robots and participants who are not attending to the instrument. As a result, attention checks in online environments are regularly presented early in the instrument (and often as the first or second question). These attention checks designed to rapidly identify low attention or responses from robots were first described by Oppenheimer, Meyvis and Davidenko (2009) and are called *instructional manipulation checks* (IMCs).

IMCs are unrelated to experimental treatments, and they are designed strictly to test attention to instructions. For example, Oppenheimer et al. (2009) describe an IMC where participants are informed that the researchers want to insure that the participants are paying attention, and participants are told not to answer the next question about sports preferences. Then participants are presented with a list of sports and asked to check all of the sports in which they are interested. Any participant who checks one or more sports is deemed to not be paying attention, and the participant is not asked to complete the remainder of the experiment or survey. As discussed earlier, this practice should not be confused with *manipulation checks*, and the purpose is strictly to reduce noise and eliminate participants from data analyses when those participants are not attending to instructions. Online studies still need *manipulation checks* when the research questions involve theoretical constructs.

Limitations of manipulation checks and approaches to overcome limitations

It is important to conduct *manipulation checks* in order to establish construct validity. However, there are circumstances where the costs of *manipulation checks* can outweigh their benefits. A primary threat posed by *manipulation checks* involves the revelation of a study's purpose and the resulting demand effects that make it difficult or impossible to rely on the results of hypotheses tests. One solution to this problem is simple. The *manipulation check* should be conducted after participants have responded to the dependent variable measures, and participants should not have any opportunity to change their responses to dependent measures after completing the *manipulation checks*. Note that attention checks could also serve to heighten participants' awareness of the goals of an experiment, and attention checks that capture whether participants have read and understood the treatments (as opposed to instructional *manipulation checks* that are not related to treatments) are also most commonly performed after participants respond to dependent variable measures.

There are situations, however, where performing *manipulation checks* after collecting dependent variable responses is not feasible. One example of this situation involves manipulations of participants' mood states. Manipulations of mood can have very short-term effects that dissipate by the time participants have responded to dependent variable measures. When the construct of interest is briefly affected by the treatment, *manipulation checks* that measure the construct after participants have responded to all dependent variables will fail to detect significant differences in the construct that are caused by the treatment.

In these situations where *manipulation checks* are needed but cannot be measured after the dependent variables, checks can be conducted during pilot testing. *Manipulation checks* performed during pilot testing can substitute for checks in the main experiment if the instrument does not change and participants are from a similar population. In addition to the ability to measure short-term effects, conducting *manipulation checks* during pilot testing creates opportunities for a wider array of measurement techniques. For example, in a small-scale pilot, the experimenter can conduct interviews with each participant or collect detailed process measures to gain a fuller understanding of the effects of treatments on constructs.

Manipulation checks also have inherent limitations that are not overcome by their timing. The most significant of these limitations is the inability of checks to disprove all plausible alternative explanations for results. *Manipulation checks* alone are insufficient to overcome challenges to a study's conclusions about causal constructs and effect constructs. Imagine that journal reviewers question the conclusion that increased audit committee objectivity causes investors to view investments in the firm more favourably. One journal reviewer argues that perceived independence of the audit committee is the real cause, and perceptions of objectivity are not actually important. Another reviewer believes that the existence of friendships between the audit committee and the CEO could weaken trust in the CEO because investors will perceive that the CEO has unduly influenced the composition of the board. *Manipulation checks* can provide evidence that the presence of friendships causes changes in perceived objectivity. In addition, statistical analyses can indicate that friendships cause changes in investor's decisions and investor decisions are related to perceptions of objectivity. But these analyses do not rule out the possibility that other causal constructs are involved.

One potential solution to the problem described in the above example involves the collection of additional *manipulation checks* that are designed to demonstrate that alternative constructs are not related to treatments. These alternative *manipulation checks* are called *confounding checks* (Wetzel 1977). The researcher could include, for example, measures to capture latent constructs such as perceived independence and trust in the CEO in the experimental instrument. If independence and trust are not influenced by the friendship treatment, then the researcher can effectively demonstrate that the alternative constructs are not causing changes in investment decisions. Thus, one important means of addressing the weaknesses of *manipulation checks* involves measuring alternative theoretical constructs that could potentially explain the causal relationships of interest. Confounding checks are powerful tools for improving construct validity, but accounting researchers have rarely employed these checks. This should change.

There are also limitations to performing confounding checks. It may not be possible to measure all plausible alternative constructs in one experiment. A researcher may be able to eliminate the most probable alternative causal constructs with the inclusion of additional measures in the experimental instrument, but there may be more challenges to conclusions about causality. Ultimately, a *manipulation check* will not resolve all disputes regarding whether the causal construct identified by the researcher is the true driver of changes to an outcome measure or if other unmeasured constructs play important roles. All behavioural researchers eventually find themselves caught in this trap because different researchers will have disparate beliefs about causal relationships, and single experiments are unlikely to convince everyone that a cause/effects relationship exists between two constructs. This weakness of *manipulation checks* is inherent to the limitations of individual experiments. Experimental research requires replication and extension, and the inability of *manipulation checks* to resolve disputes about causality is often best overcome with additional experimentation. When there are reasonable alternative explanations for relationships between causal constructs, additional experimentation and replication can rule out these explanations by controlling for the alternative constructs.

In my opinion, the absolute necessity of additional experimentation and replication represents one of the greatest threats to the future of accounting research. Accounting journals are reluctant and often unwilling to publish replications and small extensions of experimental studies. This is in contrast to archival accounting research, which often involves minor variations to prior studies, such as the addition of a new variable to an existing model or a change in measurement methods for a variable of interest. In order to understand causal constructs, we need to demonstrate convergent validity through replication. Subtle changes to manipulations across a series of experiments can effectively rule out alternative interpretations and yield more reliable theory. High-ranking accounting journals require experimental research to reach a very high "contribution bar" that can prohibit replication due to the inherent lack of novelty. Yet the foundation of experimental work in fields such as psychology, medicine, physics, etc. is replication and extension. Replications are needed precisely because individual experiments and *manipulation checks* cannot rule out all alternative explanations. Reviewers and editors of accounting journals need to promote replication, and researchers need to place more emphasis on the importance of quality *manipulation checks* to theory development.

References

Goodman, J., Cryder, C. and Cheema, A., 2013, 'Data collection in a flat world: The strengths and weaknesses of Mechanical Turk samples', *Journal of Behavioral Decision Making* 26, 213–224.

O'Keefe, D., 2003, 'Message properties, mediating states, and manipulation checks: Claims, evidence, and data analysis in experimental persuasive message effects research', *Communication Theory* 13(3), 251–274.

Oppenheimer, D., Meyvis, T. and Davidenko, N., 2009, 'Instructional manipulation checks: Detecting satisficing to increase statistical power', *Journal of Experimental Social Psychology* 45, 867–872.

Sansone, C., Morf, C. and Panter, A., 2004, *The Sage Handbook of Methods in Social Psychology*, Sage Publications, Inc., London.

Shadish, W., Cook, T. and Campbell, D., 2002, *Experimental and Quasi-Experimental Designs for Generalized Causal Inference*, Houghton Mifflin, Boston, MA.

Sigall, H. and Mills, J., 1998, 'Measures of independent variables and mediators are useful in social psychology experiments: But are they necessary?', *Personality and Social Psychology Review* 2, 218–226.

Wetzel, C., 1977, 'Manipulation checks: A reply to Kidd', *Representative Research in Social Psychology* 8(2), 88–93.

11

Social desirability in Behavioural Accounting Research

Radzi Jidin and Gary S. Monroe

The importance of considering social desirability bias

The validity and usefulness of findings involving self-reported data revolve around the truthfulness of responses provided by the participants, particularly if there may be socially sensitive issues involved in the responses. Self-report methodologies include experiments, surveys, verbal protocols and interviews. Data gathered through these methodologies are frequently subject to various response biases (Paulhus 1991; Fisher and Katz 2000). Social desirability bias is one of the most pervasive sources of response biases (Paulhus 1991; King and Bruner 2000; Fisher and Katz 2000; Tourangeau and Yan 2007). Social desirability bias "reflects the tendency on behalf of the subject to deny socially undesirable traits and to claim socially desirable ones, and the tendency to say things which place the speaker in a favourable light" (Nederhof 1985: 264). The tendency is "independent of their actual attitudes and true behaviours respectively" (Krumpal 2013: 2028). Participants' tendency to present themselves in the most favourable manner relative to prevailing social norms may lead them "to stretch the truth in an effort to make a good impression" (Martin and Nagao 1989: 72).

Social desirability bias is more likely to influence the validity of research involving socially sensitive issues that have social and normative implications (King and Bruner 2000; Kreuter, Presser and Tourangeau 2008; Krumpal 2013). These include issues related to drug use (Tourangeau and Yan 2007), domestic violence (Saunders 1991; Babcock, Costa, Green and Eckhardt 2004), abortion (Jones and Forrest 1992), levels of physical activity (Adam et al. 2005), dental care (Gordon 1987; Sanzone et al. 2013), religiosity (Presser and Stinson 1998) and ethical decision-making (Randall and Fernandes 1991; Cohen, Pant and Sharp 2001; Chung and Monroe 2003). Challenges and difficulties in preventing, identifying and controlling for social desirability bias have been widely acknowledged and documented in prior studies. This is especially true for research in the psychology and social sciences domains. There is a large stream of research in those domains that investigates various issues related to the bias. Yet, there are only a limited number of studies in accounting and auditing that systematically address potential contamination from this bias (e.g., Cohen et al. 2001; Chung and Monroe 2003).

As discussed above, social desirability bias distorts participants' responses in a socially desirable direction. Hence, the prevailing social norms determine what constitutes socially desirable or undesirable behaviours. In studies involving professionals such as accountants and auditors, the norms that constitute socially desirable behaviours may be viewed from two different perspectives. They are: social norms prevailing in the general society; or specific norms and traits expected from those in the profession. What is socially desirable from the profession's perspective may not necessarily be desirable or relevant from the general public's perspective. Take the concept of professional skepticism in auditing as an example. It is highly desirable that auditors exercise an appropriate level of skepticism when evaluating evidence provided by the client's management. However, such behaviour may not be relevant or may not be seen as desirable from the general public's point of view. This is because a high level of skepticism towards others is generally construed as a sign of distrust (Harding, Azim, Jidin and Muir 2016). The fact that the bias is context specific (Kreuter et al. 2008) makes it necessary for research in accounting and auditing to systematically examine the potential influence of social desirability bias on the validity of the findings.

Social desirability bias is an important issue in behavioural research because it may affect the validity of research when it is present. Validity is affected because the presence of social desirability bias may influence the relationships between the variables of interest. Ganster, Hennessey and Luthans (1983) provide three explanations as to why the presence of social desirability bias could be problematic.[1] First, it could produce spurious observed correlations between the independent and dependent variables. These false correlations occur when the social desirability bias is correlated with both dependent and independent variables. Hence, the observed correlations between these variables are not due to the sharing of variance in the constructs of interest. Instead, it is because both variables share the variance in social desirability bias. Second, social desirability bias could mask the relationship between the independent and dependent variables. The suppression effect would hinder the detection of the real correlations between the constructs of interest. In the third situation, social desirability bias is not correlated with either the dependent or independent variables. Instead, it interacts with one or more of the independent variables. Here, social desirability bias plays a moderating role. That is, the correlation between the independent and dependent variables is contingent upon the participant's level of social desirability bias. This bias is quite often present in behavioural research involving socially sensitive issues. For example, Fernandes and Randall (1992) investigate the roles of social desirability bias in influencing the relationships between independent and dependent variables in ethics research. The authors detected some form of social desirability bias in 63% of the 90 relationships examined. In investigating the three explanations, Fernandes and Randall (1992) find limited evidence of spuriousness and suppression effects. Instead, social desirability bias is most frequently found to play a moderating role.

Measuring social desirability bias

In order to effectively address issues related to social desirability bias, researchers need to be able to appropriately measure the bias. One of the most commonly used approaches to measure the bias is through the use of social desirability scales. There are a variety of measurement scales available that can easily be integrated into a research instrument. However, researchers need to carefully evaluate the strengths and weaknesses associated with the scale of interest before deciding to adopt it. This section reviews some of the scales frequently used to measure social desirability bias.[2] One of these scales is the Marlowe-Crowne social desirability scale (Crowne and Marlowe 1960, 1964).[3] This unidimensional scale considers social desirability bias as a personality trait, that is, the need for social approval. The original scale is comprised of 33 general items where participants need to provide "True" or "False" responses (Crowne and Marlowe 1960).

The higher the score on the scale, the higher the need for social approval, thereby, the higher the social desirability bias. Given the length of Marlowe-Crowne scale, a number of subsequent studies devised short form versions of the scale (e.g., Strahan and Gerbasi 1972; Reynolds 1982; Ballard 1992).[4] The use of abbreviated scales reduces the time taken by participants to complete the instrument; however, it has been argued that in some cases the abbreviated scales do not adequately capture the dimensions reflected in the full version of the Marlowe-Crowne scale (Fischer and Fick 1993; Barger 2002). Based on an analysis of six abbreviated scales, Fischer and Fick (1993: 423) assert that the scale devised by Strahan and Gerbasi (1972) "would seem to be the scale of choice". They argue that the scale "has high internal consistency and is highly correlated with the standard 33-item original scale" (Fischer and Fick 1993: 423). Andrews and Meyer (2003) on the other hand argue that a shorter 13-item scale proposed by Reynolds (1982) is a better alternative as it has good psychometric properties and is highly correlated with the scores on the original 33-item scale.

A number of researchers dispute the unidimensionality of the Marlowe-Crowne social desirability scale (Millham 1974; Paulhus 1984; Zerbe and Paulhus 1987; Barger 2002). They argue that the scale comprises two conceptually and empirically distinct factors (Millham 1974; Paulhus 1984; Zerbe and Paulhus 1987). Two two-component models commonly discussed in the literature are the attribution and denial model (Millham 1974; Ramanaiah and Martin 1980), and the self-deception and impression-management model (Paulhus 1984; Zerbe and Paulhus 1987; Paulhus 1991). In the first model, attribution refers to the tendency to attribute socially desirable but improbable statements to oneself whereas denial refers to the tendency to deny socially undesirable but highly probable statements about oneself (Millham 1974). In the second model, self-deception relates to an "unconscious tendency to see oneself in a favourable light", while impression management refers to "conscious presentation of a false front, such as deliberately falsifying test responses to create a favourable impressions" (Zerbe and Paulhus 1987: 253). Of these two models, the self-deception and impression-management model is more widely used in the literature to address social desirability bias (Li and Bagger 2007; Spector 2004).

One apparent difference between the self-deception and impression-management constructs is the motivation behind them. While self-deception involves "positively biased but honestly believed self-description" (Li and Bagger 2007), impression management is a "purposeful tailoring of responses to impress an audience" (Paulhus and John 1998). Given that self-deception is a relatively stable personality trait, it should not be considered as a contaminant and need not be controlled (Zerbe and Paulhus 1987; Paulhus and John 1998). Impression management on the other hand is a deliberate bias, hence, should be controlled (Paulhus 1984; Paulhus and John 1998). Paulhus (1984) argues that the Marlowe-Crowne scale simultaneously measures self-deception and impression management. However, there are many items in the scale that load on both factors, which makes it difficult to split the scale into two subscales (Paulhus 1984; Zerbe and Paulhus 1987). Therefore, Paulhus (1984, 1991) developed a 40-item Balanced Inventory of Desirable Responding (BIDR) scale. This scale is comprised of two 20-item subscales that are used to measure self-deception and impression management respectively. Researchers can add the 40 items to arrive at the overall measure of social desirability bias. The overall measure correlates highly with the Marlowe-Crowne social desirability scale (Paulhus 1991). Although this scale is longer than the Marlowe-Crowne social desirability scale, one of the advantages of BIDR is that researchers can choose either to use the full 40-item scale to measure overall social desirability bias or use only one of the 20-item subscales to measure self-deception and impression management. Although there are a number of other scales that have been developed to identify and measure social desirability bias, those scales have not been widely used in published research.[5]

Despite their usefulness, there are potential limitations associated with the use of those scales. Apart from the length, Fisher (2000) outlines two other general characteristics of social desirability scales that limit their application in studies involving self-report data. First, participants may find some of the items in the scales inappropriate or even offensive. For example, BIDR includes item such as "I have sometimes doubted my ability as a lover" while Marlowe-Crowne incorporates items such as "There have been occasions when I felt like smashing things" (Fisher 2000). The inclusion of such items may lower overall response rates and increase the likelihood of missing data (Fisher 2000). Second, some of the items in the scales are too general to be diagnostic. Those items ignore situational and sub-group differences in norms (Fisher 2000). Other than these limitations, researchers also need to be aware that the scales are developed to measure dispositional bias. That is, they consider social desirability bias as a personality trait. Given these limitations, it is incumbent upon researchers to assess the appropriateness of using any of these scales in their study.

Social desirability bias has also been measured by taking the difference in participants' responses to direct and indirect questions regarding an item of interest (Jurgensen 1978; Fisher 1993; Cohen et al. 1998, 2001; Chung and Monroe 2003). For the direct question, participants are asked to state their beliefs about or evaluation of an item. The question is expressed in the first-person wording. For indirect questioning, participants are asked to envisage how others would respond to the item. In this case, the question is asked in the third-person wording. For example, in direct questioning, participants are asked "Would you do it?" while for indirect questioning they are asked "Would your peers do it?" (Cohen et al. 1998) or they are asked to indicate "The probability that I would undertake the same action is high (1) ... low (7)" and "The probability that my peers would undertake the same action is high (1) ... low (7)" (Chung and Monroe 2003). The only difference between the direct and indirect questioning is the use of first-person and third-person wording. Comparison of participants' responses to direct and indirect questions allows researchers to assess the existence of social desirability bias. The larger the difference, the greater the social desirability bias (Cohen et al. 1998, 2001; Chung and Monroe 2003).

Despite the relative ease with which the direct and indirect questioning approach can be integrated into a research instrument, there are several limitations associated with this approach that need to be taken into consideration. First, the approach measures social desirability bias from a situational perspective. That is, it measures social desirability in the context of the contemporaneous environment. For example, some scenarios provided to participants may invoke more or less social desirability bias than other scenarios. It does not, however, measure social desirability bias as a personality trait. Therefore, the application is only limited to the measuring of situational social desirability bias. Second, the simultaneous use of direct and indirect questions may lead to a problem of "demand characteristics", which is also known as "demand effects" (Orne 1959; Weber and Cook 1972; Pany and Reckers 1987). Demand effects refer to the situation where participants are aware of what the researcher is trying to investigate and therefore respond in the manner that they believe that the researcher desires (Orne 1959; Pany and Reckers 1987). Third, participants may find it perplexing to answer the indirect question because it requires participants to predict what others would do or think and they may not be able to do this (Fisher 1993). Fourth, the extent to which answers to indirect questions reflect information about the self is questionable (Fisher 1993; Fisher and Tellis 1998).

Social desirability bias in accounting- and auditing-related research

Based on the framework discussed in the previous sections, we review accounting- and auditing-related literature that addresses issues related to social desirability bias. Our initial review of the literature reveals that the approach used to measure the bias and the depth of the analysis varies considerably across studies. Therefore, for each study that we review in this section, we focus our discussion on two aspects of each study: (a) the measurement of social desirability bias and (b) the use of social desirability bias variables in the analysis. In terms of social desirability bias measures, our review of the literature reveals a limited use of social desirability scales. Recall that such scales are developed to measure the social desirability bias trait in individuals. In investigating the influence of moral philosophy on the ethical belief of auditors, Kung and Huang (2013) include a short version of Marlowe-Crowne scale in their survey instrument. The authors use an abbreviated 13-items scale developed by Reynolds (1982). Their initial analysis reveals that social desirability bias is correlated with auditors' ethical beliefs. To examine the influence of social desirability bias on their findings, the authors eliminated data from participants with social desirability scores above seven points and re-ran the analysis. The results remained qualitatively similar, therefore, they conclude that auditors' ethical belief is not susceptible to social desirability bias.

When examining the relationship between organizational justice and accountants' turnover intentions, Parker and Kohlmeyer (2005: 362) examine whether social desirability bias influences the relationship between the two variables. Social desirability bias is measured "using a scale adopted from Crowne and Marlowe (1964)". The authors, however, do not specifically mention which form of the Marlowe-Crowne scales they used in their study.[6] To check for the existence of social desirability bias, the authors correlate the score from the social desirability scale with the dependent variables. The authors then conclude that social desirability bias does not influence their findings and that correcting for social desirability bias is not required in their study.[7]

Ryan (2001) investigates the relationship between accountants' level of moral reasoning and their organizational citizenship behaviour and look at whether social desirability bias influences the relationship. The author includes a short version (six-item) of the Marlowe-Crowne scale in the survey instrument. Like Parker and Kohlmeyer (2005), Ryan (2001) does not explain which of the 33 original items from the Marlowe-Crowne scale were included or the basis of the selection. Social desirability bias is included as one of the covariates in the regression model. The results indicate that social desirability bias is a significant covariate; however, no further discussion related to social desirability bias is provided. There was no analysis of the potential interaction between social desirability bias and the independent variable of interest reported in the paper.

Aranya and Wheeler (1986) conduct a survey to investigate the association between accountants' personality types and their work commitment. These variables are measured using a number of different scales. The original Marlow-Crowne social desirability bias scale was included in the research instrument to ascertain whether the various scales used in the study are measuring social desirability bias or measuring the construct that the scales purported to measure. Given a low correlation between the social desirability bias score and the other scales, the authors conclude that those other scales capture the relevant construct that they supposed to capture. No further analysis about social desirability bias was provided by the authors.

In order to control for potential social desirability bias when investigating the effects of ethical climate on auditors' perceptions of organizational-professional conflict and organizational commitment, Shafer (2009) includes an impression-management scale in his survey instrument. As discussed in the previous section, the impression-management scale is a component of the BIDR scale. Shafer (2009) finds that impression management is highly correlated with the dependent variables and three out of four measures of the independent variable. The results indicate that participants biased their report of organizational-professional conflict downward and their effective organizational commitment upward. In order to address the bias, the author includes the impression-management variable in all regression models. The findings indicate that impression management only has a significant negative effect on the reported organizational-professional conflict. However, the author does not investigate the potential influence of an interaction between impression management and the other independent variables on the dependent variable.

Larkin (2000) conducts a survey to investigate the roles of age, gender, employment experience and peer group on the ability of internal auditors to identify ethical and unethical behaviour. In controlling for social desirability bias, 17 items from the Marlow-Crowne scale were included in the instrument. The author asserts that these 17 items are the ones that deal with ethical beliefs. However, no further justification is provided as to why these items were chosen. Other than a conclusion that there is no influence of social desirability bias in the study, the author does not discuss how the measure is used in the analysis. Further, the dependent variable in Larkin (2000) is the participants' assessment of the acceptability of the scenarios in six vignettes provided to them. Apart from that, participants are also required to indicate their assessment of how most internal auditors would assess the scenarios in the vignettes. Recall our discussion above that one approach to measure social desirability bias is by taking the difference in participants' response to direct and indirect questioning. Interestingly, the author does not use the difference as a measure of social desirability bias. Hence, despite the findings that there are significant differences between participants' responses to direct and indirect questioning, the author concludes that the study found that social desirability bias had no effect on the results.

There are a number of other studies in the accounting- and auditing-related domain that measure social desirability bias using the difference between participants' responses to direct and indirect questions. Studies that pioneered this approach in the accounting- and auditing-related literature are those by Cohen et al. (1995, 1996, 1998, 2001). Cohen et al. (1995) is one of the earliest studies to adopt this approach. The study looks at international differences in ethical decision-making of auditors from three different cultures, Latin America, Japan and the United States. The authors also look at whether there are differences in the level of social desirability bias between the three groups. Based on the scenario in the vignettes provided to them, participants are required to indicate "the probability that I would undertake the action". They are also required to indicate "the probability that my peers or colleagues would perform the action". The results indicate that auditors believed that they would act more ethically than their colleagues. Their findings also indicate that the magnitude of the bias varies between countries.

Chung and Monroe (2003) examine the relationship between social desirability bias and accountants' ethical evaluation. They also look at the influence of gender and religiosity (and the interaction between these two variables) on the level of social desirability bias. Chung and Monroe (2003) use a similar approach to Cohen et al. (1995, 1996, 1998, 2001) to capture social desirability bias. Based on the vignettes presented to them, participants were asked to indicate the probability that they would undertake the same action and their perception of the probability that their peers would undertake the same action. The results indicate that accountants demonstrate higher social desirability bias when the situation encountered is more unethical compared to when the situation is less unethical. The findings also show the main effects of gender and religiosity (and the interaction between the two) on the bias.

Cohen et al. (1996) examine the usefulness and generalizability of a multidimensional ethics scale (MES) in evaluating auditors' ethical decision-making processes. One aspect of the study involves an analysis of whether the multidimensional measure[8] provides better explanatory power of ethical intention than the unidimensional measure (i.e., "Is it ethical?"). Ethical intention is measured by asking participants to indicate the likelihood that they would undertake the same action as the actor in the vignettes provided to them. The authors acknowledge the need to control for social desirability bias and they include a second question asking participants to indicate the likelihood that their peers would undertake the same action. A comparison of the participants' responses to those two questions indicates the existence of social desirability bias in all vignettes. A correlation between social desirability bias and the evaluation of ethicality of the action in the vignettes indicates that actions perceived as least ethical showed the highest desirability bias. Despite the findings, the authors do not include social desirability bias as a covariate in the multidimensional and unidimensional models. As a consequence, the extent to which social desirability bias influences the results of the study remains unknown.

Cohen et al. (1998) examine the effect of gender and academic discipline diversity on ethical evaluation, ethical intentions and ethical orientation. In order to control for a potential social desirability bias, Cohen et al. (1998) measure ethical intention using two questions that are framed in the first-person and third-person wording perspective. In order to test for the relationship between social desirability bias and the two independent variables, the authors ran gender-by-discipline ANCOVAs with social desirability bias as the dependent variable. Their results indicate that female participants show a higher level of social desirability bias than male participants. To control for potential contamination of social desirability bias on the main findings, the authors re-ran their ANCOVAs by including social desirability bias as one of the covariates. The results indicate that the bias covariate is highly significant and the overall results remain qualitatively the same.

Cohen et al. (2001) examine the differences in individuals' ethical decision-making between business students and accounting professionals. One aspects of ethical decision-making that the authors examine is the intention to perform questionable acts depicted in seven vignettes. Similar to Cohen et al. (1995, 1996, 1998), intention is measured using two items framed in the first-person and third-person wording perspective. Participants were asked to indicate the likelihood that they would do the action and the likelihood that their colleagues would do the action. In detecting the potential existence of social desirability bias, the authors compare participants' responses to "Would you do it?" and "Would your peers do it?" questions. The results confirmed the existence of the bias. In order to control for potential confounding effects of social desirability bias on the results of the study, they re-ran the analysis including the bias variable as one of the covariates. The analysis indicates that the covariate is significant; however, the initial results remain unchanged even after controlling for this covariate.

In an experiment, Shafer and Morris (2004) asked auditors to estimate the likelihood that they would acquiesce to a fraud perpetrated by a client's senior management. They also asked their participants to indicate the likelihood that a typical CPA employed in a similar position would do so. They report a significance difference between the two measures indicating the existence of social desirability bias. Despite this, no further step was taken by the authors to address the issue. In their analysis, participants' own assessment is used as the dependent variable and there is no control over the potential influence of social desirability bias. The authors only recognize social desirability bias as one of the limitations of their study.

Curtis (2006) conducted an experiment to examine the influence of an individual auditor's mood on his or her willingness to report the unethical action of a colleague.[9] Curtis is of the view that "participants might be reluctant to answer a 'first person' whistle-blowing question honestly or could be subject to social desirability bias" (Curtis 2006: 196). Hence, apart from indicating their whistle-blowing intention, participants were also asked to indicate the likelihood that other auditors would report the unethical action. Multivariate Analysis of Variance (MANOVA) with two dependent variables (personal reporting intentions and others' reporting intention) was used to analyze the results. In addition, Analysis of Variance (ANOVA) was conducted separately for each of the dependent variables. Interestingly, although the ANOVA results for the two dependent variables are different, the author does not provide further explanation. The ANOVA results show that the MANOVA findings are mainly driven by the results for the other auditors' reporting intention. These findings when combined with the fact that the mean for the other auditors' reporting intention is higher than personal reporting intention provide interesting insights on the potential existence of social desirability bias. However, the author provides no further discussion about the potential influence of this bias on their results.

Patel (2003) examines the influence of culture on accountants' likelihood of engaging in whistle-blowing using a sample of auditors from Australia, Malaysia and India. In identifying the potential influence of social desirability bias, the author asked the participants to indicate whether they would make the same decision as the actor in the scenarios provided to them and whether their colleagues would make the same decision. In testing for the influence of culture on accountants' likelihood to engage in whistle-blowing, Patel also checked for the existence of social desirability bias in the responses. The results indicate that participants in all three samples report that they are more likely to engage in whistle-blowing than their colleagues, which indicates the existence of social desirability bias. Apart from acknowledging the existence of the bias, there is no further discussion about the bias provided in the paper.

In a survey examining the effects of perceived audit firm ethical culture on auditors' ethical evaluation and intention to engage in various time pressure-induced dysfunctional behaviours, Sweeney, Arnold and Pierce (2010) consider the potential influence of social desirability bias on the validity of their findings. Apart from indicating their ethical evaluation and intention to act decision, which is the main measure for their dependent variable, participants were also asked for their perceptions about typical opinions and behaviours of other individuals (i.e., auditors at their employment level). After analyzing their results using the main measure, the authors conduct an additional analysis using the second measure as the dependent variable. The results remain qualitatively similar. The authors conclude that the findings are largely unaffected by social desirability bias and the initial findings based on participants' own responses remain.

Overall, the above discussion demonstrates the variation in which social desirability bias has been measured and analyzed in the accounting and auditing literature. Of these studies, only Cohen et al. (1995) and Chung and Monroe (2003) specifically consider social desirability as the main variable of interest. Our review demonstrates that the use of social desirability scales in the accounting and auditing is somewhat limited. These scales are mainly used in studies using a survey approach. Many studies in accounting and auditing measure social desirability bias by taking the difference between participants' response to questions framed in the first- and third-person wording. Apart from the differences in the way social desirability bias is measured, the depth of the analysis also varies considerably. For example, there are studies that measured social desirability bias but did not consider the potential influence of the bias in details when analyzing the results. In addition, several studies that discovered the existence of social desirability bias took no further steps to address the issue.

Recall that both types of social desirability measures have their own limitations. For example, the inclusion of a social desirability scale would increase the length of the research instrument. The use of questions framed in the first-party and third-party wording on the other hand may create a demand effect. Given the costs associated with the inclusion of social desirability measure in the research instrument, researchers must carefully evaluate the need to measure the bias. It would be counterproductive for researchers to measure the bias but then not consider the bias when evaluating the results. In the next section, we suggest some of the steps that researchers may want to follow when considering social desirability bias in accounting- and auditing-related research.

Considering and addressing social desirability bias in accounting- and auditing-related research: suggestions and recommendation

There are a number of procedures that should be considered when dealing with issues related to social desirability bias. First, researchers need to decide whether their study considers social desirability bias as the main variable of interest or as a control variable to validate findings regarding the main variable of interest. As mentioned above, two studies that look at social desirability bias as the main variable of interest are Cohen et al. (1995) and Chung and Monroe (2003). If the main objective is to examine the bias itself, either as dependent or independent variable, then researchers could choose to use one or both of the two approaches to measure the bias. That is, by adopting any of the social desirability scales or by measuring the difference in participants' response to the questions couched in the first- and third-party wording. In choosing the most appropriate approach, researchers need to consider the context of their study. They also need to assess the strength and weaknesses of each approach. The procedures for analyzing the data depend on the research questions that the study is addressing.

If the major concern is with the potential influence of the bias on the main findings, then researchers need to carefully evaluate whether it is really necessary to control for the bias. This is particularly important given the potential costs associated with the measuring it. To do so, researchers need to decide whether the issue to be investigated is considered as a socially sensitive issue. The sensitivity should be evaluated from the perspectives of the profession as well as from the perspectives of the general public. If the issue is considered sensitive from the profession's perspective, then it is crucial for the researchers to control for social desirability bias. If, on the other hand, the issue is considered sensitive from the general public's point of view, researchers need to see how relevant such sensitivity is to those in the professions. In evaluating the sensitivity of any issue, researchers need to look at the potential social and normative implications of the issue on the participants (King and Bruner 2000; Kreuter et al. 2008; Krumpal 2013).

Once it has been decided that it is a sensitive issue, researchers then need to consider whether they want to control for social desirability bias from a situational perspective, a trait perspective or from both perspectives. The perspective chosen would influence the selection of the measure of social desirability bias that would be used in the research instrument. Researchers who would like to control for a social desirability bias trait can adopt one of the social desirability scales. The decision on which scale to be used depends on the context of their study. For example, researchers who consider social desirability bias as a unidimensional construct may choose to adopt the Marlowe-Crowne scale or the abbreviated version of it. However, those who consider social desirability bias as a two-dimensional construct and would like to see how each dimension influences their findings may choose to adopt the BIDR scale. If the researchers want to control for social desirability bias from a situational perspective, then the difference in participants' response to direct and indirect questions can be used as the measure.

After the bias has been measured using the chosen approach, researchers need to consider this bias when analyzing the results. In order to check for the potential confounding effect of the bias, researchers need to correlate the bias measure with the dependent variable of interest. This is one of the most frequently used approaches in studies discussed in the previous section (e.g., Kung and Huang 2013; Parker and Kohlmeyer 2005; Shafer 2009). If the social desirability bias score is significantly correlated with the dependent variable, then there are a number of procedures that can be adopted to deal it. For studies that use a social desirability scale, researchers could eliminate data from participants with social desirability scores above a certain threshold level and re-run the analysis without those participants. If the results of the new analysis remain qualitatively the same as the initial results, then further correction for social desirability bias is not required. This method was adopted by Kung and Huang (2013). Another procedure that can be used is to include the social desirability bias score as a covariate in the model used to test the hypothesis. As we discussed in the previous section, this is one of the most common procedures (e.g., Shafer 2009; Cohen et al. 1998). Further, based on the suggestion by Ganster et al. (1983) and Fernandes and Randall (1992), researchers should also investigate the interaction between social desirability bias and the independent variables of interest. None of the studies discussed in the previous section investigate this potential interaction. Another appropriate procedure to deal with social desirability bias is to adopt the method used in Sweeney et al. (2010). This method can be used for studies that measure the bias using the difference between questions framed in the first-person and third-person wordings. Here, researchers first perform the analysis using the main measure and conduct another analysis using the second measure. If the results for these two analyses remain the same, no further correction for social desirability bias is necessary.

Notes

1 Refer to Ganster et al. (1983) for a detailed discussion on this issue.
2 For a more detail review of scales that can be used to measure social desirability bias, refer to Paulhus (1991) and King and Bruner (2000).
3 The earliest social desirability bias scale is the 79-item scale developed by Edwards (1957). However, this scale is not as widely used as Marlowe-Crowne social desirability scale.
4 Refer to Barger (2002) and Fischer and Fick (1993) for discussions about short forms of the Marlowe-Crowne social desirability scale.
5 Paulhus (1991) discussed a number of the scales including Edwards' social desirability scale (Edwards 1957), MMPI Lie Scale (Hathaway and McKinley 1951), MMPI K scale (Meehl and Hathaway 1946), RD-16 (Schuessller, Hittle and Cardascia 1978) and Children's social desirability scale (Crandall, Crandall and Katkovsky 1965).
6 They noted that "for further detail, readers may contact the authors" (Parker and Kohlmeyer 2005: 362).
7 The authors do not provide much information about the analysis apart from mentioning that in a footnote that they use the techniques proposed by Smith (1967) and Anderson, Warner and Spencer (1984). Those two studies identify the potential influence of social desirability bias by correlating the scores on bias scales with the dependent variables. If they are not significantly correlated, then it is assumed that social desirability bias does not influence the findings. If there are significant correlations, then necessary corrections need to be made. Smith (1967) uses hierarchical regression to assess whether correcting for social desirability bias would add significantly to the predictability of the model.
8 The measure is comprised of four dimensions: moral equity, contractual, utilitarian and relativism.
9 The author used senior accounting students as surrogates for auditors.

References

Adam, S., Matthews, S., Ebbeling, C., Moore, C., Cunningham, J., Fulton, J. and Herbert, J., 2005, 'The effect of social desirability and social approval on self-reports of physical activity', *American Journal of Epidemiology* 161(4), 389–398.

Anderson, C.D., Warner, J.L. and Spencer, C.C., 1984, 'Inflation bias in self-assessment examinations: Implications for valid employee selection', *Journal of Applied Psychology* 69(4), 574–580.

Andrews, P. and Meyer, R.G., 2003, 'Marlowe-Crowne social desirability scale and short form C: Forensic norms', *Journal of Clinical Psychology* 59(4), 483–492.

Aranya, N. and Wheeler, J.T., 1986, 'Accountants' personality types and their commitment to organization and profession', *Contemporary Accounting Research* 30(1), 184–199.

Babcock, J., Costa, D., Green, C. and Eckhardt, C., 2004, 'What situations induce intimate partner violence? A reliability and validity study of the Proximal Antecedents to Violent Episodes (PAVE) scale', *Journal of Family Psychology* 18(3), 433–442.

Ballard, R., 1992, 'Short forms of the Marlowe-Crowne social desirability scale', *Psychological Reports* 71, 1155–1160.

Barger, S.D., 2002, 'The Marlowe-Crowne affair: Short forms, psychometric structure, and social desirability', *Journal of Personality Assessment* 79(2), 286–305.

Chung, J. and Monroe, G.S., 2003, 'Exploring social desirability bias', *Journal of Business Ethics* 44(4), 291–302.

Cohen, J.R., Pant, L.W. and Sharp, D.J., 1995, 'An exploratory examination of international differences in auditors' ethical perceptions', *Behavioral Research in Accounting* 7, 37–64.

Cohen, J.R., Pant, L.W. and Sharp, D.J., 1996, 'Measuring the ethical awareness and ethical orientation of Canadian auditors', *Behavioral Research in Accounting* 8(Supplement), 98–119.

Cohen, J.R., Pant, L.W. and Sharp, D.J., 1998, 'The effect of gender and academic discipline diversity on the ethical evaluations, ethical intentions and ethical orientation of potential public accounting recruits', *Accounting Horizons* 12(3), 250–270.

Cohen, J.R., Pant, L.W. and Sharp, D.J., 2001, 'An examination of differences in ethical-decision making between Canadian business students and accounting professionals', *Journal of Business Ethics* 30(4), 319–336.

Crandall, V.C., Crandall, V.J. and Katkovsky, W., 1965, 'A children's social desirability questionnaire', *Journal of Consulting Psychology* 29, 27–36.

Crowne, D.P. and Marlowe, D., 1960, 'A new scale of social desirability independent of psychopathology', *Journal of Consulting Psychology* 24, 349–354.

Crowne, D.P. and Marlowe, D., 1964, *The Approval Motive*, John Wiley & Sons, New York.

Curtis, M.B., 2006, 'Are audit-related ethical decisions dependent upon mood?', *Journal of Business Ethics* 68(2), 191–209.

Edwards, A.L., 1957, *The Social Desirability Variable in Personality Assessment and Research*, Dryden Press, New York.

Fernandes, M.F. and Randall, D.M., 1992, 'The nature of social desirability response effects in ethics research', *Business Ethics Quarterly* 2(2), 183–205.

Fischer, D.G. and Fick, C., 1993, 'Measuring social desirability: Short forms of the Marlowe-Crowne social desirability scale', *Educational and Psychological Measurement* 53, 417–423.

Fisher, R.J., 1993, 'Social desirability bias and validity of indirect questioning', *Journal of Consumer Research* 20(2), 303–315.

Fisher, R.J., 2000, 'The future of social-desirability bias research in marketing', *Psychology & Marketing* 17(3), 73–77.

Fisher, R.J. and Katz, J.E., 2000, 'Social-desirability bias and the validity of self-reported values', *Psychology & Marketing* 17(2), 105–120.

Fisher, R.J. and Tellis, G.J., 1998, 'Removing social desirability bias with indirect questioning: Is the cure worse than the disease?', *Advances in Consumer Research* 25(1), 563–567.

Ganster, D.C., Hennessey, H.W. and Luthans, F., 1983, 'Social desirability response effects: Three alternative models', *The Academy of Management Journal* 26(2), 321–331.

Gordon, R.A., 1987, 'Desirability bias: A demonstration and technique for its reduction', *Teaching of Psychology* 14(1), 40–42.

Harding, N., Azim, M., Jidin, R. and Muir, J., (2016), 'A consideration of literature on trust and distrust as they relate to auditor professional scepticism', *Australian Accounting Review* 26(3), 243–254.

Hathaway, S.R. and McKinley, J.C., 1951, *The MMPI Manual*, Psychological Corporation, New York.

Jones, E.L. and Forrest, J.D., 1992, 'Underreporting of abortion in surveys of U.S. women: 1976 to 1988', *Demography* 29(1), 113–126.

Jurgensen, C.E., 1978, 'Job preferences (What makes a job good or bad?)', *Journal of Applied Psychology* 63(3), 267–276.

King, M.F. and Bruner, G.C., 2000, 'Social desirability bias: A neglected aspect of validity testing', *Psychology & Marketing* 17(2), 79–103.

Kreuter, F., Presser, S. and Tourangeau, R., 2008, 'Social desirability bias in CATI, IVR and web surveys: The effects of mode and questions sensitivity', *Public Opinion Quarterly* 72(5), 847–865.

Krumpal, I., 2013, 'Determinants of social desirability bias in sensitive surveys: A literature review', *Quality and Quantity* 47(4), 2025–2047.

Kung, F.-H. and Huang, C.L., 2013, 'Auditors' moral philosophies and ethical beliefs', *Management Decision* 51(3), 479–500.

Larkin, J.M., 2000, 'The ability of internal auditors to identify ethical dilemmas', *Journal of Business Ethics* 23(4), 401–409.

Li, A. and Bagger, J., 2007, 'The Balanced Inventory of Desirable Responding (BIDR): A reliability generalization study', *Educational and Psychological Measurement* 67(3), 525–544.

Martin, C.L. and Nagao, D.H., 1989, 'Some effects of computerized interviewing on job applicant responses', *Journal of Applied Psychology* 74(1), 72–80.

Meehl, P.E. and Hathaway, S.R., 1946, 'The K factors as a suppressor variable in the Minnesota multiphasic personality inventory', *Journal of Applied Psychology* 30, 525–564.

Millham, J., 1974, 'Two components of need for approval score and their relationship to cheating following success and failure', *Journal of Research in Personality* 8, 378–392.

Nederhof, A.J., 1985, 'Methods of coping with social desirability bias: A review', *European Journal of Social Psychology* 15, 263–280.

Orne, M.T., 1959, 'The nature of hypnosis: Artifact and essence', *The Journal of Abnormal and Social Psychology* 58(3), 277–299.

Pany, K. and Reckers, P.M.J., 1987, 'Within- vs. between-subjects experimental designs: A study of demand effects', *Auditing: A Journal of Practice and Theory* 7(1), 39–53.

Parker, R.J. and Kohlmeyer, J.M., 2005, 'Organizational justice and turnover in public accounting firms: A research note', *Accounting, Organizations and Society* 30(4), 357–369.

Patel, C., 2003, 'Some cross-cultural evidence on whistle-blowing as an internal control mechanism', *Journal of International Accounting Research* 2(1), 69–96.

Paulhus, D.L., 1984, 'Two-component models of socially desirable responding', *Journal of Personality and Social Psychology* 46(3), 598–609.

Paulhus, D.L., 1991, 'Measurement and control of response bias', in J.P. Robinson, P.R. Shaver and L.S. Wrightsman (eds.), *Measures of Personality and Social Psychological Attitudes*, 17–59, Academic Press, San Diego.

Paulhus, D.L. and John, O.P., 1998, 'Egoistic and moralistic biases in self-perception: The interplay of self-deceptive styles with basic traits and motives', *Journal of Personality* 66(6), 1025–1060.

Presser, S. and Stinson, L., 1998, 'Data collection mode and social desirability bias in self-reported religious attendance', *American Sociological Review* 63(1), 137–145.

Ramanaiah, N.V. and Martin, H.J., 1980, 'On the two dimensional nature of the Marlowe-Crowne social desirability scale', *Journal of Personality Assessment* 44, 507–514.

Randall, D.M. and Fernandes, M.F., 1991, 'The social desirability response bias in ethics research', *Journal of Business Ethics* 10(11), 805–817.

Reynolds, W.M., 1982, 'Development of reliable and valid short forms of the Marlowe-Crowne social desirability bias scale', *Journal of Clinical Psychology* 38(1), 119–125.

Ryan, J.J., 2001, 'Moral reasoning as a determinant of organizational citizenship behaviours: A study in the public accounting profession', *Journal of Business Ethics* 33(3), 233–244.

Sanzone, L.A., Lee, J.Y., Divaris, K., DeWalt, D.A., Baker, A.D. and Vann, W.F., 2013, 'A cross sectional study examining social desirability bias in caregiver reporting of children's oral health behaviors', *BMC Oral Health* 13(24), 1–9.

Saunders, D.G., 1991, 'Procedures for adjusting self-reports of violence or social desirability bias', *Journal of Interpersonal Violence* 6(3), 336–344.

Schuessller, K., Hittle, D. and Cardascia, J., 1978, 'Measuring responding desirably with attitude-opinion items', *Social Psychology* 41, 224–235.

Shafer, W.E., 2009, 'Ethical climate, organizational-professional conflict and organizational commitment', *Accounting, Auditing and Accountability Journal* 22(7), 1087–1110.

Shafer, W.E. and Morris, R.E., 2004, 'An exploratory study of auditor perceptions of sanction threats', *Research in Accounting Regulation* 17, 209–231.

Smith, D., 1967, 'Correcting for social desirability response sets in opinion-attitude survey research', *The Public Opinion Quarterly* 31(1), 87–94.

Spector, P.E., 2004, 'Social desirability bias', in M.S. Lewis-Beck, A. Bryman and T.F. Liao (eds.), *The SAGE Encyclopedia of Social Science Research Methods*, 1045–1046, Sage Publications, Thousand Oaks, CA.

Strahan, R. and Gerbasi, K.C., 1972, 'Short, homogeneous versions of the Marlowe – Crowne social desirability scale', *Journal of Clinical Psychology* 28, 191–193.

Sweeney, B., Arnold, D. and Pierce, B., 2010, 'The impact of perceived ethical culture of the firm and demographic variables on auditors' ethical evaluation and intention to ace decisions', *Journal of Business Ethics* 93(4), 531–551.

Tourangeau, R. and Yan, T., 2007, 'Sensitive questions in surveys', *Psychological Bulletin* 133, 859–883.

Weber, S.J. and Cook, T.D., 1972, 'Subject effects in laboratory research: An examination of subject roles, demand characteristics and valid inference', *Psychological Bulletin* 77, 273–295.

Zerbe, W.J. and Paulhus, D.L., 1987, 'Socially desirable responding in organizational behaviour: A reconception', *The Academy of Management Review* 12(2), 250–264.

Section 4
Study design choices (Link 4a)

12

'Moving beyond the lab'

Building on experimental accounting researchers' core competencies to expand methodological diversity in accounting research

Steven E. Salterio and Pujawati Mariestha (Estha) Gondowijoyo

Introduction

When one hears the term, Behavioural Accounting Research (BAR), especially in the context of English-speaking countries, the default assumption is that the research method involves carefully controlled, psychology-based (or more rarely, economics-based) laboratory experiments. Experiments in accounting and auditing explicitly manipulate a small number of variables based on carefully specified theories. Their main aim is to show causal inferences about the influence of the hypothesized cognitive or social variables on the participant's judgment (Libby, Bloomfield and Nelson 2002). According to survey of research methods studied by US based doctoral students, experiments are the second largest accounting research method in the USA (Kinney 2003; Brink, Glasscock and Wier 2012). Our casual empiricism suggests that experimental accounting research is only rivalled by interpretivist field research as the method of choice for researchers who are not committed to archival-based markets research. As discussed elsewhere in this book (see especially Chapter 2 on the predictive validity framework), the strengths of the experimental method for identifying cause and effect and generalizing this causal relationship via theory are unparalleled in the accounting researcher's tool kit.

What do we mean by experimental researchers 'moving beyond the lab'? We focus on two research methods (experiential surveys and qualitative interview-based field studies) that enable the researcher to develop systematically theory-based and informed evidence about current substantive fields of accounting practice. These methods have been proven to be publishable in rigorous accounting academic journals and we argue that behavioural accounting experimental researchers (what we call "BAR researchers" hereafter) are especially well positioned to carry out this type of experience-based research (what we call 'experiential research' hereafter to refer to these methods collectively).

So why should BAR researchers not just continue their lab-based research? In other words, why should they desire (or aspire) to apply their core competencies 'beyond the lab'? The recent history of management accounting research provides one clue to the answer to this question. In their book, *Relevance Lost: The Rise and Fall of Management Accounting*, Johnson and Kaplan (1987) contend that in their pursuit of rigour, management accounting researchers ended up studying problems that had neither immediate relevance to practitioners nor a long-term impact on practice (i.e., through building a foundation for future research that can contribute to practice). To maintain the relevance of their research, management accounting researchers became the first in accounting to adopt one of the experience-based methods – the qualitative field study method – that we consider at length in the second part of this chapter.

Another clue to the answer to this question is the well-documented ongoing worries that accounting research is not having sufficient (or as skeptics might say "any") effect on either other academic disciplines or practice. This worry is evidenced by the American Accounting Association's *ad hoc* committee on research impact (AAA Research Impact Task Force 2009) that was set up to assess the impact of academic accounting research. The Task Force noted that while accounting research had affected practice, its effects were uneven and tended to be concentrated in the areas where there was greater engagement with the field (i.e., auditing and management accounting research).

Putting these two clues together, we argue that the BAR researcher who moves outside the comfort of their laboratory to study the experiences of practitioners ends up being a more empowered researcher who can participate readily in a full-cycle approach to research (Chatman and Flynn 2005). This cycle starts with observing and documenting interesting practice phenomena via experiential research methods. Experiential research aids in formalizing the implications of these observations via causal theories that are the traditional domain of the BAR researcher who then relies on these theories to test these hypothesized causal relationships via laboratory experiments (Chatman and Flynn 2005).[1]

Venturing 'beyond the lab' allows BAR researchers to increase their relative contribution to accounting academic research beyond their colleagues who stay in the lab. As Malsch and Salterio (2016) observe in audit research, the relatively small number of experiential studies (e.g., Gibbins, Salterio and Webb 2001) published over the last 15 years are disproportionately represented among the set of studies that have been denoted by the research community as outstanding contributions as we document later in this chapter.

Furthermore, there seems to be an increased appetite for experiential research in areas of accounting where it has been rarely employed. Indeed, one of the stated objectives of the American Accounting Association's (AAA) Financial Reporting Section recently established section journal, *Journal of Financial Reporting*, is to "encourage the publication of field research in financial reporting" (Financial Accounting and Reporting 2016). The AAA Audit Section journal, *Auditing: A Journal of Practice & Theory*, in its first editor-chosen lead article recently published a paper that discusses how to evaluate audit field research (Malsch and Salterio 2016) adding to a special section that it had devoted to field research in 2015. Finally, Soltes (2014) in the *Journal of Accounting Research* has called for market-based archival accounting research results and their interpretation to be validated with field evidence. Soltes (2014) provides a compelling example where he examined the institutional details, the study's results and the interpretation of the results of Dichev, Graham, Harvey and Rajgopal's (2013) research. Based on his field research, Soltes's (2014) informants provide a very different understanding of the institutional details that led Soltes to a substantially different interpretation of the study's results from that advanced by the authors.

The purpose of this chapter is to discuss how psychology-based BAR researchers can leverage their core competencies to carry out research "beyond the lab".[2] We organize our chapter with this objective in mind. First, we explain five core competencies that most BAR researchers develop in their doctoral training, which we argue they can readily transfer to experiential accounting research. We then introduce the two main experiential research methods: experiential surveys and qualitative field studies. We focus on these two experiential methods because these techniques – in combination with mixed-methods approaches (e.g., random sample-based surveys combined with qualitative field interviews) – have been used to carry out groundbreaking research that has been published in top accounting journals (e.g., Gibbins, Salterio and Webb [2001] on auditor and client management negotiations). We also demonstrate how researchers can leverage these five core experimental competencies to carrying out experiential surveys and qualitative field research, illustrating our discussion with specific examples from published studies.[3] We conclude our chapter with a discussion of challenges that BAR researchers may face in applying their core competencies to experiential research.

The core competencies of an experimental accounting researcher

Table 12.1 summarizes what we see as the core competencies of the BAR researcher that permit them to cross from experimental research to experiential survey and positivist qualitative field research.[4] These five competencies represent a package of skills that we argue the BAR research

Table 12.1 Core competencies of an experimental accounting researcher

Competency	Description
1 **Theory**: Familiarity with a broad range of theories	Most BAR researchers in accounting take three or more psychology theory courses (e.g., judgment and decision-making, memory and learning, social psychology, cognitive neuroscience) or other psychology theory-based business schools courses (e.g., consumer decision-making, negotiations, organizational behaviour at the micro or meso level) in addition to having a solid basis in microeconomic theory.
	Section 2 of this book provides an excellent introduction to the many theoretical perspectives that BAR researchers have available to them including judgment and decision-making (Chapter 4), social psychology (Chapter 5), ethical frameworks (Chapter 6), stakeholder and legitimacy frameworks (Chapter 7) and agency theory or economic frameworks (Chapter 8).
2 **Engagement with practice**: knowledge of context in which practice problems occur	BAR researchers often come from a practice background (e.g., audit, financial management, control, etc.) or interact extensively with practitioners (e.g., auditors, company accounting managers, tax experts, etc.). They are cognizant of the importance of context (see Gibbins 2001 on role of context in BAR) and are well aware that mundane realism (Swieringa and Weick 1982) does not make an experiment more externally valid.
	Hence, BAR researchers have a history of interacting with practitioners to ensure that their experimental settings capture key aspects of the context they study. However, these interactions are normally not the focus on the research and hence they are just mentioned in passing as part of the research methods section (e.g., McCracken, Salterio and Schmidt 2011: 138; Tan and Yip-Ow 2001: 669).

(Continued)

Table 12.1 (Continued)

Competency	Description
3 **Practitioner participants**: selection of appropriate "subjects"	Psychology-based BAR experimental research for the most part has utilized practitioner participants or close substitutes to take part in their experiments (discussions about student subjects as proxies for actual decision makers dates back to at least Abdel-Khalik [1974]). Hence, the ability to gain access to practitioners and manage relationships that allow for access are a core competency of a BAR researcher. Furthermore, since the early 1990s BAR researchers (Libby 1989, 1995) have been sensitive to matching the participants to the task being carried out (see Elliott, Hodge, Kennedy, and Pronk [2007] for an empirical study of appropriate participant selection in financial accounting experimental research). Section 5 of this book discusses the ethical consent (Chapter 19) and participant recruitment challenges (Chapter 20) that BAR researchers encounter.
4 **Ex ante instrument design focus**: once an experiment is "run", the experimenter cannot go back and fix it except by running a completely new experiment.	BAR researchers know that they need to anticipate as many contingencies as possible before running an experiment. The BAR researcher's motto "once done, can't be undone" (adapted from Shakespeare's 1606 Macbeth where Lady Macbeth says, "what's done cannot be undone" in Act V, Scene 1) serves as a reminder that, unlike archival researchers, they cannot readily add variables to their studies without incurring the cost of rerunning the entire experiment. Hence, BAR researcher carefully develops their experimental instruments, pretest them extensively on fellow researchers and students, and expose them to comment to a handful of practitioners prior to running an experiment live. For an example of extensive ex ante instrument design and development, see Gibbins, McCracken and Salterio (2010: 584–588). Section 3 of this book provides an introduction to the planning issues that are associated with carrying out experimental accounting research (see especially Chapter 10). Section 4 provides an introduction of the design choices that affect various BAR methods (see especially Chapters 13 and 14).
5 **Measurement**: the challenge of ensuring experimenters are measuring what they think they are measuring.	Unlike archival researchers who are limited to what is recorded in the database, BAR researchers can, in principle, measure what they want to. Indeed, they have the freedom to ask participants to respond to almost any question they can think of (subject to time and ethical constraints). However, they learned from psychology researchers that self-insight of participants is often low (e.g., Wilson and Dunn 2004) and that asking the question "why" often leads to retrospective sense-making that had little to do with the factors that actually influenced the judgment (Leary and Kowalski 1990; Schwarz and Oyserman 2001; Fisher and Katz 2000; Wilson and Dunn 2004). Further, whether participants interpreted the experimental instrument the way that the researcher thought it would be interpreted is of concern (Schwarz and Oyserman 2001). Hence, BAR researchers have been cautious with the construct validity of their measures including the possibility of social desirability response biases in their research. They are also cognizant to the need of conducting manipulation and comprehension checks to gather evidence that their participants interpreted the instruments the same way the experimenter intended. These issues are introduced in Section 3 of this book.

can be applied to experiential research. To develop this list, we examined various sources that discuss experimental research in accounting including:

• Textbooks on experimental and field research in accounting (Bonner 2008; Smith 2011).
• Monographs examining various facets of accounting experimental research (e.g., Arnold and Sutton 1997; Ashton and Ashton 1995; Ashton 1982; Libby 1981).
• Subject matter area reviews focusing on experimental perspectives (e.g., tax [Davis 1995], auditing [Solomon and Trotman 2003], management accounting [Sprinkle 2003] and financial accounting [Libby et al. 2002]).
• Previous methods focusing on accounting literature reviews (e.g., Kotchetova and Salterio 2004; Peecher and Solomon 2001; Tan 2001; Trotman 2001).

We then matched the competencies identified by these sources to the skill set required for experiential survey research (e.g., Gibbins 2001; Gibbins and Qu 2005) and field studies (e.g., Malsch and Salterio 2016; Atkinson and Shaffir 1998). This leads us to identify five core competencies of BAR researcher that we argue are transferrable to experiential research.[5]

Experiential surveys

Accounting researchers have employed survey research methods in several ways (see Chapter 15), for example:

1. To collect organizational level data from individual informants within the organization to study accounting issues where public archival data is not available (e.g., Naranjo-Gil and Hartmann 2007; Maas and Matějka 2009; Soltes 2014).
2. To generate random samples from specified populations in a way that facilitates generalization to the population (e.g., Graham, Harvey and Rajgopal 2005).
3. To obtain random samples so as to evaluate opinions about specific issues (e.g., Ballas and Theoharakis [2003] on the accounting research community's view of the academic accounting journal quality).

We focus on one adaption of these survey research applications – the experiential survey method.

Experiential survey method

We focus on the experiential survey, a method which roots back to the critical incident technique from the 1950s (see Flanagan 1954). The critical incident technique is "a set of procedures for collecting direct observations of human behaviour . . . (particularly that which have) special significance" (327). The technique is appropriate to use when the incident being recalled is highly memorable (even when it is not spectacular), such that a significant amount of cognitive processing is carried out at the time the incident occurred and significant details about the incident are stored in long-term memory (Flanagan 1954). Flanagan (1954) suggests that the critical incident technique requires five major steps: defining aims, ex ante planning data collection, collecting data in ways that immunize collection biases, analyzing the data (e.g., development of codes or having respondent self-code data) and interpreting the data.

There are at least two studies that have examined the reliability and validity of the critical incident technique (e.g., Andersson and Nilsson 1964; Ronan and Latham 1974). These studies concluded that "the information collected by this method is both reliable and valid" (Andersson and Nilsson 1964: 402) and that "the reliability and content validity of the critical incident methodology are satisfactory" (Ronan and Latham 1974: 61).

A detailed introduction to the use of this method is found in several sources (e.g., Butterfield, Borgen, Amundson and Maglio 2005; Woolsey 1986). Gibbins (2001) and Gibbins and Qu (2005) provide an excellent introduction for accounting research done using this technique. They suggest that the key features of an accounting experiential survey are:

- Participants with experience and/or expertise relevant to the research issues report on their own experiences (no question requires the participant to make assumptions or to speculate on the experiences of others).
- Extensive pilot testing ensures that the questions are clear and sensible in context to the participants. The aim is to create a questionnaire that is effective and efficient in gathering necessary information, according to the theory developed by the authors.
- Participants choose and describe examples of situations they have experienced. The participants identify their own examples that then become the primary data in the study instead of researchers providing the participants an example to react to (as in a laboratory experiment).
- The participant provides examples with only minimal context guidance from the researcher. Other than a few definitions and an initial structure to orient the participant to the topics that the researcher wants the participant to recall, the researcher provides no further information to reduce the potential for demand effects in the participants' choice of incidents to recall. Further, the researcher provides an easy and explicit exit point for participants who do not have such incidents in their memory.
- Researchers collect participant's examples before posing questions about who the respondent is and what type of firm or entity the respondent works in. Again, the goal is to reduce demand effects as well as to create some commitment by participants to providing their example prior to eliciting demographic information that might dampen response rates.
- The questions eliciting details about the participant's examples and the associated pre-specified responses are structured in terms of the researcher's theory or expectations about important issues (i.e., guided by theory as in a laboratory experiment).
- The survey's questions may vary in order or style to provide data on order effects or question format effects. The aim is to detect biased response patterns (if any).
- Demographic questions are used to gather data about the participant, their organization or their client (in the case of auditing), and to determine whether the participants have the characteristics sought and if these characteristics cause variance in the types of examples they provided.

Adapted from Gibbins (2001: 229)[6]

Table 12.2 provides examples of accounting research that have used the experiential survey method. Topics include the auditor-client management negotiation process (e.g., Gibbins et al. 2001; Gibbins, McCracken and Salterio 2007), the audit file review process (Gibbins and Trotman 2002; Emby and Favere-Marchesi 2010) and inputs into the auditor's judgment process (e.g., Emby and Gibbins 1987; Gibbins and Newton 1994; Rennie, Kopp and Lemon 2010). While the experiential survey method has been predominantly used to study process issues (e.g., the negotiation process, the review process, etc.), occasionally experiential surveys have focused on a specific audit issue or output (e.g., discovery by auditors of client earnings management attempts in Nelson, Elliott and Tarpley [2002]).

Table 12.2 Experiential survey-based research in accounting examples*

Audit

Emby, C. and Favere-Marchesi, M., 2010, 'Review partners and engagement partners: The interaction process in engagement quality review'.

Gibbins, M., Salterio, S. and Webb, A., 2001, 'Evidence about auditor-client management negotiation concerning client's financial reporting'.

Gibbins, M. and Trotman, K. T., 2002, 'Audit review: Managers' interpersonal expectations and conduct of the review'.

Herda, D. N. and Lavelle, J. J., 2012, 'Auditor commitment to privately held clients and its effect on value-added audit service'.

Nelson, M. W., Elliott, J. A. and Tarpley, R. L., 2002, 'Evidence from auditors about managers' and auditors' earnings management decisions'.

Rennie, M. D., Kopp, L. S. and Lemon, W. M., 2010, 'Exploring trust and the auditor-client relationship: Factors influencing the auditor's trust of a client representative'.

Chief Financial Officers

Gibbins, M., McCracken, S. A. and Salterio, S. E., 2005, 'Negotiations over accounting issues: The congruency of audit partner and chief financial officer recalls'.

Gibbins, M., McCracken, S. A. and Salterio, S. E., 2007, 'The Chief Financial Officer's perspective on auditor-client negotiations'.

Financial analysts and investors

Brazel, J. F., Jones, K. L., Thayer, J. and Warne, R. C., 2015, 'Understanding investor perceptions of financial statement fraud and their use of red flags: Evidence from the field'.

De Jong, A., Mertens, G., Van der Poel, M. and Van Dijk, R., 2014, 'How does earnings management influence investor's perceptions of firm value? Survey evidence from financial analysts'.

Public accounting more broadly

Emby, C. and Gibbins, M., 1987, 'Good judgment in public accounting: Quality and justification'.

Gibbins, M. and Newton, J. D., 1994, 'An empirical exploration of complex accountability in public accounting'.

Tax

Bobek, D. D. and Radtke, R. R., 2007, 'An experiential investigation of tax professionals' ethical environments'.

* For full citation see reference list.

We observe that there is strong evidence to support the contention we made in the introduction that experiential survey research is disproportionately represented among the article set that is acknowledged by the accounting academy as influential. The 2008 Notable Contribution to the Audit Literature Award from the AAA Audit Section that went to an experiential survey study exploring an auditor–client management negotiation (i.e., Gibbins et al. 2001) provides just one example of the impact of such research on the broader accounting research community. In addition, experiential surveys have also enriched significant experimental research streams on justification (e.g., Koonce, Anderson and Marchant 1995), accountability (see Hayne and Salterio [2014] for review) and auditor–client management negotiations (see Salterio [2012] and Brown and Wright [2008] for reviews). To date most experiential survey research has focused on audit issues (Gibbins 2001). However, there is no principled reason why researchers cannot apply the method to other domains of accounting research. Examples of application of this method to non–auditor-participants include studies of chief financial officers (see Gibbins et al. 2007), financial analysts (see De Jong, Mertens, van der Poel and Van Dijk [2014] for a limited attempt to use this method), investors (see Brazel, Jones, Thayer and Warne 2015) and tax professionals (see Bobek and Radtke 2007).

BAR researcher's core competencies and experiential surveys

This section discusses the identified core competencies of the BAR researcher that can be applied in carrying out experiential surveys. More importantly, we illustrate how experiential survey researchers employ these BAR-based competencies using relevant examples from published research.

The BAR researcher has considerable experience in using theory to design experimental instruments that reflect the theory being tested. The BAR researcher's goal is to design a research instrument (normally a case-based instrument) that evokes enough context to allow participants to react as they would in a practice setting. In BAR research, theory guides modifications to the instrument (often a case) across different treatment groups. This use of theory is very similar to experiential researchers designing surveys that generalize based on theory (i.e., they do not generalize to the population based on random samples of potential respondents). Hence familiarity with theory and its careful ex ante specification is important to the experiential survey researcher just as it is to the BAR researchers. As an example, in their experiential survey of audit partners about their involvement in negotiating with client management for adjustments to financial statements, Gibbins et al. (2001) developed theory to guide their research based on the vast literature in psychology, economics and sociology on negotiation process. This theorization, combined with the incorporation of institutional knowledge of auditing provided structure for their experiential survey.

The BAR researcher requires an in-depth knowledge of practice to develop a critical understanding of the institutional context in which their participants are embedded. This understanding allows BAR researchers to design experimental case materials that, while abstracted from the real world, include key institutional features that enable their participants to draw on their practical expertise when responding to the experimental questions.

Similar to the BAR researchers, researchers design experiential surveys based on an in-depth knowledge of practice. First, the experiential survey researcher needs to identify a set of responses to the questions they pose that takes into account the range of real-world examples that the study's participants may recall. Hence, experiential survey researchers require an in-depth understanding of the institutional context in order to provide a complete set of possible responses in the research questionnaire. For example, to develop their experiential survey, Gibbins et al. (2001) carried out a focus group with a large number of accounting standard setters on the emerging issues committee, conducted in-depth interviews with audit partners, pretested the instrument with five audit partners and conducted an extensive debriefing interview with these partners. All of these activities were undertaken to ensure that as many potential responses as possible were provided to survey recipients.

Second, the BAR researcher exhibits great concern about matching participant experience to experimental task (see Libby 1989 and Libby and Luft 1993). Similarly, the experiential survey researcher ensures that participants have the requisite knowledge and experience that allows them to provide meaningful examples to the researcher. However, in the experiential survey context, this match is even more important as the researcher relies on the participant to have several incidents that they might recall based on the cue provided by the researcher. For example, Gibbins et al. (2001) detected the potential for differential responses between audit managers and partners in the interviews that they conducted with audit partners and managers prior to administering their experiential survey. To ensure that their research findings were valid, Gibbins et al. (2001) included in their participant pool only audit partners with extensive negotiation experience. Without this careful matching, the conclusions that Gibbins et al. (2001) reached on audit partners' negotiation process models likely would have been very different.[7]

The BAR researcher is also very familiar with the dictum "once done, can't be undone" (adapted from Shakespeare [1606]) when "running" an experiment. Unlike an archival researcher that can go back to a database to collect a subsequently discovered missing variable required for the analysis, the BAR researcher cannot go back to their participants and ask them to answer another question several months later. Similarly, after the researcher sends the experiential survey to the participant, it is not possible for the researcher to go back to add other questions or to provide additional response choices. Hence, the BAR researcher's care with ex ante instrument design issues transfers over into the care that the researcher must take in designing an experiential survey instrument.

BAR researchers worry about demand effects from their theory-justified differences in manipulations between treatment conditions. Experiential survey researchers also need to ensure that theory-driven question and response choices remain uncontaminated by demand effects. Consequently, experiential survey researchers carry out many steps that are analogous to the approaches employed by BAR researchers in developing their research instruments. BAR researchers carry out pilot studies, frequently employing student surrogates for the actual decision maker to ensure that the case-based instrument is understandable and that the theoretically grounded manipulations they embed in the case generate some reactions. In the Gibbins et al. (2001) experiential survey study, the researchers carried out interviews, focus groups and pretesting with the respondents (who were asked to think aloud while answering the survey questions) in an attempt to reduce the possibility that the survey's questions provided cues that would lead to participants merely affirming of the researchers' theory-based negotiation process model.[8] Specifically, Gibbins et al. (2001) pretested their questionnaire with five audit partners to ensure that (a) there was a common understanding between the researchers and the audit partners of what the questions meant and (b) the questionnaire's pre-formatted responses (set up to allow participants to respond by ticking boxes or indicating responses on scales) allowed for a full range of potential responses. Both experiential survey and BAR researchers' pretests are primarily aimed to develop a common understanding with their participants.

However, pretesting or piloting serves slightly different goals across these two methods. BAR researchers seek to ensure that the theoretically driven manipulation that they embed in their case generates reaction from their participants. Conversely, experiential survey researchers want assurance about the completeness of the researcher-provided response set.

The BAR researcher often collects an extensive amount of information in the final sections of their research instrument (i.e., after elicitation of the dependent variable). These include covariates or mediating variables, manipulation and comprehension check measures, other variables that may be useful to rule out alternative explanations of their results as well as demographic and experience data (particularly in the case of experienced participants). The experiential researcher also collects a large amount of information normally by requiring the participant to select – by ticking a box or marking a scale – a response about the issue under study. However, one important difference in instrument design between the two approaches is the provision in experiential surveys of multiple carefully selected opportunities for participants to elaborate on their box ticking and scaled responses using qualitative responses. The researcher identifies specific questions during the pretests or pilot study where participants indicate a wish to elaborate on the boxes they had ticked or the scaled response given. However, the researcher chooses this format only when it appears that valuable insights from such elaborations will be elicited. Further, one of the advantages of box ticking and scaled responses in experiential surveys over interview-based field studies (see the next section) is that it allows the participant to code their own response rather than the researcher attempting to code a dense interview transcript.

In summary, the five core competencies of the BAR researcher that we identified earlier can be readily transferred to carrying out experiential surveys. From using theory to allow for ex- ante planning and as the basis for generalization, the selection of appropriate participants, to the construction of the survey itself, the BAR researcher's skill set can be readily applied – in a complementary way – to the experiential survey research.

Qualitative field studies

The term "qualitative field study" refers to an overall set of methods used to study practice directly in context (Malsch and Salterio 2016). Qualitative methods can include research interviews, group discussions, direct observation of organizational actors and actions, as well as being an organizational participant and observer (Patton 1990; Savin-Baden and Major 2013).[9] We focus on the interview-based field study in this chapter, as it is the dominant method employed in carrying out positivist (defined below) accounting field research. Indeed, while we note that theory testing can be done employing field research methods (see Yin [2014] for details on theory testing qualitative methods and Johnston, Leach and Liu [1999] for an example of such research), most field research relies on induction or a "bottom up" research approach (e.g., Holland, Holyoak, Nisbett and Thagard 1989).[10] With an inductive approach, the researcher focuses on examining "data" from specific instances, and attempts to develop theories or to match patterns observed in the data to existing theory leading to a better understanding of the phenomenon (Holland et al. 1989). To date, nearly all qualitative field research using interview methods in accounting employs an inductive approach to understanding the context (Malsch and Salterio 2016).

As noted earlier, interpretivist field research rivals only experimental research as a method of choice for studying accounting-related topics among researchers who do not employ archival methods. Nonetheless, the former is relatively unknown in the USA with only a handful of prominent exceptions (e.g., the research stream by Mark Covaleski and Mark Dirsmith, as summarized in Dirsmith, Covaleski, and Samuel [2014]). Given the prominence of interpretivist accounting field research, we start by briefly explaining the differences between positivist interpretivist research in our Table 12.3 (that we adapt from Power and Gendron's 2015 Table 12.1). Our goal is to increase the awareness of the BAR researcher about this alternative approach to field research prior to describing in-depth how the BAR researcher's core competencies transfer to carrying out positivist interview-based field research.[11]

Underlying the differences between the positivist and interpretivist approaches are two different ways that researchers approach the nature of knowledge about the world. The positivist researcher's primary concern is to generalize by developing cause-and-effects-based theories of some phenomena of interest. By studying data inductively, as is done with most field studies in accounting, the researcher develops causal theories (e.g., Eisenhardt 1989). Positivists believe that theories are the best current explanation for a phenomenon and they consider that an objective researcher employing objective research instruments has a better chance to get closer to the truth – a truth that is out there to be discovered. In sum, the primary goal of positivist researchers is to discover the best causal explanation for a phenomenon, an explanation that remains true until falsification occurs leading to that theory's replacement with one that has greater explanatory power.

In contrast, the interpretivist researcher believes that social reality is constantly emergent and subjectively constructed: "all actions have meaning and intention that are retrospectively

Table 12.3 Differences of emphasis in positivist and interpretive inductive research[*]

	Positivist	Interpretive
Research aims	Aimed at empirical generalization by theorization about causes and effects	Aimed at empirical examination of global concerns and relating the particulars of the research context back to those global concerns
Methodological focus	Breadth	Depth
Analytical emphasis	Analyzing relations of cause and effect	Analyzing complexity of human behaviour
Favoured type of explanation	Prediction	In-depth understanding
Viewpoint on social reality	Reality is external to the mind	Reality is socially constructed
Viewpoint on researcher's objectivity	Objectivity of the researcher and the research process is stressed	Subjective interpretation by the researcher permeates the research processes
Viewpoint on methodological flexibility	Flexibility is constrained in the name of objectivity	Flexibility is considered as a hallmark of research
Style of writing	Aimed at conciseness	Aimed at accounting for the complexity of real-world phenomena

[*] Malsch and Salterio (2016) proposed this adaption in their Table 2 based on Table 1 originally found in Power and Gendron (2015).

endowed and that are grounded in social and historical practices" (Chua 1986: 615). Under this view, culture, social context, language and/or history will shape people's perceptions and hence influence their construction of shared knowledge. Thus, analyzing the "reality" of human behaviours implies that one has to first deconstruct the apparent objectivity of reality by tracking down its social, cultural, political, linguistic or historical underpinnings.

Given this brief explanation of the differences between positivist and interpretivist research methodologies one can see why we suggest that BAR researchers, with their emphasis on cause and effect theories and theory testing, are much more intellectually in tune with positivist than interpretivist field researchers. It is important to emphasize that we do not claim that BAR researchers cannot learn much from the techniques employed by the interpretivist field researcher (see Malsch and Salterio [2016] for an illustration). However, we contend that the accompanying intellectual superstructure required by a new researcher to understand how interpretivist field research employs theory requires a considerable investment that will likely not come naturally to most BAR researchers.[12]

The qualitative field study method

Detailed descriptions about qualitative field study methods are found in several sources (e.g., Yin 2014; albeit for the latest edition of this 1984 classic introduction to field research he calls it case study research). Table 12.4 provides a list of field research method articles from management accounting (Panel A) where positivist field research was being done contemporaneously with early interpretivist fieldwork, as well as selected field methods articles published in other business disciplines (Panel B).[13]

Table 12.4 Positivist field research methods resources*

Within accounting methods resources

Atkinson, A. A. and Shaffir, W., 1998, 'Standards for field research in management accounting'.

Lillis, A. M., 1999, 'A framework for the analysis of interview data from multiple field research sites'.

Lillis, A. M. and Mundy, J., 2005, 'Cross-sectional field studies in management accounting research-closing the gaps between surveys and case studies'.

Soltes, E., 2014, 'Incorporating field data into archival research'.

Young, S. M., 1999, 'Field research methods in management accounting'.

Broader research methods sources

Doz, Y., 2011, 'Qualitative research for international business'.

Dubé, L. and Paré, G., 2003, 'Rigor in information systems positivist case research: Current practices, trends, and recommendations'.

Eisenhardt, K. M., 1989, 'Building theories from case study research'.

Eisenhardt, K. M. and Graebner, M. E., 2007, 'Theory building from cases: Opportunities and challenges'.

Yin, R. K., 2014, *Case Study Research: Design and Methods* (5th ed.).

*Adapted from Malsch and Salterio (2016) Table 3 Panel A. See reference list for full citation.

Malsch and Salterio (2016) note that in positivist qualitative field research (hereafter qualitative field research) each researcher has to deal with at least four key issues in planning their research:[14]

- Who are the appropriate informants? How do you locate them? How does the researcher motivate them to take part in the study?
- How much engagement between the researcher and informants is needed to provide sufficient evidence about the issue being investigated (or the "sample size" issue)?
- How does the researcher carry out the research so that high quality of the engagement between the field researcher and the informants occurs? How can the researcher assure that trustworthy responses are obtained and that the informant is not just supplying the answer the researcher wants?
- How can the researcher mobilize the evidence from the field that comes from qualitative interviews, observations, etc. to contribute to the understanding of the phenomenon of interest?

Further, with respect to the role of theory in qualitative field research, Malsch and Salterio (2016) note that theory tends to be deployed using one or more of these approaches:

- Theory is developed or revised to provide deeper insights into potential cause and effect relationships (e.g., Eisenhardt 1989).
- Theory as a means of explaining field observations or accounts (see Yin 1984: Ch. 3).
- Theory as a means to diagnose the root cause(s) that lead to the behaviour seen in the field (see for example Griffith, Hammersley and Kadous 2015).

Table 12.5 provides examples of accounting research using qualitative field research methods. Other than in management accounting, field research studies have tended to be relatively rare

Table 12.5 Examples of positivist accounting qualitative field research studies*

Auditing

Dowling, C. and Leech, S., 2014, 'A Big-4 firm's use of information technology to control the audit process: How an audit support system is changing auditor behavior'.

Fiolleau, K., Hoang, K., Jamal, K. and Sunder, S., 2013, 'How do regulatory reforms to enhance auditor independence work in practice?'

Griffith, E. E., Hammersley, J. S. and Kadous, K., 2015, 'Audits of complex estimates as verification of management numbers: How institutional pressures shape practice'.

Hirst, D. E. and Koonce, L., 1996, 'Audit analytical procedures: A field investigation'.

Salterio, S. E. and Denham, R., 1997, 'Accounting consultation units: An organizational memory analysis'.

Trompeter, G. and Wright, A., 2010, 'The world has changed – have analytical procedure practices?'

Trotman, A. J. and Trotman, K. T., 2013, 'Internal audit's role in GHG emissions and energy reporting: Evidence from audit committees, senior accountants, and internal auditors'.

Westermann, K., Bedard, J. and Earley, C., 2015, 'Learning the "craft" of auditing: A dynamic view of auditors' on-the-job learning'.

Wolf, F. M., 1981, 'The nature of managerial work: An investigation of the work of the audit manager'.

Corporate Governance

Beasley, M. S., Carcello, J. V., Hermanson, D. R. and Neal, V., 2009, 'The audit committee oversight process'.

Clune, R., Hermanson, D. R., Tompkins, J. G. and Ye, Z. S., 2014, 'The nominating committee process: A qualitative examination of board independence and formalization'.

Cohen, J., Krishnamoorthy, G. and Wright, A. M., 2002, 'Corporate governance and the audit process'.

Cohen, J., Krishnamoorthy, G. and Wright, A., 2010, 'Corporate governance in the post-Sarbanes-Oxley era: Auditors' experiences'.

Hermanson, D. R., Tompkins, J. G., Veliyath, R. and Ye, Z. S., 2012, 'The compensation committee process'.

Management Control Systems

Anderson, S. W., Christ, M. H., Dekker, H. C. and Sedatole, K. L., 2013, 'The use of management controls to mitigate risk in strategic alliances: Field and survey evidence'.

Campbell, D., Epstein, M. J. and Martinez-Jerez, F. A., 2011, 'The learning effects of monitoring'.

Davila, T., 2000, 'An empirical study on the drivers of management control systems' design in new product development'.

Merchant, K. A., 1990, 'The effects of financial controls on data manipulation and management myopia'.

Mundy, J., 2010, 'Creating dynamic tensions through a balanced use of management control systems'.

Wouters, M. and Roijmans, D., 2011, 'Using prototypes to induce experimentation and knowledge integration in the development of enabling accounting information'.

Cost systems and budgeting

Brüggen, A., Krishnan, R. and Sedatole, K. L., 2011, 'Drivers and consequences of short-term production decisions: Evidence from the auto industry'.

Kaplan, R. S., 1998, 'Innovation action research: Creating new management theory and practice'.

Merchant, K. A. and Manzoni, J.-F., 1989, 'The achievability of budget targets in profit centers: A field study'.

Moll, J. and Hoque, Z., 2011, 'Budgeting for legitimacy: The case of an Australian university'.

Management accounting applications including enterprise risk management

Huelsbeck, D. P., Merchant, K. A. and Sandino, T., 2011, 'On testing business models'.

Mikes, A., 2011, 'From counting risk to making risk count: Boundary-work in risk management'.

Rowe, C., Shields, M. D. and Birnberg, J. G., 2012, 'Hardening soft accounting information: Games for planning organizational change'.

Schloetzer, J. D., 2012, 'Process integration and information sharing in supply chains'.

* See reference list for full citation.

until this century (see Wolf [1981] for a counter-example). Key topics that accounting field researchers have examined to date include:

- Audit practices and standards implementation (e.g., for analytical procedures see Hirst and Koonce [1996]; Trompeter and Wright [2010]; for complex estimates see Griffith et al. [2015]).
- The intersection of audit corporate governance (e.g., Cohen, Krishnamoorthy and Wright 2002, 2010).
- Corporate governance practices (e.g., Clune, Hermanson, Tompkins and Ye [2014] on nominating committees).
- Audit firm-level support for practice offices (e.g., Dowling and Leech 2014; Salterio and Denham 1997).
- Management control systems (e.g., Campbell, Epstein and Martinez-Jerez 2011; Mundy 2010; Merchant 1990).
- Budget systems (e.g., Moll and Hoque 2011; Merchant and Manzoni 1989).
- Cost systems and cost drivers (e.g., Brüggen, Krishnan and Sedatole 2011; Kaplan 1998).
- Risk management systems (e.g., Mikes 2011).

Evidence of the impact of interview-based field studies on the accounting academy includes the 2002 Notable Contribution to the Audit Literature Award from the AAA Audit Section (the second of such award ever) being awarded to Hirst and Koonce's (1996) qualitative interview-based field study on analytical procedures published in *Contemporary Accounting Research*. The 2012 Award went to Cohen, Krishnamoorthy and Wright's (2002) qualitative interview-based study on how corporate governance's impact on the audit process provides further evidence of the influence of this research method. In management accounting, the 2015 Notable Contribution to Management Accounting Literature Award from AAA Management Accounting Section went to Mundy's (2010) positivist field study on how organizations balance controlling and enabling uses of management control systems. Similarly, the Management Accounting Section's 2012 Greatest Impact on Practice Award winner was Brüggen, Krishnan and Sedatole's (2011) mixed-method paper that included field interviews (along with quantitative analysis of within-firm collected archival data). Lastly, Graham, Harvey and Rajgopol's (2005) mixed-methods field study in financial accounting employing a random sample survey as well as field interviews won the AAA's association wide 2007 Notable Contribution to Accounting Research Award.

Management accounting researchers were the first accounting researchers to embrace qualitative interview-based field research methods (see Merchant and Van der Stede [2006] for a review of field research accounting), though there has been a great increase in the number of audit and corporate governance field studies recently. Indeed, the first literature review of positivist management accounting field research dates back to the early 1990s (Ferreira and Merchant 1992). In financial reporting, since the publication of Graham et al. (2005) referred to earlier, there have been several financial accounting mixed-method studies. These studies normally employ interviews to provide a richer context to the authors' interpretation of the survey questions (e.g., Dichev, Graham, Harvey and Rajgopal 2013; De Jong et al. 2014). However, mixed-methods studies can also feature archival data paired with field interviews (e.g., Yoo and Pae [2017] combine archival analyst forecast data with analyst interviews), providing more depth to the findings of the archival study. Hence, while pure qualitative field studies in financial accounting are rare, researchers are employing qualitative interview-based field research methods as part of mixed-method research to develop richer insights of the issue of interest.

BAR researchers' core competencies and qualitative field studies

We argue that the five identified core competencies of BAR researchers enable them to conduct qualitative field study research with relatively low barriers to entry as opposed to the costs incurred by researchers with archival or analytical training. First, similar to the central role that theory plays in an experiment for the BAR researcher, theory also plays a central role in positivist qualitative field research (Power and Gendron 2015). Similar to an ex ante theory-based hypothesis developed by that BAR researcher in an experiment, awareness of theories that prior studies have used to explore the current phenomenon of interest helps field researchers develop baseline expectations about cause and effect relationships. In interview-based studies these theoretically driven baseline expectations become the benchmark against which the field researchers will revise their beliefs as they iteratively collect and analyze their field data (Atkinson and Shaffir 1998; Ahrens and Dent 1998). In addition, theory also serves as a lens through which field researchers define what is interesting and important during both data collection and data analysis stage of the research (Atkinson and Shaffir 1998).

The BAR researchers use theory extensively in their experimental work allowing them to develop familiarity with the four key facets of theory, that is: what (the factors in the theory), how (the relationship between these factors), why (explanation of underlying dynamics) and when (boundary condition) (Whetten 1989). This familiarity with theory's underlying structure also enables field researchers to structure to their data collection and carry out analysis of the rich field data.

Similarly, the BAR researcher's awareness of multiple theoretical perspectives from psychology to economics to sociology also sensitizes them to the fact that different theories can lead to different predictions about the same observed data pattern. Such knowledge is useful to the field researcher who has to often draw on multiple theories to understand the different, incomplete or conflicting interpretations of their field data (Ihantola and Kihn 2011). This theoretical awareness constrains field researchers from developing a premature conclusion until a coherent relationship emerges in their pattern-matching process during their data analysis (Ahrens and Dent 1998). For example, in Cohen et al.'s (2002) field study of corporate governance and its impact on the audit process, the authors entered the field with a strong agency theory view of the audit committee's role in monitoring the auditor. However, as they gathered evidence in the field they found that the agency theory perspective alone could not account for many of their observations. Hence, they incorporated aspects of institutional and resource dependency theories to explain processes of corporate governance and its effect on the audit process. Subsequent research in this area echoed the finding that a multi-theory perspective was needed to explain most of the applied governance settings examined (see for example Beasley, Carcello, Hermanson and Neal 2009; Clune et al. 2014; Cohen et al. 2010; Hermanson, Tompkins, Veliyath and Ye 2012).

As noted in the experiential survey section, the BAR researcher has substantial engagement with the practice community. Such engagement aids field researchers to identify key issues that practitioners are grappling with (Ferreira and Merchant 1992) which potentially require more study in the field (Lillis 2008). In addition, BAR researchers' awareness of the institutional contexts that their experimental participants are embedded in would aid them as field researchers in developing the questions they pose to their informants and more readily understand the informants' responses. For example, Cohen et al.'s (2002) close engagement with practice allowed them to juxtapose the diverging theoretical views of corporate governance (i.e., agency theory-based view in the accounting and finance literature, and the institutional view in the management literature), and the existing lack of professional audit guidance on how to assess the strength of corporate governance. This understanding aided them in formulating their research questions about how auditors integrate their assessment of their clients' corporate governance strength into the audit planning process and their related audit judgments.

Further, the BAR researchers' experimental background trains them to abstract away the unnecessary details of context (Swieringa and Weick 1982). This allows BAR researchers who carry out interview-based field research to have a greater ease in filtering and systematizing what they hear and observe in the field than researchers who do not have similar sensitivity to the role played by accounting context. For example, Cohen et al.'s (2002) background as BAR researchers with their close engagement with practice enabled them to identify instances "when questions took (them) down an important path" (581) given their sensitivity to context.

The BAR researchers' competence in recruiting practitioner participants for experiments also helps not only recruit but also develop trust and rapport with their potential informants in a qualitative field study (Atkinson and Shaffir 1998). These BAR-access approaches can also aid them in securing (the often elusive) access to the field research site(s) (Anderson and Widener 2006) and managing engagement with the field. As noted before, the BAR researcher has a thorough understanding of the research context and of matching their participants to their experimental task. Hence, the field researcher can put their BAR competencies to good use in identifying potential sources of information and informants at the sites (Yin 1984) as well as to match the number of sites and their level of analysis to the research questions (Lillis 2008; Anderson and Widener 2006).

BAR researchers' training in developing a thorough, ex ante planning of experimental protocols will be directly useful when developing field protocols to guide an interview-based study. The field researcher needs to develop – in advance – guidelines on how to cope with multiple contingencies that may occur in the field over the course of the study (Yin 1984). Further, the field researcher needs to plan carefully a set of non-directive questions and probes that ensure complete coverage of themes of interests (Lillis 1999) without leading to demand effects. Again these skills are very similar to that of the BAR researcher in attempting to construct experiments that avoid demand effects.

BAR researchers develop experimental manipulations and questions to operationalize underlying constructs, such as dependent variables, in their experiments. Strong BAR research exhibits attention to pretesting and pilot studies (see Gibbins, McCracken and Salterio [2010] as an example where the development of the measure instrument in that experiment took literally hundreds of student participants prior to the conclusion that it was a valid measure). The planning that underlies this experimental preparation is similar to the field researcher's interview protocol development. Indeed, the importance of ex ante preparation for field studies is highlighted by Yin's (1984) recommendation that field researchers conduct a pilot case study. Westermann, Bedard and Earley (2015) provide an excellent example of thorough, ex ante development of their qualitative interview protocol. They report carefully developing their questions for their interviews with audit partners based on prior literature, feedback of the audit firms' partners and a senior manager, in advance of pretesting their preliminary list of questions on a retired partner for clarity and completeness.

Lastly, the BAR researchers' sensitivity to different sources of measurement biases is also transferrable to qualitative interview-based field research. As we noted in Table 12.1, the BAR researchers are highly aware of the possible incongruence between their and their participants' interpretation of events and information. This means that the BAR researchers will be highly sensitive to situational cues that could change the interpretation of either the information provided by their respondents, or their own observations in the field (Ahrens and Dent 1998).

The BAR researchers' awareness of potential lack of reliability of respondents' self-report data (Schwarz and Oyserman 2001) will also serve them well in interview-based fieldwork. To illustrate, Dowling and Leech (2014: 234) provided a thorough disclosure of various steps that they took to minimize measurement bias in their study of Big-4 audit firms' change management processes associated with implementing new audit process-based information technology. The researchers collected and iteratively analyzed archival and interview data. In addition, to ensure that their interviewees' responses reflect their opinions (instead of what they thought their superiors would want them to report), the researchers – among many other steps that they implemented – ensured that each interview group consisted of only auditors of the same rank.

In summary, the five BAR researchers' core competencies that we have identified transfer readily to interview-based field studies in accounting. From having a variety of theoretical perspectives that help them recognize patterns in the evidence they gather, to the ability to manage interactions with practitioners, the BAR researcher's competencies can be transferred to carry out high-quality field study research.

Discussion and conclusions

The purpose of this chapter has been to highlight how an identified subset of the BAR researcher's core competencies can be readily leveraged into conducting experiential research, specifically, experiential survey- and qualitative field research-employed interviews. However, we acknowledge that there are challenges and costs that BAR researchers face when they embrace new-to-them experiential research approaches.[15] We will discuss some of these challenges as we conclude our chapter.

The costs of undertaking experiential research

Most BAR researchers would perceive that the most salient cost to transferring their core competencies to experiential research is the loss of the experimenter's main claim of competitive advantage vis-a-vis archival researchers: the ability of a well-designed experiment to detect cause and effect relationships (Shadish, Cook and Campbell 2002; Shields 2012). As BAR researchers consider moving into the realm of experiential survey research, they implicitly move into an area where they can only gather associational evidence. Because each participant in an experiential survey provides her or his own example in response to the survey cues, researchers lose the experimental advantage of random assignment of participants to experimental treatment conditions. This loss of experimental control means they no longer have the basis for detecting a causal relationship, a main advantage of the experimental method.[16] Indeed, BAR researchers who transition to experiential survey research have to be content with observing associations within their survey data. Similarly, while interview-based field studies allow for potential identification of causal relationships, such settings by their very nature allow for limited generalization. This limitation occurs because the observed causal relationships might simply be idiosyncratic to the specific field setting.

Second, while we argue that many of the BAR researchers' core experimental competencies are transferable to experiential research, embracing a new experiential method does require the BAR researcher to learn new research skills.[17] The administration of survey research is different from implementing a fully controlled laboratory-based experiment, particularly because survey respondents no longer sit in front of the researchers and/or their assistants (and generally comply with the latter's requests).[18] Nevertheless, we acknowledge that BAR researchers who have experience distributing their experimental instruments online or through key organizational contacts will have substantially lower barriers to embracing the experiential survey method than a more laboratory-focused BAR researcher will face. Irrespective of whether the BAR researcher has experience with administering experiments at a distance (e.g., via the internet), or not, the new experiential survey researcher is well advised to study best practices in survey research. Approaches to survey design such as Dillman's Tailored Design method (see Dillman 1978 and updated by Dillman, Smyth and Christian 2014), aid in the development of clear and coherent survey instruments, and more importantly, lead to high-quality responses at acceptable response rates.

Qualitative field studies' interview-based approach will also present multiple challenges to BAR researchers. First, they need to resist the urge to design their interview protocol as a series of exclusively scaled and tick box responses that are elicited in person rather than by questionnaire.[19] In addition, engaging in qualitative field study is likely to change the nature and the extent of the BAR researchers' interaction with practitioners. Instead of having a relatively informal consultation about experimental settings and materials, they now need to carefully elicit and document practitioners' responses. The need to set up recording equipment (if permission to record is given by the respondents), take notes during interviews, record observations in the field and immediately document one's reflections after each interview or observation period requires a rigorous, disciplined approach to interactions that is not likely required during informal discussions with practitioners. In addition, the need to analyze and look for patterns in qualitative data requires a very different skill set compared to the coding of quantitative experimental responses. Indeed, as the number of respondents grows beyond a relatively modest number, the field researcher often needs to utilize qualitative data analysis software (e.g., Atlasti 2016, see http://atlasti.com/qualitative-data-analysis-software/) to manage the very large amount of text-based data that accumulates quickly during interviews. This software allows the researcher to rearrange data to look at respondents' answers from different perspectives, and document the emerging patterns from their analyses.[20]

Experiential research is open to attacks by others in academia who view the research as "merely" a descriptive research that is worthy of − at best − a practice note in a second-tier academic journal, or an article in a journal targeted at bridging the academic practitioner gap (e.g., *Accounting Horizons* in the US, *Accounting Perspectives* in Canada and *Accounting in Europe*). Some would even argue that such research does not have a place in the top-tier basic research journals. While the numerous examples cited in this chapter demonstrate that such research can be published in rigorous, top-tier accounting research journals, the review process can be long and difficult. This happens because the researcher often needs to educate the editor and reviewers about the norms of experiential surveys or qualitative field studies as part of the review process of their submitted article.[21] Indeed, explaining why their experiential research methods are rigorous and what the appropriate evaluation criteria are for their research can be difficult even with well-meaning reviewers. When editors select reviewers who are not familiar with the experiential methods, there is a tendency (particularly in qualitative field studies) to push the theory out of the paper and highlight the descriptive materials. Nevertheless, authors following this descriptive approach often end up with, after several rounds of review, rejection due to lack of perceived academic content; a content that has been counselled out of the paper by the review process. The publication of papers that provide some guidance to editors and reviewers (e.g., Malsch and Salterio 2016) on the appropriate quality norms to assess this research will alleviate these challenges to some extent.

Finally, ensuring a coherent write-up of experiential research findings requires more of a story telling ability (Daft 1995) than producing a rigorous and precise description of the statistical results that the BAR researcher is accustomed to. Similarly, the explanation of the experiential research contribution to future academic research and practice also requires more thought and reflection than the vague "implications for practice" discussions frequently found in published experimental research. This lack of structure (or "formula") in the presentation of experiential research findings can be challenging for the BAR researcher (see Pratt 2009).

Concluding remarks

We argue in this chapter that the BAR researcher has a set of core competencies that are transferable to carry out experiential research. Careful examination of Tables 12.2 and 12.5 finds many examples of BAR researchers who have made the leap. Many familiar experimental accounting researchers, such as Jeff Cohen, Mike Gibbins, Karim Jamal, Ranjani Krishnan, Steve Salterio, Mike Shields, Jane Thayer, Ken Trotman, Alan Webb, Arnie Wright and others are authors of one or more of the studies documented in these tables (which are not intended to be exhaustive, but illustrative of the set of research published). Examination of these tables provides ample evidence to support our suggestion that experimental core competencies are transferable to experiential research.[22]

Nevertheless, in the relatively more mature experiential research area of management accounting, there are researchers who focus their primary research method on field research. Researchers such as Tony Davila, Robert Kaplan, Ken Merchant and Wim Van der Stede have made their research careers using primarily field-based experiential methods. It is an open question whether such specialization will become the norm in the future in the newly emerging areas of audit and financial accounting experiential research, and whether it will continue to be further entrenched in management accounting research.

At present, to use an old adage from the east coast of Canada, "the first in the field gets the biggest potatoes." With the relative paucity of experiential research, there is an opportunity for BAR researchers who move into the experiential research space to distinguish themselves from their uni-method focused peers. Indeed, the ability to carry out a well-designed and carefully motivated experiential research study complements BAR researchers' ability to cleanly test causal relationships in their experimental research. This full-cycle research capability positions them to make a greater contribution to theory and practice than they can make with another experimental study.

Notes

1 The fourth stage of the cycle, the further validating of these causal relationships through the potential for interventions practice, can also involve field studies.

2 The psychology-based BAR researcher has a distinct advantage over the experimental economics BAR researcher in venturing 'beyond the lab'. This is because experimental economics BAR researchers are taught to avoid context (sometimes at all costs). For example, they are taught to focus on student participants as these students' financial circumstances mean that they will respond well to the incentive amount that researchers can afford to offer in the laboratory. Hence, our arguments are more applicable to the psychology-based BAR researchers than to the experimental economics BAR researchers. This does not mean that experimental economics BAR researchers cannot lever their skills into the experiential research; it only means that the barriers they will face in doing so are somewhat higher.

3 We note that there are key differences between using random sample surveys of populations to gather data from which conclusions can be generalized to the entire population and what we call experiential surveys. This distinction will be explained later in this chapter. We will also explain the distinction between interpretivist and positivist field studies and why we believe that BAR researchers are better positioned to carry out positivist than interpretivist field research.

4 We do not mean that archival, analytical and survey researchers cannot carry out experiential research. Indeed, we acknowledge that non-BAR researchers could potentially have developed some of the same

competencies that BAR researchers have acquired. Nonetheless, we argue that it is the complementarities of the competencies (i.e., the skill set) which allow the BAR researcher lower transaction costs in learning to use experiential research methods.

5 This is not to argue that these are the only core competencies of the BAR researcher but rather they are the ones that are important to experiential research and that we believe are transferable to that research.

6 This approach covers the key questions that the critical incident techniques attempt to answer (Schluter, Seaton and Chaboyer 2008):

- What preceded and contributed to the incident?
- What did the person or people do or not do that had an effect?
- What was the outcome or result?
- What made this action effective or ineffective?
- What could have made the action more effective?

7 Indeed, in a latter theory-testing experimental paper McCracken, Salterio and Schmidt (2011) showed that managers provided a different pattern of responses to the same negotiation experimental case compared to partners.

8 The pretest approach of Gibbins et al. (2001) of having these partners verbalize what they were thinking about out loud is loosely analogous to verbal protocol research (see Ericsson and Simon [1993], and see Anderson [1985] for an example of how this is applied to accounting research).

9 Soltes (2014) reminds us that field research in accounting can include the use of archival data gathered in the field to carry out quantitative analysis. Our focus is mainly on qualitative field study (e.g., field interviews), though we acknowledge that some of the mixed-method studies complemented their qualitative field interview with quantitative analysis using field archival data (e.g., Malina, Nørreklit and Selto 2007).

10 Deductive research is also known as "top down" research. It can simply be described as following the researchers' reasoning: from basic premises to hypotheses to empirical tests of hypotheses. Experiments are clearly an example of deductive research where hypotheses are deduced from theoretical assumptions, and then tested by experimental instruments with limited manipulations that reflect theoretical concerns. Experiential surveys are primarily deductive to the extent that they are guided by theory. However, the experiential survey allows more flexibility for induction to take place since specific instances are elicited from participants and attention is paid to collecting responses that go beyond the set specified by the theory in the survey instrument. Hence, while not as robustly inductive in the way that most field research is, experiential surveys have more aspects of inductive research than experimental research does.

11 There are several papers in the accounting literature that introduce the basic difference in assumptions between positivist and interpretive research dating back to Chua's (1986) paper introducing these ideas to a North American readership. More recent discussions of similar issues have appeared in *Accounting Horizons* (e.g., Chapman 2012; Cooper and Morgan 2008) and in *Auditing: A Journal of Practice & Theory* (e.g., Power and Gendron 2015).

12 This is not to say there is no theoretical overlap between interpretive field research and experimental researcher competencies. See for example Chapter 7 of this book that examines stakeholder and legitimacy theories in BAR research. These theories, starting in the early 1980s, have spawned significant interpretivist research in accounting (for recent examples of using these theories in an interpretivist manner see Gendron and Barrett [2004]; Gallhofer, Haslam, Barrett and Gendron 2006).

13 For further explanation of how qualitative field research method can be applied in BAR, see Chapters 16 and 17 of this book.

14 Adapted from Malsch and Salterio (2016) who examine this issue in terms of audit research. See Lillis and Mundy (2005) and Young (1999) for congruent concerns developed from management accounting field research.

15 To this end, the BAR researcher can choose to find a co-author who has more experience in conducting experiential research when doing his or her first few studies.

16 See Campbell, Stanley and Gage (1963) for the many advantages in detecting causality that random assignment of participants to experimental treatments allows to occur.

17 While the BAR researcher's core competencies are transferrable to experiential research, they need to be careful in determining the extent to which these competencies should be applied when doing the experiential research. To illustrate, designing an experimental instrument requires careful abstraction of unnecessary institutional details. However, too much abstraction of contextual details when doing qualitative field research means that the researcher may miss interesting insights that could have been gathered from the qualitative field evidence.

18 Orne (1962) provided the following anecdote that serves as an interesting illustration to the degree of control that BAR researchers enjoy in their 'laboratory', but likely to lose when administering an experiential survey. "A number of casual acquaintances were asked . . . to perform five push-ups. Their response tended to be amazement, incredulity and the question 'Why?' Another similar group of individuals were asked whether they would take part in an experiment. . . . They too were asked to perform five push-ups. Their typical response was 'Where?'" (777).

19 If the researchers are interested only in eliciting such responses, they should consider the experiential survey rather than a qualitative field study.

20 The experience of the senior author of this paper is that investment in a qualitative data analysis software pays off once the number of respondents moves into the low double figures and often is helpful with smaller numbers of respondents depending on the detail of the data.

21 This can be done, for example, using a thorough description of a research method that clearly demonstrates how the methods employed are consistent with best practices. Indeed, the methods section could be elaborated on in a separate appendix, albeit with the expectation that eventually the appendix would be dropped from the paper, providing an extended opportunity to demonstrate the rigour of the experiential method employed.

22 We noted that there are also a smaller group of researchers whose initial training was in the archival method, but who have subsequently made the leap to the experiential research realm (e.g., Joe Carcello, Danna Hermanson).

References

AAA Research Impact Task Force, 2009, 'The impact of academic accounting research on professional practice: An analysis by the AAA Research Impact Task Force', *Accounting Horizons* 23(4), 411–456.

Abdel-Khalik, A.R., 1974, 'On the efficiency of subject surrogation in accounting research', *The Accounting Review*, 49, 743–750.

Ahrens, T. and Dent, J.F., 1998, 'Accounting and organizations: Realizing the richness of field research', *Journal of Management Accounting Research* 10, 1–39.

Anderson, M.J., 1985, 'Some evidence on the effect of verbalization on process: A methodological note', *Journal of Accounting Research* 23(2), 843–852.

Anderson, S.W., Christ, M.H., Dekker, H.C. and Sedatole, K.L., 2013, 'The use of management controls to mitigate risk in strategic alliances: Field and survey evidence', *Journal of Management Accounting Research* 26(1), 1–32.

Anderson, S.W. and Widener, S.K., 2006, 'Doing quantitative field research in management accounting', *Handbooks of Management Accounting Research* 1, 319–341.

Andersson, B.-E. and Nilsson, S.-G., 1964, 'Studies in the reliability and validity of the critical incident technique', *Journal of Applied Psychology* 48(6), 398.

Arnold, V. and Sutton, S.G., 1997, *Behavioral Accounting Research: Foundations and Frontiers*, American Accounting Association, Sarasota, FL.

Ashton, R.H., 1982, 'Human information processing in accounting', *Studies in Accounting Research No. 17*, American Accounting Association, Sarasota, FL.

Ashton, R.H. and Ashton, A.H., 1995, *Judgment and Decision-Making Research in Accounting and Auditing*, Cambridge University Press, Cambridge.

Atkinson, A.A. and Shaffir, W., 1998, 'Standards for field research in management accounting', *Journal of Management Accounting Research* 10, 41.

Atlasti, 2016, *Qualitative Data Analysis Software: What Is Qualitative Data Analysis Software?* viewed 25 January 2016, from http://atlasti.com/qualitative-data-analysis-software/.

Ballas, A. and Theoharakis, V., 2003, 'Exploring diversity in accounting through faculty journal perceptions', *Contemporary Accounting Research* 20(4), 619–644.

Beasley, M.S., Carcello, J.V., Hermanson, D.R. and Neal, V., 2009, 'The audit committee oversight process', *Contemporary Accounting Research* 26(1), 65–122.

Bobek, D.D. and Radtke, R.R., 2007, 'An experiential investigation of tax professionals' ethical environments', *Journal of the American Taxation Association* 29(2), 63–84.

Bonner, S.E., 2008, *Judgment and Decision Making in Accounting*, Prentice Hall, Upper Saddle River, NJ.

Brazel, J.F., Jones, K.L., Thayer, J. and Warne, R.C., 2015, 'Understanding investor perceptions of financial statement fraud and their use of red flags: Evidence from the field', *Review of Accounting Studies* 20(4), 1373–1406.

Brink, A.G., Glasscock, R. and Wier, B., 2012, 'The current state of accounting Ph.D. programs in the United States', *Issues in Accounting Education* 27(4), 917–942.

Brown, H.L. and Wright, A.M., 2008, 'Negotiation research in auditing', *Accounting Horizons* 22(1), 91–109.

Brüggen, A., Krishnan, R. and Sedatole, K.L., 2011, 'Drivers and consequences of short-term production decisions: Evidence from the auto industry', *Contemporary Accounting Research* 28(1), 83–123.

Bruns, W.J. and Kaplan, R. S. (eds.), 1987, *Accounting & Management: Field Study Perspectives*, Harvard Business Press, Boston.

Butterfield, L.D., Borgen, W.E., Amundson, N.E. and Maglio, A.-S.T., 2005, 'Fifty years of the critical incident technique: 1954–2004 and beyond', *Qualitative Research* 5(4), 475–497.

Campbell, D., Epstein, M.J. and Martinez-Jerez, F.A., 2011, 'The learning effects of monitoring', *The Accounting Review* 86(6), 1909–1934.

Campbell, D.T., Stanley, J.C. and Gage, N.L., 1963, *Experimental and Quasi-Experimental Designs for Research*, Houghton Mifflin, Boston, MA.

Chapman, C.S., 2012, 'Framing the issue of research quality in a context of research diversity', *Accounting Horizons* 26(4), 821–831.

Chatman, J.A. and Flynn, F.J., 2005, 'Full-cycle micro-organizational behavior research', *Organization Science* 16(4), 434–447.

Chua, W.F., 1986, 'Radical developments in accounting thought', *Accounting Review*, 601–632.

Clune, R., Hermanson, D.R., Tompkins, J.G. and Ye, Z.S., 2014, 'The nominating committee process: A qualitative examination of board independence and formalization', *Contemporary Accounting Research* 31(3), 748–786.

Cohen, J., Krishnamoorthy, G. and Wright, A.M., 2002, 'Corporate governance and the audit process', *Contemporary Accounting Research* 19(4), 573–594.

Cohen, J., Krishnamoorthy, G. and Wright, A., 2010, 'Corporate governance in the post-Sarbanes-Oxley era: Auditors' experiences', *Contemporary Accounting Research* 27(3), 751–786.

Cooper, D.J. and Morgan, W., 2008, 'Case study research in accounting', *Accounting Horizons* 22(2), 159–178.

Daft, R.L., 1995, 'Why I recommended that your manuscript be rejected', in L.L. Cummings and P.J. Frost (eds.), *Publishing in the Organizational Sciences*, 164–183, Sage Publications, London.

Davila, T., 2000, 'An empirical study on the drivers of management control systems' design in new product development', *Accounting, Organizations and Society* 25(4), 383–409.

Davis, J.S., 1995, *Behavioral Tax Research: Prospects and Judgment Calls*, American Taxation Association.

De Jong, A., Mertens, G., Van der Poel, M. and Van Dijk, R., 2014, 'How does earnings management influence investor's perceptions of firm value? Survey evidence from financial analysts', *Review of Accounting Studies* 19(2), 606–627.

Dichev, I. D., Graham, J. R., Harvey, C. R. and Rajgopal, S. (2013). 'Earnings quality: evidence from the field', *Journal of Accounting and Economics* 56(2), 1–33..

Dillman, D.A., 1978, *Mail and Telephone Surveys* (3rd ed.), Wiley Interscience, Hoboken, NJ.

Dillman, D.A., Smyth, J.D. and Christian, L.M., 2014, *Internet, Phone, Mail, and Mixed-Mode Surveys: The Tailored Design Method*, John Wiley & Sons, Hoboken, NJ.

Dirsmith, M.W., Covaleski, M.A. and Samuel, S., 2014, 'On being professional in the 21st century: An empirically informed essay', *Auditing: A Journal of Practice & Theory* 34(2), 167–200.

Dowling, C. and Leech, S., 2014, 'A Big-4 firm's use of information technology to control the audit process: How an audit support system is changing auditor behavior', *Contemporary Accounting Research* 31(1), 230–252.

Doz, Y., 2011, 'Qualitative research for international business', *Journal of International Business Studies* 42(5), 582–590.

Dubé, L. and Paré, G., 2003, 'Rigor in information systems positivist case research: Current practices, trends, and recommendations', *MIS Quarterly* 27(4), 597–636.

Eisenhardt, K.M., 1989, 'Building theories from case study research', *Academy of Management Review* 14(4), 532–550.

Eisenhardt, K.M. and Graebner, M.E., 2007, 'Theory building from cases: Opportunities and challenges', *Academy of Management Journal* 50(1), 25–32.

Elliott, W.B., Hodge, F.D., Kennedy, J.J. and Pronk, M., 2007, 'Are MBA students a good proxy for nonprofessional investors?', *The Accounting Review* 82(1), 139–168.

Emby, C. and Favere-Marchesi, M., 2010, 'Review partners and engagement partners: The interaction process in engagement quality review', *Auditing: A Journal of Practice & Theory* 29(2), 215–232.

Emby, C. and Gibbins, M., 1987, 'Good judgment in public accounting: Quality and justification', *Contemporary Accounting Research* 4(1), 287–313.

Ericsson, K.A. and Simon, H.A., 1993, *Protocol Analysis: Verbal Reports as Data*, MIT Press, Cambridge.

Ferreira, L.D. and Merchant, K.A., 1992, 'Field research in management accounting and control: A review and evaluation', *Accounting, Auditing & Accountability Journal* 5(4), 3–34.

Financial Accounting and Reporting, 2016, *About the Journal of Financial Reporting*, viewed 13 January 2016, from http://www2.aaahq.org/fars/JFR_about.cfm.

Fiolleau, K., Hoang, K., Jamal, K. and Sunder, S., 2013, 'How do regulatory reforms to enhance auditor independence work in practice?', *Contemporary Accounting Research* 30(3), 864–890.

Fisher, R. and Katz, J., 2000, 'Social-desirability bias and the validity of self-reported values', *Psychology & Marketing* 17(2), 105–120.

Flanagan, J.C., 1954, 'The critical incident technique', *Psychological Bulletin* 51(4), 327–358.

Gallhofer, S., Haslam, J., Barrett, M. and Gendron, Y., 2006, 'WebTrust and the "commercialistic auditor": The unrealized vision of developing auditor trustworthiness in cyberspace, *Accounting, Auditing & Accountability Journal* 19(5), 631–662.

Gendron, Y. and Barrett, M., 2004, 'Professionalization in action: Accountants' attempt at building a network of support for the webtrust seal of assurance', *Contemporary Accounting Research* 21(3), 563–602.

Gibbins, M., 2001, 'Incorporating context into the study of judgment and expertise in public accounting', *International Journal of Auditing* 5(3), 225–236.

Gibbins, M., McCracken, S.A. and Salterio, S.E., 2005, 'Negotiations over accounting issues: The congruency of audit partner and chief financial officer recalls', *Auditing: A Journal of Practice & Theory* 24(s-1), 171–193.

Gibbins, M., McCracken, S.A. and Salterio, S.E., 2007, 'The Chief Financial Officer's perspective on auditor-client negotiations', *Contemporary Accounting Research* 24(2), 387–422.

Gibbins, M., McCracken, S.A. and Salterio, S.E., 2010, 'The auditor's strategy selection for negotiation with management: Flexibility of initial accounting position and nature of the relationship', *Accounting, Organizations and Society* 35(6), 579–595.

Gibbins, M. and Newton, J.D., 1994, 'An empirical exploration of complex accountability in public accounting', *Journal of Accounting Research* 32(2), 165–186.

Gibbins, M. and Qu, S.Q., 2005, 'Eliciting experts' context knowledge with theory-based experiential questionnaires', *Behavioral Research in Accounting* 17(1), 71–88.

Gibbins, M., Salterio, S. and Webb, A., 2001, 'Evidence about auditor-client management negotiation concerning client's financial reporting', *Journal of Accounting Research* 39(3), 535–563.

Gibbins, M. and Trotman, K.T., 2002, 'Audit review: Managers' interpersonal expectations and conduct of the review', *Contemporary Accounting Research* 19(3), 411–444.

Graham, J.R., Harvey, C.R. and Rajgopal, S., 2005, 'The economic implications of corporate financial reporting', *Journal of Accounting and Economics* 40(1), 3–73.

Griffith, E.E., Hammersley, J.S. and Kadous, K., 2015, 'Audits of complex estimates as verification of management numbers: How institutional pressures shape practice', *Contemporary Accounting Research* 32(3), 833–863.

Hayne, C. and Salterio, S.E., 2014, 'Accounting and auditing', in M. Bovens, R.E. Goodin and T. Schillemans (eds.), *The Oxford Handbook of Public Accountability*, 421–440, Oxford University Press, Oxford, UK.

Herda, D.N. and Lavelle, J.J., 2012, 'Auditor commitment to privately held clients and its effect on value-added audit service', *Auditing: A Journal of Practice & Theory* 32(1), 113–137.

Hermanson, D.R., Tompkins, J.G., Veliyath, R. and Ye, Z.S., 2012, 'The compensation committee process', *Contemporary Accounting Research* 29(3), 666–709.

Hirst, D.E. and Koonce, L., 1996, 'Audit analytical procedures: A field investigation', *Contemporary Accounting Research* 13(2), 457–486.

Holland, J.H., Holyoak, K.J., Nisbett, R.E. and Thagard, P.R., 1989, *Induction: Processes of Inference, Learning, and Discovery*, MIT Press, Cambridge, MA.

Huelsbeck, D.P., Merchant, K.A. and Sandino, T., 2011, 'On testing business models', *The Accounting Review* 86(5), 1631–1654.

Ihantola, E. and Kihn, L., 2011, 'Threats to validity and reliability in mixed methods accounting research', *Qualitative Research in Accounting and Management* 8(1), 39–58.

Johnson, H.T. and Kaplan, R.S., 1987, *Relevance Lost: The Rise and Fall of Management Accounting*, Harvard Business School Press, Boston, MA.

Johnston, W.J., Leach, M.P. and Liu, A.H., 1999, 'Theory testing using case studies in business-to-business research', *Industrial Marketing Management* 28(3), 201–213.

Kaplan, R.S., 1998, 'Innovation action research: Creating new management theory and practice', *Journal of Management Accounting Research* 10, 89–118.

Kinney, W.R., 2003, 'New accounting scholars – does it matter what we teach them?', *Issues in Accounting Education* 18(1), 37–47.

Koonce, L., Anderson, U. and Marchant, G., 1995, 'Justification of decisions in auditing', *Journal of Accounting Research* 33(2), 369–384.

Kotchetova, N. and Salterio, S., 2004, 'Judgment and decision-making accounting research: A quest to improve the production, certification, and use of accounting information', in D.J. Koehler and N. Harvey (eds.), *Blackwell Handbook of Judgment and Decision Making*, 547–566, John Wiley & Sons, Hoboken, NJ.

Leary, M.R. and Kowalski, R.M., 1990, 'Impression management: A literature review and two-component model', *Psychological Bulletin* 107(1), 34–47.

Libby, R., 1981, *Accounting and Human Information Processing: Theory and Applications*, Prentice Hall, Upper Saddle River, NJ.

Libby, R., 1989, 'Experimental research and the distinctive features of accounting settings', in T. Frecka (ed.), *The State of Accounting Research as We Enter the 1990s*, 126–147, University of Illinois, Urbana, IL.

Libby, R., 1995, 'The role of knowledge and memory in audit judgment', in A.H. Ashton and R.H. Ashton (eds.), *Judgment and Decision-Making Research in Accounting and Auditing*, 176–206, Cambridge University Press Cambridge.

Libby, R., Bloomfield, R. and Nelson, M.W., 2002, 'Experimental research in financial accounting', *Accounting, Organizations and Society* 27(8), 775–810.

Libby, R. and Luft, J., 1993, 'Determinants of judgment performance in accounting settings: Ability, knowledge, motivation, and environment', *Accounting, Organizations and Society* 18(5), 425–450.

Lillis, A.M., 1999, 'A framework for the analysis of interview data from multiple field research sites', *Accounting and Finance* 39(1), 79–105.

Lillis, A.M., 2008, 'Qualitative management accounting research: Rationale, pitfalls and potential: A comment on Vaivio (2008)', *Qualitative Research in Accounting & Management* 5(3), 239–246.

Lillis, A.M. and Mundy, J., 2005, 'Cross-sectional field studies in management accounting research-closing the gaps between surveys and case studies', *Journal of Management Accounting Research* 17(1), 119–141.

Maas, V.S. and Matějka, M., 2009, 'Balancing the dual responsibilities of business unit controllers: Field and survey evidence', *The Accounting Review* 84(4), 1233–1253.

Malina, M.A., Nørreklit, H.S. and Selto, F.H., 2007, 'Relations among measures, climate of control, and performance measurement models', *Contemporary Accounting Research* 24(3), 935–982.

Malsch, B. and Salterio, S.E., 2016, '"Doing good field research": Assessing the quality of audit field research', *Auditing: A Journal of Practice & Theory* 35(1), 1–22.

McCracken, S., Salterio, S.E. and Schmidt, R.N., 2011, 'Do managers intend to use the same negotiation strategies as partners?', *Behavioral Research in Accounting* 23(1), 131–160.

Merchant, K.A., 1990, 'The effects of financial controls on data manipulation and management myopia', *Accounting, Organizations and Society* 15(4), 297–313.

Merchant, K.A. and Manzoni, J.-F., 1989, 'The achievability of budget targets in profit centers: A field study', *The Accounting Review* 64(3), 539–558.

Merchant, K. and Van der Stede, W., 2006, 'Field-based research in accounting: Accomplishments and prospects', *Behavioral Research in Accounting* 18(1), 117–134.

Mikes, A., 2011, 'From counting risk to making risk count: Boundary-work in risk management', *Accounting, Organizations and Society* 36(4), 226–245.

Moll, J. and Hoque, Z., 2011, 'Budgeting for legitimacy: The case of an Australian university', *Accounting, Organizations and Society* 36(2), 86–101.

Mundy, J., 2010, 'Creating dynamic tensions through a balanced use of management control systems', *Accounting, Organizations and Society* 35(5), F.499–523.

Naranjo-Gil, D. and Hartmann, F., 2007, 'Management accounting systems, top management team heterogeneity and strategic change', *Accounting, Organizations and Society* 32(7–8), 735–756.

Nelson, M.W., Elliott, J.A. and Tarpley, R.L., 2002, 'Evidence from auditors about managers' and auditors' earnings management decisions', *The Accounting Review* 77(1), 175–202.

Orne, M.T., 1962, 'On the social psychology of the psychological experiment: With particular reference to demand characteristics and their implications', *American Psychologist* 17(11), 776–783.

Patton, M.Q., 1990. *Qualitative Evaluation nd Research Methods*, Sage Publications, Inc., Thousand Oaks, CA.

Peecher, M.E. and Solomon, I., 2001, 'Theory and experimentation in studies of audit judgments and decisions: Avoiding common research traps', *International Journal of Auditing* 5(3), 193–203.

Power, M.K. and Gendron, Y., 2015, 'Qualitative research in auditing: A methodological roadmap', *Auditing: A Journal of Practice & Theory* 34(2), 147–165.

Pratt, M.G., 2009, 'For the lack of boilerplate: Tips on writing up (and reviewing) qualitative research', *Academy of Management Journal* 52(5), 856–862.

Rennie, M.D., Kopp, L.S. and Lemon, W.M., 2010, 'Exploring trust and the auditor-client relationship: Factors influencing the auditor's trust of a client representative', *Auditing: A Journal of Practice & Theory* 29(1), 279–293.

Ronan, W.W. and Latham, G.P., 1974, 'The reliability and validity of the critical incident technique: A closer look', *Studies in Personnel Psychology* 6(1), 53–64.

Rowe, C., Shields, M.D. and Birnberg, J.G., 2012, 'Hardening soft accounting information: Games for planning organizational change', *Accounting, Organizations and Society* 37(4), 260–279.

Salterio, S.E., 2012, 'Fifteen years in the trenches: Auditor – client negotiations exposed and explored', *Accounting & Finance* 52(1), 233–286.

Salterio, S.E. and Denham, R., 1997, 'Accounting consultation units: An organizational memory analysis', *Contemporary Accounting Research* 14(4), 669–691.

Savin-Baden, M. and Major, C.H., 2013, *Qualitative Research: The Essential Guide to Theory and Practice*, Routledge, London.

Schloetzer, J.D., 2012, 'Process integration and information sharing in supply chains', *The Accounting Review* 87(3), 1005–1032.

Schluter, J., Seaton, P. and Chaboyer, W., 2008, 'Critical incident technique: A user's guide for nurse researchers', *Journal of Advanced Nursing* 61(1), 107–114.

Schwarz, N. and Oyserman, D., 2001, 'Asking questions about behavior: Cognition, communication, and questionnaire construction', *American Journal of Evaluation* 22(2), 127–160.

Shadish, W.R., Cook, T.D. and Campbell, D.T., 2002, *Experimental and Quasi-Experimental Designs*, Houghton Mifflin Company, Boston, MA.

Shakespeare, W., 1606, *Macbeth*.

Shields, M.D., 2012, 'Understanding management accounting: Benefits and costs of experimental research', *Journal of Management Accounting Studies* 2(1), 15–38.

Smith, M., 2011, *Research Methods in Accounting* (2nd ed.), Sage Publication Inc., Thousand Oaks, CA.

Solomon, I. and Trotman, K.T., 2003, 'Experimental judgment and decision research in auditing: The first 25 years of AOS', *Accounting, Organizations and Society* 28(4), 395–412.

Soltes, E., 2014, 'Incorporating field data into archival research', *Journal of Accounting Research* 52(2), 521–540.

Sprinkle, G.B., 2003, 'Perspectives on experimental research in managerial accounting', *Accounting, Organizations and Society* 28(2), 287–318.

Swieringa, R.J. and Weick, K.E., 1982, 'An assessment of laboratory experiments in accounting', *Journal of Accounting Research* 20(Supplement), 56–101.

Tan, H., T., 2001, 'Methodological issues in measuring knowledge effects', *International Journal of Auditing* 5(3), 215–224.

Tan, H.-T. and Yip-Ow, J., 2001, 'Are reviewers' judgements influenced by memo structure and conclusions documented in audit workpapers?', *Contemporary Accounting Research* 18(4), 663–678.

Trompeter, G. and Wright, A., 2010, 'The world has changed – have analytical procedure practices?', *Contemporary Accounting Research* 27(2), 350–350.

Trotman, A.J. and Trotman, K.T., 2013, 'Internal audit's role in GHG emissions and energy reporting: Evidence from audit committees, senior accountants, and internal auditors', *Auditing: A Journal of Practice & Theory* 34(1), 199–230.

Trotman, K.T., 2001, 'Design issues in audit JDM experiments', *International Journal of Auditing* 5(3), 181–192.

Westermann, K., Bedard, J. and Earley, C., 2015, 'Learning the "craft" of auditing: A dynamic view of auditors' on-the-job learning', *Contemporary Accounting Research* 32(3), 864–896.

Whetten, D.A., 1989, 'What constitutes a theoretical contribution?', *Academy of Management Review* 14(4), 490–495.

Wilson, T.D. and Dunn, J., 2004, 'Self-knowledge: Its limits, value, and potential for improvement', *Annual Review of Psychology* 55, 1–26.

Wolf, F.M., 1981, 'The nature of managerial work: An investigation of the work of the audit manager', *The Accounting Review* (October 1), 861–881.

Woolsey, L.K., 1986, 'The critical incident technique: An innovative qualitative method of research', *Canadian Journal of Counselling and Psychotherapy* 20(4), 242–254.

Wouters, M. and Roijmans, D., 2011, 'Using prototypes to induce experimentation and knowledge integration in the development of enabling accounting information', *Contemporary Accounting Research* 28(2), 708–736.

Yin, R.K., 1984., *Case Study Research: Design and Methods*, Sage Publications, London.

Yin, R.K., 2014, *Case Study Research: Design and Methods* (5th ed.), Sage Publications, London.

Yoo, C.-Y. and Pae, J., 2017, 'Do analysts strategically employ cash flow forecast revisions to offset negative earnings forecast revisions?', *European Accounting Review* 26(2), 193–214.

Young, S.M., 1999, 'Field research methods in management accounting', *Accounting Horizons* 13(1), 76–84.

13

Maximizing the contribution of JDM-style experiments in accounting

Kathryn Kadous and Yuepin (Daniel) Zhou

Introduction

Accounting professionals' judgment plays a large role in what accounting numbers are reported and how they are used both within and outside the firm. For example, management accountants determine how to allocate resources and costs within a company, whether and how to tie compensation to worker performance, and how that performance is measured. Financial accountants and auditors determine the content of financial reports and the associated audit reports. For example, they decide when to recognize revenue from a complex contract, whether to impair assets from a recent acquisition, how to assess the fair value measurement of an asset with no ready market, how much of a tax reserve can be reversed this year, and the seriousness of a discovered weakness in internal controls. These judgments and decisions, in turn, affect economic outcomes for workers, managers, investors and creditors.

While researchers can study these important judgments using a variety of methods, judgment and decision-making (JDM) experiments provide unique value in determining the causal antecedents of important accounting judgments and providing insights into the judgment process. This chapter considers how researchers can maximize the contribution of their JDM-style experiments in accounting settings.[1] We begin with a discussion of the purpose and benefits of JDM studies in accounting, including what makes a JDM study an accounting JDM study. We then provide advice on developing high-impact accounting JDM research.

Purpose and benefits of JDM experiments in accounting

The primary comparative advantage of experiments lies in their ability to provide high-quality inferences about causal relationships (i.e., high internal validity). Establishing causality depends on demonstrating three criteria: the cause and the effect covary, the cause preceding the effect and no plausible alternative explanations (e.g., see Trochim, Donnelly and Arora 2015). Identifying which variables are causes and which are effects can be difficult in the natural world, but experimenters control the timing of the administration of the independent variable and the measurement of the dependent variable, and thus it is typically easy to determine that the theorized cause precedes the effect in an experiment. In addition, experimenters have the ability to manipulate constructs cleanly and to randomly assign individuals to experimental conditions. These features imply that experiments have strong "all else equal" conditions – that is, the only difference between conditions is the manipulated construct – which allows high confidence that the manipulated construct caused the observed effect. Thus, experiments allow for high-quality inferences about the directional impact of independent constructs on dependent constructs, and the primary purpose of JDM experimental research in accounting is to test generalizable theory about judgment and decision-making in accounting contexts.

A second advantage of JDM experimental methods lies in their ability to test the process leading to judgments and decisions. That is, with careful planning, researchers can sometimes insert into their experiment measures that unobtrusively capture participants' decision processes. For example, researchers might measure which information a participant views, the order in which a participant completes tasks, how long a participant takes to come to a judgment, and so forth. Process measures can provide corroboration of a theoretical account for an effect, providing a deeper understanding of the judgment than would be observed from analyzing decision outcomes alone. Process measures can also help to rule out potential alternative explanations that arise for the main result.[2] In any case, experiments that collect meaningful data about process provide high-quality evidence about *how and why* particular characteristics of the decision maker, the decision task and/or the decision context influence judgments and decisions. Thus, a secondary purpose of JDM experimental research in accounting is to provide insight into the decision process underlying JDM in accounting contexts.

A common criticism of experiments is that they lack external validity and thus are weak in generalizability. While there is some truth to this criticism, the nature of the limitation is not well understood. The limitation arises mainly from the fact that experimenters typically must choose one or a few values of their independent constructs to include in their experiments. To the extent that the types and strengths of the manipulations in the experiment are not representative of the types and strengths of the construct in the natural setting of interest, we cannot generalize effect sizes or relative effect sizes from experimental results. Thus, it is typically not very meaningful to extrapolate the size of the impact of an experimental manipulation to a real-world setting (Libby and Luft 1993). For example, if an experimental manipulation of accountability to a client causes auditors to be 30% more likely to agree with the client's aggressive reporting decisions, we can generalize that accountability to a client affects auditors' judgments in a particular direction, but we cannot have any certainty that the impact is 30% in the natural setting.[3]

This limitation is typically not limiting in practice because most experiments are designed to test for directional effects, rather than for the magnitude of effects. Importantly, there are other ways in which well-designed, theory-based experiments are a better basis for generalizing than are descriptive studies. For example, while a descriptive study based on archival data can perhaps best tell us what financial reporting decisions are made in a particular market under a particular set of constraints (legal, technological and otherwise) for a particular period of time, theory-based experiments can provide evidence that allows us to predict how such decisions would be made across a broader set of conditions – in other markets populated by individuals with different characteristics, under different constraints and at different times. The key is to keep in mind that *theories* are generalizable, not results.

This is not to say that generalizing is easy – experiments necessarily exclude certain contextual factors that potentially impinge on the judgments of interest, so the process of generalizing requires careful thought. But if the results are viewed through the lens of relevant theory, they provide a solid basis for generalizing to multiple contexts. For example, experiments supporting the idea that investors evaluate a firm's use of derivatives more favourably when the firm's decision to use derivatives is consistent (versus inconsistent) with industry norms deepens our understanding about the conditions under which investors react favourably or unfavourably to firms' business decisions, such as derivative use (Koonce, Miller and Winchel 2015).

In sum, high-quality JDM-style experiments have high inferential value and produce generalizable theory. A reasonable next question is "What makes them accounting experiments?" That is, how do we know when a study based on JDM theory makes a significant contribution to the accounting literature and should be published in an accounting journal, rather than a journal in some other field?

We propose that experimental researchers contribute to the accounting literature by developing and testing generalizable theory about decision-making *by accounting professionals* (auditors, CFOs, controllers, tax professionals, etc.) and/or about decision-making *using accounting information*. Relevant users of accounting information include analysts, investors and others who rely on external financial reports to make decisions about the company, as well as managers who rely on internal accounting information to manage the company.

One might ask how much accounting JDM research is needed, given the large amount of JDM research outside of accounting. The JDM literature beyond accounting is vast, but little of it examines the complex and unique conditions that characterize professional accounting settings. For example, JDM research in psychology, marketing and management tends to consider decisions of broad applicability (e.g., consumer purchasing decisions, hiring decisions) and often employs undergraduate students, online workers or other non-specialist groups as participants in stark, simple tasks. It typically does not consider expert decision makers, complex information sets, unstructured decision tasks, conflicting incentives or the like. There may be important features of a decision maker or decision context (or "constellations" of features [Solomon and Shields 2007]) that are not contemplated by the psychology research but are critical in accounting settings. Sometimes these features critical to understanding accounting decision-making are also individually important to the more basic research, but they are not always prioritized. As a result, researchers who seek to improve accounting decisions cannot rely on general JDM researchers to answer the questions for us – we need to address the questions that are of greatest importance to our field, regardless of whether other fields prioritize them. Thus, accounting researchers are in the best position to identify important drivers and moderators of accounting decisions, but we are also in a good position to contribute to the more general JDM literature through our institutional knowledge of more complex decision settings.

Conducting high-quality, impactful JDM research in accounting

The remainder of this chapter outlines a methodology for developing high-quality, impactful JDM research projects. While it is difficult to determine at the outset whether an experiment will yield interesting results and whether a research project will result in an impactful paper, researchers can take actions to maximize their chances of success. We discuss five important actions towards this goal in this section. In our discussion, we characterize these actions as steps; however, the "steps" are not necessarily sequential, but are in fact overlapping. These steps are summarized in Figure 13.1 and are discussed, in turn, below.

Step 1: gain deep knowledge

Conducting JDM research in accounting is difficult because it requires the researchers to amass knowledge and expertise across several areas. While a JDM researcher in psychology may be able to focus on a small set of theories and employ a stark decision context, JDM researchers in accounting typically are interested in more complex judgments that occur in specific contexts.

Step 1: Gain deep knowledge
- Be an expert in relevant theories
- Understand the institutional (accounting) setting
- Make connections between theories and the accounting setting of interest

Step 2: Address (an important piece of) a big question
- Find a big question that researchers and practitioners care about
- Isolate an important piece of the big question
- Recheck that the question has a meaningful connection to a real-world problem

Step 3: Follow the basic principles of good design
- Formulate hypotheses in advance
- Manipulate only your construct of interest
- Control for everything else
- Get enough observations to conduct a powerful test

Step 4: Honor the decision problem
- Use the right participant group
- Retain important task complexity and structure
- Use a dependent measure with ecological validity

Step 5: Learn something new
- Extend theory to a new decision setting
- Study conditions that do not exist or are under-represented in the natural world
- Test the process's underlying judgment and decision-making

Figure 13.1 Steps for conducting impactful JDM research in accounting

Accounting researchers typically need to combine or extend simpler theories to account for important contextual elements of the accounting environment (e.g., incentive structure, accountabilities and other institutional features), characteristics of expert decision makers (e.g., their specialized knowledge, their motives) and/or unique task features (e.g., the specific types of complexities involved, ambiguity). This means that, to be successful, JDM researchers in accounting must be experts in a fairly large set of relevant psychological theories, as well as in the task and decision setting of interest. The researcher has to know all of these components well in order to see the connections among various theories and between those theories and relevant institutional features of accounting settings. Seeing these connections is what allows researchers to appropriately apply and extend existing theories so that they are useful in the accounting context.

For example, consider a researcher interested in how auditors incorporate the advice they routinely receive from peers and specialists into their judgments. There is a wealth of JDM research on how advice is incorporated into final judgments, but nearly all of it examines how advice is used in answering general knowledge questions (a simple objective task) (Bonaccio and Dalal 2006). None of this research considers how advice is incorporated into complex judgments with significant ambiguity, such as assessments of the reasonableness of accounting estimates, though we know that these conditions (complexity, ambiguity) impact decisions and decision process. None of it considers how highly knowledgeable decision makers with potentially conflicting incentives to be right, to finish the job within budget and to support their client's and/or superior's preferred outcome use advice, though we also know that knowledge and incentives influence decision and decision process.[4] A deep understanding of both the theoretical realm and the applied setting enables researchers who are interested in use of advice in an accounting setting to identify the "gaps" between the existing theories and the accounting setting of interest, and ultimately combine and extend the theories to explain judgment in the accounting setting.

Gaining deep knowledge of theory and settings is also necessary for insight into whether and how the constructs map into the accounting setting. Understanding the mapping allows for meaningful extensions of existing theory, allowing for unique contributions to accounting, but also for meaningful contributions back to the discipline underlying the theory. Deep knowledge of relevant theory can also prevent unsuccessful attempts at applying theory to situations it cannot explain and the resulting frustration that comes along with unintelligible data.

A deep understanding of the prior literature is also useful in developing successful, impactful research projects. A researcher's understanding of the constructs at work and the theoretical mechanisms that drive them will be enhanced by knowledge of other researchers' findings relevant to those constructs and mechanisms. In addition, prior research can provide ideas about how to best manipulate and measure various constructs. If a researcher wants to manipulate a given construct, and the prior work that has manipulated it did so cleanly and in a way that translates into the setting of interest, it is sensible to use what has worked previously. Similarly, if prior research has developed a reliable measure of a construct, researchers can rely on the prior work rather than validating a new measure (or worse, using a new measure without validation).

In sum, developing deep knowledge of relevant JDM theories, accounting contexts, accounting tasks and prior literatures sets a researcher up for success by helping the researcher to identify meaningful research questions, by allowing the researcher insight into possible theoretical solutions to those questions and by pointing to validated measures and manipulations that can both save time and increase the quality of the experiment.

Step 2: address (an important piece of) a big question

A second key to conducting successful JDM research in accounting is to examine research questions that people care about. If you can shed light on a problem that is important to accounting practice and to other researchers in your field, your work is more likely to be impactful. This advice may seem obvious, but it is something that is easy to forget once a project is started and the researcher becomes attached to a planned project.

How does one find a big question to address? First, a researcher can keep abreast of current working research in his or her area by reading new working papers, attending talks by the top people in the field, and talking with peers about what interests them and what they are working on. What big problems are people in your area addressing? Do you have a unique insight into these problems (because you followed step #1!)? Do you have a potentially better way to address these problems (because you followed step #1!)? Second, one can ascertain what the leaders in the applied field care about by reading practitioner literature, attending talks by top practitioners, or seeking out contacts in practice. In either case, a variety of issues will come up, and the task is to identify common themes. Often, these themes will revolve around consequential tasks that managers, accountants, regulators or investors struggle with. For example, in management accounting, firms struggle with the use of subjective performance measures, and research has studied factors that influence how managers measure and use subjective performance evaluations (e.g., Bailey, Hecht and Towry 2011; Bol and Smith 2011). This represents an issue with important real-world implications that has benefited much from research recently. In auditing, regulators and practitioners struggle with audit testing of management estimates. Research has accordingly focused on developing insight into auditors' performance of this task and interventions to improve that performance (Cannon and Bedard 2016; Griffith, Hammersley and Kadous 2015; Griffith, Hammersley, Kadous and Young 2015; Rasso 2015).

Some researchers take the advice to focus on a big question to mean that they must address a "broad" question and find "the" answer to that broad question. A broad question is not typically answerable by a single empirical study, and that is particularly true if that study is an experiment. Because the strength of experiments is in isolating and testing causal relationships, well-designed experiments will necessarily examine only a few variables and a few relationships at a time. Successful studies isolate an important piece of a big question. Researchers can accomplish this by starting with an important question and "checking in" with themselves periodically as the project is evolving to ensure that the focus of the study remains on an important piece of the puzzle.

For example, the question "How do disclosure formats affect investor judgments?" is too broad to study in a meaningful way. When narrowing this question to develop testable hypotheses, a researcher might consider how the question maps into prior research and existing theories, what theoretical constructs are key, and whether these constructs relate to important aspects of the problem. Since the answer to such a broad question is almost certainly "it depends", a researcher might find it useful to consider the key contingencies (e.g., content, linguistic features, timing of the disclosure or features of the investors). For example, some issues to consider include: What disclosure formats are often used in practice? Why did these formats become popular? Are features of these formats likely to draw attention to one type of information or another? Are they likely to induce a particular decision strategy? Will these effects improve the quality of decision-making or make it worse? Might the disclosures be more effective for some investors if they were in different formats? What problems do managers worry about in terms of investor understanding of these disclosures?

Once the researcher has identified a potential research question, it is sensible to recheck that the question has a meaningful connection to a real-world problem. This doesn't mean that the research project will immediately solve a real-world problem, but it does mean that it will enlighten readers about some important aspect of that problem or a potential solution. For example, a demonstration that readability of the disclosure has a greater impact on investors' judgment when disclosure contains inconsistent performance measures does not provide a comprehensive view of how disclosure formats affect investors' judgment, but it does provide important insights into, for example, why managers may have incentives to selectively make disclosure with unfavourable implication more difficult to read (Tan, Wang and Zhou 2015).

Finally, it is important to keep in mind that the ultimate goals of accounting JDM research are to understand and to improve judgment and decision-making (Bonner 2008; Maines 1995). This does not imply that each study needs to demonstrate a decision problem (i.e., "irrationality") in order to make a contribution. Better understanding how important judgments and decisions are made is a valuable end in itself. It also does not imply that a study need develop a methodology or tool that business can use immediately in order to be valuable. While some studies may develop tools for immediate application, most studies will advance our understanding of accountants' decision-making and decision-making using accounting information by providing evidence about causal relationships and decision process.[5] As several others have noted, science is cumulative, and understanding decision processes is a key step to improving decisions (Bonner 2008; Weber and Johnson 2009).

Step 3: follow the basic principles of good design

Once the researcher has identified an important question to which she can meaningfully apply her theoretical and practical knowledge, the next step is to practice good design. Rather than provide a comprehensive discussion of good experimental design, which is available in various research methods texts (e.g., see Kerlinger and Lee 1999; Shadish, Cook and Campbell 2002; Trochim et al. 2015), we focus on four key aspects of design that are particularly important for research that is situated in an applied (context-rich) setting: (a) formulate hypotheses in advance, (b) manipulate (only!) your construct of interest, (c) control for everything else and (d) get enough observations to conduct a powerful test. These design guidelines set the project up for success by increasing the chances that the experiment will identify important, replicable effects. They may also save time that would be spent trying to interpret messy data.

Formulate hypotheses in advance

Hypotheses are relational propositions that are deduced from theory. Formulating testable hypotheses is a key step in the scientific process. The scientific method, and, in particular, statistical significance testing, assumes that hypotheses are specified in advance of observation. Researchers who work the other way around – who observe the data and then capitalize on observed relationships to generate hypotheses, ex post – run the risk of overgeneralizing from chance observations. In other words, statistically significant effects associated with ex post hypotheses are less likely to represent true effects, and less likely to be replicable. Thus, formulating hypotheses in advance helps to control for Type I errors, i.e., incorrectly rejecting a true null hypothesis.

Hypotheses play another important role – they direct the research design process. For example, hypotheses inform important steps such as designing materials and providing the appropriate context for testing. Well thought-out hypotheses can set up a study for success. It is tempting to believe that the hard work in research lies in identifying an interesting question, and that once the research question has been identified, one can manipulate the independent variables and the magic will happen. While occasionally a researcher might get lucky following this procedure, successful experiments are typically carefully designed to test the specific hypotheses of interest.

In order to formulate specific hypotheses, a researcher is compelled to think carefully about the independent constructs of interest and how they might best be operationalized, the relevant dependent constructs and how they might be measured, and the conditions under which the hypothesis is expected to hold. Deliberate, focused attention to these design steps increases the study's chances for success. The importance of getting these details right is magnified in an applied field, such as accounting, in which tasks and decision settings are rich and varied.

For example, a researcher who studies self-control theory and wants to demonstrate that cognitive depletion will worsen auditors' JDM would not be well served by simply selecting a popular experimental task for auditors, providing a relevant manipulation and observing what happens. Such a study might be successful if the researcher has good intuition and good luck, but a more reliable approach involves going deeper into theory and making the intuition explicit. In the example given, relevant questions include: Exactly how and why will depletion affect cognitive processing? Which cognitive processes are impacted and which are not? For which audit tasks are the impacted processes critical to success? That is, where will these processing differences translate into performance differences? Of these impacted tasks, are any particularly consequential? For example, have auditors demonstrated unsatisfactory performance in them? This knowledge must then be combined with knowledge of the context in which the task is normally performed (e.g., motivation, accountability, distractions, etc.) in order to fully assess how and under what conditions the hypothesized relationship would manifest. A researcher who has thought through all of these issues is more likely to identify a meaningful judgment task with real-world importance that needs improvement, to design an experiment that will be able to demonstrate this improvement if the causal relationship is true and to capture the process by which the improvement occurs. She will also have very specific, testable hypotheses.

When designing the experiment to test these well thought-out hypotheses, it is helpful to use the simplest design that matches the setting of interest. This is difficult to do in an applied setting, as there are typically numerous potential boundary conditions and qualifiers in the natural settings, and it is tempting to manipulate these additional variables, as well. However, resource constraints typically prevent this. Thinking through the potential moderators and boundary conditions will be useful in identifying the conditions most representative of the problematic state. For example, if a researcher expects that a particular type of training will improve managers' task performance, it is important that the researcher consider, when designing the study, whether the positive impact of the training also depends on other factors such as managers' knowledge, experience, personality traits or task characteristics. A review of the prior literature may suggest that some of those factors are predicted to interact with the independent variable. A natural follow-up question is then whether the potential moderator should be included in the study. For example, would it be interesting to show that performance improvement after training is larger for less experienced managers than for more experienced managers because the more experienced managers already perform quite well on the task prior to the training? Would the training be expected to be more effective for some tasks than others? Research design choices such as these depend, in part, on power and resource availability issues (discussed below). Regardless, identifying good design choices requires a thorough understanding of the relevant literature, the task and the institutional setting. Developing specific hypotheses helps ensure that the design matches the theory and the setting, and so the project will ultimately provide meaningful evidence about the research question.

Another important benefit of generating hypotheses in advance is that doing so allows the researcher to graph expected results. This practice serves multiple purposes. First, seeing a display of the expected results can help researchers determine whether the hypotheses are "interesting". In our experience, it is not uncommon for researchers to get carried away with testing an interesting theory and fail to realize that the specific hypotheses they are proposing are either not unique or do not capture an important implication of the theory. Drawing a simple graph can prevent these problems by forcing researchers to consider what they can (and cannot!) conclude if their hypotheses are supported.

Second, the display, in conjunction with a power analysis (discussed below), can help researchers determine whether the study has a reasonable chance of finding support for the hypotheses if they are true. For example, standard statistical methods such as traditional analysis of variance are not a good tool for testing for many specific patterns of cell means (e.g., Rosnow and Rosenthal 1996), but the use of more appropriate contrast methods requires greater depth of theorizing and additional statistical considerations (Guggenmos, Piercey and Agoglia 2016). To the extent expectations are not readily testable with standard methods, researchers can evaluate whether alternative methods are available.

Finally, graphing expected results can often help the researcher to sharpen hypotheses or think about important moderators that were not adequately considered in the original hypothesis development. For example, the researcher may be unable to draw the graph for a two-factor experiment without specifying a level of a third variable. This will prompt the researcher to consider whether the third variable should be manipulated or held constant at the appropriate level and, ultimately, whether the study should be pursued, given limited applicability of the hypothesis. Thus, drawing a graph of expected results can help researchers to avoid costly mistakes and can sharpen theory development.

Manipulate (only!) your construct of interest

To maximize the comparative advantage of experiments, researchers should design the experiment to ensure that the causal relationship of interest is tested in a way that allows for high-quality inferences. Using a strong manipulation is generally preferred, but it is perhaps even more important to use a "clean" or unconfounded manipulation. This step is more difficult in applied settings such as accounting, and it is a particular stumbling block for accounting researchers who want to simultaneously test a theory and conclude directly about the wording of an accounting standard or some other institutional feature that does not map cleanly into the theoretical construct. We encourage researchers in this position to very clearly define their constructs of interest. This can make designing a manipulation straightforward – once the construct is clearly defined, it may be a matter of varying only the necessary words relating to that construct. Where possible, researchers should consider using previously validated manipulations. For example, in auditing there are well-validated means of manipulating engagement risk (e.g., Hackenbrack and Nelson 1996), accountability (e.g., Kennedy 1993) and supervisor preferences (Peecher 1996). The psychology literature is also a good source of previously validated manipulations (e.g., ambient affect, [Forgas and George 2001]).

In some cases, tried and true manipulations are not available or do not apply to the setting of interest, and researchers must develop new manipulations. When doing so, researchers may benefit from use of pilot testing. Pilot testing allows researchers to find answers to questions such as whether participants pay attention and react to the manipulation, whether the manipulation is sufficiently strong and whether the manipulation is "clean" versus impacts other constructs that are not of interest.

Researchers must take special care to avoid introducing confounds when manipulating psychological constructs. For example, if the construct is a psychological one that can be primed nonconsciously, such as a social identity, a mindset or a goal, the researcher may feel pressure to make the manipulation more "realistic" by incorporating it into decision aids or task instructions that resemble those that currently appear in the natural setting instead of following the prior research. The researcher should carefully think through the costs and benefits of embedding the manipulation in decision aids or instructions if validated manipulations are available. Often, the scientific benefits of doing so are negligible, while the costs are high (see also Griffith, Kadous and Young 2016).

Realism may be valuable, for instance, if a validated manipulation would be so jarring as to prevent participants from engaging in their normal decision processes when performing the experimental task. This is unlikely to occur when the question of interest relates to whether and how a primed construct influences task performance because priming manipulations typically occurs before, rather than during, task performance and does not disrupt normal task performance. Situating the manipulation in the task, on the other hand, will disrupt natural task performance. If the manipulation is further altered to look more realistic by altering case instructions across conditions, the researcher loses control of the construct being manipulated, typically by confounding it with other constructs (e.g., related to documentation). This can lead to unexpected effects, and, more importantly, to an inability to attribute changes in dependent measures to the construct of interest.

For example, a researcher priming a particular mindset using a validated manipulation can be confident she is manipulating the desired construct. However, a researcher who designs a decision aid incorporating ideas from the mindset literature cannot be sure that she has manipulated the desired mindset, and that researcher must also be concerned she has manipulated documentation and/or framing and/or other constructs. This causes inference problems. While the first researcher can infer how the particular mindset (a theoretical construct) influences task performance, the second researcher can only infer how her particular decision aid (an operationalization) influences task performance. Using a "clean", validated manipulation helps to ensure that the experiment addresses the constructs of interest. This is necessary to ensure the experiment tests the causal relationship it was intended to test and produces generalizable knowledge.

Control for everything else

Once the right manipulation is selected or designed, researchers can further increase their chances of conducting a successful study by designing the study to maximize the signal-to-noise ratio, or the chances that the effect will stand out from random error. We previously mentioned that a strong, clean manipulation is critical. In addition, the researcher should attempt to control for everything other than the manipulation of interest in designing a study and testing hypotheses. There are at least four methods of control: randomly assigning participants to conditions, fixing variables, stratifying the sample and employing covariates.

When used with a design that includes an appropriate control condition, random assignment of participants to conditions is the researcher's most important tool for making high-quality inferences. Because random assignment provides every participant with an equal chance of being assigned to a given condition, any variables associated with the participants (age, experience, gender, etc.) that can affect the dependent variable are spread equally across conditions in expectation. This allows researchers to make comparisons across conditions in which only the manipulations of interest differ across conditions.

Random assignment to conditions should always be used, if possible. It allows for conceptually persuasive comparisons across conditions, as noted above. Moreover, by spreading the effects of nuisance variables across conditions, it facilitates statistical isolation of the effect of the manipulation (systematic variance) from the effects of otherwise uncontrolled variables (error variance) (e.g., see Kerlinger and Lee 1999). It accomplishes control for "everything else" without the researcher having to know exactly what constitutes "everything else".

While random assignment of participants to conditions provides experimental control in the sense of allowing the researcher to separate the impact of the independent variable from the impact of other variables, it leaves the impact of those nuisance variables in the error variance, which reduces the power of tests of hypotheses. Therefore, if the researcher can identify variables associated with participants that are associated with the dependent variable and are not of theoretical interest, these can be controlled for more specifically.

Two alternatives for this additional control are to fix or stratify across variables that are expected to impact the dependent variable, but are not strictly of interest to the researcher. In each case, deep knowledge of the decision setting will aid the researcher in determining what variables are candidates for these methods of control. For example, if the target task is only performed by accountants with at least two years of relevant work experience, then it is sensible to fix the participants' work experience at a minimum of two years. Similarly, if the task is necessarily performed under particular conditions (say, high accountability), and the effect of those conditions is not of interest to the study, it makes sense to fix those conditions, as well. Alternatively, if accountants working for different sized firms or investors with different sized portfolios are expected to react to the independent variables in the same way, but to have different baseline levels of the dependent measure, stratifying the sample by firm or portfolio size (and assigning participants randomly to conditions within each strata) will be helpful. In the first case (fixing), the variability due to the nuisance variables is eliminated by focusing the sample on one level of the nuisance variable. In the second case (stratification), the variability can be statistically associated with a blocking variable and removed from the error variance, increasing the power of hypothesis tests.

Use of these methods requires researchers to have measures of nuisance variables and the ability to assign participants to conditions based on these variables, ex ante. This is not always feasible. Knowledge of relevant theories and the setting can also help researchers to identify candidates for variables that can be measured and included in the analysis, ex post, as covariates. Like other nuisance variables, candidates for covariates are typically variables associated with the participants that are expected to affect the dependent variable, but are not of theoretical interest. For example, if the dependent variable is likely to be associated with individual characteristics of participants (personality traits, intelligence, particular types of knowledge or experience, attitudes towards risk, pre-study attitudes or assessments, etc.), and these individual differences do not interact with the independent variable in models for the dependent variable, the individual difference measures are candidates for use as covariates. Including them in the model will reduce error variance and improve the power of tests of hypotheses.

That said, accounting researchers employing covariates should take care to ensure that the conceptual and statistical assumptions underlying their use are met. Effective covariates are related to the dependent variable (if not, there is no value in including them) but unrelated to the independent variables. This implies that covariates should be measured prior to the study or should not be affected by the study. For example, measures of personality traits, knowledge or experience levels, or stable attitudes will not likely be influenced by the study. On the other hand, use of covariates that represent reactions to the experimental materials, such as assessments of misstatement risk or management integrity, the participant's mood, time spent on task, etc., is typically not appropriate.[6] The main concern with such covariates is that they can be influenced by the independent variables, and, if they are, including them in the model will divert part of the variance attributable to the independent variables to the covariate, instead, and thus the goal of the sharpening hypotheses tests is not achieved (e.g., Neter, Kutner, Nachtsheim and Wasserman 1996).

The analysis of covariance model also assumes that covariates do not interact with independent variables. If this assumption does not hold, and the covariate is included without interaction terms, results of tests of hypotheses will be inaccurate and potentially misleading. To avoid these issues, researchers should verify that proposed covariates are not statistically associated with independent variables and do not interact with independent variables in modelling the dependent variable. Again, the best way to do this is to use variables that are collected prior to the study or that will not be influenced by the study.

Get enough observations to conduct a powerful test

Finally, experiments based on small samples can have insufficient power to identify effects of the independent variable, even when those effects are present. Thus, it is important to obtain a sample large enough to conduct powerful tests of hypotheses. This is, of course, easier said than done, especially when accounting or investing professionals are needed as participants. Obtaining professional participants is costly; however, conducting underpowered experiments that have little chance of finding effects and little chance of resulting in publishable papers is also costly. For this reason, it is sensible to use a power calculation to determine the minimum appropriate sample size when planning an experiment (e.g., see Keppel and Wickens 2004: 169–177; or Kerlinger and Lee 1999: 295–299). Such a calculation may reveal that the originally planned study is not feasible or that a reallocation of participants across studies is needed.

An additional risk of small-sample experiments is that they can lead to false identification of relationships that do not exist in the larger population. This can occur because smaller samples are less likely to be representative of the population than are large samples. Thus, a statistically significant effect observed in a small sample is less likely to represent a true effect, and less likely to be replicable (Button et al. 2013). In sum, making thoughtful, intentional design choices can increase a study's chances of identifying important, significant and replicable effects and save valuable time that would otherwise be spent trying to interpret or salvage poor data.

Step 4: honour the decision problem

Once the researcher has identified a meaningful research question and established a solid set of hypotheses and basic research design, it is a good time to reassess additional design issues to ensure that the problem is addressed in a productive way. The researcher should keep in mind the real-world decision problem of interest and make choices consistent with solving that decision problem. We call this "honouring the decision problem". A variety of choices can be impacted here, but we focus on three decision rules: use the right participant group, retain important task complexity and structure and use a dependent measure with ecological validity.[7] Again, the researcher must rely on her knowledge and understanding of relevant theories and the decision setting of interest to execute these decision rules well.

Which participant group to use can be a thorny problem. As others have noted, accounting research need not always sample directly from the population of interest to provide useful, meaningful results (Elliott, Hodge, Kennedy and Pronk 2007; Libby, Bloomfield and Nelson 2002; Peecher and Solomon 2001). For example, graduate or undergraduate students can sometimes be appropriate substitutes for more difficult to obtain participant groups. We encourage researchers to consider their theory in determining the ideal participant group for a study. If the theory implicates characteristics of the decision maker (e.g., knowledge, experience, understanding of a setting, personality traits, etc.), participants should match the population of interest, at least on these important dimensions. Similarly, if the study relies on professionals (auditors, analysts, etc.) using the decision processes or attending to the incentives in place in their natural setting, then participants should be drawn from the group of interest. On the other hand, if the theory is a general decision-making theory that does not depend on these characteristics, then students or a group drawn from the general population will be at least as appropriate as a group of professionals.

In applied decision settings, researchers are typically interested in describing and improving upon the judgments and decisions of those who typically make the judgments in the real world. This situation implies that researchers should retain theory-relevant task complexity and structure in their experiments. Task complexity and task structure have profound effects on the judgment and decision processes used in completing tasks (e.g., Bonner 2008; Wood, Mento and Locke 1987). Researchers seeking to examine (or influence) the process used in the natural setting will obtain the most meaningful results if they replicate the complexity and structure in their experimental instruments, insofar as it is relevant to the research question. For example, examining performance in complex tasks that require decision makers to incorporate information from various sources may require experimental tasks with multiple sources of information. Likewise, examining tasks that are typically performed in a deliberate, analytical way may require providing participants with access to the numerical information and the tools they normally use to complete the task.

The advice to include relevant task complexity and structure does not imply that every aspect of the natural task need be reflected in the experimental task or that the experimental materials include the vast amount of information that would be available in the real world. This sort of mundane realism is not helpful and can interfere with the quality of inference if it requires incorporating distracting context with impacts that are difficult to hold constant across conditions or information that would typically be ignored in the real-world setting. It can also limit the sample size, as participants are typically less willing to engage in longer experiments. The goal is to replicate the deep structure of the task and to provide enough context and structure that (a) the theory can be tested and (b) participants will engage the processes that they normally use in practice in your experimental task.

Finally, researchers examining important real-world decision problems would do well to use an ecologically valid dependent variable. For example, if one is interested in how auditors make conclusions about particular types of accounts, the researcher might ask for an audit conclusion in its natural form (rather than in a multiple-choice question or on a Likert scale) and code dependent measures from that conclusion. Such dependent variables are typically meaningful, in that they represent decisions made by real-world decision makers. Their use enhances the potential contribution of the study in at least two ways. First, it puts pressure on the researcher to really think through how the theory applies to the setting, increasing the chances of a successful experiment. Second, it works in concert with retaining task structure and complexity to ensure that decision makers use the same decision processes they would use when doing the task on the job. If the final decision or product is something other than what participants normally do on the job, this may alter how participants get there. In sum, this step increases the researcher's chances of learning something important to the setting of interest.

Step 5: learn something new

A final step is to design the experiment so as to learn something new. In terms of theory and setting, accounting researchers can contribute back to psychology and other basic disciplines by extending theory to a complex setting or to expert decision makers or both. For example, theories about mindsets suggest, but do not go so far as to predict, how a deliberative mindset might affect cognitive processing on complex tasks. Accounting researchers have extended this relatively high-level theory, making it useful for predicting which complex accounting tasks will benefit most from decision makers being in a deliberative mindset (Griffith, Hammersley, Kadous and Young 2015). Accounting researchers can also contribute by extending theory with modifiers of previously identified effects that are important to the accounting setting. For example, Nelson and Rupar (2015) extend the ratio bias effect documented in prior psychology research by identifying two important boundary conditions in the accounting context – investors' awareness of managerial discretion and their cognitive capacity. These theoretical extensions constitute a contribution to the discipline that theory is drawn from as well as to accounting. Because researchers in the underlying discipline are not familiar with the accounting setting and typically have non-expert participants and simpler questions to ask, it is unlikely they would prioritize these important questions. Accounting researchers thus have the opportunity to contribute to multiple literatures.

In terms of method, experiments allow researchers to independently manipulate constructs to create conditions that do not exist or that are under-represented in the natural world.[8] This means that experiments allow researchers to identify separate effects of constructs that are typically confounded in nature, and they allow for ex ante tests of policies and interventions that have not yet been put in place. For example, accounting researchers have shown that certain proposed regulations, such as lowering disclosure thresholds and accounting for lease renewal options, could have unintended consequences for investors' and managers' behaviours (e.g., Fanning, Agoglia and Piercey 2015; Hales, Venkataraman and Wilks 2012).

Experiments can also be designed to test decision process. Developing an understanding of the how and why behind judgment and decision-making effects is perhaps the best way to extend theory and generate new theory. Doing so provides valuable information for applied decision settings as well as for future theoretical applications. For example, understanding whether a manipulation makes decision makers apply more effort versus use of a different cognitive strategy is useful in determining the conditions under which the manipulation will and will not improve JDM quality.

Methods of collecting data on decision process range from asking participants about their process in the post-experimental questionnaire (e.g., "How deeply did you think about management's estimate?", "How hard did you work on the task?" or "Briefly explain how you generated your answer.") to gathering relatively unobtrusive indicators of cognitive processing (e.g., time spent on various types of information, order that information was viewed). A concern with asking participants about their decision process is that they may lack insight into it. This is particularly true with "why" questions. As others have noted, decision makers can typically generate plausible reasons for their decisions, but the reasons are often incorrect and/or incomplete (Anderson 2005; Nisbett and Wilson 1977). In general, unobtrusive measures provide better inferential value.

One effective method for testing cognitive processes in experimental research involves asking for an open-ended response to an information set, and then coding the responses for cognitive complexity or specific types of processing. This method requires rich ex ante theory because the researcher must be able to determine in advance how participants' responses can be coded to test the theory. The method has been used to provide evidence about how auditors construct problem representations, including the extent to which they elaborate on information and abstract from the basic facts to overriding concepts (Christ 1993; Griffith 2016) and whether they can identify misstatements based on incomplete cue patterns (Hammersley 2006).

Alternatively, a researcher can design a study such that she can infer decision process from responses. For example, a study can be designed such that a highly effortful process results in one response and a less effortful process results in a different response (Clor-Proell and Maines 2014; Mocadlo 2016). Alternatively, issues requiring different types of cognitive processing can be seeded into experimental material and the researcher can learn about process by testing whether different sets of items are identified in different experimental conditions. These methods can be combined for powerful, unobtrusive tests of process. For example, researchers can seed errors that require different types of processing to identify in experimental materials, ask an open-ended question that gets at problems identified (for example, an audit conclusion memo), and code responses for seeded problem items requiring different types and amounts of processing. This method has been successfully applied in auditing contexts to determine that putting auditors in a deliberative mindset improves their identification of biased accounting estimates by increasing their ability to identify and incorporate conflicting information into their analyses (Griffith, Hammersley, Kadous and Young 2015) and that making auditors' intrinsic motivation for their jobs salient improves their judgment about unreasonable complex estimates by improving their depth and breadth of information processing (Kadous and Zhou 2016).

Testing the decision process provides more convincing evidence that the proposed theory is responsible for the observed results. However, it is worth emphasizing that testing process requires careful assessment of what constitutes an appropriate process measure for the study. Good process measures are directly relevant to theory, are measured relatively unobtrusively (so that the participants do not use them to attempt to explain a decision), and truly get at process, rather than outcome. Modelling "process" with variables that capture an alternative version of the dependent measure or a variable mechanically related to the dependent variable does not provide the additional insights that true examination of process provides. Researchers should carefully think through what consists of a convincing set of evidence for establishing the predicted process to readers.

Conclusion

JDM research in accounting develops and tests generalizable theory about decision-making by accounting professionals and/or about decision-making using accounting information. JDM-style experiments allow for high-quality inferences about causal relationships and to understand the underlying process of how decisions are being made. That said, impactful JDM research does not just happen – impactful studies require significant background effort and planning. We describe a methodology that will help JDM researchers maximize the contribution of their research. Specifically, we recommend that JDM researchers (a) gain deep knowledge of relevant theories and the accounting setting of interest; (b) address (an important piece of) a big question; (c) follow the basic principles of good design, including formulating hypotheses in advance, manipulating key constructs cleanly while controlling for everything else and obtaining enough observations to conduct powerful tests; (d) honour the decision problem by using the appropriate participants, task, and dependent measures and (e) learn something new by extending theory via new variables or settings or by examining decision process.

The five steps that we outline are not exhaustive and, in fact, will not always flow in sequential order. Rather, they represent a set of overlapping considerations that researchers will need to address iteratively. Our goal in providing the steps is to emphasize issues that we find to be of particular importance in designing high-quality, impactful JDM research in the complex applied field of accounting. An important conclusion that can be drawn from our discussion is that high-quality, impactful research does not just happen – it is carefully and extensively planned.

Notes

1 The chapter assumes that readers have a basic understanding of experimental design, including the strengths and weaknesses of various types of experimental designs (e.g., single group pretest/posttest, two-groups posttest only, factorial) and the importance and value of random assignment of participants to conditions (see Shadish, Cook and Campbell 2002; Trochim, Donnelly and Arora 2015, for treatment of this material).

2 It is sometimes difficult to measure process unobtrusively. In this case, conducting a carefully planned series of experiments can achieve the same goals (Spencer, Zanna and Fong 2005).

3 A second issue limiting generalizability is that an experiment necessarily examines a small piece of a complex professional judgment. Thus, to the extent that the experiment controls for or abstracts away from potential modifiers of the theoretical effect, we cannot generalize directly to settings with these features without relying on other research. In such cases, we can turn to theory, logic or other empirical results for guidance, or we can conduct additional studies. For example, many audit JDM experiments examine audit seniors' judgments, but in the natural setting these judgments are typically reviewed by a manager before they are finalized. This situation may not be problematic for generalizing if, for example, the theorized effect does not rely on experience or knowledge, and so will occur for the manager as well as the senior, or if the theorized effect involves the senior failing to consider (and pass along to the manager so that she can consider) a critical piece of information. In the latter case, the manager is unlikely to "see" what is missing (Rich, Solomon and Trotman 1997).

4 See Kadous, Leiby and Peecher (2013) and Knechel and Leiby (2016) for extensions of advice-taking theory that incorporate important institutional features of the audit setting and generate new theory and findings that contribute to psychology research, as well as to accounting research.

5 It may appear that studies focusing on theoretical relationships without developing readily usable tools are less valuable to practice, but this is not necessarily true. As we discuss in detail later, a study focused on maintaining high internal validity is more readily generalizable to various practical settings than a study focused on developing a practical decision aid. The former provides practitioners with useful information about what factors influence decision quality and how the manipulation used in the experiment can be customized to suit in various settings; whereas the latter provides ambiguous information about the causal mechanism and is not generalizable beyond the specific intervention used as a manipulation in the study.

6 An exception occurs when the analysis is part of a path or mediation analysis getting at process.

7 A fourth consideration could be to retain important incentives and motives from the natural decision setting, including the trade-offs and conflicts that arise from those incentives and motives. We omit this consideration from our list only because we observe that these issues are currently the focus of much research in auditing and in managerial accounting, and, as a result, they are often incorporated more directly in JDM studies. When these issues are not the focus of the study, however, we encourage researchers to honour the decision problem by retaining these features, as well.

8 It is important to note that while it may seem straightforward to design an experiment that tests the effects of a proposed regulatory change, the same principles of good design apply. In particular, the results of ex ante tests of non-existent or under-represented conditions are most meaningful and generalizable if the study tests theory underlying these effects, and thus provides high-quality inference about causal relationship at work. That is, it is typically not possible to test the precise form of the proposed change in the relevant setting and with the relevant players, so generalization of theory is required.

References

Anderson, J.R., 2005, *Cognitive Psychology and Its Implications* (6th ed.), Worth Publishers, Princeton, NJ.

Bailey, W.J., Hecht, G. and Towry, K.L., 2011, 'Dividing the pie: The influence of managerial discretion extent on bonus pool allocation', *Contemporary Accounting Research* 28(5), 1562–1584.

Bol, J.C. and Smith, S.D., 2011, 'Spillover effects in subjective performance evaluation: Bias and the asymmetric influence of controllability', *The Accounting Review* 86(4), 1213–1230.

Bonaccio, S. and Dalal, R.S., 2006, 'Advice taking and decision-making: An integrative literature review, and implications for the organizational sciences', *Organizational Behavior and Human Decision Processes* 101(2), 127–151.

Bonner, S.E., 2008, *Judgment and Decision Making in Accounting*, Pearson/Prentice Hall, Upper Saddle River, NJ.

Button, K.S., Ioannidis, J.P.A., Mokrysz, C., Nosek, B.A., Flint, J., Robinson, E.S.J. and Munafo, M.R., 2013, 'Power failure: Why small sample size undermines the reliability of neuroscience', *National Review of Neuroscience* 14(5), 365–376.

Cannon, N. and Bedard, J.C., 2016, 'Auditing challenging fair value measurements: Evidence from the field', *The Accounting Review* (May 1).

Christ, M.Y., 1993, 'Evidence on the nature of audit planning problem representations: An examination of auditor free recalls', *The Accounting Review* 68(2), 304–322.

Clor-Proell, S.M. and Maines, L.A., 2014, 'The impact of recognition versus disclosure on financial information: A preparer's perspective', *Journal of Accounting Research* 52(3), 671–701.

Elliott, W.B., Hodge, F.D., Kennedy, J.J. and Pronk, M., 2007, 'Are M.B.A. students a good proxy for nonprofessional investors?', *The Accounting Review* 82(1), 139–168.

Fanning, K., Agoglia, C.P. and Piercey, M.D., 2015, 'Unintended consequences of lowering disclosure thresholds', *The Accounting Review* 90(1), 301–320.

Forgas, J.P. and George, J.M., 2001, 'Affective influences on judgments and behavior in organizations: An information processing perspective', *Organizational Behavior and Human Decision Processes* 86(1), 3–34.

Griffith, E.E., 2016, 'When do auditors use specialists' work to develop richer problem representations of complex estimates?', *SSRN*, http://ssrn.com/abstract=2837962.

Griffith, E.E., Hammersley, J.S. and Kadous, K., 2015, 'Audits of complex estimates as verification of management numbers: How institutional pressures shape practice', *Contemporary Accounting Research* 32(3), 833–863.

Griffith, E.E., Hammersley, J.S., Kadous, K. and Young, D., 2015, 'Auditor mindsets and audits of complex estimates', *Journal of Accounting Research* 53(1), 49–77.

Griffith, E.E., Kadous, K. and Young, D., 2016, 'How insights from the "new" JDM research can improve auditor judgment: Fundamental research questions and methodological advice', *Auditing: A Journal of Practice & Theory* 35(2), 1–22.

Guggenmos, R.D., Piercey, M.D. and Agoglia, C.P., 2016, 'Making sense of custom contrast analysis: Seven takeaways and a new approach', *SSRN*, http://ssrn.com/abstract=2797514.

Hackenbrack, K. and Nelson, M.W., 1996, 'Auditors' incentives and their application of financial accounting standards', *The Accounting Review* 71(1), 43–59.

Hales, J.W., Venkataraman, S. and Wilks, T.J., 2012. 'Accounting for lease renewal options: The informational effects of unit of account choices', *The Accounting Review* 87(1), 173–197.

Hammersley, J.S., 2006, 'Pattern identification and industry-specialist auditors', *The Accounting Review* 81(2), 309–336.

Kadous, K., Leiby, J. and Peecher, M.E., 2010, 'How do auditors weight informal contrary advice? The joint influence of advisor social bond and advice justifiability', *The Accounting Review* 88(6), 2061–2087.

Kadous, K. and Zhou, Y.D., 2016, 'How does intrinsic motivation improve auditor judgment in complex audit tasks?', *SSRN*, http://ssrn.com/abstract=2576984.

Kennedy, J., 1993, 'Debiasing audit judgment with accountability: A framework and experimental results', *Journal of Accounting Research* 31(2), 231–245.

Keppel, G. and Wickens, T.D., 2004, *Design and Analysis: A Researcher's Handbook* (4th ed.), Prentice Hall, Upper Saddle River, NJ.

Kerlinger, F. and Lee, H., 1999, *Foundations of Behavioral Research* (4th ed.), Wadsworth, Belmont, CA.

Knechel, W.R. and Leiby, J., 2016, 'If you want my advice: Status motives and audit consultations about accounting estimates', *Journal of Accounting Research* 54(5), 1231–1394.

Koonce, L., Miller, J. and Winchel, J., 2015, 'The effects of norms on investor reactions to derivative use', *Contemporary Accounting Research* 32(4), 1529–1554.

Libby, R., Bloomfield, R. and Nelson, M.W., 2002, 'Experimental research in financial accounting', *Accounting, Organizations and Society* 27(8), 775–810.

Libby, R. and Luft, J., 1993, 'Determinants of judgment performance in accounting settings: Ability, knowledge, motivation, and environment', *Accounting, Organizations and Society* 18(5), 425–450.

Maines, L.A., 1995, 'Judgment and decision-making research in financial accounting: A review and analysis', in R.H. Ashton and A.H. Ashton (eds.), *Judgment and Decision-Making Research in Accounting and Auditing*, 76–101, Cambridge University Press, Cambridge.

Mocadlo, R., 2016, 'How do auditors order their tasks, and how does task ordering affect performance?', *Working Paper*.

Nelson, M.W. and Rupar, K.K., 2015, 'Numerical formats within risk disclosures and the moderating effect of investors' concerns about management discretion', *The Accounting Review* 90(3), 1149–1168.

Neter, J., Kutner, M.H., Nachtsheim, C.J. and Wasserman, W., 1996, *Applied Linear Statistical Models* (4th ed.), McGraw-Hill/Irwin, New York City.

Nisbett, R.E. and Wilson, T.D., 1977, 'Telling more than we can know: Verbal reports on mental processes', *Psychological Review* 84(3), 231–259.

Peecher, M.E., 1996, 'The influence of auditors' justification processes on their decisions: A cognitive model and experimental evidence', *Journal of Accounting Research* 34(1), 125–140.

Peecher, M.E. and Solomon, I., 2001, 'Theory and experimentation in studies of audit judgments and decisions: Avoiding common research traps', *International Journal of Auditing* 5(3), 193–203.

Rasso, J.T., 2015, 'Construal instructions and professional skepticism in evaluating complex estimates', *Accounting, Organizations and Society* 46, 44–55.

Rich, J.S., Solomon, I. and Trotman, K.T., 1997, 'The audit review process: A characterization from the persuasion perspective', *Accounting, Organizations and Society* 22(5), 481–505.

Rosnow, R.L. and Rosenthal, R., 1996, 'Contrasts and interactions redux: Five easy pieces', *Psychological Science* 7(4), 253–257.

Shadish, W.R., Cook, T.D. and Campbell, D.T., 2002, *Experimental and Quasi-Experimental Designs for Generalized Causal Inference*, Houghton, Mifflin, Boston, MA.

Solomon, I. and Shields, M.D., 2007, 'Judgment and decision-making research in auditing', in *Judgment and Decision-Making Research in Accounting and Auditing*, in R.H. Ashton and A.H. Ashton (eds.), 137–175, Cambridge University Press, Cambridge.

Spencer, S.J., Zanna, M.P. and Fong, G.T., 2005, 'Establishing a causal chain: Why experiments are often more effective than mediational analyses in examining psychological processes', *Journal of Personality and Social Psychology* 89(6), 845–851.

Tan, H.-T., Wang, E.Y. and Zhou, B., 2015, 'How does readability influence investors' judgments? Consistency of benchmark performance matters', *The Accounting Review* 90(1), 371–393.

Trochim, W., Donnelly, J.P. and Arora, K., 2015, *Research Methods: The Essential Knowledge Base* (2nd ed.), Cengage Learning, Belmont, CA.

Weber, E.U. and Johnson, E.J., 2009, 'Mindful judgment and decision making', *Annual Review of Psychology* 60, 53–85.

Wood, R.E., Mento, A.J. and Locke, E.A., 1987, 'Task complexity as a moderator of goal effects: A meta-analysis', *Journal of Applied Psychology* 72(3), 416–425.

14

Experimental economics

A primer for accounting researchers

Bryan K. Church and Lucy F. Ackert

Introduction

This chapter provides an overview of the significance and suitability of experimental economics to accounting research. We aim to identify and discuss fundamental issues that underlie the use of an experimental economics method, including advantages of the method, underlying theoretical paradigms, design choices and implications. We define an experimental economics method as one that employs a controlled laboratory setting and performance-contingent incentives to study individuals' behaviour, interactive (group) outcomes and market outcomes.[1] The method allows the researcher to create *real* economic environments with *real* economic actors (Berg, Coursey and Dickhaut 1990: 857). Thus, participants' behaviour in the laboratory maps into personal economic well-being. An experimental economics method differs from conventional judgment and decision-making studies, administered in the laboratory, by introducing performance-contingent incentives.

Accounting researchers readily recognize that an experimental economics method is well suited for theory testing (e.g., Berg et al. 1990; Moser 1998; Mukherji 1996). The method can be used to determine whether a theoretical model predicts individual behaviour and aggregate outcomes, and in some cases, the linkages between the two. Accounting researchers typically investigate whether individuals' behaviour conforms to the tenets of standard economic theory, most notably self-interest (e.g., Evans, Hannan, Krishnan and Moser 2001). Studies of strategic interactions focus on whether outcomes are consistent with game-theoretic predictions (e.g., Yu 2011). Studies of asset markets appeal to well-accepted economic theories, including rational expectations equilibrium, noisy rational expectations equilibrium and Bayesian Nash equilibrium (Ackert, Church and Zhang 2016). The theories provide a baseline to gauge market outcomes. In addition, accounting researchers frequently introduce psychological variables into experimental designs, positing why economic theories might not be supported (e.g., Church, Hannan and Kuang 2012, 2014).

Smith, Schatzberg and Waller (1987) point out that the use of an experimental economics method often stimulates scrutiny of extant theory. Indeed, the process of designing an experiment can lead to the identification of ambiguities, omissions or unrealistic assumptions in the underlying theory, with two potential outcomes. The researcher may actively engage in theory development, subsequently testing the revised theory (e.g., Schatzberg and Sevcik 1994). Alternatively, the researcher may determine that the theoretical drawback provides a basis to introduce an experimental variable – one that has not been considered previously. The researcher can test the effect of the variable and/or assess the theory's robustness (e.g., Baiman and Lewis 1989; DeJong, Forsythe and Uecker 1985).

An experimental economics method allows the researcher to investigate the effects of altering institutional arrangements, which is particularly worthwhile in addressing policy-related issues (e.g., Alm and Jacobson 2007; Berg 1994; Kachelmeier and King 2002). Along these lines, experimental economics is applicable to a wide spectrum of accounting-policy issues. For example, auditing researchers examine liability regimes (Dopuch and King 1992; Wallin 1992; Yu 2011), financial accounting researchers investigate disclosure regimes (Bloomfield and Wilks 2000; Elliott, Hobson and White 2015; King and Wallin 1990, 1991), managerial accounting researchers study control systems (Christ, Emett, Summers and Wood 2012; Tayler and Bloomfield 2011) and tax researchers probe enforcement (audit) regimes (Alm and McKee 2006; Beck, Davis and Jung 1992). Experimental findings provide evidence as to whether altering institutional arrangements are likely to produce results in line with policymakers' goals or, conversely, trigger unintended consequences.

Finally, the results of experimental economics studies serve as a basis to modify existing theory. As mentioned earlier, accounting researchers have considerable interest in psychological variables, and such variables potentially explain departures from economic theory. In fact, theorists have begun incorporating the effects of psychological variables into analytical models (e.g., Barberis, Shleifer and Vishny 1998; Davis, Hecht and Perkins 2003; Fischer and Huddart 2008; Mittendorf 2006). The findings of experimental economics studies provide a basis to incorporate psychological variables into existing models, which then can be tested. The results of experimental economics studies also can complement archival findings, potentially shedding light on observed anomalies (e.g., Calegari and Fargher 1997).

Our goal is to demonstrate, throughout this chapter, that experimental economics is a powerful tool to address an assortment of accounting issues. The remainder of the chapter is organized as follows. First, we trace the emergence of experimental economics research in the accounting literature. Second, we discuss the essential elements used in an experimental economics method, emphasizing specific facets that give it a comparative advantage over other research methods, and then, we underscore important points to consider in choosing topical issues to study. Third, we elaborate on economics- versus psychology-based theoretical approaches and offer examples from prior research. Fourth, we outline important design choices that should be considered in developing and conducting an experimental economics study.[2] Lastly, we offer concluding remarks.

History of experimental economics in the accounting literature

We briefly summarize the appearance of experimental economics in the accounting literature, with the focus being on studies that entail a laboratory investigation *and* monetary incentives tied to participants' performance. Early on, Ansari (1976) published a study in the *Journal of Accounting Research* examining employee behaviour in a production setting. In the study, participants' (employees) perform an experimental task, for which they receive performance-contingent payment, and interact with researcher confederates. Nearly a decade later, two studies appeared in the *Journal of Accounting Research* analyzing behaviour in laboratory markets (DeJong, Forsythe and Uecker 1985; DeJong, Forsythe, Lundholm and Uecker 1985). Both studies investigate principal-agent relationships and incorporate mechanisms designed to mitigate agents' moral hazard, including liability regime, disclosure regime and costly investigation. Overview articles soon followed in *Auditing: A Journal of Practice & Theory* (Smith et al. 1987) and the *Journal of the American Taxation Association* (Davis and Swenson 1988), espousing the importance and applicability of experimental economics to auditing and tax research, respectively, with suggestions for future study.[3]

Subsequently, the Research Foundation of the Certified General Accountants' Association of Canada provided funding and published two research monographs, both employing an experimental economics method. Berg, Daley, Gigler and Kanodia (1990) investigate the communication of private, non-verifiable information in principal-agent settings, and Dopuch and King (1991a) probe the demand for audit services as a credibility-enhancing mechanism.[4] At about the same time, *The Accounting Review* published two research forums comprised of papers using experimental economics to study, first, negotiation behaviour and outcomes (Chalos and Haka 1990; Elias 1990) and, second, the demand and supply of audit services (Dopuch and King 1992; Wallin 1992). Both forums include remarks from well-established scholars (Murnighan and Bazerman 1990; Boatsman, Grasso, Ormiston and Renau 1992; DeJong and Forsythe 1992).

The use of experimental economics in the literature continued to grow in the 1990s, as researchers studied a multitude of issues, encompassing auditing, financial accounting, managerial accounting and taxes. According to Callahan, Gabriel and Sainty (2006: 73–74), 64 papers using an experimental economics method were published across 14 accounting outlets during the 1990s, including the top six accounting journals (*Accounting, Organizations and Society*, *The Accounting Review*, *Contemporary Accounting Research*, *Journal of Accounting and Economics*, *Journal of Accounting Research* and *Review of Accounting Studies*), four section journals of the American Accounting Association (*Auditing: A Journal of Practice & Theory*, *Behavioral Research in Accounting*, *Journal of the American Taxation Association* and *Journal of Management Accounting Research*) and four other recognized journals (*Abacus*, *Journal of Accounting, Auditing & Finance*, *Journal of Accounting and Public Policy* and *National Tax Journal*).[5] In the 2000s, a wide range of issues continued to be addressed, spanning the sub-disciplines of accounting. We extend the data (publication counts) reported in Callahan et al. (2006) as a means to gauge the rate of publications in the 2000s.[6] From 2000–2014, we identify 96 papers that use an experimental economics method, representing 11 of the 14 journals noted above. The publication rate is very similar to that observed in the 1990s.

Over the past 25 years (1990–2014), we find an average of 6.40 papers published per year in the aforementioned journals, ranging from two to 13 per year, with a standard deviation of 2.52. While not large, the number is by no means trivial, and it is reasonably stable over time. Thus, the use of experimental economics in accounting research appears to be alive and well.

Why use an experimental economics method?

Creating a microeconomic system in the laboratory

An experimental economics approach allows the researcher to create a controlled microeconomic system, comprised of an environment, an institution and agent behaviour (Smith 1982). The environment represents the basic experimental setup, such as the background (e.g., asset market setting, production setting or reporting setting), the number of participants, a set of commodities or resources and participants' characteristics (technology, knowledge and preferences). The institution specifies the rules that govern participants' behaviour, including communication and exchange. Thus, the institution dictates what is allowable, and how participants' actions translate into monetary payoffs.

Induced value theory is a fundamental tenet of experimental economics that enables the researcher to ensure that participants are suitably motivated. It provides a means to enrich the study of accounting phenomena by incorporating economic outcomes. Decisions that involve accounting information frequently have economic consequences, and theories that underlie accounting phenomena typically put forth economic reasons. So, including economic outcomes is essential to studying many accounting issues. The crux of induced value theory is that a reward structure can be created to induce values so that participants' behaviour is linked to monetary payoffs. For example, participants' holdings of an experimental commodity can be tied to monetary rewards such that increasing holdings increases rewards. Participants are aware of the linkages and prefer greater to lesser payoffs (Smith 1976). In addition, payoffs are sufficient to outweigh the subjective costs of participating, including cognitive effort, time and boredom (Smith 1982). Returning to our example, as long as participants prefer more money to less, they exhibit monotonically increasing preferences in the experimental commodity. By inducing values, the researcher neutralizes participants' homegrown preferences and exerts control over experimental preferences. This aspect is critical because it provides a basis to isolate causal relationships, which is imperative for theory development and testing.

Within the environment and the institution, agents' behaviour is observed and measured. A dynamic social process emerges, which produces individual as well as aggregate (system-wide) outcomes. To illustrate, we refer to Ackert, Church and Zhang (2004), a study that examines market outcomes and linkages to individuals' behaviour. The study includes two distinct phases. In the first phase, the environment is an asset market that consists of a series of trading periods. Each market is comprised of seven or eight participants, who are endowed with cash and certificates. The certificates confer a period-end liquidating dividend, and a subset of participants pay a tax on dividend earnings. Participants who are taxed have an incentive to sell certificates, whereas those who are not taxed have an incentive to buy.[7] The institution is an oral double auction, where participants post offers to buy or sell certificates. Outstanding offers stand until accepted or replaced by better ones. At the beginning of each period, participants decide whether to acquire a costly forecast of asset value and, then, trading commences. The asset market provides data on market prices, forecast acquisition decisions and trading activity (bids, asks and transactions).

Following the completion of the trading periods, a second phase begins. The environment is an individual prediction task. Forecasts of asset value are displayed sequentially along with prior history, and participants predict the period-end liquidating dividend. The forecast-generating process is the same as that used in the asset market (phase one). The institution specifies the rule that determines participants' payment ($0.25 for each prediction within ±100 of the liquidating dividend). The prediction task provides data on participants' ability to successfully use forecasts, providing insight into whether they understand the forecast-generating process.

The experimental setup, described above, allows the researchers to investigate several issues linked to agents' behaviour. The asset market data are used to compare the closing price per period to theoretical benchmarks, with implications for market efficiency and information dissemination. Market prices and trading activity are scrutinized to probe price formation, including the speed of information dissemination. Participants' forecast acquisition decisions and trading activity shed light on the role of informed versus uninformed agents in shaping market outcomes. The prediction task provides evidence on agents' ability, which can be tied back to market outcomes. Ackert et al. (2004) refer to agents who are able to successfully use forecasts to predict asset value as smart traders. The study's findings indicate that asset price tends to approach an informed price, sometimes sporadically, over the course of a trading period and that roughly three to five transactions are needed to achieve an efficient price. Further, a sufficient number of smart informed traders are required to produce an informed price. We will return to this issue later. The detailed insights into the connections between individual behaviour and market outcomes would not be possible without the use of an experimental economics approach.

We note one other feature that is common to countless experimental economics studies, repeated trials. Agents' behaviour often is erratic over the initial periods of an experiment, especially in complex settings. Repeated trials allow participants to become familiar with the environment and the institution. The noise associated with agents' learning usually dissipates upon repeated exposure so that behaviour stabilizes. For instance, in the first phase of Ackert et al. (2004), participants complete 12 four-minute trading periods. The authors plot the data and note that asset-price behaviour (i.e., conformance to theoretical predictions) improves over the course of a session, suggesting that repeated trials promote learning. Other measures can be taken to ensure that participants become accustomed to the environment and comprehend the institutional details. Researchers can include quiz questions that cover the instructions (Church et al. 2012, 2014), practice periods (e.g., Dopuch, King and Wallin 1989; King 1996) and even practice markets (Magilke, Mayhew and Pike 2009; Mayhew 2001). Hales and Williamson (2010) include practice periods in which participants make decisions in the different experimental roles, giving them insight into how behaviour affects each role. Researchers also typically replicate experimental conditions to provide additional comfort. For instance, Ackert et al. (2004) conduct three asset markets per condition, and King (1996) includes five sessions per condition, where each replication comprises a unique cohort of participants. All in all, repeated trials and replication bolster one's ability to draw reliable inferences from data collected using an experimental economics method.

Comparative advantages in choosing topical areas of study

A chief advantage of using an experimental economics approach is control. A specific facet is that the researcher can systematically vary features of the environment and the institutional arrangements to gauge the effects on individual behaviour and market outcomes. The topical issue being studied determines the experimental manipulations. Ackert et al. (2004) are interested in agents' ability to use unbiased versus biased forecasts and how such ability impacts market outcomes. The researchers vary the forecast-generating process between sessions such that forecasts of asset value are unbiased (mean zero error term) or biased (nonzero error term). The nature of biased forecasts is systematic – a constant is either added to (upward bias) or subtracted from (downward bias) the error term.[8] In addition, the unbiased forecasts are designed to have greater variability than the biased forecasts, meaning that the latter are more informative – as long as participants can adjust for the bias (take out the constant term).

Ackert et al. (2004) find that participants have much more difficulty using biased forecasts, even though the bias is systematic, as compared to unbiased forecasts (see also Ackert, Church and Shehata 1996, 1997). In addition, the study's findings indicate that the forecast-generating process affects the composition of traders necessary to achieve an efficient, informed price. Asset price properly reflects unbiased forecasts, in general, as long as the market includes at least two smart informed traders with sufficient capacity to influence market outcomes.[9] When forecasts are biased, however, at least three informed traders with sufficient capacity are needed to produce a comparable result. The findings are noteworthy because theoretical research suggests that competitive pressures generated by having two informed traders may not be sufficient to fully reveal private information (e.g., Foster and Viswanathan 1996; Kyle 1985, 1989).

A key strength of experimental economics (as well as conventional judgment and decision-making studies) is that the method permits the researcher to capture information that otherwise is not available. For example, in Ackert et al. (2004) the researchers are able to track informed traders (identity and number), classify them (by ability to understand the forecast-generating process and capacity to influence market outcomes), and pinpoint traders' actions and the resulting outcomes. By maintaining control over participants' characteristics and isolating behaviour, the researcher gains access to a wealth of data. Other methods would face a myriad of problems and empirical challenges to collect such data.

An experimental economics approach is particularly well suited for topical issues that involve heterogeneous agents. Naturally occurring settings frequently are comprised of different types of agents. For example, some auditors in the marketplace invest in state-of-the-art technologies, which affect the quality of their services. Managers may possess proprietary information or advanced technologies, which impact their chances of being self-sustaining and profitable. Investors vary along a continuum from novice to sophisticated and, further, include informed and liquidity traders. An experimental economics approach enables the researcher to (a) exogenously impose the makeup of agents' types or (b) elicit measures that can be used to classify agents. A handful of studies have been conducted along these lines. For instance, Calegari, Schatzberg and Sevcik (1998) *manipulate* (exogenously impose) auditor type by instilling disagreements over the resolution of a client-reporting issue: that is, auditors are endowed with different private signals as a means to establish disparity in beliefs. The authors find that heterogeneity among auditors is a necessary condition for independence impairment. By comparison, Church et al. (2014) sort manager-participants based on preferences for honesty. Their experiment includes two phases, with the first phase being used to *classify* manager-participants as having low, moderate or high preferences for honesty.[10] In the second phase, the authors document that such classification is associated with manager-participants' behaviour (see also Hales, Wang and Williamson 2015). The findings are consistent with theoretical research, which suggests that managers vary in their preferences for honesty (e.g., Koford and Penno 1992; Luft 1997; Mittendorf 2006).

An experimental economics approach also permits the researcher to manipulate institutional arrangements, which can be especially relevant for tackling policy-related issues, including implications for social welfare (see also Alm and Jacobson 2007; Berg 1994; Kachelmeier and King 2002). A laboratory setting enables the researcher to investigate the effects of a change in accounting policy *before* such change occurs, thereby providing evidence of the potential ramifications (see also McDaniel and Hand 1996). As an example, policymakers have long debated the merits of mandatory audit-firm rotation (e.g., Commission on Auditors' Responsibilities 1978; Division for CPA Firms 1992; Public Company Accounting Oversight Board 2011). Yet, such a regulatory regime has never been imposed in the United States and, thus, field data are not available. An experimental economics approach is well equipped to address this issue, with the benefit of being able to create a microeconomic system that requires audit-firm rotation.

Several studies investigate audit-firm rotation using an experimental economics approach. Dopuch, King and Schwartz (2002) find that mandatory rotation reduces auditor-participants' willingness to issue biased reports, promoting independence. Wang and Tuttle (2009) conclude that mandatory rotation leads to negotiation outcomes that are more in line with auditor preferences than manager preferences. Bowlin, Hobson and Piercey (2015) find that audit quality improves with mandatory rotation, but only when auditors frame their assessments of managers' representations as potentially honest (i.e., focusing on why managers' representations are believable). Absent mandatory rotation, audit quality is enhanced as long as auditors frame their assessments of managers' representations as potentially dishonest (i.e., focusing on why managers' representations are not believable). The results of Bowlin et al. suggest that bolstering auditors' professional skepticism can be an effective means to promote audit quality in the current regulatory environment (i.e., one in which mandatory audit firm rotation is not required). These findings are relevant to policymakers.

Theoretical paradigms

Studies using an experimental economics method traditionally have appealed to germane economic theories. Early studies focus on tests of neoclassical economic theories, with *homo economicus* being the underlying theme (e.g., DeJong et al. 1985; DeJong et al. 1985; Dopuch, et al. 1989).[11] Over time, however, psychological theories have been introduced, providing insight into why behaviour deviates from the tenets of rationality (e.g., Church et al. 2012, 2014; Coletti, Sedatole and Towry 2005; King 2002), even being applied to studies of market outcomes (e.g., Ganguly, Kagel and Moser 1994, 2000; Ackert, Charupat, Deaves and Kluger 2009). Nowadays, some studies rely almost exclusively on psychological theories (e.g., Wang and Tuttle 2009; Church, Peytcheva, Yu and Singtokul 2015). The underlying theoretical paradigm often is associated with the unit of analysis, be it individuals' behaviour, interactive (group) outcomes or market outcomes. Below, we organize our discussion of theoretical underpinnings based on the unit of analysis.

Individuals' behaviour

Studies of individuals often use the standard neoclassical economic model as a baseline to evaluate observed behaviour. The gist is that individuals have known and stable preferences; they have complete information when choosing among alternatives; and they make choices so as to maximize expected utility in a world of uncertainty.[12] According to Callahan et al. (2006), many, many studies examine individual behaviour across the sub-disciplines of accounting. To illustrate, we focus on Evans et al. (2001), a study at the forefront of honesty research in accounting. This work has been influential and stimulated much additional work, and in 2006 Evans et al. was the recipient of a Notable Contributions to the Accounting Literature Award.

Evans et al. (2001) investigate manager-participants' preferences for honesty and wealth and whether truthfulness increases the value of communication. The focus of the study is individual behaviour. Manager-participants are endowed with private information about actual production costs and then prompted to report budgeted costs to corporate headquarters. The budget is automatically approved, actual costs are incurred and participants keep the difference between the reported and actual costs. The institutional arrangement is a trust contract, whereby corporate headquarters expects the manager to report honestly: the manager's pay is based on the reported cost. Corporate headquarters has no way of knowing whether the reported cost is truthful, so dishonest reporting does not have any negative repercussions. Under these conditions, participants report the maximum allowable cost as long as they do not experience disutility from lying. The experimental findings, however, indicate that a relatively small percentage of participants make reporting choices that maximize wealth, suggesting that honesty matters (i.e., participants experience disutility from misreporting).

Other theoretical models incorporate preferences for honesty. Koford and Penno (1992) assert that individuals' type (e.g., truth teller or liar) determines whether they report honestly or economically. Baiman and Lewis (1989) posit that individuals have an honesty threshold that dictates reporting behaviour: individuals report honestly below the threshold, and otherwise, they report so to maximize wealth (non-truthfully). The theoretical predictions are not borne out by the data. Roughly 50% of the participants make reporting choices that are partially honest (between honest and wealth maximizing).

Evans et al. (2001) also investigate manager-participants' reporting choices under a modified trust contract. Importantly, the contract includes a production hurdle such that production does not take place if the reported cost exceeds the hurdle cost. The production hurdle represents a key feature that is included in the optimal contract from an agency theory perspective (Antle and Fellingham 1995). In the experimental setting, the production hurdle reduces manager-participants' wealth-maximizing reported cost. The findings indicate that, with a modified trust contract, more reporting choices are in line with economic predictions (wealth maximization). Nevertheless, nearly 25% of participants report amounts that are partially honest, again suggesting that honesty matters.[13]

As mentioned earlier, Evans et al. (2001) spurred much additional research on honesty and individual behaviour. Many studies rely on psychological theories and examine behavioural factors that underlie reporting choices. For instance, Hannan, Rankin and Towry (2006) create a reporting environment that involves face-to-face communication,[14] and they manipulate the presence and precision of an information system. The face-to-face setting introduces concerns about how reporting choices are perceived by others. Because honesty is a commonly accepted norm of behaviour, it may promote truthful reporting choices. The authors contend that participants trade-off the benefits of appearing honest (impression management) with the benefits of misrepresentation (economic well-being). The study's findings suggest that under certain conditions impression-management concerns are brought to the forefront, whereas under other conditions economic well-being is paramount. The dominant consideration, in turn, drives reporting choices.

A multitude of honesty studies appear in the accounting literature. The emphasis typically is whether specific factors tilt behaviour toward honest or economic reporting choices. Accordingly, both economic and psychological theories play important roles in honesty research, including integrating theories from different paradigms. The same can be said of the bulk of accounting-based, experimental economics studies that target individual behaviour (e.g., Church et al. 2014; Hobson and Kachelemeier 2005).

Interactive outcomes

Studies of interactive outcomes involve at least two participants, typically with competing incentives, who make active decisions. Many studies specify two active player roles, representing principal-agent dyads, which include manager-auditor and owner-manager pairings. Participants generally choose from a small set of actions (e.g., low or high, invest or do not invest, disagree or agree). Participants' choices affect the likelihood of an outcome, which in turn impacts payoffs. Game-theoretic models provide the basis to predict behaviour, although some studies incorporate psychological theories (e.g., King 2002).

In an early accounting study, DeJong, Forsythe and Uecker (1985: 754) examine "whether an elementary equilibrium model of the principal-agent relationship could be operationalized in a laboratory setting." The focus is whether behaviour aligns with game-theoretic predictions. In the experimental setting, the principal can hire an agent to reduce the likelihood of a loss. Several agents submit sealed offers, and the principal decides whether to accept an offer, establishing a principal-agent dyad. If an agent is hired, a service level is chosen.[15] The principal's payoff is determined by a random draw from an outcome distribution, where a different distribution is used conditioned on the agent's service level. In equilibrium, the predictions are straightforward: the agent supplies the service level that maximizes the principal's expected wealth, and the agent's fee (price) equals the expected cost of providing services. DeJong, Forsythe and Uecker (1985) conduct two sets of markets, which differ in the number of service levels available: three levels versus five.[16] The experimental findings are consistent with the equilibrium predictions in markets with three service levels, but not in markets with five. Notably, with fewer service levels, the environment is simplified, reducing agents' cognitive load. In turn, agents are better able to isolate optimal actions, leading to behaviour that conforms with equilibrium predictions.

Many studies follow in the footsteps of DeJong, Forsythe, Lundholm et al. (1985), and some even incorporate *three* active player roles (e.g., Dopuch and King 1991b; Fatemi 2012; Hales and Williamson 2010; Kachelmeier 1991; Magilke et al. 2009; Mayhew 2001; Mayhew and Pike 2004). In these studies, multi-period settings introduce reputational concerns, and as a consequence, multiple game-theoretic equilibria exist. Researchers often focus on pure strategy equilibria, as benchmarks, to gauge behaviour and outcomes. For example, studies on auditor reputation consider two extreme pure strategies, a lemons equilibrium and a reputation equilibrium (Mayhew 2001; Mayhew and Pike 2004). Researchers also posit the effects of behavioural factors, which may cause outcomes to move toward (or away from) a specific equilibrium. For instance, King (2002) asserts that auditor-participants place too much trust in managers' cheap talk,[17] leading to suboptimal effort choices. He manipulates auditor-participants' group affiliation as a way of introducing social pressure to conform to group norms. King finds that strong group affiliation reinforces a norm of diligence such that auditor-participants ignore managers' cheap talk, and in turn, their effort choices are more in line with the Nash equilibrium.

Other studies on interactive outcomes employ a simpler approach, akin to the prisoner's dilemma. Dyads are formed and a bi-matrix game is administered. Paired participants simultaneously choose an action, and the combination of choices determines participants' payoffs. As an example, Bowlin, Hales and Kachelmeier (2009) create manager-auditor dyads. The manager chooses among actions that represent cautious or aggressive reporting, and the auditor chooses among actions that represent diligent or lax effort. The game-theoretic prediction is a mixed-strategy equilibrium. The experimental design also manipulates whether manager-participants have prior experience in the auditor's role: some participants switch roles (from auditor to manager) over the course of the experiment. By manipulating prior experience, the researchers consider psychological theory: prior experience as an auditor can lead to social-projection bias, which affects the manager's propensity to choose cautious versus aggressive reporting.

Research on interactive outcomes has developed similar to that on individual behaviour, with increasing application of psychological theories, largely based in social psychology and social cognition. Such research, however, continues to rely extensively on underlying economic theory, largely because such theory has a fundamental concern with economic efficiencies and wealth effects. Game-theoretic predictions provide a means to formalize how interacting dyads affect social welfare.

Market outcomes

Studies on market outcomes analyze asset prices. Participants are endowed with cash and/or certificates and permitted to transact (buy and sell) with one another. The market institution generally is a double auction market or a call market. Researchers test whether asset prices converge to economic predictions or, if not, reflect individual biases. These studies also delve into price formation and linkages to individual behaviour (see our earlier discussion of Ackert et al. 2004). Other studies look at treatment effects on asset prices, including convergence of prices to economic predictions.

Economic theory provides a basis to identify asset-price benchmarks, which enables researchers to gauge the extent to which accounting information is impounded in period-end price.

Some studies investigate information dissemination and market efficiencies. For example, a goal might be to determine whether private information is fully reflected in closing price, where the benchmark is a full-information price as suggested by a rational expectations equilibrium (e.g., Ackert et al. 2004). Price formation also can be examined to shed light on the speed of information dissemination, with implications for theoretical underpinnings, including models that rely on a Bayesian Nash equilibrium and a noisy rational expectations equilibrium. Researchers appeal to economic theory to investigate conditions (e.g., number of informed traders) that underlie price formation and market inefficiencies (Ackert et al. 2016; Bossaerts, Frydman and Ledyard 2014). Many studies of market outcomes produce findings that are in line with economic theory (e.g., Bossaerts and Plott 2004; Copland and Friedman 1992; Jamal, Maier and Sunder 2015; Sunder and Jamal 1996; Waller, Shapiro and Sevcik 1999). A notable exception is markets on long-lived assets, the so-called bubbles markets first reported by Smith, Suchanek and Williams (1988). The mispricing observed in these markets suggests trader irrationality (Ackert et al. 2009; Lei, Noussair and Plott 2001).

Some studies ascribe price inefficiencies to traders' cognitive biases and processing limitations. The implication is that psychological theory provides a way to understand market outcomes. This line of research investigates whether individual biases persist in the marketplace, using psychological theory. Ganguly, Kagel and Moser (1994, 2000) compare asset price with competing benchmarks (i.e., economic versus psychological predictions). The authors examine whether price adjustments are in line with Bayesian updating or individual biases, specifically base rate fallacy. Economic theory implies that traders incorporate new information in line with the laws of statistics and probability, leading to a Bayesian price prediction. Psychological theory, on the other hand, suggests that individuals are prone to overlook or underweight base rate information, leading to a biased price. Ganguly, Kagel and Moser provide evidence that base rate fallacy carries over to asset price, especially when markets include traders who are susceptible to the bias. Other studies produce similar findings, applying psychological theories that take into account well-documented biases (e.g., Bloomfield, Libby and Nelson 2003; Burton, Coller and Tuttle 2006; Tuttle, Coller and Burton 1996).

Another line of research investigates the effect of information disclosure on market outcomes (e.g., Bloomfield and Wilks 2000; Coller 1996; Dietrich, Kachelmeier, Kleinmuntz and Linsmeier 2001; Elliott et al. 2015; Hobson 2011). Research in this area considers specific characteristics of accounting disclosures, appealing to economic theory as well as psychological theory. For example, Coller (1996) considers the effect of information uncertainty and variability on price adjustments, relying on an economic model (Holthausen and Verrecchia 1988) to hypothesize asset-price reaction. Bloomfield and Wilks (2000) investigate disclosure quality (i.e., the reduction in uncertainty due to disclosure), relying primarily on economic theory. Others apply psychological theories to predict effects. Dietrich et al. (2001) investigate different ways to present supplemental information on oil and gas reserves, and Elliott et al. (2015) look at reactions to various earnings metrics. These studies suggest that asset price is more likely to properly impound value-relevant information when disclosures are easily understood, highlighting asset-price implications.[18]

All in all, the theoretical paradigms that are applied to research on market outcomes closely parallel those applied to research on interactive outcomes. Psychological theories are being introduced more frequently in studies of market outcomes; however, the economic perspective still dominates. We note that economic theory offers a ready means to identify relevant benchmarks, and researchers are compelled to investigate factors that promote market efficiency (e.g., Ackert, Charupat, Church and Deaves 2006; Dietrich et al. 2001; Elliott et al. 2015).

Design choices

Numerous design choices are involved in any experimental economics study. With careful choices, the experimenter can induce a reward structure that counteracts homegrown preferences and controls experimental preferences. In developing experimental materials, issues related to internal and external validity must be considered. Below, we organize our discussion of design choices around examples of issues associated with developing and conducting an experimental economics study. Of course, we cannot cover the many dimensions of an experimental design in one chapter and, thus, focus on some critical aspects that are commonly encountered.

Internal validity

An experimental economics method permits the study of important research questions that cannot be examined in naturally occurring settings. The variables of interest can be systematically manipulated, while holding constant extraneous variables. Design choices are critical to instilling confidence in the validity of the identified causal relationships, referred to as internal validity. A critical requirement is to fashion a design so that participants' behaviour in the laboratory maps into personal economic well-being.

The researcher exercises care to ensure that threats to internal validity are contained. Experimental participants typically are randomly assigned to treatments. The researcher is cognizant of the potential impact of recent newsworthy events. For example, it may unwise to conduct an experimental asset market immediately following a market crash or a large change in the Dow Jones Industrial Average! Further, if an unanticipated incident occurs during an experimental session (e.g., a participant exclaims loudly or inadvertently reveals private information), the data may need to be discarded due to the potential confounding influence. In computerized environments, a server failure may prematurely terminate a session. The researcher strives for procedural regularity to allow replication. To this end, experimental instructions can be posted online or placed in an appendix to the paper. To allow replication and promote participant understanding, the experimental instructions need to be clearly and carefully written so that all aspects of the experiment are fully detailed. The instructions should be consistently delivered across sessions and treatments. Recent scandals in the psychology discipline surrounding data fraud highlight the importance of replicability to the general research community (Wineman 2013). Likewise, the accounting community has become all too familiar with the perils of data fraud (Stone 2015).

With attention to detail an experimental economics method is well suited for theory testing, though risk preferences are an important extraneous variable that can complicate matters (Selto and Cooper 1990). Participants typically make decisions in uncertain environments, where predictions depend on risk tolerance and preferences can have unexpected effects on the targeted relationships. The researcher strives for a well-designed experiment that isolates the question of interest without the necessity of additional assumptions regarding the form of risk preferences. Facing a joint hypothesis problem, one can attempt to induce risk neutrality with the two-stage lottery used by Berg, Daley, Dickhaut and O'Brien (1986), among others. Unfortunately, the empirical evidence suggests that this procedure may not be effective in inducing risk neutrality (Davis and Holt 1993: 472–476). Another possible approach is to measure risk preferences at the beginning of the experiment. Participants could then be sorted into groups based on observed attitudes or, alternatively, preferences could be controlled ex post in the data analysis. Risk tolerance can be elicited in a number of ways, including the lottery-menu approach proposed by

Holt and Laury (2002) and the endowment-investment task suggested by Gneezy and Potters (1997).[19] Measuring and controlling risk preferences represents a significant challenge for those using an experimental economics approach.

Dealing with the issue of risk preferences is further complicated when outcomes depend on the decisions of others. In interactive settings the researcher is particularly challenged to provide evidence supporting the robustness of results. One potential approach is to use a computerized agent to control one side of the interaction. For example, Calegari et al. (1998) test predictions of an audit pricing model in laboratory markets. Their goal is to examine auditor independence and audit pricing under two conditions: agreement versus disagreement among auditors on the appropriateness of a client's preferred reporting strategy. Calegari et al. recognize that cooperative behaviour between the auditor and client could impact the independence-pricing relationship. Thus, in a control treatment, the client is a robot with decisions programmed to be consistent with the theoretical model. Calegari et al. conclude that the client-robot markets yield support for the model's predictions that disagreement among auditors is a necessary condition for independence impairment. However, in markets with a human client, auditors sometimes exhibit impaired judgment even with agreement among auditors on reporting strategies. Thus, the authors conclude that, while the behaviour and preferences of a computerized agent are controllable, the ability to generalize to a naturally occurring environment is limited.

External validity

An experiment, like a model, is an abstraction from the real world (naturally occurring environments). When developing a protocol, the researcher should think carefully about the laboratory environment so that insights from the experiment pertain to the natural ecology. Due to the nature of the discipline, accounting researchers value realism. However, some realism may not be central to the question of interest. Friedman and Sunder (1994: 17) encourage experimentalists to create simple economic environments because "simplicity promotes salience and reduces ambiguities." They also encourage the use of neutral wording so that participants' rewards derive from the incentives designed by the experimenter, rather than uncontrolled influences. While economists historically argue against contextual richness, accounting researchers should evaluate whether such realism is desirable, contingent on a study's objective.

Swieringa and Weick (1982) differentiate mundane and experimental realism. Mundane realism refers to the extent that the experiment reflects the real world, whereas experimental realism includes features of the experiment that are believed and that compel participants to act in meaningful ways. Real-world factors that are not central to the theoretical paradigm may actually detract from research because, to the extent that they are incomplete, nonessential factors may evoke incomplete responses. On the other hand, contextual richness may be an important element of the design if one's goal is to better understand the impact of an accounting context on decision-making. Swieringa and Weick (1982: 57) remark that "mundane realism may make verification and discovery more difficult and less instructive in some experimental situations, but may be beneficial in testing complex theories and in providing common meanings in other experimental situations." Trade-offs arise in choosing between abstract and context-rich settings, and such trade-offs should be evaluated on a case-by-case basis (Haynes and Kachelmeier 1998). To illustrate we next turn to an example of a research study that has taken the abstract route and another that introduces a rich context to better isolate the question of interest in a particular framework.

Bowlin et al. (2015) motivate the use of an abstract environment to investigate the link between auditor rotation and audit quality. In their game-theoretic-strategic setting, the authors examine whether auditor rotation impacts the quality of an audit differently depending on the auditor's decision frame. The auditor takes an honesty (dishonesty) frame when asked to assess whether managerial reports are honest (dishonest). The results suggest that rotation increases audit quality in the honesty frame, but actually *decreases* quality in the dishonesty frame. Bowlin et al. choose an abstract environment with neutral wording because the behaviour they wish to examine derives from economic and strategic forces that are not shaped by contextual features.

Another important feature of Bowlin et al.'s (2015) design is their participant pool. Study participants are undergraduate students because expertise is not a factor that impacts the relationships studied. More specifically, the theory that underlies the hypotheses does not rely on the development of a knowledge base. As Libby, Bloomfield and Nelson (2002) argue, a student participant pool is appropriate when studying questions related to general cognitive behaviour or economic forces. The use of a more experienced participant pool could actually lead to negative externalities. Not only do the costs increase for the researcher, but more sophisticated participants could potentially bring unrelated beliefs to the experiment, which are not appropriate to the particular context (Haynes and Kachelmeier 1998).

In other cases, contextual richness and an experienced participant pool may be appropriate to the research question. For example, Bloomfield et al. (2003) include key aspects of the target environment. They report that their research participants rely too much on past earnings information when asked to predict future return on equity. Though overreliance on unreliable information is a commonly reported cognitive error, an abstract environment was not chosen. Bloomfield et al. (2003) argue that a rich context is an important aspect of their design because the context, in combination with experience, alters how information patterns are evaluated by participants. For experienced people, knowledge structures that are stored in memory are triggered by a rich context. Thus, a contextually rich environment provides cues that are appropriate for the task at hand. In this case, the added context might actually eliminate the reliance on uninformative data. Participants in Bloomfield et al. (2003) are MBA students who have developed some expertise in accounting and finance. They intentionally are given limited information so that they must draw on their education and experience to predict future performance. Bloomfield et al. report that one type of cognitive error can lead to under- or overreaction to past earnings depending on the structure of earnings information. Their findings provide important insights into market participants' responses to earnings information. Research along these lines is crucial to understanding market anomalies, as documented in the archival literature.

In sum, when designing an experimental economics study like those described above, one must devote significant ex ante effort to design choices. We encourage researchers to remember that the purpose of an experiment is not to simulate the real world. Rather, the goal is to study accounting phenomenon, test theory and provide a basis for new theoretical models.

Concluding remarks

Throughout this chapter, we have strived to demonstrate the usefulness and applicability of experimental economics to accounting research. We trace the origins in accounting back to Ansari (1976), though such studies did not begin to appear regularly in the literature until the late 1980s. Experimental economics studies have been a small, but ever-present force in accounting research for nearly 30 years! Such studies investigate individual behaviour, interactive (group) outcomes and market outcomes across a wide variety of accounting issues.

As discussed, an experimental economics approach has comparative advantages over other methods in addressing certain research questions. We maintain that such an approach is particularly well suited to address questions that involve heterogeneous agents (e.g., informed versus uninformed agents, truth tellers versus liars, high-quality versus low-quality auditors, etc.) and policy-related issues (e.g., regulatory regime, reporting regime, tax regime, etc.). We encourage future study along these lines.

In this chapter, we have tried to give the reader sufficient background to appreciate accounting-related, experimental economics studies. Our hope is that some readers will follow along the path of those who have conducted such studies and published in accounting journals. Without question, experimental economics is a powerful tool that can be applied to many, many issues in auditing, financial accounting, managerial accounting and taxes.

Acknowledgements: We gratefully acknowledge the helpful comments of Jeff Hales, Adam Vitalis and Donnie Young.

Notes

1 Our definition is consistent with that of Callahan, Gabriel and Sainty (2006). Others (e.g., Kachelmeier and King 2002) define an experimental economics approach as one that involves a multi-person interactive setting with competitive incentives.

2 For more extensive background on the use of experimental economics, as a research method in general, we refer the interested reader to Davis and Holt (1993); Friedman and Sunder (1994); Kagel and Roth (1997) and Bardsley, Cubitt, Loomes, Moffatt, Starmer and Sugden (2009).

3 A handful of other papers appeared in the latter part of the 1980s. One stream of research looks at issues involving the effect of performance-contingent contracts on budgetary reporting and task performance (Baiman and Lewis 1989; Chow, Cooper and Waller 1988; Shields and Waller 1988; Waller and Chow 1985; Young, Shields and Wolf 1988). DeJong, Forsythe, Kim and Uecker (1989) investigate the effect of transfer-pricing mechanisms on negotiated agreements and misreporting. Dopuch, King and Wallin (1989) study the effect of the demand for audit services on economic efficiencies. Finally, Swenson (1988, 1989) examines the effect of tax regime on workers' productivity, total tax payments and individuals' demand for risky assets.

4 This monograph extends Dopuch et al. (1989). A fundamental difference is the inclusion of a human player as the auditor, which adds a layer of complexity to the design. In the earlier study, the auditor is computerized and, thus, not subject to moral hazard. Kachelmeier (1991) also investigates auditors' moral hazard.

5 The count only includes papers that report experimental results, thereby excluding discussion articles, overviews and commentaries.

6 Callahan et al. (2006) present publication data through 2006. We follow that study's search procedures to identify additional publications from 2007–2014 in the set of 14 journals. We find that three journals did not publish papers using experimental economics in the 2000s, including *Abacus, Journal of Accounting and Economics* and *Journal of Accounting, Auditing & Finance*. Please note that our search procedure did not include other journals outside of those originally identified in Callahan et al.

7 Certificates are less valuable to participants who are taxed on dividend earnings because payoffs are lower (i.e., net of taxes).

8 Within a session, biased forecasts are always biased in the same direction: that is, upward in some sessions and downward in other sessions. By holding the direction of the bias constant within a session, its effect on behaviour can be isolated.

9 Sufficient capacity to influence market outcomes refers to participants' ability to engage in transactions. Each period participants are endowed with cash and certificates. The endowments are such that participants can buy as many certificates as others are willing to sell, but they can only sell up to four certificates. Hence, participants who are buyers (not taxed on dividend earnings) have a greater capacity to influence market outcomes than participants who are sellers (taxed on dividend earnings).

10 An alternative approach would be to administer a personality inventory beforehand, allowing classification of participants before assigning them to experimental conditions. The benefit of this approach is that a stable measure of personality may be identified and used as a basis for classification. A potential drawback is that the dimension of personality may not systematically or meaningfully impact behaviour in the experimental setting.

11 Ansari (1976) is a notable exception, focusing on behavioural factors that influence employee satisfaction and productivity.

12 Von Neumann and Morgenstern (1944) use expected utility theory to define rational economic behaviour under uncertainty. For an overview of the theory see Ackert and Deaves (2010).

13 Partially honest reporting choices suggest that the disutility from lying is linked to the magnitude of misrepresentation. Indeed, research outside of accounting puts forth a theory that is consistent with partial honesty, referred to as self-concept maintenance (Mazar, Amir and Airely 2008). The theory suggests that lying is permissible as long as it does not undermine self-concept. Individuals are dishonest up to a point, which allows them to reap the rewards from misrepresentation and still maintain a positive self-concept. In a reporting setting, misrepresentation that is less than the maximum allowable amount improves one's economic well-being, but it also preserves self-concept. Mazar et al. conduct a series of experiments and provide findings that are consistent with their theory.

14 Face-to-face communication involves a superior-subordinate dyad. The subordinate represents a division manager who submits a budget report. The superior, on the other hand, represents a higher-level manager or corporate headquarters. In the study, the superior is present (an actual person), but plays a passive role (automatically approves the subordinate's budget).

15 The agent's services reduce the likelihood that the principal suffers a loss. Further, the agent may be held liable for losses incurred. If an agent is not hired, the principal faces a higher likelihood of loss, which is always borne by the principal.

16 The equilibrium predictions are not affected by the change in the number of service levels. By varying the number of service levels, the authors are able to assess the robustness of the game-theoretic predictions.

17 Farrell (1987) defines cheap talk as communication that is costless, nonbinding and non-verifiable.

18 Along these lines, Ackert et al. (1996) provide evidence that individuals have difficulty processing value-relevant information (i.e., inferring implications for asset value). The study's findings suggest that individuals prefer processed to unprocessed information, even though the value implications of the information are identical. The processed information is just easier to use (i.e., the value implications are more readily apparent).

19 See, for example, Ackert, Church and Qi (2015) who use the lottery-menu and endowment-investment tasks to control for risk in a study designed to isolate factors that impact individuals' portfolio selection.

References

Ackert, L.F., Charupat, N., Church, B.K. and Deaves, R., 2006, 'Margins, short selling, and lotteries in experimental asset markets', *Southern Economics Journal* 73(2), 419–436.

Ackert, L.F., Charupat, N., Deaves, R. and Kluger, B.D., 2009, 'Probability judgment error and speculation in laboratory asset market bubbles', *Journal of Financial and Quantitative Analysis* 44(3), 719–744.

Ackert, L.F., Church, B.K. and Qi, L., 2015, 'An experimental examination of portfolio choice', *Review of Finance* 20(4), 1427–1447.

Ackert, L.F., Church, B.K. and Shehata, M., 1996, 'What affects individuals' decisions to acquire forecasted information?', *Contemporary Accounting Research* 13(2), 379–399.

Ackert, L.F., Church, B.K. and Shehata, M., 1997, 'An experimental examination of the effects of forecast bias on individuals' use of forecasted information', *Journal of Accounting Research* 35(1), 25–42.

Ackert, L.F., Church, B.K. and Zhang, P., 2004, 'Asset prices and informed traders' abilities: Evidence from experimental asset markets', *Accounting, Organizations and Society* 29(7), 609–626.

Ackert, L.F., Church, B.K. and Zhang, P., 2016, 'Costly information acquisition in experimental asset markets: Spending too much, trading too little, and losing your shirt', *Working paper*, Georgia Tech.

Ackert, L.F. and Deaves, R., 2010, *Behavioral Finance: Psychology, Decision-Making, and Markets*, South-Western Cengage Learning, Mason, OH.

Alm, J. and Jacobson, S., 2007, 'Using laboratory experiments in public economics', *National Tax Journal* 60(1), 129–152.

Alm, J. and McKee, M., 2006, 'Audit certainty, audit productivity, and taxpayer compliance', *National Tax Journal* 59(4), 801–816.

Ansari, S.L., 1976, 'Behavioral factors in variance control: Report on a laboratory experiment', *Journal of Accounting Research* 14(2), 189–211.

Antle, R. and Fellingham, J., 1995, 'Informational rents and preferences among information systems in a model of resource allocation', *Journal of Accounting Research* 33(Supplement), 41–58.

Baiman, S. and Lewis, B.L., 1989, 'An experiment testing the behavioral equivalence of strategically equivalent employment contracts', *Journal of Accounting Research* 27(1), 1–20.

Barberis, N., Shleifer, A. and Vishny, R., 1998, 'A model of investor sentiment', *Journal of Financial Economics* 49(3), 307–343.

Bardsley, N., Cubitt, R., Loomes, G., Moffatt, P., Starmer, C. and Sugden, R., 2009, *Experimental Economics: Rethinking the Rules*, Princeton University Press, Princeton, NJ.

Beck, P., Davis, J. and Jung, W.-O., 1992, 'Experimental evidence on an economic model of taxpayer aggression under strategic and nonstrategic audits', *Contemporary Accounting Research* 9(1), 86–112.

Berg, J., 1994, 'Using experimental economics to resolve accounting dilemmas', *Contemporary Accounting Research* 10(2), 547–556.

Berg, J., Coursey, D. and Dickhaut, J., 1990, 'Experimental methods in accounting: A discussion of recurring issues', *Contemporary Accounting Research* 6(2), 825–849.

Berg, J., Daley, L., Dickhaut, J. and O'Brien, J., 1986, 'Controlling preferences for lotteries on units of experimental exchange', *Quarterly Journal of Economics* 101(2), 281–306.

Berg, J., Daley, L., Gigler, F. and Kanodia, C., 1990, *The Value of Communication in Agency Contracts: Theory and Experimental Evidence, Research Monograph Number 16*, The Certified General Accountants' Research Foundation, Vancouver, BC.

Bloomfield, R., Libby, R. and Nelson, M., 2003, 'Do investors overrely on old elements of the earnings time series?', *Contemporary Accounting Research* 20(1), 1–31.

Bloomfield, R. and Wilks, J., 2000, 'Disclosure effects in the laboratory: Liquidity, depth, and the cost of capital', *The Accounting Review* 75(1), 13–41.

Boatsman, J., Grasso, L., Ormiston, M. and Renau, J., 1992, 'A perspective on the use of laboratory market experimentation in auditing research', *The Accounting Review* 67(1), 148–156.

Bossaerts, P., Frydman, C. and Ledyard, J., 2014, 'Speed of information revelation and eventual price quality in markets with insiders: Comparing two theories', *Review of Finance* 18(1), 1–22.

Bossaerts, P. and Plott, C., 2004, 'Basic principles of asset-pricing theory: Evidence from large-scale experimental financial markets', *Review of Finance* 8(2), 135–169.

Bowlin, K., Hales, J. and Kachelmeier, S., 2009, 'Experimental evidence of how prior experience as an auditor influences managers' strategic reporting decisions', *Review of Accounting Studies* 14(1), 63–87.

Bowlin, K., Hobson, J. and Piercey, M., 2015, 'The effects of auditor rotation, professional skepticism, and interactions with managers on audit quality', *The Accounting Review* 90(4), 1363–1393.

Burton, F., Coller, M. and Tuttle, B., 2006, 'Market responses to qualitative information from a group polarization perspective', *Accounting, Organizations and Society* 31(2), 107–127.

Calegari, M. and Fargher, N., 1997, 'Evidence that prices do not fully reflect the implications of current earnings for future earnings: An experimental markets approach', *Contemporary Accounting Research* 14(3), 397–433.

Calegari, M., Schatzberg, J. and Sevcik, G., 1998, 'Experimental evidence of differential auditor pricing and reporting strategies', *The Accounting Review* 73(2), 255–275.

Callahan, C., Gabriel, E. and Sainty, B., 2006, 'A review and classification of experimental economics research in accounting', *Journal of Accounting Literature* 25, 59–126.

Chalos, P. and Haka, S., 1990, 'Transfer pricing under bilateral bargaining', *The Accounting Review* 65(3), 624–641.

Chow, C., Cooper, J. and Waller, W., 1988, 'Participative budgeting: Effects of a truth-inducing pay scheme and information asymmetry on slack and performance', *The Accounting Review* 63(1), 111–122.

Christ, M., Emett, S., Summers, S. and Wood, D., 2012, 'The effects of preventive and detective controls on employee motivation and performance', *Contemporary Accounting Research* 29(2), 432–452.

Church, B.K., Hannan, R.L. and Kuang, X., 2012, 'Shared interest and honesty in budget reporting', *Accounting, Organizations and Society* 37(3), 155–167.

Church, B.K., Hannan, R.L. and Kuang, X., 2014, 'Information acquisition and opportunistic behavior in managerial reporting', *Contemporary Accounting Research* 31(2), 398–419.

Church, B.K., Peytcheva, M., Yu, W. and Singtokul, O.-A., 2015, 'Perspective taking in auditor-manager interactions: An experimental investigation of auditor behavior', *Accounting, Organizations and Society* 45(August), 40–51.

Coletti, A., Sedatole, K. and Towry, K., 2005, 'The effect of control systems on trust and cooperation in collaborative environments', *The Accounting Review* 80(2), 477–500.

Coller, M., 1996. 'Information, noise, and asset prices: An experimental study', *Review of Accounting Studies* 1(1), 35–50.

Commission on Auditors' Responsibilities, 1978, *Report, Conclusions, and Recommendations*, Commission on Auditors' Responsibilities, New York.

Copland, T. and Friedman, D., 1992, 'The market value of information: Some experimental results', *Journal of Business* 65(2), 241–266.

Davis, D. and Holt, C., 1993, *Experimental Economics*, Princeton University Press, Princeton, NJ.

Davis, J., Hecht, G. and Perkins, J., 2003, 'Social behaviors, enforcement, and tax compliance dynamics', *The Accounting Review* 78(1), 39–69.

Davis, J. and Swenson, C., 1988, 'The role of experimental economics in tax policy research', *Journal of the American Taxation Association* 10(1), 40–59.

DeJong, D. and Forsythe, R., 1992, 'A perspective on the use of laboratory market experimentation in auditing research', *The Accounting Review* 67(1), 157–170.

DeJong, D., Forsythe, R., Kim, J. and Uecker, W., 1989, 'A laboratory investigation of alternative transfer pricing mechanisms', *Accounting, Organizations and Society* 14(1/2), 41–64.

DeJong, D., Forsythe, R., Lundholm, R. and Uecker, W., 1985, 'A laboratory investigation of the moral hazard problem in an agency relationship', *Journal of Accounting Research* 23(Supplement), 81–123.

DeJong, D., Forsythe, R. and Uecker, W., 1985, 'The methodology of laboratory markets and its implications for agency research in accounting and auditing', *Journal of Accounting Research* 23(2), 753–793.

Dietrich, D., Kachelmeier, S., Kleinmuntz, D. and Linsmeier, T., 2001, 'Market efficiency, bounded rationality, and supplemental business reporting disclosures', *Journal of Accounting Research* 39(2), 243–268.

Division for CPA Firms, 1992, *Statement of Position Regarding Mandatory Rotation of Audit Firms of Publicly Held Companies*, American Institute of Certified Public Accountants, New York.

Dopuch, N. and King, R., 1991a, 'The effect of MAS on auditors' independence: An experimental markets study', *Journal of Accounting Research* 29(Supplement), 60–98.

Dopuch, N. and King, R., 1991b, *Experimental tests of auditing as a credibility generating mechanism, Research Monograph Number 19*, The Certified General Accountants' Research Foundation, Vancouver, BC.

Dopuch, N. and King, R., 1992, 'Negligence versus strict liability regimes in auditing: An experimental investigation', *The Accounting Review* 67(1), 97–120.

Dopuch, N., King, R. and Schwartz, R., 2002, 'An experimental investigation of retention and rotation requirements', *Journal of Accounting Research* 39(1), 93–117.

Dopuch, N., King, R. and Wallin, D., 1989, 'The use of experimental markets in auditing research: Some initial findings', *Auditing: A Journal of Practice & Theory* 8(Supplement), 98–127.

Elias, N., 1990, 'The effects of financial information symmetry on conflict resolution: An experiment in the context of labor negotiations', *The Accounting Review* 65(3), 606–623.

Elliott, W.B., Hobson, J. and White, B., 2015, 'Earnings metrics, information processing, and price efficiency in laboratory markets', *Journal of Accounting Research* 53(3), 555–592.

Evans, J.H., Hannan, R.L., Krishnan, R. and Moser, D., 2001, 'Honesty in managerial reporting', *The Accounting Review* 76(4), 537–559.

Farrell, J., 1987, 'Cheap talk, coordination, and entry', *Rand Journal of Economics* 18(1), 34–39.

Fatemi, D., 2012, 'An experimental investigation of the influence of audit fee structure and auditor selection rights on auditor independence and client investment decisions', *Auditing: A Journal of Practice & Theory* 31(3), 75–94.

Fischer, P. and Huddart, S., 2008, 'Optimal contracting with endogenous social norms', *American Economic Review* 98(4), 1459–1475.

Foster, F.D. and Viswanathan, S., 1996, 'Strategic trading when agents forecast the forecasts of others', *Journal of Finance* 51(4), 1437–1478.

Friedman, D. and Sunder, S., 1994, *Experimental Methods: A Primer for Economists*, Cambridge University Press, New York.

Ganguly, A., Kagel, J. and Moser, D., 1994, 'The effects of biases in probability judgments on market prices', *Accounting, Organizations and Society* 19(8), 675–700.

Ganguly, A., Kagel, J. and Moser, D., 2000, 'Do asset market prices reflect traders' judgment biases?', *Journal of Risk and Uncertainty* 20(3), 219–245.

Gneezy, U. and Potters, J., 1997, 'An experiment on risk taking and evaluation periods', *Quarterly Journal of Economics* 112(2), 631–645.

Hales, J., Wang, L. and Williamson, M., 2015, 'Selection benefits of stock-based compensation for the rank-and-file', *The Accounting Review* 90(4), 1497–1516.

Hales, J. and Williamson, M., 2010, 'Implicit employment contracts: The limits of management reputation for promoting firm productivity', *Journal of Accounting Research* 48(1), 51–80.

Hannan, R.L., Rankin, F.W. and Towry, K., 2006, 'The effect of information systems on honesty in managerial reporting: A behavioral perspective', *Contemporary Accounting Research* 23(4), 885–918.

Haynes, C. and Kachelmeier, S., 1998, 'The effects of accounting contexts on accounting decisions: A synthesis of cognitive and economic perspectives in accounting experimentation', *Journal of Accounting Literature* 17, 97–136.

Hobson, J., 2011, 'Do the benefits of reducing accounting complexity persist in markets prone to bubble?', *Contemporary Accounting Research* 28(3), 959–989.

Hobson, J. and Kachelemeier, S., 2005, 'Strategic disclosure of risky prospects: A laboratory experiment', *The Accounting Review* 80(3), 825–846.

Holt, C. and Laury, S., 2002, 'Risk aversion and incentive effects', *American Economic Review* 95(3), 1644–1655.

Holthausen, R. and Verrecchia, R., 1988, 'The effect of sequential information releases on the variance of price changes in an intertemporal multi-asset market', *Journal of Accounting Research* 26(1), 82–106.

Jamal, K., Maier, M. and Sunder, S., 2015, 'Simple agents, intelligent markets', *Working paper*, Yale University Press, New Haven, CT.

Kachelmeier, S., 1991, 'A laboratory market investigation of the demand for strategic auditing', *Auditing: A Journal of Practice & Theory* 10(Supplement), 25–48.

Kachelmeier, S. and King, R., 2002, 'Using laboratory experiments to evaluate accounting policy issues', *Accounting Horizons* 16(3), 219–232.

Kagel, J. and Roth, A., 1997, *The Handbook of Experimental Economics*, Princeton University Press, Princeton, NJ.

King, R., 1996, 'Reputation formation for reliable reporting: An experimental investigation', *The Accounting Review* 71(3), 375–396.

King, R., 2002, 'An experimental investigation of self-serving biases in an auditing trust game: The effect of group affiliation', *The Accounting Review* 77(2), 265–284.

King, R. and Wallin, D., 1990, 'The effects of antifraud rules and ex post verifiability on managerial disclosures', *Contemporary Accounting Research* 6(2), 859–892.

King, R. and Wallin, D., 1991, 'Market-induced information disclosures: An experimental markets investigation', *Contemporary Accounting Research* 8(1), 170–197.

Koford, K. and Penno, M., 1992, 'Accounting, principal-agent theory, and self-interested behavior', in N. Bowie and R. Freeman (eds.), *Ethics and Agency Theory*, 127–142, Oxford University Press, Oxford.

Kyle, A.S., 1985, 'Continuous auctions and insider trading', *Econometrica* 53(6), 1315–1335.

Kyle, A.S., 1989, 'Informed speculation with imperfect competition', *Review of Economic Studies* 56(3), 317–355.

Lei, V., Noussair, C. and Plott, C., 2001, 'Nonspeculative bubbles in experimental asset markets: Lack of common knowledge of rationality versus actual irrationality', *Econometrica* 69(4), 831–859.

Libby, R., Bloomfield, R. and Nelson, M., 2002, 'Experimental research in financial accounting', *Accounting, Organizations, and Society* 27(8), 775–810.

Luft, J., 1997, 'Fairness, ethics, and the effects of management accounting on transaction costs', *Journal of Management Accounting Research* 9, 199–216.

Magilke, M., Mayhew, B. and Pike, J., 2009, 'Are independent audit committee members objective? Experimental evidence', *The Accounting Review* 84(6), 1959–1981.

Mayhew, B., 2001, 'Auditor reputation building', *Journal of Accounting Research* 39(3), 599–617.

Mayhew, B. and Pike, J., 2004, 'Does investor selection of auditors enhance auditor independence?', *The Accounting Review* 79(3), 797–822.

Mazar, N., Amir, O. and Airely, D., 2008, 'The dishonesty on honest people: A theory of self-concept maintenance', *Journal of Marketing Research* 45(6), 633–644.

McDaniel, L. and Hand, J., 1996, 'The value of experimental methods for practice-relevant accounting research', *Contemporary Accounting Research* 13(1), 339–351.

Mittendorf, B., 2006, 'Capital budgeting when managers value both honesty and perquisites', *Journal of Management Accounting Research* 18, 77–95.

Moser, D., 1998, 'Using an experimental economics approach in behavioral accounting research', *Behavioral Research in Accounting* 10(Supplement), 94–110.

Mukherji, A., 1996, 'The handbook of experimental economics: A review essay', *Behavioral Research in Accounting* 8, 217–231.

Murnighan, J. and Bazerman, M., 1990, 'A perspective on negotiation research in accounting and auditing', *The Accounting Review* 65(3), 642–657.

Public Company Accounting Oversight Board, 2011, *Concept Release on Auditor Independence and Audit Firm Rotation*, Public Company Accounting Oversight Board, Washington, DC.

Schatzberg, J. and Sevcik, G., 1994, 'A multiperiod model and experimental evidence of independence and "lowballing"', *Contemporary Accounting Research* 11(1), 137–174.

Selto, F. and Cooper, J., 1990, 'Control of risk attitude in experimental accounting research', *Journal of Accounting Literature* 9, 229–264.

Shields, M. and Waller, M., 1988, 'A behavioral study of accounting variables in performance incentive contracts', *Accounting, Organizations and Society* 13(6), 581–594.

Smith, V., 1976, 'Experimental economics: Induced value theory', *American Economic Review* 66(2), 274–279.

Smith, V., 1982, 'Microeconomic systems as an experimental science', *American Economic Review* 72(5), 923–955.

Smith, V., Schatzberg, J. and Waller, W., 1987, 'Experimental economics and auditing', *Auditing: A Journal of Practice & Theory* 7(1), 71–93.

Smith, V., Suchanek, G. and Williams, A., 1988, 'Bubbles, crashes, and endogenous expectations in experimental spot asset markets', *Econometrica* 56(5), 1119–1151.

Stone, D., 2015, 'Post-Hunton: Reclaiming our integrity and literature', *Journal of Information Systems* 29(2), 211–227.

Sunder, S. and Jamal, K., 1996, 'Bayesian equilibrium in double auctions populated by biased heuristic traders', *Journal of Economic Behavior and Organization* 31(2), 273–291.

Swenson, C., 1988, 'Taxpayer behavior in response to taxation: An experimental analysis', *Journal of Accounting and Public Policy* 7(1), 1–28.

Swenson, C., 1989, 'Tax regimes and the demand for risky assets: Some experimental market evidence', *Journal of the American Taxation Association* 11(1), 54–76.

Swieringa, R. and Weick, K., 1982, 'An assessment of laboratory experiments in accounting', *Journal of Accounting Research* 20(Supplement), 56–101.

Tayler, W. and Bloomfield, R., 2011, 'Norms, conformity, and controls', *Journal of Accounting Research* 49(3), 750–793.

Tuttle, B., Coller, M. and Burton, F., 1996, 'An examination of market efficiency: Information order effects in a laboratory market', *Accounting, Organizations and Society* 22(1), 89–103.

Von Neumann, J. and Morgenstern, O., 1944, *Theory of Games and Economic Behavior*, Princeton University Press, Princeton, NJ.

Waller, W. and Chow, C., 1985, 'The self-selection and effort effects of standard-based employment contracts: A framework and some empirical evidence', *The Accounting Review* 60(3), 458–476.

Waller, W., Shapiro, B. and Sevcik, G., 1999, 'Do cost-based pricing biases persist in laboratory markets', *Accounting, Organizations and Society* 24(8), 717–739.

Wallin, D., 1992, 'Legal recourse and the demand for auditing', *The Accounting Review* 67(1), 121–147.

Wang, K. and Tuttle, B., 2009, 'The impact of auditor rotation on audit-client negotiation', *Accounting, Organizations and Society* 34(2), 222–243.

Wineman, L., 2013, 'Interesting results? Can they be replicated?', *Monitor on Psychology, American Psychological Association* 44(2), 38.

Young, S., Shields, M. and Wolf, G., 1988, 'Manufacturing controls and performance: An experiment', *Accounting, Organizations and Society* 13(6), 607–618.

Yu, H.-C., 2011, 'Legal systems and auditor independence', *Review of Accounting Studies* 16(2), 377–411.

15

Survey research

Facts and perceptions

J.F.M.G. (Jan) Bouwens

Introduction

Survey questionnaires can be powerful instruments to directly measure accounting-related phenomena. Yet, due to the potential for measurement error, many economics-based researchers do not believe that results based on survey evidence are valid (Bertrand and Mullainathan 2001). These researchers argue that perceptual responses to survey questions contain significant measurement error and thus, may not capture the underlying construct of interest. This chapter makes some recommendations on the design of survey instruments to allow behavioural researchers in accounting to gather survey evidence while reducing measurement error, defined as the difference between a measured value and its true value.

Measurement error can be random (i.e., noise) or systematic (i.e., bias). Random measurement error will not affect the mean values of the observed variables, only the variability of the observations around the mean. Random error can be controlled by using larger samples. Systematic measurement error, or bias, must be addressed directly in the design of the survey instrument. Potential sources of systematic error that can be addressed through survey instrument design include question order, use of double-barrelled questions, question ambiguity, cognitive limitations, social limitations and attitudinal limitations of the survey respondents. To further enhance their relevance, we need to measure the variables of interest with a variety of instruments so that we can assess how reliable our measures are and to what extent we are capturing the constructs of interest (i.e., their validity).

An illustration of potential sources of measurement error in questionnaires

This section aims to illustrate the challenges to survey-based research design using a study conducted by the International Federation of Accountants (IFAC 2015). I hasten to say that the problems I observe in the IFAC study would apply as well to many studies using the survey method to create a database, including studies published in academic journals in accounting.

In 2015, IFAC was interested to learn the extent to which regulation was impacting firm innovation. To explore this question, IFAC (2016: 17) issued a survey with the central question being, "How significant is the regulation that impacts your organization's (a) costs of doing business; (b) opportunity to grow and; (c) opportunity to innovate." According to the results, 80% of respondents reported that regulation impacted their costs of doing business either significantly or very significantly, 66% reported regulation impacted their opportunity to grow either significantly or very significantly and 63% reported that regulation impacted their opportunity to innovate either significantly or very significantly. In addition, the respondents were asked "Going forward five years, how much more or less significant do you expect the impact of regulation to be for your organization overall?" (19). To that question, 83% of respondents reported that the impact was expected to be more significant (48.6%) or much more significant (36.1%) than in the past. The respondents were reported to be working in accounting, financial services and a wide range of other industry and commercial sectors.

The critical question to ask in designing surveys is whether or not responses to survey questions provide insight into the research question, which in the IFAC case is "what is the extent to which regulation affects innovation?" To that end, I subject the IFAC survey to the Socratic method (see for instance, Vlastos 1985). This entails asking a sequence of questions to reveal general, commonly held truths and beliefs, and to subsequently scrutinize them so as to determine their consistency. The Socratic method is comprised of taking questions in two stages: "What does the individual making a statement mean?" and "Is this statement true?"

Stage 1

As applied to the IFAC case, the first stage requires an assessment of what an individual means when (s)he states that regulation is impacting the firm's opportunity to innovate. Specifically, I evaluate the question: "how significant is the regulation that impacts your organization's opportunity to innovate?" When responding to this question, the respondent will have to make a series of assessments, given that the question is comprised of two notions, regulation and innovation.

The notion of regulation involves an assessment of the level of regulation and what exactly regulation entails. What is the magnitude of regulation in general, and in the industry in which the respondent's firm operates? Personal characteristics or opinions may impact how the respondent perceives the question. For example, does the respondent consider regulation as something good (i.e., an instrument to level the playing field), or as something bad (i.e., regulation is a purposeless hurdle to overcome).

Stage 2

The second stage involves an assessment of the extent of opportunity for innovation. Is the respondent referring to the full investment opportunity set, or to the extent to which (s)he is able to fund projects, or the extent to which investments in innovation are possible in her/his own unit? In addition, how the question is framed (i.e., the scope of investment opportunity as seen by the respondent) will cause further variation in the answers respondents provide.

Other factors, including recent events, also are likely to affect the answers the respondent provides. For instance, if one of his/her investments in innovation recently failed, this is likely to impact their response to the survey, and may also impact the reliability of his/her responses.

For each survey question it is therefore true that:

Measured variable = True value + *Error*

In the case of our example:

Measured Opportunity for Innovation = True Opportunity for Innovation + *Error*

Hence, the notion of innovation opportunity will inevitably be measured with systematic error. In the next section, I present some main sources of this error and some steps one can take to mitigate the impact of this type of error.

Sources of systematic error

Double-barrelled questions

In the example from the IFAC survey, two separate considerations were included in a single question: regulation *and* innovation. This is an example of a double-barrelled question, which by including two notions in one question creates error that we cannot unravel. The double-barrel question can be easily avoided by asking two questions instead (Olson 2008; Earl and Benaquisto 2009; Bryman and Bell 2011).

Ambiguity in survey questions

Another issue with the IFAC survey question emerges from the ambiguity included in questions that stem from the use of the term "impact". In the IFAC survey, the respondent is asked to assess how regulation impacts innovation opportunities; however, the term "impact" may mean different things to different respondents. For example, "impact" may be positive or negative, and may or may not encompass causality. To eliminate the ambiguity, the questions could separately ask about A and B and calculate the correlation between A and B (controlling for other factors that may impact innovation opportunities and/or regulation).

Cognitive limitations

Cognitive limitations reflect the inherent limitation in individuals' intellectual processing capacity, which may be triggered by the order of questions, phrasing and particular number or signal words in the survey questions. The order "primes" their thinking as it were. For instance, as Bertrand and Mullainathan (2001) suggest, if we ask:

1   How happy are you with life in general?
2   How often do you go out on a date?

We will get different answers compared to when we ask the same question in the opposite order:

1   How often do you go out on a date?
2   How happy are you with life in general?

Bertrand and Mullainathan (2001) find that the answers to these questions are correlated if respondents are presented with these questions in the second order, while no correlation exists when these questions are presented in the first order.

People also appear to suffer from logical inconsistencies. Possibly the query on how often people go on a date makes them happy at that very moment. This positive feeling, in turn, increases the likelihood that they will assess themselves as happier with life in general. This phenomenon is also referred to as priming; an implicit memory effect in which exposure to one stimulus influences the response to another stimulus (Meyer and Schvaneveldt 1971).

People also give different answers conditional on whether a statement is framed in a positive or negative way (e.g., Tversky and Kahneman 1971). For example, if respondents are asked (a) should speeches against democracy be forbidden, 50% of respondents say YES while if respondents are asked (b) should speeches against democracy be allowed, 75% of respondents say NO.

Number also appears to anchor individual's responses to questions (Kahneman 2011). For instance, Bertrand and Mullainathan (2001) find that when respondents are asked how much time they spend watching TV, it matters whether the researcher presents the respondent with a scale that (a) starts with 30 minutes and goes up in 30 minute intervals to 4.5 hours of TV watching or (b) a scale that starts with 2.5 hours or less and goes up in 30 minute intervals to 4.5 hours of TV watching. In the first case, 16% claim to watch TV for more than 2.5 hours per day while in the second case, 32% of the respondents make this claim. When starting the scale at the low end with 2.5 hours, people seem to feel fewer restrictions in saying that they watch over 2.5 hours of TV a day. In fact, any number referred to in a survey question can lead the respondent to use that particular number as a reference point.

Social limitations

Survey responses are also impacted by the fact that people have a desire to be evaluated as socially responsible people and thus want to provide socially desirable answers (see also Chapter 11 of this volume).

Attitudinal limitations

People do not want their shortcomings to be exposed (Bertrand and Mullainathan 2001). For instance, when they are presented with a technique to solve a puzzle and are subsequently asked to solve that puzzle, they are likely to claim that they themselves found out how to solve the puzzle. They also give their opinion on topics they have no knowledge of. For instance, most people are prepared to give their opinion on how the government should deal with government deficit. However, only a small fraction of these people can give an informed opinion.

Common method bias

A potential concern with survey-based research is that people may be inclined to put in less effort than desired to diligently fill in a questionnaire. In addition, people differ in their willingness to exert effort. There are several reasons why people are likely to put in little effort in answering a survey questionnaire. There is relatively little to win or lose with providing (in) accurate answers. For instance, if people really have to think about a question, they easily give up. As a consequence, when presented with a problem where a respondent is required to go back in memory, it is less likely that he/she will. People also have the inclination to consider a specific attribute as a main feature. The weight that he/she puts on the particular feature is going to affect all of the answers. For instance, if the questionnaire refers to an individual, the respondent may evaluate the person as being "outstanding" with regard to one particular attribute. This may cause the respondent to rate other attributes more positively than warranted by the facts (i.e., the halo effect). In other words, the rating of that one attribute "spills over" to influence the evaluation of other attributes. This inclination also extends to questions that look similar to the respondent. Once they decide that the answer to question X is high, all answers may be perceived as pointing in the same high direction. This phenomenon is referred to as common method bias (Podsakoff, MacKenzie, Lee and Podsakoff 2003).

Remedies for the issues raised

In this section, I will discuss how one can deal with wording, framing and priming issues. In the section that follows I will pay special attention to conditions where biases in the measures make it impossible to conclude anything based on a survey. I will give some solutions to that problem as well.

Some remedies to deal with common biases

In this section, I identify both procedural and statistical remedies to mitigate the adverse effects of common biases. To that end, I follow the recommendations of Podsakoff et al. (2003). I illustrate the use of these remedies through reference to a behavioural accounting study by Abernethy, Bouwens and van Lent (2013) (hereafter ABL).

One procedural remedy to deal with order and priming issues is to separate the measurement of dependent and independent variables by placing questionnaire items at the maximum distance from each other and by using different response formats. For instance, in ABL, pay-for-performance sensitivity questions appear later in the questionnaire than questions about performance measures so as to mitigate the anchoring effect.

In addition, one can assure the respondent's anonymity so as to reduce evaluation apprehension. Respondents can also be advised that there are no "right or wrong answers" and that they should answer questions honestly. Such procedures are put in place "to make people less likely to edit their responses to socially desirable, lenient, acquiescent, and consistent with how they think the researcher wants them to respond" (ABL), thus reducing common method bias. ABL protects the respondent anonymity and reduces evaluation apprehension by assuring respondents that there are no right or wrong answers and that they should answer questions honestly. An additional issue is that some scale items are more susceptible to common method bias. Specifically, similar end points and formats in Likert scales are likely to cause common method bias and anchoring effects (similar to the TV watching example above).

To deal with common method bias and anchoring, one can alternate Likert scales in terms of their end points and formats. Harman's (1967) single factor test can be applied to evaluate the extent to which common method variance exists in the data. If present, then either a single factor will emerge from a list of items that are theoretically unrelated, or one factor will account for the majority of covariance among (all of) the independent variables included in the model of interest.

An example of this approach is in ABL and in Bouwens and Van Lent (2007). They conduct factor analyses on each multi-item measure separately and on all latent variables with multiple items jointly and show that the constructs are one-dimensional and exhibit a "clean" factor structure (i.e., each item loads on the factor it is theoretically associated with and not significantly on any other factor). The joint factor analysis also allowed them to assess the potential for common rater bias (Harman 1967). The fact that the items did not appear as one factor assures that the sample does not suffer from common rater bias. However, a more convincing test would be to ask the same question to different respondents who work in the same business unit. However, it appears to be very difficult to collect such data in one firm.

Table 15.1 Instrument used to gauge the latent construct of interdependence

	No impact at all			Some impact		A very significant impact		
(a) To what extent do your unit's actions impact on work carried out in **other** organizational units of your firm?	1	2	3	4	5	6	7	n/a
(b) To what extent do actions of managers of other units of the firm impact work carried out in **your** particular unit?	1	2	3	4	5	6	7	n/a
(c) What percentage of your total production is delivered to other organizational units of your firm?	___%							
(d) What percentage of your total production uses inputs acquired from other organizational units of your firm?	___%							

Validity

Reliability refers to the stability of the measure, over time, and between raters. While a measure must be reliable, we also want to make sure that the variable we are interested in is captured by the measure we administer, i.e., that the measure is valid. If, for instance we are interested in how much activities of two departments are related to each other, we need to develop a measure that allows us to gauge their interdependence. For example, Keating (1997) introduced an instrument to capture the notion of inter-dependence (Abernethy, Bouwens, and Van Lent 2004). This instrument will be used to propose three methods that researchers can apply to evaluate the validity of the instruments they use: face validity, chain of evidence and convergent validity. The methods I discuss are based on ideas put forward by Brownell (1995). The set of questions reproduced in Table 15.1 will be used to elaborate on these methods.

Item (a) gauges how much decisions made in the respondent's unit impact other units. This measure purportedly includes not only the supply of products/services to other units, but also planning decision and information exchange. Item (b) gauges the opposite of item (a), that is how much is the work of other units impacting the work performed in the respondent's unit. Items (c) and (d) are trying to capture how much product is supplied from (to) the respondent's unit. The latter two items will be used to examine the validity of the Keating (1997) instrument.

Face validity

Most researchers using a survey have only one chance to collect their data. It is therefore impor-tant to assure that the instrument is valid before going into the field. To that end, the researcher can create a team of experts that examine instrument validity. We could present the list of words in a panel, e.g., dynamism, environments, complexity, synergy, etc. Respondents could be asked to rank the words according to how well they represent the underlying meaning of the ques-tion, or example, "To what extent do your unit's actions impact on work carried out in **other** organizational units of your firm?"

Chain of evidence

In the case where respondents from only one firm are surveyed, the researcher could try to collect data that provide evidence of the level of interdependence between firm units. Sources that spring to mind are: internal supplies, budget reports, transfer-pricing information and the like. This data could subsequently be examined to see whether it matches up with the evidence collected through the survey.

Convergent/discriminant validity

Convergent validity (and its converse discriminant validity) refers to the notion that different people should rate measures that purportedly capture the same (different) underlying variable the same (differently), and that the same people should observe that different measures that supposedly pick up different constructs are indeed recognized as instruments that capture a different construct. A sophisticated way of testing convergent validity was presented by Lawler (1967). His multitrait-multimethod approach comprises a series of steps to assess construct validity. He proposes that the same instrument focusing on the same event/firm unit is administered to two respondents. Then he suggests that two instruments are administered so that both convey the latent construct, but that they differ in what dimension they are emphasizing. In other words, the researcher administers similar instruments (multitraits). The idea would be that for the instrument to be valid, it should at least show some relation with the similar instrument. At the same time the correlation between the two instruments should not amount to one given that the dimensions the two instruments touch on are different. The idea is that different people should converge on the extent to which the same measures are indeed labelled as the same measure and that they also agree on the observation that different measures capture a different construct. At the same time, this method evaluates whether the same person appreciates the fact that different measures are indeed recognized as being different (discriminant validity).

In our case, we have two instruments that measure the level of interdependence (Table 15.1, instrument *a* and *b*), and we have two instruments that are related to interdependence, but these measures focus on another dimension: deliveries of goods/services (Table 15.1, instrument *c* and *d*). The first set of measures (a and b) gauge the level of interaction between firm units, while the second set of measures (*c* and *d*) emphasize supply of internal production only. The attractive feature of items *c* and *d* is that they are more objective (that require the respondent to recall a hard number) than *a* and *b* (that require an assessment of how much impact units impose on each other). That is, *a* and *b* are likely to contain higher levels of measurement error than *c* and *d*. On the other hand, *a* and *b* arguably capture a broader range of dimensions of interdependence than items *c* and *d*.

With multiple raters and several instruments, we can conduct three tests proposed by Lawler (1967) and Brownell (1995). Specifically, (a) we can test whether different respondents believe that the same instrument represents the same thing, (b) we can test whether the same person believes that the measures are different but related and 3) we can test whether different respondents agree that different measures are related (yet that they are at the same time recognized as being different). We can use simple correlation analysis to examine the relationships between the measures.

I show the results of this exercise in Table 15.2, where managers and controllers of business units represent multi-raters. We first a) test what is the correlation of instruments used by different respondents. We then b) estimate the correlation between two different instruments administered to one respondent and finally, c) calculate the correlation between the answers two different respondents give on two similar instruments. According to the theory, we should observe the following pattern: CORR (I)] CORR (II)] CORR (III). Inspection of Table 15.2 confirms this pattern. In other words, the "impact instrument" meets the test of convergent validity. Indeed, different raters agree to a large extent on how much impact their unit has on

Table 15.2 Multitrait-multimethod matrix

		Manager		Controller	
		a. Influence	c. Supply	a. Influence	c. Supply
Manager	a. Influence	1.0			
	c. Supply	0.56	1.0		
Controller	a. Influence	0.75	0.2	1.0	
	c. Supply	0.2	0.77	0.50	1.0

0.75   Test I: Same construct, different respondents

0.56   Test II and IV: Different but related constructs, same respondents

0.2   Test III: Different but related constructs, different respondents

other units in the same firm (Table 15.2 item *a*: CORR=0.75). The same rater confirms a positive relation between impact and internal delivery (Table 15.2 items *a* and *c*: CORR=0.56). Different raters confirm some relation between items *a* and *c*, but the correlation is lower than the other correlations (Table 15.2 items *a* and *c*: CORR=0.2).

Only one respondent

In most cases, we do not get to administer our instrument to two respondents for each unit. We therefore can only rely on test II above with different, but related constructs and the same respondents. This means that we have to make sure that the survey design allows such tests of validity. This means that we have to ask a similar question more than once to be able to make that analysis. In the case of interdependence, we have question *c (d)* to verify the validity of question *a (b)*. In addition, we can use question *a* to verify the validity of question *b* as it is likely that when unit one impacts unit two, unit two also impacts unit one.

Testing models: when facts are better than perceptions

In this section, I will discuss situations where perceptions in questionnaires pose a serious threat to the validity of a study. I will argue that especially omitted correlated variable issues impose a major threat to the identification of models that include variables that are measured using surveys. This problem can be circumvented, provided that the dependent variable is measured as a fact, rather than as a perception. By fact I refer to a number recorded in the company database or a survey measure asking the respondent to remember a verifiable situation, such as: "How large were sales in 2015?" or "How much did your sales grow as a percentage compared to 2016?" A measure gauging a fact differs from a measure gauging a perception in that the latter requires the respondent to make an assessment of a situation, for instance: "On a scale ranging from 1–5, how volatile is the environment?" or "Please rate, on a scale ranging from 1–5, the extent to which you agree with the statement that people in your firm are just out for themselves." I will argue below that a variable measured as a perception can be used as independent variable, but may be less appropriate as a dependent variable.

The problem

Recall the IFAC question: "How significant is the regulation that impacts your organization's opportunity to innovate?" The Likert scale used by IFAC varies between not significant at all, not significant, neutral, significant and very significant. As discussed above, we know that it is problematic to use a double-barrelled question so we split the questions into two subquestions and ask respondents:

1   What is the level of regulation in your industry?
    and
2   How much opportunity do you have to innovate?

Likert scales are used to rate levels of regulation and innovation, and the scale is comprised of the following anchors: 1. not at all, 2. very little, 3. some, 4. a lot, 5. very much.

We know that both measures will contain measurement error because the respondent must assess the level of regulation and his/her investment in innovation. But let us put that critique aside for the moment and present a model that allows us to test this relation. In that case, the following model would constitute a test of whether regulation impacts the number of opportunities a respondent observes to innovate:

$$INN = c + bREG + error \qquad (1)$$

Where,
REG = Level of regulation;
INN = Opportunity to innovate.
In equation 1, we try to explain a situation: the opportunity to innovate. Given that a survey instrument is used, the explanatory variable will contain measurement error. This error term is unlikely to represent noise (i.e., mean of the error term is not zero) because answers to questions potentially contain bias. In our case, the fact that we position our regulation question first, will likely *prime* the respondent to recall associations with regulation when answering the question about innovation opportunities.

Now, let us assume that the level of overconfidence [O] of the respondent is positively associated with both the innovation and regulation responses. This means that when overconfidence goes up, so will our measures of regulation and innovation.

Of course, [O] is only one factor that causes measurement error to surface:

Measured INN = True INN + Error(i) and
Measured REG = True REG + Error (r).

Since [O] is related to INN and REG, [O] is also related to both Error (i) and Error (r). Since we regress the measured INN on the measured REG, we know that the error terms are related through

[O]. As a consequence, the relation between INN and REG may be completely spurious and there is no way that we can unravel the error terms so as to attribute them unless we control for overconfidence. However, even if we could control for overconfidence, the relation would potentially be equally spurious if the respondent is primed at some point with a reference, for instance if the respondent has been asked at some point to provide information about the actions local governments took.

Estimation of equation 1 results in:

Omitted correlated variable: overconfidence

$$INN + error = c + b \ (REG + error) + model \ error \qquad\qquad (1a)$$

The fact that innovation and regulation are related through common measurement error is called an *omitted correlated variable* problem. The problem is present because the variables INN and REG have an explanatory variable in common that is missing. In our case the omitted correlated variable is overconfidence, and may also include other factors not identified nor controlled for.

To control for this issue, it is preferable that an instrumental variable is added that is related to REG so as to reduce measurement error. This would result in an unbiased measure of innovation: INN★ (see Bertrand and Mullainathan 2001). In this case the TRUE model would look like this:

$$INN★ = a + bREG + \delta Z + error \qquad\qquad (2)$$

Where,
REG = Perceived Regulation;
INN★ = Opportunity to innovate;
Z = variable related to REG and measured INN

Model 2 measures REG with error and the impact of that error is mitigated with the introduction of Z.

The model estimate would be more accurate (contain less error) if it were possible to include the Z variable for situations where INN is measured as a perception, as it would constitute a de facto control for the error the measures of REG and INN have in common. That case would allow for interpretation of coefficient b, albeit that it would be biased to the extent that INN contains measurement error. But, the fact of the matter is that it proves to be difficult if not impossible in practice to include Z in our model. As in reality INN is measured as a perception too, and the error in REG is most likely to be related to INN through [O], we are stuck. Since variable Z is absent, we fall back to estimating equation 1. This means that it is difficult if not impossible to interpret the coefficient on b as it is entirely possible that b reflects the relation between measurement error in REG and INN (equation 1a).

Dependent variable as fact rather than perception

One way to address the measurement error problem is to use a dependent variable that is a (near) fact, rather than a perception. Thus, the ideal model would look like equation 3. In that case, we can use a perception to explain real behaviour (Y = *the planned investment in innovation next year as a percentage of this year's investments*, for example), rather than explaining one perception using other perceptual measures. In this case, it is possible to use a measure that reflects perceived regulation and perceived innovation opportunities.

$$Y_{it} = \alpha + \beta REG + \theta INN + \delta Z + error \qquad (3)$$

Where,

Z = economic conditions facing the firm

Y = the planned investments of next year as a percentage of this year's investments

In many cases, it will be difficult (if not impossible) to find an instrument like Z that compensates for potential measurement error in the attitudes REG and INN. I therefore propose to test the following model:

$$Y_{it} = \alpha + \beta REG + \theta INN + error \qquad (4)$$

While Z is still unavailable, model 4 will yield a more reliable estimation than one based on equation 1. That is, the coefficients of β and θ will be biased since the unobserved Z will be related to INN and REG. This can occur as both coefficients of β and θ reflect the true effects of INN and REG on planned investments as well as the relation between investments with measurement error in REG and INN. This is true as Y represents a rather hard number since we do not ask the respondent to make some assessment, but rather ask him or her to give a number. Note that this measure would be even better if the real investment could be obtained from the company's financial records. However, that is not always possible in the case of a survey.

The estimate thus captures (true) attitude Y and other factors that determine how attitude is reported (error). The relation between REG and INN and thus the potential effect of omitted correlated variables that impact REG and INN surfaces in the error term. Interpretation of β and θ, however, is still possible assuming that measurement problems are not dominant (e.g., when the correlation between the measures of REG and INN exceeds 0.9).

In sum, using perceptions as *independent* variables in a model is not so much of a problem. Fatal problems can arise when the *dependent* variable is a perception. Such models can only be tested as long as an instrument can be included in the model that reduces the measurement error present because the measures reflect perceptions. More specifically, the instrument should reduce the error present in the measured independent variable (model 2), through the use of an objective observation (if possible a fact), rather than a perception.

Conclusion

In this chapter, I argue that we can learn from data that we collect with questionnaires. In order to create conditions where learning from survey research becomes feasible, I recommend that researchers take much care to prevent, where possible, measurement error.

I paid special attention to how we can best model a study based on a questionnaire. I demonstrate the difficulties faced by researchers when using a dependent variable that is measured as a perception rather than as an objective observation and offer several potential remedies to this and other potential causes of measurement error in surveys.

References

Abernethy, M.A., Bouwens, J. and Van Lent, L., 2004, 'Determinants of control system design in divisionalized firms', *The Accounting Review* 79(3), 545–570.

Abernethy, M.A., Bouwens, J. and Van Lent, L., 2013, 'The role of performance measures in the intertemporal decisions of business unit managers', *Contemporary Accounting Research* 30(3), 925–961.

Bertrand, M. and Mullainathan, S., 2001, 'Economics and social behavior: Do people mean what they say? Implications for subjective survey data', *American Economic Review* 91(2), 67–72.

Bouwens, J. and Van Lent, L., 2007, 'Assessing the performance of business unit managers', *Journal of Accounting Research* 45(4), 667–697.

Brownell, P., 1995, *Research Methods in Management Accounting*, Coopers & Lybrand and Accounting Association of Australia, New Zealand.

Bryman, A. and Bell, E., 2011, *Business Research Methods*, Oxford University Press, Oxford.

Earl, R.B. and Benaquisto, L., 2009, *Fundamentals of Social Research*, Nelson Education Ltd., Scarborough, Ontario.

Harman, Gilbert H., 1967, 'Psychological aspects of the theory of syntax', *The Journal of Philosophy,* 64(2), 75–87.

International Federation of Accountants (IFAC), 2015, *IFAC Regulatory Survey: Regulation and Growth*, viewed September 2015, from www.ifac.org/system/files/publications/files/Global-Regulation-Survey.pdf.

International Federation of Accountants (IFAC), 2016, *IFAC Global SMP Survey: 2015 results*, from https://www.ifac.org/publications-resources/ifac-global-smp-survey-2015-results.

Kahneman, D., 2011, *Thinking Fast and Slow*, Farrar Straus and Giroux, New York.

Keating, A. S., 1997, 'Determinants of divisional performance evaluation practices', *Journal of Accounting and Economics* 24(3), 243–274.

Lawler III, E.E., 1967, 'The Multitrait-Multirater approach to measuring managerial job performance', *Journal of Applied Psychology* 51(5), 369–445.

Meyer, D.E. and Schvaneveldt, R.W., 1971, 'Facilitation in recognizing pairs of words: Evidence of a dependence between retrieval operations', *Journal of Experimental Psychology* 90, 227–234.

Olson, K., 2008, 'Double-barreled question', in P. Lavrakas (ed.), *Encyclopedia of Survey Research Methods*, 211, Sage Publications, Thousand Oaks, CA. doi: http://dx.doi.org/10.4135/9781412963947.n145.

Podsakoff, P., MacKenzie, S., Lee, J. and Podsakoff, N., 2003, 'Common method biases in behavioral research: A critical review of the literature and recommended remedies', *Journal of Applied Psychology* 88(5), 879–903.

Vlastos, G., 1985, 'Socrates' disavowal of knowledge', *The Philosophical Quarterly* 35(138), 1–31.

16

The field research method as applied to Behavioural Accounting Research

Interviews and observation

Matthew Hall and Martin Messner

Introduction

Interviews and observation are two prominent, important and well-established research methods in the social sciences. In this chapter, we focus on the use of interviews and observation as part of field research methods, and will discuss how they can (and could be) applied in Behavioural Accounting Research.

As with any research method, the use and usefulness of interviews and observation cannot be discussed independently from methodological considerations. In particular, interviews and observation are means of data collection, but the way in which data are collected, and the status of these data, will differ depending on the methodological position taken by the researcher (Silverman 2014; Alvesson 2003, 2011). We cannot offer a comprehensive discussion of methodology here (see e.g., Neuman 2000) but will focus on one issue that we consider particularly important for the purpose of this chapter. This concerns the types of findings that researchers seek to generate.

We suggest thinking here of a continuum. At one end there are researchers who are interested in detecting *broad tendencies* or patterns in social phenomena to produce claims about 'what is likely to be the case'. In order to do so, they will abstract from social phenomena and inscribe them into 'variables' that can be subjected to statistical testing. The objective of such testing is to identify the isolated effects of individual variables. This approach to social reality is inspired by the scientific model of the natural sciences and adopts many of its methodological principles. Researchers thereby mainly rely on archival, experimental or survey data. If they use interviews and/or observation to collect data, they tend to do so in a very structured way, so as to elicit answers that can be transformed into 'data points' without much ambiguity.

At the other end of the continuum, we find researchers who are interested in the *details* of how the social world is produced and kept together. Much like anthropologists who immerse themselves in a foreign culture, they will delve into the empirical field and try to capture as best as possible the complexity of the social world. They tend to treat social phenomena as part of a context from which they assume their meaning and significance, and they seek a holistic understanding of how different phenomena hang together. Interviews and observation are popular research methods for such researchers as they can provide rich accounts of the complexity of the social world. Rather than strongly abstracting from these accounts, rese.archers use the 'phenomenological detail' (Flyvbjerg 2001: 85) contained in these accounts to authentically convey to the reader how the social world works.

These two approaches are sometimes referred to as 'quantitative' and 'qualitative', respectively, but it is important in our view to see this as a continuum rather than two incommensurable positions. For instance, while a 'qualitative case study' (e.g., Chenhall, Hall and Smith 2010) is typically rich on details of organizational practice, a 'qualitative cross-sectional interview study' (e.g., Kraus and Lind 2010) will more strongly abstract from some of these details in order to effectively compare and contrast interview accounts across cases. This may still be done in a 'qualitative way', i.e., without resorting to quantification and statistical testing, but it will be inspired by the idea of detecting patterns and tendencies within the 'sample'.

It is also important to recognize that there is quite some diversity *within* those studies that address the details of how the social world works. This diversity reflects further methodological choices that go along with different theoretical perspectives and worldviews. One such choice, for instance, relates to whether researchers foreground the power of social structures or the agency of individual actors when explaining social phenomena (cf., Giddens 1984). Some theoretical perspectives emphasize the role of structures or discourses that work upon individual actors and influence their behaviour (e.g., Foucault 1981; DiMaggio and Powell 1991; Bourdieu 1992). Interviews and observation may then be used to identify the contents of such discourses or structures and how they condition people's actions.

Other theoretical perspectives highlight the active part that human actors play in constructing and maintaining social reality (e.g., Garfinkel 1967; Joas 1997) and hence suggest a use of interviews and observation to trace such construction work. And even within this latter type of studies, there are further methodological differences to acknowledge. For instance, while some researchers seek to understand the construction of reality mainly by inquiring into what happens in actors' minds (e.g., Schütz 1967; Berger and Luckmann 1967), others approach the production of social reality more in terms of what actors do, i.e., how they connect to other entities (actors, objects) within their environment (e.g., Latour 2005).

Differences in theoretical perspective are likely to be reflected not only in the type of interview questions asked and observations carried out but also in the analysis of the data. As Ahrens and Chapman (2006: 820) point out, "[d]ata are not untainted slices of objective reality but aspects of recorded activity that a study finds significant for theoretical reasons." Different theoretical assumptions will produce different accounts of reality, in part because of differences in the interview and observational data collected, in part because of different ways to 'read' these data. With these methodological considerations in mind, we now turn to discuss the use of interviews and observations, respectively, in Behavioural Accounting Research.

Interviews

Interviews are an established method in the social sciences (Benney and Hughes 1956). The term 'interview' is commonly used to denote a conversation with someone from the field that goes beyond an informal chat and provides data to use as input in one's research project. Interviews are usually agreed upon in advance and follow a certain protocol. This typically involves explaining the purpose of the interview, how the interview will proceed and how the data will eventually be used. Since interviews may contain 'sensitive' information, such as what interviewees think about other members of their organization, researchers need to be transparent about their intended use of interview data.

Typically, interviewees are guaranteed that their testimonies will be treated in an anonymous way, and most publications feature neither the real names of organizations nor of individuals. Moreover, in contrast to observations, interviews require that interviewees 'step out' of their professional routine and dedicate some time to reflect upon and talk about their work. Interviews are therefore time consuming for interviewees, which might make it difficult to arrange them and which means that valuable interview time has to be spent wisely.

How to structure interviews?

While interviews are more formal than a chat at the coffee machine, there is quite some variation in how interviews proceed. Typically, interviews are differentiated with respect to their degree of structure, i.e., into structured interviews, semi-structured interviews and unstructured interviews (Bryman and Bell 2011: 467). Highly structured interviews follow a predetermined and detailed questionnaire from which the researcher does not deviate. Semi-structured interviews are typically based on an interview 'guideline' which outlines the broad direction the interview should take but leaves some flexibility in what is asked and how it is asked. Unstructured interviews are not facilitated by any guideline and are therefore rather unpredictable in terms of how they proceed.

It is helpful in our view to see structure as having both a theoretical and an empirical dimension. On the one hand, structure refers to the level of *theoretical* motivation behind interview questions. Interviews that are highly theoretically structured focus on examining or 'testing' particular theoretical ideas or hypotheses, i.e., they follow a deductive research approach. In contrast, interviews that are theoretically unstructured feature only empirical questions allowing the interviewer to obtain an understanding of what is the case, without particular theoretical ideas in mind. They thus follow an inductive approach.

On the other hand, structure also refers to the level of empirical detail covered by the prepared interview questions. Some interviews will feature a detailed questionnaire covering different empirical issues, while others will be conducted on the basis of one broad empirical question, where the answer is then followed up with *ad hoc* questions by the interviewer. When an interview is highly structured in theoretical terms, it typically also has a detailed empirical structure, as the theoretical interest is translated into a set of specific questions. This is not necessarily true the other way round, however, as a detailed questionnaire may also serve purely inductive purposes, i.e., to generate an understanding of the field without particular theoretical ideas in mind.

The choice with respect to the degree of theoretical and empirical structure will depend on the general design of the research study as well as on the purpose of the particular interview within that study. When a research study adopts a deductive approach, i.e., starts with a precise theoretical ambition and with clarity about the key theoretical constructs, then the interviews used for data collection will likely reflect this deductive approach. That is, they will tend to be highly structured in theoretical (and empirical) terms. In contrast, when a study adopts a more inductive approach, leaving key theoretical constructs open to discovery within the field, then interviews will tend to be less structured in theoretical terms, so as to allow new constructs to emerge from the interview. For instance, in a case study on the introduction of a new performance measurement system (PMS), the researcher may deductively 'test' alternative explanations for why the PMS was introduced (e.g., for economic reasons, for micro-political reasons, to gain legitimacy, etc.), in which case it would make sense to ask specific questions to see which of these reasons apply. Alternatively, the researcher may want to adopt a more inductive style and perhaps discover new explanations for the introduction of PMS that could not be deductively generated from the literature. In this case, a rather open question such as "How did it come to the introduction of the PMS?" may be the best starting point, followed by more specific questions probing further into the interviewee's answer.

As mentioned above, a key feature of qualitative research is that it seeks to generate an intimate understanding of the complexity of social and organizational life. Qualitative researchers are typically interested in the details of how the social world is produced and kept together, and they want to provide a holistic understanding of how different phenomena hang together. In order to do so, a purely deductive approach, in which certain theoretical ideas are 'tested', is unusual. Rather, researchers will dedicate an important part of their field research to inductively develop an understanding of what is the case. At the same time, qualitative research seeks to produce theoretically meaningful explanations of why things are as they are. Researchers will hence also inquire into the field deductively, using theoretical concepts and perspectives that guide them in their exploration of an otherwise messy complexity. In other words, qualitative research typically combines deductive and inductive elements (e.g., Ahrens and Chapman 2006; Lukka and Modell 2010).

How exactly the deductive and inductive elements are balanced will depend on the research design. Single case studies score particularly high on 'depth' regarding the understanding of phenomena, which is facilitated by a strong inductive element in data collection. In a single case study, the researcher often lets herself be 'guided' by her initial observations (inductive) and only later in the process will narrow down data collection and analysis to particular themes that are deemed to be of theoretical interest (deductive). In comparison, a cross-sectional interview study with CFOs from different firms will likely follow a more deductive approach from the outset. This is because it is hardly possible to make iterations in this case, i.e., to go back to earlier interviewees and ask them anew about themes that came up in later interviews. Nevertheless, the choice of an interview study in such a case (as opposed to, for instance, a survey) suggests that some inductive element will be at work as well. That is, a researcher will typically expect also in a cross-sectional interview study that some interesting issues will emerge from the interviews that the researcher had not envisaged before.

The alternation between deductive and inductive elements in case studies may be visible both across interviews and within interviews. It is common that interviews conducted in the early stages of a case study project will be rather inductive in nature, so as to create an understanding of what is going on. Such inductive inquiry usually generates observations that researchers can relate to theoretical concerns. For instance, when asking a manager to elaborate on the reasons for introducing a new PMS, the answer may contain elements that suggest micro-political reasons for the introduction.[1] The researcher may then wish to follow up on this theme by using her knowledge of the literature on micro-political behaviour to see whether the particular case can contribute to enriching our understanding of PMS and micro-political behaviour, or whether it 'simply' confirms what others have already said about this. In this way, researchers can use interviews to inductively generate different 'leads', which are then followed up in a more deductive manner. The same logic may apply within interviews, where some questions are used to 'test' the usefulness of particular theoretical perspectives, while others are saved for generating new leads that could then be followed up in later interviews.

A similar point can be made for the degree of empirical structure. Early interviews will often be used to generate a broad understanding of what is the case in the field. This will allow the researcher to draft a preliminary story. Reading through one's interview transcripts and writing up a story typically generates new questions relating to specific 'gaps' within this story. These can then be followed up by later interviews. For instance, having conducted a few rather weakly structured interviews on the introduction of a new PMS, the researcher may feel the need to obtain further knowledge on particular steps in the introduction process that previous interviewees have only briefly commented upon. Such questions can then be raised in subsequent interviews, turning these interviews into more strongly structured ones from an empirical point of view.

What to use interviews for?

In what follows, we will provide a few examples for how researchers in accounting have used interviews in their studies. We thereby select studies that are interested in capturing the details and complexity of accounting practice and that use interviews (alone or in combination with other methods) to produce *rich* accounts of such practice. How exactly these studies mobilize interviews depends on the particular theoretical concerns that they address and on the types of findings they seek to generate.

Jordan and Messner (2012) examine reactions to the introduction of a new performance measurement system in a manufacturing firm. Their key theoretical interest is with the incompleteness of performance measures and with the conditions under which such incompleteness becomes a 'problem' for middle managers. Hence, an important part of their paper is dedicated to describing the beliefs, interpretations and judgments of managers, i.e., way in which managers *make sense* of performance measures. For instance, the authors quote one manager saying: "Personally, *I don't see* this project as having the ultimate aim to increase the performance on this indicator." Another one commented: "[The new COO] defined goals that were provocative. . . . *For me, it was clear that*, if we have no growth, this is not going to happen." And a third one said: "The targets are, I would say, very visionary . . . at first glance, *they appeared* unattainable" (our emphasis). These three quotes exemplify how interviews are used in this study to convey to the reader how managers felt about the new performance measures and corresponding targets. In the spirit of interpretive research, the key concern here is with understanding managers' attitudes vis-à-vis the measures and the reasons for these attitudes. Jordan and Messner suggest that the problem of incompleteness cannot be assessed by only considering the design characteristics of PMS; managers' personal accounts are needed to understand how these design characteristics impacted their work.

A similar use of interviews is made by Guénin-Paracini, Malsch, and Paillé (2014) who combine interviews with extensive ethnographic observation to highlight experiences of fear in the audit process. Given their interest in this emotion, which the authors theorize by drawing upon a psychodynamic perspective, the personal accounts of the interviewees obviously become crucial for finding out how auditors experience such fear during the audit process. In other words, interviews are used here again in a strongly interpretive spirit, so as to 'access' the minds of employees. For instance, Guénin-Paracini et al. quote one auditor saying:

> In the accounts of a large company, there are hundreds of thousands of recorded operations. . . . When you think about it . . ., *it makes you feel* all dizzy! Because what you're being asked to do is to put your finger on a mistake deemed to be significant in what is essentially a gigantic hotchpotch. . . . *It's a bit like* looking for a needle in a haystack. Where's the mistake? That is the question! It could be anywhere . . . everywhere and nowhere.
>
> *(272, our emphasis)*

Note how the interviewee reports upon her 'feelings' and how she mobilizes a metaphor to give the interviewer an idea of the extent of uncertainty involved in her work. In so doing, she makes accessible to someone else what is essentially a personal experience that would be hard to uncover and account for with more impersonal research methods such as a questionnaire.

While Jordan and Messner (2012) and Guénin-Paracini et al. (2014) both use interviews within a single case study, other studies mobilize them in a cross-sectional setting. For instance, Carter and Spence (2014) conducted 32 interviews with audit partners or senior auditors to find out what it takes to become an audit partner in a large audit firm. Their interest is not so much with the viewpoints, interpretations or emotions of these auditors, but rather with the underlying 'rules of the game' in the field. Hence, interviews are used here to access insiders' knowledge about the field and the types of capital needed to become a successful auditor. For example, the authors quote one partner saying: "[I]t is more important to be a relationship person that somebody else likes and gets on with . . . someone they [clients] can trust and who they like to spend time with. You don't get that from a one-dimensional geek who just wants to read books" (969). Because many of the interviewees have successfully climbed the career ladder and because they are in a position to decide upon others' career advancement, such individual statements are more than just personal viewpoints. Interviewees become representatives of the profession or at least of the key players (Big 4) in the profession. Compared to the studies by Jordan and Messner (2012) and Guénin-Paracini et al. (2014), respectively, this study therefore mobilizes interviews more strongly to learn about *structural* characteristics of the field, which is in line with the theoretical perspective chosen by the authors (i.e., Bourdieu's theory of fields).

In some studies, the use of interviews becomes so closely intertwined with a description of events and actions that the interpretive act that interviewees engage in moves almost entirely to the background. This is the case, for instance, in Miller and O'Leary's (1994) study of the restructuring of manufacturing at a Caterpillar plant. Miller and O'Leary were concerned with tracing the details of how a manufacturing plant was reorganized in the name of economic efficiency. Their goal was not to highlight how different actors made sense of, or felt about, these changes. Rather, they used interviews mostly to learn about the events and actions as such, i.e., to trace the 'facts' that happened in the plant (cf. Ahrens and Chapman 2006). Such use of interviews is not uncommon even in studies that explicitly take an interpretive perspective. For instance, Jordan and Messner use material from interviews to reconstruct what happened in the case firm when the performance measures were introduced. The authors use interview material to explain that

> [i]n each plant, selected middle managers and engineers were asked to form project groups and to start working on the implementation of the four performance indicators. This work started in May 2008 with separate working groups for each indicator. The COO and his team provided definitions for these indicators and set objectives ultimately.
>
> *(ibid., 549)*

Clearly, the authors present these events as 'facts' rather than as matters of interpretation. Indeed, most interpretive studies will use interview data not only for examining the interpretive act that interviewees engage in, but also for reconstructing what 'really happened' in the organization. However, it may happen that the reader challenges such seemingly objective accounts. Comments such as "Is this the general view of what happened or rather the perspective of top management only?" suggest that there is sometimes a fine line between what researchers can take for granted as a 'fact' and what needs closer scrutiny from an interpretive point of view. More generally, when an interviewee speaks of the world, there are always (at least) two possible readings of their accounts: a realist one and an interpretive one. The former focuses on the characteristics of the reality that the interviewee comments upon, while the latter one focuses on the subject that speaks.[2] Depending on the theoretical focus and methodological assumptions, a given study may lean more strongly towards either of these readings.

Observation

Observation has served as a foundation source of human knowledge as long as people have been interested in studying the social and natural phenomena around them (Adler and Adler 1994). It is a method of inquiry focused on using the human senses to make a record of phenomena as they unfold in the field. The field is where the researcher actively witnesses the phenomena they are studying in action (Adler and Adler 1994), with a major purpose to learn about events, actions or encounters in specific settings or situations as they actually unfold (Charmaz 2014). Observation thus draws the researcher into the phenomenological complexity of the world where actions, relations and consequences are observed as they happen (Adler and Adler 1994). In this way, observation is distinctive to other methods such as surveys and experiments because it directly engages with the lives and experiences of the people being studied, seeking to witness how those people perceive, act and feel in order to understand those perceptions, actions and feelings more fully (Lofland, Snow, Anderson and Lofland 2006). It is focused not just on what people do but also on understanding the meaning and function of the activities, decisions and actions people undertake in the context in which they are embedded (Atkinson and Hammersley 1994; Lofland et al. 2006). Observation also engages all of the human senses, where making a record can involve noting what a setting, action or decision looks, sounds, smells, feels and even tastes like (Creswell 2013; Adler and Adler 1994; Corbin and Strauss 2015).

Why use observation?

A prime reason for using observational methods is to focus on analyzing actions, situations or decisions as they occur. Interviews, for example, can make people's accounts of practices and events accessible rather than the actual practices themselves because they contain a mix of how the practice occurs and how it should occur (Flick 2014). People may also say they are doing one thing but in practice do something else (Corbin and Strauss 2015). In contrast, observation can help the researcher to achieve intimate familiarity with the actions and orientations of people and the practices and activities they are engaged in (Lofland et al. 2006).

Observation is also important because people may not always be aware of how to articulate what it is they do (Corbin and Strauss 2015). For example, Ahrens and Mollona (2007) use observation in order to study aspects of organizational control that organization members could not report on and to uncover differences between what they say and what they do. Observation can also help to uncover the tacit and cultural knowledge people use to interpret their experience and generate behaviour (Spradley 1980). In particular, it can provide maximum ability to understand the motives, beliefs, emotions and customs that can frame and shape behaviour (Lincoln and Guba 1985; Spradley 1980). For example, Guénin-Paracini et al. (2014) used detailed observation of several audit engagements to uncover and analyze the role of fear in the audit process.

A further strength of observational methods relates to an ability to retain flexibility and be open to the emergence of new insights and knowledge. This is because theory development and data analysis are typically iterative with observational methods (Lofland et al. 2006), rather than the linear process of theory to data collection and analysis found in more deductive research. As such, instead of working with predetermined categories as specified by theory, observers can develop theories and alter problems/questions as the researcher gains greater knowledge of the subjects and practices under observation (Jorgensen 1989). This provides more opportunity to develop insights into new realities or new ways of looking at old realities (Adler and Adler 1994). For example, Guénin-Paracini et al. (2014) used their field observations to go beyond the primarily cognitive understandings of audit and develop new insights about the role of emotions in the audit process.

Observational methods can help researchers to collect data that goes beyond talk (Flick 2014), such as nonverbal cues, and salient details of the context. For example, a researcher interested in understanding performance evaluation could ask an informant for a verbal description of a performance evaluation meeting, but could also observe that meeting directly, collecting data not only about what is said, but the setting and space of the room, the interpersonal dynamics between participants, and the feelings expressed, trying to provide a layered description of the unfolding activities (Ahrens and Mollona 2007). This can be particularly important where nonverbal behaviour conflicts with verbal behaviour, thus raising questions about candour and completeness that would otherwise go unnoticed or unquestioned (Lincoln and Guba 1985).

Observation can also be advantageous for analyzing certain types of research questions. For example, it is suited to research questions where little is known about a phenomenon, such as a new accounting practice, or a new domain of accounting work. It is also beneficial where research interest is focused on human meanings and interpersonal interactions, such as understanding the characteristics of a supportive relationship between junior and senior management accountants or auditors. Perhaps most pertinent for accounting research, observation is very useful when the object of analysis is a practice, process or encounter and how it is organized and unfolds in particular socio-cultural contexts (Flick 2014; Jorgensen 1989). For example, observation could be used to study practices such as how management accountants develop performance measures, how auditors evaluate fair value estimates, or how financial analysts use financial statements in making buy/sell recommendations. It could also examine encounters, such as what happens when management and auditors disagree on a financial statement estimate, what happens when two performance measures give conflicting signals about divisional performance or what happens when management accountants from different cultural and education backgrounds have to work together.

What to observe?

The question of what to observe is largely driven by the research question and interests of the researcher. However, as mentioned above, observation is typically oriented to exploring social phenomena rather than setting out to test hypotheses (Atkinson and Hammersley 1994). As such, the researcher typically enters the field with a general research question in mind, where initial observations can be very unstructured with an aim of developing a sense of what is salient or important (Lincoln and Guba 1985). The task of selecting topics and questions for further observation and analysis typically occur during the course of the research itself (Lofland et al. 2006). The extent of observation carried out is typically driven by an overarching objective to be able to describe comprehensively and exhaustively a phenomenon of interest (Jorgensen 1989), often with a focus on a few cases or a single case. For example, Ahrens and Mollona (2007) examined organizational control in a single steel mill, and Chenhall, Hall and Smith (2016) analyzed the development of a new performance measurement system in a single development project.

Initial observations tend to be descriptive, with the aim of grasping the field's complexity and developing more specific questions (Spradley 1980). This can help the researcher to develop more focused observations, narrowing in on particular processes or problems or issues most essential for the research question (Spradley 1980). Focused observation can be accompanied by more selective observation, where the researcher seeks further evidence or examples of practices and processes found in focused observation (Spradley 1980).

The scope of the research project will also influence what is observed. A researcher may be focused on a particular practice, judgment or set of people (e.g., an incentive system, a specific audit judgment, a specific type of accountant) and so observations are directed at these aspects only. In contrast, the researcher may be interested in understanding a total way of life (of an accountant or auditor, for example) or a total system (such as an organization) and so observations are broad ranging and comprehensive, often involving extended periods in the field (Spradley 1980).

Sampling is used in observation but serves a different purpose. In particular, whether a case is 'representative' of some larger population is not especially relevant (Jorgensen 1989) as the interest is in maximizing the scope and range of information obtained on the phenomena of interest (Lincoln and Guba 1985). As such, sampling can involve deliberate attempts to select extreme or deviant cases (Flick 2014), such as highly successful or extreme failure cases. For example, in a study of how financial analysts use financial statements, a researcher could try to observe very successful and very unsuccessful analysts, or analysts who have a reputation for using unorthodox methods. A researcher can also try to maximize variation, selecting cases that are as different as possible in order to understand the range of differentiation of the phenomena (Flick 2014). For example, a study of how auditors evaluate fair value estimates could observe very junior and very senior auditors, or very consequential or inconsequential estimates or auditors with extensive vs. little industry knowledge. A researcher may also select cases based on the intensity with which the phenomenon occurs (Flick 2014). For example, a study examining how management accountants develop performance measures could focus on observing the very initial stages in the development of a new performance measurement system where the intensity of the process is likely to be heightened. Practical considerations, such as ease of access, cost and time of travel, and opportunities to make repeated observations, also play a role in what cases to observe (Flick 2014; Spradley 1980).

What role will the researcher take in the field?

As observation involves being present in the field, a researcher must decide what type of role(s) he/she will assume during the course of the research. In particular, a researcher must decide on the extent to which he/she will participate in the action and events taking place in the field itself. This can be considered along a continuum ranging from a researcher not being seen or noticed by the people under study (a complete observer) to being fully engaged with the situation and people being observed (a complete participant) (Flick 2014; Creswell 2013; Jorgensen 1989; Spradley 1980; Adler and Adler 1994; Atkinson and Hammersley 1994).

Researchers unfamiliar with observational methods may initially gravitate towards the complete observer end of the spectrum out of a desire to avoid disturbing or influencing the field. This default strategy, however, is associated with an understanding of observational methods based on notions of objectivity and independence more usually employed in quantitative research (Flick 2014). In contrast, stronger participation in the field can allow the researcher to gain an insider's understanding by learning to experience it as the members do (Charmaz 2014), which can be vital for forming an accurate appraisal and understanding of the situations under study (Adler and Adler 1994). For example, understanding the experience and practice of organizational control can involve working alongside participants as well as participating in their social activities such as drinks at the pub and fishing expeditions (Ahrens and Mollona 2007). In contrast, being a complete observer can lead to problems in analyzing data and assessing interpretations because the researcher is less able to gain knowledge of the interior perspective of the field and its participants (Flick 2014). Furthermore, being an active participant can allow a researcher to ask questions and gather data an observer could not (Charmaz 2014). This is because participation can help generate trust between the researcher and participants, as well as provide the insider knowledge necessary to ask certain questions.

Importantly, the field, and the researcher's involvement in it, is a dynamic and evolving social setting. As such, the researcher as observer must develop an ongoing reflexive awareness regarding his/her role in and 'closeness' to the field as the research unfolds. A useful analogy is that of the 'martian' and the 'convert' (Lofland et al. 2006). The 'martian' is like a stranger in the field, seeking to grasp it with fresh eyes, seeing the field outside the frame of its participants. This can involve maintaining the distance of the professional stranger in order to develop knowledge that can transcend the everyday understandings of the field itself (Flick 2014). In contrast, the 'convert' aims to be immersed ever more deeply in the field so that what is going on can be revealed directly. As above, this can be important in obtaining data and an understanding of it only available from deep immersion in the field. As both roles are important, the sensitive observer tries to take on both or either role as the research demands rather than sticking steadfast to one or the other throughout the period of observation (Lofland et al. 2006).

The observer must also consider his/her role in relation to the participants in the field. This involves consideration of 'who' the researcher is in contrast to 'who' the participants are (Lofland et al. 2006). This typically centres on how 'similar' or 'different' the researcher is seen to be in comparison to the participants. For example, consider a study involving observation of a group of trainee auditors. A Ph.D. student with acknowledged experience in a similar audit firm and of a similar age might be perceived by the trainee auditors as 'similar'. In contrast, a senior professor who is a very well-known audit expert and considerably older than the audit trainees may be perceived as 'different'. These perceptions are important because they can affect the ability of the observer to collect data. For example, being seen as different to participants can raise problems in being able to acquire rich data (Lofland et al. 2006). However, being seen as different or as an 'outsider' can also be advantageous in being able to ask 'stupid' questions an insider could not, not being accountable to the typical in-group demands, and being more aware of and sensitive to relational processes an insider might take for granted (Lofland et al. 2006).

Of particular relevance for behavioural accounting researchers is how the observer's expertise is interpreted in the field (cf., Charmaz 2014). On the one hand, being seen to have relevant expertise or experience can help make the researcher come across as a credible participant and avoid being positioned as an immature trainee to be avoided (Charmaz 2014). For example, our Ph.D. student who has a professional accounting designation or relevant work experience is likely to be seen as a credible participant by other qualified accountants. However, there are also dangers of being seen and treated as an expert, as this can prevent the researcher from becoming an insider and regular participant in the field (Charmaz 2014). For example, our highly regarded senior professor may be seen as and thus take on the role of 'the expert', even to the point of trainee accountants coming to her with technical audit questions or career advice.

How to make an observational record?

As observational methods are typically used to understand the phenomenological complexity of particular situations, events or experiences, creating an observational record should focus on collecting the richest possible data. This necessitates collecting a wide and diverse range of information over a relatively prolonged period of time in a persistent and systematic manner (Lofland et al. 2006).

The classic medium for making a record is the researcher's field notes (Flick 2014). For example, Ahrens and Mollona's (2007) field notes totalled more than 2000 pages, which involved taking extensive notes on the shop floor of the steel mill and transcribing key observations and conversations after work. Field notes include details about what is happening and what is being said, but should also focus on recording nonverbal cues, and salient details of the context. This can include making a record of sounds, smells, touch and even tastes. Furthermore, field notes should try to record details of the meaning associated with the actions being studied and to understand the contexts in which those actions are embedded (Lofland et al. 2006).

Spradley (1980) provides a useful distinction between four different kinds of field notes: the condensed account, the expanded account, the fieldwork journal, and analysis and interpretation. The researcher's field notes represent a condensed version of what is taking place, as it is not humanly possible to write down everything participants say or everything going on. As such, the condensed account typically consists of snapshots of events recorded as phrases, or even single words, written down by the researcher as events unfold. The expanded account fleshes out the details of the phrases and single words, trying to record longer verbatim statements and more lengthy descriptions of events. For greater accuracy and completeness, it should be completed as soon as possible, for example, by turning hand written notes into an expanded account on a word processor each evening after making field observations (e.g., Chenhall, Hall and Smith 2016).

The condensed and expanded accounts are focused on making a record of observations of participants and the field setting. In contrast, the fieldwork journal is focused on the researcher making a record of his/her own experiences in the field, including personal feelings, problems, mistakes or successes, particularly as they relate to interactions with participants. As the researcher as observer is part of the field setting, the fieldwork journal is extremely important in enabling the researcher to reflect on how observations (as recorded in the condensed and expanded accounts) have been influenced by his/her own feelings and experiences. The fourth type of note making, analysis and interpretation, involves making a record of the researcher's insights, ideas, themes or meanings that come to mind during the data collection process. These notes may be sparked by a particularly interesting or unusual event or statement, or seeing a connection between an experience in the field and a particular theoretical idea or concept.

Researchers can also draw on other media to make an observational record. For example, the words spoken during conversations, meetings or events could be recorded using a digital audio recorder, with the recording then fully or partially transcribed for analysis. Taking photographs could facilitate making a record of a particular space or location or an entire field setting. Utilizing technological advances, researchers are increasingly using video recordings to make a record of moving visual images and audio (e.g., Smets, Burke, Jarzabkowski and Spee 2014; Jarzabkowski, Bednarek and Spee 2015). This has the advantage of enabling the researcher to freeze interactions and examine them repeatedly, to use multiple observers, and to capture behavioural nuances more precisely (Adler and Adler 1994).

Conclusion

In this chapter, we analyzed the role and use of interviews and observation in Behavioural Accounting Research broadly conceived. We discussed how the use of interviews and observation depends upon the types of findings that researchers seek to generate about social phenomena, for example, detecting broad tendencies or patterns, or analyzing the details of how social phenomena are produced and sustained. Relatedly, the behavioural accounting researcher using interviews and observation must tackle a variety of important research design choices, such as how and how much to structure interviews, and how and how much to participate in field observations. Given their long and established history in the wider social sciences, interview and observational methods can provide the behavioural accounting researcher with valuable and potentially unique insights into the relations between accounting and human behaviour.

Notes

1 In a cross-sectional qualitative study, 'pilot interviews' can fulfill a similar purpose.
2 A third reading foregrounds the dynamics of the interview situation itself (Alvesson 2003; 2011). Interviews are social situations where 'truth' is co-produced by the interviewer and the interviewee. Interviewees' accounts may therefore be influenced by the interviewer and by the particular setting or context of the interview. Such a reading of an interview sensitizes, for instance, for impression-management tactics that interviewees may apply.

References

Adler, P.A. and Adler, P., 1994, 'Observational techniques', in N.K. Denzin and Y.S. Lincoln (eds.), *Handbook of Qualitative Research*, 377–392, Sage Publications, Thousand Oaks, CA.

Ahrens, T. and Chapman, C.S., 2006, 'Doing qualitative research in management accounting: Positioning data to contribute to theory', *Accounting, Organizations and Society* 31, 819–841.

Ahrens, T. and Mollona, M., 2007, 'Organisational control as cultural practice – a shop floor ethnography of a Sheffield steel mill', *Accounting, Organizations and Society* 32, 305–331.

Alvesson, M., 2003, 'Beyond neopositivists, romantics, and localists: A reflexive approach to interviews in organizational research', *Academy of Management Review* 28(1), 13–33.

Alvesson, M, 2011, *Interpreting Interviews*, Sage Publications, London.

Atkinson, P. and Hammersley, M., 1994, 'Ethnography and participant observation', in N.K. Denzin and Y.S. Lincoln (eds.), *Handbook of Qualitative Research*, 248–261, Sage Publications, Thousand Oaks, CA.

Benney, M. and Hughes, E.C., 1956, 'Of sociology and the interview: Editorial preface', *American Journal of Sociology* 52(2), 137–142.

Berger, P. and Luckmann, T., 1967, *The Social Construction of Reality: A Treatise in the Sociology of Knowledge*, Anchor Books, Garden City, NY.

Bourdieu, P., 1992, *The Logic of Practice*, Stanford University Press, Stanford.

Bryman, A. and Bell, E., 2011, *Business Research Methods* (3rd ed.), Oxford University Press, Oxford.

Carter, C. and Spence, C., 2014, 'Being a successful professional: An exploration of who makes partner in the Big 4', *Contemporary Accounting Research* 31(4), 949–981.

Charmaz, K., 2014, *Constructing Grounded Theory* (2nd ed.), Sage Publications, London.

Chenhall, R.H., Hall, M. and Smith, D., 2010, 'Social capital and management control systems: A study of a non-government organization', *Accounting, Organizations and Society* 35(8), 737–756.

Chenhall, R., Hall, M. and Smith, D., 2016, 'The expressive role of performance measurement systems: a field study of a mental health development project', *Accounting, Organizations and Society*, 1–62.

Corbin, J.M. and Strauss, A., 2015, *Basics of Qualitative Research: Techniques and Procedures for Grounded Theory* (4th ed.), Sage Publications, London.

Creswell, J.W., 2013, *Qualitative Inquiry and Research Design: Choosing Among Five Approaches* (3rd ed.), London, Sage Publications.

DiMaggio, P.J. and Powell, W.W. (ed.), 1991, *The New Institutionalism in Organizational Analysis*, University of Chicago Press, Chicago and London.

Flick, U., 2014, *An Introduction to Qualitative Research* (5th ed.), Sage Publications, London.

Flyvbjerg, B., 2001, *Making Social Science Matter: Why Social Inquiry Fails and How It Can Succeed Again*, Cambridge University Press, Cambridge.

Foucault, M., 1981, 'The order of discourse' (I. McLeod, Trans.), in R. Young (ed.), *Untying the Text: A Post-Structuralist Reader*, 48–78, Routledge & Kegan Paul, London and New York.

Garfinkel, H., 1967, *Studies in Ethnomethodology*, Polity Press, Cambridge.

Giddens, A., 1984, *The Constitution of Society: Outline of the Theory of Structuration*, Polity Press, Cambridge.

Guénin-Paracini, H., Malsch, B. and Paillé, A., 2014, 'Fear and risk in the audit process', *Accounting, Organizations and Society* 39(4), 264–288.

Jarzabkowski, P., Bednarek, R. and Spee, P., 2015, *Making a Market for Acts of God: The Practice of Risk-Trading in the Global Reinsurance Industry*, Oxford University Press, Oxford.

Joas, H., 1997, *The Creativity of Action*, University of Chicago Press, Chicago.

Jordan, S. and Messner, M., 2012, 'Enabling control and the problem of incomplete performance indicators', *Accounting, Organizations and Society* 37(8), 544–564.

Jorgensen, D.L., 1989, *Participant Observation: A Methodology for Human Studies*, Sage Publications, Thousand Oaks, CA.

Kraus, K. and Lind, J., 2010, 'The impact of the corporate balanced scorecard on corporate control – a research note', *Management Accounting Research* 21(4), 265–277.

Latour, B., 2005, *Reassembling the Social: An Introduction to Actor-Network-Theory*, Oxford University Press, Oxford.

Lincoln, Y.S. and Guba, E.G., 1985, *Naturalistic Inquiry*, Sage Publications, Newbury Park, CA.

Lofland, J., Snow, D., Anderson, L. and Lofland, L.H., 2006, *Analyzing Social Settings: A Guide to Qualitative Observation and Analysis*, Wadsworth, Belmont, CA.

Lukka, K. and Modell, S., 2010, 'Validation in interpretive management accounting research', *Accounting, Organizations and Society* 35(4), 462–477.

Miller, P. and O'Leary, T., 1994, 'Accounting, "Economic Citizenship" and the spatial reordering of manufacture', *Accounting, Organizations and Society* 19(1), 15–43.

Neuman, W.L., 2000, *Social Research Methods: Qualitative and Quantitative Approaches* (4th ed.), Allyn and Bacon, Boston, MA.

Schütz, A., 1967, *The Phenomenology of the Social World*, Northwestern University Press, Evanston, IL.

Silverman, D., 2014, *Interpreting Qualitative Data* (5th ed.), Sage Publications, London.

Smets, M., Burke, G., Jarzabkowski, P. and Spee, P., 2014, 'Charting new territory for organizational ethnography: Insights from a team-based video ethnography of reinsurance trading', *Journal of Organizational Ethnography* 3(1), 10–26.

Spradley, J.P., 1980, *Participant Observation*, Holt, Rinehart and Winston, New York.

17

The field research method as applied to Behavioural Accounting Research

Case studies

Ariela Caglio and Angelo Ditillo

Introduction

The case study is a research approach characterized by a systematic and organized way to produce knowledge about a topic. It requires an in-depth and contextually informed examination of a given domain. It focuses on particular organizations, events or situations by scrutinizing the activities and experiences of the subjects involved, as well as the setting in which these activities and experiences take place (Stake, Denzin and Lincoln 2000; Cooper and Morgan 2008). It may assume the logic of scientific empiricism as well as that of phenomenological analysis, which regards social phenomena as more specific and ambiguous than clearly definable and replicable (Van Maanen 1979).

Through the case study approach, the researcher seeks to minimize the distance between indicated and indicator, between theory and data, between context and action. She attempts to gather and record the necessary raw data *in vivo*, in proximity to the point of origin, expressed figuratively as brackets put around a temporal and spatial social domain, which is intended to be investigated (Van Maanen 1979).[1]

Case research offers the possibility to study and understand accounting in its practical setting. Its sensitivity to context allows researchers to take into consideration questions that may not be contemplated in other research approaches (Cooper and Morgan 2008). In fact, case-based research relies on the idea that we can improve our knowledge of reality by developing theories that illuminate individual observations in their context, thus supporting a holistic approach (Ryan, Scapens and Theobald et al. 2002). In addition, case studies are particularly useful when studying multifaceted phenomena where many variables are involved (Cooper and Morgan 2008). Case studies embrace specificity and avoid thinning out the data beyond the point where they lose their distinctive meaning and become bland (Ahrens and Chapman 2007). Another specific characteristic of case-based research is that it is especially suitable when a theory is not well developed or when existing theories are incomplete (Otley and Berry 1998; Ryan et al. 2002). Moreover, whereas large sample studies tend to assume temporal stability and emphasize equilibrium, case studies can be used to understand discontinuity and disequilibrium, and to learn from shocks that interrupt routines (Cooper and Morgan 2008). Finally, case studies are particularly useful in highlighting practical questions and issues, and subsequently in providing guidance for solving concrete problems: in this sense, case studies can be an answer to accounting research's partial success in generating useful knowledge that could also be relevant to practitioners (Reiter and Williams 2002).

Why case studies

The case study is suitable to investigate (Cooper and Morgan 2008):

- Complex and dynamic situations in which many variables (including those that cannot be easily quantified) play a role. This is for example the case of the contribution by Alvesson and Kärreman (2004), who investigate a variety of forms of management control in a large management consultancy company. They show that various formal control devices focusing on financial issues as well as human resources do not comply that well with the bureaucratic-technocratic logic they rest upon and are, on the contrary, identified as non-obvious sources of socio-ideological control. The paper emphasizes the interface between different forms of control and argues for a more symbolic, meaning-focusing view of bureaucratic and output control. The complexity of the organization and the difficulty to measure the socio-ideological mode of control made the choice of the case study particularly suitable to study this phenomenon. In fact, case study researchers tend to analyze the unfolding of social processes in conjunction with the pure social structures that are often the main and sole focus of other research approaches (Van Maanen 1979). This is important because given that the field functions as a "powerful disciplinary force: assertive, demanding, even coercive" (Geertz 1995: 119), "insistent" on the logic of its specific functioning, case study researchers, by investigating social processes, are able to go beyond the perceptions and reports of the individuals, and unveil deeper, unaware and more hidden social dynamics (Ahrens and Chapman 2007). This requires a specific ability of the case study researcher to read between the lines and collect and reconcile data from a plurality of sources. This is, for example, the case of the contribution of Revellino and Mouritsen (2009), who studied the relations between control and innovation and their co-development. They showed that the multiplicity of controls changed and adapted to the innovation as the innovation unfolded. They were able to unveil that controls were part of the innovation more likely than an external device to make it transparent, thanks to their deep analysis of the innovation process.
- Situations in which the context is crucial because it has an impact on the phenomenon under investigation (and the phenomenon may also influence the context). Case study researchers claim strongly to know very little about what a specific behavioural episode means, until they have developed an understanding of the context in which the behaviour takes place and attempted to interpret that behaviour from the position of the originator. Such contextual comprehension is unlikely to be generated unless a direct, first-hand and more or less intimate knowledge of a research setting is collected (Van Maanen 1979). One example of this is represented by the work of Ahrens (1997), who showed that the organizational functioning of accounting depends on its combination with other forms of organizational knowledge in talk depending on the context. By contrasting British and German organizations he showed how British management accountants questioned the commercial acumen of the work of line managers in contrast to German management accountants.

- Actual practices, including the features of relevant experiences that may be unusual or infrequent. Case study researchers attempt to describe, decode, translate and understand the meaning, not the frequency, of these practices occurring in the social world. The data they collect are symbolic, cryptic and reflexive standing for nothing so much as their ability to generate a meaningful interpretation and reaction. "When crossing the street, for example, the sight of a ten-ton truck bearing down on us leads to an immediate and presumably prudent action. We do not stop to first ask how fast the truck is travelling, from where did it come, how often does this occur, or what is the driver's intention. We move. Our study of the truck involves little more than a quick scan, a glance up the road which reveals to most of us a menacing symbol of such power that a speedy, undeliberated response is mandatory" (Van Maanen 1979: 521). Similarly, case study researchers aim to identify the various elements and signals embedded in practices and understand their meaning, elements and symbols that elicit specific and immediate responses by individuals. This requires that researchers develop careful descriptions of the daily routines and of the concerns of the subjects involved, over a rather lengthy period of time (Van Maanen 1979: 523–524). One example of studying actual practices is represented by Mouritsen, Hansen and Hansen (2001), who studied inter-organizational management control practices and showed that they do not merely capture a state of affairs to be modelled. In contrast, these practices are associated with multiple aspects of the firm's life and generate effects on strategic, technological and organizational aspects.

Types of case studies

Case studies appear to have a number of potential roles to play, and different types of case studies can be undertaken depending on their purpose (Otley and Berry 1998).

Exploratory case studies are used to support the development of theoretical statements from observations. This is not to say that such observations are theory free. Actually, the observations that are sought, the phenomena that are perceived and the interpretations given to them are all affected by the researcher's theoretical position. However, this position is modified because of the way in which observations have caused it to change.

In some circumstances, exploratory case studies are also used in conjunction with other research approaches.[2] They may then represent a preliminary investigation that is intended to develop hypotheses about the reasons for particular practices. These hypotheses are then tested subsequently in larger-scale studies at a later stage. The purpose of such subsequent investigation is to produce statistical generalizations about observed practices (Ryan et al. 2002). Davila (2000), for example, followed this logic and conducted some exploratory case studies to develop some hypotheses that were statistically tested, on the characteristics and roles of management control systems in the context of product development. This specific use of exploratory case study does not, however, mean that these case studies may not have a validity on their own.

Illustrative case studies are used to provide a description of a real-world situation, which is interpreted and explained in the light of the specific theoretical standpoint adopted. This may be the case when a certain theory is used to explain new or innovative practices or to interpret practices used in a specific context by particular organizations and which have never been studied before with that perspective (Ryan et al. 2002). This is for example what Jørgensen and Messner (2009) did when they used the theoretical lenses of coercive and enabling forms of bureaucracy to study how enabling control is adopted in the particular setting of new product development.

Critical case studies are those cases that are used to falsify theory by providing an observed domain, which is inconsistent with a set of theoretical statements. In this case the data may suggest that a theory is not suitable to explain certain phenomena and requires modification. They may also suggest potential ways in which the theory can be changed, enriched and become more comprehensive. One example of this is represented by Thrane (2007), who suggested the need to overcome cybernetic conceptions of inter-organizational control to illustrate how this control can shift between fundamentally different behaviours and orders within a short span of time. By using a systems approach he showed how management controls may dynamically become a source of instability rather than stability and a source of emergent, unintended order.

The various forms of case study described above can take the form of *single* or *multiple-case studies*. The choice between the two implies solving a trade-off between the deep understanding of particular social setting and the benefits of comparative insights. A part from the obvious circumstance in which the single case is chosen because there is an interest in studying a particular organization that has some elements of uniqueness – e.g., how scientific researchers are controlled and rewarded at CERN – single case studies are also used to study the characteristics of exceptional cases, those that in statistical analysis would be eliminated because considered as outliers (Dyer and Wilkins 1991). For example, if the interest is in understanding the complexity of how to successfully control product development, it would be probably more useful to study in depth how this is done in Apple, rather than looking at common elements that Apple shares with more ordinary organizations. Also Miller and O'Leary (1998) stressed the insights that can be obtained from in-depth, longitudinal case studies. One example of attempting to understand the complexity of a certain phenomenon in a specific organization is provided by Abernethy and Chua (1996), who conducted a longitudinal study of a large, public teaching hospital in Australia, to develop an understanding of the factors shaping the design and operation of accounting control systems. On the contrary, multiple case studies are more convenient to develop more comprehensive theories. Different cases, in fact, often emphasize complementary aspects of a certain phenomenon and by piecing together the individual patterns, a more complete theoretical picture may emerge (Eisenhardt 1991). This is what Caglio and Ditillo (2008) did to study the control systems and the management accounting information exchanges in inter-organizational relationships. The comparative analysis of these case studies highlighted the key variables that explained the accounting and control choices adopted by collaborating partners. Finally, an intermediate solution among these two extremes would be to focus on comparisons within the same organizational context, in an attempt to achieve at the same time deepness and comprehensiveness. This is, for example, what Ditillo (2004) did in his work on management control systems in knowledge-intensive firms, where he studied the characteristics of controls by comparing three software development projects characterized by different types of knowledge complexity.

Theorizing through case studies

Theorizing in case studies means observing and analyzing directly a certain phenomenon (even if only provisionally) and to make sense of the observed behaviours that fall within the selected research domain. It involves alternating explorative phases and reflective pauses; interfaces at which the researcher moves from the present to the distant in an attempt to recast the local as well as the general. Developing the theory means answering the following questions: What is happening? What does it mean? What patterns are unveiled? How are my tentative expectations changed by the evidence? How can the analysis lead to more general theoretical arguments? What concepts and relationships can be adopted to generate a more enduring explanation of a certain phenomenon (Baxter and Chua 1998)?

The process of theorizing changes depending on the specific research perspective selected to investigate the social world. This perspective depends on the philosophical assumptions about the empirical world, a certain view about the knowledge and the models of human intentions and rationality, as well as about how individuals relate to one another and to society as a whole. On the basis of these assumptions three different research perspectives can be identified: functionalist, interpretative and critical (Burren and Morgan 1979; Chua 1986).

Each of these perspectives implies a different assumption about the relationship between the theory and the empirical domain. In the functionalist perspective, the researcher looks for means-end relationships, in an attempt to identify those observations of the most 'efficient and effective' means to achieve a certain end of the decision maker. However, the researcher does not involve herself with moral judgments about the decision maker's needs or goals. In the interpretative perspective, the researcher has the objective to reveal what individuals do when they decide and behave as they do. She does so by illustrating the symbolic structure and taken-for-granted themes which shape the social world in which individuals operate. The aim is to enrich the understanding of the meaning of the individuals' actions and apprehend new languages, behaviours and forms of social interaction, thus enhancing the ability of individuals to mutually communicate and adjust to each other (Chua 1986). One example of this perspective is represented by Fernandez-Revuelta Perez and Robson (1999), who studied the introduction of 'budgetary participation' in a division of a European subsidiary of a large North American car manufacturer. They provide a revealing instance of the roles of formal budget participation as a ritual of control and legitimation without the substantive involvement of middle managers and illustrated the introduction of decoupling and organizational hypocrisy alongside the introduction of budget participation.

Finally, in the critical perspective, the researcher is concerned with unveiling the existing restrictive conditions of individuals' existence and action, with the objective of demonstrating that the supposedly existing objective and universal social laws are but expressions of particular forms of domination and ideology. In this way the researcher tries to identify paths of social change so that injustice and inequities may be removed (Chua 1986). One example of this logic can be found in Ezzamel, Willmott and Worthington (2004) where the authors investigate the role of accounting in management-labour relations in a context of manufacturing process reorganization, and explained the impact of introducing different accounting techniques on labour conditions. Conducting a rigorous case study requires awareness of which of these perspectives is adopted, with all the implications in terms of the theoretical references to use to develop theory and of the methods for collecting, analyzing and interpreting data.

The research perspective adopted has also some implications for the way in which the dialogue between the theory and the field is conducted. With the functionalist perspective, very often expectations are developed from the literature a priori, and they tend to be presented and discussed as subject to ongoing development, depending on the progression of the fieldwork. For this reason, they are often indicated as 'propositions' and not as 'hypotheses', given that these latter normally imply a clearly and tightly defined set of theoretical expectations. Hypotheses are developed from existing contributions and are subject to test against empirical observation (data). And this clear and tight definition of expectations and subsequent empirical tests rarely occur in case studies. On the contrary, in case studies propositions are developed but they may be discarded or refined during field visits. This is because the data collected may be suggestive of a different way to interpret them (Ahrens and Chapman 2007). This is for example the logic adopted in Ditillo (2012). This paper reports a framework to explain how management control systems foster knowledge transfer between organizational units in knowledge-intensive firms. The data collected interpreted with the combination of network theory and knowledge network research suggested that the design of management control systems takes into consideration the various forms of relationships between individuals (strong/weak, direct/indirect) that are activated by these systems and that are necessary to transfer various forms of knowledge characterized by different levels of causal ambiguity and relatedness. The work reports a set of propositions that were revised and fine-tuned during field visits.

Long field visits may lead to a familiarity that may allow researchers to collect or construct very rare, very detailed or otherwise remarkable evidence that may in turn be functional to refining propositions. This familiarity, however, is not usually described in the published work, but that does not mean that it is not there. It simply means that the linearity with which the dialogue between the theory and the data is described in the final manuscript is in fact the result of an iterative process characterized by continuous improvement of theoretical expectations and data interpretations. This is the common path adopted by functionalist case study researchers. In contrast, with interpretive and critical perspectives the dialogue between the theory and the field is different. The theory provides the general framework and categories to explore various aspects of the field. But these aspects are not objectively real, rather they are subjectively developed through the interaction of the subjects involved. As a result more specific categories to structure the data collected are developed during the fieldwork, and these categories are very contexts specific, given that they have emerged from definite organizational domains, but alluding to more widely spread practices (Ahrens and Chapman 2007).

Generalizing from case studies

Dealing with the issue of generalization in social sciences requires the recognition of an important premise: the difficulty of predicting human behaviour. Thus, social researchers face a crucial dilemma when trying to extend their conclusions beyond the specific context they are analyzing. On the one hand, they would like to make valid generalizations of individuals' behaviours with the purpose of providing insights on how to engage in convenient social interaction with others. On the other hand, they cannot neglect the independence and freedom individuals have to choose their courses of action, i.e., they cannot overlook their unpredictability. So any consideration of generalization in case studies should start from the idea that generalizations in social sciences may exist, but in a significantly weaker form than hard sciences. This consideration is even stronger for case study researchers that adopt an interpretive or a critical perspective. In fact, given that these researchers presume that the meaning of human behaviours is socially constructed, they propose the absence of trans-temporal and trans-spatial regularities in any unconditional sense. Despite this fact, one may assume the existence of at least some social structures containing some certain, though, transient regularities (Humphrey and Scapens 1992; Lukka and Kasanen 1995).

So what kind of generalization is possible from case studies? First of all, it is possible to say that it is not a generalization based on statistical inference. Rather it is a form of 'theoretical' or 'analytic' generalization. These two labels imply gaining generalizability from interpreting case findings through, or against, existing theories or a systematic induction deriving from comparative case analysis (Chua 1989; Eisenhardt 1989; Eisenhardt 1991; Lukka and Kasanen 1995).

There are different ways of realizing 'theoretical' or 'analytic' generalizations. The common element of these different ways is the attempt to explain individual observations with their specific wholeness and integrity, by using a holistic approach (Ryan et al. 2002). One mode is using case studies to apply a certain theory in new contexts so that the theory is likely to be refined and/or modified and through this process the theory is generalized (Ryan et al. 2002). This is what happens for example when the study of new cases leads to additional new important determinants of a specific phenomenon. The contribution by Cristofoli, Liguori, Sicilia and Steccolini (2010) achieved this objective when, by analyzing the field, they showed that the management controls adopted in public-private inter-organizational relationships depended not only on the organizational variables characterizing transactions but also on the political visibility of the public service provided by the outsourcers. Another way of realizing generalization is to use case studies to identify the real (causal, teleological or other) tendencies and determinants that explain a certain phenomenon (Whitley 1984; Lukka and Kasanen 1995). For example, Caglio and Ditillo (2012b) illustrate the role of individuals in explaining open book accounting. The deep analysis of the case, supported by theory, allowed to analytically generalize, and extend beyond the single case analyzed, the role and importance of individuals in sharing accounting information between partner organizations.

Doing case research: on collecting, analyzing and reporting case evidence

Case-based research requires specific methodological choices on how to collect, analyze and report case evidence. It has to be noticed up front that as Baxter and Chua (1998: 69) argue – borrowing a metaphor from Turner (1988) – doing case research is like cooking a strudel. Following the recipe of the Austrian strudel-making competition's winner is not enough to get a delicious strudel: cooks develop a significant amount of tacit knowledge and culinary skills as a result of their hands-on experience. In the same way as cooking, doing case research and becoming a competent case researcher require a significant amount of direct investigation and adaptation in the field. It is thus very difficult to articulate the craft of doing case research: what can be done in a book is to try to outline some practical issues, while acknowledging that case-based research is more than a method, a mechanical procedure that needs to be followed.

It is also important to underline that doing a case study not only involves a craft-like element but it also implies enacting a meta-theory of accounting research. Hence, not only is the role of case-based research dependent upon the epistemological stance taken by the researcher, as already explained in the previous sections, but also are the ensuing practical issues (Otley and Berry 1998). Thus, articulating the fundamentals of collecting, analyzing and reporting case evidence is further complicated by the fact that there might be differences in the way researchers approach the inquiry in the field depending on whether they follow the logic of scientific empiricism or phenomenological analysis. In fact, mainstream accounting researchers are usually interested in case studies as a way to explore topics and generate ideas and hypotheses that will then be tested in large-scale statistical studies for subsequently developing theories. On the contrary, for interpretive or critical researchers, case studies themselves are central in the theory development process (Ryan et al. 2002) and are used to explain the presumed relations and patterns that are too complex for surveys or experimental strategies (Yin 2009). Besides, reality is conceived as emergent, subjective and constructed; therefore, the field is not simply part of the empirical world, but is also shaped by the interests of the investigator (Ahrens and Chapman 2007). Thus, the orientation of the researcher significantly influences the researchers' strategies and the ways in which practical issues in case-based research are approached and resolved. For example, the interview can be more or less structured and mobilized towards functionalist (clarify and uncover an objective reality) or interpretive-critical ends (a method for expressing social reality) depending on the notion of reality of the researcher. Or, again: case studies are often required to justify their findings in terms of research validity and reliability and, for this purpose, the use of research protocols designed to eliminate any bias is usually recommended (Yin 2009). However, this is a rather functionalist stance. On the contrary, when the researcher actively works to understand the ways in which different actors comprehend reality in an ongoing exchange process, having such analytical checklists can even be counterproductive (Ahrens and Chapman 2007).

Notwithstanding these premises, some important steps need to be followed to develop a 'case study in the making', i.e., selecting a case and getting access, preparing to approach the case study, collecting evidence, assessing and explaining evidence and, finally, reporting case evidence.

Selecting a case and getting access

Gaining access to the field is an art (Baxter and Chua 1998), where access means not only the possibility of interviewing people, but also the opportunity to view and analyze proprietary documents as well as to observe the functioning of an organization and experience some aspects of organizational life. In fact, differently from other methods where researchers work *outside* organizations, case research is carried on *within* organizations. This first step, i.e., gaining access, goes in parallel with case selection and is fundamental as it has a lot of consequences on the following steps of a case study. The worst situation would be designing a research study having in mind a case that turns out not to be feasible, or starting to collect data and realizing that the case is not an instance of what the researcher planned to study. This initial phase needs to be approached very carefully.

Researchers may use different strategies in this respect. Theoretical sampling takes into consideration all the potentially interesting organizations that would offer a rich source of information (Baxter and Chua 1998). The organizations included in the sample are defined based on a set of operational criteria (aligned with the specific research question of the researcher), whereby they will be considered as eligible to serve as potential cases. The subsequent screening to define which organizations to target is usually done based on an a priori collection of some documentation regarding each of the organizations included in the initial sample, e.g., from archival sources, from statistical databases. These target organizations are then contacted for getting access, starting from the one (or the ones, if doing a multiple-case study) that is most likely to yield the best data (Yin 2009). For example, as a first step to understanding accounting information flows in the context of inter-organizational relationships, Caglio and Ditillo (2012b) collected some exploratory evidence on eight firms. Their goal was, on the one hand, to gather a diverse set of experiences on the enabling conditions of accounting information flows in inter-firm relationships and, on the other hand, to identify a firm suitable for further investigation. By leveraging on the information emerging from the preliminary data collection, the authors decided to study a case in depth, and, among the ones included in the initial sample, they selected the firm that seemed to be the most interesting in terms of the main enabling conditions of inter-organizational accounting information exchanges. In other situations, selecting a case and gaining access to the field completely overlap, because the researcher aims at investigating a research topic that requires getting access to a unique or revelatory case. In other situations, again, these two steps coincide for the reason that the researcher has some special arrangement or opportunity of pervasively accessing a specific organization. For example, Busco and Quattrone (2014), exploring the multiple roles of the balanced scorecard (BSC) in a large corporation operating in the oil and gas industry, stated that the choice of the site in which the case study developed was driven by many reasons but also by practicality. In fact, the company was chosen because it provided the researchers with extensive access to written and visual material (e.g., slides utilized in presentations concerning BSC implementation, guidelines, minutes of meetings and consultants' documents) that were crucial given the specific aim of the authors, i.e., understanding the power of inscriptions in the context of BSC implementation.

In any case, it should be noted that access is provisional and must be continually negotiated and re-negotiated (especially in longitudinal research studies). A researcher must always demonstrate her credibility and cultivate a deep relationship with the people within the organization she aims to study. There can also be situations where access can be endangered by changed organizational circumstances, e.g., a merger, a key informant moving from her organizational position. In these situations, having nurtured the rapport between the observer and the observed, for example creating relationships with different informants, becomes critical to retain access to the field (Baxter and Chua 1998).

Preparing to approach the case study

The research question is the compass of any case researcher as it points to the substantial elements of the field evidence that are to be chased and investigated. So it is important to articulate such question as much as possible in order to be able to thereby derive a tentative research plan and define the resources needed to complete the case study. This preliminary step is also instrumental to evidence collection, as the research question will provide clues to the researcher about where to look for data and which substantive aspects of practice need to be examined in depth, especially when the data collection process stalls. The researcher will be prompted by the research question to look for field experiences that may enable a better understanding of her research topic and to actively seek useful data also in unexpected places (Baxter and Chua 1998).

Reviewing the existing literature and the available theories should also be done as a preparatory step to define a list of things, issues and incidents to search for while collecting evidence. In this respect, the preparation to interviews is particularly important. There are different approaches the researcher can use for interviews and these require different forms of preparation (Yin 2009). The structured interviews' approach is when the researcher asks each informant the same series of questions. The ordering and phrasing of the questions are the same from interview to interview and are to be formally defined prior to the interviews. The preparation of structured interviews requires a clear understanding of the topic under study: therefore, structured interviews are best used when the literature is highly developed. When the researcher aims at using semi-structured interviews, she needs to develop an interview guide, e.g., a list of questions and topics that need to be covered, usually in a specific order. The researcher follows the list but is also aiming at following topical paths as the conversation evolves. For example, Dekker (2004), studying an alliance's governance structure, opted for semi-structured interviews with boundary spanners of both partners involved in the design of the governance structure and in the operation of the alliance. The author used an interview protocol based on his theoretical framework, at the same time leaving ample room for the interviewees to discuss what in their perceptions was important. Finally, the unstructured interviews' approach is when the researcher and the informants engage in a formal interview but there is no guide or list for questions. The researcher has a well-defined plan in mind regarding the focus and aims of the interviews and builds an ongoing relationship with the informants, getting them to communicate and express themselves in their own way. Unstructured interviews are used to identify new ways of understanding the topic under study and hold the greatest potential for open-ended interaction between the researcher and the key informants.

Prior to the collection of case evidence, it is also desirable to obtain formal approval of the research plan from the organization under study. Moreover, at this stage, the researcher would need to take care to gain informed consent from the people who will take part in the case study and try, in this way, to solicit their volunteerism in participating in the research. Special precautions might also be needed to guarantee that the privacy and confidentiality of the participants will be protected and that they will not be put in any undesirable position (Yin 2009).

Collecting evidence

Case research usually involves the use of multiple sources of evidence including not only interviews but also observing actions and meetings; collecting artefacts, such as formal documents and reports and using questionnaires to obtain evidence from a number of people in a consistent way (Ryan et al. 2002). A unique feature of case-based research is its potential for combining structured and unstructured data which can result in a great variation of information (Ahrens and Chapman 2007). For example, Chenhall, Hall and Smith (2013) studied a non-government organization and the internal debates over the design and operation of a performance measurement system. The authors conducted 32 interviews, which were digitally recorded and transcribed, and, where this was not possible, they took extensive notes during the interview and further notes were then written-up on the same day. They also attended meetings, observed day-to-day work practices, collected internal and publicly available documents and participated in lunches and after-work drinks. Due to the location of the non-government organization staff around the world, some interviews were also conducted via telephone.

Therefore, to get started with gathering evidence, it is crucial for the researcher to make sure that she can leverage different potential sources of information. This can be done by carefully structuring the relationships with the potential informants from the very early stages of the evidence collection. If it is true that researchers usually gain access to an organization through one person, cultivating relationships with diverse key informants is also fundamental. In practical terms, it would be advisable to choose, as the first person to interview, a potential gatekeeper (Baxter and Chua 1998), e.g., someone who is able to introduce the researcher to other organizational participants involved in activities of research interest. For example, Caglio (2003) studied the adoption of a new Enterprise Resource Planning (ERP) system, and how it challenged the definition of the roles of accountants within a pharmaceutical company. The author gained access to the company through the chief financial officer (CFO) who was also the leader of the ERP implementation project. She was then introduced by the project leader to the other team members and was therefore able to interview all the relevant actors of the implementation process, including the most important key users of the new ERP system. Similarly, Kornberger, Justesen and Mouritsen (2011) used a "snowballing technique" to recruit interviewees from different levels and divisions in their ethnographic study of a Big 4 Firm.

Expanding the potential sources of evidence means also targeting at being invited to attend meetings that are held on areas and topics of interest for the researcher. It is certainly more effective to be personally involved in such meetings rather than having to rely on the recollections of others who were present on the minutes of those meetings. If the researcher is particularly lucky, she can be allowed to participate in the life of the organization and observe organizational issues and events unfolding for a certain time, as if she were part of the organization itself. Ditillo (2004), for example, could spend 20 days full-time over a period of two months in a software company to study the role of management control systems in a knowledge-intensive company thus being able to participate as an observer in three different software development projects.

While being very open to multiple sources of evidence, the case researcher needs to be extremely disciplined in order to benefit from such informational richness and not get lost in the abundance of accumulated evidence. This does not mean that the researcher should rely on a rigid formula to guide her inquiry, but rather on systematized routines for data collection to ensure methodological rigour (Baxter and Chua 1998) and to prevent her from being overwhelmed by the quantity and complexity of field evidence. Hence, when authorized, interviews and meetings should be tape-recorded. All evidence collected should be classified and kept in an ordered manner for subsequent analysis. Notes by the researcher should be added every time new evidence is collected, as soon as possible thereafter, to record, for example, informal signals, such as casual comments, the tone of certain answers and special body attitudes. In fact, such informal evidence might suggest new issues to be explored as well as the credibility of formal answers (Ryan et al. 2002).

Assessing and explaining evidence

To assess their evidence, case researchers do not test against some predetermined statistical standards of significance and legitimacy. They rather develop schemas and models and apply these in the field, in an iterative process that requires also the revision of such frameworks, until they can explain the patterns of behaviours and actions observed. As noted by Dent (1991), it is only through successive rounds of analyzing notes and collected evidence that the researcher improves her understanding such that subsequent data become predictable: the job of connecting case evidence and theory to the research question requires discipline and patience.

Of course, like other scholars, also case-based researchers are worried about having 'reliable' data and they take care of this, for example, by using multiple sources of information – 'triangulation' (Yin 2009) – and by relying on systematized routines to collect and analyze evidence (as illustrated in the preceding pages). But the 'usual' issues of data reliability and validity take on a different significance in case-based research. Certainly, triangulation as well as case protocols and routines are important, but, ultimately, it is the plausibility of the whole narrative what counts. Ryan et al. (2002) note that as reliability implies an independent and impersonal investigator and validity assumes an objective reality, these notions are not meaningful in interpretive and critical research. They rather propose the notions of: 'procedural reliability', i.e., the fact that the researcher has employed appropriate and reliable research procedures; 'transferability' of the case study findings, i.e., theoretical generalizability; and, finally, 'contextual validity', i.e., the credibility of the case study evidence and the conclusions that are drawn from such evidence (Ryan et al. 2002: 155–156). The goal of a case researcher is thus to make her explanation trustworthy (Covaleski, Dirsmith, Heian and Samuel 1998; Ahrens and Chapman 2007). In this sense, when assessing and explaining evidence, a case researcher needs to make sure that the theoretical framework she has developed thoroughly explains the patterns of behaviours observed. Therefore, when needed, she needs to revise her framework to take into account emerging patterns or events that might question previous interpretations instead of reaffirming them. The research problem, the theory and the field evidence influence each other during the research process where the researcher's job is to iteratively try to generate a plausible fit between problem, theory and data (Ahrens and Chapman 2007: 313). Therefore, assessing and explaining evidence in case-based research is the result of an ongoing process of theorizing, of theoretical repositioning and concepts' redefinition aimed at gaining a multifaceted understanding of the topic under study and at achieving 'fit' between theory, methodology and field domain; otherwise the researcher is confronted with the so-what question (Ahrens and Chapman 2007). The veracity of case researchers' explanations depends on their conceptual solidity, on their consistency and their revelation value (Baxter and Chua 1998: 74).

Reporting case evidence

The writing of a case study is a difficult and time-consuming process. Difficult, because the reporting of case evidence involves the construction of a story: writing up a case study is a creative and literary act, whereby the investigator needs to produce a convincing text. Time consuming, because there is always more going on in the field than the researcher can report in a publication: the case study has to be constructed from a mass of field notes, transcriptions, data and reports (Ryan et al. 2002).

Apart from being gifted with special language skills, there are some golden rules that a scholar can follow when writing a case study. First of all, in reporting case evidence, it is vital to preserve the multifaceted stories told by informants and to demonstrate that the researcher's account retains the informants' interpretations and experiences of reality. The verbatim quotes are very useful for this purpose as they convey authenticity in the final research report and help the researcher to demonstrate that her interpretation is substantiated by direct case evidence. To convince the reader, it is also important to describe and provide details about the multiple kinds of evidence collected, e.g., the people interviewed, the duration of the interviews, the meetings attended, the documents and reports analyzed, etc. This is to show how deeply and how extensively the investigator has been involved in the case reality she is describing and explaining. The textual account should also be provocative: when reporting case evidence, selective plausibility needs to be avoided, i.e., the researcher should not emphasize in the writing only that evidence that fits her theoretical framework. Sometimes, there is a natural bias to see only what the researcher expects to see: for this reason, it is a good practice to revise notes in search of evidence that would contradict initial expectations and mobilize such evidence in the writing up to raise new ideas and add to theory (Ryan et al. 2002). Of course, this is also a question of academic honesty. Finally, in the write-up, it is absolutely fundamental that the issues raised by the case are explicitly linked back with the theory developed and with the reviewed literature (and with propositions when present) to substantiate the original theoretical framework but also to draw out new theoretical insights.

In conclusion, the methodological choices presented above, although described as sequential steps of a case study in the making, are in effect the result of an iterative and combined process that might include also reflective pauses, tensions and changes. It is the task of the researcher to practice case studies by choosing a consistent research approach and at the same time being flexible enough to grasp opportunities that the field may offer.

Pride and prejudice of case study research

Although case-based research has gained acceptance in accounting, authors of case studies frequently feel the need to 'apologize' – for instance, for a lack of statistical generalizability of their findings – or they feel compelled to defend the appropriateness of their research approach. That is the reason why, in conclusion, it is useful to summarize the potentials of case studies in order to contribute to facing some still existing prejudices against case-based research.

As argued in this chapter, case studies allow the collection and analysis of qualitative data,

> which are attractive for many reasons: they are rich, full, earthy, holistic, "real"; their face validity seems unimpeachable; they preserve chronological flow where that is important, and suffer minimally from retrospective distortion; and they, in principle, offer a far more precise way to assess causality in organizational affairs than arcane efforts like cross-lagged correlations (after all, intensive fieldwork contains dozens of "waves" of data collection, not just two or three).
>
> *(Miles 1979)*

Moreover, despite the prejudice that case studies are an easy means to conduct research, collecting and analyzing qualitative data is a highly labour-intensive and time-consuming process:

the wide range of phenomena to be captured, the recorded amount of notes, the time required for write-up and analysis can be overwhelming. Finally, being a qualitative researcher demands sharpness in identifying important details, interpersonal ability to interact with the subjects, elegance in approaching the field, acumen and originality in analyzing and interpreting data.

Having said this, it is important to underline that quantitative research is not the evil twin of qualitative, case-based research (Van Maanen 1998). Case-based research has its own strengths and weaknesses. Whether it is appropriate or preferred to other methods will depend upon the research question, the topic under study as well as upon the methodological and epistemological position of the researcher.

Notes

1 Throughout this chapter, we report some examples of papers based on case studies. We draw on them as illustrative of specific aspects of the case study methodology and not as ideal types or perfect benchmarks. In addition, we refer to the accounting field to provide our examples, yet our arguments and reflections are valid also for other areas in the wider fields of social sciences.
2 One of these approaches is the Grounded Theory introduced by Glaser and Strauss (1967), intended as a theory whose development is based on "how well data fit conceptual categories identified by an observer, by how well the categories explain or predict ongoing interpretations, and by how relevant the categories are to the core issues being observed" (Suddaby 2006: 634).

References

Abernethy, M. and Chua, W.F., 1996, 'A field study of control system "redesign": The impact of institutional processes on strategic choice', *Contemporary Accounting Research* 13(2), 569–606.
Ahrens, T., 1997, 'Talking accounting: An ethnography of management knowledge in British and German Brewers', *Accounting, Organizations and Society* 22(7), 617–637.
Ahrens, T. and Chapman, C.S., 2007, 'Doing qualitative field research in management accounting: Positioning data to contribute to theory', in C.S. Chapman, A.G. Hopwood and M.E. Shields (eds.), *Handbook of Management Accounting Research*, 299–318, Elsevier, Amsterdam.
Alvesson, M. and Kärreman, D., 2004, 'Interfaces of control: Technocratic and socio-ideological control in a global management consultancy firm', *Accounting, Organizations and Society* 29, 423–444.
Baxter, J.A. and Chua, W.F., 1998, 'Doing field research: Practice and meta-theory in counterpoint', *Journal of Management Accounting Research* 10, 69–87.
Burren, G. and Morgan, G., 1979, *Sociological paradigms and organizational analysis, elements of the sociology of corporate life*, Heinemann Educational Books, Portsmouth, NH.
Busco, C. and Quattrone, P., 2014, 'Exploring how the balanced scorecard engages and unfolds: Articulating the visual power of accounting inscriptions', *Contemporary Accounting Research* 32(3), 1236–1262.
Caglio, A., 2003, 'Enterprise resource planning systems and accountants: Towards hybridisation', *European Accounting Review* 12(1), 123–153.
Caglio, A. and Ditillo, A., 2008, *Controlling Collaboration Between Firms: How to Build and Maintain Successful Relationships with External Partners*, CIMA-Elsevier, Oxford, UK.
Caglio, A. and Ditillo, A., 2012a, 'Interdependence and accounting information exchanges in inter-firm relationships', *Journal of Management and Governance* 16(1), 57–80.
Caglio, A. and Ditillo, A., 2012b, 'Opening the black box of management accounting information exchanges in buyer-supplier relationships', *Management Accounting Research* 23, 61–78.
Chenhall, R.H., Hall, M. and Smith, D., 2013, 'Performance measurement, modes of evaluation and the development of compromising accounts', *Accounting, Organizations and Society* 38(4), 268–287.
Chua, W.F., 1986, 'Radical development in accounting thoughts', *The Accounting Review* LXI(4), 601–632.
Chua, W.F., 1989, 'Interpreting sociology and management accounting research – a critical review', *Accounting, Auditing and Accountability Journal* 2(1), 59–79.
Cooper, D.J. and Morgan, W., 2008, 'Case study research in accounting', *Accounting Horizons* 22(2), 159–178.

Covaleski, M.A., Dirsmith, M.W., Heian, J.B. and Samuel, S., 1998, 'The calculated and the avowed: Techniques of discipline and struggles over identity in Big Six public accounting firms', *Administrative Science Quarterly* 43(2), 293–327.

Cristofoli, D., Liguori, M.A., Sicilia, M.F. and Steccolini, I., 2010, 'Do environmental and task characteristics matter in the control of externalized local public services? Unveiling the relevance of party characteristics and citizens' offstage voice', *Accounting, Auditing and Accountability Journal* 23(3), 350–372.

Davila, T., 2000, 'An empirical study of the drivers of management controls systems' design in new product development', *Accounting, Organizations and Society* 25, 383–409.

Dekker, H., 2004, 'Control of inter-organizational relationships: Evidence on appropriation concerns and coordination requirements', *Accounting, Organizations and Society* 29, 27–49.

Dent, J.F., 1991, 'Accounting and organizational cultures: A field study of the emergence of new organizational reality', *Accounting, Organizations and Society* 16, 705–732.

Ditillo, A., 2004, 'Dealing with uncertainty in knowledge-intensive firms: The role of management control systems as knowledge integration mechanisms', *Accounting, Organizations and Society* 29, 401–421.

Ditillo, A., 2012, 'Designing management control systems to foster knowledge transfer in knowledge-intensive firms: A network-based approach', *European Accounting Review* 21(3), 425–450.

Dyer, W.G. and Wilkins, A.L., 1991, 'Better stories, not better constructs, to generate better theory: A rejoinder to Eisenhardt', *Academy of Management Review* 16(3), 613–619.

Eisenhardt, K.M., 1989, 'Building theories from case study research', *Academy of Management Review* 14(4), 532–550.

Eisenhardt, K.M., 1991, 'Better stories and better constructs: The case for rigor and comparative logic', *Academy of Management Review* 16(3), 620–627.

Ezzamel, M., Willmott, H. and Worthington, F., 2004, 'Accounting and management-labour relations: The politics of production in the 'factory with a problem', *Accounting, Organizations and Society* 29, 269–302.

Fernandez-Revuelta Perez, L. and Robson, K., 1999, 'Ritual legitimation, de-coupling and the budgetary process: Managing organizational hypocrisies in a multinational company', *Management Accounting Research* 10, 383–407.

Geertz, C., 1995, *After the Fact: Two Countries, Four Decades, One Anthropologist*, Harvard University Press, Cambridge.

Glaser, B.S. and Strauss, A. (1967). *The Discovery of Grounded Theory*, Aldine Publishing Company, Chicago.

Humphrey, C. and Scapens, R., 1992, 'Theories and case studies: Limitation or liberation (or a case of accounting theory not becoming what it was not)', *Working paper 92/4*, University of Manchester, Manchester.

Jørgensen, B. and Messner, M., 2009, 'Management control in new product development: The dynamics of managing flexibility and efficiency', *Journal of Management Accounting Research* 21, 99–124.

Kornberger, M., Justesen, L. and Mouritsen, J., 2011, 'When you make manager, we put a big mountain in front of you: An ethnography of managers in a Big 4 accounting firm', *Accounting, Organizations and Society* 36(8), 514–533.

Lukka, K. and Kasanen, E., 1995, 'The problem of generalizability: Anecdotes and evidence in accounting research', *Accounting, Auditing & Accountability Journal* 8(5), 71–90.

Miles, M.B., 1979, 'Qualitative data as an attractive nuisance: The problem of analysis', *Administrative Science Quarterly* 24(4), 590–601.

Miller, P. and O'Leary, T., 1998, 'Finding things out', *Accounting, Organizations and Society* 23(7), 709–714.

Mouritsen, J., Hansen, A. and Hansen, C.Ø., 2001, 'Inter-organizational control and organizational competencies: Episodes around target cost management/functional analysis and open book accounting', *Management Accounting Research* 12, 221–244.

Otley, D.T. and Berry, A.J., 1998, 'Case study research in management accounting and control', *Accounting Education* 7, 105–127.

Reiter, S.A. and Williams, P.F., 2002, 'The structure and progressivity of accounting research: The crisis in the academy revisited', *Accounting, Organizations and Society* 27(6), 575–607.

Revellino, S. and Mouritsen, J., 2009, 'The multiplicity of controls and the making of innovation', *European Accounting Review* 18(2), 341–369.

Ryan, B., Scapens, R.W. and Theobald, M., 2002, *Research Method and Methodology in Finance and Accounting*, Thompson, London, UK.

Stake, R.E., Denzin, N. and Lincoln, Y., 2000, *Handbook of Qualitative Research*, Sage Publications, Thousand Oaks, CA.

Suddaby, R., 2006, 'From the editors: What grounded theory is not', *Academy of Management Journal* 49(4), 633–642.

Thrane, S., 2007, 'The complexity of management accounting change: Bifurcation and oscillationin schizophrenic organizational systems', *Management Accounting Research* 18, 248–272.

Turner, B.A., 1988, 'Connoisseurship in the study of organizational cultures', in A. Bryman (ed.), *Doing Research in Organizations*, 108–122, Routledge, London.

Van Maanen, J., 1998, 'Editor's introduction: Different strokes', in J. Van Maanen (ed.), *Qualitative Studies of Organizations*, 9–33, Sage Publications, Thousand Oaks, CA.

Van Maanen, J.V., 1979, 'Reclaiming qualitative methods for organizational research: A preface', *Administrative Science Quarterly* 24(4), 520–526.

Whitley, R., 1984, 'The scientific status of management research as a practically-oriented social science', *Journal of Management Studies* 21(4), 369–390.

Yin, R.K., 2009, *Case Study Research: Design and Methods*, Sage Publications Inc, Thousand Oaks, CA.

18

New technologies for behavioural accounting experiments

Kristian Rotaru, Axel K.-D. Schulz and Dennis D. Fehrenbacher

> *Attacking the bigger issue of ultimate causation in accounting requires that we gather direct evidence on how accounting alters decision-making within the brain . . . . Recent technological innovations now used widely by neuroscientists offer an opportunity to get a more direct look at what occurs in the brain while economic decisions are being made.*
>
> G.B. Waymire (2014: 2011–2012)

Introduction

Over the past several years, the study of neurocognitive mechanisms of decision-making has gained increased prominence in the research literature resulting in a novel body of interdisciplinary research borrowing and mixing constructs, theories, tools and measurement techniques from a number of disciplines, including psychophysiology and neuroscience, and leading to the emergence of novel hybrid disciplines. This has led to the rise of a range of hybrid social science disciplines, giving birth to the emerging fields of neuroeconomics (Camerer, Loewenstein and Prelec 2005; Loewenstein, Rick and Cohen 2008), neuromarketing (Lee, Broderick and Chamberlain 2007; Fugate 2007), decision neuroscience (Shiv, Loewenstein, Bechara, Damasio and Damasio 2005; Bossaerts and Murawski 2015), neurofinance (Vasile and Sebastian 2007; Frydman, Barberis, Camerer, Bossaerts and Rangel 2014), neuro-information systems (neuroIS) (Dimoka et al. 2010; Riedl, Davis and Hevner 2014) and more recently neuroaccounting (Dickhaut, Basu, McCabe and Waymire 2010; Birnberg and Ganguly 2012; Farrell, Goh and White 2014; Barton, Berns and Brooks 2014; Waymire 2014).

Being termed as "neuromania" by some (Legrenzi and Umiltà 2011), the phenomenon continues to grow, resulting in a number of well-equipped laboratories appearing in business schools, or as collaborative efforts between business and medical schools. The outcomes of the multidisciplinary research produced in such collaborative settings are getting increasingly accepted by the top journals in the relevant fields of social science, such as *Management Science* (Smith, Dickhaut, McCabe and Pardo 2002), the *Journal of Finance* (Bruguier, Quartz and Bossaerts 2010), *Management Information Systems Quarterly* (Dimoka et al. 2010) and more recently, *The Accounting Review* (Farrell et al. 2014) and *Journal of Accounting Research* (Chen, Jermias and Panggabean 2016).

The purpose of this chapter is to discuss some of the neuropsychological tools that have entered or are about to enter the accounting research field. It is not meant to be an exhaustive list of technologies but rather a reference point for researchers interested in using new technologies as part of their toolset.[1] The chapter will focus on how these technologies may assist in identifying neurophysiological correlates associated with various decision-making conditions or cognitive states of individual decision makers. Relevant accounting studies will be included, although the majority of studies are from related fields, which reflects the recent entry of accounting research in this area. Current limitations will be highlighted along with suggestions for future research.[2]

Neurophysiological research in accounting: a new level of analysis

Behavioural research in accounting examining the judgment and decision-making of individuals has a long tradition (Ashton and Ashton 1995; Libby, Bloomfield and Nelson 2002; Bonner 2008). Understanding the cognitive process by which an individual arrives at a judgment or decision lies at the heart of this inquiry. While cognitive theories have underpinned a majority of judgment and decision-making studies in accounting research, until recently (e.g., Barton et al. 2014; Farrell et al. 2014), testing of these theories has relied primarily on self-reported process measures. Traditional cognitive research accepts the difficulty of observing the cognitive process and therefore treats cognition as a "black box" (Birnberg and Ganguly 2012; Camerer et al. 2005), and uses theory to map expected relationships between observed inputs and outputs.

An alternative to treating the cognitive process as a "black box" is to measure biological responses of decision makers while they perform a specific task. For example, a number of recent studies in accounting and other social science disciplines has been performed at the neurological/physiological (or simply, neurophysiological) level of analysis. The connection to the biological roots of cognitive processes allows for new insights into the neurological correlates of observed judgment and decision outcomes.

There are several different neurophysiological tools or technologies that will warrant in-depth discussion. Overall, the choice of the technologies discussed in this chapter is determined either by the wide adoption of the technology (for instance, functional magnetic resonance imaging) and/or by the authors' experience in using the technology for the purposes of neuroaccounting research.[3] Following the framework suggested by Riedl and Léger (2016) for categorizing neurophysiological tools, the technologies discussed in this chapter will be structured according to their measurement of the *peripheral nervous system* (eye tracking, cognitive pupillometry, skin conductance) or the *central nervous system* (electroencephalography, functional magnetic resonance imaging). Each is discussed in turn below.

Technologies for recording the activity of the peripheral nervous system

In this section, a number of techniques for measuring aspects of the peripheral nervous system are going to be discussed. Specifically, the techniques discussed in this section include eye tracking, pupillometry and skin conductance level. These techniques have been reported to be correlated with attention, anxiety and other motivational states.

Eye tracking and pupillometry

Accountants engage in many tasks that require the processing of visual information as accounting information is often transmitted in written form. To process visual information, we point the fovea of our eye, that is, the small depression in the retina of the eye where visual acuity is highest, at the areas from which we expect to acquire the necessary information. We spend a fraction of a second on a particular area and then move on to focus on another area of interest. Another fraction of a second is spent to focus on this new area, then we move on again.

Our eye movement is not smooth. Instead, it consists of sequences of fixations, the time spent focusing on one spot, and saccades, the movement between two fixations (Wedel and Pieters 2008; Dodge 1900). Short fixations have been defined to be shorter than 150 ms, medium fixations ≥ 150 ms and [500 ms and long fixations ≥ 500 ms (Velichkovsky 1999), while saccades occur roughly about three times every second (Tatler, Kirtley, Macdonald, Mitchell and Savage 2014).

The utility of such eye movements in adding to the understanding of human behaviour has been acknowledged by many disciplines, including accounting, psychology and marketing (Tatler et al. 2014; Fehrenbacher, Schulz and Rotaru 2015; Chen et al. 2016). For accounting researchers in particular, mapping eye movements while managers, auditors or accountants make decisions can potentially enhance the understanding of accounting-related judgment and decision-making.

Along with eye movements, the modern eye-tracking technology can also capture information about the pupillary response. The pupil is the opening located in the centre of the iris of the eye that permits light to reach the retina, thereby facilitating vision (Sirois and Brisson 2014). Apart from the pupillary light reflex (i.e., the pupil tends to dilate in dark conditions and constrict in bright conditions), pupils dilate when participants are in conditions of increased attention and/or emotional or cognitive arousal (Kahneman 1973).

Pupillometry is the study of dilation and constriction in pupil diameter as a function of cognitive processing and thereby can be used as an index of arousal and implicit processing (Sirois and Brisson 2014). Of particular interest in pupillometry has been the size, and change in size, of the pupil for particular stimuli. Depending on environmental conditions or internal state of the individual, pupil diameter may vary significantly: from 1.5 to 9 mm (Lowenstein and Loewenfeld 1962). A more substantial variation of the pupil diameter is observed under light reflex, while the response to increased/decreased attention or cognitive processing is usually subtler (Sirois and Brisson 2014). The average pupil diameter under normal light conditions is 3 mm, however the diameter of the pupil under such conditions may still vary significantly across individuals (Wyatt 1995). The reaction time for stimulation of the pupil is about 200 ms (Lowenstein and Loewenfeld 1962). Pupil dilation level, measured as increase in pupil size from baseline to laboratory tasks requiring mental processing of information, is a relevant neurophysiological marker of emotional arousal, stress or cognitive processing and attentional effort (Hess and Polt 1964; Kahneman 1973).

Technology for eye tracking

Multiple technological solutions for eye tracking are currently available on the market. These differ in terms of their mobility (portable or stationary), sampling rate (the number of observations per second the technology is able to capture) and other characteristics. A comprehensive review of the fundamentals of eye tracking is provided in Holmqvist et al. (2011). Further, the handbook by Liversedge, Gilchrist and Everling (2011) contains an outline of the research directions in eye-tracking research. As examples of portable and stationary eye-tracking devices are depicted in Figure 18.1. Figure 18.2 demonstrates a typical setup for an experiment involving the use of cognitive pupillometry.

Figure 18.1a   Portable eye-tracking device: Tobii Pro Glasses 2 (sampling rate: 50 Hz to 100 Hz)

Figure 18.1b   Stationary eye-tracking device: Tobii TX300 (sampling rate: 300 Hz)

Height-adjustable forehead and chin rests are highly useful for ensuring high-quality data capturing and for addressing the risks of breaks in the recording of data. This relates to the use of the eye-tracker when capturing such gaze data as fixation durations and fixation counts, but is particularly critical when conducting cognitive pupillometry assessment. For the latter, it is important that the experimenter allows for as many controls and adjustments of participants' physical position as possible: height-adjustable chairs, table desk, forehead and chin rests.

Figure 18.2 The use of the eye-tracker while recording pupillary response

Attention studies in accounting

Since we are not fully aware of our erratic eye movements, we do not have full control over them (Wedel and Pieters 2008). However, we have some control and thus, eye movements are regularly used as a proxy for what individuals attend and pay attention to. Attention can be described according to two aspects: selective aspects of attention and intensive aspects of attention (Kahneman 1973).

Empirical evidence has shown that individuals selectively attend to some stimuli in preference to others. Accounting research has dealt with this aspect governing individual choice and has called for research examining selective information processing in more depth (e.g., Shields 1980, 1983; Birnberg and Shields 1984; Kennedy 1993; Lipe and Salterio 2000; Luft and Shields 2009; Lachmann, Stefani and Wöhrmann 2015; Peterson, Schmardebeck and Wilks 2015). The study of selectivity can be further extended by the use of eye-tracking technology. For instance, researchers can observe which stimuli are fixated on (and how often they are fixated on) and which stimuli are ignored. Accounting research has used eye-tracking technology to study whether or not certain measures in a balanced scorecard are attended to or not (e.g., Dalla Via, van Rinsum and Perego 2016), whether particular items on a balance sheet are visually examined (e.g., Grigg and Griffin 2014) during the judgment and decision process or whether prior impressions influence selectivity in attention (Kramer and Maas 2016).

The intensity of attention is one of the measures captured in eye-tracking research (Liversedge et al. 2011). Typically, the level of intensity of attention can be measured using individual's fixation duration on an area of interest (AOI) as a proxy. The longer the fixation duration, the higher the intensity of attention tends to be. With regards to eye tracking, fixation duration can only be an approximation of attention, as individuals may look at something while thinking something else. Fixation duration has also been suggested to be an approximation for System 1 versus System 2 thinking (Horstmann, Ahlgrimm and Glöckner 2009; Kahneman 2011). For example, Fehrenbacher et al. (2015) use fixation duration to study System 1 vs. System 2 thinking in biased processing of subjective information in a performance evaluation setting.

An alternative way of reliably measuring attention (attentional effort) was proposed by Hecht, Rotaru, Schulz, Towry and Webb (2016) in one of the first accounting studies to use cognitive pupillometry. Specifically, they introduce pupillometry to accounting researchers as a technique to measure effort intensity, while isolating this construct from effort duration. Based on the adaptation of Chow's (1983) letter decoding task, this study demonstrated the differential effect of incentive scheme (piece rate vs. fixed rate) on the level of pupil dilation. In line with existing literature (Kahneman 1973), this allowed the authors to draw inferences regarding the role of incentive scheme in directing attentional effort when individuals perform an information search task. Moreover, the study confirmed that a positive and significant relationship exists between the level of pupil dilation and performance on an effort intensive task.

Design considerations

Calibration is an important step in the operation of eye trackers. It is important that the system accurately measures and represents where individuals look and is usually performed before the actual experiment starts. Different eye-tracking systems provide different levels of calibration accuracy. It is important to ensure that the calibration accuracy is appropriate for the research question being examined.

How data is to be analyzed is also of importance. As the amount of raw data collected during the recording phase is relatively large, systems vary widely in terms of the tools they provide for users to extract particular data sets of interest from the raw data. Where particular systems do not provide a particular tool, the researcher must revert back to the raw data and individually extract the relevant data of interest. This requires programming knowledge. The latter is particularly relevant for pupillometry data, which currently can only be analyzed using raw data.

Another consideration is the area of the screen relevant to the research question. Here some eye-tracking systems allow the researcher to define the regions of the screen that are of particular interest (namely, the AOIs) and hence extract observations of eye movement that relate to this area from the raw data. This could include how many times the subject's eyes were located in the AOI, how much time elapsed before the eyes were located in the AOI, or how frequently the eyes were in the AOI.

Finally, another consideration relates to parameters associated with an eye-tracking event. Threshold levels related to what constitutes a fixation and a saccade have been discussed in the eye-tracking literature. These may differ for particular tasks. For example, threshold levels for when a fixation starts and ends have been recommended to be relatively low (≥ 60 ms, Rayner 1998; Radach, Huestegge and Reilly 2008; Holmqvist et al. 2011) for reading tasks. For saccades the threshold level for velocity (how fast the eye needs to move before a movement is considered to be a saccade) needs to be considered. For instance, the setting of this parameter to 30 visual degrees per second has been shown to be adequate with various levels of noise when using the IV-T filter (Olsen 2012; Olsen and Matos 2012).

Visualizing eye-tracking and pupillometry data

Prior to formal statistical testing researchers may wish to visually explore the fixations and saccades in their data. This can help researchers to get an intuitive understanding of how individuals processed the data in the AOI. Some visualizations may also be calculated in a pooled way using several participants, e.g., participants in a particular experimental condition. Visualizations can normally not be used to analyze data in a quantitative fashion but may help researchers to gain and communicate an understanding of the data at hand in a descriptive way (Bojko 2009).

Two types of visualizations are gaze plots and heat maps. In gaze plots each fixation is represented by a circle. Each circle is numbered indicating the position of a particular fixation in a sequence: the larger the circle, the longer the duration of a single fixation. For instance, Grigg and Griffin (2014) used gaze plots to explore how individuals process balance sheets.

In heat maps colour-coding is used to indicate the distribution of attention, i.e., the amount of time an individual or a group of individuals fixated on a particular spot, within an AOI. A usual convention is that the redder the colour-coding, the longer the fixation duration. If only red colour-coding is used, the fixation duration is at or above a particular (high) threshold. Green colour-coding indicates that a participant fixates an area less than a particular (low) threshold. Yellow colour-coding indicates a fixation duration in between the two thresholds. If a participant does not fixate on an area, no colour-coding is used. Fehrenbacher et al. (2015) use this colour-coding to document the fixation duration of certain participants and explain the link drawn to System 1 and System 2 processing.

Different from the more common eye-tracking measures, pupil dilation data is more commonly visualized as a time series. A sample of the smoothed pupil dilation data collected as part of the study by Hecht et al. (2016) is presented in Figure 18.3. Specifically, the time series reflects the smoothed pupil dilation data (right and left eyes) collected during one three-minute production round (letter decoding session) for two individuals (Figures 18.3a and 18.3b). On each graph (Figures 18.3a and 18.3b), the two time series represent the changes of the left and right pupil size (in mm). Vertical lines represent the instances of letter decodes by the individual. Comparing the data in Figures 18.3a and 18.3b, one can observe a higher variation of the pupil dilation level in Figure 18.3b compared to 18.3a. Overall, the intensity of cognitive processing for the participant in Figure 18.3b is higher than for the participant in Figure 18.3a. Based on this data, one can also draw the inference that the participant in Figure 18.3b is more engaged in the task than the participant in Figure 18.3a, regardless of the mean absolute level of the pupil dilation which may vary significantly across individuals.

Figure 18.3a   Pupil dilation data. Example of a data set showing low-level cognitive activation

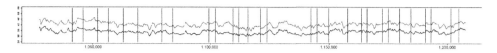

Figure 18.3b Pupil dilation data. Example of a data set showing high-level cognitive activation

In summary, eye-tracking and cognitive pupillometry technologies can provide account-ing researchers with an additional tool to better understand judgment and decision-making in accounting-related tasks. Due to the dynamic eye-brain communication, eye behaviour can be used as a proxy for people's thinking, attention and effort (Kahneman 1973, 2011; Van Gompel, Fischer, Murray and Hill 2007; Hecht et al. 2016) and may shed light on ques-tions such as how accountants process financial statements, how incentives are associated with effort and performance or on whether different thinking styles influence accounting judgments.

Skin conductance

Skin conductance level reactivity is a physiological marker of the level of arousal associated with attending to stressful or challenging tasks (Andreassi and Filipovic 2006; Naqvi and Bechara 2006). Skin conductance measurement is a conventional technique used in many behavioural laboratories to capture physiological data associated with decision-making. The effect of changes to skin conductance may be observed in a variety of environmental contexts faced by decision makers. For example, novelty of experience, anticipation of an outcome, decision-making under risk or ambiguity, deception of others or surprise (Riedl and Léger 2016; Andreassi and Filipovic 2006) are associated with increased levels of skin conductance.

In the context of affective decision-making research in particular, it is important to note that the measure of skin conductance level reactivity is also a marker of the neurophysiological motivational system known as the behavioural inhibition system. This system governs sensitivity to aversive circumstances or avoidance of such circumstances (Beauchaine 2001; Fowles 1987). The function of this system is to inhibit behaviours when aversive consequences are anticipated (Gray 1987). In line with the Somatic Marker Hypothesis, introduced by Bechara and Damasio (2005), the decision-making process is influenced by marker signals that express themselves in emotions and feelings. Thus, the activation of the behavioural inhibition system, and thereby an increase in skin conductance level reactivity, is typically observed, in the context when individu-als are presented with affectively charged stimuli.

Technology

Two types of devices are commonly used to measure skin conductance level: gel devices that require the application of the isotonic electrode gel to reduce impedance and enhance the precision of measurement; and the 'dry electrode' devices which allow measurements simply by attaching Velcro bands to fingers of the subject's hands whose electrodermal activity is measured. In Figure 18.4. a picture of such device produced by Shimmer is presented. To assure high qual-ity of measurement when taking measurement with a device similar to the one represented in Figure 18.4, it is recommended to place Velcro bands with the electrodes on the volar surfaces of distal phalanges (bones that make up the fingers; normally, the index and the middle finger) of the non-dominant hand.

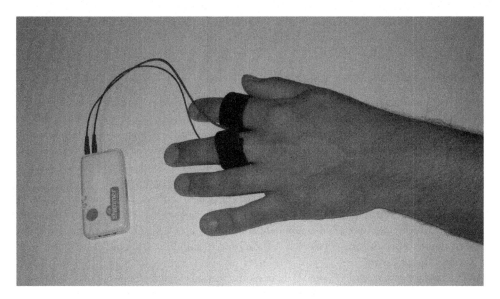

Figure 18.4   An example of a skin conductance-level device (Shimmer3 GSR+ Unit)

Affect studies using skin conductance technology

There are a number of studies in accounting investigating the role of affect in decision-making (Moreno, Kida and Smith 2002; Bhattacharjee and Moreno 2002; Sullivan and Kida 1995). However, to the authors' knowledge there are none that have made use of the skin galvanic measurement. In contrast, within the adjacent field of neuro-information systems, research in this area has been dynamic. For example, Léger, Riedl and vom Brocke (2014b) conducted a laboratory study to test differences in emotional response between expert and novice users of enterprise resource planning systems. Léger, Davis, Cronan and Perret (2014a) justified their use of skin conductance level in capturing users' emotional responses during enterprise resource planning decision-making by arguing that emotions quite often do not reach users' awareness and therefore a self-reported measure of emotional involvement would not be useful in such a context. Using skin conductance measure of emotional, or affective decision-making, the authors confirm the significant effect of user emotion upon enterprise resource planning information sourcing behaviour, as well as the moderating role of user experience in the relationship between user emotion and enterprise resource planning information sourcing behaviour.

Design considerations

When designing a study that involves the use of skin conductance measurement, one needs to be aware of the delay between stimulus and expected skin conductance response. The skin conductance response, also known as stimulus elicited response, is normally observed in the window from 0.8 to 4 seconds from stimulus onset. After this time, the observed changes in skin conductance are characterized as non-specific, or spontaneous response, which cannot be directly associated with the presented stimulus. A further necessary characteristic of the stimulus elicited response is the minimum response amplitude of the signal. At minimum, the response amplitude of the signal generally needs to be equal or exceed 0.02 micro Siemens (Andreassi and Filipovic 2006).

Visualizing skin conductance data

As part of a small experimental study, Dokumentov (2015) asked participants to watch a series of short videos which was followed by a short demographic questionnaire. The videos differed in terms of their visual narrative (nature *versus* social contexts) and, arguably, the inherent level of emotional intensity. Specifically, the first and the third videos presented slow and relaxing narratives of nature and rain with almost no action. The second video showed a famous pre-race warm-up (World Junior Track and Field Championships, Barcelona 2012), which involved dancing of Australian hurdler Michelle Jenneke. The video had two rather different parts: (a) seconds 1–94 are "warm-up dancing" and (b) seconds 95–114 are the actual race, which Jenneke won. The fourth video was a Nike commercial in the style of a horror movie. That video also had two quite different parts: (a) seconds 1–14 related to running a bath and (b) seconds 15–54 relate the "horror" part.

The data set presented in Figure 18.5, demonstrates strong differences in skin conductance level reactivity related to each of the four videos (six individual themes). The data shows that Videos 1 and 3 had the expected relaxing effect, while the "race" part of the Video 2 and the "horror" part of the last video demonstrated a strong level of arousal, arguably brought about by emotional intensity and fear. In line with the Somatic Marker Hypothesis (Bechara and Damasio 2005), the results confirm the value of collecting the data on neurophysiological markers of arousal in order to understand the actual response to a variety of stimuli administered to the participants.

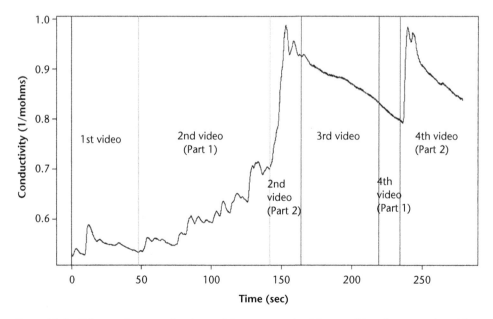

Figure 18.5 Skin conductance level reactivity measured while watching four popular videos separated into six distinctive themes

Technologies for recording the activity of the central nervous system

In this section, two brain imaging techniques which are relevant to the research conducted in the accounting field are discussed: electroencephalography (EEG) and functional magnetic resonance imaging (fMRI). Fundamental to providing insight into judgment and decision-making in accounting is the development of an understanding of how the brain processes the information presented. Historically, the tools that potentially permit direct measurement of brain activity have not been readily accessible to researchers in the domain of accounting, rather they have been restricted to medical researchers. However, these research tools are becoming more readily available to accounting researchers as these technologies, and in particular the EEG, are becoming available in business school laboratories.

Electroencephalography (EEG)

EEG is a brain imaging technique facilitating the measurement and interpretation of the central nervous system activity via the recording of the brain's electrical activity at the surface of the skull (Berger 1929). More specifically, EEG measures electrical activity of neurons within the cerebral cortex (i.e., on the outside of the brain) (Pascual-Marqui, Michel and Lehmann 1994).

Technology

Modern EEG systems are composed of electrodes, normally placed on the scalp using a cap (see Figure 18.6) or a net, the amplifiers, analog-to-digital converter, and a computer to record the collected data (Riedl and Léger 2016). When the amplifier changes the analog current to digital form, the resulting digital representation of the signal may be recorded with the different sampling rate. The sampling rate of modern EEG amplifiers ranges between 256 and 8,192 samples per second (Chapin and Russell-Chapin 2013).

One of the distinctive properties of the EEG is its ability to detect very rapid changes in the electrical activity of the brain, which occur in the range of milliseconds. From the temporal resolution perspective EEG is still considered to be more advanced than more novel methods of brain imaging compared to functional magnetic resonance imaging (fMRI) (Riedl and Léger 2016). Spatial resolution is considered to be one of the weaknesses of the EEG method (compared to fMRI, for example), although the modern analytical methods have significantly improved the functionality of EEG, in terms of source localization.

EEG studies relevant to accounting research

Currently, there are no EEG studies published in the accounting literature that the authors are aware of. However, observing the pattern in other social science disciplines, such as neuromarketing, neuroeconomics or neuroIS and considering the relatively low cost of this technology (compared to, for example, fMRI) this is likely to change in due time.

In a review dedicated to the use of electroencephalography as a research tool in the information systems discipline, Müller-Putz, Riedl and Wriessnegger (2015) made reference to the two special issues dedicated to neuroIS that appeared in two mainstream IS journals: the *Journal of Management Information Systems* (*JMIS*, Volume 30, Issue 4) and the *Journal of the Association for Information Systems* (*JAIS*, Volume 15, Issue 10). In the *JMIS* special issue, five out of six

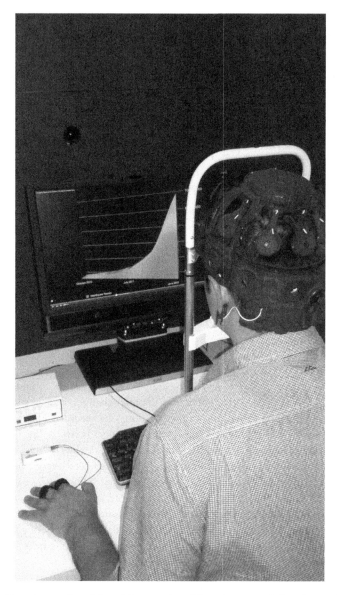

Figure 18.6a Experimental multimodal setup involving the use of dry electrode EEG device DSI-24, skin conductance device Shimmer3 GSR+, and Tobii TX300 eye-tracking system

papers applied EEG technology, while in JAIS, two out of three special issue papers adopted this method. Below we briefly outline a number of studies from these special issues most relevant for the judgment and decision-making research in accounting.

In a neuro-information systems research study that involved the use of EEG in a controlled laboratory setting, Vance, Anderson, Kirwan and Eargle (2014) showed that the differences in neural responses to positive and negative feedback strongly predict users' information security behaviour, and specifically, that the EEG measures are a robust predictor of information security

Figure 18.6b Experimental multimodal setup involving the use of dry electrode EEG device DSI-24 and Tobii T120 eye-tracking system (sampling rate: 120 Hz)

behaviour. The predictive validity of the EEG measures was compared to that of self-reported measures of information security risk perceptions. The results indicated that while EEG measures significantly predicted behaviour in both salient and non-salient conditions, self-reported measures were ineffective in predicting security behaviours under a condition in which information security was not salient.

Gregor, Lin, Gedeon, Riaz and Zhu (2014) studied the influence of emotions on e-loyalty. Among other findings, this study shows that the suggested EEG measure has some predictive power for an outcome such as e-loyalty. In a study of neurophysiological correlates of cognitive absorption in the context of IS training, Léger et al. (2014a) found that subjects with high EEG Alpha and low EEG Beta frequency bands reported being more cognitively absorbed than subjects who did not display these characteristics. In a multimodal experimental study that synchronously captured the EEG and eye-tracking data, Léger et al. (2014c) demonstrated the distinctive differences between neurophysiological responses associated with the following cognitive processes: the attentional reaction to email pop-up notification, the cognitive processing of the email pop-up notification, and the motor planning activity involved in opening or not the email.

Design considerations

One important design consideration is the level of precision necessary for the research questions being investigated. While EEG has its origins in medical research, from the 1960s onwards alternative nonclinical uses of EEG recording and analyses were reported including the study of EEG correlates and associated psychological effects of transcendental meditation (Wallace 1970). For example, EEG technology was used to administer experimental designs based on the principles of (bio-) and neuro-feedback where neurophysiological signals, such EEG frequency and band power, were used to continuously control the parameters of the virtual environment (e.g., game character speed and mobility) in real time (Pope and Palsson 2001). Such nonclinical approaches to EEG data recording and analysis required less precision than some clinical trials. In clinical research, high-density 128-, 256-, or even 512 EEG channel sensor arrays (e.g., Alotaiby, El-Samie, Alshebeili and Ahmad 2015; Schwabedal and Kantz 2016) are conventionally used to measure patients' EEG activity. Such high-density EEG devices are commonly used for localizing the source of electrical activity of the brain.

Until the early 1990s EEG data could not be used to construct sufficiently reliable visualizations for three-dimensional (3D) topography of the electric neuronal activity. However, this problem was addressed with the introduction of source localization, a novel technique for EEG. Source localization methods (e.g., Pascual-Marqui et al. 1994; Pascual-Marqui et al. 2002; Jatoi, Kamel, Malik, Faye and Begum 2014), while non-trivial, can be used for assessing functional dynamic connectivity in the brain – a property not available with more traditional methods of EEG data analysis. On the other hand, EEG devices designed specifically for brain-computer interface games (Ahn, Lee, Choi and Jun 2014) may be very basic and contain just a single electrode. A small number of electrodes may be appropriate for special circumstances where there is no need to record very localized activity or to analyze accurately the distribution of more diffuse activity within the cerebral cortex.

Another design consideration is the type of material the EEG electrodes are made of. EEG devices can be broadly categorized into two groups: gel-based devices (conventional technology using conductive electrode gel for optimal impedance and data quality) or more innovative dry electrode devices which do not require gel, but for this reason run a higher risk of suboptimal quality of the measured signals. One of the advantages of the dry electrode technology for accounting experiments is that it is less demanding from the point of view of calibration time and it brings less discomfort to the participants since no electrode gel needs to be applied to their scalps. Research in the area of brain-computer interaction (Guger, Krausz, Allison and Edlinger 2012) compared the performance of gel-based and dry electrode EEG systems in the context of a copy-spelling task using a specific component of the EEG waveform elicited in the process of decision-making (namely, the so called P300, or P3, wave). The findings showed that dry electrode EEG devices yielded classification accuracies that were similar to those obtained with gel EEG devices.

Visualization and analysis of EEG data

Given the high sampling rate of the EEG devices and the high susceptibility of collected EEG data to the undesirable influences of the physiological and non-physiological factors, the first step in analyzing the raw EEG data is the removal of these various artefacts which are not subject to experimental treatment. The most commonly reported artefacts are the ones associated with eye blinks and eye movements, muscle artefacts and the heartbeat (e.g., Müller-Putz et al. 2015).

A number of statistical approaches have been suggested to help filter out the undesirable influence of artefacts. A brief overview of the most widely used analytical techniques, including Fast Fourier Transform and Event Related Potential (ERP) is provided in Müller-Putz et al. (2015) and Riedl and Léger (2016). A structured overview of the method and its various applications is found in the handbook by Luck and Kappenman (2011). In terms of interpretation of EEG results, particularly relevant is Müller-Putz et al.'s overview of a range of theoretical constructs and associated EEG measures. For example, the constructs that can be captured by ongoing EEG measurement include: mental load, affective processes, cognitive processes, positive affect, negative affect, memory performance, cognitive workload, fatigue and task difficulty. On the other hand, constructs captured using ERPs (waveform electrical brain responses to an external stimulae) include: selective attention, the state of arousal, discriminative processing, cognitive matching, detection of the target stimuli, detection of a deviation of a concrete stimulus from an expectation, attention, motivation, memory, reward value, semantic processes, unconscious mental categorization and perception of erroneous events.

Functional Magnetic Resonance Imaging (fMRI)

Among all brain imaging methods functional magnetic resonance imaging (fMRI), which is a non-invasive way to assess brain function (Ogawa, Lee, Kay and Tank 1990), has been most widely used in neuroaccounting research. The method was originated by Ogawa et al. (1990) who discovered the positive relationship between neural activity and oxygenated blood level in response to heightened demand by neurons. Oxygenated blood has different magnetic properties from deoxygenated blood. Thus, by measuring changes in blood oxygenation, or the Blood Oxygenation Level Dependent (BOLD) signal, fMRI measures, in an indirect manner, the activity of specific brain regions.

Only three neuroaccounting studies have been published to date, specifically Barton et al. (2014), Farrell et al. (2014) and Hartmann, Godec, Repovs, Slana and Slapnicar (2015) using fMRI to test theories of managerial judgment and decision-making.[4] Barton et al. (2014) used fMRI when testing individual investors' reaction to corporate earnings news after the investors took a long or a short position in the stock of 60 publicly traded companies. Consistent with prospect theory, they found the asymmetric response (activation) in the ventral striatum region of the brain to positive and negative earnings surprises. Farrell et al. (2014) used fMRI to test the effect of performance-based incentives in mitigating the adverse influence of emotions in managerial decision-making. The authors found the support for their theory and specifically that performance-based incentives inducing System 2 processing is associated with more rational decision-making.

Finally, Hartmann et al. (2015) measured and analyzed participants' brain activity using fMRI while they performed a series of computer-based tasks. The authors set out to measure the participants' ability to assess information under different time pressures and types of distractions. In particular, the researchers distinguished between cases where managers received a monetary reward for speed and accuracy and scenarios where managers experienced social pressure to perform well. Their findings showed that while monetary incentives and social pressure result in people working harder, their performance seemed not to improve for work that required vigilance and attention. Based on the obtained fMRI results one of the conclusions put forward in their study was that individuals are bounded by their individual biological limits to improve at certain types of work, which implied the need to search for more flexible approaches to measure and reword work performance.

It is important to note that the interpretation of data acquired through neurophysiological instruments, and in particular, via brain imaging devices, is a challenge not only to novice researchers but also to professionals in neuroimaging. Considering the highly complex technical and analytical nature of the apparatus associated with fMRI studies and the increased interest in fMRI technology within a number of social science disciplines, Dimoka (2012) published a set of guidelines on how to conduct a fMRI study in social science research. In her study, each of the four basic phases for conducting an fMRI study – (a) formulating research questions; (b) designing the fMRI protocol; (c) analyzing fMRI data; (d) interpreting and reporting fMRI results – are decomposed into a number of steps which are very relevant in supporting procedural integrity when designing an fMRI study. The description of each of the aforementioned phases are accompanied by an extensive set of guidelines which are relevant to accounting researchers considering the use of fMRI in their research.

Conclusions and future directions

The new technologies presented in this chapter offer challenges to accounting researchers who have traditionally little or no formal training in these areas. Some technologies are likely to be more challenging than others. For example, the technologies of eye tracking and skin galvanic response are more easily learned than those measuring the activity of the central nervous system (such as EEG and fMRI). Additional training is also required for learning the software and data analysis techniques associated with these new technologies. Some techniques, such as observation of pupil dilation, require analysis at the raw data level. Other analysis involves the use of specialized software.

Meeting the challenges posed by the new technologies can take many different forms. Prior research in accounting and related disciplines provide more limited general guidance, while reference books and manufacturer documentation provide more detailed technology specific guidance. This can often be sufficient to provide entry into the field. For more advanced technologies collaboration with researchers in the related area might be the most fruitful avenue. A good example in the fMRI space is Farrell et al. (2014) which included a medical researcher. Whilst such collaborations bring with them their own challenges, it also provides exciting opportunities to broaden our field of accounting research.

At the very minimum accounting researchers need to avoid underestimating the steepness of the learning curve associated with many of the technologies covered in this chapter. And the potential value of undertaking this learning to accounting research is reflected in the increasing number of researchers using neurophysiological tools (at this stage, predominantly fMRI and eye tracking) for testing theories in accounting. Contributing to this trend is the increased diversity of neurophysiological tools potentially available to neuroaccounting researchers as well as the decrease in costs associated with the use of them. Functional magnetic resonance imaging is one of the most expensive tools discussed in this chapter with other technologies being considerably cheaper.

For accounting research the availability of a multimodal '360-degree' measurement of the judgment and decision process facilitated by these technologies has the potential to provide substantial advantages over current approaches based on input and output measures in combination with self-reported measures.

Notes

1 For instance, technologies unlikely to be adopted by accounting research in the near future include such invasive neurophysiological technologies as single-neuron measurement (Camerer et al. 2005) and Transcranial Direct-Current Stimulation (Horvath, Forte and Carter 2015a, b).
2 Other technologies which may have applicability to accounting research but are beyond the scope of this chapter include the Electrocardiogram (EKG), Facial Muscular Movement, Electromyogram (EMG), Positron Emission Tomography (PET), Functional Near-Infrared Spectroscopy (FNIRS) and Transcranial Magnetic Stimulation (TMS). These technologies are outlined in Riedl and Léger (2016).
3 The tools discussed in this chapter are not meant to be comprehensive. More comprehensive reviews of a variety neurophysiological tools in the context of social science research more generally can be found in Riedl and Léger (2016) and Dimoka et al. (2010).
4 The challenges of using such sophisticated technologies as fMRI for the accounting researchers are well described in Birnberg and Ganguly (2012).

References

Ahn, M., Lee, M., Choi, J. and Jun, S.C., 2014, 'A review of brain-computer interface games and an opinion survey from researchers, developers and users', *Sensors* 14(8), 14601–14633.

Alotaiby, T., El-Samie, F.E.A., Alshebeili, S.A. and Ahmad, I., 2015, 'A review of channel selection algorithms for EEG signal processing', *EURASIP Journal on Advances in Signal Processing* 2015(1), 1–21.

Andreassi, J.L. and Filipovic, S.R., 2006, *Psychophysiology: Human Behavior and Physiological Response*, Elsevier, Philadelphia.

Ashton, R.H. and Ashton, A.H., 1995, *Judgment and Decision-Making Research in Accounting and Auditing*, Cambridge University Press, Cambridge.

Barton, J., Berns, G.S. and Brooks, A.M., 2014, 'The neuroscience behind the stock market's reaction to corporate earnings news', *The Accounting Review* 89(6), 1945–1977.

Beauchaine, T., 2001, 'Vagal tone, development, and Gray's motivational theory: Toward an integrated model of autonomic nervous system functioning in psychopathology', *Development and Psychopathology* 13(2), 183–214.

Bechara, A. and Damasio, A.R., 2005, 'The somatic marker hypothesis: A neural theory of economic decision', *Games and Economic Behavior* 52(2), 336–372.

Berger, H., 1929, 'Über das elektrenkephalogramm des menschen', *European Archives of Psychiatry and Clinical Neuroscience* 87(1), 527–570.

Bhattacharjee, S. and Moreno, K., 2002, 'The impact of affective information on the professional judgments of more experienced and less experienced auditors', *Journal of Behavioral Decision Making* 15(4), 361–377.

Birnberg, J.G. and Ganguly, A.R., 2012, 'Is neuroaccounting waiting in the wings? An essay', *Accounting, Organizations and Society* 37(1), 1–13.

Birnberg, J.G. and Shields, M.D., 1984, 'The role of attention and memory in accounting decisions', *Accounting, Organizations and Society* 9(3–4), 365–382.

Bojko, A., 2009, 'Informative or misleading? Heatmaps deconstructed', in J.A. Jacko (ed.), *Human-Computer Interaction, Part I, HCII*, 30–39, Springer-Verlag, Berlin.

Bonner, S.E., 2008, *Judgment and Decision Making in Accounting*, Prentice Hall, Upper Saddle River, NJ.

Bossaerts, P. and Murawski, C., 2015, 'From behavioural economics to neuroeconomics to decision neuroscience: The ascent of biology in research on human decision making', *Current Opinion in Behavioral Sciences* 5, 37–42.

Bruguier, A.J., Quartz, S.R. and Bossaerts, P., 2010, 'Exploring the nature of "trader intuition"', *The Journal of Finance* 65(5), 1703–1723.

Camerer, C., Loewenstein, G. and Prelec, D., 2005, 'Neuroeconomics: How neuroscience can inform economics', *Journal of Economic Literature* 43, 9–64.

Chapin, T.J. and Russell-Chapin, L.A., 2013, *Neurotherapy and Neurofeedback: Brain-Based Treatment for Psychological and Behavioral Problems*, Routledge, London.

Chen, Y., Jermias, J. and Panggabean, T., 2016, 'The role of visual attention in the managerial judgment of balanced-scorecard performance evaluation: Insights from using an eye-tracking device', *Journal of Accounting Research* 54(1), 113–145.

Chow, C.W., 1983, 'The effect of job standard tightness and compensation scheme on performance: An exploration of linkages', *The Accounting Review* 58(4), 667–685.

DallaVia, N., van Rinsum, M. and Perego, P., 2016, 'The influence of accountability and balanced scorecard framing on investment decisions', paper presented at the American Accounting Association, Management Accounting Section Meeting, Dallas, USA, January 7–9.

Dickhaut, J., Basu, S., McCabe, K. and Waymire, G., 2010, 'Neuroaccounting: Consilience between the biologically evolved brain and culturally evolved accounting principles', *Accounting Horizons* 24(2), 221–255.

Dimoka, A., 2012, 'How To Conduct A Functional Magnetic Resonance (FMRI) Study In Social Science Research', *MIS Quarterly* 36(3), 811–840.

Dimoka, A., Banker, R.D., Benbasat, I., Davis, F.D., Dennis, A.R., Gefen, D., Gupta, A., Ischebeck, A., Kenning, P., Pavlou, P.A. and Müller-Putz, G., 2010, 'On the use of neurophysiological tools in IS research: Developing a research agenda for NeuroIS', *MIS Quarterly* 36(3), 679–702.

Dokumentov, A. (2015). 'Measuring arousal: Demographic differences in emotional response to popular videos', *Working paper*, Monash Business Behavioural Laboratory, Monash University.

Dodge, R., 1900, 'Visual perception during eye movements', *Psychological Review* 7, 454–465.

Farrell, A.M., Goh, J.O. and White, B.J., 2014, 'The effect of performance-based incentive contracts on System 1 and System 2 processing in affective decision contexts: fMRI and behavioral evidence', *The Accounting Review* 89(6), 1979–2010.

Fehrenbacher, D.D., Schulz, A.K. and Rotaru, K., 2015, 'The moderating role of information processing systems on the spill-over effect in subjective performance evaluation', *SSRN* 2675956.

Fowles, D.C., 1987, 'Application of a behavioral theory of motivation to the concepts of anxiety and impulsivity', *Journal of Research in Personality* 21(4), 417–435.

Frydman, C., Barberis, N., Camerer, C., Bossaerts, P. and Rangel, A., 2014, 'Using neural data to test a theory of investor behavior: An application to realization utility', *The Journal of Finance* 69(2), 907–946.

Fugate, D.L., 2007, 'Neuromarketing: A layman's look at neuroscience and its potential application to marketing practice', *Journal of Consumer Marketing* 24(7), 385–394.

Gray, J.A., 1987, *The Psychology of Fear and Stress* (Vol. 5), CUP Archive.

Gregor, S., Lin, A.C., Gedeon, T., Riaz, A. and Zhu, D., 2014, 'Neuroscience and a nomological network for the understanding and assessment of emotions in information systems research', *Journal of Management Information Systems* 30(4), 13–48.

Grigg, L. and Griffin, A.L., 2014, 'A role for eye-tracking research in accounting and financial reporting?', in *Current Trends in Eye Tracking Research*, 225–230, Springer International Publishing, Cham, Switzerland.

Guger, C., Krausz, G., Allison, B.Z. and Edlinger, G., 2012, 'Comparison of dry and gel based electrodes for p300 brain-computer interfaces', *Frontiers in Neuroscience* 6(60), 1–7.

Hartmann, F., Godec, M., Repovs, G., Slana, A. and Slapnicar, S., 2015, 'Incentives, accountability and myopic decision making: A neuroscientific investigation', Chartered Institute of Management Accountants (CIMA) report, www.cimaglobal.com/Documents/Thought_leadership_docs/09-07-2015-Incentives-Accountability-and-Myopic-Decision-Making.pdf.

Hecht, G., Rotaru, K., Schulz, A., Towry, K. and Webb, A. 2016, 'Decoding effort', *Working paper*.

Hess, E.H. and Polt, J.M., 1964, 'Pupil size in relation to mental activity during simple problem-solving', *Science* 143, 1190–1192.

Holmqvist, K., Nyström, M., Andersson, R., Dewhurst, R., Halszka, J. and van de Weijer, J., 2011, *Eye Tracking: A Comprehensive Guide to Methods and Measures*, Oxford University Press, Oxford.

Horstmann, N., Ahlgrimm, A. and Glöckner, A., 2009. 'How Distinct are Intuition and Deliberation? An Eye-Tracking Analysis of Instruction-Induced Decision Modes', *Max Planck Institute for Research on Collective Goods* (10).

Horvath, J.C., Forte, J.D. and Carter, O., 2015a, 'Quantitative review finds no evidence of cognitive effects in healthy populations from single-session transcranial direct current stimulation (tDCS)', *Brain Stimulation* 8(3), 535–550.

Horvath, J.C., Forte, J.D. and Carter, O., 2015b, 'Evidence that transcranial direct current stimulation (tDCS) generates little-to-no reliable neurophysiologic effect beyond MEP amplitude modulation in healthy human subjects: A systematic review', *Neuropsychologia* 66, 213–236.

Jatoi, M.A., Kamel, N., Malik, A.S., Faye, I. and Begum, T., 2014, 'A survey of methods used for source localization using EEG signals', *Biomedical Signal Processing and Control* 11, 42–52.

Kahneman, D., 1973, *Attention and Effort*, Prentice Hall, Englewood Cliffs, NJ.

Kahneman, D., 2011, *Thinking, Fast and Slow*, Palgrave Macmillan, New York.

Kennedy, J., 1993, 'Debiasing audit judgment with accountability: A framework and experimental results', *Journal of Accounting Research* 31(2), 231–245.

Kramer, S. and Maas, V.S. 2016, 'Information search and information processing in subjective performance evaluation: Evidence from an eye tracking experiment', *SSRN* 2457941.

Lachmann, M., Stefani, U. and Wöhrmann, A., 2015, 'Fair value accounting for liabilities: Presentation format of credit risk changes and individual information processing', *Accounting, Organizations and Society* 41, 21–38.

Lee, N., Broderick, A.J. and Chamberlain, L., 2007, 'What is 'neuromarketing'? A discussion and agenda for future research', *International Journal of Psychophysiology* 63(2), 199–204.

Léger, P.-M., Davis, F.D., Cronan, T.P. and Perret, J., 2014a, 'Neurophysiological correlates of cognitive absorption in an enactive training context', *Computers in Human Behavior* 34, 273–283.

Léger, P.-M., Riedl, R. and vom Brocke, J., 2014b, 'Emotions and ERP information sourcing: The moderating role of expertise', *Industrial Management & Data Systems* 114, 456–471.

Léger, P.-M., Sénecal, S., Courtemanche, F., de Guinea, A.O., Titah, R., Fredette, M. and Labonte-LeMoyne, É., 2014c, 'Precision is in the eye of the beholder: Application of eye fixation-related potentials to information systems research', *Journal of the Association for Information Systems* 15(10), 651–678.

Legrenzi, P. and Umiltà, C., 2011, *Neuromania: On the Limits of Brain Science*, Oxford University Press, Oxford.

Libby, R., Bloomfield, R. and Nelson, M.W., 2002, 'Experimental research in financial accounting', *Accounting, Organizations and Society* 27(8), 775–810.

Lipe, M.G. and Salterio, S.E., 2000, 'The balanced scorecard: Judgmental effects of common and unique performance measures', *The Accounting Review* 75(3), 283–298.

Liversedge, S., Gilchrist, I. and Everling, S. (eds.), 2011, *The Oxford Handbook of Eye Movements*, Oxford University Press, Oxford.

Loewenstein, G., Rick, S. and Cohen, J.D., 2008, 'Neuroeconomics', *Annual Review of Psychology* 59, 647–672.

Lowenstein, O. and Loewenfeld, I.E., 1962, 'The pupil', in H. Davsoned (ed.), *The Eye: Muscular Mechanisms* (Vol. 3), 231–267, Academic Press, New York.

Luck, S.J. and Kappenman, E.S. (eds.), 2011, *The Oxford Handbook of Event-Related Potential Components*, Oxford University Press, Oxford, UK.

Luft, J. and Shields, M.D., 2009, *Psychology Models of Management Accounting*, Now Publishers, Hanover, NH.

Moreno, K., Kida, T. and Smith, J.F., 2002, 'The impact of affective reactions on risky decision making in accounting contexts', *Journal of Accounting Research* 40(5), 1331–1349.

Müller-Putz, G.R., Riedl, R. and Wriessnegger, S.C., 2015, 'Electroencephalography (EEG) as a research tool in the information systems discipline: Foundations, measurement, and applications', *Communications of the Association for Information Systems* 37(1), 911–948.

Naqvi, N.H. and Bechara, A., 2006, 'Skin conductance: A psychophysiological approach to the study of decision making', in T. Russell and M.S. Gazzaniga (eds.), *Methods in Mind*, 103–122, MIT Press, Cambridge/London.

Ogawa, S., Lee, T.M., Kay, A.R. and Tank, D.W., 1990, 'Brain magnetic resonance imaging with contrast dependent on blood oxygenation', *Proceedings of the National Academy of Sciences* 87(24), 9868–9872.

Olsen, A., 2012, *Tobii I-VT Fixation Filter – Algorithm Description*, tobii.com.

Olsen, A. and Matos, R., 2012, 'Identifying parameter values for an I-VT fixation filter suitable for handling data sampled with various sampling frequencies', Proceedings of the symposium on eye tracking research & applications – ETRA Santa Barbara, CA.

Pascual-Marqui, R.D., Esslen, M., Kochi, K. and Lehmann, D., 2002, 'Functional mapping of electric neuronal activity with zero localization error: Standardized low resolution brain electromagnetic tomography (sLORETA)', *Methods Findings in Experimental and Clinical Pharmacology D* 24, 5–12.

Pascual-Marqui, R.D., Michel, C.M. and Lehmann, D., 1994, 'Low resolution electromagnetic tomography: A new method for localizing electrical activity in the brain', *International Journal of Psychophysiology* 18(1), 49–65.

Peterson, K., Schmardebeck, R. and Wilks, T.J., 2015, 'The earnings quality and information processing effects of accounting consistency', *The Accounting Review* 90(6), 2483–2514.

Pope, A.T. and Palsson, O.S., 2001, 'Helping video games rewire our minds', Technical report, NASA Langley Research Center, Hampton, VA.

Radach, R., Huestegge, L. and Reilly, R., 2008, 'The role of global top-down factors in local eye-movement control in reading', *Psychological Research* 72(6), 675–688.

Rayner, K., 1998, 'Eye movements in reading and information processing: 20 years of research', *Psychological Bulletin* 124(3), 372–422.

Riedl, R., Davis, F.D. and Hevner, A.R., 2014, 'Towards a NeuroIS research methodology: Intensifying the discussion on methods, tools, and measurement', *Journal for the Association for Information Systems* 15(10), 1–35.

Riedl, R. and Léger, P.-M., 2016, 'Tools in neuroIS research: An overview', in R. Riedl and P.-M. Léger (eds.), *Fundamentals of NeuroIS*, 47–72, Springer, Berlin Heidelberg.

Schwabedal, J.T. and Kantz, H., 2016, 'Optimal extraction of collective oscillations from unreliable measurements', *Physical Review Letters* 116(10), 104101.

Shields, M.D., 1980, 'Some effects of information load on search patterns used to analyze performance reports', *Accounting, Organizations and Society* 5(4), 429–442.

Shields, M.D., 1983, 'Effects of information supply and demand on judgment accuracy: Evidence from corporate managers', *Accounting Review* 58(2), 284–303.

Shiv, B., Loewenstein, G., Bechara, A., Damasio, H. and Damasio, A.R., 2005, 'Investment behavior and the negative side of emotion', *Psychological Science* 16(6), 435–439.

Sirois, S. and Brisson, J., 2014, 'Pupillometry', *Wiley Interdisciplinary Reviews: Cognitive Science* 5(6), 679–692.

Smith, K., Dickhaut, J., McCabe, K. and Pardo, J.V., 2002, 'Neuronal substrates for choice under ambiguity, risk, gains, and losses', *Management Science* 48(6), 711–718.

Sullivan, K. and Kida, T., 1995, 'The effect of multiple reference points and prior gains and losses on managers' risky decision making', *Organizational Behavior and Human Decision Processes* 64(1), 76–83.

Tatler, B.W., Kirtley, C., Macdonald, R.G., Mitchell, K.M. and Savage, S.W., 2014, 'The active eye: Perspectives on eye movement research', in M. Horsley, N. Toon, B. Knight and R. Reilly (eds.), *Current Trends in Eye Tracking Research*, 3–16, Springer International Publishing, Cham, Switzerland.

Van Gompel, R., Fischer, M., Murray, W. and Hill, R., 2007, *Eye Movement Research: Insights Into Mind and Brain*, Elsevier Science, The Netherlands.

Vance, A., Anderson, B.B., Kirwan, C.B. and Eargle, D., 2014, 'Using measures of risk perception to predict information security behavior: Insights from electroencephalography (EEG)', *Journal of the Association for Information Systems* 15(10), 679–722.

Vasile, D. and Sebastian, T.C., 2007, 'Neurofinance – getting an insight into the trader's mind', *Neuroscience* 27(31), 8159–8160.

Velichkovsky, B.M., 1999, 'From levels of processing to stratification of cognition: Converging evidence from three domains of research', in B.H. Challis and B.M. Velichkovsky (eds.), *Stratification in Cognition and Consciousness*, 203–235, John Benjamins Publishing Company, Amsterdam, The Netherlands.

Wallace, R.K., 1970, 'Physiological effects of transcendental meditation', *Science* 167(3926), 1751–1754.

Waymire, G.B., 2014, 'Neuroscience and ultimate causation in accounting research', *The Accounting Review* 89(6), 2011–2019.

Wedel, M. and Pieters, R., 2008, *Eye Tracking for Visual Marketing*, Now Publishers Inc., Tilburg, The Netherlands.

Wyatt, H.J., 1995, 'The form of the human pupil', *Vision Research* 35(14), 2021–2036.

Section 5

Study implementation (Link 4b)

19

The ethics of Behavioural Accounting Research

Mary Marshall and Robin R. Radtke

Introduction

Behavioural Accounting Research is an area replete with ethical considerations. Any research study including interaction between researchers and study participants requires ethical awareness of potential issues of concern. This includes experiments, surveys and field studies such as interviews, observation and case analysis. While it could be argued the potential ethical concerns may be the greatest in experimental manipulations, questions asked via surveys or interviews can also raise ethical issues. All types of Behavioural Accounting Research require careful planning, preparation and execution to ensure ethical research practices are being followed.

Also of concern is the publication process itself. Authors, reviewers and editors all play a crucial role in maintaining research integrity. While responsibility for research study execution and analysis lies with authors, reviewers and editors also carry primary responsibilities to be fair and free from bias. Many opportunities for unethical behaviour on the part of all three parties exist throughout the publication process. Only when all parties involved make strides to ensure they are upholding their ethical responsibilities will the entirety of the publication process operate in an ethical manner.

The purpose of this chapter is to examine the importance and history of ethics review, discuss ethical issues involved in the publication process and delve into a set of specific issues associated with research design ethics. Taken in combination, these topics provide the reader with a broad picture of the many angles of ethical consideration involved in publishing Behavioural Accounting Research.

The remainder of this chapter is organized as follows. The next section introduces the need for ethics review, after first delineating several examples of poor research ethics. "A brief history of ethics review guidelines" catalogues the multiple sources for ethics review guidelines. "The ethics of the publication process" section investigates the many potential ethical issues that may arise in the publication process for the different parties involved: authors, reviewers and editors. In the next section, selected topics regarding research design ethics are investigated with the goal of informing the reader of many considerations to keep in mind when embarking on a Behavioural Accounting Research study. The final section includes concluding thoughts regarding the importance of a focus on ethical research practices.

Why do we need ethics review?

There are many types of behavioural accounting studies that include some sort of interaction with human subjects. One such type is experimental accounting research, which by design manipulates the experiences of human participants. Often, experimenters are testing for psychological processes, cognitive mechanisms and the use of heuristic biases by creating environments to activate specific processes, mechanisms or biases. This process can present ethical concerns, especially if a manipulation or treatment has the potential to cause harm to participants. Although experimental ethics originated in the medical sciences, experimenters in the social sciences also face ethical concerns associated with experimental design. Other types of Behavioural Accounting Research, including surveys and field studies based on interviews, observation and case analysis, while not including manipulations or treatments, nevertheless, still present ethical concerns based on such considerations as question type and phrasing. By focusing on research ethics as part of the design, data collection, write-up and review process, behavioural accounting researchers can ensure that they maintain the integrity of their research, which increases the usefulness and informativeness of study findings.

Classic experiments that generated the need for research ethics review

Ethics review has not always been a focus of research studies involving human subjects and history provides several examples of harmful research tactics that produced serious negative effects.[1] This section discusses several examples of poor research ethics. For example, in the notorious Stanford Prison Experiment, college students were recruited by Stanford University researchers to participate in a research study and earn $15 per day (Zimbardo 1971). Several weeks after answering a newspaper advertisement seeking volunteers to study the psychological effects of prison life, the 'suspects' were arrested at their homes and taken to the Palo Alto Police Department. The 'prisoners' were then transported to the Stanford County Jail where they were processed and issued a uniform. The experiment took place in the basement of Stanford University's Psychology Department building, where the other half of the recruited students were assigned to be prison 'guards' within the newly fashioned prison.

While participating in the experiment, students quickly adapted to their assigned roles. Prisoners focused on organizing a social structure, including developing grievance procedures and selecting leaders. Guards focused on imposing their authority, which led many to become increasingly controlling and abusive. Although the experiment produced interesting observations regarding prisoner behaviour, the experimental design introduced several ethical concerns. Students voluntarily participated in the study, but the 'suspects' were publicly arrested by officers within their community. Such a public embarrassment could have influenced participants' future reputations within the community. In addition, many of the students adapted to their roles very quickly, and thoroughly, which may have produced potential psychological damage beyond the experiment. In fact, prisoner #8612 was begrudgingly released 'after suffering from acute emotional disturbance, disorganized thinking, uncontrollable crying, screaming and rage' (Zimbardo 1971: 8).

Another example, the Milgram experiment, tested whether people will violate their personal conscience because an authority figure instructed them to do so (Milgram 1963). Specifically, participants were asked to fill the role of 'teacher' and were told to use electric shocks to punish their 'learner' for incorrect responses. Many participants blindly followed the instructions and delivered shocks to a learner that they believed were increasing in severity. The study demonstrated that people will follow orders from an authority figure even if doing so violated their personal conscience. Although this is an interesting research question, several components of the experiment included ethical questions. Participants were volunteers; however, they were deceived by the experimenter because they were unaware that the 'learner' was a confederate who was not actually being shocked. This deception was especially heinous because the experimenters reinforced the perception that the shocks were real by giving each participant a low shock at the beginning of the experiment. As a result, participants experienced serious psychological trauma that was visible both during and after the experiment.

Although experimental accounting studies generally focus on psychology-based research questions, many experimental ethics concerns arose from medical experiments. Studies of medical disease and treatments are very informative, but they can inflict physical harm both through exposure to disease and withholding of treatment. For example, medical experiments in Nazi Germany exposed prisoners to exhaustive testing and evaluation, including exposure to disease, varying experimental treatments and examination of differences between Nordic and other populations (Greenberg and Folger 1988). Specifically, German physicians conducted experiments using low-pressure chambers, freezing temperatures and varying levels of water potability to better understand whether soldiers could survive in extreme conditions. In addition, some camps focused on pharmaceuticals, including infectious disease vaccination, mustard gas antidotes and bone-grafting experiments. In order to test vaccinations and treatments, physicians first exposed the prisoners to harmful diseases, toxic chemicals or broken bones. As a result, many prisoners were subjected to treatment that would be considered torture by modern standards. Further, many of these experiments used race as a control group and were intended to advance Nazi Germany's theories of racial supremacy.

Additionally, the Tuskegee experiment presented serious ethical concerns when it enrolled nearly 600 African-American males in rural Alabama to study the effects of syphilis (Jones 1981). Although participants were told they were receiving free health care, those with the disease were never treated, even after penicillin was approved during the study. Withholding treatment not only affected the participants, but it also influenced the quality of life of spouses and children, both present and future. Although researchers gained valuable insight into the progression of the disease, the decision to withhold treatment from participants led to discussion about the ethical treatment of subjects. This decision was especially heinous because participants were unaware that treatment was withheld, which may have prevented them from seeking medical treatment elsewhere and likely led the infected individuals to unknowingly spread the disease.

In contrast to other types of psychology-based research, experimental research in accounting generally presents fewer possibilities to inflict harm on participants. Nevertheless, common experimental issues from the past can inform research design in behavioural accounting studies. It is important to ensure that accounting studies follow the same set of ethical principles as other disciplines. In addition, ethical considerations can influence design choices. For example, avoiding deception is a good practice, both related to ethics and construct development. The next section examines research ethics guidelines as they have evolved over time.

A brief history of ethics review guidelines

As early as 1947, various governing bodies began producing guidelines for ethical research using human subjects. The Nuremberg Code, which was developed after the Nuremberg Trials at the close of World War II, outlined ten principles for experimentation primarily focused on avoiding pain and suffering of human subjects and the necessity of the experimentation (US Department of Health and Human Services 1949). Nearly 20 years later, the World Medical Association issued the Declaration of Helsinki (World Medical Association 1964). Focused on medical experimentation, the Declaration of Helsinki incorporated many rules similar to those in the Nuremberg Code but focused heavily on a physician's role as experimenter. Similarly, the 1979 Belmont Report outlined principles, and accompanying guidelines of application, for biomedical and behavioural research (US Department of Health, Education, and Welfare 1979). The Belmont Report summarized many of the principles from earlier guidelines, including respect for persons, beneficence and justice, and added more concrete applications, such as informed consent, assessment of risk and benefits and selection of subjects. These efforts to build guidelines for ethical experimental research created the foundation of the current rules used in the United States.

Additional standards for ethical research have also been developed more recently. In 1991, several agencies within the federal government codified the Federal Policy for the Protection of Human Subjects, which is known as the "Common Rule" (US Department of Health and Human Services 1991). The Common Rule codified principles from the Belmont Report into regulations for agencies across the federal government, with special attention added for protection of pregnant women, fetuses, prisoners and children. In 2005, the United Nations Educational, Scientific and Cultural Organization (UNESCO) introduced the Universal Declaration on Bioethics and Human Rights, which focused on applying principles of ethical research to the bioethics field (UNESCO 2005). The American Psychological Association's Ethical Principles and Code of Conduct (2010) also serves as a baseline for many potential ethical issues in Behavioural Accounting Research.

Current US regulations for ethical research using human subjects are based on the Belmont Report, the Common Rule and institutional review board (IRB) policies. Ethical guidance for researchers in the European Union broadly parallels that of the US (European Union 2013). Guidance resources across a wide array of worldwide countries are provided by the Office for Human Research Protections (US Department of Health and Human Services 2016). Additionally, agencies, educational institutions and non-profit organizations within the US all have their own IRBs that oversee the approval process for research using human subjects and attempt to identify potential issues prior to implementation.[2]

Wherever researchers are located around the globe, they are required to meet all relevant accepted ethical standards before carrying out research projects and publishing results. The current US process involves several safeguards in attempts to ensure ethical research practices. In addition, behavioural researchers complete regular training on human subjects research and reviewers are expected to identify potentially unethical design and/or implementation choices in the peer review process. By ensuring that all of the parties involved are aware of ethical research expectations, the current system strives to maintain the integrity and informativeness of research findings, while also ensuring humane treatment of human subjects.

The ethics of the publication process

The publication process involves multiple parties including the author, reviewers, journal editors and IRBs. While each of these parties has an ethical responsibility to uphold research integrity, each also has personal interests that may interfere with this responsibility. Since publishing in high-quality journals is paramount for many accounting faculty, the importance of the publication process functioning in an ethical manner is essential. Although Payne (2000) suggests that each researcher makes his/her own choices with respect to appropriate research behaviour, several other studies have examined specific types of activities with the goal of assessing their acceptability (e.g., Borkowski and Welsh 1998; Meyer and McMahon 2004; Bailey, Hermanson and Louwers 2008). Responsibilities and potential unethical behaviour of authors, reviewers and editors are now discussed.

Authors' responsibilities

Authors ultimately hold primary responsibility for the ethical research integrity of their work. This includes many components such as initial review of methodology, receiving IRB approval, ethical treatment of subjects, and truthful reporting of data and results. With an ever increasing 'publish or perish' mentality at many universities, it is easy to see the potential temptations authors face. Moizer (2009: 289–290) points out several of these possible transgressions:

- Identical manuscripts should not be sent simultaneously to two journals (Von Glinow and Novell 1982; Calabrese and Roberts 2004).
- Publishing two papers which have considerable overlap is acceptable to UK accounting academics provided there are different audiences (e.g., professional and academic), but not acceptable where the audiences are the same (Brinn, Jones and Pendlebury 1998).
- Deriving multiple publications from a single set of data should be allowed only (a) if it is not possible to write a single integrative article that is clear, digestible and meaningful and (b) the multiple articles have distinct purposes (Fine and Kurdek 1994).
- Colleagues should only be shown as authors if they have contributed to the research (Sherrell, Hair and Griffin 1989).
- Papers should not replicate other researchers' methodology without giving due credit (Brinn et al. 1998).

Reviewers' responsibilities

The role of peer review, in general, is to aid in improving a paper prior to journal submission. Moizer (2009) suggests that motivations of reviewers are problematic, as there is generally no direct benefit associated with providing a review, while the process itself can be time consuming. With respect to ethical responsibilities of reviewers, a primary concern is to be fair and free from bias (Borkowski and Welsh 1998). This is generally somewhat dependent on a blind review, although it has been noted that with small, well-connected research communities and the prevalence of pre-publication online outlets for accounting manuscripts, it is often easy for a reviewer to identify authors (Bailey et al. 2008). Other potentially unethical reviewer actions include: pursuing an idea from a rejected manuscript (Meyer and McMahon 2004), excessive time delays (Borkowski and Welsh 1998), selfish or cliquish acts (including "a reviewer rejects a paper to 'get even' with an apparent author who is believed to have previously caused one of the reviewer's papers to be rejected" [Bailey et al. 2008: 63]) and violating the spirit of the review process (including "a reviewer positively reviews a manuscript to encourage research in the reviewer's area" [Bailey et al. 2008: 64]).

Perceptions of university accounting faculty of the seriousness of these potentially unethical reviewer actions vary widely. Bailey at al. (2008: 63) report that "A reviewer intentionally drags out the review process so as to allow his or her own paper on the same topic a better chance of acceptance" was viewed the most negatively among their survey items, while "A reviewer reveals his or her identity to the author after the manuscript has been accepted or rejected" was viewed as the least problematic. Interestingly, at least two accounting journals give Outstanding Reviewer Awards: *The Journal of Accounting Education* and *Accounting Education: An International Journal*. The *Journal of Accounting Education* states: "Consideration for the award will include the depth and comprehensiveness of the reviews submitted, submission timeliness, and the role of the submitted reviews in the faculty-development process" (Stout 2015). While this sort of recognition may incrementally aid in procuring fair and unbiased reviews, Bailey et al.

(2008) report that different types of dysfunctional reviewer behaviours are somewhat frequently observed and are also considered to be both relatively prevalent and serious.

Editors' responsibilities

Borkowski and Welsh (1998) suggest authors want editors to be unbiased "gatekeepers" and the accounting research community would certainly hope editors are neutral and fair, and also work hard to prevent excessive delays in the review process. Selecting reviewers who are considered friendly or hostile to bias acceptance/rejection, as well as showing favouritism to friends are among the unethical practices editors engage in according to Sherrell et al. (1989). Laband and Piette (1994: 197) investigated "author's personal ties to the editor" within 28 top economics journals in 1984 and conclude that while most of the time high-quality/high-impact manuscripts are accepted and published, "It seems possible, if not probable, that part of the implicit compensation offered to journal editors is the opportunity to publish low-quality papers, relatively speaking, written by professional friends (including himself) and allies" (202). Other examples of unethical editor behaviour include "An editor succumbs to pressure from a prominent author to accept a paper despite unfavorable reviews" and "An incoming journal editor forces authors with papers far into the review process (third or fourth round) under the previous editor to start the review process over with new reviewers" (Bailey et al. 2008: 63). While most of the dysfunctional editor behaviours investigated by Bailey et al. (2008) are not perceived to occur frequently, "An editor allows a slow reviewer to hold up the review process for an unreasonable period of time" was observed by 67% of study participants.

Institutional review board responsibilities

While mentioned last in this section, the responsibility of an IRB for the ethical integrity of a research study chronologically occurs toward the beginning of the research process. As mentioned previously, IRBs oversee the approval process for behavioural research using human subjects and help to identify potential issues prior to implementation. IRBs also require compliance from institutional researchers, with noncompliance risking the threat of offenders being barred from engaging in future research activities.

Selected topics regarding research design ethics

Recognizing and avoiding deception

Deception is a critical design issue associated with many of the experiments discussed earlier in this chapter. For example, participants in the Tuskeegee experiment believed that they were receiving medical care, but the researchers were merely observing the progression of the disease. Similarly, participants in the Milgram experiments were told that they would be inflicting increasing levels of electric shock to their 'learners', but the electric shock machine was fake. In both the Tuskeegee and Milgram experiments, these deceptive tactics led to stronger experimental results. Subsequent scrutiny of these experimental methods, however, determined the costs exceeded the rewards, and hence, deception is not allowed by the principles implemented by the Belmont Report and Common Rule. In other disciplines, such as marketing and psychology, some extent of deception is acceptable if the researcher sufficiently debriefs participants upon completion of the experiment.

Deception in accounting research is widely condemned based on the American Psychological Association's Ethical Principles and Code of Conduct (2010), which includes the following:

1 Psychologists do not conduct a study involving deception unless they have determined that the use of deceptive techniques is justified by the study's significant prospective scientific, educational or applied value and that effective nondeceptive alternative procedures are not feasible.
2 Psychologists do not deceive prospective participants about research that is reasonably expected to cause physical pain or severe emotional distress.
3 Psychologists explain any deception that is an integral feature of the design and conduct of an experiment to participants as early as is feasible, preferably at the conclusion of their participation, but no later than at the conclusion of the data collection, and permit participants to withdraw their data.

Deception in accounting research was widely discussed following the publication of Lord's (1992) study involving deception of audit managers. Lord (1992) suggested that he "temporarily" deceived the "pressure" group subjects into believing that a senior partner in their audit firm would evaluate their performance on the experimental task. This study was widely debated in the accounting academic community and both Dopuch (1992) and Gibbins (1992) offered published discussions. Dopuch (1992) suggested that the potential pool of auditor subjects may shrink in response to the knowledge that deception was used in the Lord (1992) experiment. Gibbins (1992) analyzed the issue from both sides and suggested both benefits and costs. Benefits included: deception is part of the experimental strategy, deception is an ethical practice, deception reduces demand effects and deception works (Gibbins 1992: 116–118). Costs included: lies are lies, deception interferes with informed consent, deception fouls the research nest and deception is unprofessional and unnecessary (Gibbins 1992: 118–119).

Hooks and Schultz (1996a) explained how they came to the conclusion that deception should be used in their previously undertaken and subsequently published study of auditors' methods for discovering fraud (Schultz and Hooks 1998). They showed that theoretical hypotheses were supported by the actual behaviour displayed by students in an experimental setting employing deception. An additional opinion-based case scenario approach not employing deception did not support these results. They concluded that "For those who do not take a moral position condemning deception in research, satisfying the necessary conditions of a sufficiently important subject; lack of effective, feasible nondeceptive designs; care for the participants; and proper procedures should be paramount" (Hooks and Schultz 1996a: 44). Krogstad (1996) critiqued their argument and clearly disagreed and Hooks and Schultz (1996b) subsequently offered a rebuttal. Although seemingly widely condemned, the topic of deception appears to still be up for debate in the opinion of some accounting researchers. Therefore, if a researcher believes deception is necessary for a study, they should carefully vet such a decision with colleagues to avoid unnecessary use of such a disputed methodology. In studies where deception appears to be necessary, careful documentation of the costs and benefits is crucial for justifying the choice.

Acceptable priming and demand effects

Priming occurs when a desired response is alluded to in some manner earlier in the research study. The American Psychological Association's Ethical Principles and Code of Conduct (2010) is mum on priming and a search for accounting research evaluating acceptable priming yields no results. In psychological research, however, a vast body of research addresses different types and effectiveness of priming methods (e.g., Herring et al. 2013). There appears to be no judgment with respect to acceptability of the usage of priming in research; however, especially strong priming is often believed to lead to demand effects. This was first introduced into accounting research discussion by Libby (1979: 41), who was concerned that "knowledge of the manipulation allows the subject to uncover the experiment's hypothesis and to behave accordingly." Cook and Campbell (1979) later described demand effects as a threat to construct validity. Arguably, the presence of demand effects can threaten a study's results; however, other scholars disagree that demand effects produce a concern.

Demand effects occur when participants are able to: (a) correctly identify the research question, (b) correctly identify the researcher's desired behaviour and (c) act according to the knowledge of the research question and researcher's desired behaviour (Shimp, Hyatt and Snyder 1991; Schepanski, Tubbs and Grimlund 1992). Schepanski et al. (1992) develop a model to demonstrate that participants are rarely able to successfully complete all three steps, which reduces the risk of demand effects. Nevertheless, researchers can produce stronger results by avoiding the use of excessive priming and limiting manipulation strength when possible.

The decision to debrief

Debriefing occurs when research participants are informed about the goals of the research study and their contribution to the study. In its early uses, debriefing involved face-to-face interactions and often aided researchers in understanding whether certain procedures were effective (Toy, Wright and Olson 2001). The American Psychological Association's Ethical Principles and Code of Conduct (2010) states the following with respect to debriefing:

1   Psychologists provide a prompt opportunity for participants to obtain appropriate information about the nature, results, and conclusions of the research, and they take reasonable steps to correct any misconceptions that participants may have of which the psychologists are aware.
2   If scientific or humane values justify delaying or withholding this information, psychologists take reasonable measures to reduce the risk of harm.
3   When psychologists become aware that research procedures have harmed a participant, they take reasonable steps to minimize the harm.

In accounting research, debriefing can take the form of a debriefing questionnaire (e.g., Libby 1975; Ponemon 1992) or a debriefing discussion (e.g., Zimmer 1980). It seems as though debriefing, per se, does not occur frequently in accounting. In consumer and marketing research, debriefing is usually discussed along with the use of deception (e.g., Toy et al. 2001; Klein and Smith 2004).

Rewriting hypotheses post-results

In general, rewriting hypotheses after data collection and analysis is viewed quite negatively. 'Twisting' of hypotheses is sometimes seen as a major offense, and if encountered during the review process can serve as a reason for rejection in scientific publications (von Schacky 2014). In management research, O'Boyle, Banks and Gonzalez-Mulé (2014) examine what they call the 'Chrysalis Effect'. They explain several ways that hypotheses are either altered to support the data or vice versa. O'Boyle et al. (2014: 7) empirically test for the Chrysalis Effect by "tracking changes in hypotheses, data, and results as a manuscript moved from defended dissertation to journal publication". They conclude that there is evidence of a Chrysalis Effect in management and applied psychology and suggest many negative implications of this practice, including a tarnished credibility in terms of both research and practice. Additional discussion of the appropriateness, and potential for, rewriting hypotheses is included in Kerr (1998) in his article on 'HARKing' (Hypothesizing After the Results are Known).

Several methods for eliminating the practice of rewriting hypotheses after data collection include an honour code for authors, open access of the original submission, publication of replication studies and enforcement of data sharing policies. Additionally, von Schacky (2014) suggests a 'bank' of hypotheses be created wherein researchers 'deposit' their hypotheses before data collection and receive a 'receipt', which can then be produced upon submission of the completed manuscript.

Informed consent and voluntary participation

The Belmont Report requires that human subjects must voluntarily participate in research studies. Informed consent represents the process of obtaining agreement from research study subjects to take part in the study. According to the Belmont Report, the informed consent process includes the three elements of information, comprehension and voluntariness. Enough information about the study, including risks and anticipated benefits to the subjects, must be provided and be readily understood. Agreement to participate must be given voluntarily, with no undue influence. Varying rules exist with respect to the different types of studies that may be undertaken (more rigorous review for studies with greater potential risk), as well as different types of participants (children and other at risk populations require additional procedures to ensure comprehension by the subjects and a lack of pressure to participate). Most accounting studies fall into the categories of either exempt or expedited review of materials, as risks associated with accounting studies are generally very low or non-existent.

Privacy and confidentiality

Researchers are generally required to ensure that data collected will be either anonymous or that confidentiality will be maintained. Originally, these principles were implemented for medical research, which has strong potential to inflict bodily harm. However, the same principles are applied to behavioural research because a poorly implemented manipulation, for example, even though hypothetical, can influence participants' well-being beyond the experiment. From a practical perspective, participants are more likely to respond honestly if researchers have assured anonymity or confidentiality.

Data collection and management

Behavioural Accounting Research results hinge on the ethical collection and management of research data. Recent scandals in several disciplines have led to increased scrutiny of data collection practices. Steen (2011a, 2011b) found that retractions of academic papers in the scientific literature has increased significantly and that this increase is driven largely by data falsification or fabrication. Data collection should be well planned and anonymous if at all possible. If it is not possible to collect data anonymously, every effort should be made to protect research participants' privacy and confidentiality. After collection, data should be stored properly to ensure its security. Additionally, all named authors should be aware of the methods used to gather, store and analyze the research data.

Conclusion

Engaging in and publishing Behavioural Accounting Research is subject to many ethical speed-bumps along the way. This chapter has delineated the importance and history of ethics review, ethical issues involved in the publication process and a set of specific issues associated with research design ethics. Taken in combination, these topics provide the reader with a broad picture of the many angles of ethical consideration involved in publishing Behavioural Accounting Research. It is ultimately important for scholars to remain aware of potential ethical challenges as an author, reviewer and editor.

Although many intentional ethical issues are egregious and obvious to scholars, unintentional ethical lapses can also hinder the behavioural research process. Authors should carefully plan their research designs to avoid unnecessary ethical concerns, such as deception, overly strong priming, careless data collection or management or alteration of hypotheses. Researchers face increasingly strong incentives to produce publishable results as quickly as possible; however, these pressures should not lead to a decreased focus on ethical research practices. Both the researcher's reputation and the study's impact require strict adherence to an ethical process.

Notes

1 This section discusses several examples of classic experiments that included questionable ethical decisions. Another interesting resource is a recent TED talk by Philip Zimbardo. It can be found at: *www.ted. com/talks/philip_zimbardo_on_the_psychology_of_evil?language=en#t-963750*.
2 Researchers outside the US may be subject to review by similar organizations which could include independent ethics committees (IEC), ethical review boards (ERB) or research ethics boards (REB).

References

American Psychological Association, 2010, *Ethical Principles of Psychologists and Code of Conduct*, viewed 18 April 2016, from www.apa.org/ethics/code/.

Bailey, C., Hermanson, D. and Louwers, T., 2008, 'An examination of the peer review process in accounting journals', *Journal of Accounting Education* 26, 55–72.

Borkowski, S. and Welsh, M., 1998, 'Ethics and the accounting publishing process: Author, reviewer, and editor issues', *Journal of Business Ethics* 17, 1785–1803.

Brinn, T., Jones, M. and Pendlebury, M., 1998, 'UK academic accountants' perceptions of research and publication practices', *British Accounting Review* 30, 313–390.

Calabrese, R. and Roberts, B., 2004, 'Self-interest and scholarly publication: The dilemma of researchers, reviewers, and editors', *The International Journal of Educational Management* 18(6), 335–341.

Cook, T. and Campbell, D., 1979, *Quasi-Experimentation: Design and Analysis Issues for Field Settings*, Boston, MA, Houghton Mifflin.

Dopuch, N., 1992, 'Another perspective on the use of deception in auditing experiments', *Auditing: A Journal of Practice & Theory* 11(2), 109–112.

European Union, 2013, *Ethics for Researchers*, viewed 18 April 2016, from http://ec.europa.eu/research/participants/data/ref/fp7/89888/ethics-for-researchers_en.pdf.

Fine, M. and Kurdek, L., 1994, 'Publishing multiple journal articles from a single data set: Issues and recommendations', *Journal of Family Psychology* 8(4), 371–379.

Gibbins, M., 1992, 'Deception: A tricky issue for behavioral research in accounting and auditing', *Auditing: A Journal of Practice & Theory* 11(2), 113–126.

Greenberg, J. and Folger, R., 1988, *Controversial Issues in Social Research Methods*, Springer-Verlag, New York.

Herring, D., White, K., Jabeen, L., Hinojos, M., Terrazas, G., Reyes, S., Taylor, J. and Crites, S., 2013, 'On the automatic activation of attitudes: A quarter century of evaluative priming research', *Psychological Bulletin* 139(5), 1062–1089.

Hooks, K. and Schultz, J., 1996a, 'Ethics and accounting research: The issue of deception', *Behavioral Research in Accounting* 8(Supplement), 25–47.

Hooks, K. and Schultz, J., 1996b, 'Response to commentary on "Ethics and accounting research: The issue of deception"', *Behavioral Research in Accounting* 8(Supplement), 53–56.

Jones, J., 1981, *Bad Blood: The Tuskegee Syphilis Experiment*, The Free Press, New York.

Kerr, N., 1998, 'HARKing: Hypothesizing after the results are known', *Personality and Social Psychology Review* 2(3), 196–217.

Klein, J. and Smith, N., 2004, 'Forewarning & debriefing as remedies to deception in consumer research: An empirical study', *Advances in Consumer Research* 31(1), 759–765.

Krogstad, J., 1996, 'Commentary on "Ethics and accounting research: The issue of deception"', *Behavioral Research in Accounting* 8(Supplement), 48–52.

Laband, D. and Piette, M., 1994, 'Favoritism versus search for good papers: Empirical evidence regarding the behavior of journal editors', *Journal of Political Economy* 102(1), 194–203.

Libby, R., 1975, 'Accounting ratios and the prediction of failure: Some behavioral evidence', *Journal of Accounting Research* 13(1), 150–161.

Libby, R., 1979, 'The impact of uncertainty reporting on the loan decision', *Journal of Accounting Research* 17(Supplement), 35–57.

Lord, A., 1992, 'Pressure: A methodological consideration for behavioral research in auditing', *Auditing: A Journal of Practice & Theory* 11(2), 89–108.

Meyer, M. and McMahon, D., 2004, 'An examination of ethical research conduct by experienced and novice accounting academics', *Issues in Accounting Education* 19(4), 413–442.

Milgram, S., 1963, 'Behavioral study of obedience', *Journal of Abnormal and Social Psychology* 67(4), 371–378.

Moizer, P., 2009, 'Publishing in accounting journals: A fair game?', *Accounting, Organizations and Society* 34, 285–304.

O'Boyle, E.H., Banks, G.C. and Gonzalez-Mulé, E., 2017, 'The chrysalis effect: How ugly initial results metamorphosize into beautiful articles', *Journal of Management* 43(2), 376–399.

Payne, S., 2000, 'Challenges for research ethics and moral knowledge construction in the applied social sciences', *Journal of Business Ethics* 26(4), 307–318.

Ponemon, L., 1992, 'Auditor underreporting of time and moral reasoning: An experimental lab study', *Contemporary Accounting Research* 9(1), 171–189.

Schepanski, A., Tubbs, R. and Grimlund, R., 1992, 'Issues of concern regarding within-and between-subjects designs in behavioral accounting research', *Journal of Accounting Literature* 11, 121–149.

Schultz, J. and Hooks, K., 1998, 'The effects of relationship and reward on reports of wrongdoing', *Auditing: A Journal of Practice & Theory* 17(2), 15–35.

Sherrell, D., Hair, J. and Griffin, M., 1989, 'Marketing academicians' perceptions of ethical research and publishing behavior', *Academy of Marketing Science Journal* 17(4), 315–324.

Shimp, T., Hyatt, E. and Snyder, D., 1991, 'A critical appraisal of demand artifacts in consumer research', *Journal of Consumer Research* 18(3), 273–283.

Steen, R., 2011a, 'Retractions in the scientific literature: Do authors deliberately commit research fraud?', *Journal of Medical Ethics* 37(2), 113–117.

Steen, R., 2011b, 'Retractions in the scientific literature: Is the incidence of research fraud increasing?', *Journal of Medical Ethics* 37(4), 249–253.

Stout, D., 2015, 'Outstanding Reviewer Award 2014', *Journal of Accounting Education* 33(1), v.

Toy, D., Wright, L. and Olson, J., 2001, 'A conceptual framework for analyzing deception and debriefing effects in marketing research', *Psychology & Marketing* 18(7), 691–719.

United Nations Educational, Scientific and Cultural Organization, 2005, *Universal Declaration on Bioethics and Human Rights*, viewed 25 April 2016, from http://portal.unesco.org/en/ev.php-URL_ID=31058&URL_DO=DO_TOPIC&URL_SECTION=201.html.

US Department of Health, Education, and Welfare, 1979, *The Belmont Report*, viewed 25 April 2016, from www.hhs.gov/ohrp/humansubjects/guidance/belmont.html.

US Department of Health & Human Services, 1949, *The Nuremberg Code*, viewed 25 April 2016, from http://ori.hhs.gov/chapter-3-The-Protection-of-Human-Subjects-nuremberg-code-directives-human-experimentation.

US Department of Health & Human Services, 1991, *Federal Policy for the Protection of Human Subjects ('common rule')*, viewed 25 April 2016, from www.hhs.gov/ohrp/humansubjects/commonrule/.

US Department of Health & Human Services, 2016, *International Compilation of Human Research Standards*, viewed 25 April 2016, from www.hhs.gov/ohrp/international/.

Von Glinow, M. and Novell, L., 1982, 'Ethical standards with organizational behaviour', *Academy of Management Journal* 25(2), 417–436.

von Schacky, C., 2014, 'Hypotheses and ethos of publication', *European Journal of Clinical Nutrition* 68, 863.

World Medical Association, 1964, *WMA Declaration of Helsinki – Ethical Principles for Medical Research Involving Human Subjects*, viewed 25 April 2016, from www.wma.net/en/30publications/10policies/b3/.

Zimbardo, P., 1971, *The Stanford Prison Experiment*, viewed 25 April 2016, from http://web.stanford.edu/dept/spec_coll/uarch/exhibits/spe/Narration.pdf.

Zimmer, I., 1980, 'A lens study of the prediction of corporate failure by bank loan officers', *Journal of Accounting Research* 18(2), 629–636.

20

Use of student and online participants in Behavioural Accounting Research

Vicky Arnold and Anis Triki

Introduction

Behavioural Accounting Research encompasses all aspects of accounting and auditing and involves the use of human participants to gain insight into the phenomenon under study. Behavioural research includes studies with data collected from experiments, quasi-experiments, fieldwork (interviews and observation), as well as surveys. The purpose of this chapter is to discuss the use of both student participants and online participants as well as the incentives used to motivate performance. This discussion is not exhaustive but provides a starting point, along with references, for researchers trying to address the frequently asked question of whether a convenience sample is appropriate to use in a behavioural accounting study. Readers should revisit most of the studies cited in this chapter to establish a solid understanding of when a convenience sample is appropriate to use.

A convenience sample is a sample that is easy to reach at a relatively low cost. This chapter focuses on two types of convenience samples: student samples and online samples such as Amazon Mechanical Turk (MTurk).[1] The focus is on these two specific types of samples because the debate of whether students are appropriate to use when conducting Behavioural Accounting Research persists and whether online participant sources such as MTurk, an option for quickly accessing real-world participants at a low cost, is a viable option for obtaining participants. The importance of sample selection is not limited to accounting research. In all disciplines, sample selection is a criterion that is heavily scrutinized and a manuscript may be rejected or more difficult to publish as a result of using a convenience sample. In an applied setting such as accounting, "journals are more reluctant to accept papers analyzing data collected from student samples because most students, except those in EMBA programs, are not employees or managers in reality" (Bello, Leung, Radebaugh, Tung and Van Witteloostuijn 2009: 361).

While convenience samples may not be appropriate to use under certain circumstances, criticisms of using convenience samples are not necessarily warranted and are often inappropriate. Criticisms are often the result of the lack of understanding of the purpose of experimental research methods (Dobbins, Lane and Steiner 1988).

Use of student participants

Academic debates about using students as surrogates in research has been expressed in various fields such as psychology (Wintre, North and Sugar 2001), logistics (Thomas 2011), social science (Peterson 2001), international business (Bello et al. 2009) and accounting (Ashton and Kramer 1980) and, at times, that debate has been particularly contentious. Some studies defend and legitimize the use of students as participants in accounting research (e.g., Ashton and Kramer 1980; Hamilton and Wright 1982). Peecher and Solomon (2001) suggest that seeking participants with real-world experience is a research trap and recommend that, unless necessary, researchers should use a student sample (see also Libby, Bloomfield and Nelson 2002). Others caution against using students and suggest that students, even MBA students, are not good surrogates for business decision makers (Abdel-Khalik 1974).

While these represent the two extreme positions, other studies take the middle ground and suggest conditions under which student surrogation is acceptable. For example, Abdolmohammadi and Wright (1987) report that the adequacy of using auditing students as surrogates for CPAs may depend on the type of task; using student surrogates may be less of an issue when the task is structured because experience has less of an effect. This middle ground is also shared by other academics. Bello et al. (2009) classify research topics using two categories: fundamental and proximate (Bello et al. 2009). Fundamental research focuses on questions about human nature and is theory driven while proximate research focuses on specific contexts such as the practice environment. For fundamental research, internal validity is an important criterion; and, for proximate research, external validity is an important criterion. Student participants are acceptable for fundamental research, but are not acceptable for proximate research (except for EMBAs). This argument is based on the idea that findings from students may not be generalizable to a non-student population (Bello et al. 2009). Similarly, Thomas (2011) argues that students are not appropriate for studies using surveys or qualitative methods because the objective is to provide generalizable results and generally require individuals with real-world experience. However, students are often appropriate for experimental research when the goal is theory testing (Thomas 2011; Kalkhoff, Youngreen, Nath and Lovaglia 2007).

Homogeneity

Students have unique characteristics and are different from the general population (Sears 1986; Wintre, North and Sugar 2001). Students are neither adult, nor adolescent and do not represent either population (Wintre et al. 2001). Student participants represent a convenience sample that is easily assessable and available at a low cost (e.g., Abdolmohammadi and Wright 1987; Liyanarachchi 2007) and non-student participants (such as auditing professionals, CEOs or financial analysts) represent a non-convenience sample that is often difficult to obtain. For experimental research, accounting students, especially upper level and masters' level accounting students represent a unique participant pool that can be used to examine many issues. Peecher and Solomon (2001) argue that accounting students are often good surrogates for practitioners unless the theory suggests that factors exist that differentiate students from practitioners.

Student samples, particularly when taken from the same university, are homogeneous, and variance due to differences such as age, experience, income or background is minimized. For experimental research, students represent one of the most homogeneous groups available (Thomas 2011). Homogeneity, which strengthens the internal validity of experimental research, is particularly important when the goal of the research is theory testing. Increased variance increases the likelihood of falsely rejecting the theoretical relationships when using a heterogeneous sample; thus, researchers conducting experimental work should seek homogeneous samples to reduce measurement errors (e.g., Kalkhoff et al. 2007). If the theorized relationships do not hold in a controlled environment using a homogeneous sample, the likelihood that the relationship will hold when applied to a more diverse population is very low. Since the goal of experimental research is to test theoretical predictions (Lucas 2003), student participants are particularly valid as long as the experiment is designed to test those theoretical cause and effect relationships and the context in which the relationships are examined are applicable to students. The nature of the research often determines whether use of students as surrogates is acceptable (Abdolmohammadi and Wright 1987; Libby et al. 2002; Lucas 2003).

Representativeness and generalizability

Opponents of using students in accounting and auditing research often argue that students are not representative of the population. However, using non-student participants, in itself, does not necessarily mean that the sample is representative of the population. Non-student samples are often obtained from a narrowly defined group, such as a local office of a single firm, and individuals have the right to opt out of participating. Thus, the resulting sample may not be more representative of the population and the findings from using a non-student convenience sample may suffer from the same issues as a convenience sample of students (Walters-York and Curatola 2000; Kalkhoff et al. 2007).

Opponents of using students also raise the generalizability concerns by highlighting that the results (effect sizes or directionality) and conclusions of a study may depend on whether the research used student or non-student participants (e.g., Peterson 2001), and use this line of reasoning to recommend caution when using students as surrogates. (For a literature review on studies that compare student to non-student sample, see Liyanarachchi 2007). However, using non-student participants, in itself, does not improve generalizability. Results may differ between two non-student samples (Greenberg 1987). Also, generalizability cannot be attained from one study. Replication is needed to reach generalizability (Liyanarachchi 2007). Therefore, "student samples provide no greater threat to external validity than typical real-world samples. The customary real-world sample can be placed under the same scrutiny for lack of formal representativeness and atypicality as the customary student sample" (Walters-York and Curatola 2000: 258).

This lack of generalizability argument also falls apart when considering the statistical properties of non-convenience samples that are arguably more representative of the target population and lead to more generalizable findings. Due to experimental issues such as attrition, both convenience and non-convenience samples have the statistical properties of a convenience sample that may not be representative of the target population (Cook and Campbell 1979; Walters-York and Curatola 2000).

> [T]he audit researcher rarely, if ever, can employ a strict and formal random sampling plan. Human subjects' requirements at universities, for example, usually mandate that both student and practitioner participants be given the option of not participating as well as the option of withdrawing from an experiment once participation has begun.
>
> *(Peecher and Solomon 2001: 200)*

Therefore, "a convenience sample of non-student, real-world subjects provides no better basis for generalizability on the grounds of formal representativeness than does a convenience sample of student subjects" (Walters-York and Curatola 2000: 247).

Mundane vs. experimental realism

In experimental research, there are two types of realism: experimental realism and mundane realism. Mundane realism exists when the experimental setting is similar to real-world events. Experimental realism exists when the experiment is realistic, attended to and taken seriously (Swieringa and Weick 1982; Dobbins et al. 1988). Experiments that use student samples are often criticized for external validity issues because of their artificiality and lack of mundane realism (Lucas 2003). Criticisms about the artificiality fail to consider that every experiment lacks mundane realism and that it is almost impossible to perfectly recreate a real-world setting (e.g., Swieringa and Weick 1982; Walters-York and Curatola 2000). In conducting experiments, what matters more is experimental realism and not mundane realism. The decision on whether to seek students or non-students should be based on reaching experimental realism and not mundane realism (Liyanarachchi 2007). Critics about the artificiality of experiments may be due to a lack of understanding about the difference between experimental and mundane realism (Swieringa and Weick 1982).

From a theoretical perspective, artificiality is an advantage. A theory cannot possibly incorporate every single factor that is present in an individual's environment, nor can it predict how all of these factors can simultaneously impact individuals' behaviour. Theories are usually focused on certain factors and artificially in experiments allow the researcher to focus on the variable of interest and exclude every other factor. In sum, "generalization of any sort can only occur through theory" (Lucas 2003: 242) and realism does not improve generalizability. Artificiality of experiments is an advantage because it allows us to focus on what is theoretically relevant (Lucas 2003).

Another interesting observation is that sometimes the real world does not exist as the research is interested in answering a "what-if" question. In that situation, artificiality is needed (Swieringa and Weick 1982) as only experimental methods can predict, ex ante, the effect of implementing a new accounting policy (or an alternative policy to an existing policy) while controlling for extraneous factors that may affect the analyses. "Only in a true experiment can we vary an existing or proposed policy alternative of interest and measure its incremental influence on decision makers, holding all other influences constant" (Kachelmeier and King 2002: 219). The value of laboratory experiments should not be judged based on its external validity since external validity is not the purpose of laboratory experiments (Dobbins et al. 1988). The goal of experiments is not generalization, but theory testing (Kalkhoff et al. 2007) and a representative sample can be sacrificed to improve internal validity (Cook and Campbell 1979). Experiments are "one of the most powerful of these methods for helping one test and refine theories about causal relationships" (Peecher and Solomon 2001: 195) and should be used to complement other research methods (Dobbins et al. 1988).

In sum, criticisms based on artificiality and lack of realism can be made to both convenience and non-convenience samples. Therefore, non-convenience samples do not necessarily provide better generalizability or external validity than convenience samples. The primary focus should be on experimental realism and making sure that participants are paying attention and are committed to the experimental material. Results from students who are committed to participate to a study are more internally valid than results from a group of practitioners that are not committed to or engaged in the study (Liyanarachchi 2007).

Incentives for motivating students

Paying participants to participate in an experiment should ensure that participants focus on the experimental task (see Bonner, Hastie, Sprinkle and Young 2000 for a review of the effects of financial incentives on performance). Two methods that are used to motivate student partici-pants are course credit and monetary payment. While course credit may not be as efficient as monetary payment, awarding course credit may ensure that participants show up and complete the experimental task, but does not ensure that they will focus their efforts and appropriately attend to the experimental task (Kalkhoff et al. 2007). However, paying participants may not always work to obtain participants' attention and full commitment either. Therefore, researchers should use attention checks to make sure that their participants are reading the materials care-fully and that they are able to understand the materials (Meade and Craig 2012). These questions will ensure that experimental realism is not compromised.

Use of online participants

As an alternative to using students, many researchers in virtually every discipline have turned to online platforms to reach non-student participants (Goodman, Cryder and Cheema 2013). As technology has advanced, online platforms such as Amazon Mechanical Turk (MTurk) have made it easy to recruit non-student samples. Over 500,000 individuals from 190 countries are MTurk workers; most are from the US and India with less than 25% from other countries (Paolacci and Chandler 2014). MTurk represents an attractive means to access a diverse pool of participants at an extremely fast rate and low price (Buhrmester, Kwang and Gosling 2011; Berinsky, Huber and Lenz 2012; Mason and Suri 2012). While several online options exist (see Brandon, Long, Loraas, Mueller-Phillips and Vansant 2014 for an extensive discussion of online participant recruitment services), MTurk has emerged as the most popular online recruitment option as an alternative to using student participants. The following discussion focuses on the extensive research conducted on the validity and reliability of MTurk participants, but it should be noted that these are issues of online participants as a whole and the discussion should be considered as relating to the broader online participant debate.

MTurk is a crowdsourcing platform where a researcher (requester) meets a participant (worker). This platform allows the researcher to introduce a task (HIT) to participants and to pay them for completing the task (see Mason and Suri 2012 for a detailed overview of MTurk). It was originally designed as an online labour market that facilitated the contact between employers and workers who would complete short, menial tasks online for very low pay. Researchers have capitalized on the online labour market as a quick source of accessing participants for a very low monetary reward. For example, MTurk participants are willing to provide their age and gender for a monetary payment of one penny (Buhrmester et al. 2011). On the other hand, the higher the monetary reward the more participants a researcher can reach (Horton, Rand and Zeckhauser 2011). While MTurk participants seem to be primarily motivated by the monetary reward offered by researchers (Horton et al. 2011), some evidence suggests that MTurk participants are also intrinsically motivated to exert effort while partici-pating in experiments (Farrell, Grenier and Leiby 2017). For example, Paolacci, Chandler and Ipeirotis (2010) reported that 40.7% of MTurk participants surveyed say that they complete MTurk tasks for entertainment. MTurk is also attractive to researchers because they can access a diverse set of participants from across North America (Buhrmester et al. 2011) as well as from other countries. In other words, MTurk participants are more representative of the population than most student participant pools (e.g., Berinsky et al. 2012).

This platform is in its infancy and represents a new opportunity for researchers to collect data from a convenience sample. While researchers from various disciplines are using MTurk more and more frequently (Goodman et al. 2013) as a source of data, questions about the validity and reliability of the data have been raised, and several studies have investigated whether using

MTurk as a participant pool is an appropriate mechanism for academic research (Paolacci et al. 2010; Buhrmester et al. 2011; Horton et al. 2011; Berinsky et al. 2012; Goodman et al. 2013; Chandler, Mueller and Paolacci 2014; Farrell et al. 2017). These concerns centre around whether the data obtained from online participants is credible and believable, which goes directly to questions of internal and external validity. Many of these concerns are similar to those regarding the use of student participants, while other issues are unique to collecting data in an online environment. These issues, along with a discussion of the existing research designed to examine these issues, are discussed in the following paragraphs.

Participant motivation and effort

A major concern that is often raised when MTurk samples are used is that participants are completing the task just for the money. Given that many tasks pay as little as a few cents, participants may complete a task as quickly as possible, paying little attention or exerting little effort in order to maximize pay. This issue becomes a bigger concern for instruments that are longer and more complex (Goodman et al. 2013).

Evidence confirms that MTurk participants are motivated by money (Paolacci et al. 2010) and that they value money more than time (Goodman et al. 2013). Participation rates are significantly higher when the compensation is greater or when the length of the instrument is shorter (Buhrmester et al. 2011). Contrary to expectations, research also shows that MTurk participants pay closer attention to detail than do other non-student samples (Berinsky et al. 2012), and exert as much as or more effort than do student samples (Farrell et al. 2017). Further, effort is not affected by the compensation when payment is based on a flat fee for completion. The amount of effort is the same under a low versus a high flat fee. On the other hand, performance-based wages induce higher effort regardless of whether the task is intrinsically interesting. Participants also exert more effort when the task is more interesting regardless of pay and these results hold when the task is more complex (Farrell et al. 2017).

While the majority of participants do tend to pay close attention and to exert effort, a small percentage of participants do not. Features embedded in MTurk can be used to motivate participants to pay attention to the task. Those features include information regarding the participant's prior approval rate and number of tasks completed.[2] When a participant (worker) completes a task, the researcher (employer) has to approve the results and authorize payment. If the results are not acceptable, then the participant is not paid. MTurk calculates an approval rate based on the number of successful tasks completed divided by total number of tasks completed. Researchers can limit access to any study to productive individuals with a strong reputation, i.e., individuals that have participated in a high number of tasks and have a high approval rate (Peer, Vosgerau and Acquisti 2013). Individuals with an approval rate $\geq$ 95% and who have more than 500 approved hits typically provide high-quality data (Peer et al. 2013). Hence, MTurk participants are motivated to keep their approval rate high in order to continue to have access to future studies, especially to those studies that are more lucrative (e.g., Berinsky et al. 2012).

Concerns of paying attention to the study materials are not unique to MTurk (Chandler et al. 2014). However, in MTurk, researchers can implement strict attention and manipulation checks and can withhold approval and payment to anyone who fails either check (Horton et al. 2011). Workers are concerned about keeping their approval rate above 95% and are cognizant of answering attention and manipulation checks correctly, which means that they tend to pay more attention than might otherwise be expected (Marder and Fritz 2015).

Honesty and integrity

Another issue that that is often expressed relates to concerns over the honesty and integrity of online workers. In a laboratory environment, the researcher can control access to the outside world during the course of an experiment. In an online environment, the researcher cannot control the environment and participants can use the internet or other resources to find answers to objective questions. Because of the low pay and anonymity, online workers may respond less truthfully, particularly when there is an incentive to report dishonestly.

Research suggests that online workers may use the internet to look up answers to objective questions when there is a financial incentive to do so. Goodman et al. (2013) compared the answers of MTurk participants to that of prior studies and found that MTurk participants performed better when asked objective questions (such as the number of countries in Africa). The authors conclude that MTurk participants may be more likely to look up answers online. When participants are specifically asked not to look up the answers, the likelihood that they do so decreased. The authors also suggest that another beneficial way to encourage participants to pay attention is to emphasize the scientific importance of the research (Goodman et al. 2013).

Farrell et al. (2017: 3) extends this prior research by examining the honesty of MTurk participants in an experimental environment and conclude that they "are willing to report their private information honestly . . . even when doing so is quite costly". Further, online workers exhibit similar honesty levels as that of student participants even when the incentive to report dishonestly is the highest. Online participants do not appear to exhibit higher levels of dishonesty than other participants. Again, reputation concerns may encourage MTurk workers to be more honest because they do not want to jeopardize their approval rate in any way.

Repeat participation

Another related concern that is often expressed is whether online participants are likely to participate in a study multiple times especially when the payment is high. Random assignment is a key element in experimental research, and is designed to ensure that groups do not differ systematically. Further, each observation should be independent and participants should not be aware of the treatment. If a participant is a repeat participant, random assignment is violated and data validity is an issue.

In order to assess the extent of the problem, Berinsky et al. (2012) collected data from 551 participants and compared IP addresses to determine whether multiple responses were originating from the same IP address. While each MTurk participant has a unique worker ID and is allowed to participate only once in each task, individuals can have multiple MTurk accounts (although that violates the MTurk agreement and is strongly discouraged) or can use a different browser to access the same experiment multiple times. The results show that less than 2.5% of responses come from the same IP addresses suggesting that repeat participation is not a significant problem. Horton et al. (2011) note that their research confirms that frequency of repeat participation is very low.

Chandler et al. (2014) takes this research a step further and compares the demographic information from responses from the same IP address. Based on demographic information provided and a comparison of responses, the results show that in many instances the responses are from different people at the same IP address. Thus, the problem may be even less than that reported by Berinsky et al. (2012).

While the problem does not appear to be extensive, researchers should take care to employ features to prevent participants from completing the instrument more than once. Further, a researcher can identify duplicate responses by collecting IP addresses and deleting any duplicate responses (or keeping the first response from an IP address). Software used for online data collection also frequently enables the researcher to disallow repeat visits from the same IP address. Interestingly, evidence suggests that the motive of some repeat participants is not money, but is a result of an inherent interest in the research (Chandler et al. 2014). Participants report that they are aware that they are participating in an experiment and that they are interested in knowing the information contained in the other versions of the instrument (treatments). Similar to suggestions by Goodman et al. (2013), asking participants not to participate a second time or reminding them of the importance of scientific research might be effective in deterring repeat participation.

Demographics and personal characteristics

When using a convenience sample, one of the primary concerns is whether the sample is representative and whether the results can be generalized. This concern is exacerbated in an online environment where little is known about the participants. When using a convenience sample of student participants, the researcher has some a priori knowledge about those students. For example, if a study uses a sample of audit students as a surrogate for auditors, a reviewer (or reader) can make several assumptions about those participants regarding level of education, age, accounting knowledge and even intelligence. No assumptions can be made about who is completing the instrument in an online environment. Thus, the question of whether the characteristics of online participants differ from the characteristics of traditional samples is an important question. Further, given that MTurk participants complete simple tasks for very small monetary amounts, it is easy to assume those participants have less education and skill than other types of samples such as students, or that "they might be unusual in ways that challenge the validity of research investigations" (Goodman et al. 2013: 213).

In order to examine this issue, several studies have compared the demographics of MTurk samples to both student and non-student samples (Behrend, Sharek, Meade and Wiebe 2011; Berinsky et al. 2012; Buhrmester et al. 2011; Goodman et al. 2013; Ross, Irani, Silberman, Zaldivar and Tomlinson (2010). The results indicate that MTurk samples are typically older than student samples, but younger than non-student adult samples. In terms of gender, MTurk samples are similar to students, but contain a larger proportion of females than do non-student adult samples. MTurk samples typically have education similar to student samples, but are more educated than non-student adult samples; in addition, MTurk participants are higher in technology related knowledge. MTurk samples are more diverse than most convenience samples in terms of race, education and profession, and are much more diverse than student samples. When compared to the non-student samples, MTurk samples are more internet savvy and more liberal (Berinsky et al. 2012). These results suggest that the MTurk samples are more representative of the general population than other convenience samples and that the results may be more generalizable.

An examination of personal characteristics indicates that, similar to students, MTurk participants value money more than time, which is different from the non-student adult samples. MTurk participants are also likely to exhibit the same biases as students. MTurk participants are more likely to have learned English as a second language than students or the general population, and exhibit lower levels of reading comprehension. Further, MTurk participants are less extraverted, less emotionally stable and have lower self-esteem than either student or non-student samples. Evidence indicates that their cognitive effort and ability is similar to non-student adult samples (Goodman et al. 2013).

Overall, prior research indicates MTurk is a reasonable option for participant pools, that the samples are as representative as other types of convenience samples, and that the results received from using those samples are generalizable. A researcher should be aware of the differences in factors such as age or gender and control for those factors if there is reason to believe that those factors might have a systematic impact on their research.

Data quality

In order to address concerns over the validity of the data, recent studies have examined the quality of the data collected via MTurk to other traditional methods of data collection (Paolacci, Chandler and Ipeirotis 2010; Behrend et al. 2011; Horton et al. 2011; Berinsky et al. 2012; Goodman et al. 2013; Crump, McDonnell and Gureckis 2013; Farrell et al. 2017; Bartneck, Duenser, Moltchanova and Zawieska 2015). The overarching research question that is addressed in this stream of research, which goes to the issue of generalizability, is: do the results from data collected from online participants differ from traditional samples?

Researchers in various disciplines including psychology, political science, accounting, economics, business, sociology, law and medicine have conducted replications of prior research to assess the quality of data collected through MTurk. In psychology, Berinsky et al. (2012) replicated three classic experiments that used both student and nationally representative samples. They reported that treatment effects observed from MTurk participants are similar to treatment effects in prior research. Similarly, Horton et al. (2011) replicated three classic experimental economics studies using MTurk participants and show that the treatment effects are similar to those achieved in prior research.[3] Crump et al. (2013) also replicated several classic behavioural studies to compare responses from MTurk participants to those obtained in a laboratory environment. The results along with results of other replications studies (Bartneck et al. 2015: Behrend et al. 2011; Farrell et al. 2017; Goodman et al. 2013; Paolacci et al. 2010) also indicate that the responses are similar to prior studies providing strong evidence that data quality is high and generally compares well to the laboratory environment. The exception noted is that online participants are not as successful at learning tasks. This may be due to the fact that MTurk samples are more diverse than student samples and may be more representative of the general population than students who are accustomed to a learning environment. In sum, findings from these studies suggest that MTurk participants represent a valid and reliable source for high-quality data.

There is one caveat that Goodman et al. (2013) note. Preliminary evidence suggests that MTurk data collected from individuals outside the US and Canada may be of lower quality than data collected from individuals within these two countries. For example, participants outside of the US and Canada are more likely to fail manipulation checks and show lower levels of reading comprehension than domestic participants. Future research is needed in this area to gain a better understanding of the pros and cons of collected data from participants outside of the US and Canada, but researchers may want to exert caution to limit data collection to domestic participants, which can be done using the controls embedded in MTurk.

Chronic participation and self-selection

Unlike students, MTurk participants can complete tasks as often as they want for as long as they want (24 hours per day for year after year); while students graduate, and are no longer part of the participant pool, MTurk participants can continue to complete experiments for years. In other words, they can become chronic participants (Chandler et al. 2014 refer to these workers as non-naïve participants). If the same people are being used repeatedly to study similar phenomenon, those responses may not be independent (Berinsky et al. 2012; Chandler et al. 2014).

Considering the size of MTurk participant pools, some argue that it is difficult to imagine that the same individuals who have responded in the past will be the same ones that respond on the next experiment. Evidence from the literature suggests that MTurk participants tend to spend a day or less per week completing instruments (Ipeirotis 2010), which decreases the likelihood of receiving responses from the same individuals. Research studies utilizing MTurk to obtain participants come from a significant number of disciplines and a huge number of academics. The research methods and questions between these studies differ, and the format and content is very diverse. Therefore, MTurk participants are unlikely to embrace these differences and become professional survey takers.

Berinsky et al. (2012) investigate this issue by examining the responses from seven different studies over a four-month period. The results indicate that most MTurk participants are not chronic users; 70% participate in only one study over this four-month period, while less than 2% participate in five or more. Further, responses of habitual respondents and non-habitual respondents are not different. With that said, evidence suggests that some MTurk participants may follow a specific researcher or a specific type of survey (Chandler et al. 2014). When a participant follows a researcher, s/he becomes used to the style of research methods and may even identify research traps that the researcher uses to exclude low-quality responses. Further, discussion boards are available to facilitate discussion about studies and plug-ins have been developed to allow workers to identify and complete tasks posted by specific researchers. From this perspective, chronic use of MTurk may be more concerning as it allows participants to have foreknowledge of the study and its purpose. While students share knowledge about studies, the problem has the potential to be more significant with online experimentation as more studies are conducted online.

Researchers can take steps to identify whether these participants have participated in one of their previous studies by tracking participants' worker IDs or IP addresses. Chandler et al. (2014) suggest using the Qualifications filter to reduce the number of chronic participants. Overall, data collected via MTurk requires some effort to "clean" the data, and researchers should spend some additional time to minimize noise in the data. These exclusion criteria should be set at an ex ante rather than employed on a post hoc basis (Chandler et al. 2014).

Conclusions

Participants are obviously a fundamental issue in the validity and reliability of behavioural research. The appropriate match of participants with the task at hand can have significant implications for the meaningfulness of the research results. However, both researchers and reviewers often attempt to assess the reasonableness of participants, not based on the research task, but based on preconceived conceptions of the importance of professional participants to research related to profession-based disciplines. This generally occurs as a result of a failure to reflect back upon the true purpose for conducting experimental research – to test theory.

This chapter first explores the viability of using students as participants in research. While students may not be applicable to research studies that emphasize external validity over internal validity (e.g., surveys and interviews), they can be preferred as participants for experimental studies where internal validity is the dominant concern. A number of issues are raised in this chapter that should be considered in the decision as to whether student participants are acceptable and desirable.

The second primary focus of this chapter is on the increasing availability and use of online participants. While there are a number of services, including marketing firms, that can facilitate access to online participants, the dominant source at this point in time is Amazon's Mechanical Turk. As a result, the vast majority of research on the validity and reliability of online participants has been conducted within the MTurk environment. Thus, the focus herein has been on this extensive body of research that examines online participants via the MTurk system, and demonstrates that such participants have proven to be equally valid, or even better than, student participant pools and general adult populations. This review of the research on online participants is critical as one of the questions most frequently posed to researchers using such participant pools are widespread concerns over the quality, validity and reliability of the data. Contrary to common perceptions, data obtained from online participants have actually proven to be of very high quality – including high validity and reliability.

Notes

1 We have chosen to discuss the use of online participants obtained via MTurk as that is currently a very popular option for obtaining non-student participants for research purposes across all academic disciplines. Most of the discussion is also applicable to other mechanisms for soliciting online participants.
2 While pre-screening features such as prior approval rate and number of tasks completed are available when using MTurk, they are not necessarily available from other vendors. Researchers should query the vendor on pre-screening methods used to insure the quality of responses for any particular study.
3 Horton et al. (2011) provide an excellent discussion of when online participants are and are not appropriate for experimental research.

References

Abdel-Khalik, A., 1974, 'On the efficiency of subject surrogation in accounting research', *The Accounting Review* 49(4), 743–750.

Abdolmohammadi, M. and Wright, A., 1987, 'An examination of the effects of experience and task complexity on audit judgments', *The Accounting Review* 62(1), 1–13.

Ashton, R. and Kramer, S., 1980, 'Students as surrogates in behavioral accounting research: Some evidence', *Journal of Accounting Research* 18(1), 1–15.

Bartneck, C., Duenser, A., Moltchanova, E. and Zawieska, K., 2015, 'Comparing the similarity of responses received from studies in Amazon's Mechanical Turk to studies conducted online and with direct recruitment', *PLOS One* 10(4), e0121595.

Behrend, T., Sharek, D., Meade, A. and Wiebe, E., 2011, 'The viability of crowdsourcing for survey research', *Behavioral Research* 43, 800–813.

Bello, D., Leung, K., Radebaugh, L., Tung, R. and Van Witteloostuijn, A., 2009, 'From the editors: Student samples in international business research', *Journal of International Business Studies* 40(3), 361–364.

Berinsky, A., Huber, G. and Lenz, G., 2012, 'Evaluating online labor markets for experimental research: Amazon.com's Mechanical Turk', *Political Analysis* 20(3), 351–368.

Bonner, S., Hastie, R., Sprinkle, G. and Young, S., 2000, 'A review of the effects of financial incentives on performance in laboratory tasks: Implications for management accounting', *Journal of Management Accounting Research* 12(1), 19–64.

Brandon, D., Long, J., Loraas, T., Mueller-Phillips, J. and Vansant, B., 2014, 'Online instrument delivery and participant recruitment services: Emerging opportunities for behavioral accounting research', *Behavioral Research in Accounting* 26(1), 1–23.

Buhrmester, M., Kwang, T. and Gosling, S., 2011, 'Amazon's Mechanical Turk: A new source of inexpensive, yet high-quality, data?' *Perspectives on Psychological Science* 6(1), 3–5.

Chandler, J., Mueller, P. and Paolacci, G., 2014, 'Nonnaïveté among Amazon Mechanical Turk workers: Consequences and solutions for behavioral researchers', *Behavior Research Methods* 46(1), 112–130.

Cook, T. and Campbell, D., 1979, *Quasi-Experimentation*, Houghton Mifflin, Boston, MA.

Crump, M., McDonnell, J. and Gureckis, T., 2013, 'Evaluating Amazon's Mechanical Turk as a tool for experimental behavioral research', *PLOS ONE* 8(3), e57410. doi:10.1371/journal.pone.0057410.

Dobbins, G., Lane, I. and Steiner, D., 1988, 'Research note: A note on the role of laboratory methodologies in applied behavioural research: Don't throw out the baby with the bath water', *Journal of Organizational Behavior* 9(3), 281–286.

Farrell, A., Grenier, J. and Leiby, J., 2017, 'Scoundrels or stars? Theory and evidence on the quality of workers in online labor markets', *The Accounting Review* 92(1), 93–114.

Goodman, J., Cryder, C. and Cheema, A., 2013, 'Data collection in a flat world: The strengths and weaknesses of Mechanical Turk samples', *Journal of Behavioral Decision Making* 26(3), 213–224.

Greenberg, J., 1987, 'The college sophomore as guinea pig: Setting the record straight', *Academy of Management Review* 12(1), 157–159.

Hamilton, R. and Wright, W., 1982, 'Internal control judgments and effects of experience: Replication and extensions', *Journal of Accounting Research* 20(2), 756–765.

Horton, J., Rand, D. and Zeckhauser, R., 2011, 'The online laboratory: Conducting experiments in a real labor market', *Experimental Economics* 14(3), 399–425.

Ipeirotis, P., 2010, 'Demographics of Mechanical Turk', *CeDER Working Paper 10–01*, New York University.

Kachelmeier, S. and King, R., 2002, 'Using laboratory experiments to evaluate accounting policy issues', *Accounting Horizons* 16(3), 219–232.

Kalkhoff, W., Youngreen, R., Nath, L. and Lovaglia, M., 2007, 'Human participants in laboratory experiments in the social sciences', in M. Webster Jr. and J. Sell (eds.), *Laboratory Experiments in the Social Sciences* (2nd ed.), 103–126, Elsevier, New York.

Libby, R., Bloomfield, R. and Nelson, M., 2002, 'Experimental research in financial accounting', *Accounting, Organizations and Society* 27(8), 775–810.

Liyanarachchi, G., 2007, 'Feasibility of using student subjects in accounting experiments: A review', *Pacific Accounting Review* 19(1), 47–67.

Lucas, J., 2003, 'Theory-testing, generalization, and the problem of external validity', *Sociological Theory* 21(3), 236–253.

Marder, J. and Fritz, M., 2015, 'The internet's hidden science factory', *PBS NewsHour*, www.pbs.org/newshour/updates/inside-amazons-hidden-science-factory/.

Mason, W. and Suri, S., 2012, 'Conducting behavioral research on Amazon's Mechanical Turk', *Behavior Research Methods* 44(1), 1–23.

Meade, A. and Craig, S., 2012, 'Identifying careless responses in survey data', *Psychological Methods* 17(3), 437–455.

Paolacci, G. and Chandler, J., 2014, 'Inside the Turk: Understanding Mechanical Turk as a participant pool', *Current Directions in Psychological Science* 23, 184–188.

Paolacci, G., Chandler, J. and Ipeirotis, P., 2010, 'Running experiments on Amazon Mechanical Turk', *Judgment and Decision Making* 5(5), 411–419.

Peecher, M. and Solomon, I., 2001, 'Theory and experimentation in studies of audit judgments and decisions: Avoiding common research traps', *International Journal of Auditing* 5(3), 193–203.

Peer, E., Vosgerau, J. and Acquisti, A., 2013, 'Reputation as a sufficient condition for data quality on amazon Mechanical Turk', *Behavioral Research Methods* 46(4), 1023–1031.

Peterson, R., 2001, 'On the use of college students in social science research: Insights from a second-order meta-analysis', *Journal of Consumer Research* 28(3), 450–461.

Ross, J., Irani, L., Silberman, M., Zaldivar, A. and Tomlinson, B., 2010, 'Who are the crowdworkers? Shifting demographics in Amazon Mechanical Turk', in *CHI EA 2010*, 2863–72, ACM Press, New York.

Sears, D., 1986, 'College sophomores in the laboratory: Influences of a narrow data base on social psychology's view of human nature', *Journal of Personality and Social Psychology* 51(3), 515–530.

Swieringa, R. and Weick, K., 1982, 'An assessment of laboratory experiments in accounting', *Journal of Accounting Research* 20, 56–101.

Thomas, R., 2011, 'When student samples make sense in logistics research', *Journal of Business Logistics* 32(3), 287–290.

Walters-York, M. and Curatola, A., 2000, 'Theoretical reflections on the use of students as surrogate subjects in behavioral experimentation', *Advances in Accounting Behavioral Research* 3, 243–263.

Wintre, M., North, C. and Sugar, L., 2001, 'Psychologists' response to criticisms about research based on undergraduate participants: A developmental perspective', *Canadian Psychology* 42(3), 216–225.

21

Improving statistical practice

Incorporating power considerations in the design of studies and reporting confidence intervals

R. Murray Lindsay and George C. Gonzalez

Introduction

If a researcher wishes to increase the chances of obtaining statistical significance, use resources wisely and design studies providing the greatest potential for increasing knowledge, then statistical power considerations need to be incorporated in the design of studies. However, all too often researchers set sample sizes on the basis of resource or subject availability and give little or no attention, at least formally, to the issue of statistical power.

This situation is perplexing. Given the importance of publication to researchers (i.e., "publish or perish") along with the well-known bias against publishing "negative result" studies (Lindsay 1994), one would think that incorporating power considerations in the design of studies would be routine. However, surveys across a variety of disciplines, including accounting (Lindsay 1993; Borkowski, Welsch and Zhang 2001), reveal that the average published study is underpowered and, in many cases, woefully so (Ellis 2010: 75); and this situation continues to persist despite countless articles drawing attention to its importance (Sedlmeier and Gigerenzer 1989; Maxwell 2004).

However, the importance of understanding power extends beyond increasing the prospects for publication. *P* values are the predominant measure used by researchers to interpret the meaningfulness and overall importance of study results (Lindsay 1993, 1995); yet, they cannot serve as an adequate gauge for the scientific or practical importance of a particular result because they conflate sample size with effect size (Lang, Rothman and Cann 1998; Rothman 1998). An understanding of power is crucial to appreciating why much more attention needs to be placed on assessing and reporting effect sizes, along with their associated confidence intervals, as a key component of good statistical practice.

The chapter is structured into four remaining sections. The next section provides a comprehensive examination of statistical power that is designed to be helpful to both the beginning and seasoned researcher. That section covers the concept and components of statistical power, its importance in designing meaningful studies and the various considerations involved in planning for power in the design stages of a study. As well, the perils of conducting retrospective (ex post) as compared to ex ante power analyses are discussed. It also draws readers' attention to the availability of computerized power analysis programs that make power analysis straightforward. We then report effect sizes and power levels along with researchers' awareness and attention to these considerations for experimental Behavioural Accounting Research published in *Behavioral Research in Accounting* (*BRIA*) during the 2010–2014 period. This is followed by a discussion recommending that confidence intervals for the effect size obtained be assessed and reported to further improve statistical practice. We end with concluding comments.

A comprehensive examination of statistical power[1]

The concept of statistical power

A good statistical test needs to consider and control two types of errors, called Type I and Type II, which are present in every study.[2] A Type I error, denoted by α, represents the probability of rejecting the null hypothesis when it is true. Typically, the null represents the hypothesis that a nil effect exists in the population, with any observed departures from 0 reflecting only chance or random factors that arise on account of sampling error. On the other hand, a Type II error, denoted by β, represents the probability of failing to reject a false null hypothesis when some specific, alternative hypothesis (as specified by the researcher) is true. Mathematically, statistical power is $1 - \beta$; it represents the probability of rejecting the null hypothesis if a precisely stated alternative hypothesis is true.

A study's power depends on three factors: (a) effect size (δ); (b) the critical level of significance (α) and (iii) sample size (N). Each will be considered in turn.

Effect size (δ)

Calculating statistical power requires the researcher to specify the degree to which the null hypothesis is false. This value assumes the status of the alternative hypothesis. A different level of power exists for each uniquely specified δ, permitting a power function to be calculated. Power and δ are related in that, all other things being equal (i.e., α and N), power increases as δ increases. Relative to α and N, changes in δ have the most dramatic influence on a study's level of power (Cumming 2012).

It is now common in the statistics literature and much less troublesome to express effect sizes using metric-free or standardized δs which incorporate a test statistic's variance into its calculation. This overcomes the problem of having to interpret effect sizes in their raw form based on the actual measurement scales used in the study. While many different effect sizes exist, in general they relate to two families (Ellis 2010): measures of association (the well-known *r* family) and measures of group differences (Cohen's *d* family). The latter expresses a difference in relation to the standard deviation of the observations ($d = [\bar{x}_1 - \bar{x}_2]/\sigma$), where $\bar{x}_1$ and $\bar{x}_2$ are the sample means expressed in their original measurement units and σ is the common within-population standard deviation.

The critical level of significance (α)

In order to reject the null hypothesis, a test statistic must lie within the tail-area rejection region corresponding to the Type I error level set by the researcher. As α decreases, the size of the rejection region decreases by lying further away from the expected value of the null hypothesis, resulting in the need to obtain a larger δ to reject the null. As a consequence, it becomes more difficult, or less probable, to reject the null. A non-directional (two-tailed) test splits the Type I error limit in half (one in each tail), therefore making the rejection region in either tail smaller (i.e., further away from the expected value of the null). Consequently, two-tailed tests have lower power levels than directional (one-tailed) tests. Based on the simulations performed by Cumming (2012), changes in α have the second greatest impact on power levels (i.e., more than sample size), particularly when small and medium effect sizes are targeted.

Sample size (N)

The importance of sample size is connected to sampling error. As Ellis (2010) explains, every sample has quirks introducing noise that result in a departure from the true population parameter. These quirks might be measurement error or the introduction of a randomizer that selects sampling units in a survey study or places them in specific groups in a laboratory study. The problem with small samples is that it is probabilistically more likely for chance – the luck of the draw – to produce results that depart materially from the true effect existing in the population from which the sample was drawn. On the other hand, these quirks are more likely to cancel each other out in larger samples, resulting in the test statistic becoming, on average, more reliable as an estimate of the population δ. Sampling error is inversely proportional to the square root of the sample size. Increases in N permit the critical (rejection) region of the test statistic to contain lower values of δ, while still maintaining the risk of committing a Type I error at the desired α level, thereby increasing the power of the test.

The manner in which δ, α and N influence power is perhaps most easily understood visually. Based on Kinney (1986), Figure 21.1 illustrates two tests with high and low statistical power. In both tests, the left-hand distribution reflects the null hypothesis ($H_o = 0$) while the right-hand

A. A high-powered test

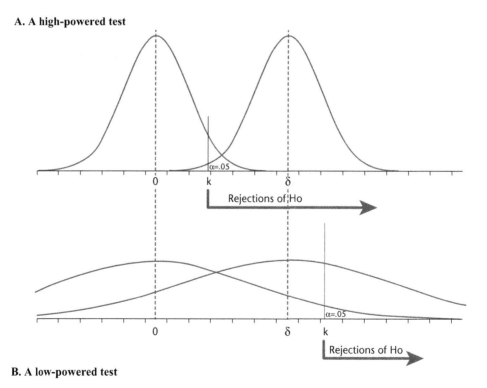

B. A low-powered test

Figure 21.1   An illustration of high- and low-powered tests*

Source: Kinney (1986)

distribution reflects the same specific departure from the null hypothesis ($H_A = \delta$). The rejection region under the H_A distribution, which begins at point k, represents the probability, over repeated sampling, that H_o will be rejected when H_A is true, i.e., the power of the test. In the low-powered test, the sampling distributions are much flatter due to the unreliability of the small sample size. This requires obtaining a much higher δ to achieve the same level of control over a Type I error as compared to the high-powered test; consequently, it becomes less probable to reject H_o. With respect to effect size, Figure 21.1 illustrates that if δ decreases (i.e., the second distribution in either the high or low-powered tests shifts to the left), the rejection area under the H_A distribution decreases, resulting in power decreasing. Finally, if α decreases (the point represented by k shifts to the right in either test), the area under the H_A distribution representing rejections of H_o also decreases, leading to a loss of power.

The importance of understanding power

It is widely appreciated in the statistical literature that p values (i.e., statistical significance) cannot serve as an adequate gauge for the scientific or practical importance of a particular result. Statistical power lies at the heart of this contention in three main ways.

First, statistical power underlies the critical distinction between statistical and scientific (or practical) significance. This distinction arises because p values are a function of both the (standardized) δ obtained and N. In particular, a test can be rendered more sensitive to quantitatively smaller (and perhaps practically or scientifically unimportant) departures from a "sharp" (exact value) null hypothesis by increasing N. As a result, the null can be rejected when, for all practical purposes, it is true. Harsha and Knapp (1990) provide an illustration of this problem in auditing.

This concern has been expressed by Bayesians in the form of a paradox that is not well understood by researchers (Lindsay 1993; Witmer and Clayton 1986). This paradox states that, for a fixed α, no matter how small, providing the prior probability of H_o is greater than zero, there always exists a large enough sample size that can result in H_o being rejected, yet produce a Bayesian posterior probability for H_o near to one as anybody would like (Johnstone 1986, 1990; Lindley 1957; Mayo 1985). The intuition behind this paradox is that although a statistically significant result is rare or infrequent under the null, it is even more infrequent under the alternative hypothesis, and thus the rejection becomes of no consequence (Berkson 1942).[3]

The upshot is that assessing the scientific or practical importance of a result requires the consideration of an alternative hypothesis to establish an interpretation baseline for assessing the scientific (or practical) importance of a result (Berkson 1942; Spielman 1974). As Lindley (1986: 503) puts it:

> There is one message that statisticians should recognize and convey to scientists: rejection of a hypothesis must be based on a comparison with alternatives. An unlikely [null] hypothesis cannot be rejected if there is no reasonable alternative to accept.

To escape this paradox, the null hypothesis should be expanded beyond a nil result to include values of δ that are not practically or scientifically meaningful (Cashen and Geiger 2004; Serlin and Lapsley 1985).

Second, negative results can be interpreted as providing convincing evidence in favour of the null *only* when the power of the test is high (Johnstone 1990). Specifically, providing a test has high power to detect a practically or theoretically important δ, and although always subject to some risk of making a Type II error, the failure to reject the null indicates no meaningful effect (as specified by the researcher) exists. This is a result that is meaningful and valuable to science (Cohen 1965; Kinney 1986; Lindsay 1994).[4] In contrast, running studies with low power jeopardizes the value of a study when statistical significance is not achieved. The result cannot be interpreted in support of the null because there is uncertainty as to whether it is due to the absence of a meaningful effect (as posited by the researcher) or simply to the study's low power (Cashen and Geiger 2004; Cox 1982). The only responsible conclusion is that further research is necessary (Cook and Campbell 1979: 40–41, 46).

Third, running studies with low power is an issue for a discipline that aspires to develop a reliable body of literature; specifically, it leads to the published literature possessing a higher incidence of Type I errors beyond what is conveyed by the α levels used in each individual study (Overall 1969; Spielman 1973; Maxwell, Kelley and Rausch 2008). This higher incidence, itself a probability, was coined by Overall (1969) as "conditional alpha probability" (α^C). α^C is derived from Bayes theorem as follows:

$$\alpha^C = \frac{\text{Prob}\left(H_o\right)\alpha}{\text{Prob}\left(H_o\right)\alpha + \text{Prob}\left(H_A\right)\left(1 - \beta\right)}$$

α^C reflects a test's (long run) proportion of incorrect rejections of H_o to total rejections of H_o, both incorrect and correct. It depends upon α, power $(1 - \beta)$, and the a priori probability that the null hypothesis is true. In examining this formulation, it is easy to verify that α^C increases as power decreases and vice versa. This result can also be seen by examining Figure 21.1. In the high-powered test, the null's critical rejection region is a very small proportion of the alternative hypothesis' probability distribution to the right of point k, whereas it is a much greater proportion in the low-powered test.

Conducting ex ante power analyses

The researcher's goal in conducting a power analysis is to design a study so that it has reasonably high power to detect scientifically (or practically) meaningful effects and low power for detecting all others. This often involves the need to employ considerable judgment. For example, the need to specify δ in advance is premised on a contradiction: if we already know the value for δ, why bother conducting the study (Murphy and Myors 2004)? As well, the required sample size necessary to have a "reasonable" amount of power is frequently beyond a researcher's means. In such situations, it becomes necessary to balance a number of considerations involved in making appropriate trade-offs between α and β. The purpose of this sub-section is to aid researchers in making such decisions consistent with the above goal.

Establishing the alternative hypothesis: effect size considerations

As previously stated, relative to α and N, changes in δ have the most dramatic influence on power (Cumming 2012). While steps can be taken to increase δ through improvements in research design (see below), in the main, once power is determined to be too low given the posited δ, the only recourse is to increase N and/or α. Consequently, establishing δ becomes the starting point in performing a power analysis.

METHODS FOR ESTIMATING EFFECT SIZE

Five different approaches exist to help researchers posit δ to serve as the study's alternative hypothesis. They can be used alone or in combination with one another. First, as a starting point, Cohen (1988) has proposed three operational definitions of δ for a variety of statistical tests using the qualitative labels, "small", "medium" and "large". These δs correspond to correlation coefficients r (Cohen's d) of approximately .10 (.20), .30 (.50), and .50 (.80), respectively. Although somewhat arbitrary, they provide reasonable guidelines because Cohen made a considered effort to use magnitudes of effect that can be expected to be encountered in the behavioural sciences. Researchers can use their subject expertise to determine which, if any, is most appropriate based on the nature of the inquiry and the research design adopted.

Second, as a starting point, and while subject to the vagaries of any measure derived from a heterogeneous database, δ can be based on the aggregate past experience of the discipline in question (Haase, Waechter and Solomon 1982).

Third, a highly useful method is to examine δs obtained in prior studies involving the same or similar variables to those of the planned investigation (Cohen 1965; Cooper 1981; Haase et al. 1982). This information is calculable even for studies that do not report effect sizes provided test statistics and sample sizes are reported (Rosenthal 1993). However, this recommendation comes with a caveat. It is well accepted in the methodological literature that δs appearing in the published literature will be biased upwards because of the bias against publishing negative results (Bangert-Drowns 1986; Schmidt 1992). A confidence interval should be calculated to determine the range of effect sizes that are statistically compatible with these reported findings. If more than one study exists, a meta-analysis should be conducted to statistically combine the results across studies (Bangert-Drowns 1986).

Fourth, the researcher can undertake a pilot study. However, as Chase and Tucker (1975: 32) write, "the typical pilot study, with its characteristic lack of control and small sample size, can provide the investigator with misleading information due to the probable lack of statistical power." Consequently, for this option to be meaningful, the pilot study should mirror the design of the proposed main study and confidence intervals should be calculated to estimate the potential variability in δ.

Finally, researchers can adopt the minimum size of effect that would be of practical usefulness to the end user of the research (Cooper 1981). For example, in a study assessing the efficacy of various treatments on group decision-making, Van de Ven and Delbecq (1974: 612) specified δs that practitioners would likely consider to be trivial or important as well as a zone of indecision where judgment would be suspended until further data became available.

RESEARCH DESIGN CONSIDERATIONS IMPACTING EFFECT SIZE

In using the above approaches, it is important to recognize that the magnitude of the effects obtained are impacted by the study's research design. Measurement error is one such consideration because it has the potential to attenuate observed effect sizes significantly (Bohrnstedt 1970). Table 21.1 illustrates the effect of measurement error on observed effect sizes and required sample sizes. For example, if the correlation existing in the population between X and Y equals 0.30 (Cohen's medium size of effect) and if the reliabilities of X and Y are both 0.80 (a common value in accounting research), then the observed correlation would be reduced to .24. Assuming a test with a desired power level of .80 and $\alpha = .05$ (two-tailed), the minimum sample size required is 133 rather than only 84 if no measurement error existed.

Measurement error introduces three considerations of relevance to our discussion. First, unless the reliabilities of the measures are taken into account, a power analysis will normally overstate the study's actual power. Second, reported δs will normally underestimate the true effect existing in the population; consequently, obtained δs should be adjusted to provide an estimate of the population effect when assessing their magnitude.[5] Finally, reported δs becomes

Table 21.1 The effect of measurement error on observed effect sizes and required sample sizes

$\sqrt{(r_{xx}r_{yy})}$	Small effect R_{xy} (true) = .10		Medium effect R_{xy} (true) = .30		Large effect R_{xy} (true) = .50	
	r_{xy} observed	Min N	r_{xy} observed	Min N	r_{xy} observed	Min N
1.0	0.10	782	0.30	84	0.50	29
0.9	0.09	966	0.27	105	0.45	36
0.8	0.08	1,224	0.24	133	0.40	46
0.7	0.07	1,599	0.21	175	0.35	61
0.6	0.06	2,177	0.18	239	0.30	84

Note: Sample sizes are based on desired power = .80 and α = .05 (two-tailed).

r_{xy} observed = r_{xy} (true) * $\sqrt{(r_{xx}r_{yy})}$, where r_{xx} and r_{yy} represent the reliability coefficients for X and Y, respectively.

Source: Ellis (2010: 67)

ambiguous to interpret if the reliabilities of measurement instruments are not available (Mitchell and Hartmann 1981). It is important that they be reported.

In addition to increasing the reliability of measures, two additional steps can be employed to increase δ. The first is to reduce error variance by introducing physical or statistical controls, adopting stratified or matched-paired sampling, or using within-subjects designs. The second is to increase the range or intensity of the independent variable (Cohen 1994; O'Grady 1982).

SIZE OF EFFECTS TO BE ENCOUNTERED IN BEHAVIOURAL RESEARCH

What size of effects are likely to be encountered in behavioural research? The literature is quite clear: we should not expect anything above very modest effect sizes; certainly, not large ones. This is due to such causes as the complexity of the human behaviour and the forces that shape it, the imprecision of our measurement tools, and the sheer logistic inability to control for multiple sources of extraneous variance in any single study (Haase et al. 1982). Haase et al. (1982) surveyed ten years of counselling research in psychology and found the median value of explained variance to be η^2 (eta squared) = .083. The authors concluded that this size of effect, when adjusted for the peculiarities of their sampling technique, was essentially the same as the figure given by Cohen (1988) for his "medium" size of effect (r = .30). Organ (1977: 48) states that statistically significant correlations greater than r = .20 are usually taken in the behavioural sciences as a signal for continued exploration and analysis. Indeed, this size of effect may even be high! Cohen (1988) argues persuasively in suggesting many relationships pursued in the "soft" behavioural sciences reflect an operational effect size of r = .10. In accounting, no such analysis has been performed. The analysis presented in the section "A power and effect size analysis of experimental behavioural accounting research" will contribute further to this literature when the effect sizes obtained in experimental Behavioural Accounting Research are reported.

Considerations for α and β

ESCHEWING STATISTICAL RITUALS

In the social and behavioural sciences, there is a tradition that has made the .05 critical level virtually sacrosanct regardless of the resulting consequences on β or power (see, e.g., Cashen and Geiger 2004; Cohen 1994; Gigerenzer 2004; Skipper, Guenther and Nass 1967). This tradition reflects the view that the costs from committing a Type I error to either society (e.g., from adopting a bad standard) or to an individual firm (e.g., from implementing an ineffective practice) are greater than those involved with making a Type II error. However, such a view can be supported only if one assumes conclusions are determined on the basis of a single study – a practice that is inconsistent with how progressive science operates (see Lindsay 1995; Lindsay and Ehrenberg 1993; Ravetz 1971; Schmidt 2009).[6]

There is no logical reason to support the use of conventional α levels (i.e., α = .05) when their adoption entails running tests with low or "too much" power (Winer 1971). Master statisticians are clear on this point. For example, Neyman and Pearson, the statisticians who invented the concept of statistical power, write that the relative importance of Type I and Type II errors is a subjective decision that lies outside the theory of statistics, one that should be left to the particular investigator to determine in each particular case (Neyman 1950: 263; Neyman and Pearson 1933/1967: 146). Similarly, Kendall and Stuart (1973: 191) write: "It is always incumbent upon the statistician to satisfy himself that, for the conditions of his problem, he is not sacrificing sensitivity in one direction to sensitivity in another."

The problem with the .05 convention is that it leads to unsupportable Type II/Type I ratios. Table 21.2 presents ratios, obtained by dividing β by α, for different levels of δ and N. An examination of Table 21.2 leads to the following observations. First, if small effect sizes are being pursued, the resulting ratios are so high for virtually any realistic sample size that there is no point in conducting such studies. Second, while matters improve substantially when attempting

Table 21.2 Ratios of Type II/Type I error rates for different levels of α, δ and n*

n	Effect sizes and critical levels of significance levels					
	r = .10 (small)		r = .30 (medium)		r = .50 (large)	
	α = .05	α = .01	α = .05	α = .01	α = .05	α = .01
10	19	99	17	96	13	88
20	19	98	15	91	7	62
30	18	98	13	83	3	38
40	18	98	10	75	2	22
50	18	97	9	67		11
60	18	97	7	59		6
70	17	96	6	52		2
80	17	96	4	44		1
90	17	95	4	38		
100	17	94	3	31		
120	16	93	2	22		
140	16	92	1	15		
160	15	91		10		
180	15	89		6		
200	14	88		4		
300	12	80				
400	10	72				
500	8	63				

Entries are to the nearest integer. Missing values are <1

* *Source:* Rosenthal and Rubin (1985)

to detect medium sizes of effect, there is still a reasonably large subset of studies where the ratio remains inappropriately large. Finally, the gross asymmetry between the two errors disappears only when large effects are operative. Unfortunately, such effects are unlikely to be common in behavioural research.

The upshot is that researchers must eschew statistical rituals if their use entails running studies with inadequate power (Gigerenzer 1998; Gigerenzer 2004). Instead, consideration should be given to the relative seriousness of the two errors as they pertain to the specific circumstances of a study, with the goal being to strike an appropriate balance that can be defended (Ellis 2010: 50; Di Stephano 2003; Labovitz 1968). Three types of considerations are involved.

One is that significance levels need to reflect the current state of theory and the degree of control provided by a study's design (Labovitz 1968). As R.A. Fisher (1959: 42), the father of the modern theory of experimentation, put it: "no scientific worker has a fixed level of significance at which from year to year, and in all circumstances, he rejects hypotheses; he rather gives his mind to each particular case in light of his evidence and his ideas" (see also Cochran 1967: 1461). For example, if there is considerable prior evidence to suggest the null hypothesis is false (i.e., an effect exists in the population), then emphasizing α to the exclusion of β is, in the words of Ellis (2010: 52), "the height of folly" because we can't make a Type I error. In this situation, the only error that can be made is a Type II error. On the other hand, there are situations where lowering α may be prudent to help prevent chance findings from being declared significant. Examples include situations where the current state of knowledge contradicts the proposed (alternative) hypothesis, the study's degree of control is modest, or when multiple tests of significance are being conducted.

A second consideration involves the degree to which a study is exploratory (Davis and Gaito 1984; Giere 1976). Consider the following example. A researcher develops a new audit procedure she believes will lead to fewer audit errors. A "pilot" study is conducted to determine whether the practice appears sufficiently promising to warrant investing in a larger and more convincing study. Assume a medium size of effect is applicable. Seventy practicing accountants matching carefully specified experience requirements agree to participate in the study. Given the difficulty of attracting such qualified participants, it does not seem wise to consider a Type I error as being six times more serious (or costly) than a Type II error (see Table 21.2). A test that is reasonably sensitive to both types of errors can shed important information on whether this new practice has promise. If it does, a larger follow-up study can be conducted to provide added protection against making a false rejection of the null. On the other hand, no such protection exists when a study is conducted with low power and a Type II error occurs, leading to Cohen's famous quotation:

> A generation of researchers could be profitably employed in repeating interesting studies which originally used inadequate sample sizes. Unfortunately, the ones most needing such repetition are least likely to have appeared in print.
>
> *(Cohen 1962: 153)*

The third consideration follows from Popper's (1963) philosophy (see Lindsay 1995). If the researcher's theory predicts the existence of a null relationship (including trivial departures from the null), then a Type II error becomes *more* important than a Type I error because a high-powered study (low β) results in a more severe test, providing a higher degree of corroboration for the theory if the prediction turns out to be correct. Recall from our earlier discussion that failing to reject the null with a low-powered study is essentially non-informative. Consequently, in such studies, power should be very high (e.g., .95 or higher) to support the conclusion that

Table 21.3 Minimum sample sizes for detecting various effect sizes at different levels of power

	Power				Power				Power				Power		
$d(\alpha_1)$	.70	.80	.90	$d(\alpha_2)$	.70	.80	.90	$r(\alpha_1)$	.70	.80	.90	$r(\alpha_2)$	.70	.80	.90
.10	1,884	2,475	3,427	.10	2,471	3,142	4,205	.10	470	616	853	.10	616	782	1,046
.20	472	620	858	.20	620	787	1,053	.20	117	153	211	.20	153	193	258
.30	211	277	382	.30	277	351	469	.25	75	97	134	.25	97	123	164
.40	120	156	216	.40	157	199	265	.30	51	67	92	.30	67	84	112
.50	77	101	139	.50	101	128	171	.35	38	49	67	.35	49	61	81
.60	54	71	97	.60	71	90	119	.40	29	37	50	.40	37	46	61
.70	40	52	72	.70	53	67	88	.45	22	29	39	.45	29	36	47
.80	31	41	55	.80	41	52	68	.50	18	23	31	.50	23	29	37
.90	25	32	44	.90	33	41	54	.60	12	15	20	.60	15	19	24
1.00	21	27	36	1.00	27	34	45	.70	9	11	14	.70	11	13	17

α_1 = one-tailed (directional) test and α_2 = two-tailed (non-directional) test. The sample sizes reported for the d statistic are combined for each independent sample ($N_1 + N_2$). The minimum number in each sample is thus half the figure shown above and rounded up to the nearest whole number.

Source: Ellis (2010: 139–140)

the effect size is negligible or trivial (Cashen and Geiger 2004; Cohen 1990). Obtaining such high levels of power without increasing α will be beyond the scope of many studies.

GUIDELINES FOR ESTABLISHING VALUES FOR A AND POWER (1- B)

If obtaining the required sample is feasible, then the researcher is advised to set α and β = .05 (i.e., power = .95). This permits the test to be equally sensitive to both types of errors. Unfortunately, such a situation is uncommon in Behavioural Accounting Research; consequently, a compromise position between α and β will often be necessary. Faul, Erdfelder, Lang and Buchner (2007) call this a "compromised power analysis", to which we now turn.

Cohen (1965, 1988) suggests, in the spirit of a guideline, that a reasonable value for power is .80 (i.e., β = .20). This policy reflects two considerations. First, Cohen (1988) believes a Type I error is more serious than a Type II error in the field of behavioural psychology based on the conventional scientific view that "failure to find is less serious than finding something that is not there." He therefore proposed that Type I errors should be considered four times more serious than Type II errors.[7] Given the standard convention of α = .05, this results in β = .20. The second and more practical reason is that sample sizes would get prohibitively large if power was in the .90+ range. This second point is uncontestable. Given the small to medium δs applicable to many behavioural research areas, Cohen's power = .80 guideline will often require the use of very large sample sizes (see Table 21.3). For example, consider a significance test where δ is posited halfway between a "small" and "medium" size of effect (i.e., r = .20). If α is set at .05 (one-tailed), a sample size of over 153 is needed for power to reach .80. Increasing power to .90 would require 211 cases.

An additional reason supporting Cohen's guideline is that it combines the best sample-power balance (Aberson 2010: 15). Aberson (2010) states the relationship between power and sample size is roughly linear when moving from power levels of .20 to .80 but nonlinear afterwards. For example, increasing power from .5 to .6, .6 to .7 and .7 to .8 reflects consistent increases of about one quarter of the sample size. However, increasing power from .8 to .9 requires an increase of approximately one-third of the sample size and from .90 to .95 requires another one quarter increase.

It is important to appreciate that Cohen's "five-eighty" convention, as it is sometimes called, was offered in the spirit of a guideline rather than as a straightjacket. It was his hope that researchers would use their informed judgment in considering the relative risk of each error and strike an appropriate balance. The following passage by Cohen (1990: 1310) is worth quoting at length:

> I think it is wise to *plan* the research. This means making tentative informed judgments about, among many other things, the size of the population effect or effects you're chasing, the level of alpha risk you want to take (conveniently, but not necessarily .05), and the power you want (usually some relatively large value like .80). These specified, it is a simple matter to determine the sample size you need. It is then a good idea to rethink your specifications. If, as is often the case, this sample size is beyond your resources, consider the possibility of reducing your power demand ... or even (heaven help us) increasing your alpha level. Or, the required sample size may be smaller than you can comfortably manage, which also should lead you to rethink and possibly revise your original specifications. This process ends when you have a credible and viable set of specifications, or when you discover that no practicable set is possible and the research as originally conceived must be abandoned.

In conclusion, faced with the constraint of realistically attainable sample sizes, and consistent with Cohen's remarks, in some cases researchers will have little choice other than to relax α to provide reasonable levels of power such as .80 (Barnard 1989; Di Stephano 2003; Giere 1976; Kendall and Stuart 1973). On this point, B.J. Winer (1971: 14), the past president of the American Statistical Association and former managing editor of the journal *Biometrika*, writes:

> The frequent use of the .05 and .01 levels of significance is a matter of convention having little scientific or logical basis. When the power of tests is likely to be low under these levels of significance, and when the type I and type II errors are of approximately equal importance, the .30 and .20 levels may be more appropriate than the .05 and .01 levels.

For those individuals equating low alphas with fact acquisition, scientific conservatism, strength of experimental effect or the meaningfulness of a result, the practice of increasing α to .10 or even .20 may appear inconceivable as this recommendation will raise conditional alpha probability (α^c). But if one adopts a more sensible view of the limited role significance tests play in science and accepts that *many* studies are required to establish facts and develop theories (Lindsay 1995; Lindsay and Ehrenberg 1993; Ravetz 1971), then such a change is entirely sensible provided it occurs in conjunction with the following general recommendations advocated by Lindsay (1993):

1   Report in the method section the output of the ex ante power analysis along with the rationale (defence) for its inputs (i.e., δ, α, and N) (Cohen 1973: 228);
2   Report the confidence interval for the effect size obtained and assess the degree of uncertainty of the estimate as indicated by the width of the interval, as discussed further in the "One further step towards improving statistical practice: assessing and reporting confidence intervals" section;
3   Recognize that the results of most studies need to be repeated in a close replication (Lindsay and Ehrenberg 1993; Hubbard and Lindsay 2013; Schmidt 2009) and
4   Combine the results of the series of replicated studies in a meta-analysis to calculate a confidence-bounded estimate of the population effect size which should be assessed for its scientific and/or practical implications (Rosenthal 1978; Schmidt 1992, 1996).

One final consideration involves situations where studies can actually have "too much" power (Johnstone 1986; Lindsay 1993). For example, capital-market research in accounting often uses archival databases that consist of thousands of data points. In such situations, care must be exercised so as not to succumb to the statistical paradox outlined earlier in the "Considerations for α and β" section. It is only the practice of fixing α at conventional levels that leads to this paradox. To avoid it, we simply need to lower α to strike an appropriate balance between α and β. As Kendall and Stuart (1973: 191) write:

> The hypothesis tested will only be rejected with probability near 1 if we keep α fixed as n increases. There is no reason why we should do this: we can determine α in any way we please, and it is rational ... to apply the gain in sensitivity (power) arising from increased sample size to the reduction of α and β. It is only the habit of fixing α at conventional levels which leads to the paradox.

In this way, a properly designed study can never have "too much" power, resulting in the sensible conclusion that more data is always preferred to less.

Retrospective (ex post) power analysis: a caution

As previously discussed, there are two potential competing explanations when a study fails to reject the null. One is that no meaningful effect (as posited by the researcher) exists and the other is that such an effect may exist but the test had too little power to detect it. The use of retrospective power analysis (RPA) is recommended in some circles as a way to eliminate the latter explanation (Hoenig and Heisey 2001). RPA involves calculating a study's "observed" power based on the sample size N, α and the actual δ obtained in the study (in contrast to the δ posited to exist in the population *before* the results are known). Statistical programs like SPSS now calculate retrospective power.

However, RPA is "fundamentally flawed" procedure (Ellis 2010). It adds nothing to the interpretation of results because the observed level of significance p determines on a one-to-one basis a test's retrospective power. Specifically, non-significant p values will *always* correspond to low "observed" statistical power so nothing is gained by its calculation (Goodman and Berlin 1994; Hoenig and Heisey 2001). Moreover, power is exclusively a *pre*-experiment probability reflecting a hypothetical set of results based on repeated sampling (Goodman and Berlin 1994). RPA ignores the existence of sampling error by making the dubious assumption that the sample's observed effect size mirrors the population effect size (Ellis 2010). The reality is that the only way to answer the question "Did the study have sufficient power" is to use an unbiased estimate of the population effect size. RPA violates this requirement because it is conditioned on a statistical decision that has already been made (i.e., do not reject the null).

Computerized power analysis programs

Once the various considerations underlying power analyses are understood, computerized power analysis programs exist to easily calculate required sample sizes as a function of α, ex ante δ and desired power $(1 - \beta)$. In addition, these programs are valuable in assisting the researcher to understand and make appropriate trade-offs among these parameters given the researcher's resources and/or availability of subjects and the circumstances of each study.[8] The G*Power3 statistical analysis program is particularly useful when performing a "compromised power analysis" (see Faul et al. 2007). This program allows users to compute both α and power $(1 - \beta)$

as a function of inputting values for ex ante δ, N (the maximum sample size available to the researcher or the actual sample size obtained) and the relative error probability $q = \beta/\alpha$, which specifies the relative importance the researcher attaches to the two errors.

A power and effect size analysis of experimental Behavioural Accounting Research

A survey was conducted for the purpose of obtaining information to determine the current state of power levels and effect sizes obtained in recent behavioural accounting experimental research. In addition, data was collected to assess researchers' awareness of the importance of these considerations and whether progress has been made since the time Lindsay (1993) conducted the first survey in accounting.

Method

Table 21.4 summarizes the outcome of the sampling protocol employed. The initial population consisted of all papers published in *Behavioral Research in Accounting* (*BRIA*) during the 2010–2014 period. This resulted in an initial population of 82 papers in ten journal issues. Non-experimental papers were then deleted from this total, resulting in 56 studies remaining. Missing information resulted in the next cut to the sample. Some studies had to be discarded because insufficient information was provided to calculate effect sizes (e.g., sample means and standard deviations, total sum of squares, sum of squares for the effect or sum of squares for the error term). The final cut involved eliminating studies from the sample if they reported statistics that were dramatically outside of the range of the statistics reported in the other papers. This protocol left 48 studies in the sample for calculating power, 33 studies for calculating Cohen's *d* for the difference in means and only 18 papers for the three ways of measuring explained variance: eta squared (η^2) (Richardson 2011), omega squared (ω^2) (Keppel 1991) and partial η^2 (Richardson 2011).

Consistent with the approach used in most power surveys, power levels were calculated based on $\alpha = .05$ (two-tailed) for Cohen's (1988) three sizes of effect: "small", "medium", and "large". Recall these δs correspond to $r = .10$, $.30$ and $.50$, respectively. For each study, the study's hypotheses were identified and the power associated with the statistical test for each hypothesis was calculated for the three sizes of effect. A study's power was based on the average of all the tests conducted.

Table 21.4 Sample size determination

	Power	Measures of effect size	
		Cohen's d	η^2 / ω^2 /partial η^2
Total number of papers published in *Behavioral Research in Accounting* during 2010–2014 period	82	82	82
Less: number of non-experimental papers	(26)	(26)	(26)
Number of experimental papers in *BRIA*, 2010–2014	56	56	56
Less: number of papers with insufficient information to calculate statistic	(0)	(16)	(32)
Number of papers for power/effect size study	56	40	24
Less: number of outliers in one or more statistics	(8)	(7)	(6)
Number of papers in the final sample	48	33	18

Results

Effect size

As revealed in Table 21.4, many papers did not report sufficient information to calculate effect sizes. This result represents not only poor data reporting practices, but also indicates many researchers are not aware of the importance of calculating and interpreting the effect size obtained from the perspective of their theory, use in practice or prior research.

Also, no progress has been made in moving beyond the emphasis placed on p values for interpreting results since the time Lindsay's (1993) survey was conducted. Not a single study reported a measure of effect size that related to the study's hypothesis. Only 1 of the 48 papers considered the magnitude of the effect obtained in interpreting their results. Consequently, 47 out of 48 papers relied on the test's p value as a proxy for the importance or scientific and/or practical meaningfulness of the results.

Turning to the size of effects obtained, Table 21.5 presents the results reflecting two different levels of analysis. In Panel A, the results are based on calculating an average effect size for each study, resulting in each paper counting equally to the calculation of the overall measure of central tendency. In Panel B, the reported measures of central tendency are based on all of the tests conducted across the studies.

Table 21.5 Results of effect size analysis

Panel A

Level of analysis: each study

Effect size		Cohen's d		Eta squared		Partial eta squared		Omega squared	
		Freq.	Cum. %	Freq.	Cum. %	Freq.	Cum. %	Freq.	Cum. %
0.00	<.10	1	3	15	83	14	78	15	83
0.10	<.20	3	12	2	94	3	94	2	94
0.20	<.30	1	15	1	100	1	100	1	100
0.30	<.40	5	30						
0.40	<.50	7	52						
0.50	<.60	5	67						
0.60	<.70	3	76						
0.70	<.80	2	82						
0.80	<.90	3	91						
0.90	<1.00	0	91						
1.00	<1.10	2	97						
1.10	<1.20	0	97						
1.20	<1.30	0	97						
1.30	<1.40	0	97						
1.40	<1.50	1	100						
n		33		18		18		18	
Median		0.49		0.05		0.07		0.04	
Mean		0.54		0.07		0.09		0.06	
σ		0.29		0.06		0.06		0.06	

(Continued)

Table 21.5 Results of effect size analysis (cont'd)

Panel B

Level of analysis: each test

Effect size		Cohen's d		Eta squared		Partial eta squared		Omega squared	
		Freq.	Cum. %	Freq.	Cum. %	Freq.	Cum. %	Freq.	Cum. %
0.00	<.10	47	17	72	79	68	76	74	82
0.10	<.20	31	28	12	92	12	89	10	93
0.20	<.30	41	43	3	96	3	92	2	96
0.30	<.40	24	52	1	97	3	96	1	97
0.40	<.50	21	59	0	97	1	97	1	98
0.50	<.60	20	66	2	99	0	97	1	99
0.60	<.70	17	73	1	100	1	98	1	100
0.70	<.80	18	79			0	98		
0.80	<.90	9	82			1	99		
0.90	<1.00	9	86			1	100		
1.00	<1.10	7	88						
1.10	<1.20	10	92						
1.20	<1.30	1	92						
1.30	<1.40	1	92						
1.40	<1.50	4	94						
1.50	<1.60	3	95						
1.60+		14	100						
n		277		91		90		90	
Median		0.38		0.04		0.05		0.03	
Mean		0.54		0.07		0.09		0.06	
σ		0.55		0.11		0.16		0.11	

Given the number of studies that had to be excluded in calculating measures of explained variance (i.e., η^2, partial η^2 and ω^2), the discussion that follows is based on Cohen's d statistic to permit more studies to be included. The median effect size obtained was .49 when the unit of analysis was at the study level (Table 21.5, Panel A). This corresponds approximately to a medium size of effect following Cohen's (1988) typology. However, when the unit of analysis was at the test level, the median effect size falls to .38 (Table 21.5, Panel B), with the standard deviation indicating a wide variance in individual test results. In particular, 28% of the tests obtained a result of $d \leq .20$ (a small size of effect) whereas 21% obtained a result of $d \geq .80$ (a large effect).

Power

Table 21.6 reports summary statistics as well as the frequency and cumulative percentage distribution of the sample's power levels for each of the three effect sizes: small, medium and large. For this analysis, each study contributed equally to the calculation of the overall measure of central tendency.

Table 21.6 Frequency and cumulative percentage distribution of studies' average power to detect small, medium and large effects

Power		Small effect		Medium effect		Large effect	
		Freq.	Cum. %	Freq.	Cum. %	Freq.	Cum. %
0.05	0.099	9	19				
0.10	0.199	28	77				
0.20	0.299	6	90	3	6		
0.30	0.399	5	100	2	10		
0.40	0.499			10	31		
0.50	0.599			8	48	1	2
0.60	0.699			4	56	3	8
0.70	0.799			7	71	1	10
0.80	0.899			7	85	12	35
0.90	0.949			4	94	7	50
0.95	0.989			0	94	5	60
.99+				3	100	19	100
n		48		48		48	
Median		.15		.63		.95	
Mean		.16		.64		.92	
σ		.08		.22		.11	

SMALL EFFECTS

The median power was only .15, reflecting, on average, that the studies reviewed had about a one in seven chance of detecting a small effect existing in the population. Under this assumption, no study had power $\geq 40\%$.

MEDIUM EFFECTS

The median power level was .63. Under this assumption, only 29% of the studies met Cohen's recommended guideline of power $\geq .80$.

LARGE EFFECTS

The median power level was .95. Under this assumption, only 10% of studies would fail to meet Cohen's recommended guideline of power $\geq .80$.

Table 21.7 reports the comparison of this study's power levels with those of earlier power surveys conducted in accounting. The present results compare closely with those of Borkowski et al. (2001) for the subset representing studies published in *BRIA*, thereby indicating no increase in power over the time period of the two studies. In contrast, considerable improvement appears to have been made since the time Lindsay's (1993) study was conducted. Power for his subset of experimental studies was considerably lower, although his study only examined planning and control articles involving budgeting whereas the present study and Borkowski et al.'s (2001) examined all areas within Behavioural Accounting Research.

Finally, only two of the 48 studies presented evidence suggesting that a formal power analysis had been conducted by the researcher. Nonetheless, this represents a slight improvement over

Table 21.7 Comparison of median power levels in accounting power surveys

Survey	Small δ	Medium δ	Large δ	Number of studies	Time period
Current study[1]	.15	.63	.95	48	2010–2014
Borkowski et al. 2001[2]	.15	.69	.78*	96	1993–1997
Borkowski et al. 2001[3]	.13	.61	.96	48	1993–1997
Lindsay 1993[4]	.14	.58	.91	43	1970–1987
Lindsay 1993[5]	.13	.41	.73	11	1970–1987

[1] Experimental studies conducted in *Behavioral Research in Accounting* (BRIA).
[2] Behavioural Accounting Research studies conducted in *Issues in Accounting Education* (IIAE), *Behavioral Research in Accounting* (BRIA), and *Journal of Management Accounting Research* (JMAR) for the 1993–1997 time period.
[3] Behavioural Accounting Research studies conducted only in *Behavioral Research in Accounting* (BRIA) for the 1993–1997 time period.
[4] All planning and control articles (surveys and experiments) involving budgeting published in *Journal of Accounting Research, The Accounting Review,* and *Accounting, Organizations, and Society* for the 1970–1987 time period.
[5] The subset of articles in Lindsay (1993) that were experiments.
* This appears to be an error as the reported mean power levels were .23, .71 and .93.

Lindsay's (1993) study where none were reported. Of the remaining 46 studies not undertaking a formal power analysis, eight studies (17%) provided evidence indicating at least some degree of researcher awareness of the concept of power in the design of their study and/or in the interpretation of the results. Once again, this represents a slight improvement over Lindsay's (1993) results where only 12% of the studies incorporated such considerations.

Discussion of results

Four main observations arise from these results. First, for the first-time behavioural accounting researchers have a starting point, crude though it may be, for conducting power analyses for their proposed study. Table 21.5 (Panel A) suggests that the average effect size (Cohen's *d*) in behavioural accounting utilizing experiments is in the range of .40 to .50, which is approaching a medium size of effect.

However, these estimates are highly likely to be overstated. The bias against publishing negative results ensures that "published studies are more powerful than those which do not reach publication, certainly not less powerful" (Cohen 1962: 152). Sampling error causes results to vary from the population δ, and dramatically so for studies with low power. For example, in 100 actual replications in psychology conducted with high power levels, the replications reported *half* the magnitude of the original effects (Open Science Collaboration 2015). Consequently, unless information exists to the contrary, it would seem prudent to posit δ no higher than halfway between a small and medium δ in a power analysis (i.e., Cohen's *d* = .4 or *r* = .20).

Second, on the basis of the finding that not a single paper reported effect sizes, we can continue to conclude, as did Lindsay (1993: 225), that "statistical significance *continues* to be the predominant measure used by many researchers to interpret the meaningfulness and overall importance of their results" despite the fact that *p* values provide a very poor gauge for doing so.

Third, only two studies provided comments that the researchers computed the power of their study. This result suggests that much more needs to be done to increase researchers' awareness of the importance of calculating power and reporting the result along with the input values underlying the calculation and their rationale.

Fourth, assuming that a medium size of effect is in operation, the median power observed was .63, resulting in the majority of studies (71%) failing to meet Cohen's recommended guideline of power ≥ .80. This result represents a considerable improvement since the time Lindsay's survey was conducted although it is relatively unchanged from Borkowski et al.'s (2001) study conducted approximately 15 years earlier. However, the situation can only be described as dire if a small δ is applicable, which is the case for 28% of the studies covered by the survey. Overall, these results indicate that compromised power analyses will be necessary in many studies to permit tests with reasonable power to be conducted.

One further step towards improving statistical practice: assessing and reporting confidence intervals

Regardless of whether our interest is in theory construction (where estimating population parameters is paramount), treatment comparison (where determining which practice or treatment is superior) and/or determining the practical importance of a result (where cost-benefit considerations arise), master statisticians are clear in stating that parameter estimation and its precision should be the primary statistic of interest; statistical significance is ancillary to this basic requirement (Cox 1982; Kempthorne 1952; Yates 1964).[9] Consequently, in addition to conducting a power analysis and reporting the level of power along with the rationale (defence) for its inputs, i.e., δ, α and N, it is strongly recommended that a confidence interval (CI) surrounding the obtained effect size be assessed and reported to further improve statistical practice. CIs are the procedure that Tukey (1960: 429) considers to be "probably the greatest ultimate importance" among all types of statistical procedures and, according to the American Psychological Association (2010: 34), "the best reporting strategy".

The standard (somewhat arbitrary) convention is to report a 95% CI. Assuming normality, homogeneity of variance and equal group sizes, a 95% CI for the difference in independent means is as follows:

$$\bar{x}_1 - \bar{x}_2 \pm t_{.975, 2n-2} \, S_p \sqrt{2/n}$$

where $\bar{x}_1$ and $\bar{x}_2$ are the sample means for each treatment group, $t_{.975, 2n-2}$ is the critical t-value corresponding to $\alpha = .05$ (two-tailed) with $2n-2$ degrees of freedom, S_p is the pooled standard deviation and n is the sample size for each group (Maxwell et al. 2008).[10] For example, using study 1 in Table 21.8 (to be discussed below), the 95% CI is typically reported as follows: the difference in means was 6.53 (95% CI, 0.53 to 12.54).

In support of this recommendation, consider the following thought experiment of the type initially proposed by Schmidt (1996) that was reported in Hubbard and Lindsay (2013). Ten independent studies (essentially reflecting close or direct replications) are proposed to examine the difference between a new and existing treatment. Unbeknownst to investigators, a population difference of 6 (11–5) in favour of the new treatment exists with a standard deviation of 12. This represents a medium size of effect (i.e., Cohen's $d = .5$). Each treatment condition has 30 subjects and statistical significance is demarcated using $\alpha = .05$ (two-tailed). Power in each study is .47 (Cohen 1988: 36). Running a simulation based on these parameters results in five studies rejecting the null and five that do not. Table 21.8 presents the results of this simulation which can be used to support several key points.

Confidence intervals facilitate cumulative science

A single study amounts to choosing randomly from an infinite sequence of possible results. A single p value provides virtually no information about this sequence (Cumming 2014). This point is particularly salient where power is low and sampling error looms large, such as in our

Table 21.8 Ten hypothetical study replications[a]

Studies	$\overline{X}_1$	$\overline{X}_2$	$\bar{x}_1 - \bar{x}_2$	t	p	Reject H_0?	95% confidence interval on differences between means	
							Lower	Upper
1	11.55	5.02	6.5	2.18	.033	Yes	0.53	12.54
2	6.67	5.29	1.4	0.40	.694	No	−5.61	8.37
3	14.41	8.67	5.7	1.91	.061	No	−0.28	11.75
4	13.09	2.43	10.7	3.25	.002	Yes	4.10	17.22
5	7.44	7.01	0.4	0.12	.902	No	−6.44	7.29
6	7.43	2.00	5.4	1.60	.114	No	−1.35	12.21
7	7.77	5.88	1.9	0.68	.499	No	−3.65	7.47
8	10.57	3.68	6.9	2.29	.026	Yes	0.86	12.93
9	16.38	4.73	11.7	4.07	.000	Yes	5.92	17.38
10	10.73	2.53	8.2	2.84	.006	Yes	2.43	13.97

[a] These results are based on random drawings from independent normal distributions with a population difference $\overline{X}_1 - \overline{X}_2 = 6$ and $\sigma = 12$, $n_A = 30$ and $n_B = 30$, $\alpha = .05$ (two-tailed), and power = 0.47.

Source: Hubbard and Lindsay (2013)

example. In all likelihood, based on NHST the ten studies would be interpreted as mixed or inconclusive, with the implication that some unknown factor moderating the effects of the new treatment remains to be discovered (Schmidt 1996). Yet, such a conclusion is not in accord with reality because we *know* a real effect exists.

Now consider the last two columns in Table 21.8 reporting the CI for each study. Notice how *every* CI includes the true population difference of 6. Notice also that all ten CIs overlap, indicating that all the studies are in statistical agreement with one another. CIs foster cumulative science because they provide a range of plausible values for consideration rather than focusing on a single outcome from the sampling error lottery (Cumming 2014; Schmidt 1996).

Confidence intervals provide an antidote against the perniciousness of power in obtaining sensible insights from the data because they provide information on the precision of an estimate

The precision or accuracy of an estimate (or conversely, its uncertainty) is revealed by the width of the confidence interval. Precision is important because not all estimates are created equal (Goodman and Berlin 1994). A wider interval leads to a less informative study because fewer possibilities can be ruled out statistically, making it more difficult to make a substantive conclusion. This is crucial when interpreting the outcome of a negative result study. As Tukey (1960: 428) writes, only with the use of CIs is it possible to convert a negative statement about significance into a positive conclusion. The conventional NHST procedure, with its focus on the *p* value obtained, completely ignores the concept of precision.

Turning to our example, assume the level of improvement of the new treatment needs to be at least 3 measurement units given its increased cost over the conventional treatment. The non-rejection decision becomes justifiable only if a study's upper CI limit fails to include the minimum threshold effect. However, in each non-rejection study, the 95% confidence interval indicates a difference of 3 is not incompatible with the data, making the "no difference" decision unsupportable. The only reasonable conclusion within each study is that additional data is required to obtain a more precise estimate of the population difference.

A symmetry exists between NHST and confidence intervals

If a NHST rejects the null at the 5% level (studies 1, 4, 8, 9 and 10), 0 will not be contained within a 95% confidence interval. On the other hand, if the NHST fails to reject the null, 0 will be included within the confidence interval (studies 2, 3, 5, 6 and 7). This symmetry is why some people argue that CIs provide all the information p values offer plus more.

In conclusion, we should avoid interpreting results by reducing them to two black and white outcomes – "reject" ($p \leq \alpha$) or "fail to reject" ($p > \alpha$). The upshot is that a researcher cannot properly evaluate the scientific value of a finding and decide next steps without assessing the estimate of the parameter of interest and its degree of statistical accuracy in relation to the particular context, goals and research questions of the study (Goodman and Berlin 1994). And this is exactly what the confidence interval approach to data analysis enables researchers to do that NHST does not.

Conclusion

The formal incorporation of statistical power in the NHST procedure is an important step towards increasing the meaningfulness of studies and improving statistical conclusion validity (see Cook and Campbell 1979: 39–50). Researchers should report in the method section the output of their ex ante power analyses along with the rationale (defence) for its inputs, i.e., δ, α, and N (Cohen 1973). However, the chapter's examination of power levels and obtained effect sizes in experimental papers published in *BRIA* during the 2010–2014 period indicate that power levels in the average study are likely to be unacceptably low if conventional levels of alpha levels (α) are used. In some situations, this may necessitate the use of compromised power analyses – where α is allowed to rise – to permit a more balanced test. While this recommendation can be expected to be controversial, there is much logic in support of this recommendation provided the guidelines presented in the chapter are followed.

Notwithstanding, conducting power analyses alone is not enough to truly improve statistical practice because p values cannot serve as an adequate gauge for assessing the scientific or practical meaning of a particular result. This contention follows from the perniciousness of statistical power in interpreting results. Consequently, it is further recommended that a confidence interval for the obtained effect size be reported and evaluated in relation to the particular context, goals and research questions of the study. At the individual study level, this recommendation will permit attaching scientific significance to negative results, help trivial results from being declared important, and indicate when further research is necessary to reach a conclusion. It will also facilitate cumulative science across studies.

The good news is that these recommendations can be easily and immediately put into practice by all researchers. Given their promise to improve statistical practice, it behooves the accounting research community to do so.

Notes

1 Portions of this section build on the earlier review by Lindsay (1993).
2 This point leads to a glaring problem with null hypothesis statistical testing. Power is neither necessary nor part of its logic. In practice, NHST follows R.A. Fisher's logic for significance tests with only lip service being placed on Neyman and Pearson's ideas on Type II errors and power (Johnstone 1986;

Spielman 1974). The intellectual and often vitriolic controversy between these statistical giants on this issue is not well known or appreciated by practicing scientists (Gigerenzer 1987; see also Lindsay 1995, text to footnote 2).

3 Later we will describe the way to overcome this issue that is crucially important to large sample size studies.

4 It should be noted that the use of high-powered tests is only one requirement for "accepting" the null. Cook, Gruder, Hennigan and Flay (1979) outline three additional criteria which must be met before the null hypothesis can be practically, although not logically, affirmed. See also Cashen and Geiger (2004) for additional requirements.

5 See O'Grady (1982) for such a formula.

6 Consider medicine where the costs of making Type I errors clearly exist to the individual (lifestyle, health) and society (in the form of potentially increased health care costs or the use of ineffective treatments). While exceptions exist (e.g., there is no other treatment for a terminal disease), recommendations on the efficacy of a new treatment protocol or change in lifestyle are normally based on the results of many, many studies. For example, the International Agency for Research on Cancer (2015) announced that processed meat is carcinogenic and red meat probably causes cancer. This announcement was made on the basis of reviewing more than 800 epidemiological studies investigating the association in many countries, from several continents, with diverse ethnicities and diets.

7 Greenwald (1975) surveyed authors and reviewers in psychology and asked them, among other things, to indicate the level of α and β they would regard as satisfactory in rejecting the null hypothesis. The average results were .046 and .274, respectively.

8 See Ellis (2010: 71, fn 22) for references to online, freeware power calculators.

9 As stated earlier, knowledge accrues on the basis of *many* studies. When a specific finding is repeatedly found statistical significance becomes a non-issue.

10 See Smithson (2003) for how to calculate confidence intervals for various tests and Kelley (2007) for a reference to a statistical package that calculates CIs for standardized effect sizes.

References

Aberson, C.L., 2010, *Applied Power Analysis for the Behavioral Sciences*, Routledge, New York.

American Psychological Association, 2010, *Publication Manual of the American Psychological Association* (6th ed.), American Psychological Association, Washington, DC.

Bangert-Drowns, R.L., 1986, 'Review of developments in meta-analytic method', *Psychological Bulletin* 99(3), 388–399.

Barnard, G.A., 1989, 'On alleged gains in power from lower *p*-values', *Statistics in Medicine* 8, 1469–1477.

Berkson, J., 1942, 'Tests of significance considered as evidence', *Journal of the American Statistical Association* 37, 285–294.

Bohrnstedt, G.W., 1970, 'Reliability and validity assessment in attitude measurement', in G. Summers (ed.), *Attitude Measurement*, 80–89, Rand McNally, Chicago.

Borkowski, S.C., Welsch, M.J. and Zhang, Q., 2001, 'An analysis of statistical power in behavioral accounting research', *Behavioral Research in Accounting* 13, 63–84.

Cashen, L.H. and Geiger, S.W., 2004, 'Statistical power and the testing of null hypotheses: A review of contemporary management research and recommendations for future studies', *Organizational Research Methods* 7(2), 151–167.

Chase, L.J. and Tucker, R.K., 1975, 'A power-analytic examination of contemporary communication research', *Speech Monographs* 42(1), 29–41.

Cochran, W.G., 1967, 'Footnote to an appreciation of R.A. Fisher', *Science* 156, 1460–1462.

Cohen, J., 1962, 'The statistical power of abnormal-social psychological research: A review', *Journal of Abnormal and Social Psychology* 65, 145–153.

Cohen, J., 1965, 'Some statistical issues in psychological research', in B.B. Wolman (ed.), *Handbook of Clinical Psychology*, 96–121, McGraw-Hill, New York.

Cohen, J., 1973, 'Statistical power analysis and research results', *American Educational Research Journal* 10, 225–229.

Cohen, J., 1988, *Statistical Power Analysis for The Behavioral Sciences* (2nd ed.), Lawrence Erlbaum, Hillsdale, NJ.

Cohen, J., 1990, 'Things I have learned (so far)', *American Psychologist* 45(12), 1304–1312.

Cohen, J., 1994, 'The earth is round (p<.05)', *American Psychologist* 49(12), 997–1003.

Cook, T.D. and Campbell, D.T., 1979, *Quasi-Experimentation: Design and Analysis Issues for Field Studies*, Rand McNally Publishing Company, Chicago.

Cook, T.D., Gruder, C.L., Hennigan, K.M. and Flay, B.R., 1979, 'History of the sleeper effect: Some logical pitfalls in accepting the null hypothesis', *Psychological Bulletin* 86, 662–679.

Cooper, H., 1981, 'On the significance of effects and the effects of significance', *Journal of Personality and Social Psychology* 41, 1013–1018.

Cox, D.R., 1982, 'Statistical significance tests', *British Journal of Clinical Pharmacology* 14, 325–331.

Cumming, G., 2012, *Understanding the New Statistics: Effect Sizes, Confidence Intervals and Meta-Analysis*, Routledge, New York.

Cumming, G., 2014, 'The new statistics: Why and how', *Psychological Science* 25(1), 7–29.

Davis, C. and Gaito, J., 1984, 'Multiple comparison procedures within experimental research', *Canadian Psychologist* 21, 1–13.

Di Stephano, J., 2003, 'How much power is enough? Against the development of an arbitrary convention for statistical power calculations', *Functional Ecology* 17(5), 707–709.

Ellis, P.D., 2010, *The Essential Guide to Effect Sizes: Statistical Power, Meta-Analysis, and the Interpretation of Research Results*, Cambridge University Press, Cambridge, UK.

Faul, F., Erdfelder, E., Lang, A. and Buchner, A., 2007, 'G★Power 3: A flexible statistical power analysis program for the social, behavioral, and biomedical sciences', *Behavior Research Methods* 39(2), 175–191.

Fisher, R.A., 1959, *Statistical Methods and Scientific Inference* (2nd ed.), Oliver & Boyd, Edinburgh.

Giere, R.N., 1976, 'Empirical probability, objective statistical methods, and scientific inquiry', in W.L. Harper and C.A. Hooker (eds.), *Foundations of Probability Theory, Statistical Inference and Statistical Theories of Science*, 2, Reidel, Dordrecht, Holland.

Gigerenzer, G., 1987, 'Probabilistic thinking and the fight against subjectivity', in L. Kruger, G. Gigerenzer and M.S. Morgan (eds.), *The Probabilistic Revolution: Ideas in the Sciences*, 2, 11–34, MIT Press, Cambridge, MA.

Gigerenzer, G., 1998, 'We need statistical thinking, not statistical rituals', *Behavioral and Brain Sciences* 21(2), 199–200.

Gigerenzer, G., 2004, 'Mindless statistics', *Journal of Socio-Economics* 33(5), 587–606.

Goodman, S.N. and Berlin, J.A., 1994, 'The use of predicted confidence intervals when planning experiments and the misuse of power when interpreting results', *Annals of Internal Medicine* 121(3), 200–206.

Greenwald, A.G., 1975, 'Consequences of prejudice against the null hypothesis', *Psychological Bulletin* 82, 1–20.

Haase, R., Waechter, D.M. and Solomon, G.S., 1982, 'How significant is a significant difference? Average effect size of research in counseling psychology', *Journal of Counseling Psychology* 29(1), 58–65.

Harsha, P.D. and Knapp, M.C., 1990, 'The use of within- and between-subjects experimental designs: A methodological note', *Behavioral Research in Accounting* 2, 50–62.

Hoenig, J.M. and Heisey, D.M., 2001, 'The abuse of power: The pervasive fallacy of power calculations for data analysis', *The American Statistician* 55(1), 19–24.

Hubbard, R. and Lindsay, R.M., 2013, 'From significant *difference* to significant *sameness*: Proposing a paradigm shift in business research', *Journal of Business Research* 66(9), 1377–1388.

International Agency for Research on Cancer, 2015, 'Carcinogenicity of consumption of red and processed meat', *The Lancet Oncology* 16(16), 1599–1600.

Johnstone, D.J., 1986, 'Tests of significance in theory and practice', *The Statistician* 35, 491–498.

Johnstone, D.J., 1990, 'Sample size and the strength of evidence: A Bayesian interpretation of binomial tests of the information content of qualified audit reports', *Abacus* 26, 17–33.

Kempthorne, O., 1952, *The Design and Analysis of Experiments*, Wiley, New York.

Kendall, M.G. and Stuart, A., 1973, *The Advanced Theory of Statistics*, 2, Charles Griffin & Co., London.

Keppel, G., 1991, *Design and Analysis: A Researcher's Handbook*, Prentice Hall, Englewood Cliffs, NJ.

Kinney, W.R., 1986, 'Empirical accounting research design for Ph.D. students', *The Accounting Review* 61(2), 338–350.

Labovitz, S., 1968, 'Criteria for selecting a significance level: A note on the sacredness of .05', *The American Sociologist* 3(3), 220–222.

Lang, J.M., Rothman, K.J. and Cann, C.I., 1998, 'That confounded p-value', *Epidemiology* 9(1), 7–8.

Lindley, D.V., 1957, 'A statistical paradox', *Biometrika* 44, 187–192.

Lindley, D.V., 1986, 'Discussion on Johnstone', *The Statistician* 35, 502–504.

Lindsay, R.M., 1993, 'Incorporating statistical power into the test of significance procedure: A methodological and empirical inquiry', *Behavioral Research in Accounting* 5, 211–236.

Lindsay, R.M., 1994, 'Publication system biases associated with the statistical testing paradigm', *Contemporary Accounting Research* (Summer), 33–57.

Lindsay, R.M., 1995, 'Reconsidering the status of tests of significance in management accounting research: An alternative criterion of adequacy', *Accounting, Organizations and Society* 20, 35–53.

Lindsay, R.M. and Ehrenberg, A.S.C., 1993, 'The design of replicated studies', *The American Statistician* 47(3), 217–228.

Maxwell, S.E., 2004, 'The persistence of unpowered studies in psychological research: Causes, consequences, and remedies', *Psychological Methods* 9(2), 147–163.

Maxwell, S.E., Kelley, K. and Rausch, J.R., 2008, 'Sample size planning for statistical power and accuracy in parameter estimation', *Annual Review of Psychology* 59, 537–563.

Mayo, D.G., 1985, 'Behavioristic, evidentialist, and learning models of statistical testing', *Philosophy of Science* 52, 493–516.

Mitchell, C. and Hartmann, D.P., 1981, 'A cautionary note on the use of omega squared to evaluate the effectiveness of behavioral treatments', *Behavioural Assessment* 3, 93–100.

Murphy, K.R. and Myors, B., 2004, *Statistical Power Analysis: A Simple and General Model for Traditional Modern Hypothesis Tests*, Lawrence Erlbaum, Mahwah, NJ.

Neyman, J., 1950, *First Course in Probability and Statistics*, Henry Holt, New York.

Neyman, J. and Pearson, E.S., 1933, 'On the problem of the most efficient tests of statistical hypotheses', *Philosophical Transactions of the Royal Society* A231, 289–237. Reprinted: in Neyman, J. and Pearson, E.S., 1967, *Joint Statistical Papers*, London, Cambridge University Press, 140–185.

O'Grady, K.E., 1982, 'Measures of expanded variance: Cautions and limitations', *Psychological Bulletin* 92, 766–777.

Open Science Collaboration, 2015, 'Estimating the reproducibility of psychological science', *Science* 349(6251), aac4716-1–aac4716-8.

Organ, D.W., 1977, 'A reappraisal and reinterpretation of the satisfaction-causes-performance hypothesis', *Academy of Management Review* 2, 46–53.

Overall, J.E., 1969, 'Classical statistical hypothesis testing within the context of Bayesian theory', *Psychological Bulletin* 71, 285–292.

Popper, K., 1963, *Conjectures and Refutations*, Routledge & Kegan Paul, London.

Ravetz, J.R., 1971, *Scientific Knowledge and Its Social Problems*, Oxford University Press, Oxford.

Richardson, J.T., 2011, 'Eta squared and partial eta squared as measures of effect size in educational research', *Educational Research Review* 6(2), 135–147.

Rosenthal, R., 1978, 'Combining results of independent studies', *Psychological Bulletin* 85, 185–193.

Rosenthal, R., 1993, 'Cumulating evidence', in G. Keren and C. Lewis (eds.), *A Handbook for Data Analysis in the Behavioral Sciences: Methodological Issues*, 519–559, Lawrence Erlbaum Associates, Hillsdale, NJ.

Rosenthal, R. and Rubin, D.B., 1985, 'Statistical analysis: Summarizing evidence versus establishing facts', *Psychological Bulletin* 97, 527–529.

Rothman, K.J., 1998, 'Writing for epidemiology', *Epidemiology* 9(3), 333–337.

Schmidt, F.L., 1992, 'What do data really mean? Research findings, meta-analysis, and cumulative knowledge in psychology', *American Psychologist* 47(10), 1173–1181.

Schmidt, F.L., 1996, 'Statistical significance testing and cumulative knowledge in psychology: Implications for the training of researchers', *Psychological Methods* 1(2), 115–129.

Schmidt, S., 2009, 'Shall we really do it again? The powerful concept of replication is neglected in the social sciences', *Review of General Psychology* 13(2), 90–100.

Sedlmeier, P. and Gigerenzer, G., 1989, 'Do studies of statistical power have an effect on the power of studies?', *Psychological Bulletin* 105(2), 309–316.

Serlin, R.C. and Lapsley, D.K., 1985, 'Rationality in psychological research: The good-enough principle', *American Psychologist* 40(1), 70–83.

Skipper, J.K., Guenther, A.L. and Nass, G., 1967, 'The sacredness of .05: A note concerning the uses of statistical levels of significance in social science', *The American Sociologist* 2, 16–18.

Smithson, M., 2003, *Confidence Intervals*, Sage Publications Inc., Thousand Oaks, CA.

Spielman, S., 1973, 'A refutation of the Neyman-Pearson theory of testing', *British Journal for the Philosophy of Science* 24(3), 201–222.

Spielman, S., 1974, 'The logic of tests of significance', *Philosophy of Science* 41(3), 211–226.

Tukey, J.W., 1960, 'Conclusions vs. decisions', *Technometrics* 4, 423–433.

Van de Ven, A.H. and Delbecq, A.L., 1974, 'The effectiveness of nominal, delphi and interactive group decision making processes', *Academy of Management Journal* 17, 605–621.

Winer, B.J., 1971, *Statistical Principles in Experimental Design* (2nd ed.), McGraw-Hill, New York.

Witmer, J.A. and Clayton, M.K., 1986, 'On objectivity and subjectivity in statistical inference: A response to Mayo', *Synthese* 67, 307–321.

Yates, F., 1964, 'Sir Ronald Fisher and the design of experiments', *Biometrics* 20(2), 307–321.

Section 6

Data analysis issues (Link 4c)

22

A modern guide to preliminary data analysis and data cleansing in Behavioural Accounting Research

Ethan G. LaMothe and Donna Bobek

Introduction

The purpose of this chapter is to review the processes related to initial handling and preparation of data prior to conducting statistical analysis. To achieve this goal, this chapter is divided into three primary sections. The next section suggests processes related to initial data handling and preparation. We then discuss cleaning up messy data, including dealing with missing data and outliers. We then review the initial steps of data analyses, including exploration of the data, as well as testing for and correcting problems with the data. Finally, we conclude.

Importantly, this chapter is not intended to be a step-by-step guide. Rather, we briefly identify and familiarize readers with considerations related to initially handling data. A number of great statistics texts discuss the topics mentioned in this chapter, and elaborate on them in much greater detail. This chapter is largely adapted from three such texts: Hair, Black, Babin and Anderson (2010), Field (2013) and Mazzocchi (2008). The sections entitled "Data handling and preparation" and "Data cleaning" in particular rely on the first two resources listed above. Texts such as these should be consulted for technical guidance when conducting the analyses suggested in this chapter. The text by Andy Field comes in editions with specific guidance for both SAS (Field and Miles 2011) and SPSS (Field 2013) and is particularly favoured by the authors.

Data handling and preparation

Prior to analyzing data, it must be properly prepared. Data preparation entails all of the procedures between the actual collection of data and any kind of analysis. While data preparation may seem like a series of mechanical steps to take before performing analyses, the authors highly recommend putting some thought into this process. The needs of the intended analyses have a great impact on how the data is handled, and carefully considering these needs will allow the data preparation process to be addressed efficiently.

Transcribing data

In the process of preparing behavioural data, sometimes the need arises to manually input data into a software-readable format.[1] This can occur for a number of reasons, but most frequently is the result of using paper instruments. Given the time required, the tedious nature of manually transcribing responses, and the likelihood of creating errors, it is best to avoid paper instruments wherever possible. We recommend using electronic research instruments developed using online survey builders such as Qualtrics or Survey Monkey. These survey builders are easy to use, provide reasonable technical support and automatically convert participant responses into a usable data set.

In some cases, researchers may be required to use paper instruments. This situation arises when access to computers is limited (e.g., field data, students during class), or the providers of participants prefer paper instruments (e.g., a CPA firm may require the use of a paper instrument if they are concerned with anonymity and the potential of collecting IP addresses). If a paper instrument is used, there are several ways to increase the likelihood of entering the data correctly. First, recognize the process of transcribing data is tedious. Break up the data set into small subsets of participants and only enter a few at a time. Second, consider getting multiple people to transcribe the data. Descriptive statistics can then be compared and used to determine if any differences exist among transcribers. Third, descriptive statistics can be used to validate the data. For example, minimum and maximum statistics quickly indicate if an invalid number was coded given a particular response scale. Other consistency checks can be run based on the nature of the data. For example, if a participant indicates he/she is an audit manager, it makes very little sense for the participant to only have six months of public accounting experience. Finally, it is always a good idea to double check a portion of the data for accuracy.

Statistics software

Once data is in a computer readable format (e.g.,. xls,. xlsx,. csv, etc.), analysis is typically conducted using specialized statistics software packages. Behavioural accounting researchers have a number of options when it comes to general statistics software including SPSS, SAS, R and STATA. However, R and STATA are infrequently used and most behavioural accounting researchers prefer to use SPSS. SPSS is a relatively intuitive software package able to handle most of the methods behavioural researchers utilize in their research. Further, SPSS uses a graphics-based interface making it easy to learn and use. However, the graphic user interface comes at a cost. In particular, researchers using SPSS have less fine control over the options for some advanced methods, leading to a "black box" problem (i.e., sometimes it is difficult to know what SPSS uses as default options).

SAS is a more powerful syntax-based general statistics software when compared to SPSS; using SAS trades off ease of use for finer control over the statistical methods. While learning the coding syntax for SAS is a large start up cost for using this software, there are a few noteworthy advantages. First, the creators of SAS provide an expansive and well-documented online user's guide. Further, many secondary resources are available online for free.[2] Second, because SAS is syntax based, the program file generated when running statistical analysis automatically documents everything. While SPSS has a syntax function, the code for each operation must be manually copied and recorded in a separate document. Finally, SAS is a more expansive software package than SPSS and can handle some statistical methods that would otherwise require an additional add-on for SPSS such as AMOS, or a specialized software package such as MPLUS, LISREL or SMART PLS.

Structure of the data set

When designing the experiment, it is important to look ahead to the data analyses to be performed. This is important not only for ensuring all of the variables are collected, but also makes it easier to know how to structure the data set. For example, the manipulations in a 2x2 between-participant experiment can be recorded in the data set as one variable with four levels or two variables with two levels each. In most cases, behavioural researchers will record the manipulations as two separate variables because doing so allows for explicit tests of interactions between manipulations. While an interaction effect can be statistically modelled in an ANOVA using a four-level independent variable, the main and interactive effects cannot be disentangled.

Variable names

Another consideration related to data structure is how variables in the data set are named. Variables should preferably be assigned names using a systematic rule to ensure variable names are easily interpreted (e.g., a single word description of the variable). However, sometimes using a systematic naming convention may not be the most practical. This is particularly the case when intuitive variable names exist. For example, "ETR" is an intuitive and common name for "effective tax rate". However using an acronym is not appropriate in other situations (e.g., when the acronym is not easily interpretable or with single word variable names). Also consider using prefixes and suffixes for common characteristics for your variables (e.g., "_R" for reverse coded variables, or "c_" for manipulation checks) to help you sort and interpret them quickly.[3]

Finally, remember to keep in mind the requirements and feature of the statistics software when naming variables. For example, SAS has certain restrictions on the characters used in a variable name and some statistical procedures, such as the PROCESS macro, have a maximum number of characters allowed for variable names. Both SPSS and SAS allow variables to be given labels to attach descriptions to variable names. These labels can be suppressed in the results of the data analysis, but can be used as quick reference to ensure the correct variables are in the data analysis. Both SPSS and SAS also allow meanings to be assigned to particular values of a variable,[4] aiding in the interpretation of results. Alternatively, variable and value labels can be recorded in a separate document called a codebook.

Transforming variables

Occasionally, it will be necessary to transform variables before they can be analyzed. For example, a series of scale items will need to be combined to have meaning, either through summing or averaging.[5] When transforming variables, it is best to leave the original variables intact. Erasing or overriding these variables can make it difficult to remember whether variables have been transformed, and what the raw data was. This is a particularly important consideration when dealing with reverse-coded variables. If the original variable is deleted, then it is easy to forget if the variable was ever reverse coded, especially when months can pass between rounds in the review process.

Another good practice to observe when transforming variables is to consistently use an intuitive naming convention for common transformation. For example, include a "_R" on the end of all reverse coded variables or a "_AVG" on the end of all averaged variables. Finally, consider keeping a cumulative log of any changes made to the data set. This change log will allow for future reproduction of the data set for analysis if it is ever lost, and can make it easier to respond to reviewer questions about the data. Going one step further, if SAS is used for data transformations, all of the changes made to the data set are automatically recorded in the SAS programming syntax file.

Data storage and access

When storing data sets, you cannot have too many redundancies. At a bare minimum, data should be stored on a computer hard drive and a backup should be kept on a separate storage device such as an external hard drive or USB flash drive. We also encourage the use of a remote backup service or a web-based cloud storage solution such as Dropbox or OneDrive. However, when using a cloud-based backup medium it is advisable to only save versions of the data set stripped of participant identification information such as IP addresses, names and contact information (if this information was collected) to ensure the privacy of participants. A second recommendation related to data storage is to maintain an original, unaltered, raw data file. This data file along with a change log described in the previous section can be used to recreate the data set used in the analysis.

In the current environment, it is also appropriate to ensure all co-authors on a project have access to the raw data used in the analysis. Each co-author should maintain their own copy of the data set and follow the recommendations above. First, data in behavioural research is far too precious to not be spread among co-authors as they all have a joint interest in the success of a research project. Spreading ownership of the data set helps protect researchers from cataclysmic loss when unfortunate events happen to a co-author. Second, in light of recent events regarding ethical research conduct in Behavioural Accounting Research, sharing data reinforces the accountability of individual co-authors. If at all possible, data collection and data analysis should be separated, but every co-author should have access to raw data.

Data cleaning

Real-world data, by its very nature, is almost always messy. Failing to appropriately clean data prior to statistical tests and analysis can potentially lead to biased and unreliable results. This section discusses two topics fundamental to cleaning data prior to analysis: missing data and outliers.

Missing data

Missing data in behavioural research can be loosely divided into two categories: missing responses and non-responses. Missing responses occur when an otherwise valid observation is incomplete because a participant fails to respond to one or more items in the instrument. For example, a participant's failure to respond to a demographic question such as his/her age constitutes a missing response. Missing responses can also arise when participants start a study, but do not complete it. This latter case is particularly problematic as a larger amount of data tends to be missing from these observations. The second broad category of missing data is called a non-response and occurs when individuals do not respond to requests to participate in the study.

Problems caused by missing data

Irrespective of the type of missing data, there are at least two different reasons why missing data can result in reduced reliability of statistical results. First, from a practical standpoint, missing data reduces the sample size available for analysis, and thus reduces the statistical power of analysis. This problem is less severe because it can usually be remedied by collecting additional data. Further, the effect of reduced sample size can even be quantified by conducting a power analysis. Second, from a substantive perspective, missing data may not arise randomly and thus may result in systematic bias. For example, if individuals with high levels of income systematically do not respond to an item about income, then the mean and variance of reported income may appear lower in the sample than in the population. These suppressed sample means and variances could in turn cause statistical tests to indicate income level is not related to some dependent variable, when in fact it is.

Testing for randomness of missing data

Systematic variation in missing data can reduce the reliability of statistical tests. Thus, the first step of addressing missing data is to determine if the data is missing randomly, or if there is a pattern to the missing data. To test for randomness, the observations should be divided into two groups based on whether or not data is missing for a particular variable. Responses can be assumed to be missing at random if there are no differences between these groups on related control variables.[6]

A special procedure is used to test for randomness in *non*-responses. Specifically, observations are divided into two groups based on when they completed the study (early versus late); then the dependent, independent and control variables can be compared between these two groups. Non-AU:responses can be assumed to have occurred randomly if no differences exist between participants in these groups.[7] Non-response bias is generally more of a concern with survey data (as opposed to experimental data with random assignment).

Dealing with missing data – deletion

Once missing data has been identified there are two ways to handle it. The first method for handling missing data is deletion. Deletion refers to the removal of observations with missing data from the analysis. Two deletion procedures are available to researchers: listwise deletion and pairwise deletion. Listwise deletion removes any observation when the observation is missing data used in *any* of the analyses. This deletion process is the most conservative technique and is frequently used in Behavioural Accounting Research. Pairwise deletion allows each test to use every valid case, even if the observation is missing data pertinent to a different test in the analysis.

In general, the authors recommend researchers use listwise deletion with respect to an observation if the data is missing for key variables in the primary analyses. Listwise deletion should always be used if the dependent variable is missing. Additionally, whenever observations with missing data are deleted (whether listwise or pairwise), researchers should note (typically in a footnote), how many observations were deleted, and the reason for the deletion.

Dealing with missing data – data imputation

The second method of handling missing data is to use data imputation. Data imputation replaces missing values with values maintaining (as close as possible) the original distribution of a variable. Imputation involves using other information available in the sample to estimate the value of missing data observations (Schafer and Graham 2002). Imputation techniques range from simple mean substitution methods where missing variable observations are replaced with the mean of valid observations to complex imputation methods relying on regression analysis or maximum likelihood estimation (Mazzocchi 2008). Often it is preferable to use multiple imputation techniques, and then the average of the values determined by these techniques is used to replace a missing value (Rubin 2003).

Given their complex nature and requirements, a complete discussion of imputation techniques is outside the scope of this chapter; readers are encouraged to consult more complete sources of information such as Hair et al. (2010) for guidance. Additionally, the authors recommend against data imputation other than in extreme circumstances. Specifically, the authors recommend data imputation should only be used when the frequency of missing data is so high deletion would substantially reduce the statistical power of the analysis *and* collecting additional responses is not possible. Further, the method and extent of imputation should be properly disclosed in the paper; along with sensitivity tests indicating what the results would be without the imputed data.[8]

Outliers

Outliers are seemingly anomalous observations because their values appear to be inconsistent with the distribution of other observations in the data set (Mazzocchi 2008). Outliers cannot easily be categorized as either beneficial or problematic (Hair et al. 2010). Outliers may be beneficial as they potentially reveal something interesting about the sample population. For example, outliers may highlight a boundary condition or may show conventional predictions perform well or fail in the presence of an extraordinary circumstance. Conversely, an outlier can be problematic, and represent the result of erroneous transcription, a misunderstanding by a participant, or the inclusion of an observation not representative of the population under study. Further, even if the outlier is representative, its inclusion in statistical testing potentially biases the estimation of relationships that exist between variables in the data.

Detecting outliers

Regardless of the reason for outliers in the data, the process of detecting outliers is straightforward. On a univariate basis, outliers are often quantitatively defined in terms of their dispersion from some measure of central tendency. Outliers are commonly quantified as all observations greater than 2.5 standard deviations from the mean (Hair et al. 2010).[9] Based on this definition, outliers can be identified by calculating a cutoff value of 2.5 standard deviations above and below the mean. Alternatively, the variable of interest can be standardized.[10] Once standardized, all observations with an absolute value greater than 2.5 are considered outliers (Field 2013). Boxplots and histograms are also helpful tools for identifying outliers (discussed in the next section of the chapter).

As sample size gets larger (approximately 80 observations or more), the cutoff should be adjusted to 4 standard deviations instead of 2.5 (Hair et al. 2010). As sample size increases, the probability of finding an observation with a value of more than 2.5 standard deviations away from the mean increases and the impact of these observations on the analysis decreases. Thus, by adjusting the cutoff, observations investigated as outliers remain those cases truly abnormal and potentially influential.

Outliers can also exist in multivariate dimensions. These outliers may be seemingly reasonable in univariate terms, but appear strange when the value of one variable is considered in relation to the value of other variables (Mazzocchi 2008). Scatterplots are often helpful in identifying multivariate outliers: these outliers will frequently appear as isolated observations separate from the groupings or patterns of the other observations. However, since scatterplots only consider two variables at a time, analyzing multivariate data can become quite cumbersome using this method as the number of variables increases. Mahalanobis D^2 is an alternative measure for detecting multivariate outliers (Hair et al. 2010). This statistic computes the multivariate distance of an observation from the mean centre of all observations (Mahalanobis 1936). Due to its statistical properties, Mahalanobis D^2 can be tested for statistical significance. Specifically, when Mahalanobis D^2 is divided by the number of variables involved, the resulting statistic is approximately distributed as a t-value. Because a t-value is standardized, the same cutoff of 2.5 for small samples and 4 for larger samples can be applied (higher values indicate a greater likelihood that the observation is an outlier).

Dealing with outliers

Once an outlier is identified, researchers face the difficult decision of what to do with it. Some sources (e.g., Hair et al. 2010) suggest that the outlier should be treated like missing data: retention, deletion or imputation. However, most researchers in behavioural accounting discount the possibility of data imputation and simply decide between retention and deletion. Even with this simple decision set, the treatment of outliers is still an open question. Some sources advocate for very selective deletion of outliers, suggesting it is only allowable when no reasonable explanation (other than error) exists for the observation (e.g., Hair et al. 2010). Other sources treat the removal of outliers as an ordinary step in the process of conducting research (e.g., Field 2013). In Behavioural Accounting Research, the authors recommend that outliers be removed for the primary analysis. However, researchers should also conduct supplemental analyses including the outliers and comment on any qualitative differences between the original and alternative analyses in a footnote.

Initial data analysis

Spending time on preliminary analyses and becoming familiar with the data allows for better decisions when conducting the primary analyses. The steps outlined in this section illustrate how to dig into the data and get a better understanding of what the responses looks like to ensure the statistical and theoretical underpinnings the analyses are based on are supported. Finally, by running the initial checks suggested in this section, behavioural researchers afford themselves a higher degree of confidence in their analyses.

Exploring data

Researchers are frequently tempted to immediately jump into statistical analysis once their data has been prepared and cleansed. However, getting familiar with the data can improve the effectiveness of the analysis and clue researchers into potential issues to explore. For example, as indicated in the previous section, various plots of the data can help researchers identify potential outliers. In addition, familiarity with the underlying data allows researchers to interpret and articulate the results of their analyses. Graphic and tabular representations of the data provide a map to guide researchers as they conduct the analysis. Without this guide, researchers will often get bogged down with the statistics, and fail to recognize and account for small details in the data.

Graphical analyses

To start, consider using graphical analysis to explore the univariate nature of the variables of interest. Of particular interest is characterizing the shape of the distribution of a variable. Two graphical representations in particular are useful for examining the shape of a distribution: histograms (see Figure 22.1) and box plots (see Figure 22.2). A histogram uses a series of bars to represent the frequency of a particular value or range of values for a single variable. A box plot,

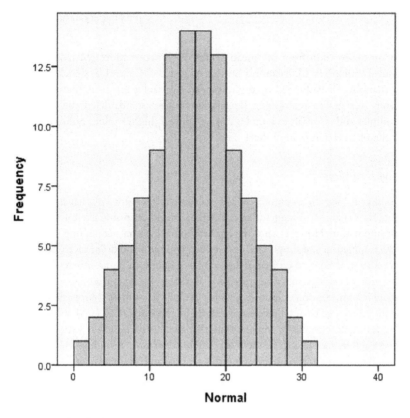

Figure 22.1   Example of a histogram

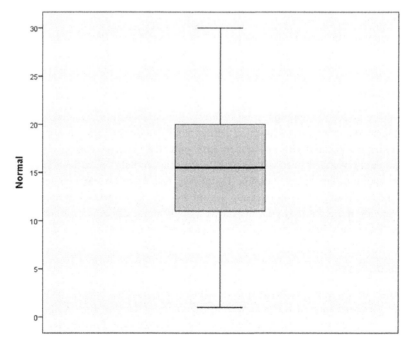

Figure 22.2   Example of a box plot

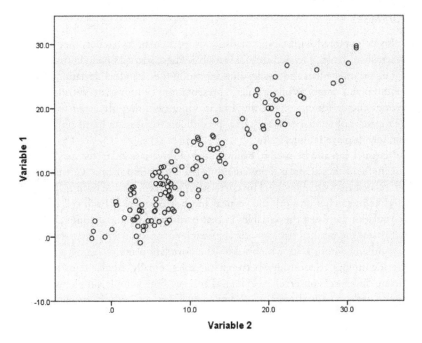

Figure 22.3   Example of a scatterplot

often called a box-whisker plot, is a graphic containing a box split into two sections and two lines protruding from the ends of the box. The outside edges of the box represent the upper and lower quartiles while the line separating the two sections of the box is drawn though the median. The "whiskers" protrude from the ends of the box and extend to the largest and smallest values within one quartile range of the box. Outliers and extreme values beyond the "whiskers" are marked with a symbol.

Scatterplots (see Figure 22.3) are the most frequently used tool for graphically examining multivariate relationships. In a scatterplot, one variable defines the horizontal axis while another defines the vertical axis, and points on the plot represent the joint values of individual observations. Scatterplots are useful for detecting relationships between variables. Specifically, a systematic pattern that appears in a scatterplot potentially indicates the form of a relationship between two variables (e.g., linear, curvilinear, etc.). In multivariate analysis with more than two variables, a matrix of scatterplots can be generated to get a general sense of the relationships that exist in the data.

Finally, graphs can be used in the analysis of group differences. When comparing group means of a variable, a very simple option is to use a bar graph. A bar graph is similar to a histogram, except instead of showing the frequency of a particular level of a variable, it shows the mean of a variable for different groups. Line graphs also display means, but use a point to represent the mean rather than a bar, and related means (i.e., within a group or within a manipulation) are linked with lines. Line graphs are also useful in behavioural research, especially when used to form an interaction plot. A more advanced comparison of groups can be graphed by replacing the bars in a bar chart with box plots. Thus, each group has a box plot displaying median values and the group distribution around those medians. These graphs in particular are helpful to behavioural researchers, who often use manipulations to create different treatment groups.

Tabular analyses

Data can also be explored with tabular statistics. In particular, researchers may find it useful to explore descriptive statistics related to each variable. These statistics include measures of central tendency (i.e., mean, median and mode) and dispersion (i.e., standard deviation, variance, minimum, maximum and range). While tabular representations of univariate statistics may not seem like an obvious choice for examining the data, in some cases they are easier to understand. For example, a measure of central tendency may be difficult to estimate based on a histogram, and more accurately displayed numerically.

Tabular statistics can also be used to examine the multivariate characteristics of the data. One of the most useful of these tabular representations is a correlation matrix. Correlation is a measure of how related two variables are. The correlation matrix is a table listing all of the variables specified by the researcher on both the vertical and horizontal axis. Each cell of the table contains the correlation between the variables in that particular row and column of the table. Most statistics programs include asterisks to indicate which correlations in the correlation matrix are significantly different from zero, which makes the correlation matrix an extremely useful tool for quickly identifying relationships between variables. Finally, tabular statistics can also help confirm group differences observed in graphical analysis. For example, simple two-sample t-tests can be used to preliminarily determine if significant differences exist between groups.

Testing for basic assumptions

The remainder of this chapter discusses procedures for detecting and correcting violations in the basic assumptions of statistical analysis. These assumptions include normality, heteroscedasticity, linearity and independence. While not every type of statistical analysis relies on these assumptions,[11] these four assumptions are the foundation of statistical analysis (Hair et al. 2010). Departures from these assumptions frequently gives rise to biased and inappropriate conclusions, thus steps must be taken if the assumptions are violated to ensure that the analysis is correct.

Normality

Normality is the primary assumption underlying statistical analysis and relates to the shape of the data distribution. Specifically, this assumption is met when the assumed distribution of a particular statistic is approximately normal. While parameter estimates are somewhat robust to violations of this assumption, approximate normality is very important in the construction of error terms, confidence intervals and tests of significance (Field 2013). When the assumption of normality is not met, these parameters tend to become less accurate. A common misconception regarding normality is that the sample data actually needs to be normally distributed.[12] However, the assumed distribution of the statistic of interest is what must be approximately normal (Field 2013). If a mean is of interest in statistical testing (e.g., testing that a mean is statistically significantly different from zero), the sampling distributions of the mean must be normally distributed.[13] No assumption is necessarily made about the distribution of the data the mean is calculated from (i.e., the sample distribution); instead the assumption is a normal distribution of means would be created if a number of samples were taken from the population.

Importantly, the effects of non-normality greatly diminish as the size of the sample increases. This occurs for two reasons. First, with a larger sample size, non-normality has smaller effect on statistical estimates. Second, the central limit theorem suggests distributions of sample statistics generally approach normality as sample size increases (Rice 2006). The sampling distribution is assumed to approach approximate normality when the sample size reaches about 50, but a commonly accepted cutoff is a sample size of 30 (Hair et al. 2010). In tests comparing multiple groups (such as ANOVA), normality is concerned with group level distributions and thus this sample size rule-of-thumb applies to each group or cell (Field 2013).

Deviations from normality

A normal distribution is characterized by the classic symmetrical bell shape, and implies the levels of the variable closest to the mean occur most often. Further, the frequency of observations decreases as the distance from the mean increases. Deviations from normality are often described by two variations in the shape of the distribution: skewness and kurtosis. Skewness refers to the balance of the distribution, and occurs when a larger proportion of observations are on one side of the mean versus the other. Distributions are positively skewed if a greater number of observations falls to the left of the mean and negatively skewed if a greater number of observations falls to the right of the mean. Kurtosis refers to the "peakedness" or "flatness" of the distribution. Distributions with a very concentrated peak are leptokurtic while relatively flat distributions without much of a peak are platykurtic. Figure 22.4 illustrates a normal distribution, skewness and kurtosis.

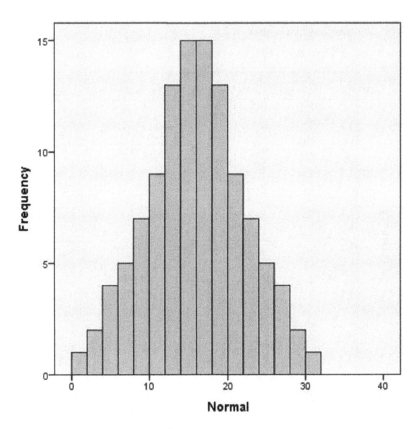

Figure 22.4a Normal distribution in a histogram

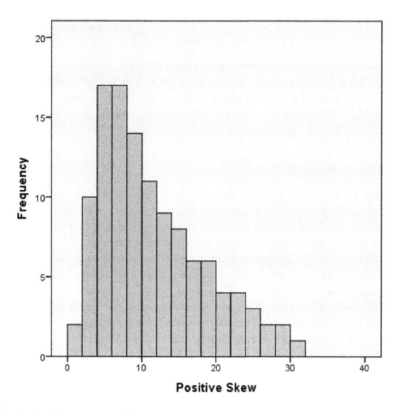

Figure 22.4b Positive skew in a histogram

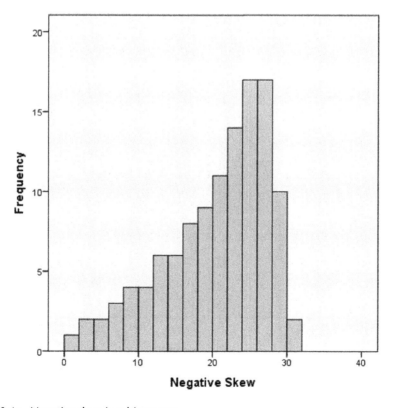

Figure 22.4c Negative skew in a histogram

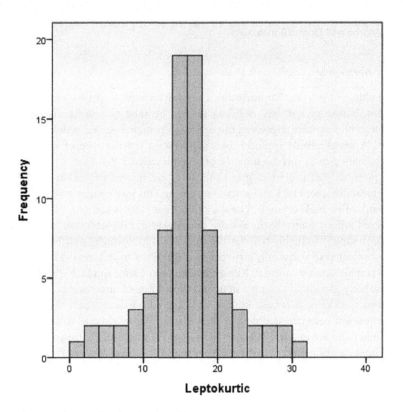

Figure 22.4d   Leptokurtic distribution in a histogram

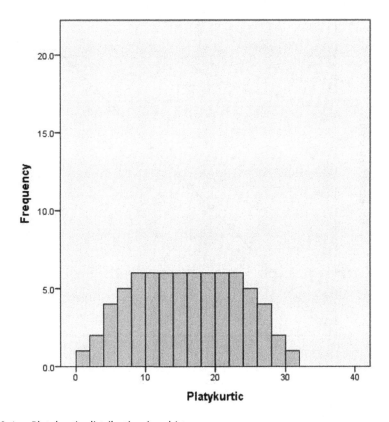

Figure 22.4e   Platykurtic distribution in a histogram

Testing for normality

There are multiple ways to test for normality. The most intuitive ways involve graphically examining the distribution of the data. A histogram can be used to visually check the shape of the distribution of a variable. However, this approach is imprecise and problematic for smaller sample sizes. A more reliable approach is to construct a specific type of scatterplot called a normal probability plot (a specific instance of a graph called a P-P plot). This plot graphs the cumulative probability of a variable against the cumulative probability of a normal distribution. A normal probability plot ranks and sorts observations and then assigns a z-score corresponding to the rank of each observation. The z-score is then plotted against a standardized z-score of the observed value. Intuitively, the z-score calculated from the observations and the rank of the observation should be highly correlated if the variable is normally distributed. This correlation can be compared to statistically significant cutoff values to quantitatively determine if the distribution is approximately normal (Kutner, Nachtsheim, Neter and Li 2005). Additionally, the normal probability plot should graph a straight diagonal line of observations (see Figure 22.5).

There are a number of other quantitative approaches to detecting non-normality. Most statistical packages will compute statistics for skewness and kurtosis along with other descriptive statistics. While there are multiple ways of calculating these statistics, most packages will create statistics centred on zero; thus, positive numbers suggest positive skewness/leptokurtosis while negative numbers indicate negative skewness/platykurtosis. Additionally, these statistics can be standardized by dividing them by their standard errors (usually provided by statistics software) and tested for conventional statistical significance by looking up their values on a z-score table

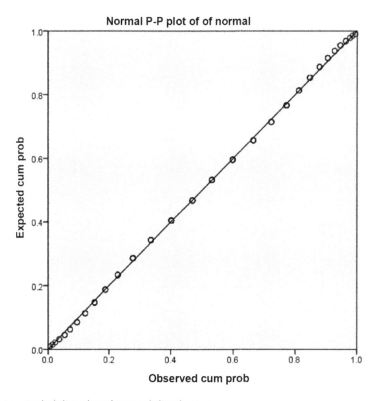

Figure 22.5a Probability plot of normal distribution

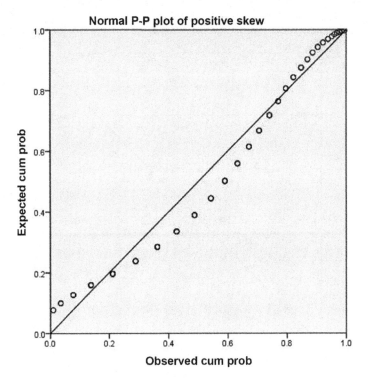

Figure 22.5b   Probability plot of positively skewed distribution

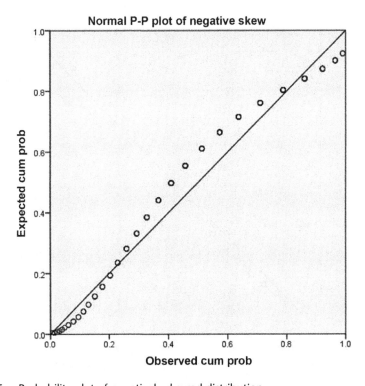

Figure 22.5c   Probability plot of negatively skewed distribution

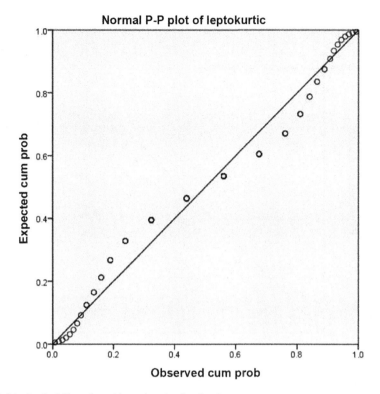

Figure 22.5d Probability plot of leptokurtic distribution

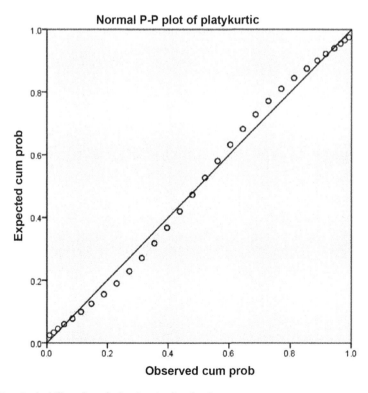

Figure 22.5e Probability plot of platykurtic distribution

(Field 2013). Kolmmogorov-Smirnov and Shapiro-Wilk tests are also common statistics computed by statistical software to quantitatively test for normality (Field 2013). These tests compare the distribution of a variable to a normal distribution and an insignificant statistic indicates the distribution of a variable is not statistically different from a normal distribution.

Correcting for non-normality

There are three common remedies to non-normal data. The first remedy is to simply collect more data. As previously mentioned, issues with normality and the biases in statistics caused by non-normal data are reduced when sample size increases. A second solution is to use analyses robust to departures from normality. Non-parametric tests (e.g., Wilcoxon Signed Rank test) do not rely on the assumption of normality and can be substituted for conventional statistical analyses (e.g., ANOVA). Another alternative is to use bootstrapping methods. These methods use multiple subsamples of the data to create robust parameter estimates. Finally, a third remedy for non-normal data is to apply transformations to the data. Data transformations can help resolve a number of data problems, and thus will be discussed in more detail at the end of this section.

Heteroscedasticity

Heteroscedasticity is an assumption related to dependence relationships, and occurs when variation in a dependent variable is non-constant across different levels of predictor variables or groups (Hair et al. 2010). Unlike violations to normality, heteroscedastic will not result in inaccurate parameter estimates. Instead, heteroscedasticity leads to biased estimates of errors in parameter estimates, and in turn may cause confidence intervals and significance testing to be inaccurate. Another term used to describe heteroscedasticity is heterogeneity of variance, and homoscedasticity or homogeneity of variance are terms used to describe when heteroscedasticity does not occur or has been appropriately controlled for. Heteroscedasticity usually arises for one of two reasons (Hair et al. 2010). First, heteroscedasticity can naturally occur in certain types of variables. For example, reported income has a well-defined lower bound (i.e., $0) but not a well-defined upper bound.[14] Second, skewed distributions in one or more variables may increase the likelihood of heteroscedasticity. To illustrate, Panel B of Figure 22.6 was created by plotting a normally distributed variable against a variable with a skewed distribution.

Detecting heteroscedasticity

Scatterplots (see Figure 22.6) are frequently used to graphically assess the possibility of heteroscedasticity when both variables are continuous. When two variables are plotted against each other in a scatterplot, heteroscedasticity is indicated by certain shapes: cones and diamonds, in particular. Heteroscedasticity is apparent when the visual distribution of the highest and lowest values of one variable along its axis is not constant as the value of the other variable changes. When the data is used to create a model, the values of the prediction residuals can also be plotted against the values of a given variable to check for heteroscedasticity. Box plots are frequently used to assess the possibility of heteroscedasticity when one of the variables is a grouping variable. Differences in the size of the boxes and whiskers between different groups potentially indicate heteroscedasticity.

The possibility of heteroscedasticity can also be assessed quantitatively. A crude test of heteroscedasticity is to order observations along one variable and divide the observations into two groups at the mean. The variance of other variables can then be calculated and compared. When the variance across these groups is similar, the possibility of heteroscedasticity decreases. A more precise test for heteroscedasticity is the Levene test (Field 2013). The Levene test is similar to

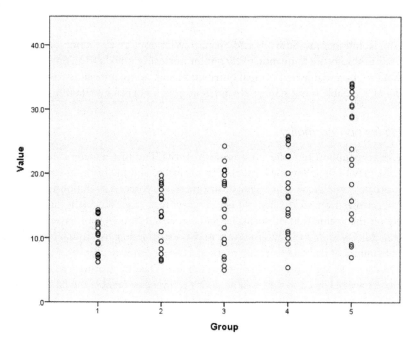

Figure 22.6a   Heteroscedasticity in group data

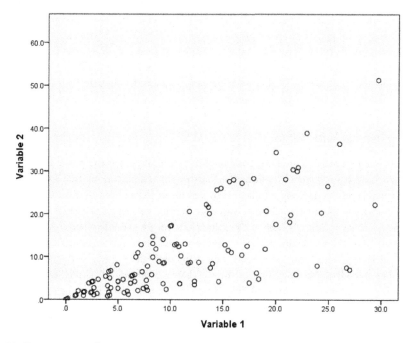

Figure 22.6b   Heteroscedasticity in continuous data

the process outlined above, just with more groups and with deviations from group means rather than variances. After deviations are determined, the Levene test conducts an ANOVA analysis to determine if the average deviation in each group differs from other groups. A statistically significant p-value indicates heteroscedasticity. However, when sample size is large, the Levene test naturally has more power and is more likely to be significant. In these cases, alternative statistics for heteroscedasticity such as Hartley's F_{max} (Hartley 1950) can be consulted (Field 2013).

Correcting for heteroscedasticity

The best option available to correct for heteroscedasticity is data transformation. While transformations may not completely eliminate heteroscedasticity, they can reduce the size of differences in variances. Again, data transformations will be discussed in greater detail at the end of this section.

Linearity

The assumption of linearity implies the dependent variable is linearly related to predictor variables (Hair et al. 2010). Importantly, this does not mean quadratic and higher-level terms cannot be used as predictors. Instead, it means a constant coefficient is able to account for the relationship between a predictor and an outcome, even if the coefficient is attributed to a quadratic or interactive term. This assumption is paramount to model building as failing to meet this assumption invalidates the model used to predict a dependent variable and reduces the detectable strength of a predictor.

Assessments of linearity typically consist of visually reviewing the data. As with heteroscedasticity, scatterplots are frequently used to detect nonlinearity. Nonlinearity is a problem if the patterns in the scatterplots seem to take on shapes other than straight lines. A more precise tool for examining linearity is to examine a scatterplot of the residuals of a model once it has been estimated. In these scatterplots, any pattern other than evenly dispersed residuals can indicate a nonlinear relationship. Correcting for violations in linearity can be achieved through transformation of variables and is discussed in greater detail at the end of this section.

Independence

Independence means the error terms for separate observation are not related (Field 2013). Independence can be violated in Behavioural Accounting Research when individual observations are systematically related to each other. This systematic relationship could occur through a circumstance in the experiment or an unobserved or uncontrolled factor. Detecting issues with independence is tricky because there must be some theoretical explanation for why errors are related. For example, distractions can lead to differences in performance; and one group of participants (e.g., one session of a multi-session experiment) may be exposed to a distraction due to some random event (e.g., construction, power outage, etc.). Other factors that may lead to a lack of independence of observations include firm effects, position within the firm, university major or even gender.

Once the theoretical source of the correlated error terms is identified, the threat of a violation of independence can be controlled. For example, the error terms for observations of accounting professional responses may be correlated because the sample includes multiple observations from the same firm. Accounting professionals from the same firm may respond more similarly to each other than to those at other firms. In this case, firm (e.g., indicator variables can be created to identify whether a participant works at firm 1, firm 2, etc.) can be included as a covariate in any statistical testing to explicitly model and therefore remove this correlation from the error terms. This approach removes the unexplained systematic variance in the error terms and allows the rest of the parameters to be more accurately estimated. If the source of correlation in the error terms cannot be or was not measured (i.e., information about the participant's firm was not recorded), or the source cannot be theoretically identifiable, then more advanced analysis techniques such as multilevel linear modelling may need to be considered (Field 2013).[15]

Data transformations

Data transformations can be helpful for correcting violations in the main assumptions for statistical analysis, but it is important to realize the benefits of applying transformations do not always outweigh the costs. In fact, there is a debate among statisticians about the appropriateness of transformations. For example, the F-test in an ANOVA analysis is generally regarded as robust to deviations from the assumptions (Glass, Peckham and Sanders 1972). Further, a number of researchers have openly debated whether transformations do more harm or good when calculating the F-statistic (Games 1983, 1984; Levine and Dunlap 1982, 1983).

By applying transformations to data, the nature of relationships between variables may be altered, but the existence of a relationship is not affected (Field 2013). Because transformations alter the relationships between variables, it is important to understand the effects of transforming data and realize transformations limit the interpretation of relationships. For example, using a log transformation converts the interpretation of a regression coefficient into terms of percentage changes.[16] In general, relationships between variables should be interpreted and discussed in terms of the untransformed variables (Hair et al. 2010). Additionally, using transformations to correct for the violation of one assumption may also resolve the violation of a second assumption. For example, heteroscedasticity is sometimes caused by non-normality in one or both of the variables in a dependence relationship; thus, transforming a skewed variable may correct for non-normality and heteroscedasticity between the two variables. Generally, transformations should be applied to independent variables before they are applied to dependent variables (Hair et al. 2010). However, a notable exception to this general rule is heteroscedasticity which can only be corrected by transforming the dependent variable (Hair et al. 2010).

A number of different transformations are available to researchers, and many of them can address the same problems. Thus, it is up to the researcher to determine the type of transformation most appropriate. Unfortunately, the best way to do this is through trial and error. Log transformations and square root transformations can both help with a number of problems including positive skewness, leptokurtoses, heteroscedasticity and nonlinearity because they have a greater effect on larger numbers than smaller numbers (Field 2013). However, log transformations cannot be applied to values of 0 or negative values. If either of these cases apply, a constant can be added to the observed values and then the variable can be transformed (e.g., log(x+1) if the minimum value of the observation is 0). Additionally, squaring a variable may help with issues of nonlinearity. Another option for reducing positive skewness, leptokurtoses, and heteroscedasticity is the inverse transformation. This is computed by dividing 1 by the value of the observation. Importantly, the inverse transformation reverses the order of the observations (the largest observation becomes the smallest), so a negative inverse transformation may be preferred. Finally, negative skew can be reduced by using any transformation reducing positive skew, but the variable should be reverse coded first. After transforming the data to correct skewness, the variable should be reverse coded again in order to return the variable to its original scale.

Ultimately, the authors recommend as a first step to applying any transformation, researchers contemplate the effect a transformation will have on their analysis. It is important to realize the point of applying any transformation to data is to help ensure that researchers draw appropriate conclusions from their analysis. To the extent transformations help attain this goal they can be very helpful tools. To the extent a particular transformation detracts from this goal, it should be avoided. Finally, the authors recommend that if data transformation is used, researchers should disclose in a footnote any qualitative differences between the primary analysis and an alternative analysis using untransformed data. For additional information about transformations, readers are directed to Hair et al. (2010, 87).

Conclusion

In summary, this chapter provides a concise review of issues researchers should consider in the preliminary stages of data analyses. We have attempted to provide non-technical and basic guidance while also referencing more thorough statistical treatises where more details are available. We hope this chapter is helpful to beginning and experienced researchers as they explore their data.

Notes

1 This chapter does not discuss practices and procedures related to transcribing and coding qualitative data. Readers are directed to the appropriate chapter of this companion.
2 For example, a number of academics, statisticians and users have provided class materials, how-to guides and examples of SAS code online.
3 Prefixes on variables names (e.g., "c_variable1") can be used for easily sorting variables by type. For example, a prefix of "c_" could indicate control variables, and sorting variables alphabetically will force all of your control variables to be grouped together. Suffixes on variable names (e.g., "variable1_r") can be used to help with interpretation. For example, in a multi-item measure, the suffix "_r" can help you distinguish which items are reverse coded, but will not interfere when sorting variables by name.
4 For example, a gender variable can have 0 labelled as male and 1 labelled as female, or a manipulation variable can have 0 labelled as a control condition and 1 labelled as a treatment condition. Labels can also be used for variables with more than two levels (e.g., 1=partner, 2=manager, 3=senior, 4=staff, etc.).
5 Statistically, averaging or summing the items of a multi-item measure will yield the same results (i.e., significance level). However, the two transformations yield different coefficients and standard errors. As a result, the interpretation of the coefficients is a key concern when deciding between these two transformations.
6 For example, consider the previous example of systematically unreported income by high income participants. A concern about participants who do not report their income level are systematically different from the rest of the sample is reduced if participants who do not report their income are statistically the same as participants who do along other dimensions related to wealth such as number of cars, size of their home, etc.
7 Readers are directed to Dillman, Smyth and Christian (2014) for advice and suggestions for creating instruments with higher response rates.
8 Hair et al. (2010) provides an extensive discussion of dealing with missing data in general and imputation techniques.
9 An alternative quantitative definition of a univariate outlier includes all observations more than 1.5 times the interquartile range above (below) the upper (lower) quartile (Mazzocchi 2008).
10 Standardizing means the variable is transformed into a z-score (i.e., =). A z-score scales responses in terms of standard deviations away from the mean of the distribution of observations. For example, a z-score of 1.5 or -1.5 indicates that an observed value is 1.5 standard deviations above or below the mean, respectively. Standardizing a variable can easily be accomplished by subtracting the mean from each observation, and then dividing by the standard deviation.

11 For example, non-parametric analyses usually rely on rank transformed data and do not assume any particular distribution of the underlying data.

12 This misconception probably arises because normally distributed sample data frequently results in normally distributed sampling and error distributions.

13 A sampling distribution is the probability distribution of a statistic (Field 2013). For example, the sampling distribution of a mean from some population can be thought of as a frequency distribution (histogram) of all the possible means from every possible sample of a given size taken from the population.

14 Further, consider the earnings of an accounting Ph.D. student and an accounting faculty member. Not only is there a large difference in the average earnings of these two groups, but the range of possible earnings of an accounting Ph.D. student is much smaller than the range of an accounting faculty.

15 For additional information about multilevel linear modelling, see Field (2013), chapter 20.

16 For example, a coefficient of 2.00 on a log transformed variable indicates a 1% change in the independent variable results in a 2 unit change in the dependent variable or a 2% change in the dependent variable if it is log transformed as well.

References

Dillman, D.A., Smyth, J.D. and Christian, L.M., 2014, *Internet, Phone, Mail, and Mixed-Mode Surveys: The Tailored Design Method*, John Wiley & Sons, Hoboken, NJ.

Field, A. and Miles, J., 2011, *Discovering Statistics Using SAS*, Sage Publications, Thousand Oaks, CA.

Field, A., 2013, *Discovering Statistics using IBM SPSS Statistics*, Sage Publications Ltd., Thousand Oaks, CA.

Games, P.A., 1983, 'Curvilinear transformations of the dependent variable', *Psychological Bulletin* 93(2), 382–387.

Games, P.A., 1984, 'Data transformations, power, and skew: A rebuttal to Levine and Dunlap', *Psychological Bulletin* 95(2), 345–347.

Glass, G.V., Peckham, P.D. and Sanders, J.R., 1972, 'Consequences of failure to meet assumptions underlying the fixed effects analyses of variance and covariance', *Review of Educational Research* 42(3), 237–288.

Hair, J.F., Black, W.C. Babin, B.J. and Anderson, R.E., 2010. *Multivariate Data Analysis* (7th ed.), Prentice Hall, Upper Saddle River, NJ.

Hartley, H.O., 1950, 'The use of range in analysis of variance', *Biometrika* 37(3/4), 143–152.

Kutner, M.H., Nachtsheim C., Neter J., and Li W., 2005, *Applied Linear Statistical Models*, McGraw-Hill Irwin, New York.

Levine, D.W. and Dunlap, W.P., 1982, 'Power of the F test with skewed data: Should one transform or not?', *Psychological Bulletin* 92(1), 272–280.

Levine, D.W. and Dunlap, W.P., 1983, 'Data transformation, power, and skew: A rejoinder to Games', *Psychological Bulletin* 93(3), 596–599.

Mahalanobis, P.C., 1936, 'On the generalized distance in statistics', *Proceedings of the National Institute of Sciences (Calcutta)* 2, 49–55.

Mazzocchi, M., 2008, *Statistics for Marketing and Consumer Research*, Sage Publications Ltd., Thousand Oaks, CA.

Rice, J., 2006, *Mathematical Statistics and Data Analysis*, Cengage Learning, Boston, MA.

Rubin, D.B., 2003, 'Discussion on multiple imputation', *International Statistical Review* 71(3), 619–625.

Schafer, J.L. and Graham, J.W., 2002, 'Missing data: Our view of the state of the art', *Psychological Methods* 7(2), 147–177.

23

Contrast coding in ANOVA and regression

Susan Pickard Ravenscroft and Frank A. Buckless

Introduction

The usual Omnibus F-tests of main and interaction effects offered by default in popular statistical packages do not calculate the most powerful, efficacious or even relevant statistics in some cases. In this chapter we examine the use of contrast coding,[1] which offers researchers more powerful and relevant tests of main and interaction effects (Buckless and Ravenscroft 1990). We demonstrate the use of contrast coding and show that while it began in the context of Analysis of Variance (ANOVA) it can be beneficial for researchers using regression analyses as well. Newer statistics textbooks (e.g., Cumming 2012) advise researchers to attend more to meaningful effects rather than to rely primarily on low p-values to claim statistical significance. Therefore, we demonstrate how contrast coding can be applied to determine effect sizes in both ANOVA and regression frameworks. When researchers provide effect sizes and consider them while evaluating obtained results, they and their readers are less likely to unwittingly join the "cult of statistical significance" (Ziliak and McCloskey 2008). Members of the "cult" share a preoccupation with obtaining p-values lower than 0.05 and considering such p-values to be in and of themselves meaningful support for a proposed alternative hypothesis.[2]

What is contrast coding?

A planned contrast is a focused test of a particular pattern of means that has one degree of freedom in the F- or t-test, as opposed to an Omnibus F-test that compares all means simultaneously (Rosenthal and Rosnow 1985). Omnibus F-testing has been compared to "playing the guitar with mittens on" (Abelson 1995: 105). Both default coding wired in to statistical packages and graduate statistical education have resulted in researchers who are "virtually automatic" (Abelson) in their impulse to analyze all 2x2 tables as two main effects and an interaction, when the more parsimonious explanation possible using a planned contrast may be more valid and relevant (McShane and Gal 2016).

Why use contrast coding?

What benefits does contrast coding offer to researchers accustomed to relying on ANOVA and/or regression results? The first benefit of using contrast coding is that doing so increases statistical power; the second is that contrast coding can provide researchers with a well-specified test that serves as a useful first step toward determining whether the effect the researcher is interested in has support and should be explored further.

The first benefit of contrast coding – increased power

In Behavioural Accounting Research the primary statistical test of relationships continues to be ANOVA. A review of the 11 issues of *Behavioral Research in Accounting* from 2010 through early 2015 inclusive reveals that ANOVA is by far the most frequently used statistical approach for hypothesis testing. Of 65 research articles results (rather than literature reviews or commentaries), the authors of 42 articles used ANOVA or its variants (ANCOVA and MANOVA) to analyze results. The next most frequently used statistical approach was structural equation modelling or path analysis.

A complicated world and complex processes are not necessarily well modelled by simplified explanations of direct effects or strictly linear relationships amongst variables. As research progresses, strongly established main effects provide the grounding for studying more complex relationships. Because statistical packages are programmed to code certain values into their statistical test routines, knowing the assumptions underlying ANOVA and regression programs is crucial to correctly interpreting results generated by those programs. Contrast coding allows researchers to change those assumptions by using appropriate coding. We apply contrast coding to several fact situations, working examples showing how contrast coding can be used in either ANOVA or regression to yield equivalent results in terms of explanatory power.

The default ANOVA coding is designed to test most powerfully main effects and a specific disordinal interaction, which assumes that the effect of Variable One increases as the effect of Variable Two decreases. We demonstrate the interaction graphically in Figure 23.1, where observed values are points and cell means are shown with lines. However, interactions are like Proteus; they can assume many forms beyond that one particular pattern. The effect of Variable One could be amplified in the presence of high levels of Variable Two, or it might be diminished. Both variables might have an effect only in the presence of the other. One could imagine many other possible variations.

We begin with a simple 2x2 between subject main effects and an interaction. In the first example, we are interested in whether performance (defined as course points earned) in Financial Accounting is affected by earlier completion of either Microeconomics or Managerial Accounting. We are also interested in any effect of where Microeconomics or Managerial Accounting was completed, i.e., earned with transfer credits or at the same university. The population data would reveal that students completing Microeconomics with transfer credits earn higher Financial Accounting points than do students completing Microeconomics at the university and that students completing Managerial Accounting at the university perform better than students transferring credits. This example demonstrates the default disordinal interaction tested in ANOVA. Figure 23.1 and Table 23.1a show the sample data of 60 students used to test whether the relationship exists. The results of the ANOVA using the data from Table 23.1a are displayed in Table 23.1b. The default coding of ANOVA is shown in Table 23.1c.

The ANOVA results for the sample show no significant main effects for either course completed or where credits were earned (credit type), but do indicate a significant interaction. This is the disordinal interaction that ANOVA is best suited to test, because the default coefficients wired in to ANOVA correlate significantly with the means in the population tested.

While the particular interaction in Figure 23.1 holds with some variables and in some circumstances, many other forms of interactions can occur and are of interest to researchers.

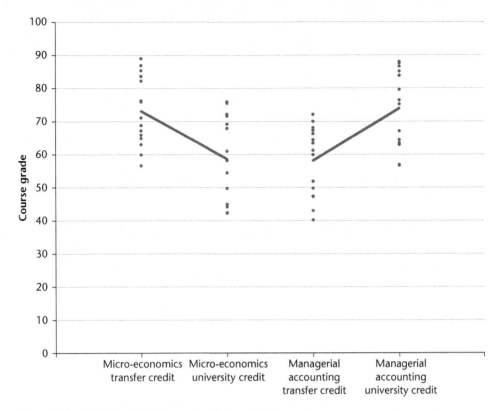

Figure 23.1 2x2 Disordinal interaction (example 1)

Table 23.1a 2x2 Disordinal interaction (example 1)

		Variable Two	
		Transfer credit	University credit
Variable One	Micro-Economics	Average = 73.10 Standard deviation = 10.45 n = 15	Average = 58.63 Standard deviation = 12.64 n = 15
	Managerial Accounting	Average = 58.15 Standard deviation = 10.55 n = 15	Average = 73.93 Standard deviation = 11.23 n = 15

Table 23.1b ANOVA analysis – 2x2 disordinal interaction (example 1) dependent variable: course points earned in Financial Accounting

Independent variable	Sum of squares	DF	Mean square	F-value	Prob.] F
Variable One (Course)	0.45	1	0.45	0.00	0.9598
Variable Two (Where Completed)	6.40	1	6.40	0.04	0.8492
Interaction Effect	3,429.22	1	3,429.22	19.55	0.0000
Error	7,086.12	56	126.54		
R2	0.326555		Omnibus F	9.05	0.0001

Table 23.1c ANOVA – 2x2 default coding

Variable One	
Microeconomics	*Managerial Accounting*
–1	1

Variable Two	
Transfer credit	University credit
–1	1

Interaction	
Microeconomics	Managerial Accounting
Transfer credit	
1	–1
University credit	
–1	1

However, when an interaction that differs structurally from the disordinal interaction in Figure 23.1 is tested using ANOVA, the statistical results can provide ambiguous results. Therefore, a significant interaction statistic is often followed up with more tests of selected means to determine the actual nature of the interaction. Whether that further investigation is done with simple effects tests or with tests of contrasts, probing the interaction post hoc is less powerful and effective and less scientifically rigorous than setting up tests of the actual hypothesized contrasts of theoretical interest in advance, by using contrast coding. Such post hoc exploration can be useful for setting up and designing future research or for exploratory work, but treating data as "supportive" of unpredicted hypotheses is itself usually unsupportable.[3]

The intuition behind the increased power of contrast coding can be demonstrated with a simple thought experiment. Imagine a 2x2x2 study with three variables; the working hypothesis is that subjects receiving a high level of Variable One combined with the high level of Variable Two and low level of Variable Three differ from all the other combinations possible, and those other seven cells tend to be clustered rather closely together. The standard ANOVA uses one degree of freedom to test each of the three main effects, one degree of freedom to test each of the three possible two-way interaction effects and one degree of freedom to test a three-way interaction effect, diffusing the sum of squares across seven tests, decreasing the power of every test and performing tests that are not theoretically interesting. A key to the increased power of contrast coding is (as we noted earlier) that each contrast has one degree of freedom and tests the hypothesized relationship. Therefore, using contrast coding improves power by increasing the sum of squares of the hypothesized relationship. Realizing that some set of contrast coefficients is assumed in any analysis can increase one's comfort in explicitly using coefficients that actually reflect one's theory. Using contrasts also reduces the likelihood that one is testing interactions that are not theoretically supported or motivated by theory. Recent examples of the use of contrast coding in accounting research include Rennekamp (2012) or Tan, Wang and Zhou (2014).[4]

Using the same independent and dependent variables, we provide a second example involving main effects but no interaction, and a third involving a one-cell interaction. Our second example assumes that students completing either Microeconomics or Managerial Accounting at the university perform better than students transferring credits, and that students completing Managerial Accounting perform better than students completing Microeconomics. This example demonstrates the default main effects tested in ANOVA. The sample data are displayed in Table 23.2a and Figure 23.2 and the ANOVA results for the sample are displayed in Table 23.2b. The ANOVA results show a significant main effect for both the course and for where the course was completed and do not show a significant interaction effect; ANOVA is well suited to test for this type of main effect pattern.

In the third example, we assume that students who complete Managerial Accounting at the university perform better than students completing Microeconomics at the university and better than students who completed either course with transfer credits. This example represents a one-cell interaction that is not well suited for testing with a traditional ANOVA. The sample data are displayed in Table 23.3a and Figure 23.3; the results of the ANOVA are displayed in Table 23.3b.

The ANOVA results for the sample show two significant main effects but does not show a significant interaction effect, because the default coding of ANOVA is not designed to test for one-cell interactions (Buckless and Ravenscroft 1990). The default coding of ANOVA (shown in Table 23.1c) for the interaction effect tests whether students completing the Microeconomics course with transfer credit or Managerial Accounting course with university credit perform better compared to students completing Microeconomics with university credit or Managerial Accounting with transfer credit (i.e., the interaction shown in example 1). The hypothesized relationship, however, is that students completing Managerial Accounting at the university will perform better in Financial Accounting than students in all three other conditions, and the performance in all three other conditions will be equivalent. The coding that tests the hypothesized one-cell effect is shown in Table 23.3c, with the results shown in Table 23.3d.

Table 23.2a 2x2 Main effects only (example 2)

		Variable Two	
		Transfer credit	University credit
Variable One	Micro-Economics	Average = 40.39 Standard deviation = 11.73 n = 15	Average = 65.63 Standard deviation = 14.22 n = 15
	Managerial Accounting	Average = 52.33 Standard deviation = 12.57 n = 15	Average = 72.83 Standard deviation = 14.27 n = 15

Table 23.2b ANOVA analysis – 2x2 main effects only (example 2) dependent variable: course points earned in Financial Accounting

Independent variable	Sum of squares	DF	Mean square	F-value	Prob.] F
Variable One (course)	1,373.77	1	1,373.77	7.83	0.0070
Variable Two (where completed)	7,850.13	1	7,850.13	44.76	0.0000
Interaction effect	84.25	1	84.25	0.48	0.4911
Error	9,822.05	56	175.39		
R2	0.486568		Omnibus F	17.69	0.0000

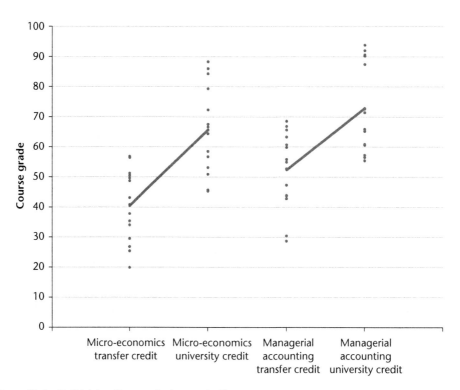

Figure 23.2 2x2 Main effects only (example 2)

Table 23.3a 2x2 One-cell interaction effect (example 3)

		Variable Two	
		Transfer credit	University credit
Variable One	Micro-Economics	Average = 46.79 Standard deviation = 15.39 n = 15	Average = 51.81 Standard deviation = 14.67 n = 15
	Managerial Accounting	Average = 52.00 Standard deviation = 12.92 n = 15	Average = 70.33 Standard deviation = 14.73 n = 15

Table 23.3b ANOVA analysis – 2x2 one-cell interaction effect (example 3) dependent variable: course points earned in Financial Accounting

Independent variable	Sum of squares	DF	Mean square	F-value	Prob.] F
Variable One (course)	2,112.27	1	2,112.27	12.04	0.0010
Variable Two (where completed)	2,046.34	1	2,046.34	11.67	0.0012
Interaction effect	664.00	1	664.00	3.79	0.0567
Error	11,701.05	56	208.95		
R^2	0.291861		Omnibus F	7.69	0.0002

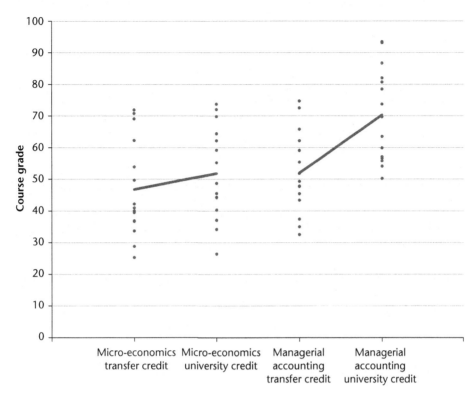

Figure 23.3 2x2 One-cell interaction effect (example 3)

Table 23.3c Model contrast coefficients – 2x2 one-cell interaction effect (example 3)

	Microeconomics	Managerial Accounting
Transfer credit	−1	−1
University credit	−1	3

Table 23.3d Contrast analysis – 2x2 one-cell interaction effect (example 3) dependent variable: course points earned in Financial Accounting

Independent variable	Sum of squares	DF	Mean square	F-value	Prob.] F
Model contrast	4,560.20	1	4,560.20	21.82	0.0000
Between-groups residual	262.41	2	131.20	0.63	0.5326
Error	11,701.05	56	208.95		

The coefficients in Table 23.3c test a one-cell interaction using a one degree of freedom test. The formula for calculating the contrast sum of squares for the one-cell interaction using the cell coding shown in Table 23.3c is as follows:

In Table 23.3d the between-groups residual (portion of between-groups sum of squares not explained by the model contrast) tests whether the other three conditions are statistically equivalent. The contrast analysis supports the expected one-cell interaction results by showing significance for the model contrast and insignificance for the between-groups residual.

Contrast coding can be especially useful (Buckless and Ravenscroft 1990; Rosenthal and Rosnow 1985; Abelson and Prentice 1997) when variables are tested at more than two levels (e.g., Cardinaels and van Veen-Dirks 2010). The greater number of levels allows testing of quadratic or cubic (or higher-order) main or interaction effects, which are further removed from the default coding of ANOVA and therefore less likely to be detected in ANOVA. To illustrate, we use a traditional ANOVA with a 3x2 between-subjects design. For this example, students could have previously completed any of three courses (Macroeconomics, Microeconomics or Managerial Accounting) and earned credits either as transfer students or at the university. In our example, students completing Managerial Accounting perform better than students completing Microeconomics who perform better than students completing Macroeconomics. In addition, students completing courses at the university perform better than students who transfer in their credits. We assume two main effects, one for the prior course and one for where the course was completed. The sample data created for this example are displayed in Table 23.4a and Figure 23.4; the results of the ANOVA displayed in Table 23.4b.

The ANOVA shows a significant main effect for where the course was completed and does not show a significant effect for the course or interaction effect. Traditional ANOVA is not well suited to test for the linear main effect of Variable One as it is an unfocused two degree of freedom test. All means are tested against all other means rather than testing for a particular pattern or relationship among multiple levels of the variable.

Table 23.4a 3x2 Linear main effect (example 4)

		Variable Two	
		Transfer credit	University credit
Variable One	Macro-Economics	Average = 46.46 Standard deviation = 15.05 n = 10	Average = 68.70 Standard deviation = 13.22 n = 10
	Micro-Economics	Average = 51.51 Standard deviation = 13.99 n = 10	Average = 75.30 Standard deviation = 14.40 n = 10
	Managerial Accounting	Average = 57.37 Standard deviation = 10.67 n = 10	Average = 76.39 Standard deviation = 14.97 n = 10

Table 23.4b ANOVA analysis – 3x2 linear main effect (example 4) dependent variable: course points earned in Financial Accounting

Independent variable	Sum of squares	DF	Mean square	F-value	Prob.] F
Variable One (course)	883.31	2	441.65	2.32	0.1081
Variable Two (where completed)	7,052.50	1	7,052.50	37.04	0.0000
Interaction effect	59.21	2	29.60	0.16	0.8564
Error	10,282.70	54	190.42		
R2	0.437419		Omnibus F	8.40	0.0001

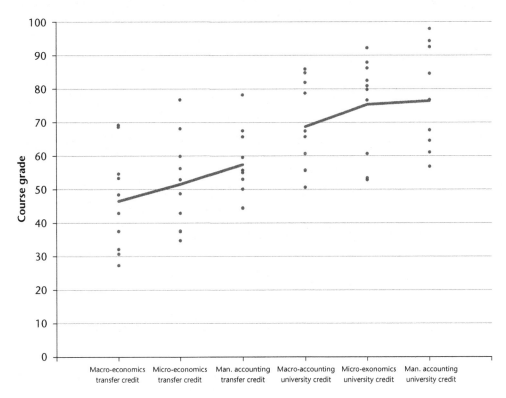

Figure 23.4 3x2 Linear main effect (example 4)

Planned contrasts allow researchers to test a more specific hypothesis than ANOVA does. In this case, we test whether students completing Managerial Accounting perform better than students completing Microeconomics who perform better than students completing Macroeconomics. We also hypothesize that students completing courses at the university perform better than students transferring credits. To show the differences from ANOVA, we present the cell coding for the contrast analysis in Table 23.4c and the results of the contrast analysis in Table 23.4d. The results support the hypothesis that students completing the Managerial Accounting Course perform better than students completing the Microeconomics Course who in turn perform better than students completing the Macroeconomics course. Students completing courses at the university perform better than students completing the courses at other universities. The between-groups residual statistically tests for nonlinear and interaction effects, which are not significant.

These examples illustrate how to apply contrast coding and demonstrate some relationships that contrast coding tests more powerfully than a traditional ANOVA does. For assistance in determining contrast coding coefficients in more complex interactions or with variables of multiple levels, we recommend Rosenthal and Rosnow (1985). Other resources for selecting contrast coding coefficients are Abelson and Prentice (1997) and Rosenthal, Rosnow and Rubin (2000). We look next at a second benefit of contrast coding.

A second benefit of contrast coding – more meaningful effect sizes

A recent article on assessing research provides an extensive checklist of points to consider. The authors (Evans, Feng, Hoffman, Moser and Van Der Stede 2015) twice recommend establishing

Table 23.4c Model contrast coefficients – 3x2 linear effects (example 4)

Variable One		
Macroeconomics	Microeconomics	Managerial Accounting
–1	0	1
Variable Two		
Transfer credit		University credit
–1		1

Table 23.4d Contrast analysis – 3x2 linear main effects (example 4) dependent variable: course points earned in Financial Accounting

Independent variable	Sum of squares	DF	Mean square	F-value	Prob.] F
1st model contrast (course)	864.90	1	864.90	4.54	0.0376
2nd model contrast (where completed)	7,052.50	1	7,052.50	37.04	0.0000
Between-groups residual	77.61	3	25.87	0.14	0.9382
Error	10,282.70	54	190.42		

and providing effect sizes, in both the "Contribution" section and in the "Interpretation of Results" section of accounting academic papers. Effect sizes are critical in evaluating research because p-values alone do not indicate whether an independent variable affects a dependent variable in meaningful or substantive ways. To determine whether a statistically significant result has meaningful import, one must look further. That further investigation can include effect sizes, confidence intervals, Bayesian analyses and meta-analyses (e.g., Abelson 1995; Cumming 2014; Ziliak and McCloskey 2008; Schwab, Abrahamson, Starbuck and Fidler 2011; Kline 2013; Hubbard 2016). Cumming defines an effect size as "an amount of anything of interest. Means, differences between means, frequencies, correlations, and many other familiar quantities are effect sizes (ESs). A p-value, however is *not* an ES" (2014: 15).

Some researchers use R squared as an effect size measure. Given that R squared is a measure of how much variance is explained by various treatments and/or the model, this comports with the ANOVA framework, which is literally the analysis of variance amongst measured variables. The presentation of R squared is helpful as a first step in deciding whether a relationship appears to exist. However, it still leaves unanswered the basic question of how much effect an independent variable or combination of independent variables has on a dependent variable, which is necessary to determine whether the results have meaningful impact, beyond having statistical significance.

Determining effect sizes in ANOVA

Output from a traditional ANOVA provides information on the sum of squares explained by each independent variable, which allows calculation of the incremental R squared associated with each independent variable. The incremental R squared can be calculated by taking the sum of squares associated with each independent variable divided by the total sum of squares. It is a measure of the strength of the association between the dependent and independent measures.

For illustration, using the ANOVA table (Table 23.2b) from the second example above, the incremental R squared for Variable One (course completed) is 0.07, calculated as (1,373.77/[1,373.77 + 7,850.13 +84.25 + 9,822.05]) and the incremental R squared for Variable Two (where the course was completed) is 0.41, calculated as (7,850.13/[1,373.77 + 7,850.13 + 84.25 + 9,822.05]). The incremental R squared calculation indicates that Variable Two (where the credits were earned) explains more of the variance in the dependent variable than Variable One (which prior course was completed).

Incremental R squared indicates whether a large amount of variance relates to a particular variable or interaction, but it does not tell us how much each independent variable impacts the dependent variable, course points earned in this example. In other words, it does not signal how substantively impactful an effect is.

Coding coefficients allow for the calculation of effect sizes that can provide more meaningful comparisons than merely reporting p-values and incremental R squared. We demonstrate effect sizes that provide direct light on the impact value of results. To do so, we use the cell coefficient codings combined with cell means, marginal means, and overall sample mean. We use the second example (Table 23.2a) to calculate effect size with a 2x2 design. The effect size calculation is based on the default ANOVA coefficient codings and the cell averages replicated from Table 23.1c and Table 23.2a in Table 23.5.

The effect size of Variable One (course completed) can be calculated by taking the sum of the second row and subtracting it from the sum of the first row and then dividing by the sum of each cell coefficient coding squared. The cell coefficient codings are shown in Table 23.1c and Table 23.5. The effect size for Variable One (course completed) is 4.79 ([52.33 + 72.83–40.39–65.63]/[1^2 + 1^2 + -1^2 + -1^2]). The effect size of Variable Two (where course completed) can be calculated by taking the sum of the second column and subtracting it from the sum of the first column and then dividing by four (the sum of the squared cell coefficient codings). The effect size for Variable Two (where course was completed) is 11.44 ([65.63 + 72.83–40.39–52.33]/[1^2 + 1^2 + -1^2 + -1^2]). The dependent variable of points in Financial Accounting has a maximum possible score of 100. The effect size tells us that students transferring credits from other universities earn 11.44 fewer points than the overall average for the Financial Accounting course and students completing the courses at the university earn 11.44 more points than the overall average. Likewise, students completing the Microeconomics course perform 4.79 points below the overall average for the Financial Accounting course and students completing the Managerial Accounting course earn 4.79 points more than the overall average. These effect sizes provide more information in determining future pre-requirement rules for the Financial Accounting course than p-values would.

Table 23.5 2x2 Main effects only (abbreviated Table 23.2a – example 2)

		Variable Two	
		Transfer credit	University credit
Variable One	Micro-Economics	Average = 40.39	Average = 65.63
		Course coefficient = –1	Course coefficient = –1
		University coefficient = –1	University coefficient = 1
	Managerial Accounting	Average = 52.33	Average = 72.83
		Course coefficient = 1	Course coefficient = 1
		University coefficient = –1	University coefficient = 1

When there are only two levels and equal observations in each cell the calculated effect size tells us how much a specific cell mean or average differs from the overall sample mean or average. The effect size calculation and interpretation are more complicated when an independent variable is tested at more than two levels or when a researcher hypothesizes relationships other than main effects or disordinal interactions. Effect sizes with orthogonal coding[5] and more than two levels represent weighted contrasts between-group means or averages. More generally, the formula to calculate the effect size with orthogonal coding can be written as follows:

$$Effect\ Size = \frac{\sum_{i=1}^{\#\ of\ Cells}\left(Cell\ Average_i\ x\ Cell\ Coding_i\right)}{\sum_{i=1}^{\#\ of\ Cells}\left(Cell\ Coding_i\right)^2}$$

Example three (Table 23.3a) will be used to illustrate the calculation of effect sizes with orthogonal contrast coefficients. Table 23.6 is an abbreviated form of the earlier Table 23.3a that also includes the cell coefficient codings shown in Table 23.3c. Based on the one-cell interaction coding the effect size is 5.03 ([46.79(-1) + 51.81(-1) + 52.00(-1) + 70.33(3)]/[-1² + -1² + -1² + 3²]). The effect size for this example tells us that students completing Managerial Accounting at the university earn 15.10 (5.033 × 3)[6] more points than the overall average for the Financial Accounting course.[7] Likewise, students in the other three cells on average earn 5.03 (5.033 × -1) fewer points than the overall average for Financial Accounting.[8]

The cell averages from the fourth example (Table 23.4a) can be used to calculate the effect size with a 3x2 design. The effect size calculation is based on the orthogonal coding and the cell averages replicated from Table 23.4c and Table 23.4b in Table 23.7. The linear effect size for the

Table 23.6 2x2 One-cell interaction effect (abbreviated Table 23.3a – example 3)

		Variable Two	
		Transfer credit	University credit
Variable One	Micro-Economics	Average = 46.79 One-cell interaction = –1	Average = 51.81 One-cell interaction = –1
	Managerial Accounting	Average = 52.00 One-cell interaction = –1	Average = 70.33 One-cell interaction = 3

Table 23.7 3x2 Linear main effect (based on Table 23.4b – example 4)

		Variable Two	
		Transfer credit	University credit
Variable One	Macro-Economics	Average = 46.46 Course coefficient = –1 University coefficient = –1	Average = 68.70 Course coefficient = –1 University coefficient = 1
	Micro-Economics	Average = 51.51 Course coefficient = 0 University coefficient = –1	Average = 75.30 Course coefficient = 0 University coefficient = 1
	Managerial Accounting	Average = 57.37 Course coefficient = 1 University coefficient = –1	Average = 76.39 Course coefficient = 1 University coefficient = 1

course completed would be calculated as follows: $([46.46(-1) + 51.51(0) + 57.37(1) + 68.70(-1) + 75.30(0) + 76.39(1)]/[-1^2 + 0^2 + 1^2 + -1^2 + 0^2 + 1^2]) = 4.65$. The interpretation of this effect size is that a student completing Macroeconomics performs 4.65 points below the combined average points earned in Financial Accounting for students completing Macroeconomics and Managerial Accounting and a student completing Managerial Accounting performs 4.65 points above the combined average points earned in Financial Accounting for students completing Macroeconomics and Managerial Accounting.[9] Notice that the effect size for this scenario with a variable with three levels compares how students completing Macroeconomics or Managerial Accounting differ from the combined average for those two groups, rather than comparing to the overall sample average. When there are more than two levels the effect size will not always represent a difference from the overall sample mean; thus researchers must make sure the effect size calculation is relevant for their tests and hypotheses.

Because only two groups exist for where credits are earned, only a linear main effect is possible. The linear effect size for where credits were earned is calculated as follows: $([46.46(-1) + 68.70(1) + 51.51(-1) + 75.30(1) + 57.37(-1) + 76.39(1)]/[-1^2 + 1^2 + -1^2 + 1^2 + -1^2 + 1^2]) = 10.84$. The interpretation of this effect size is that a student transferring credits earns 10.84 fewer points than the overall average points earned in Financial Accounting and a student completing credits at the university earns 10.84 points above the overall sample average.[10]

Contrast coding and regression analysis

Behavioural researchers most often use ANOVA in part because such research typically involves fixed-effect manipulated variables, which are tested at selected levels. Regression is routinely used when variables are measured rather than manipulated, most typically in archival research. However, when regression analysis is used in behavioural research, planned contrasts can be applied. Regression coding does have advantages over ANOVA because of the direct and intuitive interpretation of regression coefficients as the practical significance of statistically significant results. Determining effect sizes is more easily done using regression rather than ANOVA. We therefore extend our discussion of contrast coding from its typical ANOVA setting to demonstrate how to apply it using regression analysis. The regression coefficients and standard errors directly enable some informal calculations of the statistical "surprise" level of the findings, helpful in determining substantive significance. They also provide a rather quick and easy test of whether the results will pass the 0.05 alpha level. One determines whether the coefficient is double or greater the standard error, a figure which is usually provided in standard statistical packages (such as SPSS, SAS and R). Regression analysis lends itself to testing planned contrasts using different coding schemes, including dummy coding, orthogonal coding and effect coding.

Regression analysis commonly involves dummy coding, in which fixed-effect independent variables and covariates are coded as zero or one. One result of this coding pattern is often overlooked; regression coefficients (if unstandardized) indicate the extent to which a change in an independent variable affects the dependent variable compared to the mean of the cell that was coded with all zeros, because the mean of the zero-coded cell is the intercept in standard regression analysis. That cell may or may not be of particular interest, but whether a difference is considered significant turns on whether and to what extent other cell means differ from that particular cell mean. Also the regression coefficients represent differences from the zero-coded cell instead of differences from the overall sample mean. This type of coding would be useful, for instance, when there is a control group receiving no treatments and researchers want to know the effect of different experimental treatments compared to the designated control (baseline) group.

Continuing with the second example of main effects only (Table 23.2a) we provide the regression output based on dummy coding in Table 23.8a. Notice that the R squared is identical to that of Table 23.2b and that the intercept equals the average for students who completed Microeconomics at another university. However, the p-values differ, because the current test shows whether each of the other three groups singly and individually differ from the average of students who completed Microeconomics at another university, i.e., the group designated as the baseline in this instance.

Compared to that baseline group, students completing Microeconomics at the University earn 11.94 more points on average; students completing Managerial Accounting at another university earn 25.25 more points on average; and students completing Managerial Accounting at the university earn 32.45 more points on average.[11] When researchers are interested in testing other comparisons among the cells, another coding scheme should be used.

While we have been using orthogonal coding in our earlier ANOVA examples, readers may be familiar with the concept of effect coding in regression analysis. When there are only two levels for any independent variable, effect coding and orthogonal coding are identical, as the coding is -1 for one level and 1 for the other level for each independent variable. Effect and orthogonal coding differ, however, when there are more than two levels of the independent variable, because orthogonal coding will assign coding values other than -1, 0 or 1. With effect coding there will be (g − 1) independent variables where g represents the number of groups or cells. One group is assigned -1 for all independent variables and is not tested against the overall sample average. A separate independent variable is included for each group or cell where 1 is assigned for the group which that independent variable is measuring and 0 for the other groups or cells included as independent variables. When cell sizes are equal, effect coding tests whether each of the (g − 1) group averages differs from the overall sample average. This type of coding would be useful, for instance, when there is a control group receiving no treatments and researchers want

Table 23.8a (Based on Table 23.2a) Regression analysis – 2x2 main effects only (example 2) dummy coding dependent variable: course points earned in Financial Accounting

Independent variable	Coefficient	Std. error	t-statistic	Prob.> |t|
Intercept (Microeconomics at other university)	40.39	3.419	33.54	0.0000
Microeconomics at university	11.94	4.836	2.46	0.0166
Managerial Accounting at other university	25.25	4.836	5.22	0.0000
Managerial Accounting at university	32.45	4.836	6.71	0.0000
R2	0.486568			

Table 23.8b (Based on Table 23.2a) Regression analysis – 2x2 main effects only (example 2) – default ANOVA orthogonal coding dependent variable: course points earned in Financial Accounting

Independent variable	Coefficient	Std. error	t-statistic	Prob.> |t|
Intercept	57.80	1.709	33.80	0.0000
Variable One (course)	4.79	1.709	2.80	0.0070
Variable Two (where completed)	11.44	1.709	6.69	0.0000
Interaction Effect	(1.19)	1.709	0.69	0.4911
R2	0.486568			

to know the effect of different experimental treatments compared to the overall sample average. Again, the coding schemes that we previously used in our examples before the regression discussion were orthogonal. Similar to effect coding when the cell sizes are equal, the intercept with orthogonal coding equals the overall sample average.[12]

Continuing with the second example previously discussed (Table 23.2a), we provide the regression output in Table 23.8b based on the default ANOVA orthogonal coding presented in Table 23.1c. Notice that the p-values are identical to the p-values reported in Table 23.2b for the respective independent variables and interaction effect. Also notice that the R squared is identical with that of Table 23.2b. When orthogonal coding with two levels for each independent variable and equal cell sizes is used the intercept coefficient equals the overall average for the dependent variable and the independent variable coefficients equal the average difference of each variable from the overall sample average. The coefficient values reported in the regression results in Table 23.8b represent the effect sizes and are identical to the effect sizes calculated in the discussion of contrast effect sizes in Table 23.5.

The third example involving a one-cell interaction (Table 23.3a) provides the regression results with contrast coding reported in Table 23.9.[13] Showing the equivalence of ANOVA and regression in this situation, the R squared is identical with that of Table 23.3b and the p-value for Managerial Accounting completed at the university compared to the other three cells is identical to that for Table 23.3d. The effect size for the one-cell interaction is also identical to the effect size calculated in the previous discussion of Table 23.6.

Next, we illustrate regression analysis and orthogonal coding for the fourth previous example (Table 23.4a), which includes three levels of previously completed courses (Macroeconomics, Microeconomics and Managerial Accounting) and two levels of where completed (transfer credit and university credit). Again, for variables with more than two levels, regression coefficients with orthogonal coding represent the weighted contrasts between-group averages. The data used in this analysis are the same as those in Table 23.4a and Figure 23.4; the complete set of orthogonal codings for this example is in Table 23.10a; and the regression results are presented in Table 23.10b. The actual relationship is that students completing Managerial Accounting perform better than students completing Microeconomics, who perform better than students completing Macroeconomics. Additionally, students completing courses at the university perform better than students transferring their credits. This example assumes two main effects, one for the course and one for where the course was completed.

Notice that we present separate p-values for the linear and quadratic effects. Because there are three courses, the relationship among the courses could take many forms such as a linear or quadratic. The coefficient coding should be assigned based on the expected relationship. Also notice

Table 23.9 (Based on Table 23.3a) Regression analysis – 2x2 one-cell interaction (example 3) – contrast coding dependent variable: course points earned in Financial Accounting

Independent variable	Coefficient	Std. error	t-statistic	Prob.> |t|
Intercept	55.23	1.866	29.60	0.0000
Managerial Accounting at university compared to other three cells	5.03	1.077	4.67	0.0000
Managerial Accounting transferred in compared to Microeconomics at university or transferred	0.90	1.524	0.53	0.5571
Microeconomics at university compared to Microeconomics transferred	2.51	2.639	0.95	0.3450
R2	0.291861			

Table 23.10a 3x2 Orthogonal coding

Variable One

		Macro-Economics	Micro-Economics	Managerial Accounting
Linear		−1	0	1
Quadratic		−1	2	−1

Variable Two

	Transfer credit	University credit
	−1	1

Interaction

		Macroeconomics	Microeconomics	Managerial Accounting
Transfer	Linear	1	0	−1
credit	Linear	−1	0	1
University	Quadratic	1	−2	1
credit	Quadratic	1	2	−1

Table 23.10b (Based on Table 23.4a and Figure 23.4) Regression analysis – 3x2 linear main effect – orthogonal coding dependent variable: course points earned in Financial Accounting

Independent Variable	Coefficient	Std. Error	t-statistic	Prob. > $|t|$
Intercept	62.62	1.781	35.15	0.0000
Variable One (course)				
Linear	4.65	2.181	2.13	0.0376
Quadratic	0.39	1.259	0.31	0.7571
Variable Two (where completed)	10.84	1.781	6.09	0.0000
Interaction effect				
Linear	(0.81)	2.181	(0.37)	0.7136
Quadratic	0.53	1.259	0.42	0.6775
$R2$	0.437419			

that the R squared is identical to that in Table 23.4b. Again, with orthogonal coding and equal cell sizes the intercept coefficient equals the overall average for the dependent variable and the independent variable coefficients equal the weighted contrasts between-group averages. As with the previous two examples the coefficient values for Variable One (Course – Linear) and Variable Two (Where Completed) are identical to the effect sizes calculated in the previous discussion of the results in Table 23.7.

Contrast coding in ANCOVA

Analysis of Covariance (ANCOVA) increases statistical power by incorporating a covariate, a continuous variable with a linear relationship to the dependent variable that reduces experimental error and thus increases the power of the experiment. ANCOVA also adjusts the estimates of the effect of the categorical independent variables for the effect of the covariate on the dependent variable. To demonstrate the use of ANCOVA, we continue with the initial example previously discussed. The categorical independent variables for this example are Microeconomics or

Managerial Accounting (Variable One) and whether the courses were completed at the university or transferred (Variable Two). We add as covariate a continuous variable, an assessment of financial accounting knowledge completed the first day of class.

We assume financial accounting knowledge is assessed on a 10-point scale and that such prior knowledge has a linear relationship with the dependent variable, i.e., performance in Financial Accounting. The actual relationship is that students completing either Microeconomics or Managerial Accounting at the university perform better than students completing the courses at another university. Additionally, students completing Managerial Accounting perform better than students completing Microeconomics. The data created for this example are displayed in Table 23.11a, Figure 23.5a, Figure 23.5b and Figure 23.5c.

ANOVA results for the sample are presented in Table 23.11b, showing a significant main effect for where the course was completed but not for the course or the interaction effect. The R squared for this analysis is 0.13 indicating a substantial amount of the sums of square is not explained by the two independent variables. Because of the large experimental error, the ANOVA analysis does not identify the relationships that actually exist.

Table 23.11a 2x2 Covariate with main effects only

Panel A: course points earned in Financial Accounting

		Variable Two	
		Transfer credit	University credit
Variable One	Micro-Economics	Average = 53.80 Standard deviation = 10.96 n = 15	Average = 64.25 Standard deviation = 9.97 n = 15
	Managerial Accounting	Average = 61.36 Standard deviation = 10.74 n = 15	Average = 62.23 Standard Deviation = 11.16 n = 15

Panel B: course points earned adjusted for the covariate

		Variable Two	
		Transfer credit	University credit
Variable One	Micro-Economics	Average = 53.45 Standard deviation = 6.30 n = 15	Average = 62.20 Standard deviation = 8.12 n = 15
	Managerial Accounting	Average = 61.29 Standard deviation = 5.89 n = 15	Average = 64.71 Standard deviation = 11.32 n = 15

Panel C: assessment of Financial Accounting knowledge (covariate)

		Variable Two	
		Transfer credit	University credit
Variable One	Micro-Economics	Average = 7.73 Standard deviation = 1.62 n = 15	Average = 8.13 Standard deviation = 1.41 n = 15
	Managerial Accounting	Average = 7.67 Standard deviation = 1.80 n = 15	Average = 7.07 Standard deviation = 1.67 n = 15

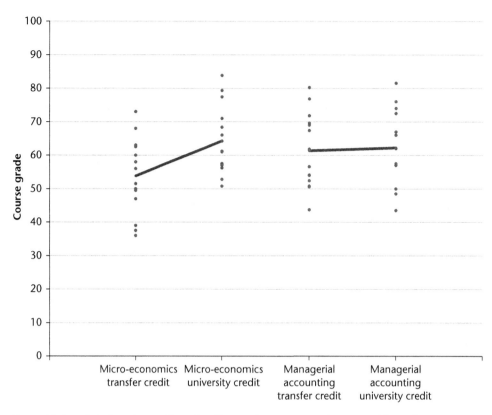

Figure 23.5a   2x2 Covariate with main effects only – course points earned by cell

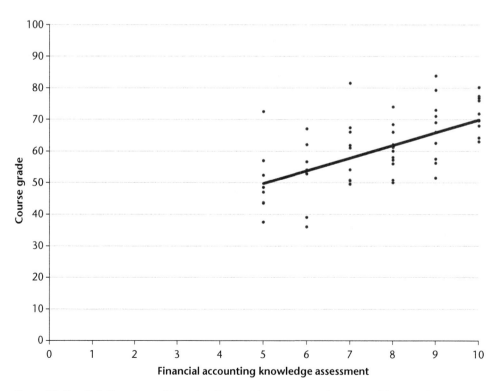

Figure 23.5b   2x2 Covariate with main effects only – course points earned by covariate

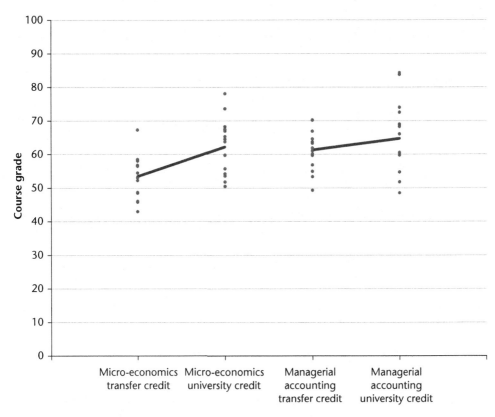

Figure 23.5c 2x2 Covariate with main effects only – course points earned adjusted for covariate

Table 23.11b ANOVA – 2x2 covariate with main effects only dependent variable: course points earned in Financial Accounting

Independent variable	Sum of squares	DF	Mean square	F- value	Prob. >F
Variable One (course)	115.09	1	115.09	1.00	0.3212
Variable Two (where completed)	481.10	1	481.10	4.19	0.0454
Interaction effect	344.16	1	344.16	3.00	0.0890
Error	6,433.13	56	114.88		
R2	0.127532		Omnibus F	1.73	0.0525

Table 23.11c ANCOVA – 2x2 covariate with main effects only dependent variable: course points earned in Financial Accounting

Independent variable	Sum of squares	DF	Mean square	F- value	Prob. >F
Covariate (knowledge assessment)	2,675.62	1	2,675.62	39.16	0.0000
Variable One (course)	388.65	1	388.65	5.69	0.0205
Variable Two (where completed)	555.25	1	555.25	8.13	0.0061
Interaction effect	104.36	1	104.36	1.53	0.2217
Error	3,757.51	55	68.32		
R2	0.490403		Omnibus F	5.11	0.0034

The ANCOVA results for the sample are presented in Table 23.11c. The ANCOVA shows a significant effect for the covariate, a significant main effect for the course, and a significant main effect for where the course was completed. Because of the reduction in the experimental error and the adjustment of the dependent variable for the impact of the covariate, both main effects are now significant and the R squared increased to 0.49. The ANCOVA analysis does not show a significant interaction effect.

Caveats

> *The emphasis on significance levels tends to obscure a fundamental distinction between the size of an effect and its statistical significance.*
>
> (Tversky and Kahneman 1971: 110)

To non-statisticians the variety of opinions about various statistical techniques and the vigour and wit with which divergent and sometimes directly conflicting positions are promoted can be an entertaining and thought-provoking surprise. Contrast coding, like other statistical "truths" has its detractors and its skeptics, who do not totally decry the approach, but offer some caveats regarding its application. The reader is referred to *Psychological Science* (Abelson 1996; Petty, Fabrigar, Wegener and Priester 1996; Rosnow and Rosenthal 1996) for a forum-type discussion which warrants careful reading about concerns and possible misapplications of contrast coding. To summarize very briefly, these authors reiterate that researchers should think carefully beforehand about which relationships they are testing, taking particular care to avoid treating a simple effect as a contrast of some more complex sort. What one hopes to find is that the R squared of a contrast is significant and the residual R squared is not. Rosnow and Rosenthal respond to Abelson's concern that contrast coding may be "too flexible" by countering that there may be more than one right answer (1996: 256) when doing research about complex phenomena. However, the liveliness of this discussion pales when considering the passion with which the general null hypothesis testing framework is discussed, excoriated, defended and debated. For more discussion of the general null hypothesis testing framework debate and resulting focus on p-values, see Cohen (1995); Hunter (1997); Kline (2013); Schwab et al. (2011) and Ziliak and McCloskey (2008). Other helpful resources are on this topic are listed in Appendix Two.

Conclusion

Contrast coding offers two general advantages to researchers over the general, unfocused Omnibus F-tests or default main and interaction effects tested in ANOVA. Contrast coding provides increased power and tests the actual relationship of interest, rather than testing an unspecified difference among several means. We began by reviewing the use of contrast coding as a way to increase statistical power and to provide approaches to determining effect size when using contrast coding. We also demonstrate how contrast coding can be used in regression analysis, which lends itself more easily to providing effect sizes, giving it an advantage over ANOVA in this regard at least. Finally, we look briefly at contrast coding in ANCOVA.

Contrast coding will not in and of itself allow researchers to avoid the conflation of statistical significance with a meaningful, substantive import. Nor does the use of contrast coding imply that researchers using null hypothesis testing frameworks create null hypotheses that are of interest and present credible alternatives. Those two issues must be addressed separately and are discussed in Chapter 21 of this volume.

Notes

1 We use the phrase 'contrast coding' as synonymous with 'contrast analysis' and 'planned contrasts'.
2 As accounting researchers rather than trained statisticians, we shall be providing guidance, illustrative examples and caveats, rather than breaking new statistical ground.
3 The derogatory acronym HARKing refers to the practice of Hypothesizing After Results are Known.
4 An expanded (but by no means exhaustive) list of academic accounting articles in which contrast coding is used is included as Appendix One.
5 Orthogonal coding, which we have been using throughout the paper, refers to coding schemes in which the independent variables are uncorrelated. In orthogonal coding the sum of the coded cell coefficients for any independent variable equals zero, and the sum of the cross products of the coded cell coefficients for all the independent variables also equals zero.
6 Since the effect size represents the weighted contrast of the Managerial Accounting at the university cell to the other three cells, the effect size must be multiplied by 3 to determine how much that cell differs from the overall sample mean.
7 The overall average for this example is 55.23 points ([(46.79 × 15) + (51.81 × 15) + (52.00 × 15) + (70.33 × 15)]/[15 + 15 + 15 +15]). The cell mean for completing the Managerial Accounting course at the university is 70.33 and the difference between the cell mean and the overall average is 15.10.
8 The overall average for students in these three cells is 50.20 points ([(46.79 × 15) + (51.81 × 15) + (52.00 × 15)]/[15 + 15 + 15]). The difference between this average and the overall average of 52.23 is 5.03.
9 The overall average for students in the Macroeconomics and Managerial Accounting cells is 62.23 ([(46.46 × 10) + (68.70 × 10) + (57.37 × 10) + (76.39 × 10)]/[10 + 10 + 10 + 10]). The average for students completing Macroeconomics is 57.58 ([(46.46 × 10) + (68.70 × 10)]/[10 + 10]) and the difference between this average and the combined average for Macroeconomics and Managerial accounting is 4.65. Likewise, the average for students completing Managerial Accounting is 66.88 ([(57.37 × 10) + (76.39 × 10)]/[10 + 10]) and the difference between this average and the combined average for Macroeconomics and Managerial Accounting is 4.65.
10 The overall average for this example is 62.62 ([(46.46 × 10) + (68.70 × 10) + (51.51 × 10) + (75.30 × 10) + (57.37 × 10) + (76.39 × 10)]/[10 + 10 + 10 + 10 + 10 + 10]). The average for students transferring credits is 51.78 ([(46.46 × 10) + (51.51 × 10) + (57.37 × 10)]/[10 + 10 + 10]) and the difference between this average and the overall average is 10.84. Likewise, the average for students completing credits at the university is 73.46 ([(68.70 × 10) + (75.30 × 10) + (75.20 × 10)]/[10 + 10 + 10]) and the difference between this average and the overall average is 10.84.
11 The average for students completing Microeconomics at the University is 52.33 and the difference between this average and the average for students completing Microeconomics at another university is 11.94. Likewise, the average for students completing Managerial Accounting at another university is 65.63 and the difference between this average and the average for students completing Microeconomics at another university is 25.25. Finally, the average for students completing Managerial Accounting at the university is 72.83 and the difference between this average and the average for students completing Microeconomics at another university is 32.45.
12 As we previously noted, with orthogonal coding and more than two levels, effect sizes (regression coefficients) represent weighted contrasts between-group means or averages and will not always represent a difference from the overall sample mean or average.
13 The overall sample average for this example is 57.80 points ([(40.39 × 15) + (65.63 × 15) + (52.33 × 15) + (72.83 × 15)]/[15 + 15 + 15 +15]).
14 The complete set of orthogonal contrast coding coefficients used for the regression analysis in Table 23.9 is:

	Transfer credit	University credit
Macroeconomics	Contrast One = −1 Contrast Two = −1 Contrast Three = −1	Contrast One = −1 Contrast Two = −1 Contrast Three = 1
Managerial Accounting	Contrast One = −1 Contrast Two = 2 Contrast Three = 0	Contrast One = 3 Contrast Two = 0 Contrast Three = 0

References

Abelson, R.P., 1995, *Statistics as Principled Argument*, Lawrence Erlbaum Associates, Hillsdale, NJ.

Abelson, R.P., 1996, 'Vulnerability of contrast tests to simpler interpretations: An addendum to Rosnow and Rosenthal', *Psychological Science* 7(4), 242–246.

Abelson, R.P. and Prentice, D.A., 1997, 'Contrast tests of interaction hypotheses', *Psychological Methods* 2(4), 315–328.

Buckless, F.A. and Ravenscroft, S.P., 1990, 'Contrast coding: A refinement of ANOVA in behavioral analysis', *The Accounting Review* 65(4), 933–945.

Cardinaels, E. and van Veen-Dirks, P.M.C., 2010, 'Financial versus non-financial information: The impact of information organization and presentation in a balanced scorecard', *Accounting, Organizations and Society* 35, 565–578.

Cohen, J., 1995, 'The earth is round (p <.05)', *American Psychologist* 49(12), 997–1003.

Cumming, G., 2012, *Understanding the New Statistics: Effect Sizes, Confidence Intervals, and Meta-Analysis*, Routledge, New York.

Cumming, G., 2014, 'The new statistics: Why and how', *Psychological Science* 25(1), 7–29.

Evans, J.H. III, Feng, M., Hoffman, V.B., Moser, D.V. and Van Der Stede, W.A., 2015, 'Points to consider when self-assessing your empirical accounting research', *Contemporary Accounting Research* 32(3), 1162–1192.

Hubbard, R., 2016, *Corrupt Research: The Case for Reconceptualizing Empirical Management and Social Science*, Sage Publications, Thousand Oaks, CA.

Hunter, J.E., 1997, 'Needed: A ban on the significance test', *Psychological Science* 8(1), 1–7.

Kline, R.B. 2013, *Beyond Significance Testing: Statistics Reform in the Behavioral Sciences* (2nd ed.), American Psychological Association, Washington, DC.

McShane, B.B. and Gal, D., 2016, 'Blinding us to the obvious? The effect of statistical training on the evaluation of evidence', *Management Science* 62(6), 1707–1718.

Petty, R.E., Fabrigar, L.R., Wegener, D.T. and Priester, J.R., 1996, 'Understanding data when interactions are present or hypothesized', *Psychological Science* 7(4), 247–252.

Rennekamp, K., 2012, 'Processing fluency and investors' reactions to disclosure readability', *Journal of Accounting Research* 50(5), 1319–1354.

Rosenthal, R. and Rosnow, R.L., 1985, *Contrast Analysis: Focused Comparisons in the Analysis of Variance*, Cambridge University Press, Cambridge, UK.

Rosenthal, R., Rosnow, R.L. and Rubin, D.B., 2000, *Contrasts and Effect Sizes in Behavioral Research: A Correlational Approach*, Cambridge University Press, Cambridge, UK.

Rosnow, R.L. and Rosenthal, R., 1996, 'Contrasts and interactions redux: Five easy pieces', *Psychological Science* 7(4), 253–257.

Schwab, A., Abrahamson, E., Starbuck, W.H. and Fidler, F., 2011, 'Researchers should make thoughtful assessments instead of null-hypothesis significance test', *Organization Science* 22(4), 1105–1120.

Tan, H.-T., Wang, E.Y. and Zhou, B., 2014, 'When the use of positive language backfires: The joint effect of tone, readability and investor sophistication on earnings judgments', *Journal of Accounting Research* 52(1), 273–302.

Tversky, A. and Kahneman, D., 1971, 'Belief in the law of small numbers', *Psychological Bulletin* 76(2), 105–110.

Ziliak, S.T. and McCloskey, D.N., 2008, *The Cult of Statistical Significance: How the Standard Error Costs Us Jobs, Justice and Lives*, University of Michigan Press, Ann Arbor.

Appendix One

Selected articles using planned contrasts

Bailey, W. J., Hecht, G. and Towry, K. L., 2011, 'Dividing the pie: The influence of managerial discretion extent on bonus pool allocation', *Contemporary Accounting Research* 28(5), 1562–1584.

Borthick, A. F., Curtis, M. B. and Sriram, R. S., 2006, 'Accelerating the acquisition of knowledge structure to improve performance in internal control reviews', *Accounting, Organizations and Society* 31(4–5), 323–342.

Cardinaels, E. and van Veen-Dirks, P.M.C., 2010, 'Financial versus non-financial information: The impact of information organization and presentation in a balanced scorecard', *Accounting, Organizations and Society* 35: 565–578.

Elliott, W. B., Krische S. D. and Peecher, M. E., 2010, 'Expected mispricing: The joint influence of accounting transparency and investor base', *Journal of Accounting Research* 48(2), 343–381.

Hannan, R. L., McPhee, G. P. and Newman, A. H., 2012, 'The effect of relative performance information on performance and effort allocation in a multi-task environment', *The Accounting Review* 88(2), 553–575.

Hoffman, V. B. and Zimbelman, M. F., 2009. 'Do strategic reasoning and brainstorming help auditors change their standard audit procedures in response to fraud risk?', *The Accounting Review* 84(3), 811–837.

Joe, J. R. and Vandervelde, S. D., 2007, 'Do auditor-provided nonaudit services improve audit effectiveness?', *Contemporary Accounting Research* 24(2), 467–487.

Khim, K., 2010, 'The effects of incentives on information exchange and decision quality in groups', *Behavioral Research in Accounting* 22(1), 43–66.

Rennekamp, K., 2012, 'Processing fluency and investors' reactions to disclosure readability', *Journal of Accounting Research* 50(5), 1319–1354.

Seyfert, N., 2010, 'RandD capitalization and reputation-driven real earnings management', *The Accounting Review* 85(2), 671–693.

Tafkov, I. D., 2013, 'Private and public relative performance information under different compensation contracts', *The Accounting Review* 88(1), 327–350.

Tan, H-T, Wang, E.Y. and Zhou, B., 2014, 'When the use of positive language backfires: The joint effect of tone, readability and investor sophistication on earnings judgments', *Journal of Accounting Research* 52(1), 273–302.

Appendix Two

Additional articles on hypothesis testing

Anderson, D. R., Burnham, K. P. and Thompson, W. L., 2000, 'Null hypothesis testing: Problems, prevalence, and an alternative', *Journal of Wildlife Management* 64(4), 912–923.

Berkson, J., 1942, 'Tests of significance considered as evidence', *Journal of the American Statistical Association* 37, 325–335.

Cohen, J., 1990, 'Things I have learned (So far)', *American Psychologist* 45(12), 1304–1312.

Gigerenzer, G., 2004, 'Mindless statistics', *The Journal of Socio-Economics* 33, 587–606.

Greenwald, A. G., Gonzalez, R., Harris, R. J. and Guthrie, D., 1996, 'Effect sizes and p values: What should be reported and what should be replicated?', *Psychophysiology* 33, 175–183.

Nickerson, R. S., 1999, 'Statistical significance testing: Useful tool or bone-headedly misguided procedure?', *Journal of Mathematical Psychology* 43, 455–471.

24

Moderation and mediation in Behavioural Accounting Research

Ian Burt and Clark Hampton

Introduction

Moderation and mediation relationships are frequently hypothesized and tested in accounting behavioural research. At their core both moderation and mediation attempt to explain the effect of an additional variable on the independent and dependent variable relationship. In this chapter, we provide an overview and discussion of moderation, mediation and moderated mediation. For each of these relationships, we first define key terms and associations. Next, we provide an introduction to the different approaches and procedures used for testing and analysis, noting issues to consider. Throughout we provide references for researchers seeking more information as well as relevant examples from accounting behavioural research.

Before proceeding, we note two points. First, our discussion of moderation, mediation and moderated mediation uses both path diagrams and regression equations. For all path diagrams and regression equations, X is the independent variable, Y is the dependent variable, MO is a moderator variable and ME is a mediator variable. Equation intercepts and residuals are denoted as i and ε, respectively. Variable coefficients in equations and path diagrams are represented by lowercase italicized letters. Second, while we introduce and briefly discuss the primary methodological assumptions specific to the estimation of moderation, mediation and moderated mediation models, we do not review the methodological assumptions of regression, analysis of variance and structural equation modelling procedures used to estimate these models. However, these assumptions are critical and should be evaluated prior to estimating moderating or mediating relationships. Regression, analysis of variance and structural equation modelling assumptions are discussed in most graduate level statistics textbooks such as Tabachnick and Fidell (2013) and Hair, Black, Babin and Anderson (2009).

Moderation

Definition

A moderator is a qualitative or quantitative variable that affects the strength and/or direction of the relationship between the independent and dependent variables. Moderation addresses the

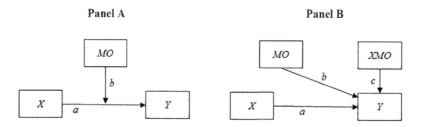

Figure 24.1　Conceptual (Panel A) and statistical estimation (Panel B) moderation model

question of when or for whom certain effects will hold (Baron and Kenny 1986; Frazier, Tix and Barron 2004). The terms moderation and interaction are used interchangeably within accounting behavioural research. However, moderation implies a theoretical basis for the assignment of independent and moderator variables, while interaction does not. Thus, all moderation effects are interactions, but not all interactions can be classified as moderation effects.

Figure 24.1 presents a conceptual (Panel A) and statistical estimation (Panel B) path diagram of a moderation model.

The statistical model in Figure 24.1 Panel B expressed as an equation is

$$Y = i + aX + bMO + cXMO + \varepsilon \tag{1},$$

where XMO, the interaction term, is the product of the independent variable, X, and the moderator variable, MO. A key assumption of Equation 1 is independence (i.e., no causal relationship) between the independent variable X and the moderator variable MO. The general test of moderation is a significant interaction coefficient, c, signifying X varies in magnitude and/or direction as a function of MO. In short, MO moderates the form of the relationship between X and the dependent variable, Y. Graphically, the moderating effect can be seen as the variation in the slope of the regression line of Y and X.

Regardless of the statistical procedure used, moderation tests typically exhibit low power. Aguinis, Boik and Pierce (2001) find that the power to detect an interaction effect is around 0.20 to 0.34 – much lower than the recommended level of 0.80 for independent variables. Consideration of the expected effect size is critical to ensure a sufficient sample is collected that enables detection of the potential moderating effect. Frazier et al. (2004) provide a discussion of other key issues relevant to detecting a moderating effect.

Moderation testing approaches

There are three widely used procedures for testing moderator effects, each of which can be adapted, to varying degrees, to facilitate different data types or research designs. These include moderated multiple regression, analysis of variance and structural equations modelling.

Moderated multiple regression

Bisbe and Otley (2004) use moderated multiple regression (MMR) to investigate the effects of innovation, moderated by management control system style of use, on performance. MMR uses hierarchical regression to evaluate the interaction term. In step 1, Equation 1 is estimated without the interaction term, XMO. Step 2 re-estimates Equation 1 with the interaction term, XMO, included. Confirmation of a moderator effect is indicated by a significant interaction term coefficient. Multiple moderators can be accommodated by including the additional independent variables and interaction terms in Equation 1.

MMR can accommodate continuous or categorical moderator variables.[1] If the moderator variable is categorical, variable coding is necessary prior to analysis. The type of coding used depends on the research questions examined. Dummy coding is used for comparisons to a reference or control group. Effects coding is used for comparisons to the grand mean. Contrast coding is used for comparisons between specific groups (Frazier et al. 2004). West, Aiken and Krull (1996) provide detailed guidance on variable coding approaches.

If the moderator variable is continuous, the resulting interaction term may exhibit multicollinearity with the independent variables included in the equation. Mean centring the independent and moderator variable prior to forming the interaction term will reduce multicollinearity and improve interpretability of the moderation effect.

Although a significant interaction term coefficient, c, provides support for the existence of moderation, it is not appropriate to use the interaction term coefficient to understand effect size. If the effect size is of interest, hierarchical regression can be used. The R^2 from a regression with the interaction term is compared to the R^2 from a regression without the interaction term, and the change is used to evaluate the effect size.

Analysis of variance

Within accounting behavioural research, Analysis of Variance (ANOVA) is frequently used to analyze experimental data when the independent variables are categorical (see for example Choi 2013; Burt 2016). In this case, the researcher is interested in the differences between categories. The interpretation of the interaction term is the same for both ANOVA and MMR, with a significant interaction term supporting moderation.

ANOVA is sometimes used when the independent variable is continuous by artificially creating categories through the use of a cut point (frequently a mean or median). However, this approach should be used with caution as artificially categorizing continuous variables can result in information loss, a reduction in power to detect interactions effects and spurious results (MacCallum Zhang, Preacher and Rucker 2002; West et al. 1996). In addition, cut points, such as mean or median values, are not necessarily stable for different samples making comparison of results across studies difficult.[2]

Structural equation modelling

Structural equation modelling (SEM) is a multivariate technique combining aspects of factor analysis and multiple regression to enable the simultaneous examination of multiple interrelated dependence relationships between variables (Hair et al. 2009). SEM offers two different ways to assess moderation: (a) multi-group moderation models and (b) interaction models.

Multi-group moderation models (also referred to as group invariance models) split the data into groups and test for group differences in the independent and dependent variable relationship. Values of the moderator variable determine group membership. Once group membership is determined, identical models are estimated for each group. Significant between-group differences for the a path coefficient (Figure 24.1 Panel A) indicate a moderator effect. The second approach, estimates the interaction term as in Equation 1 and Figure 24.1 Panel B. A significant interaction term coefficient, c, indicates a moderation effect. For detailed descriptions and discussions of using SEM for testing moderation effects see Marsh, Wen, Nagengast and Hau (2012), Lin, Wen, Marsh and Lin et al. (2010) and Byrne (2008).

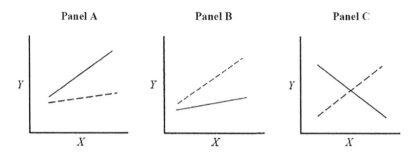

Figure 24.2 Enhancing (Panel A), buffering (Panel B) and antagonistic (Panel C) interaction graphs

The primary advantage of using SEM for moderation testing is the ability to include both measured and latent variables in the model. If latent variables are included, measurement error associated with latent variable estimation can also be estimated. The primary disadvantage of moderation testing with SEM is the need for relatively larger sample sizes, which can be difficult to obtain in experimental settings. This is especially true for multi-group moderation models where each group model requires a sufficient sample size for estimation (e.g., 150–200 cases per group). In addition, relative to MMR and ANOVA, the statistical assumptions of SEM are more restrictive.[3]

Interaction forms

Regardless of the statistical approach used, confirmation of a significant interaction does not explain the direction or form of the interaction (e.g., whether MO negatively or positively moderates the impact of X on Y). There are three main moderating interaction forms: (a) enhancing interactions (both moderating and independent variables make the independent variable effect stronger and the increase is greater than the additive effect), (b) buffering interactions (moderating variable makes the independent variable effect weaker) and (c) antagonistic interactions (moderating variable and independent variable have the same effect, but in opposite directions) (Frazier et al. 2004). Graphs for enhancing, buffering and antagonistic interactions are shown in Figure 24.2 Panels A through C respectively. Again, theory is important to predict the specific form of the interaction. Graphing is useful to gain an initial understanding of the interaction form, but additional testing is necessary to confirm this form. Because the use of grouping variables is common in accounting behavioural research, simple effects and interaction contrasts are useful in understanding the form of the interaction.

Simple effects focus on the effect of the independent variable on the dependent variable at specific levels of the moderator variable. Simple effects split the data by the moderator variable and test the difference between independent variable groups. Therefore, looking at the simple effects at each level of the moderator allows the researcher to understand specifically how the moderator affects the X and Y relationship. If the moderator is continuous, specific values of research interest can be selected for testing or, as discussed by Aiken and West (1991), the mean and values ± 1 standard deviation from the mean can be analyzed.

While simple effects allow the evaluation of the conditional effect of the moderator on the independent to dependent variable relationship, the determination of whether these differences represent a moderation effect is best examined with interaction contrasts. Interaction contrasts decompose the larger interaction into a series of 2x2 contrasts each with 1 degree of freedom to identify exactly where the effects of the independent variable differ at different levels of the moderator. "For an interaction effect to exist in a moderator framework, the effect of the focal

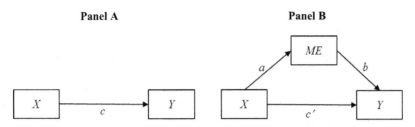

Figure 24.3 Simple mediation model

independent variable must differ depending on the level of the moderator variable" (Jaccard and Turrisi 2003: 6). Interaction contrasts are especially useful when there are more than two levels of the moderating variable. Jaccard and Turrisi (2003) provide a detailed discussion and examples of estimating simple effects and interaction contrasts.[4]

Mediation

Definition

A mediator is defined as an intervening variable that establishes how or why one variable predicts or causes an outcome variable (Frazier et al. 2004). Thus, mediation represents a causal process best investigated using data from controlled experimental settings or time-series analysis. Figure 24.3 Panel B depicts a simple mediation model, also referred to as a single mediator model. A simple mediation model contains one independent, one dependent and one mediator variable. For purposes of our discussion, we assume the independent variable is either continuous or dichotomous, the mediator and dependent variables are continuous, and the simple mediation model is not embedded within a larger model.

Mediation decomposes the causal path from the independent variable (X) to the dependent variable (Y), called the total effect (Figure 24.3 Panel A path c), into two causal paths, the indirect effect and the direct effect. The indirect effect is composed of the two paths (Figure 24.3 Panel B paths a and b) linking X to Y through the mediator variable (ME). The indirect effect is estimated as the product term of ab. The direct effect is the path linking X to Y (Figure 24.3 Panel B path c'). For a simple mediation model estimated using multiple regression,[5] the total effect equals direct effect plus indirect effect or $c = c' + ab$ (Baron and Kenny 1986; MacKinnon 2008). The arrows connecting the variables represent the causal sequence of the mediation relationship.

Mediation assumes the existence of an $X \rightarrow ME \rightarrow Y$ causal sequence, which cannot be unequivocally determined or supported solely by statistical analysis. As Mathieu and Taylor (2006: 1032) note "inferences of mediation are founded first and foremost in terms of theory, research design, and the construct validity of measures employed, and second in terms of statistical evidence of relationships." Thus, in addition to regression assumptions, simple mediation analysis also incorporates the following causal assumptions (Fairchild and MacKinnon 2009):

- Correct specification of causal order (i.e., $X \rightarrow ME \rightarrow Y$),
- No reverse causality (i.e., $Y \rightarrow ME$),
- No independent and mediator variable interaction effects.

Testing simple mediation

Baron and Kenny (1986) is the seminal reference for providing a causal steps strategy for testing simple mediation models.[6] Their approach decomposes and tests mediation using the following regression equations:

$$(Y = i + cX + \varepsilon \text{ Figure 24.3 Panel A)} \tag{2},$$
$$(ME = i + aX + \varepsilon \text{ Figure 24.3 Panel B)} \tag{3},$$
$$(Y = i + c'X + bME + \varepsilon \text{ Figure 24.3 Panel B)} \tag{4}.$$

Under the causal steps strategy, three conditions are necessary to provided statistical support for mediation:

1 *Condition 1*: X predicts $Y - c$ in Equation 2 is significant,
2 *Condition 2*: X predicts $ME - a$ in Equation 3 is significant,
3 *Condition 3*: ME predicts Y controlling for the effect of X on $Y - b$ in Equation 4 is significant.

In addition, if the results of Equations 2 through 4 support mediation, the effects of X on Y in Equation 2 should be greater than the effects of X on Y in Equation 4, or $c] c'$ (Figure 24.3 Panels A and B). When c is significant and c' is not significant, full mediation exists indicating the effects of X on Y are fully transmitted through ME. Conversely, when c is significant and c' remains significant after controlling for the effects of the mediator, partial mediation exists implying the effects of X on Y are not fully transmitted through ME.

Conditions 2 and 3 are necessary for supporting the existence of mediation. However, there is debate concerning the necessity of Condition 1. Some methodologists (Baron and Kenny 1986; Preacher and Hayes 2004; Mathieu and Taylor 2006) advocate using the term indirect effects instead of mediation if Condition 1 is not met. Mathieu and Taylor (2006) provide an overview and discussion of the conceptual and statistical distinction between indirect effects and mediation when Condition 1 is not met. Others (Kenny, Kashy and Bolger 1998; MacKinnon, Lockwood, Hoffman, West and Sheets 2002; Zhao, Lynch and Chen 2010) use the term mediation whether or not Condition 1 is met. While intuitive that a significant $X{\rightarrow}Y$ relationship to be mediated should exist prior to testing for the effects of an intervening variable, there are several reasons Condition 1 may not be met. For example, inconsistent mediation (also referred to as suppression) can result in a non-significant total effect (MacKinnon, Krull and Lockwood 2000; Shrout and Bolger 2002). Inconsistent mediation occurs when the direct effect, (c' in Figure 24.3) is opposite in sign from the indirect effect (the product of the a and b paths in Figure 24.3). If inconsistent mediation exists, the total effect ($c = c' + ab$) may be non-significant due to the opposing signs of the direct and indirect effects. Other potential causes for non-significant total effects include omitted variables (e.g., unspecified mediators or moderators) and confounding variables. Zhao et al. (2010) discuss the inadvisability of requiring a significant total effect as a requirement for testing mediation. Conceptual and methodological debate continues concerning the necessity of establishing a significant $X{\rightarrow}Y$ relationship prior to testing for mediation. In the interim, if a significant $X{\rightarrow}Y$ relationship does not exist prior to testing for mediation (i.e., Condition 1 is not met), we advise researchers to investigate and discuss both the theoretical and statistical reasons for the absence of this relationship.

The causal steps strategy continues to be used in accounting behavioural research. For example, Newman and Tafkov (2014) use this technique for supplementary analysis when investigating the effects of relative performance information in tournament settings. However, MacKinnon et al. (2002) discuss several potential issues with this approach. First, a joint test of Conditions 1, 2 and 3 is not provided. Second, an estimate of the size and significance of the indirect effect (the *ab* product term) is not directly produced or evaluated. Third, the causal steps strategy is difficult to apply when a mediation relationship is embedded in a larger model or when multiple mediators exist.

Other simple mediation testing approaches

MacKinnon et al. (2002) identify and evaluate 14 mediation testing procedures. Unlike the causal steps strategy, most of these approaches do not focus on the individual paths in the mediation model. Instead, the indirect effect is investigated using the product term *ab*. We do not review and discuss each of these 14 approaches, but instead focus on the approaches frequently used or with potential for use in accounting behavioural research.

Product of coefficients test

The product of coefficients test estimates and evaluates the significance of the indirect effect by dividing the *ab* product term by its standard error. There are several variations of the product of coefficient test. Equation 5 is the second-order exact solution (Aroian 1947),

$$\text{z-score} = \frac{ab}{\sqrt{a^2 s_b^2 + b^2 s_a^2 + s_a^2 s_b^2}} \tag{5}$$

where *a* and *b* are the indirect path coefficients and s_a and s_b are the associated standard errors. The unbiased solution (Goodman 1960) subtracts the $s_a^2 s_b^2$ term, while the first-order solution (Sobel 1982) excludes the $s_a^2 s_b^2$ term. The choice of which product of coefficient test to use is largely determined by researcher preference, as the differences in estimates typically have negligible effects on results. Regardless of the variation used, the resulting z-score is compared to a standard normal distribution to evaluate significance (Baron and Kenny 1986).

Within accounting behavioural research, Sobel's (Sobel 1982) first-order solution, referred to as the Sobel Test, is the most frequently used product of coefficients test (see for example Kachelmeier, Majors and Williamson 2014). The Sobel Test is well understood, widely accepted and relatively simple to use. In addition, results obtained from estimating Equations 2 and 3 of the causal steps strategy serve as input to the Sobel Test equation. A concern with all versions of the product of coefficients test, especially with smaller sample sizes, is the use of the standard normal distribution (Preacher and Hayes 2008). If mediation exists, the product of random normal variables with positive means will tend to have positive skew and the product of random normal variables with means of opposite signs will tend to have negative skew (Bollen and Stine 1992; MacKinnon et al. 2002; Shrout and Bolger 2002), resulting in meditation tests with low power and potentially inaccurate results (Shrout and Bolger 2002; Preacher and Hayes 2004).

Bootstrapping

Bootstrapping is a non-parametric approach that makes no assumptions about the shape of the distribution of variables or the distribution of the *ab* product term. According to Preacher and Hayes (2004: 722):

> bootstrapping is accomplished by taking a large number of samples of size *n* (where *n* is the original sample size) from the data, *sampling with replacement*, and computing the indirect

effect, *ab*, in each sample. Assume . . . that 1,000 bootstrap samples have been requested. The point estimate of *ab* is simply the mean *ab* computed over the 1,000 samples and the estimated standard error is the standard deviation of the 1,000 *ab* estimates.

Because bootstrapping uses resampling, product term and standard error, estimates will vary depending on the number of bootstrap resamples constructed. However, this variation will diminish as the number of resamples increases (Preacher, Rucker and Hayes 2007). Hayes (2009) recommends estimating at least 5,000 bootstrap resamples.

Testing mediation relationships using a bootstrapping procedure provides a means to address potential non-normal distribution issues associated with the product of coefficients test. In addition to making no distribution assumptions, bootstrapping offers other benefits relevant to accounting behavioural researchers. First, because bootstrapping is not based on large-sample theory, it can be applied to smaller sample sizes typically encountered in accounting behavioural research. Second, bootstrapping allows the construction of asymmetric confidence intervals for point estimates of the indirect effect. Finally, PROCESS (Hayes 2013), an extensive bundle of macros for SPSS and SAS, is freely available. PROCESS automates bootstrapping estimation for mediation analysis and can facilitate multi-categorical independent variables (Hayes and Preacher 2014). In addition, PROCESS enables the application of bootstrapping techniques to moderation analysis (Hayes 2015a). The capabilities and functionality of PROCESS are extensive, well documented (Hayes 2013) and expanding. Burt (2016) uses bootstrapping techniques to estimate a moderated mediation model (discussed below) examining differences in internal and external auditors' ability to obtain information on material control weaknesses. Given the benefits of bootstrapping, we encourage accounting behavioural researchers to adopt this approach for testing mediation relationships.

Structural equation modelling

SEM is the preferred approach for estimating and testing mediation relationships embedded within larger models. SEM offers a flexible approach to testing mediation relationships (Preacher and Hayes 2008). SEM programs typically incorporate bootstrapping capabilities and product of coefficients procedures for estimating the significance of the indirect effect. Latent variables estimated using multi-item scales to incorporate the effects of measurement error can also be analyzed. In addition to evaluating mediation effects, SEM also produces a number of indices useful for evaluating how well the model reproduces sample data correlations. Ullman (2006) provides an introduction to SEM estimation while Kline (2011) discusses SEM estimation, including mediation analysis, in greater detail and depth. While mediation testing with SEM offers numerous advantages, the previously noted issues of large sample size requirements and more restrictive statistical assumptions remain a challenge. However, numerous accounting behavioural researchers (e.g., Baines and Langfield-Smith 2003; Presslee, Vance and Webb 2013; Kadous, Koonce and Thayer 2012) are using SEM to investigate mediation relationships using survey, field study and experimental data.

Complex mediation models

Simple mediation models are the most common type of mediation analysis performed in accounting behavioural research. However, more complex mediation models exist that are also applicable to accounting behavioural research. We provide a brief overview of two complex forms of mediation relationships: multiple mediation models and serial mediation models, and references for complex mediation precipitated by the use of binary and categorical variables. While more complex, the equations used to estimate these models are variations and combinations of the basic mediation equations previously discussed. Further details about multiple mediation and sequential mediation, including the development of the equations and examples, are outlined in MacKinnon (2000), Preacher and Hayes (2008) and Taylor, MacKinnon and Tein (2008).

Multiple mediator models

Multiple mediator models contain two or more mediators linking the independent and dependent variables. Figure 24.4 depicts a multiple mediator model where ME_1 and ME_2 mediate the relationship between X and Y.

As shown in Figure 24.4, the product terms *ab* and *de* represent the specific indirect effects of X on Y through ME_1 and ME_2 respectively. The total indirect effect is the sum of the specific indirect effects (i.e., *ab* + *de*) or $c - c'$. The c' path is the direct effect of X on Y controlling for the effects of the mediators, ME_1 and ME_2. The total effect of X on Y is calculated as $c = c' + (ab + de)$. If additional mediators are included in the model, the additional product terms are added to the above equations (Preacher and Hayes 2008). Multiple mediator models are typically estimated and tested using SEM in conjunction with either the product of coefficients or bootstrapping procedure for standard error estimation. Many accounting behavioural research studies using SEM to examine mediation relationships are in fact evaluating multiple mediator models (e.g., Presslee, Vance and Webb 2013; Kadous et al. 2012).

Regardless of the statistical approach used, a key difference between simple mediation models and multiple mediator models is the interpretation of specific indirect effects. Because the mediators in a multiple mediator model are likely correlated, specific indirect effects represent the ability of a mediator to mediate the relationship between X and Y conditional on the inclusion of other mediators in the model (Preacher and Hayes 2008).

Sequential mediation

Sequential mediation describes a linked series or chain of at least two mediators intervening between the independent and dependent variables. Figure 24.5 depicts a sequential mediation model.

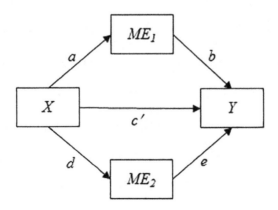

Figure 24.4   Multiple mediator model

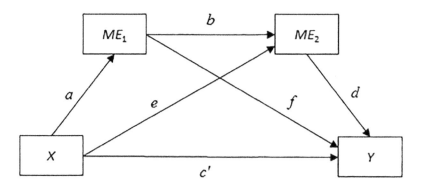

Figure 24.5 Sequential mediation model

Sequential mediation models allow the testing of a number of indirect effects, both specific and in combination. Mediated effects are derived from the product terms of the coefficients for each of the relevant paths in the mediational chain. The sequential indirect effect, representing the effects of X on Y through ME_1 and ME_2, is the *abd* product term. The specific indirect effect of X on Y through ME_1 is the *af* product term. The specific indirect effect of X on Y through ME_2 is the *ed* product term. The total indirect effect of X on Y is the sum of the sequential indirect and the specific indirect effects, *abd* + *af* + *ed*. The direct effect of X on Y controlling for both mediators is c'. Finally, the total effect of X on Y can be estimated as the sum of the total indirect effect and the direct effect, or $c = (abd + af + ed) + c'$ where c denotes the total effect. Indirect effects passing through a single mediator can also be estimated. For example, the indirect effect of X on Y passing through ME_2 is *abd* + *ed* (Taylor et al. 2008: 242–243).

Sequential mediation models are typically estimated and tested using SEM in conjunction with either the product of coefficients or bootstrapping procedure for standard error estimation. The casual order assumption is a concern when testing sequential mediation models. Taylor et al. (2008: 265) note "regression coefficients for the relations among the two mediators and the dependent variable are not direct estimates of causal effects." Thus, theory, research design and prior literature are critical to supporting the causal order assumption in sequential mediation models. To our knowledge, no accounting behavioural researchers have specifically investigated sequential mediation relationships.

Mediation involving categorical variables

Our prior discussion of mediation assumes the mediator and dependent variable are continuous, while the independent variable is assumed to be either dichotomous or continuous. However, mediation can be analyzed under other variable measurement assumptions. While detailed discussion of mediation involving categorical variables is beyond the scope of this chapter, we can recommend several useful resources for readers who wish to know more. For example, Hayes and Preacher (2014) discuss mediation analysis for categorical independent variables. MacKinnon and Dwyer (1993) and Li, Schneider and Bennett (2007) provide discussion and guidance on estimating models with binary and categorical variables. Finally, Iacobucci (2012) proposes and discusses a framework for evaluating mediation models with combinations of continuous, dichotomous and categorical independent, mediator and dependent variables. MacKinnon and Cox (2012) and Feinberg (2012) provide critiques and suggestions on Iacobucci's (2012) proposed approach.

Moderated mediation and mediated moderation

Moderation and mediation can be combined to form a number of different models, collectively referred to as moderated mediation. For example, the *a* or *b* paths in Figure 24.3 Panel B could be moderated, either individually or in combination, by one or more moderators operating individually or in combination. In addition, the *c'* path could also be moderated in conjunction with the *a* and/or *b* paths. Given the variety of potential moderated mediation models, correct model specification based on theory is critical. In addition, moderated mediation models incorporate the statistical assumptions of moderation, mediation and regression. Burt (2016) provides an example of estimating and evaluating a moderated mediation model with accounting behavioural research data.

Moderated mediation describes a mediated effect that varies as a function of a moderator variable (Preacher et al. 2007). The conceptual and statistical estimation path diagrams for a first-stage moderated mediation model are shown in Figure 24.6 Panels A and B, respectively.

The model in Figure 24.6 Panel B expressed as a series of equations is:

$$M = i + aX + dMO + eXMO + \varepsilon \qquad (6),$$

$$Y = i + c'X + bME + \varepsilon \qquad (7),$$

where *XMO* is the interaction term indicating *MO* moderates the first stage, *X* to *ME*, of the indirect effect. The various forms of moderated mediation models use different, but related, sets of equations for estimation and testing. We focus our discussion on the estimation and testing of a first-stage moderated mediation model with continuous independent, dependent and mediator variables and a continuous or dichotomous moderator variable. For information on estimating other forms of moderated mediation models, see Edwards and Lambert (2007), Preacher et al. (2007) and Hayes (2015b).

A first-stage model can also be used to investigate mediated moderation – a special case of moderated mediation. Mediated moderation describes the transmission of a moderating effect through a mediator variable. For a first-stage model, moderated mediation and mediated moderation are analytically equivalent. Whether the *X* to *ME* path is moderated or the *XMO*

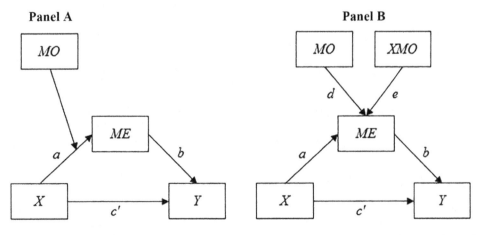

Figure 24.6 First-stage conceptual (Panel A) and statistical estimation (Panel B) moderated mediation model

interaction term is mediated is determined by theory, conceptual framing and research focus (Edwards and Lambert 2007). Muller, Judd and Yzerbyt (2005) provide a detailed discussion of the similarities and differences between moderated mediation and mediated moderation.

There are several approaches for estimating moderated mediation models. The sub-group approach is typically used with a dichotomous moderator representing different group assignments. Separate mediation models are estimated for each group. If the mediation effect varies between groups, evidence of moderated mediation exists. Typically, the product of coefficients procedure or bootstrapping is used to test mediation relationships within each group. Because separate mediation models are estimated for each group, the group analysis approach is typically a low-power technique. MacKinnon (2008) and Edwards and Lambert (2007) discuss estimating moderated mediation with the group analysis approach.

The modified causal steps strategy (Edwards and Lambert 2007; Muller et al. 2005) is a variation of causal steps strategy that incorporates moderation. Applying this approach to the statistical estimation model in Figure 24.6 Panel B, evidence for moderated mediation exists if both the e and b paths are significant. However, whether the indirect effect (i.e., the ab product term) is moderated cannot be definitely determined. As Fairchild and MacKinnon (2009) discuss, moderation of an individual path of the indirect effect does not imply moderation of the complete indirect effect. Muller et al. (2005) and Edwards and Lambert (2007) discuss estimating and testing moderated mediation with the modified causal steps strategy.

Extending the work of Preacher et al. (2007) and Edwards and Lambert (2007), Hayes (2015b) proposes the index of moderated mediation. The index of moderated mediation estimates the effect of a moderator on the indirect effect (i.e., the ab product term). For the moderated mediation model in Figure 24.6 Panel B, the indirect effect of X on Y through ME (denoted as ω in Equation 8) is the sum of the indirect effect and the moderated indirect effect from Equations 6 and 7:

$$\omega = ab + ebMO \tag{8}$$

which is a line with intercept ab and slope eb. For a first-stage moderated mediation model, the eb product term is the index of moderated mediation (Hayes 2015b: 4). If the index of moderated mediation is different from zero, the indirect effect is systematically larger or smaller for some values of MO than other values of MO (Hayes 2015b: 4–5). The significance of the index of moderated mediation can be evaluated using the product of coefficients or bootstrapping techniques. If the index of moderated mediation is significant, specific moderator values can be substituted into Equation 8 to investigate the form of the interaction effect.

Conclusions

Moderation and mediation analysis probe the effects of additional variables on the relationship between independent and dependent variables. Both techniques allow accounting behavioural researchers to gain additional insight and understanding. Moderation allows the researcher to understand for whom or when certain effects will hold, while mediation focuses on understanding how or why causal effects are transmitted. Moderated mediation combines both moderation and mediation to examine questions about the "when or for whom" of the "how or why" (Hayes 2015b).

In this chapter, we presented an overview of moderation, mediation and moderated mediation. We discussed the frequently used techniques and approaches for investigating moderation, mediation and moderated mediation in accounting behavioural research. In addition, we provided information on the critical issues and assumptions of the techniques and approaches presented.

Our presentation and discussion are by no means comprehensive. The methodologies for investing moderation, mediation and especially moderated mediation are evolving and, depending on the research context, frequently complex. We encourage researchers to invest the time and effort to gain a more comprehensive knowledge of the techniques discussed. The references cited throughout this chapter provide an initial starting point.

Notes

1 We do not discuss estimating and testing interaction effects with logistic regression. For an introduction to this topic, see Jaccard (2001).
2 See Chapter 23 in this volume for a more general overview of the use of ANOVA in behavioural accounting research.
3 See Chapter 25 in this volume for an overview of the use of SEM in behavioural accounting research.
4 Chapter 23 also provides a general overview of simple effects analysis that the reader may find helpful.
5 Testing mediation with ANOVA or its related techniques is possible; however, these approaches have several methodological shortcomings (Fiske, Kenny and Taylor 1982) and have been largely replaced in the methodological literature by regression-based procedures.
6 As of 2015, Google Scholar shows over 50,000 citations for Baron and Kenny (1986).

References

Aguinis, H., Boik, W.R.J. and Pierce, C.A., 2001, 'A generalized solution for approximating the power to detect effects of categorical moderator variables using multiple regression', *Organizational Research Methods* 4(4), 291–323.

Aiken, L.S. and West, S.G., 1991, *Multiple Regression: Testing and Interpreting Interactions*, Sage Publications Inc., Thousand Oaks, CA.

Aroian, L.A., 1947, 'The probability function of the product of two normally distributed variables', *The Annals of Mathematical Statistics* 18(2), 265–271.

Baines, A. and Langfield-Smith, K., 2003, 'Antecedents to management accounting change: A structural equation approach', *Accounting Organizations and Society* 28(7), 675–698.

Baron, R.M. and Kenny, D.A., 1986, 'The moderator-mediator variable distinction in social psychological research: Conceptual, strategic, and statistical considerations', *Journal of Personality and Social Psychology* 51(6), 1173–1182.

Bisbe, J. and Otley, D., 2004, 'The effects of the interactive use of management control systems on product innovation', *Accounting Organizations and Society* 29(8), 709–737.

Bollen, K.A. and Stine, R.A., 1992, 'Bootstrapping goodness-of-fit measures in structural equation models', *Sociological Methods and Research* 21(2), 205–229.

Burt, I., 2016, 'An understanding of the differences between internal and external auditors in obtaining information about internal control weaknesses', *Journal of Management Accounting Research* 28(3), 83–99.

Byrne, B.M., 2008, 'Testing for multigroup equivalence of a measuring instrument: A walk through the process', *Psicothema* 20(4), 872–882.

Choi, J., 2013, 'Can offering a signing bonus motivate effort? Experimental evidence of the moderating effects of labor market competition', *The Accounting Review* 89(2), 545–570.

Edwards, J.R. and Lambert, L.S., 2007, 'Methods for integrating moderation and mediation: A general analytical framework using moderated path analysis', *Psychological Methods* 12(1), 1–22.

Fairchild, A.J. and MacKinnon, D.P., 2009, 'A general model for testing mediation and moderation effects', *Prevention Science* 10(2), 89–99.

Feinberg, F.M., 2012, 'Mediation analysis and categorical variables: Some further frontiers', *Journal of Consumer Psychology* 22(4), 595–598.

Fiske, S.T., Kenny, D.A. and Taylor, S.E., 1982, 'Structural models for the mediation of salience effects on attribution', *Journal of Experimental Social Psychology* 18(2), 105–127.

Frazier, P.A., Tix, A.P. and Barron, K.E., 2004, 'Testing moderator and mediator effects in counseling psychology research', *Journal of Counseling Psychology* 51(1), 115–134.

Goodman, L.A., 1960, 'On the exact variance of products', *Journal of the American Statistical Association* 55(292), 708–713.

Hair, J.A., Black, W.C., Babin, B.J. and Anderson, R.E., 2009, *Multivariate Data Analysis* (7th ed.), Pearson, Upper Saddle River, NJ.

Hayes, A.F., 2009, 'Beyond Baron and Kenny: Statistical mediation analysis in the new millennium', *Communication Monographs* 76(4), 408–420.

Hayes, A.F., 2013, *Introduction to Mediation, Moderation, and Conditional Process Analysis: A Regression-Based Approach*, The Guilford Press, New York.

Hayes, A.F., 2015a, *Hacking PROCESS to Estimate a Simple Moderation Model With a Three-Category Moderator*, viewed 23 March 2015, from http://afhayes.com/public/quadratichack.pdf.

Hayes, A.F., 2015b, 'An index and test of linear moderated mediation', *Multivariate Behavioral Research* 50(1), 1–22.

Hayes, A.F. and Preacher, K.J., 2014, 'Statistical mediation analysis with a multicategorical independent variable', *British Journal of Mathematical and Statistical Psychology* 67(3), 451–470.

Iacobucci, D., 2012, 'Mediation analysis and categorical variables: The final frontier', *Journal of Consumer Psychology* 22(4), 582–594.

Jaccard, J., 2001, *Interaction Effects in Logistic Regression*, Sage Publications Inc., Thousand Oaks, CA.

Jaccard, J. and Turrisi, R., 2003, *Interaction Effects in Multiple Regression* (2nd ed.), Sage Publications, Thousand Oaks, CA.

Kachelmeier, S.J., Majors, T. and Williamson, M.G., 2014, 'Does intent modify risk-based auditing?', *The Accounting Review* 89(6), 2181–2201.

Kadous, K., Koonce, L. and Thayer, J.M., 2012, 'Do financial statement users judge relevance based on properties of reliability?', *The Accounting Review* 87(4), 1335–1356.

Kenny, D.A., Kashy, D.A. and Bolger, N., 1998, 'Data analysis in social psychology', in D. Gilbert, S. Fiske and G. Lindzey (eds.), *Handbook of Social Psychology* (4th ed.), 1, 233–265, McGraw-Hill, New York.

Kline, R.B., 2011, *Principles and Practice of Structural Equation Modeling* (3rd ed.), The Guilford Press, New York.

Li, Y., Schneider, J.A. and Bennett, D.A., 2007, 'Estimation of the mediation effect with a binary mediator', *Statistics in Medicine* 26(18), 3398–3414.

Lin, G.-C., Wen, Z., Marsh, H.W. and Lin, H.-S., 2010, 'Structural equation models of latent interactions: Clarification of the orthogonalizing and double-mean-centering strategies', *Structural Equation Modeling: A Multidisciplinary Journal* 17(3), 374–391.

MacCallum, R.C., Zhang, S., Preacher, K.J. and Rucker, D.D., 2002, 'On the practice of dichotomization of quantitative variables', *Psychological Methods* 7(1), 19–40.

MacKinnon, D.P., 2000, 'Contrasts in multiple mediator models', in J.S. Rose, L. Chassin, C.C. Presson and S.J. Sherman (eds.), *Multivariate Applications in Substance Use Research: New Methods for New Questions*, 141–160, Lawrence Erlbaum Associates, Mahwah, NJ.

MacKinnon, D.P., 2008, *Introduction to Statistical Mediation Analysis*, Lawrence Erlbaum Associates, Mahwah, NJ.

MacKinnon, D.P. and Cox, M.G., 2012, 'Commentary on "Mediation analysis and categorical variables: The final frontier" by Dawn Iacobucci', *Journal of Consumer Psychology* 22(4), 600–602.

MacKinnon, D.P. and Dwyer, J.H., 1993, 'Estimating mediated effects in prevention studies', *Evaluation Review* 17(2), 144–158.

MacKinnon, D.P., Krull, J.L. and Lockwood, C.M., 2000, 'Equivalence of the mediation, confounding and suppression effect', *Prevention Science* 1(4), 173–181.

MacKinnon, D.P., Lockwood, C.M., Hoffman, J.M., West, S.G. and Sheets, V., 2002, 'A comparison of methods to test mediation and other intervening variable effects', *Psychological Methods* 7(1), 83–104.

Marsh, H.W., Wen, Z., Nagengast, B. and Hau, K.-T., 2012, 'Structural equation models of latent interactions', in R.H. Hoyle (ed.), *Handbook of Structural Equation Modeling*, 436–458, The Guilford Press, New York.

Mathieu, J.E. and Taylor, S.R., 2006, 'Clarifying the conditions and decision points for mediational type interference in organization behavior', *Journal of Organizational Behavior* 27(8), 1031–1056.

Muller, D. C., Judd, M. and Yzerbyt, V.Y., 2005, 'When moderation is mediated and mediation is moderated', *Journal of Personality and Social Psychology* 89(6), 852–863.

Newman, A.H. and Tafkov, I.D., 2014, 'Relative performance information in tournaments with different prize structures', *Accounting Organizations and Society* 39(5), 348–361.

Preacher, K.J. and Hayes, A.F., 2004, 'SPSS and SAS procedures for estimating indirect effects in simple mediation models', *Behavior Research Methods, Instruments, & Computers* 36(4), 717–731.

Preacher, K.J. and Hayes, A.F., 2008, 'Asymptotic and resampling strategies for assessing and comparing indirect effect in multiple mediator models', *Behavior Research Methods* 40(3), 879–891.

Preacher, K.J., Rucker, D.D. and Hayes, A.F., 2007, 'Addressing moderated mediation hypotheses: Theory, methods, and prescriptions', *Multivariate Behavioral Research* 42(1), 185–227.

Presslee, A., Vance, T.W. and Webb, R.A., 2013, 'The effects of reward type on employee goal setting, goal commitment, and performance', *The Accounting Review* 88(5), 1805–1831.

Shrout, P.E. and Bolger, N., 2002, 'Mediation in experimental and nonexperimental studies: New procedures and recommendations', *Psychological Methods* 7(4), 422–445.

Sobel, M.E., 1982, 'Asymptotic confidence intervals for indirect effects in structural equation models', *Sociological Methodology* 13, 290–312.

Tabachnick, B.G. and Fidell, L.S., 2013, *Using Multivariate Statistics* (6th ed.), Pearson, Upper Saddle River, NJ.

Taylor, A.B., MacKinnon, D.P. and Tein, J.-Y., 2008, 'Tests of the three-path mediated effect', *Organizational Research Methods* 11(2), 241–269.

Ullman, J.B., 2006, 'Structural equation modeling: Reviewing the basics and moving forward', *Journal of Personality Assessment* 87(1), 35–50.

West, S.G., Aiken, L.S. and Krull, J.L., 1996, 'Experimental personality designs: Analyzing categorical by continuous variable interactions', *Journal of Personality* 64(1), 1–42.

Zhao, X., Lynch, J.G. Jr. and Chen, Q., 2010, 'Reconsidering Baron and Kenny: Myths and truths about mediation analysis', *Journal of Consumer Research* 37(2), 197–206.

25

Structural equation modelling in Behavioural Accounting Research

Jonathan Farrar and Lan Guo

Introduction: different approaches to SEM

Structural equation modelling (SEM) refers to a collection of statistical techniques that allow a set of relations between one or more independent variables (IVs), and one or more dependent variables (DVs), to be examined simultaneously. Both IVs and DVs can be measured variables (directly observed) or latent variables (theoretical constructs that are not directly observed). In SEM, causal processes are represented by a series of regression equations, and are illustrated pictorially to provide a visual representation of the constructs being studied. Statistically, SEM is an extension of general linear modelling (GLM) procedures, such as ANOVA and multiple regression analysis.

There are several different approaches to SEM. The most common is a covariance-based full SEM approach, which involves evaluating two models: a measurement model and a structural model. A measurement model specifies how latent variables are measured using indicator variables, and is analyzed using confirmatory factor analysis (CFA).[1] Once the measurement of the latent constructs is psychometrically sound, the researcher can proceed to evaluate the structural model (Anderson and Gerbing 1988).

The structural model depicts the directional influences or causal relations among multiple latent constructs. The estimation of the structural model usually involves three iterative processes. First, researchers identify the optimal structural model by conducting a series of difference tests among alternative models, including the theoretical model and models that have been altered based on theoretical and/or statistical considerations (cf., the decision-tree framework for the sequential difference tests recommended by Anderson and Gerbing 1988). Second, an assessment of the optimal structural model is made through an examination of multiple goodness-of-fit indices, including those assessing the overall model fit, the incremental fit compared to a baseline model and the fit adjusted for the complexity of the model (Hair, Anderson, Tatham and Black 1998). Finally, researchers use estimated regression weights from the optimal structural model to test the hypothetical linkages among latent variables.

Other common SEM approaches include covariance-based partial aggregation, path analysis and variance-based partial least squares (PLS) analysis. SEM approaches differ in terms of the number of models to be evaluated (a measurement model and a structural model, or a structural model only); model specification (e.g., whether indicators are reflective or formative[2] in

Table 25.1 Common SEM techniques

SEM technique	Model specification	Estimation process	When to use	Accounting example
Covariance-based full SEM	Measurement model tests relationship between latent variables and their *reflective* indicators; structural model then analyzes relationships among latent variables	Covariance-based (i.e., to minimize the difference between observed and predicted covariance matrices)	Data is multivariate normally distributed; indicators of latent variables are reflective in nature; reasonably large sample size to ensure a sample-size-to-parameter ratio of 10 or higher; model is confirmatory	Wentzel (2002)
Covariance-based partial aggregation form of SEM	Scale scores are used as the single-item *reflective* indicators of the latent variables; structural model analyzes relationships among latent variables	Covariance-based	Data is multivariate normally distributed; indicators of latent variables are reflective in nature; reasonably small sample size due to smaller number of parameters to be estimated; model is confirmatory	Cadez and Guilding (2008)
Path analysis	No measurement model is estimated and scale scores are used to proxy for the latent variables (without accounting for measurement errors); path model analyzes structural relationships among measured variables	Covariance-based	Data is multivariate normally distributed; reasonably small sample size due to smaller number of parameter to be estimated; some variables are categorical and thus the estimation of the measurement model is unnecessary; model is confirmatory	Drake, Wong and Salter (2007)
Partial least squares (PLS)	Measurement model tests relationship between latent variables and their *reflective* or *formative* indicators; structural model analyzes relationships among latent variables	Variance-based (i.e., to maximize variance of the dependent variable explained by the independent variables)	Data can be non-normally distributed; indicators of latent variables can be both reflective and formative; reasonably small sample size is sufficient; model can be both confirmatory and exploratory	Pondeville, Swaen and De Rongé (2013)

nature); estimation process (covariance-based or variance-based) and conditions under which each approach is most suitable (in terms of, for example, the distribution of data, sample size and whether the model is confirmatory or exploratory).[3] These approaches are contrasted and summarized in Table 25.1. For example, as shown in Table 25.1, covariance-based full SEM, covariance-based partial aggregation and path analysis are used when data is normally distributed, whereas PLS analysis can be used when data is non-normally distributed.

In Table 25.1, we also identify one accounting study that uses each of these SEM approaches.[4] These studies may be useful as a reference source so that researchers can better understand why a particular approach is suitable and how it is conducted. For example, Wentzel (2002) uses covariance-based full SEM because she analyzes relationships among latent variables, which she first measured. Her data was normally distributed, and her sample size was relatively large. Covariance-based full SEM is the predominant SEM method in accounting (Smith and Langfield-Smith 2004), but the other approaches may also be useful. For example, Cadez and Guilding (2008) use the covariance-based partial aggregation form of SEM, which averages scores of all indicators of any given factor rather than using the indicators themselves in the model. This method increases the model's parsimony by decreasing the number of parameters to be estimated. Drake, Wong and Salter (2007) use path analysis because they had a relatively small sample size and their main independent variables were categorical. Pondeville, Swaen and De Rongé (2013) use a PLS approach because they had a relatively small sample size and their data was not normally distributed.

In the sections that follow, we limit our discussion to *covariance*-based SEM approaches, including full and partial aggregation forms of SEM as well as path analysis. Lee, Petter, Fayard and Robinson (2011) discusses the differences between covariance-based and variance-based SEM approaches (PLS in particular) and provides a review of accounting studies that use the latter.

Why use SEM?

Why use SEM? In short, SEM can overcome the major disadvantages of GLM procedures such as ANOVA and multiple regression analysis. We explain further below.

- Measurement error in variables is a serious problem for the estimation of regression models. Error in dependent variables will bias R^2 and standardized regression coefficients, and error in independent variables will also bias unstandardized regression estimates. These errors in turn will adversely affect estimates and conclusions (Oberski and Satorra 2013). However, in SEM (with the exception of path analysis), relations among variables are theoretically free of measurement error because the errors are estimated and corrected, leaving only common variance (Ullman 2006).
- Regression models are unable to provide separate estimates of relations between latent constructs and their indicators. Conversely, SEM can be used to assess the psychometric properties of the measures of latent constructs, and subsequently study the relations among latent constructs (Tomarken and Waller 2005; Ullman 2006).
- It is difficult to assess the fit of data to a hypothesized model using multiple regression, since the fit has to be assessed on model components on an equation-by-equation basis. Conversely, SEM provides a wide variety of global fit indices that allow researchers to evaluate the fit of data of a simple or complex model. Furthermore, by using chi-square difference tests and comparing goodness-of-fit indices, researchers can easily evaluate the fit of data among alternative models (Tomarken and Waller 2005).

Many SEM software packages are available, including AMOS (compatible with SPSS), CALIS (compatible with SAS), EQS, LISREL and Mplus. Psychology professor emerita Barbara Byrne has written a number of textbooks for learning SEM with different software applications, including Amos (Byrne 2010), EQS (Byrne 2006), LISREL (Byrne 1998) and Mplus (Byrne 2012).

Examples of accounting research using SEM

SEM has become increasingly popular in the behavioural sciences (Burnett and Williams 2005), and correspondingly in Behavioural Accounting Research (Birnberg 2011). Using ABI/Inform, we identified 75 articles in 11 leading accounting journals over the past 20 years (1995–2014) in which SEM analysis was used.[5] Forty-four (59%) of these were published in the year 2005 or later, which is evidence of the gradual acceptance and utilization of this methodology by behavioural accounting researchers.

This section provides examples of recent and important accounting papers that have used SEM. We selected the two papers with the most Google Scholar citations from each of the accounting sub-disciplines of financial accounting, management accounting, auditing and tax, published from the years 2005 to 2014. These examples are to demonstrate to the readers how different SEM techniques can be used to study different research topics and to analyze different types of data.

Financial accounting

Gillet and Uddin (2005) investigate various factors contributing to chief financial officers' (CFOs) intentions to engage in fraudulent financial reporting. The authors use a modified version of Ajzen and Fishbein's (1980) theory of reasoned action, and apply it to the fraudulent reporting context. The antecedents to fraudulent reporting intentions they examine include attitude, compensation structure, company size and subjective norm. The authors collect survey data from 139 CFOs of publicly traded firms. Their main finding is that CFO attitude toward fraudulent reporting is the most important predictor of fraudulent reporting intentions. A full SEM approach is used to examine the relations among ten latent constructs.

Chen and Tan (2013) is an experimental study of 89 MBA students. It examines how prior exposure to an analyst's name and performance may affect investors' judgment relating to the analyst's credibility and earnings estimates. The authors show that exposure to an analyst's name and prior performance jointly affects perceived analyst credibility, which in turn affects investors' willingness to rely on analyst's future reports, as well as investors' earnings estimates. Although the main hypotheses are tested using ANOVA, path analysis is used to confirm that the exposure effect on investors' judgments and decisions is indeed due to the underlying decision process they posit.

Management accounting

Widener (2007) tests the 'levers of control' framework (Simons 2000). This framework posits that strategic uncertainties and risks determine the choice and use of four control systems (i.e., beliefs system, boundary system, diagnostic controls, interactive controls), which in turn affects organizational performance through the use of management attention and organizational learning. Her study is based on survey data from 122 CFOs of US public firms, and her results support her theoretical predictions. Due to the relatively small sample size and model complexity, she employs path analysis to test base and alternative structural models after establishing the validity of the measurement model.

Cadez and Guilding (2008) adopt a contingency theory approach to examine the relation between strategic management accounting (Simmonds 1981) and firm performance. Specifically, they assess how company performance is affected by the appropriate fit between the strategic management accounting system and four contingency factors (strategy type, deliberate strategy formulation, market orientation and company size). Using survey responses from 193 large Slovenian companies, they find that there is no universally appropriate strategic management accounting system. A partial aggregation form of SEM is adopted because some latent constructs are multidimensional and indicators are thus aggregated by factor.

Auditing

Using a social identity theory framework (Turner, Hogg, Oakes, Reicher and Wetherell 1987), Bamber and Iyer (2007) test a model of the auditor-client relationship. The variable of interest is auditor's acquiescence to the position preferred by the client. Based on survey responses from 252 practicing auditors, Bamber and Iyer (2007) find that auditors' identification with their clients is positively associated with their acquiescence to the client-preferred position, whereas auditors' experience and their professional identification are negatively associated with such acquiescence. A full SEM approach is adopted. Because the data includes both continuous and ordinal variables, a polyserial correlation matrix is used as input data. This issue is discussed further in endnote 6.

Deumes, Schelleman, Vander Bauwhede and Vanstraelen (2012) explore the relation between audit firm governance disclosure transparency and audit quality. Using publicly available data of 103 audit firms in four European countries, they study variation in governance disclosure transparency across audit firms, as well as its association with audit quality. Although they find differences in the extent and type of governance disclosures among their sample firms, they do not find that these disclosures significantly impacted audit quality. They undertake two SEM techniques in their paper: first, they confirm the factor structure of a new construct (transparency report disclosure score) using CFA; and second, they test the relations between the disclosure score and its antecedents using path analysis.

Tax

Henderson and Kaplan (2005) investigate the role of ethical beliefs on tax compliance behaviour. Fifty-five taxpayers responded to two hypothetical tax scenarios and answered other attitudinal and demographic questions. The researchers find that individuals' general ethical beliefs (ethical orientations in particular) affect tax compliance behaviour indirectly, through contextual ethical beliefs. Despite the small sample size, a full SEM approach is adopted to test the hypothesized relationships.

Blanthorne and Kaplan (2008) explore the relations among opportunity to underreport taxable income, social norms, ethical beliefs and underreporting behaviour. Survey results from 355 taxpayers indicate that high opportunity taxpayers judged evasion as less unethical than low opportunity taxpayers, and that ethical beliefs mediate the relation between opportunity, social norms and underreporting. The authors also adopt a full SEM approach.

Summary

The papers reviewed in this section cover a wide range of topics. They also utilize different SEM techniques for different purposes, such as validating factor structure of new constructs with

CFA, testing relations among multiple latent variables using full SEM, and analyzing psychological decision processes using path analysis to supplement main results. Data sources are also diverse and include survey, experimental and archival data.

SEM reporting practices

In general, SEM reporting suffers from inconsistent reporting practices (e.g., MacCallum and Austin 2000, Shook, Ketchen, Hult and Kacmar 2004, Shah and Goldstein 2006). Likewise, in the accounting literature, three papers provide detailed evidence that accounting studies using SEM contain shortcomings (Smith and Langfield-Smith 2004; Henri 2007; Rodgers and Guiral 2011). The shortcomings pertain to the sample itself (such as a sample size that is too small); construct measurement (such as missing descriptions of the reliability and validity of measurement models); the structural model (such as no rationale for the choice of fit statistics) and model respecification (little to no discussion about if and why a structural model was respecified).

Next, we review the observations provided by these papers, and subsequently provide suggestions on SEM reporting practices designed to correct or alleviate these and other shortcomings we identify.

Empirical evidence on SEM reporting practices in the accounting literature

Smith and Langfield-Smith (2004) and Henri (2007) critically reviewed management accounting studies using SEM. Smith and Langfield-Smith (2004) reviewed 20 studies from 1980 to 2001 across ten leading accounting journals. Among other shortcomings, they found that authors tended not to specify their estimation techniques, did not refer to the normality or non-normality of their data, had small sample sizes and were inconsistent in their choice of goodness-of-fit indices. Henri (2007) reviewed 41 studies from 1980 to 2005 across 14 accounting journals. He also noted important information that is missing in many studies. Such information includes but is not limited to information about sample distribution, statistical power, assessment of measurement model, estimation method, justifications for model respecification and the selection of equivalent models.

Rodgers and Guiral (2011) examined 66 studies in different accounting disciplines from 1992 through 2008, across 11 leading accounting journals, for evidence of model misspecification. Their analysis focuses on the improper classification of reflective vs. formative measurement model in particular (for a brief discussion see the next section). They found that 52 out of the 66 studies may have suffered from misspecification bias, i.e., constructs that should have been modelled as formative were modelled as reflective.

In the 75 SEM papers we identified, we noticed many of the same omissions, inconsistencies and problems that these authors elucidated. Consequently, we believe it is useful to develop a set of "SEM best practice reporting guidelines" for behavioural accounting researchers. Following a set of reporting guidelines will improve comparability and reproducibility of accounting studies that use SEM techniques.

SEM best practice reporting guidelines

In Table 25.2 we present a set of guidelines which we recommend behavioural accounting researchers follow when reporting SEM results. We constructed these guidelines based on suggestions made by Smith and Langfield-Smith (2004), Henri (2007), Rodgers and Guiral (2011),

Table 25.2 SEM reporting guidelines for Behavioural Accounting Research

Important SEM issue		Guidelines and/or rationale
Sample	• Sample size	• Minimum number is between 100 and 200 responses (Smith and Langfield-Smith 2004; Henri 2007), although it may vary according to the number of variables • The ratio of responses to number of parameters to be estimated (N:q ratio) should be at least 10:1, ideally 20:1 when maximum likelihood is used (Kline 2016) • Sample size impacts statistical power (Henri 2007)
	• Distribution of data	• Distribution of data (e.g., multivariate normality) determines what transformation procedures and estimation method should be used (Thompson 2000; McDonald and Ho 2002; Kline 2016) • Refer to Hampton (2015) for different approaches to take when data are not multivariate normal
Construct measurement	• Reflective vs. formative model	• Correctly depict constructs as reflective or formative to reduce model misspecification bias (Rodgers and Guiral 2011)
	• Validity of measurement model	• Measurement model should be explicitly tested and described in terms of reliability, convergent validity and divergent validity before structural model can be estimated (Henri 2007)
	• Number of items	• Number of items per latent variable (or number of items per factor for multidimensional latent variables) should be at least three (Ding et al. 1995; Blanthorne et al. 2006; Kline 2016)
Structural model	• Choice of fit statistics	• Fit statistics should be chosen purposefully, with explanation of their implication, because fit statistics vary depending on their purpose (Henri 2007): • overall fit (e.g., RMSEA, chi-square test, SRMR, GFI) • incremental fit compared to a baseline model (e.g., CFI) • fit adjusted for the number of variables in the model (e.g., PGFI) • There is a threshold value for each statistic that should be met for the goodness-of-fit to be supported (Kline 2016)

Important SEM issue		Guidelines and/or rationale
	• Report R² values	• R² values provide a relevant measure of fit for each structural equation (or each DV) which complements path coefficients (Henri 2007)
	• Report unstandardized estimates	• Unstandardized estimates permit comparisons across different samples (Lomax 2007)
	• Test equivalent models	• Theoretically plausible alternative models should be discussed and compared to alleviate confirmation bias (McDonald and Ho 2002; Kline 2016)
Model respecifications	• Justify model respecification	• Model respecifications should be justified to help readers understand how and why a final model was selected (Thompson 2000; Kline 2016). Specifically: ○ the specific paths or covariances added or dropped ○ theoretical reasons for adding or dropping each of them ○ statistics consulted in respecifying the model, and the value changes of these statistics

as well as Ding, Velicer and Harlow (1995), Thompson (2000), McDonald and Ho (2002), Blanthorne, Jones-Farmer and Almer (2006), Lomax (2007) and Kline (2016). For each of these guidelines, we specify the recommendation and provide succinct rationale for it.

Two issues relating to the sample are sample size and distribution of data. A minimum suggested sample size is between 100 and 200. Furthermore, when the maximum likelihood estimation method is used (the most commonly used estimation method), the ratio of responses to the number of parameters to be estimated (i.e., model parameters that require statistical estimates) should be at least 10:1 and ideally 20:1. Thus, the minimum sample size could be greater than 100 or 200, depending on the complexity of the model. As well, how the data is distributed (e.g., multivariate normality) determines what transformation procedures (e.g., Box-Cox transformations) and estimation method (e.g., maximum likelihood) must be used, so researchers should assess how their data is distributed, and comment on why this data distribution led to their choice of transformation procedures as well as estimation method.[6] Otherwise, researchers may have used an incorrect estimation technique, unbeknownst to reviewers and other readers.

Regarding construct measurement, researchers should ensure that their constructs are correctly modelled as reflective or formative. In a reflective model, a latent construct exists independent of the measures; the direction of causality is from the construct to the items or indicators that measure the construct; and items/indicators should have high positive inter-correlations. In contrast, in a formative model, a latent construct is formed from, and does not exist independent of, the measures; the direction of causality is from the items/indicators to the construct and items/indicators can have any pattern of inter-correlations as long as they have the same directional relationship (Coltman et al. 2008; Rodgers and Guiral 2011). A model may suffer from misspecification bias if the constructs are incorrectly modelled.

We also suggest that behavioural accounting researchers describe how they assessed the psychometric properties of the constructs in terms of scale reliability, convergent validity and divergent validity. Otherwise, the resulting model may lack construct validity. As well, there should be at least three items to measure any one latent variable. Having less than three items may result in an under-identified model (i.e., a model in which it is impossible to uniquely estimate parameters; Kline 2016), and may adversely impact the goodness-of-fit statistics (Ding et al. 1995).

Regarding a structural model, to alleviate confirmation bias, researchers should discuss any plausible alternative model, with the rationale for choosing the model they did. In addition, when researchers describe the results of their structural model, the fit statistics should be chosen carefully, and the rationale for the fit statistics should be provided, since there are many possible fit statistics, and the purpose of each differs. As well, the benchmark value for the fit statistic should be given if known (such as from a SEM textbook like Kline 2016), and the results compared to the benchmark, to provide some degree of assurance over the robustness of the model fit. Otherwise, it is possible for researchers to hide the fact that their model may not be well-fitting by choosing a statistic that may not be relevant, or by failing to report the benchmark value.

We also suggest that researchers report the R^2 value for each structural equation (or DV), since this value provides a measure of fit for each structural equation (or DV) that is not captured by the overall model fit indices. Finally, we suggest that researchers report unstandardized estimates (in addition to standardized estimates), since unstandardized estimates permit comparisons across different samples, whereas standardized estimates are more appropriate when comparing effects within a given sample.

If a structural model was respecified (e.g., paths or covariances added or dropped), researchers should provide both theoretical and statistical justifications, and illustrate how the respecified model compares to the theoretical model in terms of model fit. Doing so will help readers understand why a final model was selected, and may also provide theoretical insights.

Future directions

Within the four sub-disciplines of accounting we reviewed, management accounting clearly dominated in terms of the usage of SEM. Of the 75 articles we identified as published in the last two decades, 43 of these were related to management accounting. There were 16 articles related to auditing, six related to tax and four related to financial accounting. The remaining six were accounting-oriented, but did not clearly fall into any of these sub-disciplines. Thus, apart from management accounting, other accounting sub-disciplines could potentially benefit from an increased use of SEM.

Kline (2016) noted that a narrow view of SEM is that SEM is inappropriate for analyzing experimental data. However, an insight that emerged from Chen and Tan (2013) was the use of SEM as a complementary mediation analysis of experimental data. Chen and Tan (2013) was an experimental study that used SEM analysis to corroborate the model tested experimentally. Experimental researchers could consider using SEM to supplement traditional ANOVA to provide insights into the thought process of the participants.

It is also useful for behavioural accounting researchers to be aware of advanced statistical techniques in SEM. For instance, SEM techniques can be used to analyze interaction effects. In path analysis, the interactive effects can be simply captured by product terms between two observed independent variables, just as in multiple regression. To test for interaction effects among *latent* variables, we encourage readers to refer to Little, Bovaird and Widaman (2006), who review different approaches to testing for interaction effects among latent constructs. Of the 75 accounting studies we identified, none tested interaction effects among latent variables.

Accounting research using SEM tends to deal with data collected from one sample during one period. Consequently, multi-group and multi-period analyses have received little attention. Among the 75 studies we surveyed, only Blanthorne and Kaplan (2008) used multi-group SEM and none employed multi-period analysis. Multi-group analysis allows researchers to compare measurement and structural models between samples, such as between countries, industries, corporations or samples of different characteristics. Multi-period SEM analysis (structured as a latent growth model) allows researchers to test relationships between variables that are measured at different time periods while adjusting for errors or common variances associated with time.[7] We encourage behavioural accounting researchers to consider multi-group and multi-period analysis.

Conclusion

In this chapter, we provided an overview of SEM as a cluster of statistical techniques for accounting researchers, and also reviewed noteworthy accounting studies from the last decade that used SEM. We discuss the use of different SEM techniques, which highlights the scope and diversity of accounting research that benefits from SEM. Additionally, given the inconsistencies and concerns with SEM reporting practices in the accounting literature, we devised a set of SEM reporting guidelines for use by behavioural accounting researchers based on a number of prior studies. Following them should produce more consistent, reproducible and robust empirical results. We also suggest future directions for behavioural accounting researchers to consider when using SEM.

We gratefully acknowledge the helpful comments of Cindy Blanthorne and both editors, as well as research assistance from Phil Walker and Chadwick Poon.

Notes

1 Broadly speaking, factor analysis is used either to identify latent constructs (or factors) underlying multiple observed variables (exploratory factor analysis or EFA), or to evaluate the adequacy of the factor structure of certain latent constructs (confirmatory factor analysis or CFA). CFA differs from EFA in that factor structures are hypothesized a priori and verified empirically rather than derived from the data (Lei and Wu 2007).

2 Rodgers and Guiral (2011) and Coltman, Devinney, Midgley and Venaik (2008) explain the difference between reflective and formative indicators (items) of latent variables.

3 The goal of covariance-based SEM is to determine whether the a priori pattern of relations depicted in the structural model is consistent with collected data. As such, it is largely a confirmatory, rather than exploratory, technique. Since it is a confirmatory technique, the relationships among the latent constructs should be based on underlying theories. In contrast, variance-based SEM, PLS for example, can be used to study exploratory models.

4 Later in the chapter, we identify a number of accounting SEM studies. We chose the examples in Table 25.1 from the same pool and selected them specifically because they very clearly exemplify the correct use of each SEM approach.

5 *Accounting, Organizations & Society*; *The Accounting Review*; *Contemporary Accounting Research*; *Auditing*; *Accounting, Auditing & Accountability Journal*; *Behavioral Research in Accounting*; *International Journal of Accounting*; *Journal of Accounting and Public Policy*; *Management Accounting Research*; *Journal of Management Accounting Research* and *Journal of the American Taxation Association*.

6 Bamber and Iyer (2007) exemplify the importance of assessing the distribution of collected data, since their data was not multivariate normal, and therefore violates a key assumption of SEM. However, these authors used SEM techniques successfully by using the polyserial correlation matrix (rather than a default variance-covariance matrix) as their input data. We refer readers to Hampton (2015), who discusses a number of approaches to estimating structural models when data is not multivariate normal.

Jonathan Farrar and Lan Guo

7 Latent growth modelling refers to a class of models for longitudinal data that can be analyzed using both SEM and other techniques such as hierarchical linear modelling. The SEM technique typically requires first, "a continuous dependent variable measured on at least three different occasions", and "scores that have the same units across time and can be said to measure the same construct at each assessment" (Kline 2016: 304).

References

Ajzen, I. and Fishbein, M., 1980, *Understanding Attitudes and Predicting Social Behavior*, Prentice Hall, Englewood Cliffs, NJ.

Anderson, J. and Gerbing, D., 1988, 'Structural equation modeling in practice: A review and recommended two-step approach', *Psychological Bulletin* 103(2), 411–423.

Bamber, E. and Iyer, V., 2007, 'Auditors' identification with their clients and its effect on auditors' objectivity', *Auditing* 26(2), 1–24.

Birnberg, J., 2011, 'A proposed framework for behavioral accounting research', *Behavioral Research in Accounting* 23(1), 1–43.

Blanthorne, C., Jones-Farmer, L. and Almer, E., 2006, 'Why you should consider SEM: A guide to getting started', *Advances in Accounting Behavioral Research* 9, 179–207.

Blanthorne, C. and Kaplan, S., 2008, 'An egocentric model of the relations among the opportunity to underreport, social norms, ethical beliefs, and underreporting behavior', *Accounting, Organizations and Society* 33(7), 684–703.

Burnett, J. and Williams, J., 2005, 'Structural equation modeling (SEM): An introduction to basic techniques and advanced issues', in R. Swanson and F. Elwood (eds.), *Research in Organizations: Foundations and Methods of Inquiry*, 143–160, Berrett-Koehler, San Francisco.

Byrne, B., 1998, *Structural Equation Modeling With LISREL, PRELIS, and SIMPLIS*, Lawrence Erlbaum Associates, Mahwah, NJ.

Byrne, B., 2006, *Structural Equation Modeling With EQS* (2nd ed.), Lawrence Erlbaum Associates, Mahwah, NJ.

Byrne, B., 2010, *Structural Equation Modeling With AMOS* (2nd ed.), Routledge, New York.

Byrne, B., 2012, *Structural Equation Modeling With Mplus*, Routledge, New York.

Cadez, S. and Guilding, C., 2008, 'An exploratory investigation of an integrated contingency model of strategic management accounting', *Accounting, Organizations and Society* 33(7), 836–863.

Chen, W. and Tan, H.-T., 2013, 'Judgment effects of familiarity with an analyst's name', *Accounting, Organizations and Society* 38(3), 214–227.

Coltman, T., Devinney, T., Midgley, D. and Venaik, S., 2008, 'Formative versus reflective measurement models: Two applications of formative measurement', *Journal of Business Research* 61(12), 1250–1262.

Deumes, R., Schelleman, C., Vander Bauwhede, H. and Vanstraelen, A., 2012, 'Audit firm governance: Do transparency reports reveal audit quality?', *Auditing: A Journal of Practice and Theory* 31(4), 193–214.

Ding, L., Velicer, W. and Harlow, L., 1995, 'Effects of estimation methods, number of indicators per factor, and improper solutions on structural equation modeling fit indices', *Structural Equation Modeling* 2(2), 119–144.

Drake, A., Wong, J. and Salter, S., 2007, 'Empowerment, motivation, and performance: Examining the impact of feedback and incentives on nonmanagement employees', *Behavioral Research in Accounting* 19, 71–89.

Gillett, P.R. and Uddin, N., 2005, 'CFO intentions of fraudulent financial reporting', *Auditing: A Journal of Practice & Theory* 24(1), 55–75.

Hair, J., Anderson, R., Tatham, R. and Black, W., 1998, *Multivariate Data Analysis With Readings* (5th ed.), Prentice Hall, Upper Saddle River, NJ.

Hampton, C., 2015, 'Estimating and reporting structural equation models with behavioral accounting data', *Behavioral Research in Accounting* 27(2), 1–34.

Henderson, B. and Kaplan, S., 2005, 'An examination of the role of ethics in tax compliance decisions', *The Journal of the American Taxation Association* 27(1), 39–72.

Henri, J.-F., 2007, 'A quantitative assessment of the reporting of structural equation modeling information: The case of management accounting research', *Journal of Accounting Literature* 26, 76–115.

Kline, R., 2016, *Principles and Practices of Structural Equation Modeling* (4th ed.), The Guilford Press, New York.

Lee, L., Petter, S., Fayard, D. and Robinson, S., 2011, 'On the use of partial least squares path modeling in accounting research', *International Journal of Accounting Information Systems* 12(4), 305–328.

Lei, P.-W. and Wu, Q., 2007, 'Introduction to structural equation modeling: Issues and practical considerations', *Educational Measurement: Issues and Practices* 26(3), 33–43.

Little, T., Bovaird, J. and Widaman, K., 2006, 'On the merits of orthogonalizing powered and product terms: Implications for modeling interactions among latent variables', *Structural Equation Modeling* 13(4), 497–519.

Lomax, R., 2007, *An Introduction to Statistical Concepts*, Lawrence Erlbaum Associates, Mahwah, NJ.

MacCallum, R. and Austin, J., 2000, 'Applications of structural equation modeling in psychological research', *Annual Review of Psychology* 51, 201–226.

McDonald, R. and Ho, M.-H., 2002, 'Principles and practice in reporting structural equation analyses', *Psychological Methods* 7(1), 64–82.

Oberski, D. and Satorra, A., 2013, 'Measurement error models with uncertainty about the error variance', *Structural Equation Modeling* 20(3), 409–428.

Pondeville, S., Swaen, V. and De Rongé, Y., 2013, 'Environmental management control systems: The role of contextual and strategic factors', *Management Accounting Research* 24(2), 317–332.

Rodgers, W. and Guiral, A., 2011, 'Potential model misspecification bias: Formative indicators enhancing theory for accounting researchers', *The International Journal of Accounting* 46(1), 25–50.

Shah, R. and Goldstein, S., 2006, 'Use of structural equation modeling in operations management research: Looking back and forward', *Journal of Operations Management* 24(2), 148–169.

Shook, C., Ketchen, D., Hult, G. and Kacmar, K., 2004, 'An assessment of the use of structural equation modeling in strategic management research', *Strategic Management Journal* 25(4), 397–404.

Simmonds, K., 1981, 'Strategic management accounting', *Management Accounting UK* 59, 26–29.

Simons, R., 2000, *Performance Management and Control Systems for Implementing Strategy*, Prentice Hall, Upper Saddle River, NJ.

Smith, D. and Langfield-Smith, K., 2004, 'Structural equation modeling in management accounting research: Critical analysis and opportunities', *Journal of Accounting Literature* 23, 49–86.

Thompson, B., 2000, 'Ten commandments of structural equation modeling', in L. Grimm and P. Yarnell (eds.), *Reading and Understanding More Multivariate Statistics*, 261–284, American Psychological Association, Washington, DC.

Tomarken, A. and Waller, N., 2005, 'Structural equation modeling: Strengths, limitations, and misconceptions', *Annual Review of Clinical Psychology* 1, 31–65.

Turner, J., Hogg, M., Oakes, P., Reicher, S. and Wetherell, M., 1987, *Rediscovering the Social Group: A Self-Categorization Theory*, Basil Blackwell, Oxford.

Ullman, J., 2006, 'Structural equation modeling: Reviewing the basics and moving forward', *Journal of Personality Assessment* 87(1), 35–50.

Wentzel, K., 2002, 'The influence of fairness perceptions and goal commitment on managers' performance in a budget setting', *Behavioral Research in Accounting* 14, 247–271.

Widener, S., 2007, 'An empirical analysis of the levers of control framework', *Accounting, Organizations and Society* 32(7), 757–788.

26

Review of specialized multivariate approaches in Behavioural Accounting Research

Jean-François Henri

Introduction

Previous chapters have addressed various statistical approaches; some have a long tradition in behavioural research (i.e., regression, analysis of covariance, mediation, moderation, factor analysis, etc.) whilst others are more recent (structural equation model, mediated moderation, etc.). The purpose of this chapter is to examine other statistical approaches that could be of interest for behavioural researchers. These techniques represent specialized multivariate approaches that have not yet been used extensively in behavioural research. Three specific techniques are examined in this study, namely (a) *logit and probit models* which are a specialized form of regression used to predict an outcome or an event displaying a finite and small number of values (often dichotomous) from a set of predictors, (b) *cluster analysis* which is used to identify groups of objects reflecting common alignment of elements and (c) *multidimensional scaling* which is an exploratory technique that transforms individual judgments of similarity or preference among objects into distances represented in multidimensional space. The aim of this chapter is not to provide an exhaustive and technical description of those statistical tools but instead to address four basic questions: What is the basic purpose of the approach? What are the pros and cons? How does it work globally? How has this approach been used so far in past accounting behavioural studies?[1]

Logit and probit models

General description

Logit (logarithm of odds) and probit (probability unit) models are a specialized form of regression used to predict an outcome or an event displaying a finite and usually small number of values (discrete or dichotomous variable) from a set of predictors that may be continuous, discrete, dichotomous or a mix (Tabachnick and Fidell 2013). These models produce an estimate of the probability that the dependent variable is equal to 1 given a set of independent variables. More specifically, both models assume that the probability of the outcome or event is linked to a linear combination of predictors (i.e., regression function) by a nonlinear function. This nonlinear function can either be (a) a logistic cumulative distribution function (logit model or logistic regression) or (b) a normal cumulative distribution function (probit model) (Ge and Whitmore 2010). In addition to this difference in the transformation applied to the proportions forming the dependent variables, logit and probit models differ mainly in their emphasis regarding the results. The logit model focuses on odd ratios while the probit model mainly emphasizes the effective values of predictors for different rates of responses (Tabachnick and Fidell 2013). Otherwise, logit and probit models are highly related (further delineation of the differences between those two models will be discussed later). Numerous past accounting studies have used logit and probit models to investigate the determinants of certain types of events such as choice of accounting methods, firm failure, bond ratings, lobbying before the Financial Accounting Standards Board (FASB) and auditors' decision (Ge and Whitmore 2010; Maddala 1991). However, as will be discussed later, less interest has been shown in behavioural studies toward these approaches, notably the probit model.

Pros and cons

The more flexible but more complex nature of logit and probit models compared to Ordinary Least Squares (OLS) regression lead to various advantages and disadvantages. Table 26.1 summarizes the main pros and cons of logit and probit models as described notably by Tabachnick and Fidell (2013), Jones and Hensher (2007) and Hoetker (2007).

Table 26.1 Main pros and cons of logit and probit models

Pros	Cons
• Theoretically attractive alternatives to OLS regression when the independent variable is discrete or continuous. • Especially useful when the distribution of responses of the outcome or event is expected to be nonlinear with one or more predictors. • Unlike OLS regression, cannot produce negative predicted probabilities. • Relatively free from restrictions, such as specific distributional form of the independent variable, heteroscedasticity and linear effects. • Capacity to analyze a mix of continuous, discrete and dichotomous predictors. • No need for weighting procedures because the coefficients are not affected by the unequal sampling rates between groups.	• The interpretation of logit/probit coefficients is more complex than OLS coefficients because the effect of a change in one variable depends on the initial probability of the event occurring. • Even more complicated, and often unintuitive, in the presence of interactions between two variables because the marginal effect of an interaction between is not reflected directly by the coefficient for their interaction. • Problems may occur when the ratio of cases to number of predictors is insufficient (sample size should commonly be ten times the number of the estimated model coefficients in each group). • Assumes a linear relationship between continuous predictors and the transformation of the dependent variables, although there are no assumptions about linear relationships among the predictors. • Unlike OLS regressions, comparing covariates' effects across groups is only valid if each group has the same amount of unobserved variations (error term).

(Continued)

Table 26.1 (Continued)

Pros	Cons
	• No direct equivalent to R^2 to provide an indication of how well the model fits the data like in OLS regressions. Various pseudo-R^2 measures are proposed, but not only will they take different values for the same model but more importantly they do not represent the percentage of variance explained as commonly interpreted in OLS regressions.
	• Basic logit/probit models are severely hampered by restrictive assumptions regarding the unobserved influences of the model and they do not adequately capture the variety of firm-specific observed and unobserved heterogeneity existing between and within firms.[i]

[i] Based on the discrete choice literature, Jones and Hensher (2007) propose three more advanced logit model structures which correct for these restrictive conditions, namely nested logit, mixed logit and latent class-MNL.

Overview and illustration of the method

A general overview of the functioning of logit and probit models in three steps is provided mainly based on the work of Tabachnick and Fidell (2013). These steps are illustrated using survey data collected from a sample of 227 small-and-medium sized enterprises (SME). The main purpose of this study is to examine the influence of personal characteristics of SME managers on the use of performance measurement systems (PMS).

Step 1: determining key parameters

Four key decisions must be made in this step. First, the researcher has to establish the number and type of outcome categories. The categories can be nominal (without order) or ordinal (with order). The number and type of predictor categories are also determined (discrete, dichotomous or continuous) as well the inclusion or not of interactions among predictors. Second, one type of inferential test has to be determined: test of model (to assess overall model fit of various models using approaches such as chi-square tests, pseudo-R^2 and classification accuracy) or test of individual predictors (to evaluate the contribution of an individual predictor to a model using a specific test such as the Wald test or the Lagrange multiplier for instance). Third, one type of regression has to be selected among three, namely (a) direct (all predictors enter the equation simultaneously), (b) sequential (the researcher specifies the order of entry of the predictors) and (c) statistical (statistical criteria guide the inclusion and removal of predictors). Fourth, the researcher determines the transformation to apply to the proportions forming the dependent variables, namely logit or probit.

In this example, the outcome is a two-category nominal variable displaying the choice of SME managers to use predominately PMS diagnostically (0) or interactively (1). The predictors are three continuous variables reflecting individual characteristics of the SME managers, namely intolerance for ambiguity, self-esteem and locus of control. For the purpose of simplicity, no interaction is considered between these characteristics, and direct regression is used. The logit model is used to evaluate the contribution of individual characteristics on the probability of using PMS diagnostically or interactively.

Step 2: deriving the logit-probit model solution

The logit and probit models are used to model which of two (or more) alternatives occurs. In our example, we argue that SME managers' decision to use predominately PMS in a diagnostic or interactive way (y_i) is linearly related to a vector of three observable individual characteristics (x_i), namely intolerance for ambiguity, self-esteem and locus of control, and other unobservable factors (error term ε_i). The probability that $y_i = 1$ is given by the equation above where β is the vector of coefficients to be estimated (Hoetker 2007).

$$P(y_i = 1x_i) = \begin{cases} \dfrac{exp(x_i'\beta)}{1 + exp(x_i'\beta)} & \text{for logit} \\ \\ \Phi(x_i'\beta) & \text{for probit where } \Phi \text{ is the cumulative density function for the standard normal} \end{cases}$$

Step 3: interpreting the results

As previously mentioned, logit and probit models differ mainly in their emphasis regarding the results as the former focuses on odd ratios whereas the latter mainly emphasizes the effective values of predictors for different rates of responses (Tabachnick and Fidell 2013). We specifically focus here on the interpretation of the results of the logit model as it has been used more intensively in behavioural studies than the probit model. The interpretation can be made mainly with the original coefficients of the predictors (representing changes in the log of the odds) or the exponentiated coefficients (representing changes in the odds) (Hair, Black, Babin and Anderson 2010). The direction can be assessed by both coefficients: (a) directly using the sign of the original coefficient (positive or negative) or (b) indirectly with the value of the exponentiated coefficient (less than 1 indicates a negative relationship, more than 1 indicates a positive relationship). The magnitude of the coefficient is commonly assessed by the exponentiated coefficient. The percentage of change in the outcome or event is obtained by subtracting 1 from the exponentiated coefficient, and multiplying the result by 100. In a review of 31 articles in leading accounting journals using the logit model for binary dependent variables, Ge and Whitmore (2010) observed that most studies only examine p-values of the estimated coefficients to test for statistical significance whilst rare attempts are made to assess the magnitude of these coefficients.

The main results of the logit model for the illustrative case are presented in Table 26.2.

In terms of statistical significance of the coefficients, the results of the Wald test suggest that only locus of control has a significant impact on the estimated probability of using PMS diagnostically or interactively $(p < .05)$. Regarding the directionality of the relationship, the sign of the original coefficient (B) coefficient or the value of the exponentiated

Table 26.2 Variables in the equation

Independent variables	B	Std. error	Wald	df	Sig	Exp(B)
Intolerance for ambiguity	.030	.255	.014	1	.907	1.030
Self-esteem	-.573	.357	2.579	1	.108	.564
Locus of control	.675	.309	4.785	1	.029	1.965
Constant	.744	1.911	.151	1	.697	2.103

coefficient (Exp(B)) is used. Intolerance for ambiguity and locus of control have a positive influence on the use of PMS interactively, whereas self-esteem has a negative impact. The magnitude of the relationships is derived from the exponentiated coefficient. The coefficient of intolerance for ambiguity and locus of control denotes respectively a 3% and 96.5% increase in the odds ratio.[2] A one-unit change in the locus of control variable will increase the odds of using PMS interactively by 96.5%. Regarding self-esteem, the results suggest a decrease of 43.6% of the odds ratio.

Review of selected behavioural accounting studies using logit and probit models

Compared to other streams of accounting research, few behavioural studies have relied on logit and probit models. Table 26.3 summarizes the main behavioural studies published in accounting journals. It is worth mentioning that all studies examined have used the logit model except one.

As suggested by Maddala 1991: 790), "there is usually not much to choose from between the logit and probit models." However, notable exceptions might explain why logit is more commonly used in accounting research than probit, and might be useful to determine which techniques should be used (Maddala 1991; Noreen 1988; Tabachnick and Fidell 2013). First,

Table 26.3 Review of selected behavioural accounting studies using logit and probit models

Study	Journal	Outcome/event variable	Predictors	Model
Keasey and Short (1990)	Accounting and Business Research	Relative burden of annual accounts (ordinal ranking variable of eight requirements)	• Incorporation of the firm • Perceived benefits from preparing annual accounts • Size of firms of accountants • General accounting needs provided by a firm of accountants • Annual accounts prepared externally by an accountants' firm • Frequency of management accounts • Size, age and turnover of the firm	Probit
Schaefer and Welker (1994)	Journal of Accounting and Public Policy	Disciplined CPAs 0=General population of CPAs 1=Disciplined CPAs for three types of violation (due care, state regulations, criminal)	• Gender • Years of audit experience • Size of firm • Membership in state society • Population of country in which office is located	Logit

Study	Journal	Outcome/event variable	Predictors	Model
Collins, Parrish and Collins (1998)	Issues in Accounting Education	Consideration of tenure at the first institution; Tenure granted at first faculty position 1=yes; 0= no	• Gender • Training • Institutional resources and expectation • Research activity	Logit
Viger, Belzile and Anandarajan (2008)	Behavioral Research in Accounting	Decision to grant a loan by loan officers 0=no 1=yes	• Format of reporting (3 types) • Overall risk rating and trend rating • Firm's overall financial condition • Firm's ability to sustain growth • Firm's ability to pay its debts	Logit
Bobek and Hatfield (2003)	Behavioral Research in Accounting	Cheating intentions 0=no cheating 1=partial cheating 2=maximum cheating	• Attitude toward cheating • Subjective norms • Perceived behavioural control • Moral obligation	Logit
Aier, Comprix, Gunlock and Lee (2005)	Accounting Horizons	Accounting errors 1=if the company restated its earnings 0=otherwise	• Years of work – chief financial officer (CFO) • Experience • Advanced degrees • Professional certification	Logit
Widener (2006)	Management Accounting Research	Use of performance measures in bonus compensation 1=plans that primarily emphasize financial measures 2=plans that use non-financial measures to complement traditional financial measures Note: A more refined classification in four groups is also provided	• Reliance on human capital within firm • Firm's pay structure	Logit
Parsons (2007)	Behavioral Research in Accounting	Donation 1=cash contribution was received 0=otherwise	• Positive financial accounting information • Voluntary SEA disclosure • Prior donor	Logit
Law (2010)	Journal of Applied Accounting Research	Accounting students' career choice 1=public accounting 2=general accounting 3=non-accounting	• Intrinsic factors • Financial reward • High school education • Gender • Flexibility of career • Parental influence	Logit

probit models are to some extent more restrictive than logit models regarding the assumption of normal distribution. In other words, the use of the logit model is commonly suggested in the cases where data are concentrated in the tails. Second, logit models are considered more convenient when the analysis is based on matched samples. Lastly, logit models are more appropriate for multinomial variables, especially in the context of unordered categories.

Cluster analysis

General description

Cluster analysis is used to identify groups of objects reflecting a common alignment of elements. The 'objects' can be persons, firms, products, practices or any other entity that can be evaluated according to a number of attributes (Hair et al. 2010). This statistical technique sorts observations into similar sets or groups for which variance among elements grouped together is minimized while between-group variance is maximized (Ketchen and Shook 1996). Cluster analysis can be used for three main purposes, namely (a) description of taxonomy or validation of typology, (b) data simplification by defining structure among observations and (c) identification of relationships not previously revealed (Hair et al. 2010). Cluster analysis is similar to factor analysis in that the objective of both analyses is to assess structure. However, factor analysis groups variables based on patterns of variation while cluster analysis groups objects on the basis of distance. There are a limited number of accounting studies that have used cluster analysis. Most of them address issues related to management accounting.

Pros and cons

Despite its ability for data simplification and structuration, cluster analysis has received considerable criticism in the literature. Table 26.4 summarizes the main pros and cons of cluster analysis as denoted notably by Ketchen and Shook (1996) and Hair et al. (2010).

Table 26.4 Main pros and cons of cluster analysis

Pros	Cons
• Useful for pattern recognition and grouping • Captures the complexity of organizational reality by providing rich descriptions of configurations • Suitable for data reduction and/or hypothesis generation, as well as exploratory or confirmatory research objectives • No specific requirements in terms of normality, linearity and homoscedasticity	• Descriptive, atheoretical and noninferential in nature • Completely dependent on the variables used which can lead to inaccurate depictions of the grouping. It cannot differentiate relevant from irrelevant variables • Clusters will always be created, which could lead to groupings being imposed where none exist • No comprehensive assessment of the efficacy of its use • Extensive reliance on researcher judgment, notably for the choice of variables and methods, the number of clusters, and the interpretation of the solution. It is considered to be as much as an art as a science • Sample size has to be sufficiently large to represent all the relevant groups

Overview and illustration of the method

A general overview of the functioning of cluster analysis in three steps is provided mainly based on the work of Hair et al. (2010) and Ketchen and Shook (1996). These steps are illustrated with survey data collected from a sample of 227 small-and-medium enterprises (SME). As mentioned in the previous section, the main purpose of this study is to examine the influence of personal characteristics of SME managers on the use of performance measurement systems (PMS).

Step 1: determining key parameters

Four key decisions must be made in this step. First, the researcher has to select the clustering variables (dimensions) along which to group the objects (observations). Three methods can be used to identify the variables, namely inductive, deductive and cognitive (Ketchen, Thomas and Snow 1993). Second, the researcher determines whether the data will be standardized or not. The trade-off is that on the one hand, standardization allows for variables to contribute equally to the definition of clusters, but on the other hand it may also eliminate meaningful differences among variables. Third, a choice has to be made among several distance measures used to create groups, notably (Squared) Euclidian distance, City-block (Manhattan) distance and Mahalanobis distance. Fourth, the rules to sort observations (clustering algorithms) have to be chosen among three possibilities: hierarchical, non-hierarchical and a combination of both approaches. Hierarchical methods include mainly five agglomerative algorithms, namely single-linkage, complete-linkage, average linkage, centroid method and Ward's method. The most common non-hierarchical approach is K-means. A two-stage procedure is commonly suggested to gain benefits from both hierarchical and non-hierarchical methods.

In our example, seven clustering variables are selected, namely (a) three continuous variables referring to individual characteristics of SME managers: intolerance for ambiguity, self-esteem and locus of control, (b) two continuous variables reflecting the use of PMS: diagnostic and interactive and (c) two continuous variables displaying the design of PMS in terms of the relative attention (%) devoted to financial and non-financial indicators. Those variables are standardized considering that differences in the range of the PMS design variable (0–100%) in comparison to the individual characteristics and PMS use (scale from 1 to 7). For the purpose of simplicity, Squared Euclidian distance is used with one hierarchical method, namely Ward's method.

Step 2: deriving the cluster solution

One of the most perplexing issues in cluster analysis is to determine the final number of clusters. The use of multiple techniques is suggested in the literature to deal with this issue (Aldenderfer and Blashfield 1984). These techniques include notably (a) analysis of dendogram, (b) two techniques based on the agglomeration coefficient, namely a graph reflecting the number of clusters against the agglomeration coefficient (the appropriate number of clusters is found at the 'elbow' of the graph), and an examination of the incremental changes in the agglomeration coefficient (the appropriate number of clusters is found at the step before a sudden jump occurs) and (c) cubic clustering criterion (CCC) whereby the appropriate number of clusters is indicated by the peaking of CCC.

For the illustrative case, the two techniques based on the agglomeration coefficients guide the selection of the final cluster solution. These techniques suggest that a two-cluster solution is the most appropriate classification. Table 26.5 contains the mean score of each variable for each cluster.

Table 26.5 Results of cluster analysis

Clustering variables	Cluster 1	Cluster 2	Sig
Individual characteristics			
Intolerance for ambiguity	3.83	3.52	**
Self-esteem	5.08	5.43	**
Locus of control	4.87	5.62	**
PMS design			
Financial	6.18	5.20	**
Non-financial	3.32	3.91	*
PMS use			
Diagnostic	4.30	5.96	**
Interactive	3.76	5.63	**
Number of cases (N)	80	147	

Note: ** $p<0.01$; * $p<0.05$

Step 3: interpreting the results

The purpose of this step is to assign a label (or name) that accurately depicts the nature of each cluster by examining the variation between each clustering variable. Given the absence of statistical tests to validate the results, it is commonly suggested to validate the cluster solution. First, solutions can be derived using different distance measures and clustering algorithms. Furthermore, split samples and hold-out samples can be used to increase the reliability and validity of the complete procedure.

The results of the illustrative case suggest the presence of two groups. The first group (n=80) contains SME managers displaying less tolerance for ambiguity, less self-esteem and external locus of control. They do not use PMS to a great extent, notably in an interactive way, and emphasize financial indicators. In sum, managers in this group are more insecure and use PMS more passively in a mechanistic fashion; this cluster could be named "mechanistic insecure". The second group (n=140) contains SME managers displaying more tolerance for ambiguity, more self-esteem and internal locus of control. They use PMS diagnostically and interactively to a great extent, and display a good mix of financial and non-financial indicators. In sum, managers in this group are more self-confident and use PMS more actively in an organic fashion, this cluster could be labelled "organic confident".

Review of selected behavioural accounting studies using cluster analysis

As with the general accounting research, few behavioural studies have relied on cluster analysis. Table 26.6 summarizes the main behavioural studies published in accounting journals.

Multidimensional scaling

General description

Multidimensional scaling (MDS), also known as perceptual mapping, comprises a series of geometric models for multidimensional representation of data (Watkins 1984). It is an exploratory technique that transforms individual judgments of *similarity* or *preference* among objects into

Table 26.6 Review of selected behavioural accounting studies using cluster analysis

Study	Journal	Objects	Clustering variables	Clusters identified
Holmes and Marsden (1996)	*Accounting Horizons*	Cultures of public accounting firms	• Affiliation • Authority • Commitment • Equity • Leadership • Normative • Participation • Performance • Reward • Teamwork	1- Elite 2- Leadership 3- Meritocratic 4- Collegial
Dimnik and Felton (2006)	*Accounting, Organizations and Society*	Accountants' image in popular cinema	• Warmth • Confidence • Vitality • Occupational status • Outlook • Appearance	1- Dreamer 2- Plodder 3- Eccentric 4- Hero 5- Villain
Seifried (2012)	*Accounting Education: An International Journal*	Teacher types or belief systems regarding teaching and learning	• Constructivist ideas • Instructional ideas • Systematic ideas	1- Constructivist orientation 2- Instructional orientation 3- Systematic type

distances represented in multidimensional space. More specifically, this technique is particularly helpful in answering two fundamental questions: (a) On what dimensions or attributes are the objects seen as differing? (b) What is the perceived position of each object on each of these dimensions (Libby 1979)? Compared to other multivariate techniques, MDS is characterized by the use of a single and overall measure of judgment. More precisely, compared to other interdependence techniques such as cluster analysis discussed previously or factor analysis, MDS differs in two main elements (Hair et al. 2010). First, as the primary emphasis is on how the individual perceives the objects, and not the objects per se, MDS can provide a solution for each individual (as well as aggregated). In other words, the individual is the unit of analysis. As evaluations of all objects are provided by each respondent, a specific solution can be obtained for each individual instead of an average solution. Second, as MDS does not use a variate, the dimensions that make up the variate are inferred by the researcher from the overall measure of judgment. Therefore, it reduces the influence of the researcher who does not have to specify the dimensions to be used to compare objects.

Past accounting research has primarily used MDS to help identify structures that would otherwise be hard to identify when examining attitudes and perceptions of accountants and users of accounting information (Watkins 1984). This approach is useful in accounting research when the researcher aims to determine the perceived relative image of a set of accounting objects based on undefined and indefinite dimensions, i.e., perceived message in audit reports, perceived information use of annual reports, the perceived attributes of accounting firms, the perception of tax complexity, etc.

Pros and cons

The flexibility and inferential nature of MDS leads to numerous advantages but also important limitations. Table 26.7 summarizes the main pros and cons of MDS as denoted notably by Hair et al. (2010) and Watkins (1984).

Overview and illustration of the method

A general overview of the functioning of MDS is provided in three main steps based on the work of Hair et al. (2010). Those steps are illustrated with the study of Libby (1979) which constitutes one of the first behavioural accounting studies to use MDS. The purpose of this study was to determine and compare the perception of auditors and bankers regarding the message intended by the audit report.

Step 1: determining key parameters

Three key decisions must be made in this step. First, the researcher must select the objects to be evaluated. The number of objects must balance two considerations. On the one hand, a small number of objects facilitates the task of the participant. On the other hand, a suggested guideline for stable solutions is to have at least four times as many objects as dimensions desired. Second, the researcher must choose the basis of evaluation, namely similarities or preferences. This distinction is important because participants may base their preferences on different dimensions from those on which they base comparisons to establish similarities. The third decision relates to the level of analysis: individual vs. group level. The individual level refers to a disaggregate

Table 26.7 Main pros and cons of MDS

Pros	Cons
• Ability to infer dimensions without the need for defined attributes, and thus reduces the influence of the researcher who does not have to specify the dimensions to be used to compare objects.	• Exploratory, subjective and tentative nature of MDS that cannot give the 'true representations' of the underlying structure.
• The respondent only has to provide an overall judgment of the objects, namely a full assessment of similarity or preference among all objects. Therefore, the dimensions used are more likely to be a natural consequence of the judgmental task.	• The researcher has no objective basis to assess the dimensions used by the respondent when providing its judgment.
• These overall judgments are relatively free from evaluative reactions on the part of the respondents. More specifically, it is problematic to word questionnaires or tests and to avoid the evaluative connotations reflected by adjectives and adverbs.	• Except generalized guidelines (nonstatistical) and a priori beliefs, little guidance is available to support decisions regarding the final solution. Therefore, this technique involves substantial judgment from the researcher.
• Production of visual representation of the individual's judgment that helps in uncovering hidden structures in the data.	• The results can be greatly influenced by the inclusion of inappropriate objects or the omission of important objects.
• No restraining assumptions on the methodology, type of data or form of the relationships among the variables.	

analysis while the group level leads to an aggregate analysis. Three common approaches of aggregate analysis are (a) aggregating before the MDS analysis, (b) aggregating individual results and (c) INDSCAL, a combination of disaggregate and aggregate analyses.

Using a laboratory experiment, Libby (1979) considers ten different types of audit reports (e.g., unqualified, two variations of uncertainty qualification and uncertainty disclaimer, two variations of the scope qualification and scope disclaimer, and the unaudited disclaimer), which leads to 45 pairs of reports to compare in order to identify a number of dimensions. He asked 30 audit partners and 28 commercial loan officers to rate the relative similarity of the messages intended by each of the pair of reports on a ten-point scale. Following the precept of the MDS, the criteria for judging the similarities were left up to the participants. Using an aggregate analysis, Libby has chosen the INDSCAL approach to analyze the data.

Step 2: deriving the MDS solution and assessing the overall fit

Based on the MDS techniques, the researcher compares the results of solutions provided for different dimensionalities (i.e., two dimensions, three dimensions, etc.). The final solution will determine the number of dimensions and the relative position of each object on those dimensions. The number of dimensions is generally determined through one (or more) of three main approaches, namely (a) subjective evaluation, (b) scree plots of stress measure and (c) index of fit. First, the subjective evaluation refers to the assessment of whether the solutions appear to be reasonable in order to obtain the best fit with the smallest number of dimensions. Second, the stress measure refers to the proportion of the variance of the disparities[3] not accounted for by the MDS model. A lower stress value indicates a better goodness-of-fit. Similar to the cluster analysis, a scree plot combining the stress value and the number of dimensions indicates the optimal number of dimensions at the 'elbow'. Lastly, an index of fit can be computed to determine how well the raw data fit the MDS model. A squared correlation index constitutes an indicator of the proportion of variance of the disparities accounted for by the MDS. Similar to R^2 in other multivariate approaches, a level of 0.60 or better is commonly considered to be acceptable.

The results presented in the study of Libby (1979) suggest a two-dimension solution which accounted for 61% of the variance. The addition of a third dimension was not considered necessary as it increased the fit of the model by only 6%. Figure 26.1 reproduces the perceptual map for all participants (specific maps have also been presented for auditors and bankers) in order to illustrate the main output of MDS. The number in the quadrants represent the ten audit reports provided to the participants along the two dimensions proposed by the MDS technique.

Step 3: interpreting the results

Identifying the underlying dimensions is not an easy task. A mix of subjective and objective procedures is commonly used in MDS studies. The description of dimensions in terms of known characteristics can be made subjectively by a visual inspection of the map by the researcher himself, a group of experts or even the respondents. Among the more objective procedures formalizing the interpretation of the results, the property fitting method (PROFIT) is probably the most widely used. This method collects attribute ratings for each object allowing the researcher to determine which attributes are the most illustrative of the dimensions.

Property fitting techniques have been used by Libby (1979). Indeed, during the second phase of the experiment, the participants were asked to rate the ten reports by the degree to which each report conveyed the message in each of 13 adjective phrases. Examples of adjective phrase are: quality of the company's financial control, riskiness of the company and quality of the

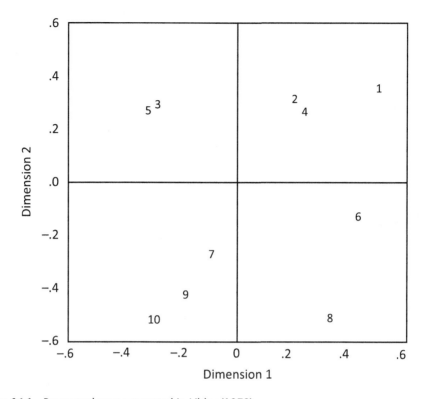

Figure 26.1   Perceptual map presented in Libby (1979)

company as a loan prospect. Libby finally labelled dimension 1 as "additional information", and dimensions 2 as "audit judgment".

Review of selected behavioural accounting studies using MDS

In addition to the study of Libby (1979), other behavioural studies published in major journals have used MDS in the past. However, it is worth mentioning that no such studies have been published in the major journals since the mid-'80s, which coincides with the publication of a critique of MDS in the Journal of Accounting Research by Watkins (1984). The purpose of the study conducted by Pratt (1982) was twofold: (a) to identify the determinants of post-cognitive structure and (b) to examine the relationships between post-cognitive structures, perceived information use and predictive accuracy. A laboratory experiment conducted on 90 participants followed three phases: a pre-treatment session, a treatment session and a post-treatment session. MDS has been used in the first and third phases in order to measure the annual report conceptual level (ARCL), one characteristic of the cognitive structure, before and after the treatment. Participants were asked to rate the relative similarity of information content provided by 12 sections of the annual report, such as income statement, president's letter, auditor's report and statistical summary of operations. The results of MDS were then used to establish links between cognitive structure, perceived information use and predictive accuracy.

Building on the experiment conducted by Libby (1979), Bailey, Bylinski and Shields (1983) had two main objectives. On the one hand, they examined differences in the perceived message between existing audit reports and those proposed by the Auditing Standards Board (ASB).

On the other hand, they assessed differences in the message perceived by two groups of readers displaying different knowledge levels regarding the audit report. Specific MDS have been conducted for groups of participants having or not having audit knowledge. Despite using a different algorithm compared to Libby, separate scree tests and R^2 analysis for each group indicated that a two-dimension solution was most appropriate. Overall, the results indicate that wording changes and knowledge level did have an effect on the perceived message.

The study of Shockley and Holt (1983) aimed to determine whether there is a differentiation in the market for audit services. MDS was used to assess banker's comparisons and ratings of big certified public accountant (CPA) firms (eight at the time) while an additional procedure was used to provide qualitative attributes along which audit firms may be differentiated. An experiment was conducted on 30 CFOs of large banks. A multidimensional rank-order method was used to obtain similarity judgment. Compared to a two-dimension solution, a three-dimension solution explains an additional 12.6% of variance (R^2) and reduces stress (similar to stress measure) from .340 to .261. The results indicate that bankers do differentiate between audit firms, notably in terms of audit firm market share and perception of audit firm conservatism (no label has been proposed for the third dimension).

The study of Milliron (1985) addressed the issue of tax complexity and involved two distinct phases. MDS has been used in the first phase to obtain an operational definition of tax complexity. Thirty prospective jurors agreed to judge the similarity of 78 pairs of tax scenarios in terms of their tax complexity. They were also asked to assess the 13 scenarios in terms of various attributes. The accepted solution contained four dimensions of tax complexity, namely (a) personal vs. financial topic, (b) low vs. high quantitativeness, (c) low vs. high misuse and (d) low vs. high readability.

Conclusion

This chapter has examined three specialized and emerging multivariate approaches that have not yet been used extensively in behavioural research, namely (a) logit and probit models, (b) cluster analysis and (c) multidimensional scaling. For each technique, four basic questions have been addressed: What is the basic purpose of the approach? What are the pros and cons? How does it work globally? How has this approach been used in past behavioural studies? Although these techniques have not been used extensively, it does not mean that they are not adequate or suitable for behavioural research. The numerous advantages of the techniques discussed throughout the chapter represent their potential to provide empirical evidence supporting various research objectives. However, their disadvantages constitute a source of concern that can be mitigated with a rigorous research design and an in-depth understanding of the approach.

In sum, logit and probit models are particularly useful when the researcher aims to predict an outcome or an event displaying a small number of values (for instance disciplined CPA or not). Cluster analysis is appropriate when the researcher intends to identify groups of objects reflecting common alignment of elements (for instance culture of public accounting firms). Multidimensional scaling is considered in order to transform individual judgments of similarity of preferences among accounting objects into distances represented in multidimensional space (for instance message intended by audit reports).

Notes

1 In order to identify the relevant studies in the accounting literature, the following search procedures have been applied. First, the articles must have been published in any accounting journal, regardless of the

publication date or the ranking of the journal. Second, the articles must have used the specific statistical approach as main or additional analysis. Third, the topic of the articles must be related to behavioural accounting (and thus, topics such as bankruptcy, takeover, earning management, reporting and accounting standards have not been considered).

2 It is worth mentioning that the results could exceed 100% because they reflect an increase in the odds, not the probabilities themselves. The odds are the probability of an event occurring to the probability of the event not happening (Hair et al. 2010). For instance, a probability of success of 60% means that the odds of success are 1.5 (0.6/0.4). In other words, success is 1.5 times more likely to happen than failure.

3 The disparities are defined as the differences in distance between objects on the perceptual map and the similarity judgment of the respondent.

References

Aier, J.K., Comprix, J., Gunlock, M.T. and Lee, D., 2005, 'The financial expertise of CFOs and accounting restatements', *Accounting Horizons* 19(3), 123–135.

Aldenderfer, M.S. and Blashfield, R.K., 1984. *Cluster Analysis*, Sage Publications, Beverly Hills, CA.

Bailey, K.E., III, Bylinski, J.H. and Shields, M.D., 1983, 'Effects of audit report wording changes on the perceived message', *Journal of Accounting Research* 21(2), 355–370.

Bobek, D.D. and Hatfield, R.C., 2003, 'An investigation of the theory of planned behavior and the role of moral obligation in tax compliance', *Behavioral Research in Accounting* 15, 13–38.

Collins, A.B., Parrish, B.K. and Collins, D.L., 1998, 'Gender and the tenure track: Some survey evidence', *Issues in Accounting Education* 13(2), 277–299.

Dimnik, T. and Felton, S., 2006, 'Accountant stereotypes in movies distributed in North America in the twentieth century', *Accounting, Organizations and Society* 31(2), 129–155.

Ge, W. and Whitmore, G.A., 2010, 'Binary response and logistic regression in recent accounting research publications: A methodological note', *Review of Quantitative Finance and Accounting* 34(1), 81–93.

Hair, J.F., Black, W.C., Babin, B.J. and Anderson, R.E., 2010, *Multivariate Data Analysis* (7th ed.), Prentice Hall, Upper Saddle River, NJ.

Hoetker, G., 2007, 'The use of logit and probit models in strategic management research: Critical issues', *Strategic Management Journal* 28(4), 331–343.

Holmes, S. and Marsden, S., 1996, 'An exploration of the espoused organizational cultures of public accounting firms', *Accounting Horizons* 10(3), 26–53.

Jones, S. and Hensher, D.A., 2007, 'Evaluating the behavioural performance of alternative logit models: An application to corporate takeovers research', *Journal of Business Finance & Accounting* 34(7/8), 1193–1220.

Keasey, K. and Short, H., 1990, 'The accounting burdens facing small firms: An empirical research note', *Accounting and Business Research* 20(80), 307.

Ketchen, D.J. and Shook, C.L., 1996, 'The application of cluster analysis in strategic management research: An analysis and critique', *Strategic Management Journal* 17, 441–458.

Ketchen, D.J., Thomas, J.B. and Snow, C.C., 1993, 'Organizational configurations and performance: A comparison of theoretical approaches', *Academy of Management Journal* 36(6), 1278–1313.

Law, P.K., 2010, 'A theory of reasoned action model of accounting students' career choice in public accounting practices in the post-Enron', *Journal of Applied Accounting Research* 11(1), 58–73.

Libby, R., 1979, 'Bankers' and auditors' perceptions of the message communicated by the audit report', *Journal of Accounting Research* 17(1), 99–122.

Maddala, G.S., 1991, 'A perspective on the use of limited-dependent and qualitative variables models in accounting research', *The Accounting Review* 68(4), 788–807.

Milliron, V.C., 1985, 'A behavioral study of the meaning and influence of tax complexity', *Journal of Accounting Research* 23(2), 794–816.

Noreen, E., 1988, 'An empirical comparison of probit and OLS regression hypothesis tests', *Journal of Accounting Research* 26(1), 119–133.

Parsons, L.M., 2007, 'The impact of financial information and voluntary disclosures on contributions to not-for-profit organizations', *Behavioral Research in Accounting* 19, 179–196.

Pratt, J., 1982, 'Post-cognitive structure: Its determinants and relationship to perceived information use and predictive accuracy', *Journal of Accounting Research* 20(1), 189–209.

Schaefer, J. and Welker, R.B., 1994, 'Distinguishing characteristics of certified public accountants disciplined for unprofessional behavior', *Journal of Accounting and Public Policy* 13(2), 97–119.

Seifried, J., 2012, 'Teachers' pedagogical beliefs at commercial schools – an empirical study in Germany', *Accounting Education* 21(5), 489–514.

Shockley, R.A. and Holt, R.N., 1983, 'A behavioral investigation of supplier differentiation in the market for audit services', *Journal of Accounting Research* 21(2), 545–564.

Tabachnick, B.G. and Fidell, L.S., 2013, *Using Multivariate Statistics* (6th ed.), Allyn & Bacon, Needham Heights, MA.

Viger, C., Belzile, R. and Anandarajan, A.A., 2008, 'Disclosure versus recognition of stock option compensation: Effect on the credit decisions of loan officers', *Behavioral Research in Accounting* 20(1), 93–113.

Watkins, P.R., 1984, 'Multidimensional scaling measurement and accounting research', *Journal of Accounting Research* 22(1), 406–411.

Widener, S.K., 2006, 'Human capital, pay structure, and the use of performance measures in bonus compensation', *Management Accounting Research* 17, 198–221.

Section 7

External validity concerns (Link 5)

27

Evaluating behavioural research in tax

An external validity framework

Andrew D. Cuccia and Anne M. Magro

Introduction

Taxes are pervasive in the world economy with different types of taxes (e.g., income, wealth-transfer, sales, employment, property and customs taxes) imposed across various jurisdictions (e.g., countries, states/provinces, counties and cities) with multiple purposes (e.g., raising revenue or influencing social and economic behaviours). Therefore, tax judgment and decision-making (JDM) in its entirety includes several types of decision makers performing a variety of judgment tasks (e.g., making compliance, investment and consumption decisions) in an environment characterized by ambiguity, complexity and risk. The depth, breadth and complexity of the tax law and the resulting effort necessary to comply with it create an ever-growing need for tax professionals to help taxpayers, both individuals and organizations, interpret and apply the law as well as comply with numerous substantiation and reporting requirements. Taxation, therefore, provides a practically important and contextually rich domain in which to study professional decision-making. The unique combination of task, decision-maker and environmental characteristics along with the complexity and significance of taxes in our society create the opportunity for behavioural tax research to make meaningful contributions to public policy, professional practice and decision theory.[1]

The ultimate goal of experimental research is external validity, the ability to generalize the relations between constructs operationalized in the laboratory to other settings. External validity may be threatened in at least two ways. First, failure to consider factors that directly impact the JDM being investigated inhibits our ability to detect the effects of other factors in which we are interested and which do impact JDM. Second, to the extent that factors that moderate the impact of the factors in which we are primarily interested are overlooked, relations that are observed in the laboratory and the theory on which they are based, may not generalize.[2] Throughout this chapter, we employ a common framework for evaluating accounting JDM research (e.g., Bonner 2008; Libby and Luft 1993; Roberts 1998) to consider factors that, if overlooked, may impact external validity. Specifically, we consider the characteristics of tax JDM tasks, the decision makers who perform them, and the environments in which those tasks are performed to guide tax researchers in assessing the generalizability of research findings for the purposes of learning about and from tax JDM. Without considering the potential effects of these factors in the planning, design and interpretation of research, the external validity and, therefore, predictive ability of the research is tenuous.

We begin by describing the general domain of tax professional JDM. We next compare and contrast the features of that domain to those applicable to the more mundane tasks and settings often examined in basic JDM research as well as to those applicable to other professional domains, including other areas of professional accounting. Finally, we consider features that may impact generalizability even across tax JDM settings. We note that most of the decision-relevant factors we discuss here, and their relation to accounting generally, are addressed elsewhere and often in much more detail.[3] Our goal is to relate these factors specifically to the tax professional setting. Similarly, although we sometimes note prior tax JDM studies that have explicitly considered a specific factor, the chapter is not intended to be a comprehensive literature review.[4] Instead, we seek to encourage a deeper understanding of the tax professional decision-making setting to help future researchers understand and enhance the predictive ability of their, as well as others', research.

The tax domain

Professional tax judgment tasks

Tax professionals help taxpayers (a) interpret and apply the tax law for the purpose of determining their legal tax liability (i.e., tax consulting), (b) meet their filing/reporting obligations (i.e., tax reporting) and (c) settle disputes with tax authorities (i.e., tax representation).[5] Tax professionals also may determine or attest to the reasonableness of tax-related disclosures included in financial statements (i.e., the tax provision). A common element of each of these tax tasks is professional tax research, research to determine the potential tax treatment of an activity or transaction.[6]

Professional tax research is commonly characterized as including the following steps: (a) establishing the facts relevant to the activity or transaction of interest, including the underlying non-tax goals of the taxpayer; (b) identifying the relevant tax issues; (c) locating and selecting relevant tax authority; (d) analyzing that authority; (e) synthesizing the facts and authority to make judgments regarding the tax consequences of the activity or transaction of interest; (f) forming reporting recommendations based on the potential tax consequences of the transaction and the non-tax goals of the taxpayer and (g) communicating the conclusions and recommendations to the taxpayer-client (e.g., Sawyers, Raabe, Whittenburg and Gill 2015). In professional firms, this process may be subject to at least one level of review before communicating a judgment and recommendation to a taxpayer-client. When performing tax research, tax professionals consult both primary authorities (those issued by the government and its agents) and secondary authorities (those issued by non-government agents to interpret primary authority). As primary authority comes from several legislative, administrative and judicial sources, and interpretations of those sources may vary, authority may at any point in time conflict and/or fail to directly address the issue being researched. Further, both primary and secondary authorities are subject to change. To help professionals conducting research identify and access currently relevant authority, commercial providers combine most primary and secondary authorities into searchable databases.

Tax research in the tax-consulting function takes place in one of two primary settings – compliance or planning. In compliance settings, a transaction or series of transactions already have been executed. In planning settings, in contrast, the transaction(s) have not yet been executed. In fact, the tax-consulting engagement may be focused both on identifying alternative ways to structure the transaction(s) to achieve economic and tax goals as well as on determining the appropriate tax positions for the transaction(s) once executed (Magro 1999). These differences add to the richness and complexity of tax professional decision-making and will be discussed in greater detail in a later section.

Professional tax decision makers

Tax professionals are a heterogeneous group with respect to education, certification, practice structure, clientele and service mix. Many work in public practice, independent from any specific taxpayer. Professionals in public accounting and tax attorneys generally have met higher-education and examination requirements to achieve certification and/or licensure.[7] National and international public accounting firms are engaged primarily by mid- and large-sized businesses and relatively high-wealth individuals to provide mainly tax consulting and representation. Smaller firms and sole proprietors are engaged primarily by smaller businesses and individuals and are more likely to provide tax reporting in addition to consulting and representation services. Other professionals, though typically not licenced accountants or attorneys, may nonetheless achieve certification by passing exams that grant them the right to represent taxpayers in administrative proceedings (e.g., enrolled agents). Finally, tax professionals can be found in large, commercially oriented firms (e.g., H&R Block) providing basic consulting and reporting services to primarily individual taxpayers.

Tax professionals also work within tax-paying and tax-reporting organizations.[8] In addition to providing tax-consulting and reporting services, these professionals also are responsible for the reporting of income taxes in the organization's financial statements based on relevant accounting standards. In such roles, the tax professional has responsibilities to both tax authorities and financial reporting regulators. Finally, tax professionals work within taxing authorities and judicial systems as revenue agents, tax attorneys and judges who administer, enforce and adjudicate the tax law. The education of these professionals may range from little advanced training to advanced degrees in tax or law.

Professional tax JDM environment

Tax professionals are subject to professional standards and government regulation as well as other potential formal and informal sanctions imposed by clients. Professional responsibilities and regulatory frameworks vary across certification/licensure status, professional affiliation and jurisdiction. Professional standards generally apply to licenced and certified tax professionals as well as those who choose to affiliate with a professional organization. These standards often include rules of conduct applicable to all within the broader profession (e.g., accounting or law) as well as rules applicable specifically to those engaged in tax practice. The former generally establish responsibilities to the public, the profession and clients for competence and trustworthiness (e.g., AICPA 2014; CPAO 2016) while the latter often also charge the professional to act as an advocate for the taxpayer-client when interpreting and applying the tax law (e.g., AICPA 2009). Academic research and professional literature suggest that tax professionals embrace this prescribed advocacy role. In an attempt to balance these potentially conflicting responsibilities to the tax system and to the taxpayer-client, professional standards may require that a minimum level of authoritative support exist before a tax position may be recommended to a taxpayer. Failure to meet professional standards can indirectly lead to financial consequences due to loss of professional certification and standing.

While professional standards are self-imposed, tax professionals also are subject to government-imposed regulations that may be applicable to many of the same behaviours as are the professional standards. However, government regulations may impose different qualitative or quantitative restrictions on that behaviour, employ different criteria for evaluation, or carry different consequences for violation including monetary fines and penalties. Finally, tax professionals' JDM may result in consequences in addition to those potentially imposed by professional organizations and government regulators. These include damage to specific client relationships and the professional's wider reputation as well as the monetary costs of malpractice claims. The tax practice literature documents substantial concern by tax professionals with managing the combination of these risks (e.g., Bandy 1996; Fiore 1998; Kahan 1996; Pascarella 1996). Interestingly, tax professionals report the non-monetary costs to be more significant to them than are monetary penalties (Collins, O'Neil and Cathey 1990). Overall, tax professionals must strive to provide the highest quality services to clients while minimizing their own risks and maximizing their long-term success in the profession (Shields, Solomon and Jackson 1995).

Generalizing from basic JDM research to professional JDM

As an applied discipline, most accounting research draws on theories developed in more basic disciplines such as economics and finance. As discussed by Jollineau and Parlee earlier in this text, most accounting JDM research relies primarily on theory and insights originating in cognitive psychology. To the extent that accounting and tax professionals are subject to the same JDM limitations as are other individuals, the insight provided by basic JDM research should provide insight into JDM in applied professional settings such as accounting as well. As such, studying JDM in an applied setting only should be necessary if the generalizability of theory and findings from the basic discipline is impacted by features of the professional JDM setting.[9]

Much research in psychology is conducted outside of, or above, the context of specific settings because such abstraction is one means of enhancing generalizability. The choice of a specific task to examine is generally based on construct validity with the goal of capturing the key elements of the theory under investigation; the practical purpose or goal of the task may be of little import. Similarly, parsimony may require that the specific attributes of the decision maker under examination and the environment in which a judgment task is performed be unrelated to performance of the task. However, as discussed in the previous section, applied settings are interesting *because* of their unique characteristics. Perhaps ironically, it is precisely the task, decision maker and environmental features that basic JDM research often ignores to enhance parsimony that potentially threaten generalizability to professional JDM.

As is often noted, the goal of professional JDM research is to learn how, and how well, a specific task is performed (e.g., Ashton 1982; Bonner 2008) and the features of the setting are of critical importance to achieve these goals. For example, professional tasks are characterized primarily by the relative complexity that results from the numerous judgment processes, types and sources of information (available from both memory and from external sources), potential outputs and dimensions of quality on which those outputs may be evaluated.[10] Professional decision makers and their relations to their tasks also differ. For example, because of task complexity and the specialized body of knowledge applicable to the professional domain, professionals may possess relatively higher levels of innate ability relevant to the tasks they perform. Unlike decision makers in more general settings, professionals often also develop domain- and task-specific expertise (Gibbins 1984). The nature and extent of that expertise depends on the decision maker's innate abilities as well as their domain- and task-specific training and experience.[11] Finally, professional JDM takes place in rich and dynamic environments that differ from other environments in systematic ways. For example, professional JDM is often made on behalf of others, influenced by professional roles and responsibilities, and subject to external oversight creating significant risks and rewards for the professional decision maker and impacting goals, incentives and motivation.

Professional settings and professional JDM are distinctive not only because of their unique characteristics but also because of the way those characteristics present in unique combinations (Solomon and Shields 1995). Decision makers may adapt to combinations of factors that impact the costs and benefits of a judgment task (Payne, Bettman and Johnson 1993). For example, both the combination of factors that cause professionals to switch from intuitive System 1 processing to more effortful and analytic System 2 processing (Jollineau and Parlee in Chapter 4 of this volume) and the benefits of switching are likely to differ from those that drive novice decision makers.

Although generalizing from basic JDM research to professional decision-making can be tenuous without explicit consideration of the distinctiveness of professional tasks, decision makers and environments, the rich and dynamic setting in which professional JDM takes place offers applied researchers opportunities to enhance the potential contribution of their own work beyond their applied discipline. Specifically, researchers in applied disciplines have the unique opportunity to speak back to the basic discipline from which they typically borrow by extending understanding of more general JDM theories and/or identifying boundary conditions that impact the external validity of those theories (Bonner 1999). In addition, because of their richness and distinctive features, applied domains such as tax can offer fertile ground for theory development as well as a valuable opportunity to conduct initial and early investigations of theory.

Generalizing from other professional JDM research to tax JDM

Because of the richness of professional settings, researchers study JDM in many applied professional domains (e.g., accounting, air traffic control, medicine). As tax JDM is a subset of accounting JDM, tax researchers understandably attempt to generalize research findings from other professional accounting settings to tax. Most accounting JDM research has examined auditors, so we focus on them here.[12] Although tax and audit decision-making share characteristics that distinguish them from more generic JDM, tax and audit JDM also differ in significant ways from each other and care should be taken before generalizing here as well.

Auditors and tax professionals are both charged with gathering evidence on which to base a judgment regarding the appropriate way to characterize financial activities of a client according to a set of rules and regulations. The auditor's primary task is to gather evidence for the purpose of attesting to the reasonableness of an auditee's financial statements. In contrast, as discussed earlier, the task underlying much tax professional JDM is professional tax research. The goal of the auditor's evidence-gathering task is assurance: detecting whether there may be problems with the information contained in a company's books and records and the system that was used to capture and measure it. In contrast, a primary goal of the tax research task is to identify opportunities, including alternate ways to structure future activities and transactions to minimize tax costs or how to report transactions. These different tasks require different types of reasoning. For example, Bonner, Davis and Jackson (1992) suggest that reasoning in auditing is primarily diagnostic, similar to medical reasoning (Libby 1985; Libby and Frederick 1990; Solomon and Shields 1995), in that auditors typically reason backward from known outcomes such as year-over-year financial statement fluctuations to possible underlying causes. Tax professionals, in contrast, employ both backward- and forward-reasoning processes in tax research depending on the decision-making context. For example, like auditors, tax professionals doing planning work reason backward from known tax and economic goals to the underlying facts that must exist to obtain those goals. However, when engaged in tax compliance, tax professionals reason forward from a set of existing facts and law to likely outcomes such as acceptable reporting positions.[13] With this emphasis on forward reasoning, tax compliance reasoning is similar to legal reasoning. The cognitive psychology literature shows that backward and forward reasoning are distinct cognitive processes that can lead to different judgments (Chi, Glaser and Rees 1982).

Similarly, although both auditors and tax professionals generally base their judgments on collected evidence, the nature and use of the evidence differs significantly. For example, audit evidence is often discreet (e.g., a confirmation of a receivable) and is interpreted only in the context of the present audit. For example, an error identified in substantive tests of details or variances discovered in analytical review are relevant directly to, and interpreted in the context of, the specific auditee and the setting in which they operate. Conversely, the evidence gathered and used by a tax professional in making a judgment is generally much richer. For example, judicial authority (i.e., a court case) might include multiple facts and address several issues. It also relates to, and must be interpreted in relation to, a taxpayer other than the client. Professionals then use analogical reasoning to look past superficial similarities and differences to identify relevant underlying principles that may transfer from the taxpayer and facts in the authority to those in the situation being researched (Magro and Nutter 2012; Marchant, Robinson, Anderson and Schadewald 1991, 1993). Differences in the nature of evidence across tax and auditing tasks will lead to the use of different information processes across those domains.

In addition to differences in the nature and use of evidence, auditors and tax professionals also gather evidence differently. Evidence gathering in auditing is often passive, accomplished by sampling from a larger population of relevant evidence.[14] Conversely, tax professionals typically seek authoritative evidence more purposefully, with greater control over which evidence is examined and incorporated into their judgments. Further, tax professionals cannot rely on a sample of relevant evidence but are charged with identifying and examining all relevant authority that may impact their final judgment. Again, the method by which evidence is gathered likely impacts the decision processes used to interpret it. For example, Cuccia and McGill (2000) demonstrate that differences in information gathering across accounting settings may cause the relevance of certain heuristics and biases to differ across those settings.

Although differences between the research task conducted by tax professionals and the tests of details and analytical-review tasks performed by auditors may seem relatively obvious, some auditing and tax tasks may appear on the surface to be structurally more analogous. For example, like tax professionals conducting tax research, auditors also may research relevant authoritative sources to determine the appropriate reporting treatment of an activity or transaction under applicable financial reporting standards. However, even these research tasks may differ in ways that impact generalizing from one to the other. For example, the governing authorities being searched and interpreted are inherently different both in their nature and organization. For example, the US Accounting Standards Codification (ASC) consolidates formerly distinct sources of financial reporting rules and regulations into a single, comprehensive source.[15] Conversely, though consolidated by publishers into a comprehensive service to facilitate the research process, the tax law remains an amalgamation of rules and principles from different, sometimes conflicting, sources. This requires tax professionals to evaluate the source and relevance of each piece of evidence/authority to assess its relative weight when making a judgment. Further, the potential complexity of a single authority as well as its relation to others will often require the tax professional to navigate back and forth between multiple primary and secondary sources included in the service or between the service and the authorities themselves. These differences suggest that the information search and evaluation processes used and, therefore, the judgments reached by auditors and tax professionals may differ in meaningful ways across seemingly similar tasks.

Because of the different tasks in which they engage and the different environments in which those tasks are performed, tax and audit professionals must bring different knowledge to their professional tasks (Bonner 1990, 2008). A common way of categorizing knowledge is by distinguishing between declarative knowledge, or knowledge of *what*, and procedural knowledge, or knowledge of *how* (Anderson 1980; Rumelhart and Norman 1981). As discussed further in the next section, declarative knowledge in accounting JDM can be further subdivided into several categories. However, the characteristics of each such category vary across accounting domains. For example, studies suggest that knowledge of accounting error base rates is necessary for expertise in analytical-review tasks (Frederick 1991; Libby 1985; Libby and Frederick 1990). Such knowledge might be considered episodic, based on memory or experience. In tax JDM, knowledge of audit base rates might be useful. As overall audit rates are regularly published and the taxing authority's interest in particular issues may be publicized, knowledge of audit rates might be considered semantic, based on facts or rules. Although both types of knowledge involve frequencies or base rates, research suggests that episodic and semantic knowledge may be organized and stored differently by a decision maker, impacting its accessibility and, therefore, the decision maker's mental processing (e.g., Chase and Simon 1973; Chi, Feltovich and Glaser 1981). Tax and audit professionals also require different procedural knowledge to perform their professional tasks. Further, by its very nature, auditing may be inherently more procedural than is tax and, therefore, rely more heavily on procedural knowledge. Although tax JDM tasks may require many procedures (e.g., the identification and documentation of authority), auditing is itself a procedure rather than a set of laws. Consequently, auditing standards themselves in large part cover the procedures underlying the audit and the auditor's responsibilities related to those procedures.

Finally, even if a tax and audit task were inherently identical, the environments in which the tasks are performed differ. For example, as discussed earlier, tax professional judgments are made most commonly in a tax-consulting setting. In this setting, tax professionals are charged by professional standards to act as client advocates. Conversely, auditors are charged to approach their task with professional skepticism (AICPA 2012). Decision makers' goals, as well as the potential consequences of their judgments, systematically impact their decision-making processes (e.g., Kunda 1990) causing otherwise similar judgment tasks to be performed differently. For example, while auditors have been found to weight more heavily evidence consistent with their role as professional skeptics (e.g., Ashton and Ashton 1990; Church 1990; Kida 1984), tax professionals have been found to weight more heavily evidence seemingly consistent with a client-preferred conclusion (e.g., Johnson 1993). Further, the consequences for substandard JDM may differ across tax and audit settings.

The above discussion notwithstanding, as tax is a sub-discipline of accounting, research examining other professional accountants can provide valuable insight into tax professional JDM. However, numerous differences across tax and other accounting decision tasks, the professionals performing them and the environments in which they are performed may nevertheless impact the generalizability of findings across accounting settings.

Generalizing across tax JDM settings

While researchers should be cautious about generalizing findings from other JDM domains to tax, similar care should be taken in generalizing within the tax domain from one context or task to another. As discussed earlier, even within the tax domain, a heterogeneous group of professionals perform a variety of tasks across many environments. It is often the interaction of these factors that impact tax professional JDM and generalizability of tax JDM research. For ease of exposition, we begin our discussion by considering how the environment in which tax JDM tasks are performed may itself impact JDM. We then discuss the potential impacts of characteristics of tax tasks and those who perform them.

Environmental factors

As described earlier, the environment provides the frame within which a decision maker interacts with a task. Even within the tax domain, the environment in which JDM takes place can vary significantly. Below we focus on differences across the compliance and planning settings as well as on client characteristics and the impact each may have on JDM.

Compliance versus planning settings

As discussed above, tax consulting is usually performed in one of two primary settings – compliance or planning. At least three key factors that differ across compliance and planning settings – complexity, ambiguity and justifiability demands (Magro 2005) – potentially impact tax JDM. Tax planning is generally characterized by greater complexity than is compliance given that planning involves (a) more judgment components, (b) more criteria on which the judgment will be evaluated and (c) greater potential to influence future transactions and tax-reporting opportunities. Tax planning involves more judgment components because the decision maker must consider the potential tax consequences of multiple potential transaction structures. Tax planning involves more judgment criteria as well because it also requires the consideration of the taxpayer's non-tax goals and how each potential transaction structure might impact those goals. Finally, the proposed structure of a transaction (e.g., choosing the legal form in which to conduct a business) may have implications for other planning opportunities and reporting choices in the future.

Ambiguity is a state of uncertainty related to (a) the imprecision or absence of information and (b) the lack of stability in information, decision alternatives, decision constraints and decision criteria (Payne et al. 1993). At the time the judgment or decision is being made, tax planning is characterized by relatively less, and less precise, information relative to tax compliance regarding judgment components and criteria, the potential impact of the chosen course of action on future events and the potential consequences of future events on the success of the chosen course of action. Specifically, tax planning involves identifying and evaluating alternative transaction structures that meet the taxpayer's goals, but some environmental factors that influence the ability to achieve these goals may be unknown, the number of possible transaction structures may be unlimited, and each potential transaction structure may have different non-tax consequences. Further, this information, as well as the taxpayer's goals and the tax law on which the planning decision is based, may change over time. Because of the heightened imprecision and ambiguity of information and more dynamic information environment, planning is more ambiguous than is compliance.

Finally, the impact of planning decisions on other current and future non-tax activities, and the ambiguity surrounding the consequences of those activities, leads to heightened justifiability demands and, therefore, risk in the tax-planning environment. A tax professional in a compliance setting likely has no culpability for the tax and non-tax consequences of the transaction that necessitates the research. Further, the tax position recommended generally involves no changes in the economic activities of the taxpayer and can often be reversed by simply filing an amended tax return. Conversely, taxpayers may initiate or modify their non-tax economic activities as the result of tax planning advice. The activities and/or transactions implemented as a result of tax planning advice may have far greater economic impact on the taxpayer than the tax savings related to them. For example, the decision to establish a business as a corporation versus a partnership not only may impact future tax liabilities but also financing options, legal liability and more. The potential consequences are magnified further as the activities implemented as a result of planning advice may be difficult to reverse or undo, and thus the tax and non-tax consequences of the transaction may be irreversible. As the provider of the advice, the tax professional may be held accountable for any negative tax or non-tax consequences of implementing or unwinding tax-planning advice, resulting in greater justifiability demands and greater practice risk (Kadous and Magro 2001).

Despite the numerous differences across the tax planning and compliance settings, the number of studies explicitly considering generalizability across these settings is limited. Magro (2005) finds that tax professionals who employ different tax research strategies across these settings are considered better decision makers. Spilker, Worsham and Prawitt (1999) report that tax preparers are more likely to exploit legal ambiguity in compliance settings but precise tax rules in planning settings. Further, as research to resolve a tax-planning problem requires more time than does research to resolve a compliance issue (Magro 1999), decision makers given the same time to complete a task in each setting may experience different levels of time pressure. Differences in time pressure are important because prior research suggests that time pressure impacts judgment processes and decisions (Spilker 1995).

Client characteristics

As noted above, tax professionals are subject to significant risks related to their provision of services to clients. Certain characteristics of the client may heighten a professional's exposure to that practice risk, causing the professional to engage in more effortful and deliberative processing to avoid the related costs (Kadous and Magro 2001).[16] Interestingly, more effortful processing may not always have positive effects on judgment. For example, Kadous et al. (2008) demonstrate that high practice risk mitigates confirmation bias. High practice risk also has been shown to mitigate the non-normative influence of client importance on the aggressiveness of tax-reporting recommendations (Vermeer and Curatola 2015). Conversely, Kadous and Magro (2001) find that enhanced mental processing in a high practice risk setting exacerbates hindsight bias.

Other variations in client characteristics also can impact JDM processes in tax. For example, client attitudes toward risk may have both direct and indirect effects on tax professional JDM. A client's risk attitudes may normatively have a direct impact on reporting recommendations as the client's willingness to accept risk should be a factor in the reporting decision. However, a client's risk attitudes also may have an indirect non-normative impact on the professional's underlying information identification, selection and weighting processes as the professional anticipates the relation of the information to the client's preferences. The economic importance of the client also may interact with other factors in tax JDM (e.g., Bobek, Hageman and Hatfield 2010; Reckers, Sanders and Wyndelts 1991; Vermeer and Curatola 2015). For example, although client importance may generally magnify the impact of the advocacy role, thereby increasing the aggressiveness of a professional's reporting recommendations, advocacy may actually lead to less aggressive recommendations at sufficiently high levels of importance (Vermeer and Curatola 2015). Like client risk attitudes, client importance also may affect indirectly the aggressiveness of recommendations by affecting the underlying information evaluation processes of the tax professional (Bobek et al. 2010).

Task features

Tax consulting, a primary tax professional task, involves multiple professional judgments and decisions. For example, tax professionals may assess the authoritative strength of a reporting position, make reporting recommendations to a client and/or make a decision about whether or not to sign a return containing the consequences of that position all within one compliance consulting engagement. These judgments and decisions are clearly related as the later rely at least in part on the earlier (e.g., judgments regarding the level of support for a reporting position will impact the recommendation made). However, knowing that they will be called upon to make a later judgment or decision can affect how tax professionals approach earlier judgments and decisions. For example, a tax professional who will ultimately prepare and sign a tax return with an uncertain position may approach the tax research process differently than will a tax professional providing tax consulting for a client who will self-prepare the return.

Further, the range of decisions available to the tax professional may differ within consulting tasks. For example, researchers often characterize tax recommendation/reporting choices as dichotomous (e.g., deduct/do not deduct or exclude/include), but reporting options actually may be more nuanced. For example, the choice may be *which* aggressive position to recommend (e.g., to deduct interest expense as a business or personal deduction) or *how* aggressive a position to take (e.g., which transfer price should be used for an intercompany transaction). Similarly, the tax professional's recommendation could condition taking an aggressive position on disclosing that position. As the number of alternatives available to a decision maker increases task complexity, it also may impact the decision processes employed and thus the ultimate judgments and/or decisions (Payne et al. 1993).

Tax professionals also perform tasks other than tax consulting including preparing the tax provision, assisting in the audit of the tax provision and representing clients before the taxing authorities or courts. Although these tasks share important features, they vary with respect to several others including the tasks' goals and structure. For example, when preparing the tax provision, the tax professional identifies book-tax differences and resolves any ambiguity with respect to uncertain tax positions, processes that parallel those commonly performed in consulting engagements (i.e., identifying the tax treatment of transactions and resolving any ambiguity surrounding that treatment). However, the goals of the tasks differ. The goal when preparing the provision is to determine the tax expense to be reported in the financial statements whereas the goal of tax consulting is to determine or impact the current and future legal liabilities actually due to the taxing authority. The difference in underlying goals may impact the basic underlying processes employed by the professional. Further, the standards for recognizing the tax benefits of UTPs in the financial statements differ from those governing the taking of a tax position for tax purposes. Although the different standards should normatively be applied independently, the existence of one may well impact the assessment of the other. Finally, the amount of tax benefits actually reported in the financial statements must be discounted based on the likelihood of the benefits being realized. Although the recognition and measurement judgments are normatively independent of each other, the measurement judgment, while not required for tax-reporting purposes, may well impact the recognition judgment.

In addition to differences in goals and structure, tax-consulting and financial-reporting tasks also differ with respect to the nature and extent of accountability to which they are subject. JDM impacting the financial statements extends the professional's accountability beyond the client to investors, creditors and the general public through the capital markets. Financial reporting JDM may be evaluated annually by external auditors and, for JDM related to public companies, by governmental regulators. Accountability for tax consulting JDM, in contrast, is typically limited to the taxpayer-client and the taxing authorities. Further, with the exception of the largest taxpayers and/or most aggressive positions, tax-consulting JDM is evaluated by the taxing authority only when the reporting decision is significant enough to attract the taxing authority's attention. With the exception of Cloyd (1995b) and Cloyd, Pratt and Stock (1996), we are aware of no studies that examine the JDM of tax professionals engaged in financial reporting or the consequences of being responsible for both tax-consulting and financial-reporting tasks concurrently.

In public accounting, tax professionals also may support the audit of the tax provision. Again, although tax consulting, preparing the tax provision and auditing the provision are similar in that all rely to some extent on professional tax research, the JDM tasks within each differ significantly. For example, tax consulting and preparing the tax provision require the tax professional to make an initial judgment regarding the level of support available for an uncertain tax position. In contrast, auditors are charged with opining on the reasonableness of a judgment made by someone else (i.e., management). The process of evaluating someone else's judgment may differ significantly from that of making the same judgment independently. For example, the evaluator may feel less need to independently search for authority or to generate alternative interpretations of the authority given that these tasks already were done. The evaluator then may have a different evidence set or use a different judgment process than they would have when making the initial judgment. Similarly, the process of evaluating the analysis justifying the initial judgment may make the reviewer relatively less able than an initial preparer to reach an alternative conclusion (Anderson, Lepper and Ross 1980; Hammersley, Kadous and Magro 1997; Heiman-Hoffman, Moser and Joseph 2010; Koonce 1992; Yip-Ow and Tan 2000).[17] Perhaps the biggest difference between tax consulting and audit support is that the tax professional in the audit-support role effectively becomes an auditor with the different professional attitudes prescribed across those roles. As discussed earlier, the tax professional is called to act as a client advocate when engaged in tax consulting. Auditors, in contrast must maintain independence and a skeptical mindset. This difference in prescribed roles raises questions about both the ability of the tax professional to navigate effectively across the tax-consulting and audit-support tasks and the comparability of tax and audit professionals performing the same audit task.

Finally, tax professionals also represent clients before taxing authorities and the courts. Like other tax tasks, representation relies on the results professional tax research. However, representation involves both unique processes and goals, requiring the professional to use the results of that research in an attempt to directly influence the judgment of a third party. The impact of several factors on tax professional judgment may be moderated in that setting. For example, a representation task may change the relative importance of the professional's accuracy and persuasion goals. While such moderating effects may be normative responses to the tasks, they also can exacerbate the biased judgment processes associated with motivated reasoning (Kunda 1990, 1999). Conversely, a perception of increased practice risk in such persuasion tasks may decrease the impact of client advocacy (Kadous et al. 2008). Further, the face-to-face negotiation involved in tax representation introduces a host of interpersonal variables that could affect JDM as highlighted in the social psychology literature (Van Kleef, de Dreu and Manstead 2006).

Representation tasks may differ from each other in several respects as well. For example, administrative proceedings (i.e., audits) may be perceived as relatively more adversarial than judicial proceedings.[18] Negotiating with an adversary and persuading a neutral party are inherently different tasks requiring different strategies. Further, regardless of the third party involved, representation tasks may differ with respect to the source of the tax position(s) in question. Professionals may feel greater commitment to the position in question, perhaps due to self-presentation concerns, as well as greater culpability in situations in which the initial position originated with the decision maker rather than with the taxpayer or another professional. Greater commitment and culpability may, in turn, impact the nature and extent of any additional research performed by the professional as well as the persuasion tactics employed. We are aware of no academic research on this important tax professional task.

Decision-maker characteristics

The variety of individuals potentially performing and/or evaluating tax JDM tasks was discussed earlier. Many JDM-related individual differences across tax professionals are systematically related to professional affiliation and are discussed elsewhere in this chapter. Others, expected to vary both within and across professional affiliations, are discussed here.

Knowledge

The importance of knowledge, including domain-specific knowledge, to task performance was discussed earlier. Given the variety of JDM tasks performed by tax accountants, several types of knowledge may be relevant to tax JDM. Further, the broad range of educational and professional backgrounds of tax professionals suggests that knowledge may vary considerably across professionals. We consider four types of knowledge that may impact the generalizability of research findings across tax tasks and decision makers – tax technical knowledge, general business knowledge, tacit managerial knowledge and institutional knowledge.

Technical knowledge of the tax law is the most studied element of tax professional knowledge. Declarative technical knowledge includes knowledge of the rules and principles included in the primary tax authorities, the specific authorities from which those rules and principles come and the relationships between them. Procedural technical knowledge includes the ability to locate relevant authority, including through the use of research databases, and the possession of a set of adaptive decision strategies that can be appropriately applied in the decision-making domain. Prior research demonstrates relations between technical tax knowledge and the identification of tax issues (Bonner et al. 1992), information search (Cloyd 1995b, 1997; Roberts and Ashton 2003; Spilker 1995), analogical reasoning (Davis and Mason 2003) and reporting recommendations (Cloyd 1995a).

Business and client knowledge includes an understanding of the business domain in general, the specific industry in which the taxpayer operates, the client being served and the potential responses of clients to the advice being rendered (Bell, Mars, Solomon and Thomas 1997). This knowledge may impact the extent and nature (i.e., the depth versus breadth) of tax research, the risk-assessment judgment and the content, form and range of recommendations made by a tax professional. Business and client knowledge is particularly, and differentially, important in planning settings relative to compliance settings. General business knowledge facilitates the identification of relevant tax issues as well as taxpayers' tax and non-tax goals at the beginning of the tax decision-making process. Later in the decision process, general business and client knowledge are key to the ability to identify possible strategies that meet the taxpayer's goals as well as the potential impacts of implementing those strategies. Few studies consider the main or moderating effects of business and client knowledge on tax JDM (but see Bonner et al. (1992) for the effects of business transaction knowledge on issue identification).

Tacit managerial knowledge (Tan and Libby 1997) is important to managing relationships both within the tax team and with the client. This knowledge is neither explicitly articulated nor taught but rather gained primarily from experience. Tacit managerial knowledge centres on knowing how to manage oneself, others and one's career (Wagner and Sternberg 1985) and becomes increasingly important as professionals progress through their careers (Abdolmoham-madi, Searfoss and Shanteau 2004; Bhamornsiri and Guinn 1991; Tan and Libby 1997). Tacit managerial knowledge may have greater impact in planning than in compliance settings because such knowledge affects both the ability (a) to communicate to various decision makers (e.g., CEOs, CFOs, audit committees) the benefits of tax planning strategies, the steps necessary to implement them and their potential consequences as well as (b) to understand the potential eco-nomic and non-economic impacts for the tax professional of delivering such advice. No studies have considered the effects of tacit managerial knowledge on tax JDM.

Institutional knowledge refers to knowledge of the environment in which tax JDM occurs (Magro 1999, 2005) and includes not only declarative knowledge about professional standards and the legal and regulatory environment in which tax practice is conducted but also procedural knowledge related to navigating that environment. For example, tax professionals in Magro (2005) who demonstrated declarative institutional knowledge of differences between tax plan-ning and compliance settings exhibited greater adaptivity in their information search strategies and better performance on the overall tax research task. Further, declarative knowledge of the audit and appeals process may moderate the impact of client advocacy on judgment. While this declarative knowledge may be acquired through education and training or experience, procedural knowledge is gained primarily through experience. For example, more experienced tax professionals have shown greater ability to employ analogical reasoning[19] and to engage in configural information processing (Magro and Nutter 2012). Both skills are key to performance in assessing the strength of tax authorities in the tax research process.

Ability

Ability is typically treated as an innate characteristic that can be affected only marginally by experience or training (Libby and Luft 1993, Bonner et al. 1992). Given common education and certification requirements, tax professionals in public accounting as well as tax attorneys and judges all likely present as relatively high-ability with low within-group variance. However, the ability of more heterogeneous groups of tax professionals such as revenue agents, enrolled agents and employees of commercial services likely vary considerably. While the highest-ability mem-bers of these groups likely match those of public accounting and judicial tax professionals, the lack of education or certification requirements for these groups suggests greater within-group variability. Tax professionals with lower levels of ability may struggle with complex, ambiguous tax tasks and may be less likely to acquire the knowledge described above as key to tax JDM.

Advocacy

Professional standards often treat client advocacy as a discrete role. For example, earlier we con-trasted the tax professional's role as advocate to the auditor's role as skeptic. However, client advocacy also can be viewed as an attitude that may be possessed to varying degrees across tax professionals.[20] Such differences may be attributable to differences in education, training and experiences as well as other individual personality traits. Therefore, client advocacy may vary across tax professionals performing the same tax task. Client advocacy also may vary across tasks or environments for a given professional. For example, Bobek et al. (2010) find that tax profession-als shift their level of advocacy in response to client-specific characteristics. This is an important consideration for generalizability as researchers generally recognize that client advocacy affects tax JDM (Cuccia 1994, 1995; Cuccia and McGill 2000; Davis and Mason 2003; Johnson 1993).

Summary

This chapter examines external validity issues in behavioural tax accounting research. Internal and construct validity, derived primarily by the ability to control the complexity of the decision environment, are often cited as the major strengths of experimental research. Nevertheless, the ultimate goal of all research, including experimental research, is external validity – the ability to generalize the relations between the constructs operationalized in a study to settings outside the confines of the study. External validity may be threatened in at least two ways. To the extent that factors that directly impact the JDM being investigated are overlooked, failure to control for them inhibits our ability to detect the effects of other factors in which we are primarily interested. To the extent that other factors that moderate the impact of factors in which we are primarily interested are overlooked, relations that are observed in the laboratory, and therefore the theory on which they are based, may not generalize. Explicitly considering external validity is especially important in rich professional JDM settings like tax. We use a common framework (e.g., Bonner 2008; Roberts 1998) to consider the impact of task, decision maker and environmental features on the external validity of tax JDM research. In so doing, we compare and contrast the features of the setting in which tax professionals operate to those applicable to the more mundane tasks and settings examined in basic JDM research as well as to those applicable to other professional domains, including those of other accounting professionals. Researchers should pay close attention to the relevance of these, as well as other domain-specific features, to the theory and/or judgments being examined before generalizing from other settings to tax or interpreting the results of tax JDM research.

Although we examine tax professional JDM specifically, we believe that many of the factors we identify are relevant to professional/applied research more generally. Regardless of the domain, however, a similar exercise can help the reader evaluate the external validity of any specific JDM study as well as identify and evaluate opportunities to make meaningful contributions to her own area of interest (Bonner 2008). For example, as tax professionals are human information processors as well as accountants, it may not be surprising that a relation predicted by theory and empirically supported in another setting, especially another accounting setting, should extend to tax accountants. Therefore, the contribution of such a study might be seen as marginal.[21] However, identifying features of the applied domain that moderate that relation makes a contribution not only to our understanding of the domain but also to the basic discipline in which the underlying theory was initially developed or examined.

Of course, as many features that vary within or across domains may impact JDM, we offer two clarifying observations. First, whereas the problems of internal validity are generally under the control of the researcher and addressable within determinable statistical limits, problems of external validity can never be fully controlled or neatly addressed (Campbell and Stanley 1963: 17). The number of factors that may pose a threat to generalizability are potentially infinite. Therefore, while researchers are generally, and rightly, held strictly accountable for internal validity, external validity problems are much less likely to represent critical flaws. Failure by the researcher to identify if or how a relation discovered in the study might apply across all possible combinations of task, decision maker and environmental features of a domain does not negate the contribution of any one study. Rather, external validity is often developed and enhanced through multiple studies over time as our understanding of the relevant theoretical constructs and domain evolves. Nonetheless, failure to consider the (moderating) impact of the most characteristic features of a domain can be just as problematic to a study in that domain as would be internal and construct validity weaknesses. Second, external validity is not synonymous with mundane realism. It is not necessary for all features of a decision environment to be replicated in an experiment in order for the research to have external validity. Although an experiment should be as realistic as necessary to motivate participants to employ the same judgment processes when performing a task in the laboratory as they would outside it, mundane realism for the sake of realism can needlessly negate many of the advantages offered by the experimental method. If, however, differential features of the task, decision maker or environment threaten the generalizability of the study, they should be controlled and examined.

Finally, we reiterate that we do not intend this chapter to be a comprehensive review of the tax JDM literature. We allude to a very small sample of that literature, chosen solely based on its relation to the points we raise. Arnold and Sutton (1997) and Bonner (2008) each provide a comprehensive synthesis of accounting JDM research. Roberts (1998) and Shields et al. (1995) both provide comprehensive literature reviews, from different perspectives, of the tax JDM literature, though much has been done since these were published. This chapter also is not meant to be an exhaustive analysis of the tax practice setting. Again, we consider a sample of potentially decision-relevant domain features that may distinguish professional tax JDM settings from other settings or from each other (i.e., that may impact external validity). Roberts (1998) and Shields et al. (1995) provide a more detailed analysis of the tax research task and its components. We do hope this analysis facilitates an appreciation of both the challenges and opportunities in studying tax JDM and fosters further interest in the field.

Notes

1 To keep the discussion in this chapter manageable, we focus on tax professional decision-making related to income taxes, although most of the issues raised apply equally across the overall tax professional decision-making domain. Taxpayer decision-making is also a ripe area for research but is not addressed in this chapter.

2 Internal and construct validity weaknesses also pose threats to external validity as they impact the ability to generalize the findings of a study to other settings. However, we focus here on external validity issues that do not stem from internal or construct validity weaknesses.

3 Arnold and Sutton (1997) and Bonner (2008) each provide a comprehensive synthesis of accounting JDM research.

4 Roberts (1998) and Shields, Solomon and Jackson (1995) provide comprehensive reviews of the behavioural tax literature.

5 Although tax reporting and representation may involve interesting JDM tasks, the vast majority of tax professional JDM research has focused on tax consulting. The relative lack of attention to tax reporting may be due to a perception that there are fewer forces that could compromise reporting-related JDM. Further, the importance of tax reporting as a professional service may be declining as technology offers taxpayers less costly options for meeting their reporting obligations on their own. Similarly, the relative lack of attention to representation may be due to the relatively small proportion of tax accountants' time spent on representation. However, we believe there is much to be learned by examining JDM in the representation setting.

6 We use the phrase 'professional tax research' to distinguish this process from 'academic tax research' – the study of the role of taxes in the economy (archival tax research) and how individuals make decisions related to tax (behavioural tax research).

7 Unlike auditing, which is restricted to those who have achieved certification and licensure, tax consulting and reporting may not require special education, certification or licensing.

8 Tax-reporting organizations include those organizations with tax-reporting requirements despite the absence of tax-paying requirements. Examples include certain not-for-profit organizations as well as partnerships, s-corporations and trusts.

9 Arnold and Sutton (1997) and Bonner (2008) provide comprehensive discussions of the impact that many variables identified in other JDM research may have on accounting JDM. Our goal is to briefly consider some factors that may distinguish professional JDM and JDM research, including accounting and tax, from other research and settings in ways that impact generalizability.

10 Task complexity is consistently believed to impact judgment quality (e.g., Wood 1986).

11 Research suggests that ability (e.g., Ackerman 1989; Hunter 1986; Sternberg 1996) and experience (e.g., Glaser and Chi 1988) can significantly impact judgment generally. Frederick and Libby (1986) and Libby and Luft (1993) consider further the factors that can impact expertise and performance in accounting.

12 Accounting research also has examined the JDM of management accountants. More recently, research has begun to examine the JDM of financial statement users.

13 This characterization of accounting reasoning processes, however, may be overly simplistic. For example, tax professionals in Magro (1999) used backward reasoning through most of the tax planning information search process but shifted to forward reasoning near the end of the process. Further, auditors employ forward-reasoning processes when they reason from known facts about a company to the likelihood that the company is a going concern. Generalization, therefore, requires consideration of precisely what decision task is being examined and what type of reasoning might be employed.

14 Though the population, sample or sample size may be purposely identified (e.g., based on relative audit risk or analytical-review procedures), the sampled items themselves are still drawn randomly.

15 International Financial Reporting Standards similarly represent a single-source set of authoritative standards covering financial reporting.

16 For example, clients who are unreasonable or uncooperative, engage in risky business activities, are unable to substantiate positions, demonstrate financial or organizational difficulties including weak controls and records, exert fee pressure, are frequently involved in litigation or in suspicious transactions or have critical personalities or questionable integrity all increase a tax professional's exposure to practice risk (Kadous and Magro 2001).

17 Professionals may review the judgments of their own subordinates as well as audit those of others. The review process is an important quality control mechanism in several settings with relatively senior-level professionals reviewing the work of staff and incorporating that work into their own conclusions. In addition to the issues discussed above, another concern may arise in these situations as the initial preparer and reviewer of the judgment share many of the same attitudes and incentives (Barrick, Cloyd and Spilker 2004; Cuccia, Magro and Whisenhunt 2016).

18 Though the court system is adversarial with respect to the defendant and plaintiff, the final disposition of the matter rests in the hands of the impartial judge rather than one of the adversaries.

19 Early studies suggested that tax professionals' ability to reason analogically did not vary with experience (Marchant et al. 1991; Marchant et al.1993). However, this result may have been obtained because the tax professionals used in the studies did not have sufficient experience to have developed the skill.

20 For example, Mason and Levy (2001) define client advocacy as the degree of loyalty the tax professional demonstrates toward the taxpayer-client.

21 Of course, insight into how a theory might map into an applied domain, or a feature in the domain, could make a significant contribution to that domain.

References

Abdolmohammadi, M., Searfoss, D. and Shanteau, J., 2004, 'An investigation of the attributes of top industry auditor specialists', *Behavioral Research in Accounting* 16, 1–17.

Ackerman, P., 1989, 'Individual differences and skill acquisition', in P. Ackerman, R. Sternberg and R. Glaser. (eds.), *Learning and Individual Differences: Advances in Theory and Research*, W.H. Freeman and Company, New York.

American Institute of Certified Public Accountants (AICPA), 2009, *Statement on Standards for Tax Services*, AIPCA, New York.

American Institute of Certified Public Accountants (AICPA), 2012, *Overall Objectives of the Independent Auditor and the Conduct of an Audit in Accordance With Generally Accepted Auditing Standards*, AU-C Section 200.

American Institute of Certified Public Accountants (AICPA), 2014, *Code of Professional Conduct and Bylaws*, AICPA, New York.

Anderson, C., Lepper, M.R. and Ross, L., 1980, 'Perseverance of social theories: The role of explanation in the persistence of discredited information', *Journal of Personality and Social Psychology* 39, 1037–1049.

Anderson, J., 1980, *Cognitive Psychology and Its Implications*, W.H. Freeman, San Francisco.

Arnold, V. and Sutton, S., 1997, *Behavioral Accounting Research: Foundations and Frontiers*, American Accounting Association, Sarasota, FL.

Ashton, A. and Ashton, R., 1990, 'Evidence responsiveness in professional judgment: Effects of positive versus negative evidence and presentation mode', *Organizational Behavior and Human Decision Processes* 46, 1–19.

Ashton, R.H., 1982, *Human information processing in accounting.* American Accounting Assn., Sarasota, FL.

Bandy, D., 1996, 'Limiting tax practice liability', *CPA Journal* (May), 46–49.

Barrick, J., Cloyd, C.B. and Spilker, B., 2004, 'The influence of biased tax research memoranda on supervisors' initial judgments in the process', *The Journal of the American Taxation Association* 26(1), 1–19.

Bell, T., Mars, F., Solomon, I. and Thomas, H., 1997, *Auditing Organizations Through a Strategic-Systems Lens: The KPMG Business Measurement Process*, KPMG, Montvale, NJ.

Bhamornsiri, S. and Guinn, R., 1991, 'The road to partnership in the "Big Six" firms: Implications for accounting education', *Issues in Accounting Education* 6(1), 9–24.

Bobek, D., Hageman, A. and Hatfield, R., 2010, 'The role of client advocacy in the development of tax advice by tax professionals', *Journal of the American Taxation Association* 32(1), 24–41.

Bonner, S., 1990, 'Experience effects in auditing: The role of task-specific knowledge', *The Accounting Review* 65, 72–92.

Bonner, S., 2008, *Judgment and Decision Making in Accounting*, Pearson Education, Upper Saddle River, NJ.

Bonner, S.E., 1999, 'Judgment and decision-making research in accounting', *Accounting Horizons* 13(4), 385–398.

Bonner, S., Davis, J. and Jackson, B., 1992, 'Expertise in corporate tax planning: The issue identification stage', *Journal of Accounting Research* 30(Supplement), 1–28.

Campbell, D. and Stanley, J., 1963, *Experimental and Quasi-Experimental Designs for Research*, Houghton Mifflin, Boston, MA.

Chartered Professional Accountants of Ontario (CPAO), 2016, *CPA Code of Professional Conduct*, viewed February 2016, from www.cpaontario.ca/Resources/Membershandbook/1011page20931.pdf.

Chase, W. and Simon, H., 1973, 'Perception in chess', *Cognitive Psychology* 4, 55–81.

Chi, M., Feltovich, P. and Glaser, R., 1981, 'Categorization and representation of physics problems by experts and novices', *Cognitive Sciences* 5(2), 121–125.

Chi, M.T.H., Glaser, R. and Rees, E., 1982, 'Expertise in problem solving', in R.J. Steinberg (ed.), *Advances in the Psychology of Human Intelligence*, 1, Lawrence Erlbaum Associates, Hillsdale, NJ.

Church, B., 1990, 'Auditors' use of confirmatory processes', *Journal of Accounting Literature* 9, 81–112.

Cloyd, C.B., 1995a, 'The effects of financial accounting conformity on recommendations of tax preparers', *The Journal of the American Taxation Association* 17(2), 50–70.

Cloyd, C.B., 1995b, 'Prior knowledge, information search behaviors, and performance in tax research tasks', *Journal of the American Taxation Association* 17(Supplement), 82–107.

Cloyd, C.B., 1997, 'Performance in tax research tasks: The joint effects of knowledge and accountability', *The Accounting Review* 72(1), 111–131.

Cloyd, C.B., Pratt, J. and Stock, T., 1996, 'The use of financial accounting choice to support aggressive tax positions: Public and private firms', *Journal of Accounting Research* 34(1), 23–43.

Collins, K., O'Neil, C. and Cathey, J., 1990, 'Tax practitioners' reactions to return preparer penalties', *Advances in Taxation* 3, 15–43.

Cuccia, A., 1994, 'The effects of increased sanctions on paid tax preparers: Integrating economic and psychological factors', *The Journal of the American Taxation Association* 16(1), 41–66.

Cuccia, A., 1995, 'Diversity in the professional tax preparation industry and potential consequences for regulation: Linking attitudes and behavior', *Advances in Taxation* 7, 73–98.

Cuccia, A., Magro, A. and Whisenhunt, A., 2016, 'The potential of the review process to detect and mitigate advocacy bias', *Working paper*, University of Oklahoma.

Cuccia, A.D. and McGill, G.A., 2000, 'The role of decision strategies in understanding professionals' susceptibility to judgment biases', *Journal of Accounting Research* 38(2), 419–435.

Davis, J. and Mason, J., 2003, 'Similarity and precedent in tax authority judgment', *The Journal of the American Taxation Association* 25(1), 53–71.

Fiore, N., 1998, 'From the tax adviser: Minimizing risks in taking on new clients', *Journal of Accountancy* 185(2), 36.

Frederick, D., 1991, 'Auditor's' representation and retrieval of internal control knowledge', *The Accounting Review* 66(2), 240–258.

Frederick, D.M. and Libby, R., 1986, 'Expertise and auditors' judgment of conjunctive events', *Journal of Accounting Research* (Autumn), 270–290.

Gibbins, M., 1984, 'Propositions about the psychology of professional judgment in public accounting', *Journal of Accounting Research* (Spring), 103–125.

Glaser, R. and Chi, M., 1988, 'Overview', in M. Chi, R. Glaser and M. Farr (eds.), *The Nature of Expertise*, Lawrence Erlbaum, Hillsdale, NJ.

Hammersley, J., Kadous, K. and Magro, A., 1997, 'Cognitive and strategic components of the explanation effect', *Organizational Behavior and Human Information Processing* 70(2), 149–158.

Heiman-Hoffman, V., Moser, D. and Joseph, J., 2010, 'The impact of an auditor's initial hypothesis on subsequent performance at identifying actual errors', *Contemporary Accounting Research* 11(2), 763–779.

Hunter, J., 1986, 'Cognitive ability, cognitive aptitudes, job knowledge and job performance', *Journal of Vocational Behavior* 29(3), 340–362.

Johnson, L., 1993, 'An empirical investigation of the effects of advocacy on preparers' evaluations of judicial evidence', *The Journal of the American Taxation Association* 15(1), 1–22.

Kadous, K. and Magro, A., 2001, 'The effects of exposure to practice risk on tax professionals' judgments and recommendations', *Contemporary Accounting Research* 18(3), 451–475.

Kadous, K., Magro, A.M. and Spilker, B.C., 2008, 'Do effects of client preference on accounting professionals' information search and subsequent judgments persist with high practice risk?', *The Accounting Review* 83(1), 133–156.

Kahan, S., 1996, 'Fire that client!', *Practical Accountant* 29(October), 46–53.

Kida, T., 1984, 'The impact of hypothesis-testing strategies on auditors' use of judgment data', *Journal of Accounting Research* (Spring), 332–340.

Koonce, L., 1992, 'Explanation and counterexplanation during audit analytical review', *The Accounting Review* 67, 59–76.

Kunda, Z., 1990, 'The case for motivated reasoning', *Psychological Bulletin* 108, 480–498.

Kunda, Z., 1999, *Social Cognition: Making Sense of People*, MIT Press, Cambridge, MA.

Libby, R., 1985, 'Availability and the generation of hypotheses in analytical review', *Journal of Accounting Research* (Autumn), 648–667.

Libby, R. and Frederick, D., 1990, 'Experience and the ability to explain audit findings', *Journal of Accounting Research* (Autumn), 348–367.

Libby, R. and Luft, J., 1993, 'Determinants of judgment performance in accounting settings: Ability, knowledge, motivation, and environment', *Accounting, Organizations and Society* 18(5), 425–450.

Magro, A.M., 1999, 'Contextual features of tax decision-making settings', *The Journal of the American Taxation Association* 21(Supplement), 63–73.

Magro, A.M., 2005, 'Knowledge, adaptivity, and performance in tax research', *The Accounting Review* 80(2), 703–722.

Magro, A.M. and Nutter, S.E., 2012, 'Evaluating the strength of evidence: How experience affects the use of analogical reasoning and configural information processing in tax', *The Accounting Review* 87(1), 291–312.

Marchant, G., Robinson, J.R., Anderson, U. and Schadewald, M., 1991, 'Analogical transfer and expertise in legal reasoning', *Organizational Behavior and Human Decision Processes* 48(2), 272–290.

Marchant, G., Robinson, J.R., Anderson, U. and Schadewald, M., 1993, 'The use of analogy in legal argument: Problem similarity, precedent, and expertise', *Organizational Behavior and Human Decision Processes* 55(1), 95–119.

Mason, D. and Levy, L., 2001, 'The use of the latent constructs method in behavioral accounting research: The measurement of client advocacy', *Advances in Taxation* 13, 123–139.

Pascarella, S., 1996, 'Client screening: How to reduce malpractice exposure', *Tax Advisor* 27(March), 179–180.

Payne, J., Bettman, J. and Johnson, E., 1993, *The Adaptive Decision Maker*, Cambridge University Press, New York.

Reckers, P., Sanders, D. and Wyndelts, R., 1991, 'An empirical investigation of factors influencing tax practitioner compliance', *The Journal of the American Taxation Association* 13(2), 30–46.

Roberts, M. and Ashton, R., 2003, 'Using declarative knowledge to improve information search performance', *The Journal of the American Taxation Association* 25(1), 21–38.

Roberts, M.L., 1998, 'Tax accountants' judgment/decision-making research: A review and synthesis', *The Journal of the American Taxation Association* 20(1), 78–121.

Rumelhart, D. and Norman, D., 1981, 'Analogical processes in learning', in J. Anderson (ed.), *Cognitive Skills and Their Acquisition*, 335–359, Lawrence Erlbaum, Hillsdale, NJ.

Sawyers, R., Raabe, W., Whittenburg, G. and Gill, S., 2015, *Federal Tax Research*, Cengage Learning, Stamford, CT.

Shields, M.D., Solomon, I. and Jackson, K.D., 1995, 'Experimental research on tax professionals' judgment and decision making', in J. Davis (ed.), *Behavioral Tax Research: Prospects and Judgment Calls*, American Taxation Association, Sarasota, FL.

Solomon, I. and Shields, M., 1995, 'Judgment and decision research in auditing', in A. Ashton and R. Ashton (eds.), *Judgment and Decision Research in Accounting and Auditing*, Cambridge University Press, New York.

Spilker, B.C., 1995, 'The effects of time pressure and knowledge on key word selection behavior in tax research', *The Accounting Review* 70(1), 49.

Spilker, B.C., Worsham Jr., R.G. and Prawitt, D.F., 1999, 'Tax professionals' interpretations of ambiguity in compliance and planning decision contexts', *The Journal of the American Taxation Association* 21(2), 75–89.

Sternberg, R., 1996, *Practical intelligence: How Practical and Creative Intelligence Determine Success in Life*, Simon and Schuster, New York.

Tan, H. and Libby, R., 1997, 'Tacit managerial versus technical knowledge as determinants of audit expertise in the field', *Journal of Accounting Research* 35(Spring), 97–113.

Van Kleef, G.A., de Due, C.K.W. and Manstead, A.S.R., 2006, 'Supplication and appeasement in conflict and negotiation: The interpersonal effects of disappointment, worry, guilt, and regret', *Journal of Personality and Social Psychology* 91, 124–142.

Vermeer, B. and Curatola, T., 2015, 'Tax professionals and antecedents to aggressive recommendations: An examination of client identification and economic importance', *Working paper*, University of Delaware.

Wagner, R.K. and Sternberg, R.J., 1985, 'Practical intelligence in real-world pursuits: The role of tacit knowledge', *Journal of Personality and Social Psychology* 49, 436–458.

Wood, R., 1986, 'Task complexity: Definition of the construct', *Organizational Behavior and Human Decision Processes* 37, 60–82.

Yip-Ow, J. and Tan, H.-T., 2000, 'Effects of the preparer's justification on the reviewer's hypothesis generation and judgment in analytical procedures', *Accounting, Organizations and Society* 25(2), 203–215.

28

Behavioural Accounting Research

A cross-cultural accounting perspective

Stephen B. Salter

Introduction

This chapter covers the theory of culture and values, why values should affect behavioural accounting, and addresses some of the criticisms of the Hofstede (1980, 1982) measures of culture.[1] We then move on to Behavioural Accounting Research (BAR) where culture has been used to explain extant behaviour. This chapter covers articles published from 1996 to early 2016. Those interested in research prior to this period should refer to Harrison and McKinnon (1999). For purposes of this chapter, BAR is defined using the Williams, Jenkins and Ingraham (2006: 787) definition as studies "relying on the methods and insights of the positive social sciences other than economics, e.g., psychology, social psychology, sociology". Cross-cultural research is defined as studies that compare national samples that are presented as having different cultural values. With the exception of the comparison of multinationals from different countries operating in a single country, it does not include single country studies. Unlike Harrison and McKinnon (1999), this chapter goes beyond the management control area to all available situations that are likely to influence human behaviour and situations where accounting and control interact with human subjects. The articles reviewed are limited to those appearing in accounting journals rated B and above in the Australian Business Deans Council (ABDC) ranking of journals. While there are other lists, this list is widely used and, unlike others, is the product of a broad consensus of academics. The articles examined here are primarily those using the Hofstede (1980) and its successors, Schwartz (1994) and House, Hanges, Javidan, Dorfman and Gupta (2004) measures of culture. It also uses the derivatives of Hofstede that are specifically targeted to accounting, i.e., Gray (1988) and Doupnik and Tsakumis (2004).

Culture and work values

In cross-cultural research, we start with the assumption that each country has a relatively unique culture. A portion of this culture is reflected in work values which have been developed over a long period of time and are influenced by the country's history. This adds an additional level of analysis in explaining an individual's behaviour which filters individual and organizational level stimuli such as rewards.

Hofstede and the impact of national culture on work values

Why and how would one society[2] differ from another? It is useful to begin with the work of Geert Hofstede.[3] Between 1967 and 1978 Hofstede collected data on employees' attitudes and values from 116,000 employees in 40 countries. This data was analyzed using factor analysis and appeared to generate four different sets of work values which were more or less powerful in each country. How these values came to be was largely explained by the geography, history and economics of the country. The two boxes on the left of Figure 28.1, External and Ecological influences, list the sources of culture.

Hofstede's (1980) model of culture was initially comprised of four value dimensions:

1   Power Distance (PD) – the extent to which the less powerful persons in a society accept inequality in power and consider it as normal;
2   Individualism (IND) – the degree to which people prefer to act as individuals rather than as members of groups. In individualist cultures a person looks primarily after his/her own interests, while in collectivist cultures people are assumed to belong to tight in-groups that protect the interests of their members in return for their loyalty;
3   Masculinity (MASC) – the degree to which masculine values such as assertiveness, performance, success and competition prevail over feminine values such as the quality of life, maintaining warm personal relationships, service, care for the weak and solidarity;

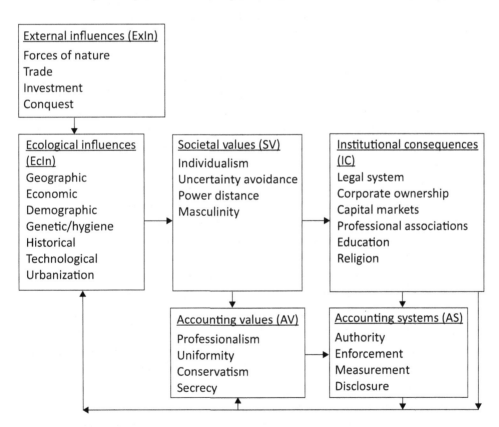

Figure 28.1   Doupnik and Tsakumis (2004) explication of Gray's 1988 framework and an inter-link with Hofstede (1982)

4   Uncertainty Avoidance (UA) – the extent to which people prefer situations which are structured or predictable.

In 1988, Hofstede and Bond added a fifth dimension, Long vs. Short-Term Orientation (Confucian Dynamism) to the original four.

Each dimension is measured at the national level starting with collecting data at the individual level and taking the median point of the whole sample as representative of the country. Hofstede (1991) refers to societal culture as the *software of the mind*, although the operating system of the mind might be a better aphorism. The individual's response is based and constrained by national values, much as the response and abilities of Microsoft Office programs are conditioned by whether the computer is running Windows 10 or Apple Mac OSX. These values influence our decisions and hence accounting outcomes.

Criticisms of Hofstede, alternatives and rebuttals

This chapter focuses on Hofstede as a primary model of culture. Hofstede's (1980) is the most cited management book with 42,185 cites. Also, Hofstede regularly updates both his data and applications thereof (Hofstede 1994; Hofstede 2003, Hofstede and Hofstede 2005; Hofstede, et al. 2010). In 2011, the series continued with the assistance of Michael Minkov (see Minkov and Hofstede 2011). The Hofstede conceptualization of national cultural values has been subject to criticisms, some of which give one pause for thought. Harrison and McKinnon (1999: 484), for example, identify the following issues to be corrected among studies using the Hofstede model.

First, they see "a failure to consider the totality of the cultural domain in the theoretical development of some studies" (484). This is typical of early studies which focus on a single dimension such as individualism to explain an outcome. Such studies often fail to address why other dimensions should not be influenced or explain the outcomes of a study or should remain dormant. Second, "The failure to attempt to account for the deferential intensity of cultural norms and values in each nation resulting in a failure to distinguish between core and peripheral values in theoretical exposition" (484). This describes a situation where no account is taken of the strength of one value versus another. For example, US historical research and documents such as the US Bill of Rights clearly indicate that individualism dominates all other values. However, other cultural dimensions are regarded as equal. Third, "A tendency to accept that culture or values can be reduced to a single score on each of the four values" (484). Some more recent studies such as Schwartz (1994), have attempted to be subtler by splitting key dimensions and having, for example, different measures of individualism. Frankly these measures do not add much to the original conception. In addition, most of the results have strong relationships with the original Hofstede values. Lastly, Harrison and McKinnon (1999: 484) criticize "an excessive reliance on the value dimensional conceptualization of culture which has produced a highly restricted conception and focus on culture, and placed critical limits on our extent of understanding". This is true of the Hofstede work and quite different from anthropology which would consider rituals, actions, icons, religions, etc., but one needs to remember that Hofstede's study was never intended to be an in-depth anthropological observation of everything in a society's culture. Instead, Hofstede, from the beginning, conducted a practical exercise in measuring work values. Perhaps the answer is simply to call Hofstede's study what it is, a description of observed work values.

Similar comments are made by others and a compilation of these comments can be seen in Table 26.1 of Baskerville-Morley (2005: 390). Baskerville-Morley further questions the validity of Hofstede's basing of his study on a single company (IBM). Baskerville-Morley also points out that using IBM, while resulting in a large total sample, resulted in a small number of participants in countries where IBM did not have a large presence. Taras, Steel and Kirkman (2012: 329–30) comment as follows:

> The study was based on a convenience sample of employees in a single American organization – IBM. As noted by Hofstede, a uni-organizational design can be advantageous as it minimizes the effects of external factors (for more details see Hofstede 1982). However, this approach can also severely limit data generalizability to the broader population. This issue is particularly problematic for Hofstede as IBM has a strong organizational culture, and its employees tend to be from a distinct demographic profile. As noted by Schwartz (1994, p. 91), "highly educated well-paid IBM employees' ability to represent the general population likely differs from country to country, with the discrepancy probably being greater, for example, in the Third World nations . . . than in industrialized Western nations".

These comments are very much like the criticisms by Baskerville (2003) and Baskerville-Morley (2005). Other issues arising from these studies include whether nation states represent a culture because they can be diverse and one can point to nations that have split apart such as Yugoslavia and other nations that hang together by the merest thread such as Belgium.

Finally, there is evidence that cultures are evolving, particularly those such as Canada and the US that take in large numbers of immigrants. Inglehart and Baker (2000) and Ralston, Gustafson, Cheung and Terpstra (1993) raise concerns as to whether or not Hofstede's indices derived from data collected in 1967–1973 are still relevant.

Taras et al. (2012) address this question using a meta-study of 451 empirical studies representing over 2,000 samples comprising over half a million individuals from 49 countries and regions. They conclude that:

> Although the reported meta-analytic indices are overall consistent with those reported by Hofstede (1980), some nations deviate from their positions in ranking tables in Hofstede's report. The difference is especially noticeable for more recent decades. For example, many Eastern European and South American countries, generally described as comparatively high Power Distance oriented and Collectivist, had lower scores on Power Distance and higher scores on Individualism, in particular for the 1990s and 2000s, than what would be expected based on Hofstede's study. Conversely, the US and some other Western nations, such as Canada and Germany, scored much lower on Individualism and higher on Power Distance compared to their scores reported by Hofstede.
>
> *(336–337)*

Taras et al. (2012) also find that when the data is divided into decades, the ability of the original Hofstede (1980) data to predict more recent economic and other indices declines.

It appears that Hofstede (1980) and subsequent publications are not perfect. They probably do not measure culture as an anthropologist sees it. The business academic interested in tools that help explain and predict the actions of organizations and their members does not see the same problems. If one understands this is a base from which to build multilevel models, then it is a good start. Hofstede is certainly aging, but still relatively accurate. One also needs to consider the alternative. As Taras et al. (2012: 340) summarize, "Unfortunately, although alternative and potentially better models of culture have been developed (e.g., House et al. 2004; Schwartz 1994; Smith et al. 1996), they have not been popular enough to generate sufficient data for meta-analysis."

Finally, we briefly look at one attempt to bypass cultural values altogether. Wong-On-Wing and Lui (2013) offer up implicit theories of causality as substitutes for Hofstede's values. They get results, but with a two-country sample, the external validity is limited.

Extending Hofstede into accounting at a theoretical level

Gray (1988) proposes that different national levels of Hofstede's (1980) social values are the progenitors of new accounting values. Accounting values are the accounting system's way of accommodating the social value base. Gray's (1988: 8) accounting-related values are Professionalism, Uniformity, Conservatism, and Secrecy and are defined as follows:

> Professionalism refers to a preference for the exercise of individual professional judgment and the maintenance of professional self-regulation. Uniformity refers to a preference for the enforcement of uniform accounting practices between companies and for the consistent use of such practices over time as opposed to flexibility in accordance with the perceived circumstances of individual companies. Conservatism refers to a preference for a cautious approach to measurement so as to cope with the uncertainty of future events as opposed to a more optimistic, laissez-faire, risk-taking approach. Finally, secrecy refers to a preference for confidentiality and the restriction of disclosure of information about the business only to those who are closely involved with its management and financing as opposed to a more transparent, open, and publicly accountable approach.

Doupnik and Tsakumis (2004: 12) describe Gray's expected connection between social values and accounting values along these lines:

1   The higher a country ranks in terms of IND and the lower it ranks in terms of UA and PD then the more likely it is to rank highly in terms of Professionalism.
2   The higher a country ranks in terms of UA and PD and the lower it ranks in terms of IND then the more likely it is to rank highly in terms of Uniformity.
3   The higher a country ranks in terms of UA and the lower it ranks in terms of IND and MASC then the more likely it is to rank highly in terms of Conservatism.
4   The higher a country ranks in terms of UA and PD and the lower it ranks in terms of IND and MASC then the more likely it is to rank highly in terms of Secrecy.

Gray's (1988) propositions are from the middle of Figure 28.1.

Doupnik and Tsakumis (2004) extend Gray's (1988) model to a series of accounting systems that might be thought of as the practical dimensions of the Gray (1988) accounting values. Doupnik and Tsakumis and others, including Schultz and Lopez (2001), Doupnik and Richter (2004), Doupnik and Riccio (2006) and Chand, Cummings and Patel (2012) use the re-envisaged Gray model in behavioural tests to determine whether accounting values, particularly conservatism and secrecy, affect financial accounting judgments. These are discussed in the "Financial reporting, culture and estimation" sub-section that follows.

Financial accounting and auditing in a cross-cultural world

The accounting literature can be divided in many ways, one of which is financial and managerial accounting. One can think of the financial world as the steps required to prepare and assure that financial statements are reliable and contain useful information for readers who are mainly external to the firm. Tests of this process are primarily done through the capital-markets literature, but there is some behavioural literature that also tests the process. This is referred to in this chapter as "Financial reporting, culture and estimation".

Financial reporting, culture and estimation

This literature stream seeks to link cultural values and responses to subsets of financial reporting. The preponderance of evidence seems to suggest that culturally conservative countries (as defined by Gray 1988) are more likely to have higher thresholds for recognizing increases in income and assets and may have some propensity to reduce the probability for recognizing negative events (Schultz and Lopez 2001; Doupnik and Tsakumis 2004; Doupnik and Riccio 2006; Chand et al. 2012). These will now be looked at in more detail.

Schultz and Lopez (2001) use an experiment to investigate the consistency of financial reporting judgments made by accountants in France, Germany and the US as they are faced with the same economic facts and similar reporting standards. Their results support the authors' expectations and Gray's (1988) conservatism hypothesis that accountants in high UA countries (France and Germany) will recommend recording warranty estimates that are higher (i.e., more cautious or conservative) than their US counterparts.

Drawing on the psychology and management literature (see for example, Beyth-Marom 1982; Hamm 1991; Wallsten, Fillebeaum and Cox 1986; Teigen and Brun 1999; Theil 2002), Doupnik and Richter (2004) hypothesize that numeric estimated probability for identical verbal probability expressions will differ between culturally different countries. Doupnik and Richter (2004: 1) believe the method is particularly useful to study cross-national interpretations of accounting standards by practicing accountants as "the assignment of probabilities to uncertainties is inherent in the application of accounting standards."

Verbal probability expressions are non-numeric expressions used in financial reporting to act as guidelines in reporting financial events. Making decisions described in these determinations requires accountants to make judgments as to what probability corresponds to the words in the verbal probability express. These terms, such as remote, probable and reasonably possible, are used to describe the likelihood of an outcome and are found in abundance on financial statements and related disclosure notes. When verbal probability expressions are embedded in accounting rules or principles and they are referred to as 'in context'. A subject might, for example, be asked to estimate the numeric probability of the word *likely* in the following extract from IAS 16.46 (2003):

> The residual value of an asset is often insignificant and can be ignored in the calculation of the depreciable amount. If the residual value is *likely* to be significant, it is estimated at the date of acquisition, or the date of any subsequent revaluation of the asset, on the basis of the realizable value prevailing at that date for similar assets.

By comparing the numeric estimated probability chosen by subjects from different countries interpreting the same verbal probability expressions, one can determine whether one national group is more or less conservative than another.

Doupnik and Richter (2004) compare participants from the US and Germany, where Germany is the conservative country. They find that "Culture affects the interpretation of positively framed verbal probability expressions" (2004: 15). German participants set a higher threshold before recognizing good news. Doupnik and Richter's findings are inconclusive as to whether German participants apply lower thresholds to recognition of liabilities and losses. Finally, they find almost no evidence that German participants need a higher threshold to write down existing assets.

Doupnik and Riccio (2006) also compare auditors in Brazil (another conservative country) and the US. Doupnik and Riccio extend Gray's (1988) measurement model to financial disclosure. The operant dimension is secrecy. Based on Gray (1988), Brazilians should be more secretive than Americans. Doupnik and Riccio confirm that, as expected, Brazilian accountants assign higher numerical probabilities than US accountants to verbal probability expressions that result in disclosures. Simply put, a result must have a higher degree of certainty to be disclosed in Brazil than the US. More recently, using student participants, Chand et al. (2012) find that those originating in conservative China are different from Anglo-Celtic Australians. As expected, the Chinese students recognize income more slowly. Interestingly, the longer Chinese students remain enrolled in Australian universities, the closer their decisions come to those made by the Anglo-Celtic Australian students.

Auditing I: professionalism and independence

This section describes cross-cultural differences in two important aspects to the audit profession, professionalism (Perera, Cummings and Chua 2012) and independence (Patel and Psaros 2000; Arnold, Bernardi, Neidermeyer and Schmee 2006; Lin and Fraser 2008). In a study of two culturally distinct countries in the South Pacific, Samoa and New Zealand, Perera et al. (2012) find major differences in the levels of accounting professionalism in the two countries. While it is true that Samoa and New Zealand are culturally different, they are also at opposite ends of the economic and development scale. It is not clear whether culture or other factors cause the difference in professionalism.

Turning to independence, three cross-cultural studies can be identified that examine how culture may affect levels and perception of auditor independence (Patel and Psaros 2000; Arnold et al. 2006; Lin and Fraser 2008). Patel and Psaros (2000) find significant differences among final year undergraduate accounting students in the UK, Australia, India and Malaysia in their perceptions of external auditors' independence. Specifically, they find that students from countries with greater political, economic and socio-cultural interactions on an ongoing basis, i.e., the UK and Australia, are likely to have greater similarities (i.e., lesser variations) in their perceptions of auditors' ability to make judgments and behave in a manner that is clearly independent of clients. Students from countries that do not have ongoing relationships, i.e., India and Malaysia, had significantly different perceptions.

Arnold et al. (2006) examine auditors from global firms located in Denmark, Ireland, Italy, Spain, Sweden, the Netherlands and the UK to study the raison d'être for doing additional work prior to signing off on an audit. They conclude that the primary factor is not culture, but the need to maintain the quality of the auditor's judgment. The secondary factor was the fear of losing the client by over auditing. However, Arnold et al. also find that Hofstede's (1980) individualism dimension is associated with both auditor judgment and fear of losing the client. In a similar vein, when examining a sample of auditors from global firms in China and the UK, Lin and Fraser (2008) find that even after controlling for the degree of specificity of accounting standards, auditor tenure, management advisory services and competition, UK participants are less likely than their Chinese counterparts to accept clients' requests for variations from recommended accounting treatments. Chinese auditors are most likely to accede in situations where their relationship with the client includes provision of management advisory services and there is significant competition. For auditors in the UK, these results are reversed.

Auditing II: culture and judgment in auditing

In this section, we look at the impact of differences in national culture on audit judgment as it relates to risk and materiality. Three of the studies, Hughes, Sander, Higgs and Cullinan (2009), O'Donnell and Prather-Kinsey (2010), and Patel and Millanta (2011) find no differences in these judgments across national cultures. Arnold, Bernardi and Neidermeyer (2001) find differences among Big 4 auditors in the scope of their reaction to materiality, but do not find a difference in the absolute score in each country.

The first study, Hughes et al. (2009), attempts to link three of Hofstede's cultural dimensions, power distance, uncertainty avoidance and individualism, to the results of analytical procedures conducted by upper level auditing students. The students are treated as a proxy for entry level auditors in Mexico and the US. Hughes et al. (2009: 33) predict that

> The high power distance, high uncertainty avoidance and lower individualism associated with Mexico suggests that auditors in that country will be less likely to conclude that there is a significant risk of material misstatement in account balances, even when industry and company events suggest such misstatements are likely.

They actually find no difference between US and Mexican students, pointing to the potential harmonization of values and judgment among auditors from these countries.

The second study, O'Donnell and Prather-Kinsey (2010), examines whether auditors from the same global audit firm in the UK, France and the US come to different conclusions when they perform analytical procedures to assess the risk of misstatement in accounts. All auditors performed analytical procedures on identical case materials and came to similar conclusions about the overall risk of misstatement. Interestingly, the auditors found that participants from different countries identified different risks as being the most dangerous. This certainly argues that different countries emphasize different statements in their risk assessment.

The third study, Patel and Millanta (2011), examines the likelihood of types of value systems on auditors adopting the "holier-than-thou" perception bias. In the "holier-than-thou" perception bias, individuals perceive themselves as acting more ethically than comparable others when confronted with ethically uncertain work-related behaviours. Using Australian and Indian professional accountants from big global audit firms, Patel and Millanta find that while the "holier-than-thou" perception bias exists among both groups of auditors, the magnitude of the bias was not significantly different between the countries.

We next turn to the issue of the impact of culture on materiality judgments. As previously discussed in the "Financial reporting, culture and estimation" section, there is some evidence that culture affects the estimation of probabilistic expressions such as "more likely than not". In auditing, a similar but crucial topic is whether an amount is material enough to disclose or do further testing. There is only one study in the area of values and materiality. Arnold et al. (2001) examine whether using the same data, experienced auditors employed by global audit firms in Denmark, Ireland, Italy, Spain, Sweden, the Netherlands, the UK and the US will classify situations as material or not. Arnold et al. find that low client-integrity ratings resulted in lower materiality estimates for all the European auditors. However, the degree of uncertainty avoidance was positively related with the actual level of the materiality threshold. Although one might have anticipated that the materiality threshold would decrease with the level of litigation, it in fact, increased.

Auditing III: internal auditing

Although internal audit has typically been seen as a newcomer in audit research, it is also affected by culture and may, in some ways, be more important to a multinational enterprise than the external audit, especially where it is assuming a crucial consulting role. Regrettably, there appears to be a relative dearth of articles in this area. Kachelmeier and Shehata (1997) investigate the premise that the effectiveness of and demand for audit-based monitoring may be sensitive to societal (cultural) factors. Using a between-subjects experiment involving 60 groups of four each (a total of 240 participants) they find a significant interaction between country and the degree of anonymity in internal reporting. They find that there is less demand for audit-based monitoring and it is less effective in communitarian/high uncertainty avoidant countries such as Hong Kong and China than in individualistic/low uncertainty avoidant countries such as Canada. Given that the purpose of the audit is as a mechanism to increase transparency, this finding mirrors Gray's (1988) proposition that the higher a country ranks in terms of uncertainty avoidance and power distance and the lower it ranks in terms of individualism and masculinity, and the more likely it is to rank highly in terms of secrecy.

Abdolmohammadi and Sarens (2011) and Abdolmohammadi (2011) explore perceptions of internal audit using data from chief audit executives from 19 countries collected by the Institute of Internal Auditors Research Foundation (Burnaby, Hass and Abdolmohammadi 2007). Similar to Kachelmeier and Shehata (1997) they conclude that countries high in uncertainty avoidance tend to use less internal audit and are less likely to comply with the Standards for the Professional Practice of Internal Auditing of the Institute of Internal Auditors. They also find evidence that the importance of performance attributes differs significantly by cultural cluster. For example, while Latin-American chief audit executives rated leadership attributes at higher levels than other cultural clusters for internal audit staff, the East-European chief audit executives assessed the importance of technical skills at higher levels than other clusters. Abdolmohammadi and Sarens is one of the few studies found to use the House et al. (2004) values of assertiveness and humane orientation. Assertiveness is defined as the degree to which individuals in organizations and societies are assertive, confrontational and aggressive in social relationships and is part of the Hofstede (1980) masculinity dimension. Humane orientation is defined as the effort and practice which a society shows in support of human beings including generosity, concern and friendliness. They find that societies that are demanding of a fair shake for all use internal audit as part of that process.

Auditing IV: ethics

Although ethics is an increasingly important topic for accountants (Kidwell, Fisher, Braun and Swanson 2013) two searches of Google Scholar using the keywords (a) accounting, ethics and Hofstede and (b) accounting, ethics and culture, find only six articles that meet the pre-defined quality filter for journals for this chapter. They are also divided into cross-national studies and studies of persons of different cultures who are working in a single country. Do cross-national differences in values affect ethical decisions? As Curtis, Conover and Chui (2012: 7) observe

> Ethics theory supports the influence of instinctive reactions on ethical behaviour, although to varying degrees. . . . Therefore, there is theoretical support for the notion that country of origin results in mental programs that result in instinctive reactions to ethically challenging situations.

Three studies are examined (Roxas and Stoneback 1997; Geiger et al. 2006; Curtis et al. 2012) and all have relatively clear cross-cultural tests of the relationship between culture and either ethical processes or behaviour and the results are mixed.

Roxas and Stoneback (1997) is the first study in the current time period. Using a nine-country sample to examine the influence of dimensions of culture on the ethical decision process (as opposed to outcomes), Roxas and Stoneback found some differences in ethical perceptions across cultures, but the results were not conclusive. Geiger et al. (2006) examine data collected from participants from eight countries and find significant variation in perceptions of right and wrong in earnings management. They find that perceptions of earnings manipulations involving the timing of operating decisions are associated with both the power distance index and the masculinity index. Regrettably, they find that the differences in aggregate perceptions across countries are not significantly associated with any one Hofstede (1991) dimension.

Curtis et al. (2012) examine the impact of national culture on ethical decision-making. Using students from China, Japan, Mexico and the US as participants, Curtis et al. test a mediation model where country of origin influences perceptions of justice and power distance. Perceptions of justice and power distance in turn influence behavioural intentions in regard to ethical dilemmas. Each of the variables (country of origin, justice perceptions, power distance perception and gender) has a significant main effect, but the mediation model works only partially. Power distance and justice partially mediate the relationship between country of origin and ethical decision-making, but the relationship depends on gender.

Three other studies in the current time period address the relationship between ethical behaviour and culture. These three studies are not cross-cultural in the pure sense of the word but use samples from different cultures in a single location. Cable and Patel (2000) find that there are significant differences in judgments between Australian and Chinese[4] participants who are students at an Australian university. Chinese are more forgiving of aggressive financial reporting than the Australian born participants. Similarly, Dunn (2006) finds that Chinese students in his sample are willing to sanction businesses and accounting-policy choices that the Canadian students in his sample consider to be inappropriate and unethical. Finally, using US citizens of different ethnicity, Cieslewicz (2015) finds that high degrees of power distance and collectivism increase the likelihood that an accounting supervisor will encourage subordinates to collude in manipulating accounting information. Uncertainty avoidance, or rule orientation, decreases the likelihood. This study is not strictly cross-cultural, but it demonstrates a new and interesting angle of this topic, i.e., using cross-cultural tools to examine within-country diversity and its effects on decisions.

Management accounting

Budgeting

One of the major areas of management accounting is budgeting. As in the domestic literature, the emphasis is first on the willingness of managers to participate and be truthful. This category includes articles that view the budgeting process as a game. The second area of emphasis examines what part the budget process plays in motivating managers and the factors that are likely to impact performance that arise from the budgetary process. In both these areas the major difference cross-nationally is the role national values play in the budget creation process and the impact budgets may or may not have on managerial performance.

A good starting overview is Derfuss (2009). Derfuss conducts a meta-study to summarize 50 years of budgetary research. He points out that it is hard to find a budgetary sub topic in which there is consensus. The meta-study standardizes different scales to a single scale and conducts an analysis of the resulting very large database. Derfuss covers both US and global research. Overall Derfuss (2009: 224) concludes:

> Contrary to recent criticisms then, budgetary participation creates value through its positive association with managers' attitudes and behaviour, though this value might not be readily measurable. Budgetary participation is indispensable, even as budget systems are adapted to changing environmental or organisational demands. Moreover, emphasising budgets as performance evaluation criteria does not inevitably lead to adverse consequences. These findings help explain why many companies do not abolish budgets, despite their acknowledged shortcomings.

For cross-cultural work Derfuss (2009: 224–225) provides the following summary:

> Many of the homogeneous relations also refer to different Anglo-American and Asian contexts, which suggests they generalise across cultures (cf. Lau and Tan 1998; Van der Stede 2003). However, knowledge is limited regarding European contexts, and no study reports correlations for African or South American settings. This gap represents a severe drawback, because perceptions of control differ even among European countries (Scheytt et al. 2003). Additional research should focus on establishing whether the findings generalise to less explored cultural contexts.

Lau and Eggleton (2004), Leach-Lopez, Stammerjohan and McNair (2008), Douglas, HassabElnaby, Norman and Wier (2007) and Stammerjohan, Leach and Stammerjohan (2015) provide some supplementation to Derfuss (2009) and examine how national culture affects budgeting participation and the creation of slack. Using a sample from Australia and Singapore, Lau and Eggleton find: (a) a significant main effect exists between national culture and budgetary participation and (b) a significant three-way interaction among national culture, performance evaluative style and information asymmetry exists that affects budgetary slack. Leach-Lopez et al. introduce a new variable, budgetary participation conflict. Budgetary participation conflict occurs when the level of budget participation experienced by a manager differs from a desired level. They find that budgetary participation conflict does not directly or indirectly affect the performance of US managers, but indirectly and negatively affects the job performance of Mexican managers.

Douglas et al. (2007) tackle a slightly different angle, i.e., the impact of multinationals on budgetary behaviour in a single country. Using a comparison of the budgeting behaviours of Egyptian managers who work for Egyptian firms and Egyptian managers who work for US firms in Egypt, they find that higher levels of budgetary participation exist for Egyptian managers working for US rather than Egyptian firms. They also find more frequent slack-creation behaviour among Egyptian managers employed by US firms. This suggests that multinationals may, through their hiring practices or other methods, encourage local employees to acculturate and become more American in their approach to budgeting.

Stammerjohan et al. (2015) use a single cultural dimension, power distance, to explain the budgetary participation to performance relationship. They argue that isolating the impact of power distance is important to this literature because participative budgeting remains a possibly underutilized management tool in high power distant countries. They find that, contrary to Hofstede (1991), the majority of managers from three supposedly high power distant countries (Mexico, Korea and China) scored in the lower half of the power distance scale. Their explanation is that the managers surveyed may not share the same high power distance tendencies of their countrymen. Stammerjohan et al. (2015) also find that managers from all countries preferred to participate in the budgetary process. Managers in traditionally high power distance countries (Mexico, Korea and China) were motivated by job relevance information while the US managers focused on job satisfaction as the mediating variable.

Stammerjohan et al.'s (2015) findings that non-US managers have much lower levels of power distance than expected is similar to the findings of Frucot and Shearon (1991). Frucot and Shearon find that Mexican managers bifurcate among a top group of anglicized upper managers and a lower group of managers who are more in line with the Mexican stereotype. Stammerjohan et al.'s sample is also quite interesting in that the majority of the participants worked in US-owned plants. As Douglas et al. (2007) point out, local employees of US firms have different attitudes and behaviours from those who work for corporations that are locally owned. This presents a significant research opportunity for samples from a large number of different countries. Also, it permits some work in the propensity of different cultures to adapt to incoming foreign firms.

Knowledge sharing

The question being asked here is do different cultures and/or specific cultural dimensions affect the truthfulness of information that is passed upward to supervisors? It includes the work of Chow, Harrison, McKinnon and Wu (1999a), Chow, Deng and Ho (2000), Salter and Schulz (2005), Salter, Schulz, Lewis and López-V. (2008) and Huerta, Salter, Lewis and Yeow (2012a). In each case the participants' culture is determined by the country where the experimental data is collected. The participants' willingness to communicate valuable but not always positive information is manipulated by offering a number of potential incentives to disclose, including anonymity and monetary reward.

Chow et al. (1999a) is considered the seminal paper in this area and is the basis of future studies (it is cited in 116 other articles). In this study, the willingness and reasons to share information of Taiwanese-Chinese and Australian participants are compared. Both quantitative and qualitative data was collected, including some quite insightful interviews. As anticipated, Australian participants, being more individualistic and low power distant were more likely to disclose information, but many individual factors affected the response. To the Taiwanese-Chinese participants there was a clear, consistent, collectivist responsibility to share, but with the injection of a supervisor there was the added factor of potential loss of face[5] and respect for the hierarchy that made it harder to determine exactly how much would be shared. The conclusion is that culture affects the willingness to share.

Similar results to Chow et al. (1999a) were found in Chow, Hwang, Liao and Wu (1998). The major results of this experiment were consistent with the prediction that Taiwanese-Chinese reported their private information more truthfully than those in the US unless a supervisor was present. The argument for this is that fear of loss of face dominated a natural truthfulness to benefit the collective enterprise.

Schulz, Salter, Lopez and Lewis (2009) also obtained similar results to Chow et al. (1999a). Using a sample of high power distance/high collectivism countries (Chile and China), Schulz et al. confirmed the importance of face in Chinese decisions. When the supervisor is present Chinese participants disclose less information. Since both Chile and China are high power distance/high collectivism countries and the Chileans have no concept of face, it appears the lower level of willingness to share information is a product of face.

Huerta, Salter et al. (2012) provide an interesting spin on the question of information sharing by changing the context from a face-to-face meeting to a computer-based knowledge management system. Data for the experiment were collected in two individualist (UK and US) and two collectivist (Chile and Mexico) countries to evaluate the influence of culture on information sharing patterns, with both successes and failures. The study finds that all participant groups share successes. Anonymity also increases the sharing of failures and participants from collectivist cultures are more likely to share failures than those from individualist countries. Interestingly, monetary incentives had no impact on sharing even among individualist countries.

Understanding and controlling for decision biases, prospect theory and framing

The phenomenon of escalation of commitment has been researched in the domestic literature from the mid-1970s onward. As Sharp and Salter (1997: 102) observe:

> The considerable project commitment escalation literature (e.g., Staw [1976]; Staw and Ross [1985]; Brockner [1992]) suggests a number of factors that could promote the excessive escalation of commitment to risky projects. Two long-established theories have recently been invoked to explain so-called escalation errors: agency theory [Jensen and Meckling 1976] and prospect theory [Kahneman and Tversky 1979]. Both theories are central to Western management thinking. For example, in accounting research alone, the assumptions of agency theory are at the heart of the very influential positive accounting theory [Watts and Zimmerman 1990].

Of the major theories explaining escalation, agency theory assumes an individualist (US) perspective is dominant. In this perspective, it is expected that an individual will seek his or her personal benefit at the expense of the company. Sharp and Salter (1997: 106) remark

> it is interesting to speculate whether agency theory could have been developed to the extent it has in any culture other than an individualist one; the very idea of rigorously modeling self-interest may not have occurred to researchers in a collectivist culture.

The second explanation of escalation is prospect theory. Kahneman and Tversky (1979: 263) define the key elements of prospect theory thus:

> An alternative theory of choice . . . in which value is assigned to gains and losses rather than to final assets and in which probabilities are replaced by decision weights. The value function is normally concave for gains, commonly convex for losses, and is generally steeper for losses than for gains. Decision weights are generally lower than the corresponding probabilities, except in the range of low probabilities. Overweighting of low probabilities may contribute to the attractiveness of both insurance and gambling.

For prospect theory, there is no clear explanation of why results might be different across countries. The perception of loss resulting from the framing of the expression or decision is not, per se, culturally bound. However, it is not unreasonable to expect that a person who is influenced by a high uncertainty avoidant culture may overreact more than one from a less uncertainty avoidant culture.

Sharp and Salter (1997), Salter and Sharp (2001), Salter, Lewis and Juarez-Valdes (2004) and Salter, Sharp and Chen (2013) explore these phenomena in great detail across North America (including Mexico) and Asia. The result of this sequence, as summarized in Salter et al. (2013: 161) is a finding that:

> The effect of negative framing (prospect theory) on escalation of commitment is significant, but unaffected by differences in national cultures. The adverse selection problem arising from agency predictions has a stronger effect in high-individualism countries than in low-individualism countries, and managers in higher long-term orientation countries are more likely to escalate projects with potential long-term payoffs.

Even small differences in individualism between the US and Canada impact the power of agency-driven escalation (Salter and Sharp 2001). Deng, Haddad and Harrison (2003) and Chow, Kohlmeyer and Wu (2007) also find that prospect theory is not culture dependent in Mexico or Taiwan.

The only research found that contradicts the universality of the framing effect from prospect theory is Huerta, Glandon and Petrides (2012). They used US and Mexican participants to examine whether automated or manual decision aid systems exacerbated or ameliorated the framing bias for each culture. Huerta, Glandon and Petrides found that for US participants, automated systems ameliorated framing biases in decision-making, but for Mexicans there was no amelioration. Huerta, Glandon and Petrides cite the ongoing distrust by Mexicans of automated systems as the reason. There does not appear to be any clear cultural reason, rather a history of lack of trust in automated systems appears to be at the heart of these differences. It would be most interesting to do a broader examination of this topic of automation in a variety of control systems and countries.

Management control systems and culture

In this section, we look at topics that are important to research in management control, but are relatively lightly represented in the extant literature. The first topic is the role of incentives in management control systems and how they are perceived and used in different cultures. This includes articles by Brody, Lin and Salter (2006), Jansen, Merchant and Van der Stede (2009), Merchant, Van der Stede, Lin and Yu (2011) and Awasthi, Chow and Wu (2001). Logically a control system in an individualist country should focus more on rewarding the individual than that from a communitarian society. In the reverse, managers in a country with a high uncertainty avoidant culture should value certain, as opposed to uncertain, rewards. Persons in a high power distance society would be expected to care less about how the rewards were determined and trust their leaders. Finally, those in a more feminine/nurturing society would require that everyone receives enough to be comfortable.

In a study of bonus versus salary payments, Brody et al. (2006) find that participants from the more individualist US provide less merit pay, less often to poor performers than the collectivist Taiwanese-Chinese. In effect in Taiwan, a highly collectivist and uncertainty avoidant country, part of the merit bonus becomes salary, guaranteeing the collective reward and certainty.

Merchant et al. (2011) compare the reward systems for auto dealers from three countries, the US, the Netherlands and China. While Jansen et al. (2009), in an earlier two-country study, had found the compensation in Dutch firms to be less incentive based than in US firms, Chinese firms were found to be much more likely to provide incentives than Dutch or even US firms. Chinese bonus plans were based less on direct performance measures, using subjective and non-financial performance measures and with more complex performance – reward functions. Like managers in the US firms, Chinese employees like incentive compensation. This was contrary to expectations built on the assumption that Chinese would be collectivist and reward sharing but reflected the similar level of masculinity in the US and China versus the Netherlands. Masculinity, for which this author prefers the term nurturing or achievement orientation, reflects what Merchant et al. (2011: 662) describe as "preferences for competitiveness, achievement and material success (traits labelled as 'masculine'), as opposed to an emphasis on relationships and quality of life (traits labelled as 'feminine')". The subjectivity of the bonuses refers to the Chinese high respect for authority or high power distance. Finally, in incentives, Awasthi et al. (2001) find that in contrasting US and Chinese participants, the US participants preferred individual work but they could be incentivized to enter and perform in groups. They were, however, still not happy about group or team participation.

A second sub-topic is documenting existing control systems. The findings here are contradictory. For example, Chow, Shields and Wu (1999b) find that employees at different home-country multinational companies, all situated in Taiwan, face different designs and uses of seven management controls tools. In contrast, using a broad sample, Van der Stede (2003) finds that corporate management control and incentive systems tend to be uniformly implemented within firms rather than reflecting local business-unit conditions.

A third sub-area is to test the impact of various management control systems cross-culturally. For example, Chow, Lindquist and Wu (2001) find the Chinese participants are more accepting of imposed high-stretch performance standards than US participants, reflecting a response to authority inherent in a high power distance culture. Patel (2003) finds that the acceptance of whistle-blowing as a control device is far more acceptable among individualist Australian accountants than more communitarian Indians and Chinese-Malaysians. Turning to an evolving control system of strategy maps, Lowe, Carmona-Moreno and Reckers (2011) find that high uncertainty avoidant Spanish participants focus on the financial portion of a strategy map and cannot be moved from this by varying the form of the strategy map. US participants, in contrast, can be persuaded to move towards a less financial, less biased view of outcomes by reformulating the strategy map. Lowe et al. link the behaviour of the Spanish participants to the high UA nature of the Spanish value system.

Conclusion

So what can one conclude after this review? First, the volume of articles since Harrison and McKinnon (1999) has increased fourfold. Even excluding single country studies and those articles in journals below the ABDC level B, this chapter reviews over 80 articles covering a huge range of topics. But have any of the Harrison and McKinnon (1999) perceived gaps in the literature been met? Fundamentally, the answer is no. There is very little evidence that researchers consider the totality of culture or the intensity of particular dimensions. Neither has the temptation to reduce culture to a series of numbers. All three major measures of culture (Hofstede 1980; House et al. 2004; Schwartz 1994) try to reduce culture to a score or number for each of the dimensions. For example, Hofstede's individualism dimension ranges from 91 in the US to 6 in Guatemala. It is difficult to conceptualize that one country may be 15 times more individualistic than another when there is evidence that small cultural differences matter (Salter and Sharp 2001). As discussed in a previous section the value, in a business setting, of using anything other than numbers for culture is minimal and so, not surprisingly, this objective has not been pursued.

Does this mean no progress has been made? Quite the contrary. We now know that culture affects a much wider range of topics, from auditing independence to escalation of commitment. Further, the Taras et al. (2012) meta-study provides additional Hofstede scores that have been updated. Similarly, Minkov and Hofstede (2011) provide re-measured cultural values.

There are still many opportunities to contribute. A good start would be to link the piecemeal issues tackled in each sub-area of accounting (i.e., internal audit, the audit process, escalation of commitment and the interpretation of verbal probability expressions including accounting principles) into a series of more holistic models. Each model would identify what components of each topic, such as auditing, are complete and what is missing. One way to accomplish this task would be to take the US/Canadian domestic research and map potentially culturally vulnerable areas. Some areas such as escalation of commitment and information sharing have been pretty much specified and tested and the picture is clear, but in audit and internal audit, the knowledge gap is huge.

Another alternative is to modify Figure 5 from Doupnik and Tsakumis (2004) which is represented by the last two boxes in Figure 28.1. Accountants Application of Financial Rules is designed for further research planned by Doupnik and Tsakumis. An equally valid application is any situation where accountants have to make judgments. This would include how to audit and the procedures to be used in the audit. Even in highly regulated markets such as the US one can make judgments. It would be even more interesting to study variations in judgments in less regulated markets. In addition, how do the auditing institutions vary between nations and to what extent does this affect judgments? Related to this is the question of private regulation. Can one argue that global audit firms form a private regulatory system? Can this really be enforced given the cultural difference of auditors?

Another open area is the need for more diversity among the countries and cultures studied. Using the stock of foreign direct investment (FDI) as an indicator,[6] countries representing 22% of the global stock of foreign direct investment are completely unrepresented. These countries include Belgium, Colombia, Finland, Indonesia, Luxembourg, Norway, Poland, the Russian Federation, Saudi Arabia, Singapore, South Africa, Sweden, Switzerland, Thailand and Turkey. Comparisons of these countries in groups or with countries about which much is known, such as the UK, would benefit the growth of knowledge. Two of these countries offer the opportunity for intra-country cultural research. Belgium and South Africa both have powerful and yet different groups interacting. In the case of Belgium, does one need to alter the control system for Flemings who are Dutch and Walloons who are French?

Even among those countries that have been the focus of research, some are under-represented, such as the UK and Brazil, and some are grossly over-represented such as Australia, China and Mexico. There are good reasons for this as Australia has a strong research tradition and a large professoriate which educates both a domestic and a large non-citizen group. China has been one of the fastest growing economies in the world and there are strong connections across the US-Mexico border. Using a slightly different measure, one might want to expand into faster growing economies such as Vietnam, India and the Philippines in Asia; Tanzania, Kenya and Ethiopia in Africa and Poland and the Czech Republic in Eastern Europe.

There is also a need for larger multi-country samples with ten or more countries. This will not be easy and would probably require larger teams than is typically tolerable in accounting journals. The alternative to this would be a meta-study, but there do not seem to be sufficient studies in any one area for this.

Lastly, and perhaps surprisingly, there is a need for more studies on the impact of acculturation. If anything, the first and second decade of the twenty-first century is the story of massive movements of populations to other countries. For Australia and Canada, these are skilled professionals from Asia; in the US it is undocumented migration from Latin America; and most recently it is Germany accepting one million refugees from the Middle East. The key question may be given our control and audit systems are based on one country's cultural values; how well will it stand up with the injection of significant numbers of persons who do not share those values?

This chapter has been a survey of models of culture and the reality of cross-cultural invest-ment and research. If I could come to a conclusion, it is that we have only just started and there is much more to do. So let us begin.

Notes

1 Hofstede has periodically updated his study, adding new countries and discussing and rebutting papers that arise. The latest issue of the full book is Hofstede, Hofstede and Minkov (2010).
2 The term society is equated with one national state in most cross-cultural literature in the business area even though theoretically there can be more than one society within a nation.
3 A thorough review of Hofstede can be found in Minkov and Hofstede (2011).
4 Defined by ethnicity and could include Chinese Australians.
5 Cardon (2009: 21) defines face as "a measure of one's position in social networks and is built up by a history of socially sanctioned behaviours. Without face, one's opportunities in the Chinese collectivist society are greatly diminished."
6 Source: UNCTAD, FDI/TNC database (www.unctad.org/fdistatistics).

References

Abdolmohammadi, M., 2011, 'Chief audit executives' assessment of internal auditors' performance attrib-utes by professional rank and cultural cluster', *Behavioral Research in Accounting* 24(1), 1–23.

Abdolmohammadi, M. and Sarens, G., 2011, 'An investigation of the association between cultural dimen-sions and variations in perceived use of and compliance with internal auditing standards in 19 coun-tries', *The International Journal of Accounting* 46(4), 365–389.

Arnold, D., Bernardi, R. and Neidermeyer, P., 2001, 'The association between European materiality esti-mates and client integrity, national culture, and litigation', *The International Journal of Accounting* 36(4), 459–483.

Arnold, D., Bernardi, R., Neidermeyer, P. and Schmee, J., 2006, 'Between country variations in the applica-tion of the principle of auditor confidentiality: A European setting', *SSRN* 1094554.

Awasthi, V., Chow, C. and Wu, A., 2001, 'Cross-cultural differences in the behavioral consequences of imposing performance evaluation and reward systems: An experimental investigation', *The International Journal of Accounting* 36(3), 291–309.

Baskerville, R., 2003, 'Hofstede never studied culture', *Accounting, Organizations and Society* 28(1), 1–14.

Baskerville-Morley, R., 2005, 'A research note: The unfinished business of culture', *Accounting, Organizations and Society* 30(4), 389–391.

Beyth-Marom, R., 1982, 'How probable is probable? A numerical translation of verbal probability expres-sions', *Journal of Forecasting* 1(3), 257–269.

Brockener, J., 1992, 'The escalation of commitment to a failing course of action', *Academy of Management Review* 17(1), 39–61.

Brody, R., Lin, S. and Salter, S., 2006, 'Merit pay, responsibility, and national values: A US-Taiwan compari-son', *Journal of International Accounting Research* 5(2), 63–79.

Burnaby, P., Hass, S. and Abdolmohammadi, M., 2007, *A Global Summary of the Common Body of Knowledge 2006*, The Institute of Internal Auditors Research Foundation, Altamonte Springs, FL.

Cable, D. and Patel, C., 2000, 'Personality and cultural influences on aggressive financial reporting practices', *Asian Review of Accounting* 8(2), 60–80.

Cardon, P., 2009, 'A model of face practices in Chinese business culture: Implications for western busi-nesspersons', *Thunderbird International Business Review* 51(1), 19–36.

Chand, P., Cummings, L. and Patel, C., 2012, 'The effect of accounting education and national culture on accounting judgments: A comparative study of Anglo-Celtic and Chinese culture', *European Accounting Review* 21(1), 153–182.

Chow, C., Deng, F. and Ho, J., 2000, 'The openness of knowledge sharing within organizations: A compara-tive study of the United States and the People's Republic of China', *Journal of Management Accounting Research* 12(1), 65–95.

Chow, C., Harrison, G., McKinnon, J. and Wu, A., 1999a, 'Cultural influences on informal information sharing in Chinese and Anglo-American organizations: An exploratory study', *Accounting, Organizations and Society* 24(7), 561–582.

Chow, C., Hwang, R., Liao, W. and Wu, A., 1998, 'National culture and subordinates' upward communication of private information', *The International Journal of Accounting* 33(3), 293–311.

Chow, C., Kohlmeyer, J. and Wu, A., 2007, 'Performance standards and managers' adoption of risky projects', *Advances in Management Accounting* 16, 63–105.

Chow, C., Lindquist, T. and Wu, A., 2001, 'National culture and the implementation of high-stretch performance standards: An exploratory study', *Behavioral Research in Accounting* 13(1), 85–109.

Chow, C., Shields, M. and Wu, A., 1999b, 'The importance of national culture in the design of and preference for management controls for multi-national operations', *Accounting, Organizations and Society* 24(5), 441–461.

Cieslewicz, J., 2015, 'Collusive accounting supervision and economic culture', *Journal of International Accounting Research* 15(1), 89–108.

Curtis, M., Conover, T. and Chui, L., 2012, 'A cross-cultural study of the influence of country of origin, justice, power distance, and gender on ethical decision making', *Journal of International Accounting Research* 11(1), 5–34.

Deng, J., Haddad, F. and Harrison, P., 2003, 'The roles of self-interest and ethical reasoning in project continuance decisions: A comparative study of US and the People's Republic of China', *Managerial Finance* 29(12), 45–56.

Derfuss, K., 2009, 'The relationship of budgetary participation and reliance on accounting performance measures with individual-level consequent variables: A meta-analysis', *European Accounting Review* 18(2), 203–239.

Douglas, P., HassabElnaby, H., Norman, C. and Wier, B., 2007, 'An investigation of ethical position and budgeting systems: Egyptian managers in US and Egyptian firms', *Journal of International Accounting, Auditing and Taxation* 16(1), 90–109.

Doupnik, T. and Riccio, E., 2006, 'The influence of conservatism and secrecy on the interpretation of verbal probability expressions in the Anglo and Latin cultural areas', *The International Journal of Accounting* 41(3), 237–261.

Doupnik, T. and Richter, M., 2004, 'The impact of culture on the interpretation of "in context" verbal probability expressions', *Journal of International Accounting Research* 3(1) 1–20.

Doupnik, T. and Tsakumis, G., 2004, 'A critical review of tests of Gray's theory of cultural relevance and suggestions for future research', *Journal of Accounting Literature* 23, 1–48.

Dunn, P., 2006, 'The role of culture and accounting education in resolving ethical business dilemmas by Chinese and Canadians', *Accounting and the Public Interest* 6(1), 116–134.

Frucot, V. and Shearon, W., 1991, 'Budgetary participation, locus of control, and Mexican managerial performance and job satisfaction', *The Accounting Review*, 80–99.

Geiger, M., O'Connell, B., Clikeman, P., Ochoa, E., Witkowski, K. and Basioudis, I., 2006, 'Perceptions of earnings management: The effects of national culture', *Advances in International Accounting* 19, 175–199.

Gray, S., 1988, 'Towards a theory of cultural influence on the development of accounting systems internationally', *Abacus* 24(1), 1–15.

Hamm, R., 1991, 'Selection of verbal probabilities: A solution for some problems of verbal probability expression', *Organizational Behavior and Human Decision Processes* 48, 193–223.

Harrison, G. and McKinnon, J., 1999, 'Cross-cultural research in management control systems design: A review of the current state', *Accounting, Organizations and Society* 24(5), 483–506.

Hofstede, G., 1980, 'Culture and organizations', *International Studies of Management & Organization* 10(4), 15–41.

Hofstede, G., 1981, 'Do American theories apply abroad? A reply to Goodstein and Hunt', *Organizational Dynamics* 10(1), 63–68.

Hofstede, G. H. 1982 [2010], *Culture's Consequences: International Differences in Work-Related Values*, Sage, Newbury Park.

Hofstede, G., 1991, *Cultures and Organizations: Software of the Mind* (Vol. 2), McGraw-Hill, Maidenhead.

Hofstede, G., 1994, 'The business of international business is culture', *International Business Review* 3(1), 1–14.

Hofstede, G., 2003, 'What is culture? A reply to Baskerville', *Accounting, Organizations and Society* 28(7), 811–813.

Hofstede, G. and Bond, M., 1988, 'The Confucius connection: From cultural roots to economic growth', *Organizational Dynamics* 16(4), 5–21.

Hofstede, G. and Hofstede, G., 2005, *Cultures and Organizations: Software of the Mind* (2nd ed.), McGraw-Hill, New York.

Hofstede, G., Hofstede, G. and Minkov, M., 2010, *Cultures and Organizations: Software of the Mind* (3rd ed.), McGraw-Hill, New York.

House, R., Hanges, P., Javidan, M., Dorfman, P. and Gupta, V., (eds.), 2004, *Culture, Leadership, and Organizations: The GLOBE Study of 62 Societies*, Sage, Thousand Oaks.

Huerta, E., Glandon, T. and Petrides, Y., 2012, 'Framing, decision-aid systems, and culture: Exploring influences on fraud investigations', *International Journal of Accounting Information Systems* 13(4), 316–333.

Huerta, E., Salter, S., Lewis, P. and Yeow, P., 2012, 'Motivating employees to share their failures in knowledge management systems: Anonymity and culture', *Journal of Information Systems* 26(2), 93–117.

Hughes, S., Sander, J., Higgs, S. and Cullinan, C., 2009, 'The impact of cultural environment on entry-level auditors' abilities to perform analytical procedures', *Journal of International Accounting, Auditing and Taxation* 18(1), 29–43.

Inglehart, R. and Baker, W., 2000, 'Modernization, cultural change, and the persistence of traditional values', *American Sociological Review* 1, 19–51.

Jansen, E., Merchant, K. and Van der Stede, W., 2009, 'National differences in incentive compensation practices: The differing roles of financial performance measurement in the United States and the Netherlands', *Accounting, Organizations and Society* 34(1), 58–84.

Kachelmeier, S. and Shehata, M., 1997, 'Internal auditing and voluntary cooperation in firms: A cross-cultural experiment', *The Accounting Review* July 1, 407–431.

Kahneman, D. and Tversky, A., 1979, 'Prospect theory: An analysis of decision under risk', *Econometrica: Journal of the Econometric Society* Mar. 1, 263–291.

Kidwell, L., Fisher, D., Braun, R. and Swanson, D., 2013, 'Developing learning objectives for accounting ethics using Bloom's taxonomy', *Accounting Education* 22(1), 44–65.

Lau, C. and Eggleton, I., 2004, 'Cultural differences in managers' propensity to create slack', *Advances in International Accounting* 17, 137–174.

Lau, C.M. and Tan, J.J., 1998, 'The impact of budget emphasis, participation and task difficulty on managerial performance: A cross-cultural study of the financial services sector', *Management Accounting Research* 9(2), 163–183.

Leach-Lopez, M., Stammerjohan, W. and McNair, F., 2008, 'Effects of budgetary participation conflict on job performance of Mexican and US managers', *Advances in Accounting* 24(1), 49–64.

Lin, K. and Fraser, I., 2008, 'Auditors' ability to resist client pressure and culture: Perceptions in China and the United Kingdom', *Journal of International Financial Management & Accounting* 19(2), 161–183.

Lowe, D., Carmona-Moreno, S. and Reckers, P., 2011, 'The influence of strategy map communications and individual differences on multidimensional performance evaluations', *Accounting and Business Research* 41(4), 375–391.

Merchant, K., Van der Stede, W., Lin, T. and Yu, Z., 2011, 'Performance measurement and incentive compensation: An empirical analysis and comparison of Chinese and Western firms' practices', *European Accounting Review* 20(4), 639–667.

Minkov, M. and Hofstede, G., 2012, 'Is national culture a meaningful concept? Cultural values delineate homogeneous national clusters of in-country regions', *Cross-Cultural Research* 46(2), 133–159.

O'Donnell, E. and Prather-Kinsey, J., 2010, 'Nationality and differences in auditor risk assessment: A research note with experimental evidence', *Accounting, Organizations and Society* 35(5), 558–564.

Patel, C., 2003, 'Some cross-cultural evidence on whistle-blowing as an internal control mechanism', *Journal of International Accounting Research* 2(1), 69–96.

Patel, C. and Millanta, B., 2011, '"Holier-than-thou" perception bias among professional accountants: A cross-cultural study', *Advances in Accounting* 27(2), 373–381.

Patel, C. and Psaros, J., 2000, 'Perceptions of external auditors' independence: Some cross-cultural evidence', *The British Accounting Review* 32(3), 311–338.

Perera, H., Cummings, L. and Chua, F., 2012, 'Cultural relativity of accounting professionalism: Evidence from New Zealand and Samoa', *Advances in Accounting* 28(1), 138–146.

Ralston, D., Gustafson, D., Cheung, F. and Terpstra, R., 1993, 'Differences in managerial values: A study of US, Hong Kong and PRC managers', *Journal of International Business Studies* 24(2), 249–275.

Roxas, M. and Stoneback, J., 1997, 'An investigation of the ethical decision-making process across varying cultures', *The International Journal of Accounting* 32(4), 503–535.

Salter, S., Lewis, P. and Juarez-Valdes, L., 2004, 'Aqui No Se Habla Agencia. An examination of the impact of adverse selection and framing in decision-making: A US/Mexico comparison', *Journal of International Financial Management & Accounting* 15(2), 93–117.

Salter, S. and Schulz, A., 2005, 'Examining the role of culture and acculturation in information sharing', *Advances in Accounting Behavioral Research* 8, 189–212.

Salter, S., Schulz, A., Lewis, P. and López-V.J.C., 2008, 'Otra empanada en la parilla: Examining the role of culture and information sharing in Chile and Australia', *Journal of International Financial Management & Accounting* 19(1), 57–72.

Salter, S. and Sharp, D., 2001, 'Agency effects and escalation of commitment: Do small national culture differences matter?', *The International Journal of Accounting* 36(1), 33–45.

Salter, S., Sharp, D. and Chen, Y., 2013, 'The moderating effects of national culture on escalation of commitment', *Advances in Accounting* 29(1), 161–169.

Scheytt, T., Soin, K. and Metz, T., 2003, 'Exploring notions of control across cultures: a narrative approach', *European Accounting Review* 12(3), 515–547.

Schultz, J. and Lopez, T., 2001, 'The impact of national influence on accounting estimates: Implications for international accounting standard-setters', *The International Journal of Accounting* 36(3), 271–290.

Schulz, A., Salter, S., Lopez, J.C. and Lewis, P., 2009, 'Revaluating face: A note on differences in private information sharing between two communitarian societies', *Journal of International Accounting Research* 8(1), 57–65.

Schwartz, S., 1994, *Beyond Individualism/Collectivism: New Cultural Dimensions of Values*, Sage Publications, Inc., Thousand Oaks, CA.

Sharp, D. and Salter, S., 1997, 'Project escalation and sunk costs: A test of the international generalizability of agency and prospect theories', *Journal of International Business Studies*, 101–121.

Smith, P.B., Dugan, S. and Trompenaars, F., 1996, 'National culture and the values of organizational employees: A dimensional analysis across 43 nations', *Journal of Cross-Cultural Psychology* 27(2), 231–264.

Stammerjohan, W., Leach, M. and Stammerjohan, C., 2015, 'The moderating effects of power distance on the budgetary participation – performance relationship', In *Advances in Management Accounting*, 103–148, Emerald Group Publishing Limited.

Staw, B.M., 1976, 'Knee-deep in the big muddy: A study of escalating commitment to a chosen course of action', *Organizational Behavior and Human Performance* 16(1), 27–44.

Staw, B.M. and Ross, J., 1985, 'Stability in the midst of change: A dispositional approach to job attitudes', *Journal of Applied Psychology* 70(3), 469.

Taras, V., Steel, P. and Kirkman, B., 2012, 'Improving national cultural indices using a longitudinal meta-analysis of Hofstede's dimensions', *Journal of World Business* 47(3), 329–341.

Teigen, K. and Brun, W., 1999, 'The directionality of verbal probability expressions: Effects on decisions, predictions, and probabilistic reasoning', *Organizational Behavior and Human Decision Processes* 80(2), 155–190.

Theil, M., 2002, 'The role of translations of verbal into numerical probability expressions in risk management: A meta-analysis', *Journal of Risk Research* 5(2), 177–186.

Van der Stede, W., 2003, 'The effect of national culture on management control and incentive system design in multi-business firms: Evidence of intracorporate isomorphism', *European Accounting Review* 12(2), 263–285.

Wallsten, T., Fillebeaum, S. and Cox, J., 1986, 'Base rate effects on the interpretation of probability and frequency expressions', *The Journal of Memory and Language* 25, 571–587.

Watts, R.L. and Zimmerman, J.L., 1990, 'Positive accounting theory: A ten year perspective', *Accounting Review* 65(1), 131–156.

Williams, P., Jenkins, J. and Ingraham, L., 2006, 'The winnowing away of behavioral accounting research in the US: The process for anointing academic elites', *Accounting, Organizations and Society* 31(8), 783–818.

Wong-On-Wing, B. and Lui, G., 2013, 'Beyond cultural values: An implicit theory approach to cross-cultural research in accounting ethics', *Behavioral Research in Accounting* 25(1), 15–36.

29

Risk management

Towards a behavioural perspective

Jeannine Jeitziner, Anette Mikes and Daniel Oyon

Introduction

It is common wisdom among finance and accounting scholars that the primary challenge of risk management is to identify and assess risks: "[I]n a well-functioning, truly enterprise-wide risk management system, all major risks would be identified, monitored, and managed on a continuous basis" (Stulz 2008: 44). Equally clear to all is how difficult this is. Yet this difficulty has largely been overlooked in the emerging strand of accounting research on risk management.

In this chapter, we review that research. Then, drawing on some seminal behaviourally and organizationally grounded studies on the development of man-made disasters, we review the less-examined behavioural challenges facing risk management at the outset. We continue from risk identification to what supposedly follows it: management control. Finally, we outline the largely normative accounting literature that addresses some of these behavioural issues and delineates avenues for future research.

Risk management: emerging concerns in accounting research

An expanding list of companies – BP, Tokyo Electric, Boeing, Bear Stearns, Lehman Brothers, Merrill Lynch, Barings Bank, Daiwa Bank, Sumitomo, Enron, Worldcom, Tyco and the Mirror Group – has become identified with failing to anticipate and manage the risks within their complex organizations. The roster of man-made disasters and their accompanying governance and corporate failures reveals the challenges of enterprise risk management. Yet while some see risk management as contributing to the problem by raising expectations it cannot fulfill, policymakers, regulators, consultants and many accounting scholars think we just need to get better at it (Kaplan 2011; National Commission 2011: 90; Ernst and Young 2012; KPMG 2013; PricewaterhouseCoopers 2015).

We already have ample regulations and prescriptive frameworks for "enlightened" risk management, including the COSO Enterprise Risk Management Framework; the ISO 31000: 2009 publication, *Risk Management – Principles and Guidelines*; and the risk disclosure recommendations in the UK Turnbull report, which were quickly incorporated into stock exchange listing rules. More recently, the US Securities and Exchange Commission has mandated that the annual proxy statements of publicly traded companies describe the board's role in risk oversight. Credit rating agencies now evaluate how firms manage risks, with Moody's and Standard & Poor's (S&P) having an explicit focus on enterprise risk management (ERM) in the energy, financial services and insurance industries (Desender and Lafuente 2012).

The academic literature on ERM has a trio of fundamental concerns: explaining the presence or lack of ERM in terms of firm-specific structural variables, identifying ERM's performance implications and understanding risk management *in situ*, as an organizational and social practice. The first two use large-sample cross-sectional research methods; the third uses small-sample or field studies.

Determinants of ERM adoption

Empirical work has studied *leverage* (Liebenberg and Hoyt 2003; Pagach and Warr 2011; Ellul and Yerramilli 2012), *size* (Colquitt, Hoyt and Lee 1999; Liebenberg and Hoyt 2003; Beasley, Clune and Hermanson 2005; Hoyt and Liebenber 2011; Pagach and Warr 2011) and *CEO incentives* (Pagach and Warr 2011; Ellul and Yerramilli 2012) as company-specific factors associated with ERM adoption. Reflecting the normative literature on the subject (COSO 2004; ISO 2009), some have examined the influence of effective corporate governance (Baxter, Bedard, Hoitash and Yezegel 2012; Ellul and Yerramilli 2012). Hypothesizing that strong *corporate governance agents* are likely to advocate ERM, Beasley et al. (2005) found that CEO and CFO support was associated with the extent of implementation, while others found the presence of an internal risk specialist to be associated with adoption (Kleffner, Lee and McGannon 2003; Beasley et al. 2005; Desender 2011; Desender and Lafuente 2010; Paape and Speklé 2012). Studies of other hypothesized determinants, such as institutional ownership and auditor influence, have yielded mixed results (Paape and Speklé 2012; Desender and Lafuente 2010; Pagach and Warr 2011). As for *regulatory pressure*, Kleffner et al. (2003) reported that Canadian companies cited compliance with Toronto Stock Exchange guidelines as the third-most-important reason (37%) for adopting ERM. Paape and Speklé (2012) also found that listing helped explain ERM implementation, but failed to find any association with the existing *governance codes* or *risk management frameworks*.

ERM and firm performance

Most financial economists are skeptical that ERM adds value since modern portfolio theory argues that shareholders can costlessly eliminate idiosyncratic risks through portfolio diversification. Any expenditure to reduce firm-specific risk, including the costs associated with a risk-management function and ERM initiatives, is therefore a negative net present value investment. Stulz (1996), however, argues that risk management can add value if it helps eliminate lower-tail outcomes. For example, it may help firms avoid the direct costs of bankruptcy and indirect costs, such as reputational loss, by reducing the likelihood and impact of extreme financial events (Pagach and Warr 2011). According to Stulz (1996), therefore, the likelihood of a lower-tail earnings outcome and the amount of firm value that could vanish in the event of financial distress can help to explain how a firm benefits from ERM. Another finance theory argument is that risk management adds value by avoiding situations in which the firm has insufficient internal funds to invest in positive net present value opportunities (Froot, Scharfstein and Stein 1993). This leads to a prediction that companies with high leverage, volatile earnings, limited cash reserves, significant firm value linked to growth options and research and development spending should benefit more from ERM (Desender and Lafuente 2010).

Beyond the academic studies, corporate governance advocates, consultants and regulators cite the many organizations that have voluntarily implemented and sustained ERM systems as evidence that they improve performance (Desender and Lafuente 2010; 2012). But can the value of ERM be "proven" by something other than the apparent demand for it? Some risk management guidance (ISO 31000) claims that ERM not only reduces the impact of negative events, but also helps to identify new opportunities. Moreover, the prescriptive guidance suggests that an ERM approach to risk management should improve resource allocation, leading to better capital efficiency, greater return on equity, lower costs of external capital and less regulatory scrutiny (Meulbroek 2002; Hoyt and Liebenberg 2011). Researchers have long sought to test these value-added hypotheses, yet measurement difficulties have kept the empirical evidence scarce, inconsistent and possibly misleading.

Pagach and Warr (2010) studied ERM's effect on long-term performance in 106 firms, mostly in the financial and utility industries, that announced the appointment of a chief risk officer (CRO). Finding no significant changes in various firm performance variables, they conclude that ERM did not add value. Gordon, Loeb and Tseng (2009), examining 112 US firms in 22 industries that disclosed their ERM activities in their 2005 regulatory filings, found an overall positive association between ERM firm performance and argued that the magnitude of the effect depended on matching the ERM system with five firm-specific factors: board monitoring, environmental uncertainty, industry competition, firm size and firm complexity. Beasley, Pagach and Warr (2008) studied the market reaction to 120 CRO announcements in the financial services, insurance and energy sectors between 1992 and 2003. They found a positive market response to announcements from the non-financial firms but a much lower association for the financial firms.

Caveat emptor

Comparing the results presented above requires caution, given their varying methods of defining and measuring ERM. For instance, Beasley et al. (2005: 527) used a simple scale to measure implementation, ranging from "no plans exist to implement ERM" to "complete ERM is in place". Liebenberg and Hoyt (2003), Beasley et al. (2008), and Hoyt and Liebenberg (2011) used the appointment of a CRO as a surrogate for ERM implementation. Hoyt and Liebenberg (2011) identified ERM programs through Lexis-Nexis SEC filings, while McShane, Nair and Rustambeko (2011) and Baxter et al. (2012) relied on S&P ERM ratings. Gordon et al. (2009) developed their own index to measure ERM maturity.

Many of the studies used simplistic variables to capture complex behaviour. For example, the single 0–1 dummy variable of ERM adoption, used by several studies, does not capture the complexity of actual implementation. Studies that rely on S&P's ERM ratings must assume that the agency's arm's-length assessment based on public information is a valid indicator of what's happening *in situ*. Further, the large-sample cross-sectional studies focus on the adoption of a particular risk management framework, but ignore how it was implemented by the management and employees. The effectiveness of risk management ultimately depends on the people who set up, coordinate and contribute to risk management processes. It is people, not frameworks, who identify, analyze and act. Their actions often require approval from the CEO and board. Hence, organizational and behavioural phenomena can cause companies that follow the same ERM framework to implement and use risk management very differently.

For example, most Wall Street financial firms had risk management functions and CROs during the expansionary period of 2002–2006, yet some failed during 2007 and 2008 while others survived quite well. Knowing that a company had a risk management department and a CRO does not predict that it also had the commitment of the CEO and board to encourage the production and dissemination of risk information or that it had the resources, leadership and support to mitigate the risks that were identified.

Likewise, statistical studies on large public databases cannot capture the fascinating variety of risk-management practices, deployed at different levels, for different purposes, by different staff groups – even by companies in the same industry. Cross-sectional empirical studies that ignore such important variation end up explaining little, especially about what works and what does not.

Research on risk management in situ

Cultural theorists have shown that risk means different things in different settings (Douglas and Wildavsky 1983; Adams 1995). In some firms, risk management focuses only on compliance with risk limits and policies. In others, it helps the organization learn about uncertainties in their strategy and their environment and convert them into "manageable risks" (Mikes 2009; Mikes, Hall and Millo 2013). Mikes (2008, 2009 and 2011) presents field-based evidence of systematic variation in risk-management practices in the financial services industry and develops the concept of calculative cultures to explain these differences. Arena, Arnaboldi and Azzone (2010) describe three comparative case studies and document a continuous and evolving interaction between pre-established management practices and ERM, which makes the latter unique to each organization. Such in-depth, small-sample or longitudinal field studies will eventually elicit a fascinating and revealing variety of context-specific practices and should, in due course, help us understand the causes and value of such variety. Over time, deductive and empirical researchers can hypothesize about and test the fit between ERM practices and different contexts and then start codifying and standardizing appropriate and contingent risk management practices (Mikes and Kaplan 2015).

But we argue that, besides building a research enterprise (Kaplan 2011), longitudinal risk-management studies could – and should – address a key behavioural concern: can risk management counter the individual and organizational biases that typically inhibit constructive thinking about risks?

Behavioural concerns: the missing link in accounting scholarship on risk management

Extensive psychological and sociological studies have documented biases – such as availability, confirmation and anchoring – that cause people to grossly underestimate the variation in possible outcomes from risky situations (Hammond, Keeney and Raiffa 2006; Kahneman, Lovallo and Sibony 2011). Especially under budget and time pressure, people often become so inured to risks that they accept deviances and near misses as false alarms or the "new normal" – a process referred to as the normalization of deviance (Vaughan 1999) – and override controls. When events begin to deviate from prior expectations, managers often double down on previous decisions and actions, "throwing good money after bad". In addition to these individual biases, groupthink arises when individuals, contemplating a course of action gathering support from a majority around them, suppress their own objections, however valid, and fall silently into line with the prevailing opinion. Such individual and collective biases explain why so many organizations overlook or misread ambiguous threats. Can risk management processes counteract them?

The development of man-made disasters

Man-made disaster theory was elaborated by Barry A. Turner in 1976 and his article, "The Organizational and Interorganizational Development of Disasters", is still one of the most important in organizational sociology. Turner discerned two distinctions between man-made disasters and accidents or incidents. First, disasters involve *large-scale losses* – death and major physical or financial destruction (Turner 1976: 379–380). Second, they come as a *surprise*, a failure of foresight, "a collapse of precautions that had hitherto been regarded as culturally adequate" (Turner 1976: 380). Thus, disasters are "neither chance events, nor 'Acts of God'" (Pidgeon and O'Leary 2000: 16); rather they result from latent errors and events that have been incubating unnoticed (Turner 1976: 381).

Turner (1976, 1978) elaborated a six-stage model, which highlights the disturbingly common sequence of events that result in disaster. Figure 29.1 summarizes the main features of Turner's model.

From an accounting and risk-management viewpoint, Turner's model means that disasters can be systematically incubated on the "dark side of organizations" (Turner 1976: 379). According to Pidgeon (1997), certain organizational preconditions can make the system vulnerable to catastrophic events. A disaster happens when those preconditions begin to interact in a complex way that modifies the situation (Pidgeon 1997), leaving established beliefs and values still in place but no longer adequate (Turner 1976).

Discussions of the incubation period (particularly in disaster post-mortems) invariably lead to a normative questioning of whether it is possible to prevent disasters by identifying incubating risks within the *recovery window*; that is, before the event that turns them into a disaster (Edmondson, Roberto, Bohmer, Ferlins and Feldman 2005). For example, in the much-studied cases of NASA's *Challenger* and *Columbia* disasters, crucial – although admittedly somewhat

Stages	Explanations
Stage 1:	Initial culturally accepted beliefs about the world and its hazards.
Notionally normal starting point	Associated precautionary norms set out in laws, codes of practices, mores and folkways.
Stage 2:	The accumulation of an unnoticed set of events, which are
Incubation period	at odds with the accepted beliefs about hazards and the norms for their avoidance.
Stage 3:	Forces itself to the attention and transforms general
Precipitating event	perceptions of Stage 2.
Stage 4:	The immediate consequences of the collapse of cultural
Onset	precautions become apparent.
Stage 5:	The immediate post-collapse situation is recognized in *ad*
Rescue and salvage – first-stage adjustment	*hoc* adjustments, which permit the work of rescue and salvage to be started.
Stage 6:	An inquiry or assessment is carried out. Beliefs and
Full cultural readjustment	precautionary norms are adjusted to fit the newly gained understanding of the world.

Figure 29.1 Turner's six-stage model

Source: Turner (1976: 381)

Complexity	Overconfidence
• **Complex** and **tightly** coupled systems lead to accidents. People do not expect the interactions of preconditions leading to failures. • **Routine procedures** cannot be applied to ill-structured problems. • **Decoy phenomenon**: attention focused on the well-structured problems rather than the ill-structured ones. • People adopt **simplifications** and **assumptions** because of information difficulties.	• **Success** can lead to **overconfidence**. Coupled with group psychological biases (e.g., groupthink), individuals let assumptions go unchallenged and tend to ignore warning signs (confirmation bias). • The psychological bias of overconfidence can lead to the **normalization of deviance** at the organizational level.

Figure 29.2 Organizational and behavioural phenomena causing rigidities of belief

ambiguous – risk-relevant information reached decision makers who failed to act upon it (Vaughan 1996; Edmondson et al. 2005). Could NASA have operated in such a way that those managers would naturally have done better?

Speaking generally rather than specifically of NASA, we believe the answer is yes. Organizations can proactively and systematically search for the types of incubating risk that erupt in man-made disasters. The focus of this search would be the rigid beliefs that the man-made disaster literature has shown to inhibit an organization's ability to challenge assumptions in the face of changing or emerging risks; that is, to wake up before it's too late. Turner offered several examples (1976: 378): "Rigidities in institutional beliefs, distracting decoy phenomena, neglect of outside complaints, multiple information-handling difficulties ... and a tendency to minimize emergent danger." Starting from this literature, we have derived two categories of behavioural phenomena that can keep an organization from seeing a disaster in the making. The first is related to *complexity*. The second concerns the psychological biases of individual and organizational *overconfidence* (see Figure 29.2).

Complexity

In the category of *complexity*, one phenomenon is the complex interactions between the preconditions to disaster mentioned before. Perrow (1984: 4–5) reflected the idea of complexity in his "normal accident theory", arguing that systems tend to create complex interactions between their components and that, in a "tightly coupled" system – in which problematic components cannot be separated or processes develop quickly and cannot be turned off – accidents are inevitable.

Turner (1976), too, addressed complexity, but focused on the complexity not of the system but of the problem itself, distinguishing between "ill-structured" and "well-structured" problems. Routine procedures can be designed to solve well-structured problems, but cannot address ill-structured ones. Easily mistaking an ill-structured problem for a well-structured one, people apply routines than can only fail. Related to this is the *decoy phenomenon*: an organizational focus on well-defined problems diverts attention from the ill-structured issues that can precipitate a disaster (Turner 1976: 388).

Based on Turner's work, Weick argued that people in organizations make simplifying assumptions so they can act collectively, but the simplifications adopted in various parts of an organization don't necessarily form a coherent whole (Weick 1998: 74). This can lead to disasters in two ways. First, when people experience gaps of information, they may choose to ignore them (Weick 1998: 74). Second, even when people try to put their individual pieces of information together, they tend to concentrate on what they have in common, suppressing what's distinct (Weick 1998: 74). Hence, a risk can incubate not only because the simplifications do not reflect reality, but also because all the members of the organization tacitly agree to make the same assumptions and ignore the same information (Weick 1998: 74).

To summarize this first category: people make mistakes either in the way they define and identify the problem or in the way they address it, as a result of the complexity of the system or of the problem.

Overconfidence

A company's success can easily convince its people that their beliefs are correct and adequate. In particular, people think that risky decisions and actions are bound to turn out well. When this overconfidence is coupled with group psychological biases (such as groupthink) and other individual risk-perception biases (such as confirmation), individuals let assumptions go unchallenged and tend to ignore warning signs. Deviances can be easily explained away, leading to the *normalization of deviance* at the organizational level (Vaughan 1996). The monster incubates unmolested. Both categories – complexity and overconfidence – reflect the fact that human behaviours are a key to risk incubation.

Implications for accounting research

From a control perspective, it can be argued that companies face decisions regarding the types and levels of risk they are willing to accept. As Turner (1976: 379) recognized, "the central difficulty. . . [is] in discovering which aspects of the current set of problems facing an organization are prudent to ignore and which should be attended to, and how an acceptable level of safety can be established as a criterion in carrying out this exercise." Weick (1998: 74) goes even further: "Organizations are defined by what they ignore."

It has been argued in the management literature that companies face three types of risk: preventable, strategic and external (Kaplan and Mikes 2012). Since preventable risks should (in principle) not be tolerated and external risks can only be managed by reducing their impact, it is strategic risks – those willingly accepted to increase returns (Kaplan and Mikes 2012) – that define a firm's "risk appetite". Indeed, strategy risks take centre stage in today's ERM frameworks and several risk appetite models have been developed in practice. For instance, the model developed by Quail (2012) elaborates on the differences between a company's target risk appetite and the risk appetite the company actually exhibits.

The prominence of the risk management discourse among corporate governance advocates and policymakers reflects the longstanding managerial preoccupation with boundary-setting and monitoring. In fact, we see reflections of Simons's "levers of control"[1] framework (Simons 1995) in the concern with risk culture (belief systems), risk appetite setting (boundary systems) and continuous monitoring (diagnostic control).

Puzzlingly to us, it seems to have been overlooked that interactive controls[2] may be equally – if not more – important to risk management. For us, a key lesson of our review of the behavioural challenges of preventing disasters is that risks cannot be reliably controlled by routine diagnostic control. Even if everyone in an organization adheres to established safety processes, this very compliance can undermine the organization's ability to handle a situation for which its routines are unsuited (Pidgeon and O'Leary 2000).

Indeed, it takes an intrusive, interrogative and interactive style of control to challenge deeply held (and synchronized) organizational assumptions, to counter overconfidence and decoy phenomena and to understand the complexity of today's organizations and ill-structured problems. The levers of control – belief, boundary and diagnostic systems – can in fact lead an organization over the cliff when they are no longer appropriate, combining to prolong rather than stop the incubation period preceding a man-made disaster. But just as strategic uncertainties can be subjected to interactive control (Simons 1995), so can beliefs, boundaries and the appropriateness of control systems be continuously questioned through interactive risk-management control systems.

Avenues for future research

More than 20 years after the emergence of the levers of control framework (Simons 1995), there is still much to learn about the architecture and use of interactive control systems, particularly for risk management. Given the pace and intensity of disruptions that many companies face, it is important to understand what interactive controls can do for risk management. We highlight three issue areas below.

The design and implementation of "intrusive and interactive" risk-management control

While Mikes and Kaplan (2015) propose the outlines of an "intrusive and interactive" risk control system, it is an empirical question whether those attributes will counter the behavioural biases that hinder risk control. We need to catalogue and understand those active and intrusive processes that can challenge assumptions about the world within and outside the organization. We also need to know more about the emerging tools of risk assessment and communication (such as risk maps, stress tests and scenarios) and the relationship of risk-management processes with other control functions, such as internal audit.

Interactive controls themselves pose many research questions. If used to examine a business model's strategic uncertainties (as Simons postulated), what kind of control mechanisms complement interactive controls in the broader dialogue on preventable and external risks? Can diagnostic controls, beliefs and boundary systems cover the non-key (but potentially incubating) uncertainties? Can interactive dialogue be extended to other issue areas, perhaps by activating different interactive controls in parallel or in sequence?

How do interactive risk controls fit into the overall control framework including belief, boundary and diagnostic control systems? What role does each have in risk management? How do we measure the effectiveness of risk management when its practice may be spread across – and dependent on – multiple levers of control?

The design and implementation of "non-punitive" reporting systems

Man-made disasters remind us that managers need to find or design a formal control system that can communicate incubating risks. This is hard to do. Should the risk dialogue be stimulated by risk-based interactive systems vertically designed between superiors and subordinates, as advocated by Simons (1995), or should the dialogue also be horizontal and cross-sectional? Under what conditions are employees more likely to participate?

To encourage everyone to participate in risk talk, some companies are setting up simple "crowd-based" reporting systems, free of any repercussion and punishment, that can host issues that other formal control systems miss. As too much unsorted input can render such a tool useless, observers are increasingly asked to jointly evaluate the information disseminated so that the most relevant issues float to the top. In some high-reliability organizations, such as hospitals and airlines, where even small mistakes can be fatal, such non-punitive control systems for risk management are gaining popularity. For scholars, they offer a promising site for descriptive and causal research that can help us understand the nature of the design parameters at play, their conditionality and the variation in crowd-based reporting systems.

Leadership and "no-blame" culture

To ensure that interactive control systems function well, leaders must encourage their people to speak freely, without fear of blame or repercussion. This is easier said than done, since most firms are hierarchical, making the "right" to speak and take part in decision processes asymmetric. Hierarchical organizations, with their need for accountability, create dependencies between superiors and subordinates that do not encourage open and detached discussion. Therefore, any kind of interactive control system involving a large part of the organization (and potentially other stakeholders) is likely to require trust and a strong commitment from governing bodies. How are such trust and commitment generated and sustained? What leadership characteristics and governance structures are more likely to foster candid dialogue? We need to investigate if and how the potentially conflicting objectives of creating a "blame-free" incident-reporting environment and an organization with strong accountability can be reconciled.

It seems humans must learn over and over that human systems work better when the peculiar strengths and weaknesses of human nature are taken into account. Now it is risk management's turn.

Notes

1 Simons (1995) distinguished four levers of control that managers can apply to execute strategy. By formalizing core values, managers can provide employees with a *belief system* that provides purpose and direction to action. By establishing limits, managers can delineate the acceptable domain of activity (*boundary systems*). Managers, of course, set targets, measure and reward achievement, and monitor progress with the help of *diagnostic controls*. Simons further argued that top managers with a clear strategic vision select one control system that addresses the firm's key strategic uncertainties and devote frequent and regular attention to it – and they use it interactively. *Interactive control systems* in turn provide signals to organizational participants about what should be monitored and where new ideas should be tested. They will be consequential in directing not only the attention of top management, but also the aspirations and concerns of subordinates. Ultimately, they influence organizational learning and action.

2 Simons (1991: 49) defines interactive control use as follows: "Based on the amount of top management attention directed to a control system, a management control system can be labelled as interactive when top managers use that system to personally and regularly involve themselves in the decisions of subordinates." Simons postulates that when systems are used interactively, four conditions are typically present: (a) The information generated by the control system is important and is on the recurring agenda addressed by the highest levels of management. (b) The control process demands frequent and regular attention from operating managers at all levels. (c) Data are interpreted and discussed in face-to-face meetings of supervisors, subordinates and peers. (d) The process relies on the continual challenge and debate of underlying data, assumptions and action plans.

References

Adams, J. 1995, *Risk*, UCL Press, London.

Arena, M., Arnaboldi, M. and Azzone, G., 2010, 'The organizational dynamics of Enterprise Risk Management', *Accounting, Organizations and Society* 35(7), 659–675.

Baxter, R., Bedard, J.C., Hoitash, R. and Yezegel, A., 2012, 'Enterprise Risk Management program quality: Determinants, value relevance, and the financial crisis', *Contemporary Accounting Research* 30(4), 1264–1295.

Beasley, M.S., Clune, R. and Hermanson, D.R., 2005, 'Enterprise risk management: An empirical analysis of factors associated with the extent of implementation', *Journal of Accounting and Public Policy* 24(6), 521–531.

Beasley, M., Pagach, D. and Warr, R., 2008, 'Information conveyed in hiring announcements of senior executives overseeing enterprise-wide risk management processes', *Journal of Accounting, Auditing and Finance* 28(3), 311–332.

Colquitt, L.L., Hoyt, R.E. and Lee, R.B., 1999, 'Integrated risk management and the role of the risk manager', *Risk Management and Insurance Review* 2(3), 43–61.

Committee of Sponsoring Organizations of the Treadway Commission (COSO), 2004, *Enterprise Risk Management Framework*, American Institute of Certified Public Accountants, New York.

Desender, K., 2011, 'On the determinants of enterprise risk management implementation', in N. Si Shi and G. Sivlius (eds.), *Enterprise IT Governance, Business Value and Performance Measurement*, IGI Global, Hershey, PA.

Desender, K. and Lafuente, E., 2010, 'The influence of board composition, audit fees and ownership concentration on enterprise risk management', *SSRN Working Paper*. Retrieved from papers. ssrn. com website.

Desender, K. and Lafuente, E., 2012, 'The role of enterprise risk management in determining audit fees: complement or substitute', in J. Abolhassan and A.G. Malliaris (eds.), *Risk Management and Corporate Governance*, Routledge (Taylor & Francis Group), New York.

Douglas, M. and Wildavsky, A., 1983. *Risk and Culture*, University of California Press, Berkeley.

Edmondson, A., Roberto, M.A., Bohmer, M.J., Ferlins, E.M. and Feldman, L.R., 2005, 'The recovery window: Organizational learning following ambiguous threats', in W.H. Starbuck and M. Farjoun (eds.), *Organization at the Limit: Lessons From the Columbia Disaster*, 220–246, Blackwell, Hoboken, NJ.

Ellul, A. and Yerramilli, V., 2012, 'Stronger risk controls, lower risk: Evidence from U.S. bank holding companies', *Journal of Finance* 68(59), 1757–1803.

Ernst and Young, 2012, *Turning Risk Into Results – How Leading Companies Use Risk Management to Fuel Better Performance*. http://www.ey.com/Publication/vwLUAssets/Turning_risk_into_results/$FILE/Turning%20risk%20into%20results_AU1082_1%20Feb%202012.pdf

Froot, K.A., Scharfstein, D.S. and Stein, J., 1993, 'Risk management: Coordinating corporate investment and financing policies', *Journal of Finance* 48(5), 1629–1658.

Gordon, L.A., Loeb, M.P. and Tseng, C.Y., 2009, 'Enterprise risk management and firm performance: A contingency perspective', *Journal of Accounting and Public Policy* 28(4), 301–327.

Hammond, J.S., Keeney, R.L. and Raiffa, H., 2006, 'The hidden traps in decision making', *Harvard Business Review* 84(1), 118–126.

Hoyt, R.E. and Liebenberg, A.P., 2011, 'The value of Enterprise Risk Management', *The Journal of Risk and Insurance* 78(4), 795–822.

International Standards Organisation (ISO), 2009, *ISO 31000:2009, Risk Management – Principles and Guidelines*, International Standards Organisation, Geneva.

Kahneman, D., Lovallo, D. and Sibony, O., 2011, 'Before you make that big decision . . .', *Harvard Business Review* 89(6), 50–60.

Kaplan, R.S., 2011, 'Accounting scholarship that advances professional knowledge and practice', *The Accounting Review* 86(2), 367–383.

Kaplan, R.S. and Mikes, A., 2012, 'Managing risks: A new framework', *Harvard Business Review* 90(6), 48–60.

Kleffner, A.E., Lee, R.B. and McGannon, B., 2003, 'The effect of corporate governance on the use of enterprise risk management: Evidence from Canada', *Risk Management and Insurance Review* 6(1), 53–73.

KPMG, 2013, *Expectations of Risk Management Outpacing Capabilities – It's Time for Action*, May.

Liebenberg, A.P. and Hoyt, R.E., 2003, 'The determinants of Enterprise Risk Management: Evidence from the appointment of Chief Risk Officers', *Risk Management and Insurance Review* 6(1), 37–52.

McShane, M.K., Nair, A. and Rustambeko, E., 2011, 'Does Enterprise Risk Management increase firm value?', *Journal of Accounting, Auditing & Finance* 26(4), 641–658.

Meulbroek, L., 2002, 'The promise and challenge of integrated risk management', *Risk Management and Insurance Review* 5(1), 55–66.

Mikes, A., 2008, 'Chief Risk Officers at crunch time: Compliance champions or business partners?', *Journal of Risk Management in Financial Institutions* 2(1), 7–25.

Mikes, A., 2009, 'Risk management and calculative cultures', *Management Accounting Research* 20(1), 18–40.

Mikes, A., 2011, 'From counting risk to making risk count: Boundary-work in risk management', *Accounting, Organizations and Society* 36(4–5), 226–245.

Mikes, A., Hall, M. and Millo, Y., 2013, 'How experts gain influence', *Harvard Business Review* 91(7–8), 70–74.

Mikes, A. and Kaplan, R.S., 2015, 'When one size doesn't fit all: Evolving directions in the research and practice of Enterprise Risk Management', *Journal of Applied Corporate Finance* 27(1), 37–41.

National Commission on the BP Deepwater Horizon Oil Spill and Offshore Drilling (National Commission), 2011, *Deep Water: The Gulf Oil Disaster and the Future of Offshore Drilling, Report to the President* (PDF file), downloaded January 2013, from www.oilspillcommission.gov/final-report.

Paape, L. and Speklé, R.F., 2012, 'The adoption and design of enterprise risk management practices: An empirical study', *European Accounting Review* 21(3), 533–564.

Pagach, D. and Warr, R., 2010, 'The effects of Enterprise Risk Management on firm performance', *SSRN Working Paper*.

Pagach, D. and Warr, R., 2011, 'The characteristics of firms that hire Chief Risk Officers', *The Journal of Risk and Insurance* 78(1), 185–211.

Perrow, C., 1984, *Normal Accidents: Living With High-Risk Technologies*, Princeton University Press, Princeton, NJ.

Pidgeon, N., 1997, 'The limits to safety? Culture, politics, learning and man-made disasters', *Journal of Contingencies and Crisis Management* 5(1), 1–14.

Pidgeon, N. and O'Leary, M., 2000, 'Man-made disasters: Why technology and organisations (sometimes) fail', *Safety Science* 34, 15–30.

PricewaterhouseCoopers, 2015, *Risk in Review – Decoding Uncertainty, Delivering Value*, April.

Quail, R., 2012, 'Defining your taste for risk', *Corporate Risk Canada*, 25–30.

Simons, R., 1991, 'Strategic orientation and top management attention to control systems', *Strategic Management Journal* 12(1), 49–62.

Simons, R., 1995, *Levers of Control: How Managers Use Innovative Control Systems to Drive Strategic Renewal*, Harvard Business School Press, Boston, MA.

Stulz, R., 1996, 'Rethinking risk management', *Journal of Applied Corporate Finance* 9(3), 8–24.

Stulz, R., 2008, 'Risk management failures: What are they and when do they happen?', *Journal of Applied Corporate Finance* 20(4), 39–49.

Turner, B.A., 1976, 'The organisational and interorganisational development of disasters', *Administrative Science Quarterly* 21, 378–397.

Turner, B.A., 1978, *Man-Made Disasters*, Wykeham Science Press, London.

Vaughan, D., 1996, *The Challenger Launch Decision: Risky Technology, Culture, and Deviance at NASA*, University of Chicago Press, Chicago.

Vaughan, D., 1999, 'The dark side of organizations: Mistakes, misconduct, and disaster', *Annual Review of Sociology* 25, 271–305.

Weick, K., 1998, 'Foresights of failure: An appreciation of Barry Turner', *Journal of Contingencies and Crisis Management* 6(2), 72–75.

Section 8

Publication considerations

30

Writing a literature review in Behavioural Accounting Research

Lindsay M. Andiola, Jean C. Bedard and Candice T. Hux

Introduction

A "literature review" is an original work that summarizes and synthesizes prior research on a particular topic. A good literature review brings readers up to date on the current state of a topic, imparts fresh insights and identifies issues that prior research has left unresolved. Literature reviews are particularly valuable when research on a topic is extensive and/or disconnected. As a result of the growth in the breadth, depth and complexity of the literature in Behavioural Accounting Research (BAR) in the past two decades (Birnberg 2011), there is significant potential for literature reviews to advance scholarship by synthesizing and connecting prior research within our discipline.[1]

In this chapter, we discuss specific rationales for writing a literature review in BAR, as well as the process of researching and preparing a literature review, including the challenges scholars may face during the process.[2] Throughout, we illustrate key points with examples from within BAR in general, and from our own experience specifically.[3] Our discussion proceeds as follows. In the next section, we consider common motivations for writing a literature review. Then, we describe the process of developing a literature review, including: determining the conceptual structure, setting parameters for the sample (i.e., the set of research that will be reviewed), categorizing and synthesizing the data, and considering validity threats. This is followed by a discussion of aspects of writing a literature review including describing the conceptual structure, explaining how the review was conducted, communicating findings and stimulating future research. We then provide concluding thoughts.

Motivation for a literature review

As with other types of research, a scholar must effectively indicate the purpose of the paper – i.e., the motivation for reviewing a particular topic (Torraco 2005; Galvan 2012). The motivation for a stand-alone literature review generally stems from meeting two main conditions: (a) the amount of research previously performed on the topic is sufficient to support an interesting analysis and (b) there is widespread interest in the topic, including relevance to real-world circumstances (e.g., Cooper 1998; Torraco 2005).

Regarding the first condition, the topics of literature reviews are limited to those for which there is a developed body of research to review, a distinction from other types of research where a study can be performed on any topic for which there is justification in theory and/or practice (Cooper 1998). The developed body of research on the topic could be either at a mature or emerging state within the accounting literature. In a review of a mature topic, the aim is "a review, critique, and the potential reconceptualization of an expanding and more diversified knowledge base of the topic as it continues to develop" (Torraco 2005: 357). A common scenario is that a BAR scholar begins to investigate a particular topic (for a dissertation or otherwise), finds a large number of disparate studies and is faced with the daunting task of organizing those studies in order to determine the potential contribution of a new study. In a mature field of inquiry, there may be dozens of papers within accounting journals, and many more in other literatures (e.g., psychology or economics) that are important to our understanding of accounting scholarship. If a literature review has not been completed on the mature topic, or significant time has elapsed since the last review, the opportunity arises for a literature review to make a contribution to knowledge. One example of a literature review that comprehensively examines a mature topic in BAR is Andiola (2014), who synthesizes auditing literature on the behavioural effects of performance feedback provided during audit review using a model and prior research from the psychology and management literatures. Prior to this study, no literature review had extensively examined the effects of formal feedback on auditor behaviours. The amount of the literature in accounting and supporting disciplines, as well as the potential to have significant implications in accounting practice, help to motivate the need for this type of literature review.

Instead of covering a mature topic, a literature review can also be "an initial or preliminary conceptualization of an emerging topic" (Torraco 2005: 357). In this scenario, a BAR scholar finds very little relevant research in the accounting domain, but there may be established theory and empirical findings in other literatures that the scholar considers connected to the topic. In this case, the value of the literature review is to introduce readers to new lines of thought. An example of a literature review on an emerging topic is Hanes (2013), who considers research relevant to geographically distributed work in auditing. Her synthesis on the topic of geographically distributed work incorporates research in management, organizational behaviour and work design to advance research on the possible impact of the changing work dynamics when audit tasks are distributed across geographic boundaries. Prior to this study, there was very limited discussion or research related to this topic within the auditing literature, but ample research in other areas. Such studies connect literature in diverse disciplines to a BAR problem presenting the current state of knowledge and suggesting future research that could advance understanding of this topic.

The second condition underlying motivation for a literature review is widespread interest and real-world impact (Torraco 2005; Galvan 2012). This condition assumes more importance for BAR as an applied discipline. In BAR, this interest and impact often stems from "hot topics" within the accounting profession, particularly topics that are the focus of regulators, practitioners and researchers. BAR scholars can often motivate the need for a literature review by citing proposed standards and business and/or popular press. For instance, Hux (2016) motivates her literature review on four different types of specialists used by auditors (i.e., in the fields of tax, systems, valuation and forensics) by citing the Public Company Accounting Oversight Board's (PCAOB) current interest in understanding the use of specialists during financial statement audits (PCAOB 2015). She identifies similarities and differences in methods and findings across the four specialist types, in order to develop topics deserving of further research. Literature reviews may also be solicited on "hot topics" by journals or regulators to assist in compiling and advancing knowledge on these topics. The PCAOB synthesis projects provide a number of "hot topic" literature review examples, including: Bratten, Gaynor, McDaniel, Montague and Sierra (2013) on auditing fair values and complex estimates; Hurtt, Brown-Liburd, Earley and Krishnamoorthy (2013) on auditor skepticism and Trompeter, Carpenter, Desai, Jones and Riley (2013) on fraud and fraud detection.[4]

In summary, BAR scholars intending to publish a stand-alone literature review should carefully consider the motivation in terms of amount of prior research on the topic and why academics, practitioners and/or regulators should care about the topic. After identifying a mature or emerging topic worthy of review and establishing a motivation to perform a stand-alone literature review, the research process can begin more formally. In the following section, we discuss stages of the process of preparing a literature review.[5]

The research process

Conducting a literature review requires a rigorous process that is similar in many ways to performing other types of research. In a literature review, each study is considered a unit of data, which is then combined with others to obtain overall findings and implications. In this section, we discuss four steps of the literature review research process that have specific distinctions from other types of research: (a) conceptualizing the structure of the literature review, which may include adopting a guiding theory or creating a model or framework; (b) determining the literature search boundaries; (c) gathering and synthesizing prior research findings and (d) considering validity threats.[6] The first three steps of the research process are often iterative in nature, as the scholar meaningfully organizes prior literature into a coherent review of the topic of interest.

Step 1: conceptual structuring

A scholar should begin conceptualizing a structure early in the literature review process because the structure impacts how the review will eventually be organized (Torraco 2005). Deciding how to organize the identified observations from prior literature is commonly one of the biggest challenges of writing a literature review. This differs from the conventional structure of most empirical work, but is integral to a well-written and clear review. The structure may develop from the patterns and relationships that emerge from reading the literature or through use of a previously developed model or theory (Torraco 2005; Galvan 2012). The objective is to select a structure that provides new insight to the reader, particularly insight that prior studies and literature reviews may not have considered.

Based on our examination of recent literature reviews in BAR and consistent with other guidance (e.g., Torraco 2005: 359), three common techniques (or a combination thereof) are used to structure a literature review: (a) a guiding theory; (b) a model (or competing models) or (c) a categorization of papers based on key characteristics of the subject matter (e.g., unit of analysis, features of the setting). First, use of a guiding theory can often create a framework in which to group research papers and to formulate a reasoned argument. For example, Peecher, Solomon and Trotman (2013) use theories on accountability from accounting, economics and psychology to develop a framework that suggests mechanisms to better motivate and incentivize audit quality improvements. Their framework focuses on two dimensions: rewards versus penalties and processes versus outcomes. They discuss theory and evidence from a range of disciplines along these dimensions, from which they can draw inferences about the effectiveness (and ineffectiveness) of existing regulatory systems.

Second, certain topics may benefit from the development and use of a model, or competing models, which provide a roadmap of the areas to be discussed within the review and/or a new way to think about a topic (Galvan 2012). For instance, Hurtt et al. (2013) develop a model of professional skepticism that builds on and complements the model developed by Nelson (2009). Their review uses the newly developed model to synthesize the research on professional skepticism into two broad categories: antecedents to skeptical judgments and antecedents to skeptical actions. Presenting a redesigned model allows the researchers to identify gaps in the literature for future investigation.

Third, the literature review may be based on factors or characteristics specific to the topic of interest. This type of literature review can be beneficial for syntheses covering a broad range of factors pertinent to the subject matter. For example, Birnberg (2011) synthesizes Behavioural Accounting Research by structuring the literature review based on the behavioural unit of the studies (i.e., individuals, small groups, organizations or the society within which accounting exists). This structure allows BAR scholars to highlight similarities across otherwise diverse research.

There are several options when deciding how to organize the literature, but from our experience it is likely that one of these options will provide greater insight or an easier roadmap for the reader to follow than others. In some cases, the best structure may not be initially evident. For instance, Andiola (2014) was originally structured based on the type of audit review (i.e., workpaper, engagement, annual). However, during the writing process it became clear that this structure was not providing the greatest insight. For example, performance feedback factors were scattered across the three separate sections in the literature review, making it a challenge for readers to easily see the patterns and relationships of these factors across studies. Therefore, the paper was re-written by grouping primary studies based on each factor in the established feedback model, which presents contextual factors (e.g., the source of feedback) and individual factors (e.g., age and gender demographics) affecting an individual's seeking and use of performance feedback. This structure allowed for better synthesis of the research in auditing, eased the identification of future research directions, and improved readers' ability to follow and understand the findings of the literature review. The challenge for a BAR scholar is deciding the best structure early on to avoid significant rewriting.

In our experience and as emphasized in the prior guidance, organizing the literature into a coherent and comprehensible structure is an effortful process, but this step is the most important to creating a clear and valuable literature review. In addition, while we and other guidance advise early conceptualization of the structure, it is not uncommon for a scholar to begin Steps 2 and 3 discussed below before deciding the most appropriate conceptual structure.

Step 2: determining literature search boundaries

There is no well-defined approach to performing a literature search; however, it is important to track how the search is conducted so the process and parameters of the search can be identified in the final paper. In order to perform a rigorous and systematic search of studies relevant to a topic, guidance suggests starting with a broad focus of the literature review and then narrowing as needed (Cooper 1998; Galvan 2012). When beginning to collect and read applicable papers, a scholar may find it helpful to start with the most recent studies related to the topic and work backward, using the reference lists of recent studies as a guide. Alternatively, a scholar may choose to start with seminal or classic papers to better understand the foundations of the literature and work forward chronologically. Key challenges during the search process include determining the extent of coverage of non-accounting literatures, and the breadth (e.g., the last decade only or experimental studies only) and/or the depth of the literature reviewed (e.g., top-tier journals only).[7] These determinations are particularly necessary after a scholar performs an initial search within the defined topic and finds that the number of papers related to the topic are too great to perform a manageable review.

First, a key challenge that BAR scholars face when determining search boundaries is whether the literature review should extend beyond the accounting literature. This decision often depends on the extent of coverage of the topic within the accounting literature and/or the conceptual structuring of the topic. For instance, professional skepticism (Hurtt et al. 2013) and fraud (Trompeter et al. 2013) are covered extensively within the accounting literature, but these topics have connections in a variety of other literatures (e.g., organizational behaviour, psychology, ethics). As such, the authors incorporated only minimal outside literature when required for supporting their discussion or providing context. In contrast, Hanes (2013) relies extensively on organizational behaviour and psychology literatures due to the lack of maturity of the literature on globalization of work within the accounting domain. In other cases, there may be a number of primary studies within accounting, but the conceptual structure is from another literature, which may require a greater review of other literature(s) to ground the topic. For example, Nolder and Riley's (2014) objective is to synthesize the growing literature on the effects of cultural diversity on auditor judgment and decision-making. But to do this, they use a framework from psychology on cross-cultural differences to organize the literature review and reference prior research from this literature as needed to frame the discussion within the auditing context. Regardless of whether the topic originated within BAR, it is important to investigate possible broader applications to other literatures before deciding whether to focus the review solely within the accounting literature or to expand the scope to other literatures.

When the initial literature search produces a large volume of relevant papers, a second challenge is to set appropriate restriction criteria for the breadth or depth of the review.[8] For instance, Messier, Simon and Smith (2013) limit breadth by identifying a seminal paper on analytical procedures as the starting point of the literature review and synthesizing the relevant research conducted over the subsequent two decades (i.e., limiting the time period). In another example, Trotman, Bauer and Humphreys (2015) limit the breadth of their review on group judgment and decision-making in auditing by including only experimental research, and limit the depth by only considering papers published in selected top accounting journals.[9]

Step 3: categorizing and synthesizing the studies

As a scholar performs a literature search and gathers papers that appear applicable to the topic under review, prior guidance indicates that certain important procedures should be performed as papers are categorized and synthesized. These include: (a) reading each paper in its entirety; (b) deconstructing each paper to identify key information and creating a system of tracking papers and (c) performing a critical analysis to identify patterns, inconsistences and deficiencies in the literature (Torraco 2005; Galvan 2012). The second procedure in this process requires breaking down each paper and categorizing key information. At this point, a scholar may find it necessary to create a tracking system of the papers to deal with the vast amount of information. The manner in which a tracking system is created is a personal preference: e.g., Cooper (1998: 26) recommends including a considerable amount of detail in a coding sheet, whereas Galvan (2012) suggests writing the details onto notecards. One approach that has worked well for us is creating a spreadsheet with separate columns for the citation, research question/objective, theory, method, sample, variables (including measurement), key findings and relationships with other papers. A challenge that can arise when summarizing findings in any tracking system is appropriately distinguishing an author's opinion from the empirical evidence. Failure to make this distinction is a common mistake in literature reviews (Galvan 2012).

As categorization of each paper continues, the scholar must continue to look for patterns and relationships among the prior studies (e.g., common findings), and begin to identify gaps and inconsistencies in the literature (Galvan 2012). This process provides input for synthesizing and critiquing the literature on the chosen topic (and perhaps sub-topics). The scholar must identify specific strengths and contributions (e.g., areas where results are consistent and together provide strong evidence of a finding), as well as deficiencies, inaccuracies or omissions (e.g., an under-studied variable or inconclusive results across studies) (Torraco 2005). As an example, Abernathy, Barnes and Stefaniak (2013) synthesize ten years of literature on the PCAOB. They start their literature review by separating identified papers on the PCAOB into four categories. By performing this step they find that only two papers focus on auditor PCAOB registration; both are archival and focus on auditor resignations or exits resulting from increased PCAOB oversight. Their categorization and understanding of key findings produced both a consistent conclusion and a deficiency in the literature, which are discussed in their paper. In sum, reading, deconstructing, categorizing and critiquing the papers relevant to the topic allow the BAR scholar to identify relationships, discrepancies and research gaps. These procedures can be laborious, but assist in streamlining the writing process of the paper.

Step 4: considering validity threats

As with empirical studies, scholars preparing literature reviews need to consider validity threats. These validity threats may occur in the literature search, during the sample analysis, and when drawing inferences from the sample. Addressing the threats can be difficult, so we offer some recommendations in this regard. The first validity threat is publication bias. Biases against publishing studies with null findings and/or contradictory findings could influence the literature review sample (Cooper 1998: 76). This validity threat is endemic to academic literature and scholars cannot readily mitigate it, but they should at least recognize it and consider how publication bias may influence their search and inferences.

Second, it is possible that a scholar could perform an unrepresentative search, where the search does not result in identifying all relevant studies. This may result in lack of generalizability of the findings. The scholar can mitigate this validity threat by performing an exhaustive search of the literature on the defined topic (Cooper 1998). One key element is the choice of search terms that define the sample. For instance, various terms may be used for a similar construct, such as "team" and "group". While "team" is more likely to be used for hierarchical groups, not all authors may use this convention. For instance, a search of *Auditing: A Journal of Practice & Theory* since 2010 yields 149 articles for "team" and 186 for "group". This example illustrates the importance of considering alternative search terms to ensure completeness. Two sources of identifying alternative terms is "keywords" chosen by authors of original papers to represent their work and talking with other scholars who are familiar with the research topic.

Third, prior guidance suggests that when reading and analyzing the identified research, scholars should assess methodological strengths and weaknesses of the studies, such as the strength of the design, the sample and the validity and consistency of variable measurements (Cooper 1998; Galvan 2012). When the validity of a study is considered unsound, scholars need to consider whether to retain or discard that study from the sample (Cooper 1998). However, methodological weaknesses in existing literature, such as differences in measurement of a single construct (e.g., audit quality), also provide an opportunity for future research to test the precision and construct validity of these measurements. Such considerations of studies' methodological strengths and weaknesses should be documented in the coding sheet or spreadsheet to support the scholar's conclusion.

Last, the nature of performing a literature review involves many decisions that affect the outcome of the review, and "integrating separate research projects into a coherent whole involves inferences as central to the validity of knowledge as the inferences involved in drawing conclusions from primary data analysis" (Cooper 1998: 2). Therefore, scholars must exercise proper care to avoid inserting their own biases when analyzing the sample and drawing inferences from the literature, and not placing undue weight on certain studies or findings. To mitigate the threat of inferential and weighting bias, scholars must diligently consider the quality of inferences and conclusions made when integrating research studies. The pervasiveness of this threat carries through to writing the literature review, as discussed in the following section.

Writing the literature review

After completing the research process, the BAR scholar should possess an extensive understanding of the topic. Transforming and communicating this understanding into a convincing and comprehensible synthesis is "a task with profound implications for the accumulation of knowledge" (Cooper 1998: 157). Therefore, when writing the literature review, the BAR scholar must give careful consideration to explaining the established conceptual structure of the review, describing the rigour of the review method (i.e., how the review was conducted) and presenting the findings and future research directions in a concise, coherent and insightful manner.[10]

First, a well-written literature review tends to introduce the conceptual structure towards the beginning of the paper. The structure serves as a guide for the literature review agenda and how the paper is organized (Torraco 2005). For example, many papers present figures early in the review discussion and organize the literature review in accordance with these figures (e.g., Abernathy et al. 2013, Peecher, Solomon and Trotman 2013). As discussed earlier in the chapter, this conceptual structuring provides the reader with a roadmap and a visual understanding of what will be discussed in the literature review and how components of the literature relate to each other.

Second, the BAR scholar must describe the literature review method and sample in enough detail for another individual to replicate the process and arrive at similar conclusions (Cooper 1998; Torraco 2005). Our examination of BAR research finds that this methodological description tends to appear in the introduction of the literature review (e.g., Abernathy et al. 2013) or in a separate methods section (e.g., Chiu, Liu and Vasarhelyi 2014). Importantly, the method description should explicitly state the literature review search parameters, including the criteria described in above. For example, to identify PCAOB-related studies, Abernathy et al. (2013) state the publication years included in the sample, and the specific databases and the distinct keywords they searched. Additionally, they note using the reference lists of the identified studies to determine other pertinent studies, giving consideration to both published and unpublished works.

In addition to the basic search parameters, the method description should state the scholar's criteria for including or discarding studies in the sample (e.g., Galvan 2012). As identified in earlier, these criteria may be based on broadening or narrowing the scope of the study (e.g., limiting the breadth) or may be based on the scholar's assessment of the validity of the study's design and findings. Regardless of the criteria, items that will not be discussed in the literature review should be noted and, if applicable, referenced to other literature reviews on that item (Galvan 2012). For example, Trotman et al. (2015) provide a thorough method description, including specific criteria for determining inclusion versus exclusion. They explain that their literature review is restricted to JDM experiments, with some attention to field studies when identifying avenues for future research. Further, they note that their literature review will not include auditor-client negotiations, and refer the reader to a recent literature review paper covering the negotiation literature.

Third, the BAR scholar should communicate and present the findings of the literature review in a concise and coherent manner. When writing a literature review, BAR scholars may feel torn between writing concisely and providing enough detail of each paper. But keep in mind, the synthesis should integrate findings from multiple studies, including several citations in a paragraph to make a point, rather than simply summarizing each study considered in the literature review (Galvan 2012). A summary table can serve as an effective means to provide an overview of the sample and data points (Cooper 1998; Torraco 2005). Many of the extant BAR literature reviews include summary tables of the studies discussed within the paper (e.g., Andiola 2014, Trompeter et al. 2013).[11] We find such tables helpful in our own work; they are readily developed from the spreadsheet tracking system mentioned in the prior section.

Other tables or figures may also be a mechanism to communicate important findings and descriptive statistics to the reader. For instance, Trotman et al. (2015) compare by topic (e.g., brainstorming) the number of published papers in the last 45 years in each of the top journals and in each of the five previous decades. These tables persuasively communicate to the reader the changes over time of the research focus and favourability of acceptance of topics to certain journals.

Lastly, writing a literature review is a creative activity aimed at providing new insight (Torraco 2005). While the scholar's conceptual structure should greatly contribute to imparting new insights, the scholar should also include avenues for future research based on that structure. There are many ways to determine areas warranting further study, such as the identified gaps in the literature or understudied areas of the conceptual structure that the scholar identifies during the research process. Additionally, the BAR scholar could talk to practitioners about factors related to the literature review topic or survey concerns or proposals raised by regulators. The ideas for future research could also stem from the objective of the journal to which the BAR scholar will submit the literature review.[12] When incorporating the future research ideas into the literature review, these ideas may be structured as research questions or propositions, a taxonomy, an alternative model or framework and/or a narrative discussion (Torraco 2005). Many of the BAR literature reviews we examined include an extensive list of specific future research questions (e.g., Bratten et al. 2013, Messier et al. 2013). By encouraging future research on the identified gaps, the academic community can work to further refine the proposed models and frameworks (e.g., as noted by Peecher et al. [2013]) and continue generating thoughtful insights, both for accounting practice and theory.

Concluding thoughts

In this chapter, we discussed the process of developing a literature review within the domain of BAR, from conceptualizing an idea through production of the paper. The social sciences literature offers several very useful guides that we have found valuable in our own work in reviewing topics relevant to BAR (Cooper 1998; Torraco 2005; and Galvan 2012); these works have differing strengths that we highlight. We build on that guidance by noting some key challenges and unique features of literature reviews, providing recent examples from BAR. We also discuss some unique aspects of writing a literature review for BAR.

Literature reviews require the same rigour as other types of research. In our experience, conceptualizing an insightful structure, determining appropriate search boundaries and critically assessing and drawing conclusions based on common and discrepant findings are often the most time-consuming and challenging tasks. In addition, deciding how to clearly present and describe the conceptual structure when writing the literature review can be taxing as this is often the section that will draw the reader into the rest of the paper (or make them want to stop reading).

We also identify certain features of literature reviews that resonate strongly within BAR. First, the evolving professional environment of accounting practice provides a constant source of new "hot topics" to motivate the need for a literature review. In addition, as BAR is an applied discipline, our reviews are often motivated by a desire to improve accounting practice by furthering academics', regulators' and/or professionals' understanding of topics of concern within the industry (e.g., current or proposed regulations, audit quality). Finally, literature reviews in accounting often borrow conceptual frameworks and theories from other literatures that enable us to make sense of our literature. However, the unique features of the accounting profession (e.g., the regulatory environment) also create the potential for a literature review in accounting to contribute to theory or extend prior frameworks or models in other literatures.

In sum, with the increase in depth, breadth and complexity of BAR, we see the literature review as an increasingly useful means of advancing our knowledge on topics important to accounting scholars, regulators and professionals. The opportunities to make future contributions to the literature through reviewing prior work appear very promising.

Notes

1 With the growth of BAR, the definition of what constitutes BAR is less clear. We adopt Birnberg's (2011: 2) definition, which identifies BAR studies as those that focus on "the actual behaviour of people ... as they interact with each other and/or their environment" in an accounting context. The most common methods used to study these behaviours include experiments, surveys and field studies, but Birnberg indicates the available methods are expanding, highlighting that it is possible for even archival data to be used to answer a question about behaviour.

2 During the course of our discussion we reference useful prior guidance for writing literature reviews in the social sciences (e.g., Cooper 1998; Torraco 2005; Galvan 2012), while considering distinctive features of applied disciplines such as accounting. The Appendix contains an annotated bibliography of these works.

3 In choosing examples we focused our search primarily on the behavioural auditing literature, our area of expertise. However, many of these literature reviews cover topics applicable to other accounting disciplines. In addition, we chose to emphasize recently published literature reviews (i.e., published between 2010 and 2015) and those in top-tier accounting journals (e.g., *Accounting, Organizations, and Society*), American Accounting Association Section journals (i.e., *Auditing: A Journal of Theory and Practice; Behavioural Research in Accounting*) and the *Journal of Accounting Literature* (which has an emphasis on literature reviews in accounting).

4 The PCAOB Synthesis Project was a project aimed to synthesize research on various topics (e.g., professional skepticism, auditor independence, internal controls over financial reporting and several others) to inform future auditing standard development and future audit research.

5 Often scholars have already performed a preliminary search of the relevant literature during the process of determining a need for a stand-alone literature review, but this process must be extended to ensure a rigorous review of possible studies to include.

6 Within BAR, the narrative literature review, in which the interpretation of findings is based primarily on the perspectives of the authors, is the most common form. However, meta-analysis is an alternative form of literature review that allows statistical conclusions to be drawn about the results from a body of literature (Greenberg 1992; Cooper 1998). Meta-analysis is used occasionally in archival accounting (e.g., Hay, Knechel and Wong 2006; Pomeroy and Thornton 2008), but appears even less frequently used in BAR (e.g., Trotman and Wood 1991) (see also Khlif and Chalmers [2015] for a comprehensive review of meta-analytic research in accounting). Given the significant increase in BAR and the infrequency of meta-analyses, this may be an area where a BAR scholar can make a significant contribution to the accounting literature. Further discussion of meta-analysis is beyond the scope of this paper, but two resources are Greenberg (1992) and Lipsey and Wilson (2001).

7 In setting the search boundaries, the scholar should carefully consider the quality of the source, focusing primarily on primary sources (i.e., empirical and theoretical works), with less emphasis on secondary

sources (i.e., the popular press and textbooks) (Galvan 2012). In addition, if the decision is made to include unpublished works, these are often available through the Social Science Research Network (SSRN) and conference programs or proceedings.

8 These parameters tend to apply to the primary literature in which the scholar is intending to review and synthesize. If the literature review uses other literatures for the conceptual structure or to provide context it appears common to cite primarily seminal papers and other studies which may improve understanding of particular concepts without strict criteria for restriction or inclusion.

9 The authors do identify a few exceptions to these criteria that they note are needed in order to present a more comprehensive synthesis of an area of research or to assist in suggesting future research directions.

10 Prior guidance offers suggestions and checklists that can be used during the editing process (see Torraco [2005: 365] and Galvan [2012: 91–109]).

11 The studies in the summary tables tend to be grouped in accordance with facets of the conceptual structure. Common features of the table include the study's citation and characteristics of the study (e.g., research method and key findings).

12 For example, the objective of *Auditing: A Journal of Practice and Theory* is to improve the practice and theory of auditing, whereas the objective of *Journal of Accounting Literature* is to advance knowledge on topics related to accounting, auditing and taxation. Therefore, the targeted journal to which the literature review will be submitted could influence or necessitate tailoring the future research ideas. In fact, the objective of the different academic journals is an important consideration not only for the future research ideas, but also when formatting and writing of the literature review. The style and format guidelines are available from the journal (typically via the journal's website).

References

Abernathy, J.L., Barnes, M. and Stefaniak, C., 2013, 'A summary of 10 years of PCAOB research: What have we learned?', *Journal of Accounting Literature* 32, 30–60.

Andiola, L.M., 2014, 'Performance feedback in the audit environment: A review and synthesis of research on the behavioral effects', *Journal of Accounting Literature* 33(1), 1–36.

Birnberg, J.G., 2011, 'A proposed framework for behavioral accounting research', *Behavioral Research in Accounting* 23(1), 1–43.

Bratten, B., Gaynor, L.M., McDaniel, L., Montague, N.R. and Sierra, G.E., 2013, 'The audit of fair values and other estimates: The effects of underlying environmental, task, and auditor-specific factors', *Auditing: A Journal of Practice & Theory* 32(Supplement), 7–44.

Chiu, V., Liu, Q. and Vasarhelyi, M.A., 2014, 'The development and intellectual structure of continuous auditing research', *Journal of Accounting Literature* 33, 37–57.

Cooper, H.M., 1998, *Synthesizing Research: A Guide for Literature Reviews*, Applied Social Research Methods Series (Vol. 2), Sage Publications, Thousand Oaks, CA.

Galvan, J., 2012, *Writing Literature Reviews: A Guide for Students of the Social and Behavioral Sciences* (5th ed.), Pyrczak, Los Angeles, CA.

Greenberg, P., 1992, 'The use of meta-analysis techniques in developing dissertation proposals: Guidelines to aid supervising faculty', *Issues in Accounting Education* 7(2), 145–163.

Hanes, D.R. (Downey), 2013, 'Geographically distributed audit work: Theoretical considerations and future directions', *Journal of Accounting Literature* 32(1), 1–29.

Hay, D.C., Knechel, W.R. and Wong, N., 2006, 'Audit fees: A meta-analysis of the effect of supply and demand attributes', *Contemporary Accounting Research* 23(1), 141–191.

Hurtt, R.K., Brown-Liburd, H., Earley, C.E. and Krishnamoorthy, G., 2013, 'Research on auditor professional skepticism: Literature synthesis and opportunities for future research', *Auditing: A Journal of Practice & Theory* 32(Supplement 1), 45–97.

Hux, C.T., 2016, 'Use of specialists on audit engagements: A research synthesis and directions for future research', *Working paper*, Bentley University.

Khlif, H. and Chalmers, K., 2015, 'A review of meta-analytic research in accounting', *Journal of Accounting Literature* 35, 1–27.

Lipsey, W. and Wilson, D., 2001, *Practical Meta Analysis*, Sage Publications: Thousand Oaks, CA.

Messier, W.F., Simon, C.A. and Smith, J.L., 2013, 'Two decades of behavioral research on analytical procedures: What have we learned?', *Auditing: A Journal of Practice & Theory* 32(1), 139–181.

Nelson, M.W., 2009, 'A model and literature review of professional skepticism in auditing', *Auditing: A Journal of Practice & Theory* 28(2), 1–34.

Nolder, C. and Riley, T.J., 2014, 'Effects of differences in national culture on auditors' judgments and decisions: A literature review of cross-cultural auditing studies from a judgment and decision making perspective', *Auditing: A Journal of Practice & Theory* 33(2), 141–164.

Peecher, M.E., Solomon, I. and Trotman, K.T., 2013, 'An accountability framework for financial statement auditors and related research questions', *Accounting, Organizations and Society* 38(8), 596–620.

Pomeroy, B. and Thornton, D.B., 2008, 'Meta-analysis and the accounting literature: The case of audit committee independence and financial reporting quality', *European Accounting Review* 17(2), 305–330.

Public Company Accounting Oversight Board (PCAOB), 2015, *The Auditor's Use of the Work of Specialists*, Staff Consultation Paper No. 2015-01, PCAOB, Washington, DC.

Torraco, R.J., 2005, 'Writing integrative literature reviews: Guidelines and examples', *Human Resource Development Review* 4(3), 356–367.

Trompeter, G.M., Carpenter, T.D., Desai, N., Jones, K.L. and Riley Jr., R.A., 2013, 'A synthesis of fraud-related research', *Auditing: A Journal of Practice & Theory* 32(Supplement 1), 287–321.

Trotman, K.T., Bauer, T.D. and Humphreys, K.A., 2015, 'Group judgment and decision making in auditing: Past and future research', *Accounting, Organizations and Society* 47, 56–72.

Trotman, K.T. and Wood, R., 1991, 'A meta-analysis of studies on internal control judgments', *Journal of Accounting Research* 29(1), 180–192.

Appendix

Annotated bibliography for literature review texts

Cooper (1998)

Cooper's textbook aims to provide researchers in social, behavioural and medical sciences with detailed guidance when conducting a literature review. Cooper discusses important considerations across five stages: (a) problem formation; (b) literature search; (c) data evaluation; (d) data analysis and (e) interpretation and presentation of findings. His discussion of the literature review process takes the form of a methodological approach that parallels the rigorous, scientific process and standards employed when performing other forms of research and inquiry. Specifically, he draws significant attention to the importance of evaluating the validity of inferences and conclusions that scholars make when integrating extant research. For example, publication bias and performing an unrepresentative search are two potential threats to search and inference validity. He emphasizes that researchers must give careful consideration to choices made during the literature search and when evaluating prior studies. Further, in the data analysis section, he outlines statistical analyses researchers can use when synthesizing extant research results (e.g., combining probabilities and effect sizes across studies, which is important for a meta-analysis). Cooper's text is a thorough reference to help researchers synthesize and write an effective literature review.

Galvan (2012)

Galvan guides the reader through the steps and considerations necessary when writing a literature review in the social and behavioural sciences. He offers a series of detailed guidelines that address the following steps: (a) determining a topic and relevant literature sources; (b) analyzing, critiquing, synthesizing and effectively organizing the literature, including explicit considerations for research employing different methodologies (quantitative versus qualitative) and (c) drafting, redrafting and editing the synthesis. He also devotes a chapter to noting key tables that could be included in the review to benefit the reader (e.g., a table of key definitions, a table of research methods and/or a table summarizing results of the studies in the sample). Throughout his discussion of these steps, Galvin draws on exemplar literature reviews from a variety of academic journals to illustrate his guidelines. His book is particularly easy to follow because it is targeted to students and individuals beginning a literature review for academic publication.

Additionally, he includes a comprehensive checklist of considerations for evaluating the importance, organization, cohesion and accuracy of the literature review. This checklist addresses common problems in writing a literature review and intends to help the review author carefully edit his/her work.

Torraco (2005)

Similar to Galvan, Torraco discusses guidelines for conducting a literature review, and offers examples to illustrate the value that reviews provide to further our understanding in a particular field. His article is separated into three sections: (a) why write a literature review; (b) organizing a literature review and (c) writing a literature review. One interesting takeaway gleaned from his discussion is that syntheses should not be a "data dump". Rather, he states that the review and critique of the extant literature should be a creative activity that yields new knowledge and insight about a topic, provides a basis for theory building, and offers future inquiry/a research agenda. Torraco also supplies the reader with a succinct checklist for organizing and writing a literature review.

31

Preparing a written review for Behavioural Accounting Research manuscripts

Jennifer Joe

Introduction

This chapter offers advice on preparing an independent peer review for behavioural research. It is focused primarily on human subjects' laboratory experimental studies where the researcher is manipulating one or more variables (independent variables) to demonstrate the effect of the manipulated variable on a variable of interest (the dependent variable). The discussion addresses how to evaluate the research contribution, theoretical development and experimental design of a study, and provides general advice on preparing scholarly reviews.

The experimental method

The vast majority of behavioural accounting studies apply the experimental method (e.g., individual laboratory studies and experimental market studies). The comparative advantage of the experimental method rests in its ability to establish cause and effect. The experimenter manipulates the independent variable (X), also referred to as the treatment variable, to determine how it impacts the dependent variable (Y), also referred to as the outcome variable, while controlling other variables. By isolating the variables of interest, this approach seeks to explain how changes in X affect Y. Accordingly, one of the keys to evaluating an experimental study is how well the researcher is able to isolate (i.e., limit changes only to) the key variable of interest while holding constant other variables that are associated with or can otherwise explain changes in the outcome variable. In other words, a well-executed study will 'turn one dial of the research machine at a time' in order to establish causation. When designing an experiment, the researcher should give careful consideration in advance to any potential variables that can vary alongside the treatment variable (X) and use that knowledge to build an experiment that will hold these potential variables (covariates) constant across all experimental conditions. Holding these other factors constant allows the independent variable to be isolated from other explanatory variables. Consequently, any changes in the dependent variable Y can be directly attributed to the independent variable. The independent reviewer should therefore critically evaluate the experimenter's choices in the construction and execution of the experiment. Below, I employ a graphical presentation of the elements associated with the experimental method, and then discuss how they can be analyzed, and issues that can arise with this research design. This graphical presentation is often referred to as "Libby boxes" within the Behavioural Accounting Research community after Robert Libby who popularized their use (see Chapter 3, this volume).

Evaluating a study's theoretical support (Link 1)

In general, researchers advocate that there is a relationship between the independent variable, X and dependent variable, Y. Kinney (1986) refers to this as "facts that will occur". Well-designed experimental studies will rely on theory as the basis for predicting the cause and effect relationship between Conceptual X and Conceptual Y. Typically, these theories come from other fields including psychology, sociology and economics. In assessing the strength of Link 1, the reviewer will want to judge the quality of the theoretical connection between Conceptual X and Y drawn by the researcher. If the research being evaluated is testing a relationship that is based on existing theory, then the reviewer will want to focus on whether or not the study accurately describes the theoretical relationship and presents a faithful representation of variables X and Y. Reviewers should also analyze whether the theory being applied is suitable and plausible in the accounting context to which it is being applied. It is important to evaluate how well the researcher has considered the unique contextual features of the accounting settings when seeking to employ a particular theory to explain an accounting "fact". For example, decision makers in accounting settings are typically adult professionals completing complex judgment and tasks. Accordingly, it would not seem immediately plausible for a researcher to apply a theory developed on the study of adolescent judgment to an accounting issue. Any researcher in this type of scenario should be called upon to explain why a theory on adolescent cognition is applicable to a setting largely characterized by professional judgment. The reviewer should carefully assess the similarities and differences between the accounting and adolescent settings to determine whether it is plausible and logical that predictions developed in an adolescent setting will hold in accounting.

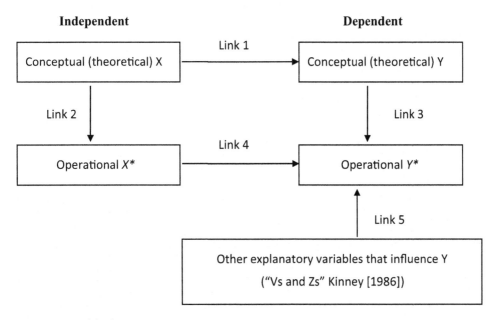

Figure 31.1 Libby boxes

Within the discipline of accounting, there are also unique contexts depending on the purpose of accounting information and role of the individuals who produce and use accounting information. For example, in managerial accounting it is important to consider economic, motivational and intrinsic factors that influence managerial decision makers. In auditing, accountability, time pressure, incentives to please the client, auditor professional reputation and legal liability are all among the potential factors that can impact auditors' judgments. Similarly, while tax professionals also face accountability and client service pressures, they do not face the high level of litigation risk that is present in the audit setting. Finally, investors and other users of financial accounting data face complex information environments that are not typical in the studies on which many psychological and economic theories are based. This list of contextual features is not meant to be exhaustive but rather to serve as an illustration of some of the factors that reviewers should consider when thinking about the applicability of a source theory to the accounting setting being investigated.

Sometimes researchers will develop new theories or extensions of existing theories. In this circumstance, the reviewer should consider the plausibility of the theoretical connection between the X and Y variables. In particular, the reviewer should analyze whether the researcher has developed logical arguments and presented adequate data to support the new theory, and whether the researcher has gathered and presented analyses of process data (measures of significant elements within the theory) to support the new theory. Further, the reviewer should assess whether the study being reviewed presents adequate data and analyses to rule out alternative explanations for the association between the dependent and independent variables that have been established in prior research and more widely accepted theories (see Link 5 discussion below).

Evaluating the study's execution of the independent and dependent variables (Link 2 and 3)

After presenting the hypothesized connection between the independent and dependent variables, the next step for behavioural researchers is to measure and test the strength of the causal link between the variables. Before this can be done, researchers must construct variables that are purported to represent the conceptual (theoretical) X and Y. These construct variables are also referred to as operational independent (X^*) and dependent (Y^*) variables. Reviewers must examine how well these operational variables capture the key aspects of the theoretical variables. For example, let's assume a researcher develops a theory and hypothesis that employee trust in management (X) leads to increased effort (Y). Assume also that the researcher measures effort as the number of correct words decoded in a word puzzle game and operationalizes trust in management by informing one group of participants that management is honest and can be trusted while informing another group that management is dishonest and cannot be trusted. A reviewer evaluating Link 2 should question whether simply telling the participants that management is honest and trustworthy invokes *feelings of trust* in management.

The reviewer should assess the extent to which the operationalized variable captures the intended theoretical construct. In this case, the concern is whether the participants actually felt more trust in management. Did the researcher measure and analyze the participant's feelings of trust in management to provide evidence that the participants actually trusted the management more in one treatment condition versus another? Assessing the manner in which the researcher measures trust is also important. Some researchers purport to present evidence that their manipulation adequately captures the conceptual variable, but instead they only offer evidence that the participants read their instructions. To illustrate, refer to the "trust-leads-to-effort" example above. If the researcher asks participants to assess the extent to which management was described as trustworthy in the experimental materials, and presents analysis of this data to indicate the degree to which the participants trusted the management, the reviewer should question the researcher's logic. In this example, a more appropriate manipulation check would be to have the participants assess the extent to which they trusted the management described in the experimental materials. For example, the researcher could utilize a well-validated scale from previous research that measures feelings or attitudes of trust to determine that the manipulation worked. The key to assessing Link 2 for behavioural studies is to determine whether the prompt that triggers the participants' behaviour (judgment) is actually one and the same as the stated conceptual (theoretical) variable.

An evaluation of Link 3 involves gauging how well the measured dependent variable (Y^*) captures the theoretical outcome variable (Y). In behavioural studies, decision process (how the judgment is made) and task performance are often the chosen measures for the operational Y^*. Task performance is typically compared to a benchmark (e.g., an expert panel or normative solution) and can be measured in many ways including: ability to predict the likelihood of going concern, ability to select the optimal mix of resources, allocating effort in some optimal way to achieve better resource allocation for the firm, estimating the likelihood of error, etc. Returning to the example of the "trust-leads-to-effort" study above, the researcher could select the total number of words decoded, the accuracy and complexity of words decoded, the proportion of correct to total words decoded, the proportion of correct words decoded to the total of possible words, and so on. The reviewer should assess how well the measure employed in the study being reviewed captures the intent of the theory on which the hypothesis is based and is faithful to the theoretical construct to which it relates. Some of these options measure both effort and accuracy (e.g., number of correct words decoded divided by total possible correct words) while others measure effort only but do not consider accuracy (e.g., number of words decoded without regard to accuracy). In evaluating the appropriateness of the operational Y^*, the reviewer would have to consider how integral accuracy is to the theory at question, and whether accuracy is an important theoretical factor in the managerial accounting context being studied. Moreover, the reviewer should determine if accuracy is being used inappropriately as a proxy for effort, leading the researcher to draw incorrect inferences about the effect of trust on effort.

Beyond the selection and construction of the operational Y^*, an important design choice that can impact the validity and quality of the inferences drawn from an experiment is the experimental task used to capture and measure the data related to the Operational Y^*. There must be a good fit between the task and the participants chosen to test the theoretical explanation between X and Y (Abdolmohammadi and Wright 1997; Nelson and Tan 2005). The reviewer should evaluate whether the participants have the knowledge and skill to perform the task (i.e., judgment or decision being made in the experiment). For studies utilizing professional participants such as auditors, tax accountants and financial analysts, ensuring that the experimental task is one that is normally performed by the study's participants will be more important than in management accounting settings where student participants' performance on abstract tasks are a typical measure of effort. Regardless of the participants' expertise, the reviewer should evaluate whether the task used in the experiment provides reasonable and reliable evidence about the types of judgments that occur in the accounting context that the researcher is seeking to study.

The level of complexity of the experimental task should also be evaluated. In general, a balance between the simplicity and external validity of the task should be considered. Reviewers should evaluate whether the task assigned is one that engages participants' attention and one that can be performed in a laboratory setting without the tools, techniques and reference materials that are routinely available to them in a natural setting. For the vast majority of experimental tasks, it is not necessary for the professional participants to have access to all of the tools and materials that are available to them in their normal working environment. However, if the experimental task requires the calculation/evaluation of a complex accounting estimate (e.g., fair value of an option) and the participants are not provided with predetermined calculations, estimation models, computers or computational tools to assist in developing the estimates, it is questionable whether the participants' judgments under those conditions provide reliable data about how the independent variables impact the dependent variable.

Evaluating the analyses and inferences (Link 4)

Researchers construct independent and dependent variables to serve as representatives of the conceptual variables. However, as discussed above, in some cases it might be difficult to achieve operational variables that are closely aligned with the conceptual variables. Further, it is not always the case that the logical connection between the operational independent and dependent variables is as strong as that of the theoretical variables for which they serve as proxies. In assessing Link 4, the reviewer should assess both the strength of the connection between operational $X^\star$ and $Y^\star$ and the plausibility of the link between the two variables. The most important aspect in evaluating Link 4 is whether the study manipulates only the independent variable of interest. The reviewer should carefully read the experimental materials to evaluate whether the differences in the experimental conditions can be attributed only to the manipulation of the independent variables of interest. To illustrate, in the trust-leads-to-effort example above, the independent variable, trust, was manipulated by stating that management can (cannot) be trusted and is honest (dishonest). A manipulation of this type is said to be confounded because the participants are exposed to two variables about management that can influence their performance: management's trustworthiness and management's honesty. As a result, any changes in effort cannot be attributed only to trust but might be due to either trust or honesty or the combination of both factors. Last, demand effects can pose a threat to the internal validity of experiments. In reviewing the experimental materials, the reviewer should evaluate whether the participants are exposed to any information that hints at the goal of the study before the dependent variables ($Y^\star$) are captured. For example, the dependent variables should be measured before the participants provide their response(s) to the manipulation check questions.

Other potential explanatory variables (Link 5)

Another critical aspect of the experimental method is the careful consideration of other factors that can influence the changes in $Y^\star$ (Kinney 1986). Because the strength of the causal inference of any study can be undermined by alternative explanations for the $X^\star$ and $Y^\star$ relation observed, the reviewer should give significant attention to other potential explanatory variables ("Vs and Zs") that are relevant for the study. In the discussion of experimental method, I noted that experimental control is achieved by manipulating only the treatment variable ($X^\star$) while holding other variables constant. Experimenters can manage the potential impact of these other explanatory variables through random assignment of participants to the treatment conditions, holding these other factors and information content constant in the experimental design, and measuring the effect of those factors on the participants' judgment in a post-experimental questionnaire and then including these measures as covariates in the analyses. The reviewer should evaluate whether the researcher has identified the relevant Vs and Zs (Link 5) from the prior literature and other theories that can influence the observed change in $Y^\star$. In assessing the strength of experimental control applied in the study, the reviewer should determine whether the participant's exposure to other explanatory variables was fixed (i.e., held constant) for all of the treatment conditions. For example, are the descriptions, location and presentation format of the potential explanatory variables consistent in the materials provided to participants in each of the experimental conditions? Was the experimental protocol uniform for all participants (e.g., media of experiment, time limit, etc.)? If not, did the researcher conduct analyses and provide evidence that these differences did not impact Y^*? Reviewers should evaluate whether the study has constructed and gathered appropriate measures of these other explanatory variables. For example, are the current measures under review consistent with the measures used in prior studies; and are they consistent with the study's theory? Last, the reviewer should evaluate whether the statistical analyses conducted appropriately control for any other explanatory variables that the reviewer judges to be important in order to isolate the treatment effect in the study.

Common "other variables" that can influence the relation between X and Y are the individual traits or attributes of the participants. Experiments typically rely on random assignment of participants to the different experimental conditions. To control for these factors. Reviewers should evaluate whether the study has measured common trait variables such as experience, knowledge, education, etc., and whether the researcher has conducted statistical tests that validate that successful random assignment was achieved. If the statistical analyses reveal that any of the relevant trait variables differ across the experimental groups, then covariance analysis (ANCOVA) can be conducted to achieve statistical equality among the experimental conditions.

Evaluating contribution

The contribution of behavioural accounting studies generally lays in the comparative advantage to establish causal inferences because, as discussed above, experimenters can manipulate X^*, while holding other factors (Vs and Zs) constant, to demonstrate its effect on Y^*. In assessing the contribution, the reviewer should evaluate the insights and importance of the causal inference being documented in the study. A key consideration is whether the causal inference being explored offers new knowledge about an accounting judgment in auditing, financial reporting, investing, lending, managerial/organizational performance or taxes. Is the study shedding new light on the decision context; is it reconciling or offering an explanation for previously conflicting results observed in the literature; is it offering a new theoretical application or behavioural explanation related to a topic that is receiving significant attention from regulators, preparers or financial statement users? Does the study make a substantive impact on any of the actors in the accounting framework – will it change the behaviour of auditors, board members, investors, lenders, managers or regulators? Finally, the reviewer might want to consider the manuscript's contribution in the context of the journal's audience and mission. However, the journal's editor is in the best position to make this evaluation.

Judgment about whether a study makes a significant contribution to the literature is often a matter of taste. One reviewer might perceive a study's ability to document judgment that differs from what was established in the prior literature to be sufficient enough to merit contribution to the literature. Another reviewer might require that any study documenting a "new" and different judgment also offer an explanation and evidence to demonstrate when the observed "new" judgment would occur and when the prior judgment can be expected to occur as the benchmark to warrant contribution to the literature. Thus, the reviewer will have to make his or her own judgment about what can be learned from the study being evaluated.

Beyond the individual taste factor, there are clearly some areas where experimental studies are not well suited to establish contribution (e.g., estimating effect sizes and magnitude of an error) and other areas where the experimental method offers a distinctive advantage. Some of these advantages include the ability to test proposed regulatory actions or potential changes to policy before implementation, the ability to test competing theories (Kerlinger and Lee 2000), the ability to disentangle and isolate the independent variable of interest from other effects that are confounded in the natural setting (including self-selection effects) and the ability to test boundary conditions for model predictions. Several review studies provide an excellent discussion of the comparative advantages of experiments and the novice reviewer can use them as a point of reference to evaluate the contribution of an experimental study (e.g., Libby, Bloomfield and Nelson 2002; Sprinkle 2003; Bonner 1999).

Qualitative/field-based studies (other behavioural methods)

Surveys

While the vast majority of behavioural studies use the experimental approach, other methods such as surveys and interviews are also common approaches to investigating research questions about how accounting information influences decision-making and resource allocation. The previous discussion on evaluating the theoretical connection between X and Y is still relevant for survey and interview studies, but there are also unique concerns for each of these research approaches, which are often more focused on being descriptive.

Reviewers of survey studies should focus on these issues that can threaten the validity of a study: the design of the survey questions, the determination of the sample, and non-response bias. The cautionary axiom "garbage in garbage out" is rather applicable in survey studies. Reviewers should carefully read the questions to assess whether they are clear and could be consistently interpreted by the research participants (respondents). Some researchers argue that failures in question design can present the largest threat to the internal validity of a survey (e.g., Litwin 1995; Diamond 2000; Van der Stede, Young and Chen 2005). Ideally, the researcher should have conducted pilot tests or cognitive interviews with representative experts from the survey population to gain comfort that the respondents can answer the questions with ease and that the terminology used in questions are consistent with respondents' understanding. Multiple questions should be designed to measure the key variables of interest, and inter-question reliability analyses should be conducted to assess whether the responses to the questions are consistent (the test-retest reliability) and capture the conceptual variable of interest (internal consistency reliability) or are due to random error. Similarly, the researcher can demonstrate reliability by using differently worded forms of a question to measure the same attribute (the alternate form reliability). Reviewers should also study the survey questions to evaluate whether the order or location of questions within a survey could have contributed to the observed dependent measures (Y^*) and therefore limit the ability to draw inferences from the study.

Because survey researchers want to generalize their results to the entire population, it is important to evaluate how representative the survey's sample is of the population at large. Most accounting studies employ convenience samples because of the challenges of obtaining qualified professional respondents. Nonetheless, reviewers should evaluate whether the researchers have taken care to explain how the sample was obtained, provide an analysis of the target population, and provide an analysis of how the sample compares on key characteristics and traits of the population. Providing these details can help readers to form their own assessment of the reliability and generalizability of the inferences that can be drawn from the sample.

Last, reviewers should focus attention on evaluating whether the study adequately addresses any response (non-response) bias. Low response rates and the attendant non-response bias are a common cause for concern in accounting studies because obtaining participation from professional participants is challenging. Response bias poses a threat to the external validity of a study because it is difficult to determine whether the effects observed are representative of the population at large or only true for the sub-group of participants who responded to the survey. Because accounting studies typically do not offer economic incentives that are significant enough to attract highly compensated accounting professionals, respondents tend to be individuals who have a strong level of intrinsic interest and value in the study. Many authors attempt to overcome the shortcomings of a low response rate by citing other studies that have a low response rate. These attempts to justify the low response rate fail to recognize and address the concern that the potential for bias in the respondent pool is a problem. Reviewers should evaluate whether the study presents data that compares the key attributes and features of the population with that of the respondents. Van der Stede et al. (2005) argue that a more detailed reporting of the steps taken to secure the survey responses is more important to establishing the validity of a survey study than is the estimation of survey error due to non-response bias.

Interview studies

Interview studies, which have increased in recent years, have the advantage of allowing research-ers to conduct more in-depth investigations of their research questions and to revise their approach and direction as new information becomes available. Interview studies are particularly informative in providing descriptive evidence about new areas or problems in accounting that can guide subsequent experimental studies. However, the absence of a rigid framework to guide the research approach makes qualitative studies vulnerable to researcher bias. Reviewers should focus on evaluating the steps taken by the researcher to ensure that the researcher's own views and positions are not inserted into the process of gathering, coding and analyzing the data. Some precautions that can be taken to limit researcher bias include: using an independent transcriber who is not a member of the research team and did not participate in the research design to document the interviews, using an independent coder who is blind to the theoretical arguments that will be presented in the study and presenting a balance of quotes and responses that is rep-resentative of the participants' responses. As in survey studies, reviewers should evaluate whether the researchers have disclosed enough information about how the participants were sampled, summarized the procedures used for transcribing and coding the data and presented sufficient data that allows readers to make their own assessment about the degree of correspondence and consistency between the interview data and the researcher's interpretation. Reviewers who are unfamiliar with field-based research can refer to Miles and Huberman (1994) and Malsch and Salterio (2015) for comprehensive discussions on evaluating qualitative research.

General issues

Last, I offer some practical advice on the preparation of a review. Refer to Table 31.1 below for a list of steps to consider when preparing a written review. Reviewers should ensure that they have set aside an adequate amount of time to complete a thoughtful, unhurried and considered review of an article. Sufficient time should be budgeted to allow the reviewer to read the article in its entirety in one sitting. Reviewing an article is a complex cognitive task; accordingly, it is difficult to maintain clarity of thought about the paper if there are other tasks competing for the reader's attention or if there are multiple interruptions. Not only is it unfair to the authors, but the review-ers are less likely to understand a study that does not receive their undivided attention. For novice reviewers, I recommend reading the manuscript twice. The first read helps the reviewer to gain an overall understanding of the study, its position in the literature and the results presented. Once the reviewer has an understanding of the paper she/he can dedicate the second reading to a detailed

Table 31.1 Steps in preparing a written review for behavioural research

Step 1. Clear your schedule and locate a quiet setting that will allow for a complete reading of the manuscript free of interruption and distraction. Schedule the review due date into your work plan to allow sufficient time to respect critical deadlines set by the editor.

Step 2. Evaluate the motivation and contribution of the article.
Possible considerations:
- Is the relationship one that advances the literature or understanding of an accounting problem?
- Has the current study under review presented its contribution in context with published and contemporaneous studies in the research area?
- Does it inform regulators or practitioners?
- Does it help to explain contradictions observed in the literature or practice?

Step 3. Evaluate the quality of Link 1.
- Is the research question clearly articulated?
- Is the relationship plausible?
- Does theory being applied have a good fit with the research question?
- Do the researchers provide an accurate and faithful representation of the theory being applied?
- Is the theoretical discussion logical?

Step 4. Evaluate the strength of the connection between the conceptual and operational variables (Links 2 and 3).
- How strong is the degree of correspondence between the operational independent variable(s) and measured dependent outcome variable(s) and the theoretical (conceptual) variables?
- Do the operational variables map with the theory?
- Read the research instrument (e.g., experimental materials, surveys, interview questions) to determine whether the description of the variables in the article correspond with the operation of the variables in the research instrument.

Step 5. Evaluate the strength of the connection between the operational independent variable(s) and the measured outcome variable(s) (Link 4).
- Is the link between the operational variables consistent with the theory being advanced in the study?
- Is the link between the operational independent and dependent variables as strong as the link and logical connection between the theoretical variables for which these operational variables serve as proxies?
- Were the independent variables the only factors that varied across the treatment conditions?
- Are the analyses focused on the appropriate measures and variables?
- Is there appropriate analysis of process variables, where necessary, to support the theoretical connection being advanced in the study?
- Is the statistical approach rigorous and appropriate for the data gathered?

Step 6. Evaluate the impact of other potential explanatory variables (Link 5).
- Were the appropriate explanatory variables considered in the research design?
- Was care taken in the research design to hold the explanatory variables constant, or are they controlled for in the statistical analysis?
- Did the researchers conduct analyses to rule out alternative explanations?

Step 7. Evaluate the appropriateness of the conclusions.
- Are the conclusions consistent with the findings and results of the statistical analyses?
- Is the author guilty of overreach?
- Are the implications of the study clearly communicated?

critical assessment of each of the links. Being armed with the knowledge of the analyses conducted and conclusions made often allows the reviewer to evaluate the theoretical arguments and research design choices with more lucidity.

Before offering your comments on concerns about the paper, reviewers should present a short summary of the study (similar to the abstract) to demonstrate their understanding and interpretation of the study. The summary helps both the editor and author(s) to gauge the reviewer's attention to and interpretation of the manuscript because there can be a disconnect between the author's view of what was accomplished in the study and the reviewer's perception of what was executed and delivered. It is also helpful if the summary provides feedback on any strengths or noteworthy aspects of the manuscript.

While there is no established format for structuring a written review, I recommend organizing your comments around five themes: contribution and motivation; theoretical discussion and hypothesis development; research design; analyses and results and appropriateness of the conclusions being drawn in the study. Organizing your comments along these lines not only helps the reviewer to be disciplined in their thoughts but also assists authors in identifying the sources of the weaknesses in their manuscript so that the appropriate remedial actions can be taken, and helps the editor in compiling comments from multiple reviewers. Some reviewers present their critical comments in the order they appear in the manuscript while others present the most serious and substantive concerns first. My preference is the latter approach and I recommend separating your critical comments into two categories: major comments which identify material threats to a successful publication of the manuscript and minor comments focused more on clarification, grammar and less technical issues that can be easily remedied.

Many reviewers approach a review with the goal of identifying the flaws to facilitate a rejection of the article rather than providing a constructive critique of the study. This approach is particularly problematic in the case of novice reviewers who fail to appreciate that no study is perfect and even well-executed studies have some weaknesses because research typically requires some trade-offs in the decision-making over design choices. For example, in qualitative and experimental studies, researchers often trade off external validity in favour of achieving internal validity. In addition, qualitative studies are more focused on being descriptive and aiding in theory development rather than testing hypotheses. A valuable reviewer will not only identify the problems in a manuscript but, where possible, will offer possible solutions to address the concerns raised. It is often helpful for a reviewer to consider whether, on balance, what can be learned from the study is significant enough to tolerate the negatives (after they have been ameliorated to the least objectionable level).

Finally, reviews are a way to contribute to learning for our entire community. Even when the reviewer's recommendation is a rejection, there are still opportunities to offer constructive recommendations to guide the authors as they continue to pursue publication at other journals. Follow the golden rule when writing your review. Avoid condescension and accusation. Do not assume that authors are dishonest or ill-informed. Instead, recognize that authors have spent considerable time thinking about and developing their research. Consequently, while it might not be immediate, over time, they will be very appreciative of constructive suggestions of how to improve their manuscript's value and the role the review process plays in enhancing the quality of their published work. Adopting a positive tone in the writing of a review makes for a more positive experience for all involved. Relatedly, it can be helpful to set the completed review aside for a day or two before submission. The intervening period provides an opportunity to contemplate what was written and the chance for a final and more detached reading of the review before it is submitted to the author(s) and editor.

Acknowledgements: *I thank Virgil Alexander, Christine Earley, Steve Fuller, Kerri-Ann Sanderson, Yi-Jing Wu and the editors for their valuable comments.*

References

Abdolmohammadi, M. and Wright, A., 1997, 'An examination of the effects of experience and task complexity on audit judgments', *The Accounting Review* 62(1), 1–13.

Bonner, S., 1999, 'Judgment and decision-making research in accounting', *Accounting Horizons* 13(4), 385–398.

Diamond, S.S., 2000, 'Reference guide on survey research', in *Reference Manual on Scientific Evidence* (2nd ed.), 229–276, The Federal Judicial Center, Washington, DC.

Kerlinger, F.N. and Lee, H.B., 2000, *Foundations of Behavioral Research* (4th ed.), Harcourt College Publishers, Holt, New York.

Kinney, W.R., 1986, 'Empirical accounting research design for Ph.D. students', *The Accounting Review* 61(2), 672–676.

Libby, R., Bloomfield, R. and Nelson, M., 2002, 'Experimental research in financial accounting', *Accounting Organizations and Society* 27(8), 775–810.

Litwin, M., 1995, *How to Measure Survey Reliability and Validity*, Sage Publications, Thousand Oaks, CA.

Malsch, B. and Salterio, S.E., 2015, 'Doing good field research:' Assessing the quality of audit field research', *Auditing: A Journal of Practice and Theory* 35(1), 1–22.

Miles, M.B. and Huberman, A.M., 1994, *Qualitative Data Analysis: An Expanded Sourcebook*, Sage Publications, Inc., Thousand Oaks, CA.

Nelson, M. and Tan, H.-T., 2005, 'Judgment and decision making research in auditing: A task, person, and interpersonal interaction perspective', *Auditing: A Journal of Practice & Theory* 24(Supplement), 41–71.

Sprinkle, G., 2003, 'Perspectives on experimental research in managerial accounting', *Accounting Organizations and Society* 28(2–3), 287–318.

Van der Stede, W., Young, S.M. and Chen, C., 2005, 'Assessing the quality of evidence in empirical management accounting research: The case of survey studies', *Accounting Organizations and Society* 30(7–8), 655–684.

32

Replication of published studies in Behavioural Accounting Research

Frank G. H. Hartmann

Before this book closes: the case for replication studies

Throughout this volume, the assumption has been that although our interest in behavioural accounting phenomena may be fundamentally intrinsic, a core purpose of engaging in any empirical study is to be read by others. The single most important way to achieve that is by disseminating pieces of our work in the form of papers in academic journals. Even if publication has become a critical and undisputed goal of scientific activity, it is good to consider that publications and the publication process serve various purposes in the scientific community. When conducting academic research, it is simply good and standard research practice to refer to existing academic sources when positioning one's own study in the field, and academic studies that have appeared in journals are a primary source. Also, when arguing for the need to address a specific research question, when building theory and deriving hypotheses, when choosing and following a certain research method and when contrasting one's results with earlier findings there is ample and explicit reference to other published studies. The reference to extant studies is important not only for these functional reasons, but also to establish oneself as an original researcher, and show how one's study relates to, but especially extends the body of knowledge captured in earlier studies. An original researcher is one who is aware of existing knowledge, shows ability to contribute to that knowledge, and who is able to present one's research as novel. Originality is an important part of what makes a good researcher.

For these reasons, the interest of behavioural accounting researchers to invest research time in replicating findings from previous studies has traditionally been limited to a couple of instances. Replication of studies can be (loosely) defined as repeating an empirical study to establish the reliability and validity of its findings within and outside the context in which those findings were originally established. Replication is, often, seen as a mere repetition of a published study, which conflicts with the aim of novelty, and is therefore dismissed as a way to allocate our resources. But before this book closes, it is important to realize the necessity of the act of replication in the scientific process. In fact, there is large agreement amongst the academic community that replication is the only single way in which a collection of individual studies become a critical mass of robust knowledge.

The remainder of this chapter presents an overview of the current debate on replication studies. The next section starts by presenting a case from the psychological management literature in which the need for replication was established and, subsequently, addressed in an original way. This well-developed example serves to illustrate how behavioural accounting researchers could learn from the 'mistakes' made, and corrected, elsewhere. The subsequent section then addresses some of the forces in the current Behavioural Accounting Research landscape that provide incentives against conducting replication studies. In contrast, the section will explore how replication may be even more important in our field, which only addresses an academic audience, but ultimately also aspires to inform an audience of accounting practitioners. In the sub-section that follows, an overview is given of the single available research paradigm in the behavioural accounting literature that contains a series of more or less systematic replication studies. The results provide a strong confirmation of the need for replication studies in our field. The chapter closes with demonstrating some ways in which replication studies may be conducted. It proposes that a critical stance towards published findings may lead to various replication studies, considering that the object of replication can be all parts of a study from research question, via statistical analyses to drawing conclusions. Such a critical stance, as the chapter will conclude, could also be seen as 'novel'.

The quest for novelty, or why good scholars may perform 'bad studies'

Recently two researchers in the field of organizational behaviour (OB) investigated the relationship between people's surnames and their hierarchical position in firms (Silberzahn and Uhlmann 2013). Trying to add to the psychological explanation of management structures in firms, the authors investigated in a Germanic context whether people with noble-sounding surnames, like Kaiser ("emperor"), König ("king") or Fürst ("prince") would hold higher-level managerial positions more frequently than people with names referring to common social positions, such as Koch ("cook"), Bauer ("farmer") and Becker ("baker"). They argued that because of a psychological process called *associative cognition*, people with names referring to high social standing would end up in roles of relative high standing. In contrast, people with names that refer to ordinary jobs would end up in roles of relatively ordinary social standing. After identifying and classifying a long list of Germanic surnames from publicly available databases, the authors performed a number of statistical analyses common to contemporary social science research. The analyses included simple bivariate correlation as well as hierarchical linear modelling, both of which have become mainstream in contemporary social research. Based on these analyses, and after inclusion of a set of control variables, the authors conclude that the data support their expectation that peoples' names are related to their hierarchical positions in firms.

This study, at first sight, seems to have little in common with studies in Behavioural Accounting Research. Even if most behavioural accounting studies are rooted in social or cognitive psychology, a study on names seems remote to the research questions of these accounting studies. Indeed, the study seems exemplary for the large amounts of studies in social psychology that are being criticized for examining the obvious at worst, or merely confirming intuitively appealing trivialities at best (Parker and Shotter 2015). However, for exactly the reason that the relationship may seem intuitive and simple, much can be learned from this study's life-cycle based on what happened after it appeared in print. In a first step, a new analysis of the original data revealed that the original relationships simply did not exist (Silberzahn, Simonsohn and Uhlmann 2014). Despite the straightforwardness of the initial study's theory, the state-of-the-art application of sampling method and statistical analysis, and the quality of the study's overall exposition, the name-effects disappeared when applying a rather simple control for *name frequency* in the data set. Due to the sampling method chosen, the proportion of people with uncommon surnames was larger in the sample, but in a nonlinear way. The linear controls applied in the study were therefore unable to correct for this sampling error, resulting in a 'finding' that was securely predicted by theory, statistically significant at common threshold levels, and robust across analyses. In a second step, the authors of the original study decided that a lesson could be learned (Silberzahn and Uhlmann 2015a). In response to the critique, they acknowledged that the flaws in their work might be related to the fact that all researchers are typically performing multiple roles when conducting research.

Researchers are inventors, who aim to create new ideas and hypotheses, but they are also optimistic statisticians, who hope to find their ideas confirmed. These two roles may be at odds with the role of the critical analyst, who tries to establish their work's robustness by ruling out alternative conclusions. As the goals of these roles conflict, Silberzahn and Uhlmann conclude that even the most honest and ethical researcher may end up drawing invalid conclusions from data. Silberzahn and Uhlmann (2015b) then took a step further than merely drawing this conclusion, by engaging in an innovative research project, aiming to show the impact of the forces and roles mentioned on research outcomes. Based on a data set comprising four major football (soccer) leagues, including a variety of data on players, scores and referee calls, they invited 29 independent research teams to show the effect of players' *skin colour* on the *chance of receiving a red card* by the referee. The outcomes of these 29 analyses was highly dispersed. Some teams concluded that dark-skinned players were 1.3 times more likely to receive a red card than light-skinned players. Other research teams did not find any significant relationship or difference. While this might have been due to differences in skills across teams, Silberzahn and Uhlmann argue that the approaches taken by all teams seemed equally justifiable. They then conclude that the approach they took to make this point, which they gave the quite contemporary label 'crowdsourcing research', was a suitable way to illustrate that research findings are contingent on multiple and consecutive choices made by researchers, which creates a variety of 'findings'.

Whereas many of these choices are made at the same moment a research question is formulated, others are made later, when methods are considered, or even during the course of the statistical analysis. The main conclusion from the work by Silberzahn and Uhlmann is that explicit consideration of the existence of alternative routes between research idea and conclusion will benefit empirical research in the social sciences. Such a critical consideration involves finding answers to questions like: What research questions do we really have? How explicit is our theory and to what extent does it specify our method? What are the degrees of freedom in applying a certain observational method? What are the degrees of freedom in finding (or seeking) statistical significance in our data?

The comparatively simple study on the relationship between skin colour and red cards reveals that much depends on the way we choose to analyze this relationship, given the degrees of freedom in design, execution and analysis. If this is the case when studying simple relationships, between highly observable constructs, what does that mean for the more complex relationships we study in behavioural accounting? We should ask ourselves this question since behavioural accounting studies typically address more complex relationships, than the bivariate one in Silberzahn and Uhlmann (2015b). More importantly, behavioural accounting studies typically involve theoretical constructs that are less naturalistic and more open to various interpretations than 'skin colour' or 'amount of red cards'. Arguably, the lessons learned in this systematic inquiry into the roots of biased studies apply to the behavioural accounting field as well.

The quest for novelty, or why good journals may publish 'bad studies'

The importance of being an original researcher has become one of the tenets of modern academic research across most disciplines, including behavioural accounting. Studies aim to be novel in the topic they address and the research question they put forward. In the review process, critical reviewers put most effort in challenging authors to especially display these characteristics, asking for a contribution beyond the confirmation of 'the already known'. Often they do so by putting effort into showing that the study is not novel, that the topic has been exhaustively studied before, or that the research question has already been answered. Although this play between authors and reviewers might suggest that the market for academic publications is subject to correcting forces, it is in fact now generally believed that this process instigates systematic market failure. This market failure can be illustrated by the presence of biases in the collection of published studies. Two such biases are especially noteworthy, since they point to a need for replication studies, while at the same time lowering the chances of replication studies being adopted for publication. These biases can be labelled the *positive findings bias* and *reputation bias*.

The *positive findings bias* indicates the tendency of journals to prefer studies that show support of hypotheses. Studies on journals' publication policies, across the whole domain of (social) science, consistently show the existence of biases towards publishing such 'positive studies'. In a recent overview of various domains of scientific inquiry, Yong (2012) reports that the proportion of such positive studies lies steadily above 70%, with economics and business approaching 90%. These numbers are in line with other fields of scientific inquiry (Armstrong 1997), suggesting that the issue is fundamental. Basu and Park (2014) analyzed the occurrence of Type I (false rejection of null hypothesis) and Type II (false acceptance of null hypothesis) errors in three major accounting journals. They report that these errors occur in respectively 11% and 22% of cases, suggesting a severe problem with reliability. This suggests a need to corroborate the validity and reliability of individual studies.

Reputation bias occurs as journals seem also biased to prefer publishing studies by authors with established reputations (Kerr, Tolliver and Petree 1977). Reputation may on the one hand be considered a relevant indicator of quality, as it is typically connected to the historical delivery of good-quality studies, or at least to good-quality *published* studies. On the other hand, however, it becomes a bias if it leads to less critical attitudes towards a study's true quality. The recent problems with the retraction of a collection of behavioural accounting papers, documented by Dickins and Schneider (2016), which again suggests that reputation bias may create the most fundamental need for replication, which is to corroborate the validity and reliability of individual studies. This is even more the case since, as Siler and Strang (2016) illustrate, papers critical of respected authors' established ideas have a significantly lower chance of being accepted for publication.

These biases present researchers with a paradox. On the one hand, they suggest a great need for replication studies. One the other hand, however, they work against the publication of such studies and thereby enhance the emphasis for novelty. Arguably, the way out of this paradox has been for individual researchers to seek novelty in detail. Especially for young researchers, or researchers whose productivity is constantly scrutinized, the risk of 'finding nothing' constitutes an effective way to constrain the study of behavioural accounting issues to the limited set of issues identified by leading and well-published scholars. In line with this suggestion, recently Basu (2012) and Moser (2012) have commented upon the current situation in (behavioural) accounting research as being *stagnant*. Research questions often do not revolve around issues that pose practitioners and academics with the largest intellectual challenge, but rather on issues that can be stylized sufficiently to be pliable for experimental analysis or for which archival data are available. A second way out of the paradox has been the tendency in Behavioural Accounting Research to study phenomena that have been well explored elsewhere. This provides a low-risk attempt at novelty, at least within the field of accounting, since for the social sciences at large such studies provide little contribution.

A very interesting illustration of this paradox, and the various ways in which researchers have addressed it, can be found in a recent paper on 'subjective performance evaluation' (Bol, Hecht and Smith 2015) and the critical commentary it received (Rinsum 2015). The first paper presents an experimental study on the way superiors use their discretion to evaluate and compensate their subordinates. Arguably, this theme is receiving increased attention in the behavioural management accounting literature, even if most of its theoretical content has been extensively explored in the OB and human resources (HR) literatures. Rinsum (2015) furthermore argues that the incremental value of the paper, and its generalizability, are limited by the experimental treatments chosen, which in combination suggest a great ground for replication study that demonstrates how this emerging paradigm overall, as well as individual studies, relate to, or add to, the larger knowledge obtained elsewhere. Nevertheless, positive findings and reputation are now creating a remarkable paradigmatic constancy. Interestingly, the tendency of behavioural management accounting studies to revisit organizational and applied psychological processes studied in OB and HR has a long tradition (Shields 2015). Already the early budgeting literature's focus on a variety of HR variables, such as *job-related tension* and *job satisfaction* contained very little accounting theory, or advancement in such theory. This paradigm is the topic of the next section.

The quest for novelty, or why good studies did not create a 'good paradigm'

To date, there is only a single case of substantial examination of the effects of the abovementioned forces and effects on theoretical progress in the field of behavioural accounting. This case concerns the enormous literature that has developed over the last decades to explore the role of budget-related performance evaluation in organizations. In fact, the study of the role of accounting budgets on the behaviour of people in organizations constituted the first real critical mass of studies, and still occupies much of the publication space in academic journals.

Arguably, this paradigm owes its existence to a failed replication. Hopwood (1972) and his Ph.D. student Otley (1978) were both followers of Hofstede's (1967) early attempt to understand the role of budgets in organizational dynamics. Hofstede had presented a study in which the accounting budgeting process was framed as a play between various stakeholders. In his view, this play was about winning or losing the budgeting game, which itself was essentially a game for gaining organizational resources to execute one's power. Hofstede had used a field study approach, using a case study methodology, consisting of a rich collection of data, including personal interviews. Hopwood (1972) replaced this method with the more efficient use of questionnaire data. In a sample of cost centre managers one of his aims was to assess how the use of budgets in managerial performance evaluation would result in a number of psychological outcomes. The expectations tested were based on role theory. Role theory is an occupational psychological theory which explains the incidence of work-related stress as a consequence of people being forced into different, partly conflicting organizational roles. The theoretical expectation in Hopwood (1972) was that strict emphasis on budget attainment would cause such "role conflict", as it would force managers to both execute their jobs, but also meet their budgetary targets, which were not necessarily aligned with job demands. Role conflict is defined as the "simultaneous occurrence of two (or more) sets of pressures such that compliance with one would make more difficult compliance with the other" (Kahn et al. 1964: 19). Emphasis on meeting the budget during periodic performance reviews would cause a conflict since the budget imperfectly represents underlying true demands of the managerial job.

What followed was a long sequence of studies investigating the generality of the findings in Hopwood's (1972) study. Notable is the first study in this sequence performed by David Otley (1978). This was a study that explicitly aimed to ascertain that the effects found in a cost centre environment, known to be using imperfect budgetary control, would also apply in a profit centre environment. This attention was evoked by Otley's (1978: 123) remark about the sample of profit-centre managers that he investigated:

> The present study was designed to eliminate technical failings in the accounting system, as far as possible, by observing the operation of a well-designed system in a type of organization that was well suited for the application of budgetary control.

Otley's findings essentially contradicted Hopwood's findings, as he found no significant relations between budget emphasis and either job-tension or negative social relations. Furthermore, Otley (1978) found positive relations between budget emphasis and managers' budgetary performance, which falsified Hopwood's suggestion that a high reliance on budgetary figures when evaluating responsibility centre managers would be universally inappropriate. Almost in parallel, researchers such as Peter Brownell and Ken Merchant investigated the impact of another variable, called *budgetary participation*. This variable, also studied by Geert Hofstede, was also scrutinized for having various effects on the outcomes variables that figured in the budgetary evaluation studies.

Otley's notion of contextual suitability of the use of budgets for performance evaluation laid the track for the explicit inclusion of contextual variables in subsequent studies, which are used to explain why the effects found do not generalize over settings, but rather depend on the situation that is studied. Each of these studies can be considered a replication and for over more than four decades, a large quantity of models has been tested, in which the two budgeting variables (budget-based evaluations and budgetary participation), are combined with contextual variables and organizational outcomes in various permutations. Already in 1991 Brownell and Dunk (1991: 703) note about this paradigm that it is the "the only organized critical mass of empirical work in management accounting". It is, to date, also the only part of behavioural management accounting research in which there is a systematic, even if not unproblematic, quantity of studies that have attempted to replicate and extend earlier studies. In addition, several review studies have evaluated the quality of this overall paradigm, the consistencies in findings, or rather lack thereof and the overall contribution of knowledge. This set of early behavioural accounting studies are, to date, the single example of a paradigmatic interest in confirming old findings through more or less systematic replication. The contradictory findings in the two budgetary evaluation studies, and the parallel interest in the effect of budgetary participation, led to a sequence of studies investigating and testing various combinations of budget-related, contextual and outcomes variables. An overview of these studies was graphically presented in Luft and Shields (2003). It evidences both the large amount of studies and accounting and other variables studied.

Recently, a collection of studies by Derfuss (2009, 2015, 2016) put this behavioural accounting paradigm to a critical test. In three related papers, Derfuss investigates the validity and research findings of the studies, using a procedure called meta-analysis. Meta-analysis is a set of methodological techniques to evaluate a body of literature in a standardized way. Its main goals are to obtain an estimate of the true strength of a relationship, test the robustness of a common research finding and to test for and investigate biases (Møller and Jennions 2001).

Derfuss's analyses consist of finding patterns in the variety (see Figure 32.1), and are of a remarkable detail, owing to the multitude of studies in this field. His conclusions directly support the importance of replication to establish the validity and reliability of research findings. Combining and contrasting various variables and relationships, he concluded that small samples had been responsible for creating statistical artefacts, which may both explain corroboration of findings across studies as well as conflicting evidence. Moreover, the choice of accounting constructs and the way they are operationalized and measured seemed a dominant factor in finding converging and diverging evidence. Also, the effect of industry on accounting variables and their relationship with performance seemed underestimated in most studies. Overall, therefore, the conclusion was that many of the individual findings, so diligently summarized and reported by Luft and Shields (2003, see Figure 32.1) do not hold for the paradigm overall.

At this moment in time, the paradigm as sketched above has lost its former level of activity, significance and impact on the behavioural accounting literature (Hartmann and Moers 1999; 2003). Budgets remain the corner stone of management accounting in firms, and continue to have an important impact on human behaviour. However, the apparent dissatisfaction with the overall achievements of this research paradigm in establishing consistent and useful truths has led to its demise. The contrast between Figure 32.1 and the conclusions from the meta-analysis performed by Derfuss, illustrate both the 'knowledge' created by the paradigm, but also the ways in which replications have been performed, which ultimately contributed to this lost popularity. The analysis presents a warning for the current building of critical mass in other topics within behavioural accounting. Consistent replication of findings, and trying to break the publication and reputation biases continue to be of great importance.

The quest for novelty or why replication studies may provide novel insights

We live in times in which there seems to be an explosion of empirical research across the sciences, as has been the case in the, relatively small, arena of Behavioural Accounting Research. Whereas robustness of findings is best served by continuous replication, the quest for novelty in the competitive international research arena at the same time seems to come at a cost to validity and reliability of studies. Fortunately, across almost all fields of science, there is a renewed interest in the validity and reliability of research findings, as well as a renewed acknowledgement that systematic threats to validity and reliability exist at various levels of the academic production model (Armstrong 1997; Ioannidis 2005; Ingre 2013; Makel and Plucker 2014). The systematic review of the budgetary research in behavioural accounting is telling us some important lessons. First, it suggests that findings differ between individual studies to an extent that our idea of having solid and fundamental knowledge in this area is severely challenged. Second, it suggests that we are inclined to overestimate the validity and reliability of individual studies. Together, it provides strong support for the idea that the kind of knowledge we aim to create via academic research requires repeated investigation and continuous corroboration. Only replication of research will result in findings that are robust across empirical settings. At the level of the individual researcher, incentives exist to strive for novel research, which may lead to implicit or explicit choices to establish novel findings. Interestingly, it is probably better understood by behavioural accounting researchers than anybody else, that a combination of data and clear economic and social incentives that determine the current research playing field are the perfect ground for engaging in data filtering, massaging or even outright faking. Clearly, the publication scandals in the social sciences may endorse a renewed appreciation of pure replication, as well as continuing the tradition of periodic review of behavioural accounting studies' progress (e.g., Hartmann 2000; Luft and Shields 2003; Shields 2015). At the level of academic journals, biases exist that also seem to work against the growth of valid and reliable knowledge. The attention that journals now devote to these issues are a sign of hope that receptivity to replication studies is increasing.

Despite agreement at large about the significance of validity and reliability at the paradigmatic level, individual researchers are constantly confronted with the choice how to allocate their resources, and how to strive for novelty, without becoming the victim of personal or institutional biases. In this last section, some conclusions are drawn that are potentially useful in addressing this question, both by individual authors and by those responsible for adoption of papers for publication in the journals they serve as editors.

First, it is important to qualify the meaning of *novelty* when talking about novel Behavioural Accounting Research, in relationship to replication. Novelty could relate to a *new phenomenon* that is studied, but also to the application of *new methods*, or to the development of *new theory*. Understanding what is new to a study is crucial in evaluating its potential quality, but questioning an individual study's novelty may help in finding ways to replicate a study. Clearly, replication studies could focus on finding connections, agreements or disagreements between behavioural accounting studies and studies on similar phenomena that have appeared in the general management literature. Most phenomena in the behavioural accounting literature, such as the incidence of subjective performance evaluation, provide an opportunity for cross-field replication. The question here would be how generic OB and HR findings, about general firms and general employees, are when replicated in accounting contexts, using *accounting* firms and *accountants* as empirical objects. As regards method, replication is currently the most underdeveloped. The original dominance of questionnaire surveys in Behavioural Accounting Research has disappeared, but methodological variety is still limited, with experimental and archival methods currently dominating. Replicating survey findings with experiments, or vice versa, seems a viable path, which exploits the strengths, weaknesses and idiosyncrasies of these methods. Finally, replication could provide new findings when the focus is on theory. A replication study can argue that findings of previous studies can be reinterpreted using alternative theoretical lenses. The current liberal and *ad hoc* mix of economic and psychology theory in Behavioural Accounting Research calls for these types of, ultimately challenging (Ioannidis 2005; Stroebe 2016), attempts to create generalizable knowledge.

Second, it is important to understand that replication is not a poor-man's view on research, but in fact is a core element of any sound discipline. Replication studies are simply essential to the progress of knowledge. Establishing robust empirical evidence for increasingly accurate theories requires that both received wisdom and achieved statistical analyses are constantly scrutinized. To acknowledge this importance, it is required that perceptions of replications as simply executing a replica of an original study are broadened to include more sophisticated forms of repetition. Such latter forms include studies that explicitly, and deliberately, change one or more original design choices to, for example, seek the boundaries of an original study's implications. In all these more advanced cases, replication requires a solid understanding of method (Miller 2009).

Third, and very much related to the previous point, is the notion that the social sciences are particularly vulnerable to validity and reliability threats, which even more supports the need for replication studies (Makel and Plucker 2014). Also in behavioural accounting, the variety of methods, the constant development of new statistics and the combination of measurement interpretation provide a strong reason to conduct replication studies, as researchers willingly or unwillingly may become victim of the large amounts of alleged freedom and possibilities in conducting their analyses. Poor understanding of statistics combined with typically large degrees of freedom in analyzing empirical data create the perfect environment where few findings are likely to be as general and robust as we believe, and in which replication studies could do great service to eradicate 'false positives'. This means that scrutinizing published work for 'flaws' has a high expected payoff.

Fourth and finally, academic research, also in the area of behavioural accounting, remains the work of humans. General fallibility, proclivity to bias and explicitly striving for reputation and recognition all contribute to the forces that confront individual researchers when competing for limited publication space. These forces may present a barrier against publication of replication studies, the crossing of which requires effort, skill and courage (Neuliep 1990). However, they also provide a fertile ground for sober and critical judgment, which are often remarkably absent in our everyday research exercises (Christenson 1983).

References

Armstrong, J.S., 1997, 'Peer review for journals: Evidence on quality control, fairness, and innovation', *Science and Engineering Ethics* 3(1), 63–84.

Basu, S., 2012, 'How can accounting researchers become more innovative?', *Accounting Horizons* 26(4), 851–870.

Basu, S. and Park, H.U., 2014, 'Publication bias in recent empirical accounting research', *Working paper.*

Bol, J. C., Hecht, G. and Smith, S.D., 2015, 'Managers' discretionary adjustments: The influence of uncontrollable events and compensation interdependence', *Contemporary Accounting Research* 32(1), 139–159.

Brownell, P. and Dunk, A.S., 1991, 'Task uncertainty and its interaction with budgetary participation and budget emphasis: Some methodological issues and empirical investigation', *Accounting, Organizations and Society* 16(8), 693–703.

Christenson, C., 1983, 'The methodology of positive accounting', *Accounting Review* Jan 1, 1–22.

Derfuss, K., 2009, 'The relationship of budgetary participation and reliance on accounting performance measures with individual-level consequent variables: A meta-analysis', *European Accounting Review* 18(2), 203–239.

Derfuss, K., 2015, 'Relating context variables to participative budgeting and evaluative use of performance measures: A meta-analysis', *Abacus* 51(2), 238–278.

Derfuss, K., 2016, 'Reconsidering the participative budgeting – performance relation: A meta-analysis regarding the impact of level of analysis, sample selection, measurement, and industry influences', *The British Accounting Review* 48(1), 17–37.

Dickins, D. and Schneider, D.K., 2016, 'Academic research in accounting: A framework for quality reviews', *Current Issues in Auditing* 10(1), A34–A46.

Hartmann, F.G., 2000, 'The appropriateness of RAPM: Toward the further development of theory', *Accounting, Organizations and Society* 25(4), 451–482.

Hartmann, F.G. and Moers, F., 1999, 'Testing contingency hypotheses in budgetary research: An evaluation of the use of moderated regression analysis', *Accounting, Organizations and Society* 24(4), 291–315.

Hartmann, F.G. and Moers, F., 2003, 'Testing contingency hypotheses in budgetary research using moderated regression analysis: A second look', *Accounting, Organizations and Society* 28(7), 803–809.

Hofstede, G., 1967. *The game of budget control–How to live with budgetary control and yet be motivated by them.* Van Gorcum, Assen.

Hopwood, A.G., 1972. 'An empirical study of the role of accounting data in performance evaluation', *Journal of Accounting Research*, pp. 156–182.

Ingre, M., 2013, 'Why small low-powered studies are worse than large high-powered studies and how to protect against "trivial" findings in research: Comment on Friston', *NeuroImage* 81, 496–498.

Ioannidis, J.P., 2005, 'Why most published research findings are false', *PLoS Med* 2(8), e124.

Kahn, R., Wolfe, D., Quinn, R., Snoek, J. and Rosenthal, R., 1964, *Organizational Stress: Studies in Role Conflict and Ambiguity*, Wiley, New York.

Kerr, S., Tolliver, J. and Petree, D., 1977, 'Manuscript characteristics which influence acceptance for management and social science journals', *Academy of Management Journal* 20(1), 132–141.

Luft, J. and Shields, M.D., 2003, 'Mapping management accounting: Graphics and guidelines for theory-consistent empirical research', *Accounting, Organizations and Society* 28(2), 169–249.

Makel, M.C. and Plucker, J.A., 2014, 'Facts are more important than novelty: Replication in the education sciences', *Educational Researcher* 43(6), 304–316.

Miller, J., 2009, 'What is the probability of replicating a statistically significant effect?', *Psychonomic Bulletin & Review* 16(4), 617–640.

Møller, A.P. and Jennions, M.D., 2001, 'Testing and adjusting for publication bias', *Trends in Ecology & Evolution* 16(10), 580–586.

Moser, D.V., 2012, 'Is accounting research stagnant?', *Accounting Horizons* 26(4), 845–850.

Neuliep, J.W., 1990, 'Editorial bias against replication research', *Journal of Social Behaviour and Personality* 5(4), 85.

Otley, D.T., 1978, 'Budget use and managerial performance', *Journal of Accounting Research*, 122–149.

Parker, I. and Shotter, J. eds., 2015, *Deconstructing Social Psychology* (Vol. 21), Psychology Press.

Rinsum, M., 2015, 'Discussion of "Managers' discretionary adjustments: The influence of uncontrollable events and compensation interdependence', *Contemporary Accounting Research* 32(1), 160–168.

Shields, M.D., 2015, 'Established management accounting knowledge', *Journal of Management Accounting Research* 27(1), 123–132.

Silberzahn, R., Simonsohn, U. and Uhlmann, E.L., 2014, 'Matched-names analysis reveals no evidence of name-meaning effects: A collaborative commentary on Silberzahn and Uhlmann, 2013', *Psychological Science* 25(7), 1504–1505.

Silberzahn, R. and Uhlmann, E.L., 2013, 'It pays to Be Herr Kaiser: Germans with noble-sounding surnames more often work as managers than as employees', *Psychological Science* 24(12), 2437–2444.

Silberzahn, R. and Uhlmann, E.L., 2015a, 'Crowdsourced research: Many hands make tight work', *Nature* 526(7572), 189.

Silberzahn, R. and Uhlmann, E.L., 2015b, *Many Analysts, One Dataset*, https://osf.io/j5v8f/.

Siler, K. and Strang, D., 2016, 'Peer review and scholarly originality let 1,000 flowers bloom, but don't step on any', *Science, Technology & Human Values* 42(2), 29–61.

Stroebe, W., 2016, 'Are most published social psychological findings false?', *Journal of Experimental Social Psychology* 66, 134–144.

Yong, E., 2012, 'In the wake of high profile controversies, psychologists are facing up to problems with replication', *Nature* 483, 298–300.

Index

Note: Page numbers in italic indicate a table and page numbers in bold indicate a figure on the corresponding page.

Printed in the United States
by Baker & Taylor Publisher Services